Eros of the Impossible

Eros of the Impossible

Impossible

The History of Psychoanalysis in Russia

Alexander Etkind

translated by
Noah and Maria Rubins

WestviewPress

A Division of HarperCollins*Publishers*

Copyright © 1997 by Westview Press, A Division of HarperCollins Publishers, Inc.

First published in Russian as *Eros nevozmozhnogo: Istoriia psikhoanaliza v. Rossi* in 1993 by Meduza.

Published in 1997 in the United States of America by Westview Press, 5500 Central Avenue, Boulder, Colorado 80301-2877, and in the United Kingdom by Westview Press, 12 Hid's Copse Road, Cumnor Hill, Oxford OX2 9JJ

Library of Congress Cataloging-in-Publication Data
Etkind, Alexander.
  [Ėros nevozmozhnogo. English]
  Eros of the impossible: the history of psychoanalysis in Russia/
Alexander M. Etkind; translated by Noah and Maria Rubins.
     p.   cm.
  Includes bibliographical references and index.
  ISBN 0-8133-2712-1
  1. Psychoanalysis—Soviet Union—History. 2. Psychoanalysis—
Russia (Federation)—History. 3. Psychoanalysis and literature.
I. Title.
BF175.E8313 1997
150.19′5′0947—dc21   97-12146
                                                                  CIP

The paper used in this publication meets the requirements of the American National Standard for Permanence of Paper for Printed Library Materials Z39.48-1984.

10   9   8   7   6   5   4   3   2   1

Contents

Acknowledgments

I sincerely thank everyone who helped me over the course of several years of work on this book.

If Alan de Mijolla (International Association of the History of Psychoanalysis, Paris) had not shown an interest in publishing a French edition of this work, it is quite possible that it never would have been completed.

In various circumstances, at times difficult ones, M. G. Yaroshevsky (Institute of the History of Natural Science and Technology of the USSR Academy of Sciences, Moscow), B. M. Firsov (Sociological Institute of the Russian Academy of Sciences, St. Petersburg), and Clemens Heller (Maison des Sciences de l'Homme, Paris) all lent me their support.

N. P. Snetkova, M. I. Spielrein, N. N. Traugott, M. I. Davydova, E. A. Luria, A. I. Lipkina, Ronald Grele, James L. Rice, Boris Kravtsov, Gennady Obatnin, Leonid Ionin, Paul Roazen, Valery Maksimenko, Yury Vinogradov, Eugenia Fischer, Ferenz Eros, Michael Molnar, Vera Proskurina, and Yelena Kostiusheva generously shared information that in some cases proved priceless.

I am especially grateful to the librarians of the Central State Archives of Russia.

I sincerely thank all who read the original Russian manuscript in its entirety or in part and aided me with their comments and their interest in the project, particularly Yefim Etkind, Yulia Kagan and Moisei Kagan, Marina Khmeleva, Igor Kon, Irina Manson, Boris Kolonitsky, Lazar Fleishman, Andrew Samuels, Natalie Zaltsman, Leonid Gozman, Lilya Mikhailova, and Yakov Gordin.

A number of clarifications and additions have been introduced in this English edition in grateful response to reviews and comments on the Russian edition from Ernest Gellner, D. S. Likhachev, James L. Rice, Irina Paperno, Eric Naiman, Andreas Trettner, Boris Paramonov, Eliot Bornstein, Svetlana Boym, Viktor Krivulin, Lesley Chamberlain, and Mariia Amelina. I wish also to thank Westview's anonymous reviewer for valuable suggestions and criticisms.

Special thanks to Rebecca Ritke for the patience and enthusiasm with which she edited the English translation.

Finally, I send gratitude separately to my daughter, Anna Etkind.

Alexander Etkind

Introduction

This is a book about Russia and written in Russia. It is a sad society whose truth is told by others, for such a tale tends to be incomplete and one-sided. History written from within a society is likewise inevitably subjective, particularly when it is written in the depths of a crisis of historic proportions; but it is just this subjectivity that is needed in a period of change. The perspective of those who have experienced any historical process directly is distorted, but it is also enriched by the wisdom of those who know where history has led.

.   .   .

Culture in Russia generally has not been so divided and particularized according to professional pursuit and academic discipline as it has been in the West. In Russia, concurrent academic and artistic cultures have always been infused with the same trends and political ideas. Thus, decadent poets, moral philosophers, and professional revolutionaries have played as great a role in the history of psychoanalysis in Russia as have physicians and psychologists.

Russian culture thrived in the decade and a half between the beginning of this century and World War I, giving rise to a stunning topography of ideas that was repeated with variations across the humanities, politics, social thought, the visual arts, and literature (particularly poetry). Russia at this time was still one of the centers of European high civilization: Although the prophets of modernist culture included those who predicted an impending decline into barbarism, Russian cities large and small were witnessing a flowering of the modern arts and sciences, as Slavophilic argumentation gradually gave way before the press of Westernization. However, the belated attempt to modernize the empire would ultimately fail. A series of military defeats, the czar's endless blundering, and popular skepticism about the possibility of real change, combined with a general premonition of catastrophe, inspired a keen interest in the esoteric and mystical and compelled people to place their faith in romantic dreams. The "eros of the impossible" was how Vyacheslav Ivanov, the leading theorist of Russian symbolism, described the mood of this age.[1] The roiling life of the intelligentsia was a source of continual surprises, from table-raising seances to Masonic rites, from the rumors of court orgies to the ever more public and more extreme political acts of Socialist Revolutionaries.

Contemporary thought hastened toward the questions of existence that marked the boundaries of knowledge, skipping across the odds and ends of life along the way. Love and death became basic, almost exclusive, concepts of human existence, the primary categories of its analysis, and melded into a kind of supernatural oneness. The intuitive perception of the unity of love and death became a constant of the culture, manifested in such disparate forms as the philosophical writings of Vladimir Solovyov, the late stories of Leo Tolstoy, the poetry of Vyacheslav Ivanov, the novels of Dmitry Merezhkovsky, the plays of Leonid Andreev, and the psychoanalytical works of Sabina Spielrein.

The writings of Friedrich Nietzsche were likewise immensely popular in turn-of-the-century Russia.[2] Nietzsche's disdain for everyday life and his insistence on reexamining the contemporary system of values exerted a far-reaching influence on Russian thought that has yet to be fully recognized. According to an authoritative witness, artist Alexander Benois, "back then, Nietzsche's ideas were seen as quite trendy and topical (just as Freud's ideas would be later)."[3] Nietzsche's impassioned sermons, despite their unsuitability for practical application, were interpreted in Russia in such a way as to provide guidance for daily life. In the words of Apollon Grigoriev, "Russian romanticism is different from foreign romanticisms in that it takes any idea, however odd or laughable, to its utmost limit, and puts it into practice, no less."[4] What for Nietzsche and the majority of his European readers was just a flight of fancy and graceful metaphor was taken in Russia as the basis for social engineering. There was a prevailing notion that the new man, the *Übermensch* whose existence would crush the outmoded conventions of common sense, should and would be created in Russia. Russian Orthodox philosophers from Vladimir Solovyov onward had called for the foundation of godmanhood on earth through the transformation of man's bestial side. This impulse was later drowned in the mystical abstraction of Rudolf Steiner's anthroposophy, which promised an easier route to the same end. In their younger years, future leaders of the Soviet intelligentsia such as Maxim Gorky, Vladimir Mayakovsky, and Anatoly Lunacharsky were strongly influenced by Nietzsche, and their late-blooming Bolshevism could well have owed more to him than to Marx. The political extremism of Russian Marxists coexisted at that time with the spiritual extremism of Nikolai Fyodorov, who demanded that all human endeavors be abandoned in favor of his "common cause," the resurrection, by means of humanity's total mastery over nature, of everyone who had ever lived. Now, almost a century later, it is easy to pass judgment on these philosophical movements, which seemed so diverse to those living at the time, and conclude that they contained a common utopianism based on total faith in science and a Nietzschean disdain for the natural or traditional order.

Novyi mir (New World), a book by Alexander Bogdanov, one of the Bolsheviks' most serious theoreticians and a psychiatrist by education, begins with epigraphs from the Bible, Marx, and Nietzsche. "Man is the bridge to the *Übermensch*," Bogdanov quoted, and continued in his own words: "Man has not yet arrived, but he is almost here, and his silhouette is clearly visible on the horizon."[5] The year was 1904.

Man as he was, was no longer an end and an absolute, but only a means toward a more advanced, future creature. As Nietzsche taught, man must be surmounted. Today, given our experiences during the past century, this idea seems not only dangerous but utterly misanthropic. At the beginning of our century, however, there were many who took it to heart: Decadent writers and Russian Orthodox theosophs, high-ranking Masons, and terrorist ideologues disagreed completely about the path that the impending transformation of man and humanity would take—mystical or scientific, aesthetic or political; but hardly anyone doubted the goal itself or the necessity of changing man's nature.

The Orthodox ideal of conciliarism (*sobornost'*)—an undemocratic form of collectivism based on a priori concord and obedience—added another layer to the Russian conception of this transformation's means and ends. The Russian spiritual tradition had developed under the variegated and, it would seem, incompatible influences of Nietzsche, Orthodoxy, and social extremism. The victorious Bolsheviks embodied this collectivist ideal in their program for the mass transformation of man, setting off down a path that was suicidal for Russian culture but that might well have been the only one open, given the cultural framework of the time.

· · ·

From the 1910s to the 1930s, psychoanalysis was an important component of Russian intellectual life. In the multicolored mosaic of a rapidly expanding culture, the unusual ideas of Sigmund Freud were assimilated quickly and without the fierce opposition they encountered in the West. In the years before World War I, psychoanalysis evoked more interest in Russia than in France, and, by some accounts, even in Germany. In Russia, Freud wrote in 1912, "there seems to be a local epidemic of psychoanalysis."[6]

The eternal Russian "longing for world culture" could be satisfied in those days, when poets Mandelstam and Pasternak, writers Ivanov and Bely, philosophers Ilyin and Shestov, and psychoanalysts Andreas-Salomé and Spielrein were able to live, study, and work abroad for years at a time. It was only the following generation that would be denied the freedom to leave their homeland and return at will. Even today it is difficult for Russians to imagine how closely the intelligentsia of that time was linked to the intellectual life of Europe, how accessible to them were the best universities, salons, and clinics in Germany, France, Austria, and Switzerland.

On returning home, the new psychoanalysts found an eager clientele in Russian society, which was freeing itself from traditional constraints with unprecedented speed. The first Russian psychoanalysts occupied prestigious positions in the medical world. They were closely involved in literary and political circles, and had their own journal, university clinic, and sanatorium. They were on their way to institutionalizing psychoanalysis according to the highest European standards. Their patients included eminent figures of the "Silver Age." Psychoanalysis, patronized in the 1910s by Emile Medtner and Ivan Ilyin, became one of the latent causes of the schism in Russian symbolism that had such a marked effect on the life and work of the movement's leaders. Under the influence of numerous translations of Freud, the word *podsoznatel'noe*, Russian for "the subconscious" (a noun specific to psychoanalysis, unlike the older, adjectival form "unconscious," or *bessoznatel'noe*, in Russian), spread like wildfire in the speech and writing of Russian intellectuals from Vyacheslav Ivanov to Konstantin Stanislavsky.

The history of psychoanalysis is surprisingly full of people from Russia, individuals who became prominent figures in the international psychoanalytical movement. Lou Andreas-Salomé, a remarkable, cosmopolitan psychoanalyst and a close friend of Freud's, became one of the brightest stars of European modernist culture, while still preserving distinct traces of Russian philosophy in her work. Russian-born Max Eitingon, Freud's closest pupil, for many years headed the International Psychoanalytic Association. Sabina Spielrein, the most romantic figure in the history of psychoanalysis, returned to Russia in 1923 in order to contribute to the creation of utopia in her homeland—and instead lived the second half of her life alone, in abject poverty and terror.

These individuals and many others, who maintained close ties with their native Russia and often returned there, formed a large contingent among Freud's earliest students, colleagues, and followers. For years, the analysts of Vienna, Zurich, and Berlin—many trained by Freud—looked after wealthy Russian patients. Like other European countries, Russia in the 1910s and 1920s began to form its own psychoanalytic tradition. Nikolai Osipov, Moisei Wulff, Tatiana Rosenthal, Mikhail Asatiani, and Leonid Droznes were all psychoanalysts who had studied or consulted with Freud, Jung, or Karl Abraham and who returned to Russia before the revolution to pursue careers as practitioners and popularizers of psychoanalysis.

Beyond that point, their fates diverged: Rosenthal killed herself in 1921. After founding the Institute of Psychiatry in Tbilisi, which still bears his name, Asatiani rejected psychoanalysis. Osipov and Wulff emigrated to the West in the 1920s. Wulff joined Eitingon in Israel to lay the foundations of psychoanalysis there. Osipov and his student Fyodor Dosuzhkov founded a local psychoanalytic movement in Prague, and to this day psychoanalysis in the Czech Republic is led by the scions of a long line of Russian analysts. In Russia itself, no second generation of psychoanalysts like the one that came of age in the West during the 1920s managed to develop.

Freud followed the chain of events in Soviet Russia intently, at first with hope, then fear, and finally desperation and revulsion. At pains to dispel the understandable impression that his *Future of an Illusion* was inspired by the Soviet experience, Freud wrote in 1927, "I have not the least intention of making judgments on the great experiment in civilization that is now in progress in the vast country that stretches between Europe and Asia."[7] But just three years later he confessed to Arnold Zweig that the events taking place in that immense nation presented him with a problem of personal significance: "What you say about the Soviet experiment strikes an answering chord in me. We have been deprived by it of a hope—and an illusion—and we have received nothing in exchange. We are moving towards dark times. . . . I am sorry for my seven grandchildren."[8] Among those with whom Freud discussed Russian issues over the decades was his patient and coauthor William Bullitt, the first U.S. ambassador to the USSR. Bullitt, in turn, left his unmistakable imprint on Mikhail Bulgakov's *The Master and Margarita,* as the reader will see in exploring with me the intertwining lives of Freud, Bullitt, and Bulgakov, in a new interpretation of this novel.

The problems addressed by nascent psychoanalysis were central to the Russian intelligentsia's quest for knowledge. One of the most original Russian thinkers, Vasily Rozanov, became notorious for his attempts to unravel the riddles of sex. Andrei Bely, the most important writer of the era, tried to reconstruct early childhood experiences in his novels, and scholars following in the footsteps of the equally renowned Vladislav Khodasevich relied heavily on psychoanalysis to understand Bely's works. Even in the Soviet period we find the same unexpected overlap: Mikhail Bakhtin, whose works of literary criticism received worldwide acclaim, carried on a dialogue with Freud throughout his life. Sergey Eisenstein, the most important Russian film director of the time, also sought treatment in psychoanalysis and used its precepts in his art.

In the early years following the Bolshevik revolution, Muscovite analysts were supported and employed in the country's highest political circles, most intensively by Leon Trotsky, whose interaction with psychoanalysis we will examine more closely in chapter 7. Psychoanalysis had a remarkable influence on the ideas that emerged during the political and social debates of the 1920s, and it also made itself felt in the development of Russian psychology for half a century thereafter. Pedology, the unique Soviet science that offered methods of transforming human nature during childhood, was founded by people who had gone through relatively serious training in psychoanalysis. The most prominent psychologist of the Soviet period, Alexander Luria, began his long pilgrimage in science as the secretary of the Russian Psychoanalytic Society. Books by Freud had a tangible impact on the works of Lev Vygotsky and Pavel Blonsky. Discussions with Spielrein, who brought the living traditions of the Vienna, Zurich, and Geneva schools of psychology to Moscow, seem to have exerted an influence on Vygotsky, Luria, and others as they formed their psychological views.[9]

The Russian medical community was less willing to accept psychoanalysis than was the general public. Although Freud's books were systematically translated into Russian from 1904 to 1930, they were rarely used in university courses on psychiatry. Ivan Pavlov's physiology and Vladimir Bekhterev's psychoneurology, locked in a struggle for supremacy in the field now known as neuroscience, periodically showed some interest in psychoanalysis but only from a safe distance. Soviet psychiatry tended toward mechanical classification and repressive methods of treatment, contrary to the principles of psychoanalysis. In Soviet psychotherapy, as befitted the spirit of the time, hypnosis was the prevailing technique.

After the fall of Trotsky, the Russian psychoanalytic tradition was rudely interrupted by Stalin's reign of terror. Some analysts found a temporary shelter in pedology; but even this escape route was closed off in 1936. Now, nearing the end of the twentieth century, the question of whether and how the psychoanalytic tradition might be revived in Russia seems nearly unanswerable.

• • •

The peculiarities of psychoanalysis lend a certain specificity to the history of the discipline. The history of psychoanalysis is a distinct sphere of research, with its own authorities, traditions, journals, and international association. A Russian reader will easily pick out differences in style and content between this book and other domestic works on the history of psychology.[10] My approach is also a departure from the view of Russian and Soviet psychology that currently dominates the works of American historians.[11]

The history of psychology and medicine, disciplines closely related to psychoanalysis, is directed toward the analysis of scientific ideas, methods, and categories. Less attention is paid to the people who created and practiced the science, to their personalities, biographies, and interrelations. In the history of psychoanalysis, the development of ideas is tightly intertwined with the lives of the people who created them. Both the ideas and the people were partially infused with the spirit of their times and partially set in opposition to the changing influences around them. I find myself most interested by what one might call the historical and, more broadly, the human context of psychoanalytic theory and practice. This context illuminates the deep continuity between the Soviet and prerevolutionary periods of Russia's intellectual history, which has so often been underestimated for political reasons. I am fascinated by the influences shared by psychoanalysis and the philosophy, literature, and art of the time; by the relationship between the substance of psychoanalysis and the lives of those who became involved in it.

The lives of analysts and patients are no less interesting (and quite possibly more interesting) than the development of their scientific ideas. The nature of analysis is such that psychoanalytical values, views, goals, means, and methods could not help but have a telling impact on these people's biographies, their words and actions, on the choices they made throughout their lives, and on their relationships with others. It was through people that the course of history influenced the essence of analytical conceptions. The interaction of ideas, people, and epochs is what interests me and motivates this history of psychoanalysis in Russia. Thus, I composed the book in such a way as to reflect the complex fabric of history: The reader will find, among chapters focused on the life and work of individuals, more general explorations of particular eras in the perception, development, and transformation of psychoanalysis in Russia.[12]

This approach will not be congenial to all readers, nor is it the only one that might have been taken; but it is an approach fully in line with the views held by many of this book's protagonists. In 1882, Nietzsche wrote to Andreas-Salomé: "My dearest Lou, your idea of bringing together philosophical ideas and the lives of their authors [is a good one]. . . . That is just the way I taught the history of ancient philosophy, and I always told my audience that a system may be discredited and dead, but if the person standing behind it is not discredited, it is impossible to kill the system."[13] Arguing with Jung, Freud concluded his history of psychoanalysis with the declaration, "Men are strong so long as they represent a strong idea; they become powerless when they oppose it."[14] For Mikhail Bakhtin, "An idea is a *living event* that unfolds in the point of dialogue where two or more conscious beings meet."[15] And as Bulgakov's devil, Woland, playfully put it, "I am a historian. There will be a most interesting occurrence at the Patriarchs' Ponds this evening!"[16]

1

At the Crossroads of Worlds and Centuries: The Life and Work of Lou Andreas-Salomé

In 1861, a girl was born in the General Staff building on Palace Square in St. Petersburg—a girl destined for fame abroad while remaining virtually unknown in her home country. Her father, Gustav von Salomé, was a Baltic German in the service of the Russian army, a Huguenot by confession. After receiving a military education in Russia, he had quickly risen through the ranks under Czar Nicholas I. His wife had been born in Russia, the descendant of Danish Germans. The couple gave their newborn daughter a Russian name—Lyolya.[1]

Lyolya lived the first twenty years of her life in St. Petersburg. Much later, speaking of her childhood, she found it difficult to identify her native tongue. Her parents spoke German, her nanny Russian, and her governess French; and Lyolya was enrolled in a private English-language school. "We felt ourselves to be Russian," Lyolya recalled, at the same time noting that the family's household servants were Tatar, Swabian, and Estonian. For her, St. Petersburg "combined the charm of Paris and Stockholm." Remembering its majestic beauty, reindeer-drawn sleighs, and ice castles on the Neva, she described it as a cosmopolitan city despite its idiosyncrasies.[2]

Lyolya's father, a general and a privy councillor, had been close to Czar Nicholas I, and he viewed the reforms of Alexander II with suspicious reservation. His six children—Lyolya was the youngest, and the only girl—grew up in an atmosphere of intellectual and political excitement such as had never before been experienced in Russia. The novels of Tolstoy and Dostoevsky were written during these decisive decades. It was also at this time that the first socialist-revolutionary movements were formed, with women playing a significant role. According to historians' calculations, 178 women were convicted in the political trials of the 1870s and 1880s. Most belonged to the "People's Will" terrorist organization, which succeeded in assassinating Alexander II on its seventh attempt, the day before he was to sign the first Russian constitution. One of the women who had played a key role in the conspiracy against the "Czar-Emancipator" was sentenced to death.[3] It is unclear to what extent Lyolya was aware of these events; but throughout her life she kept a photograph of Vera Zasulich, a revolutionary who was acquitted by a jury after her attempt to assassinate the mayor of St. Petersburg that same year. The case became a political cause célèbre throughout Europe, and Zasulich was described by one French journal as the most popular person on the continent.

Lyolya was very close to her father and brothers. Later she would recall that she was so accustomed to the company of older men in her childhood that when she went abroad "the whole world seemed populated by brothers."[4] Judging from her memoirs, she was also an independent, introspective, and dreamy child. She never played with dolls but was constantly inventing stories: She spoke with the flowers that grew in the gardens at Peterhof, where she spent each summer, and she made up stories about people she saw in the streets. She remembered that it took her a long while to believe that mirrors faithfully reproduced her image, as she did not feel separated from the world around her. The world was probably kind to her. But her memoirs are also marked by childhood rows with her mother. Her reminiscences include her childhood faith in God and the early loss of that faith. Lyolya seems not to have felt burdened by protestant rituals and to have believed in God only to the extent that she found belief necessary. At some point in her childhood, God disappeared; but there remained a "darkly awakening sensation, never again ceasing . . . of immeasurable comradeship . . . with everything that exists."[5]

First Encounter

This idyllic childhood—if such it was—appears to have ended when Lyolya was seventeen. She had written to a certain Pastor Gillot, whom she did not know but whose sermons interested her, introducing herself boldly:

> The person writing you, Herr Pastor, is a 17-year-old girl who is lonely in the midst of her family and surroundings, lonely in the sense that no one shares her views, let alone shares her longing for fuller knowledge. Perhaps it is my whole way of thinking that isolates me from most girls of my age and from our circle—there is scarcely anything worse for a young girl, here, than to differ from the rule in her likes and dislikes, in her character and her ideas. But it is so bitter to close everything up in oneself because one would otherwise give offence, bitter to stand so wholly alone because one lacks that easy-going agreeable manner which wins people's trust and love.[6]

The pastor must have answered politely, as the two subsequently met. This meeting was the first in a series of encounters that would change Lyolya's life. Gillot loaded her down with lessons in philosophy, religious history, Dutch, and other subjects that he deemed important. The main protagonists in their discussions were Kant and Spinoza. He also freed her from the intense dreams she found so onerous, in a way that she would understand only later—by forcing her to relate them to him in minute detail.

Lyolya concealed her meetings with Gillot from her parents; one can well imagine how difficult and stormy this as yet unnamed process was for the introverted, passionate young woman. She later recalled how she saw God in Gillot and how she bowed down to him as if before God himself. The two became increasingly intimate, and one day, Lyolya reported, she lost consciousness as she sat in the pastor's lap.

In 1879, Lyolya's father died, and Gillot instructed her to tell her mother about their lessons. After meeting with her mother, Gillot proposed marriage to Lyolya. The girl was in shock; for her, the experience was like losing God a second time. "With a single blow, what I had worshipped dropped out of my heart and senses and became alien."[7] For many years afterward, sexual intimacy with her would be impossible; Gillot was but the first in a long line of men who would be enraptured with this girl and brought to desperation by her stubborn refusal of physical intimacy, linked as it was with her extraordinary beauty.

The romance with Gillot ended when Lyolya had a row with her mother, refused confirmation, and developed a pulmonary condition. Travel abroad was the recommended solution. Gillot helped her obtain a passport, which was difficult due to her lack of religious affiliation. Her passport was stamped with her new name: Lou. It was under this name that she would go down in history.

Something Almost Unwomanly

Lou found herself in Zurich with her mother. For a time, she studied philosophy at the university. The professor who taught the history of religion there described her as "a fundamentally pure being who had, however, with exceptional energy concentrated solely on mental development." He even saw this as "something almost unwomanly."[8] Another memoirist recalled her as "a lovable, winning, genuinely feminine being . . . who has renounced all the means that women use and has taken up the weapons with which men conduct the battle of life."[9] In photographs that survive from that time, Fräulein Salomé looks haughty and very pretty: a coal-black dress, hair pulled straight back, a pale, concentrated face. The girl had just turned twenty, and she had come to Europe for the first time.

Once again her health gave out, and her mother took her to Italy. In Rome, Lou met the famous Malwida von Meysenbug, a writer and passionate advocate of women's liberation, devoted to the establishment of new, "honorable" relations between the sexes. Malwida was a close friend and longtime correspondent of Alexander Herzen's; she raised his daughter and had lived for an extended period in his house in London. A quarter-century before the events at hand, Herzen wrote, "I would like to test Mademoiselle Meysenbug and take her in. She is unusually intelligent and very educated . . . fantastically ugly and thirty-seven years old."[10]

In her *Memoirs of an Idealist*, von Meysenbug recalled her desire to found an educational union that would lead adults of both sexes toward the free development of their spirituality, "so that they might then enter the world as sowers of a new, inspired culture."[11] Within the framework of Malwida's project, the familiar forms of the cultural salon were combined with the recently instigated search for the new man and new relations between people. It was not a matter of theory; for Malwida, as for some of her contemporaries and many who were to follow, this idea was thoroughly practical. It was possible to create a new human being. For this to happen, all that was needed was . . . The completion of this formula was an important and perhaps a defining aspect of modernist culture.

A frequent guest in Malwida's salon was Friedrich Nietzsche. His interlocutor, a thirty-two-year-old Jewish philosopher named Paul Rée, was the author of several books on moral philosophy in which he demonstrated the applicability of the principles of ethics to practicality, rationality, and Darwinism. Rée was also a passionate and totally impractical person, hysterically ashamed of his Jewish identity, prone to attacks of irrational melancholy, and unable to rein in his love of roulette.

In Malwida's words, her project was received with intense enthusiasm by the two men. Nietzsche and Rée were ready to participate on the spot as lecturers. Malwida was convinced that this would attract a large number of young women to whom she could devote particular attention, in order to make them into noble defenders of female emancipation.[12]

Lou, however, did not become a feminist in Italy, just as she had not become a revolutionary in Russia. She went her own way, cutting across the intellectual trends of her time, assimilating something from each, and moving on in the direction dictated by her subtle intellectual curiosity and equally refined feminine intuition.

Rée met Lou during a lecture he was giving to a group of educated young ladies in Malwida's salon. He fell in love with her right away, and although he considered it irrational to marry and produce children in such a horrid world, he hurriedly asked for her hand. Lou rejected him just as firmly as she had Gillot a short time earlier, but now she felt strong enough to do more than that. There was no need to run from a man who proved incapable of controlling his emotions; better to conquer those emotions in him, to force him to crush them just as she had crushed them in herself. As a reward, Rée was allowed to continue seeing Lou and even to live with her.

The girl reasoned that if Rée were to eliminate all possessive feelings toward her, they would be able to live together through their common spiritual interests. Public opinion did not concern her. Rée, once again violating the principles of his own moral philosophy, agreed. It remained only to overcome other sources of understandable resistance: Lou's mother, Pastor Gillot, and even Malwida von Meysenbug, whose ideas were no longer sufficiently up-to-date. As Lou wrote to Gillot,

> Malwida too is opposed to our plan. . . . But it has been clear to me for a long time now that basically we always have something different in mind, even where we agree. Her usual way of expressing herself is: "we" may not do this or that, or "we" must accomplish this or that—and I've no idea who this "we" actually is—some ideal or philosophical party, probably—but I myself know only of "I."[13]

In 1882, the year he met Lou, Nietzsche was on the threshold of yet another in a long series of discoveries; this one would lead to his creative zenith and then to his final ruin. He had been seriously ill with a malady that physicians and historians have been unable to diagnose. Some think Nietzsche suffered from syphilis, while others (such as Odessa physician I. K. Khmelevsky, who devoted an entire research project to the subject[14]) assert that his degenerative paralysis had a different cause. In any case, by the time he met Lou, Nietzsche was practically blind and was continually tormented by headaches, which he soothed with an ever increasing dose of narcotics and frequent changes of scenery. His illness was cyclical, and during the periods of reprieve he wrote ceaselessly and voluminously. He was lonely despite a close attachment to his sister Elisabeth. Several times he had asked his friends to find him a wife; with the onset of blindness, he urgently needed at least a secretary. There were rumors that he had never been with a woman. In sum, he was a man singularly unlike his favorite hero, the *Übermensch*. He was a romantic who lived vicariously through his diseased but remarkable mind.

That spring, however, Nietzsche was feeling better than ever. When Rée and then Meysenbug wrote to him about Lou, he read his own subtext in their words: "Do greet that Russian girl for me, if you see any sense in it: I have a passion for this kind of soul. . . . Considering what I intend to do in the next years, it's essential. Marriage is an entirely different story; I could agree to two years of it at most,"[15] he answered Rée lightly, little suspecting what was to come.

The three of them met in Rome in April 1882. Nietzsche read to Lou and Rée from his recently completed book, *Joyful Wisdom*, the most life-affirming of his works, in which he lauded the strength and magnificence of the extraordinary man of the future, the *Übermensch*. Man as he was, was not enough for Nietzsche. "It is a different ideal that draws us, a marvelous, seductive, and potentially dangerous ideal . . . , in comparison with which all the lofty things by which the people justly gauge their values would be no more than baseness, humiliation, danger, or at the very least a mere means of self-preservation." He added with remarkable accuracy that his ideal often seemed nearly inhuman.[16] Nietzsche had little time left in which to see his ideal come to fruition: A tragedy awaited him; but in Rome he experienced only a melodrama—his meeting with Lou.

Together the three traveled through the mountains of northern Italy and Switzerland and prepared to set up housekeeping together in Paris. They joined forces to successfully repel an attack by Lou's mother, who, horrified by her daughter's lifestyle, had enlisted Lou's favorite brother, Yevgeny, in an attempt to take her back to Russia.

Don't Forget the Whip!

A remarkable photograph was taken during those days in Lucerne. It shows Nietzsche and Rée standing harnessed to a cart in which Lou sits, with a whip in her hand, against the backdrop of the Alps. Rée's pose is confident, that of a man who feels utterly at ease. Nietzsche, with his huge mustache, trains his unseeing eyes on the distant horizon. There is no mockery in Lou's face, although it was she who had choreographed this little sketch; indeed, this was serious business. It was less than a year later, after his painful breakup with Lou, that Nietzsche would compose the celebrated line, "You go to women? Don't forget the whip!"

As she brandished her whip, Lou dreamed of building a small intellectual commune, "as holy as the Trinity," where men who had relinquished their claims on her would channel their demands into common spiritual pursuits that would allow her an equal role. Rée accepted this plan. She called him "Brother Rée" and praised him for his "unearthly kindness." For his part, Rée referred to himself as "your little house"[17] in his letters to her. In Lou's new life, Rée truly took the place of her former, brother-filled home. Her relationship with Nietzsche, however, was entirely different.

In August 1882, Lou wrote to Rée,

> Talking with Nietzsche is very exciting, as you know. But there is a special fascination if you encounter like thoughts, like sentiments and ideas—we understand each other perfectly. Once he said to me in amazement: "I think the only difference between us is that of age. We have lived alike and thought alike." It is only because we are so much alike that he reacts so violently to the differences between us, or what seem to him differences. That is why he is so upset. If two people are so unalike, as you and I, they are pleased when they discover points of agreement. But if they are as alike as Nietzsche and I, they suffer from their differences.[18]

For his part, Nietzsche wrote that "it is unlikely that there has ever been more philosophical openness between anyone" than between Lou and him. He described her this way to his friend Peter Gast: "She is a Russian general's daughter, twenty years old, keen as an eagle, brave as a lion, and yet a very girlish child who may well not live long ... She's amazingly ripe and ready for *my* way of thinking ... Besides, she has an unbelievably firm character and knows exactly what she wants—without consulting or caring about the world's opinion."[19] One can only guess how Zarathustra would have spoken if Nietzsche's relationship with Lou had taken another course; but he seemed then to be standing on the threshold of completely different discoveries.

It is possible that Nietzsche's sexual libido was just as repressed as were Lou's still unawakened feelings and that for this reason they took such pleasure in their intimate sharing of the rarefied heights of the spirit. In any case, experts on this question agree with Nietzsche's sister, Elisabeth, that his feelings for Lou were the strongest he had ever experienced toward any woman. The lovestruck Nietzsche sent a letter of formal proposal to Lou's mother in St. Petersburg and for a time, broke off contact with his own mother and sister, who hated Lou. This rupture with his family was an act of heroism on Nietzsche's part, worthy of his philosophy but impossible to maintain for long. Little more than a year passed before Nietzsche was cursing Lou, once again influenced by his sister.

> If I am leaving you, it is only thanks to your horrible disposition ... Not only have you hurt me, you have hurt everyone who loves me ... I did not create the world, nor did I create Lou. If I had created you, I would have given you better health and something else which is much more important than health— maybe a little love for me.[20]

Yet, the threats of a decisive breakup at times gave way to second thoughts:

> Dearest Lou and Rée, don't worry about my flashes of paranoia and injured pride. Even if I someday take my own life in a fit of melancholy, there should be no reason for sadness. I want you both to know that I am no more than a semi-lunatic, tortured by headaches and driven batty by loneliness. I have achieved this rational understanding of the situation, as I now consider it, after taking a solid dose of opium, the only thing that saves me from despair.[21]

It was, indeed, on the exalted heights of despair that Nietzsche penned his magnum opus, *Thus Spoke Zarathustra*. The first part of the work, from which the following passages are taken, was written in just ten days. "What is the ape to man? A laughing-stock or else a thing of painful shame. And just that shall man be to the Superman: a laughing-stock or else a thing of painful shame."[22] The superman, Nietzsche's *Übermensch,* is the earth's meaning and purpose, while man is just a muddy stream. Only an ocean can take in a muddy stream without becoming impure: "Look, I teach you the Superman: he is that sea into whose depths your great contempt can descend."[23] People's contempt for themselves, the author's contempt for people, and the author's contempt for himself would one day dissolve without a trace in the glorious new creation.

As his sister, Elisabeth, recalled, "Some cruel fate decided that at just that time, when my brother's health had improved somewhat, he had to pass through harsh personal trials. He experienced deep disappointment in friendship . . . and for the first time he knew loneliness."[24] According to Elisabeth, the image of Zarathustra was the embodiment of Nietzsche's dream of the perfect friend that he had been unable to find during his latter years; but she wrote this for public consumption. In private correspondence, written in November of the same year (1882), she expressed herself more directly: "[Lou] uses Fritz' maxims so artfully to tie his arms behind his back. I have to admit, she is truly the incarnation of my brother's philosophy."

Peter Gast, a friend of Nietzsche's and a neutral observer of his romance with Lou, told a similar story but with greater detachment.

> For some time Nietzsche was really enchanted by Lou. He saw in her somebody quite extraordinary. Lou's intelligence, as well as her femininity, carried him to the heights of ecstasy. Out of his illusion about Lou grew his mood for Zarathustra. The mood is indeed entirely Nietzsche's own but, nevertheless, that it was Lou through whom he was propelled into such Himalayan heights of feeling makes her an object of reverence.[25]

Could it be that Nietzsche found his *Übermensch* in a twenty-year-old Russian girl, and Zarathustra, the missing "perfect friend," was an encoded version of the beautiful Lou? It is difficult to say just how literally we should take this interpretation. It seems clear, however, that it was love for Lou, love unrealized and unspent, that aroused the bonfire of emotion in Nietzsche that still smolders in the pages of his book. In her monograph on Nietzsche's philosophy, Lou herself would tell it this way: "When Nietzsche no longer forces his spirit, when he freely expresses his emotions, it becomes clear what kind of torture surrounded him, one can hear the cry for self-destruction. . . . In total desperation, he seeks within and without the saving ideal that is diametrically opposed to his internal essence."[26]

While Nietzsche sought his *Übermensch*, Elisabeth devoted her life to appropriating first her brother, then his legacy, and in the process lent her own peculiar interpretation to his work. Her brother fought her attempts at usurpal, at first; but with the increasing weight of his suffering he became more and more dependent on her and less able to defend himself and his work. Elisabeth's hatred of those who were exceptionally close to Friedrich seems to have become intertwined with her hatred of Jews: She did all she

could to ruin Rée, apparently because of his Jewishness; and later she asserted that Lou, too, was Jewish. In 1885, Elisabeth married Bernhard
Förster, an activist in the German nationalist movement. He was famous
for having collected a quarter of a million signatures on a petition to
Bismarck demanding that he ban the entry of Jews into Germany and fire
them from government service. When he failed in his homeland, Förster
and his wife left for Paraguay to build a new Germany there. His misman-
agement led to a revolt of the settlers, and he shot himself in June 1889.
Elisabeth returned home and occupied herself with her brother's legacy, as
he had just passed away in a psychiatric hospital (where he had been
treated by Otto Binswanger, the uncle of Ludwig Binswanger, a close friend
of Freud's). Thus, it is not surprising that the posthumous collection of
Nietzsche's unfinished manuscripts entitled *Will to Power* was later found
by historians to be a hoax, and Elisabeth Förster-Nietzsche identified as the
source of the primitive and racist *Übermensch* that would later be accepted
and canonized by the Nazis. It was Elisabeth's efforts, not Friedrich's, that
culminated in Adolf Hitler's 1935 pilgrimage to the Nietzsche archives in
Weimar. Racism was foreign to Nietzsche, and anti-Semitism even more so:
His *Übermensch* was purely hypothetical—not so much a myth as the
framework for a myth, a challenge without any prescriptions. As for the
question of race, Nietzsche never considered himself a German, instead as-
sociating his lineage and uncommon last name with the Polish gentry.

In Russia, Nietzsche was viewed as a romantic and a prophet. "It could
be that in Nietzsche we see the romantic desire to accept the whole world"
and to find the "presence of the infinite in the finite," philologist Victor
Zhirmunsky wrote in 1914. Romantics "bring life and poetry together; the
life of a poet is like verse; life in the era of romanticism is subject to poetic
emotion. . . . Experience becomes the subject of poetic expression, and
through this expression the experience takes on form and sense."
According to Zhirmunsky's exacting formula, this could have been a kind
of "mass delirium"; "but from a psychological standpoint, in any case,
delirium is a state of consciousness like any other."[27]

In the light of such romanticism, the love between Nietzsche and Salomé
could end only one way. Unfolding as it did amid Alpine peaks and
Mediterranean resorts, the story of the couple's relationship recalls Russian
romantic literature. Before he met Lou, Nietzsche had read Lermontov and
had written to a friend about the writer's work, "this totally unfamiliar
country and disappointment in the Western spirit are so marvellously described, with Russian naïveté and the wisdom of an adolescent."[28] The exoticism of Russian life was no obstacle to his identifying the same familiar
problems in Lermontov as in Milton or Novalis. In Nietzsche's letters from
the time of his romance with young Lou, however, there is no mention of
Russian naïveté and immaturity. Lou was well prepared. Nietzsche's feel-

ings were subject to rules she knew well—the international code of romantic experience, by which happiness is unattainable, love intertwines with death, and in the end a person is significant only as the shadow of eternity.

It is possible that Nietzsche's rave review of Lermontov applies to the Russian author's most surprising creation, written a half-century before *Zarathustra* but strangely reminiscent of the later work. Banned by the czar's censors, the epic poem *Demon* came out in Germany before it was ever published in Russia, and it was translated into German many times (first in 1852 by Friedrich von Bodenstedt, who was personally acquainted with both Lermontov and Nietzsche[29]). *Demon* contains the same striking, nearly absurd romanticism found in Nietzsche's famous work: a poetics of loneliness and disdain for everyday life, dreams of resurrection through love, and a lack of interest in the technical details that would make the dream come true. Perhaps the author of *Zarathustra* was amazed to find himself in the Russian poem's strange hero, surprised to find his own dreams, worries, and guilt. The heroes of Lermontov and Nietzsche are dark symbols of the masculine creative essence invading the settled feminine routine from without, full of premonitions of "new life." These characters are descendants of the classic devils of Goethe and Byron and relatives of the new demons of Russian literature—Dostoevsky's devils and Bulgakov's Woland.

One need but open Lermontov's *Demon* to discover how love stories begin and end in romantic culture. Lermontov's hero, a creature of incomprehensible nature, was neither god nor man:

> *the ill he sowed in his existence*
> *brought no delight, His technique scored*
> *. . . yet evil left him deeply bored.*[30]

He would have lived on in this fashion, had he not met the mortal woman who transformed his being:

> *emotion started on discourses*
> *in language he used to know*
> *Was this a sign of new begetting?*[31]

He tells the beautiful woman of his uncommon ideas and arouses her thoughts with his "strange and prophetic dream." Finally, he seduces her with the transformation that is coming over him:

> *If you could guess, if you could know*
> *how much it costs in tribulation*
> *to expect no praise for evil, no*
> *prize for good deeds.*[32]

But the satisfaction of his demonic passion leads only to the girl's destruction.

Twenty years after Nietzsche and Salomé met, the idea outlined in
Demon (and paralleled in Pushkin's "Egyptian Nights"), that love and
death are one and the same, would become a dominant theme throughout
"decadent" Russian culture. The idea was deemed to have originated with
Nietzsche, but it slipped smoothly into the Russian context, saturated as it
was with both traditional and newly revived romanticism. I have explored
this development in greater depth in the chapter that follows.

It is interesting that in each story, tragedy came to the hero through an
exotic, foreign woman—an easy focal point for unfulfillable expectations.
For the Demon it was a daughter of the Caucasus and for Nietzsche a
Russian; however, Lou differed from Lermontov's Tamara, if only in that
her contact with the Demon was not to be the last in her life.

Zarathustra Gets Married

After Lou's breakup with Nietzsche, she and Rée lived together in Berlin.
Many of the people who passed through their salon were part of the intellectual elite of Europe or were preparing to enter that circle, such as
Hermann Ebbinghaus, one of the founders of experimental psychology, and
Ferdinand Tönnies, the most important German sociologist of the fin-de-
siècle. All attempted to woo Lou, and each was rejected in turn. It was
about this time that an episode took place involving playwright Frank
Wedekind, who was famous for his scandalously erotic plays. When he first
met Lou at a party, she seemed easy prey; but when he took her to his
home, he came face to face with such striking resistance that the next
morning he paid her a visit in a frock coat, bearing flowers. According to
legend, Wedekind got his revenge in the end by making Lou the heroine of
his famous play "Lulu."

For three years, Salomé and Rée managed to preserve the state of asexual, intellectual partnership that Lou wanted so badly and that it would
seem was acceptable to Rée. When they finally parted ways, Rée was ago-
nized. He abandoned his work in moral philosophy and became a physician in a small German village. The local inhabitants considered him a
saint: He lived as a hermit and provided free treatment, offering patients
hospitalization at his own expense in Berlin and Breslau and smuggling in
food and wine for them under his clothes. Although his whole life he talked
of suicide, Rée died during a walk in the mountains. This, however, happened much later, in 1901.

Biographers who have studied everything Lou left behind and fabricated
all sorts of life stories based on this material nonetheless seem unable to explain why she married Fred Andreas, a forty-year-old expert in Oriental languages, in June 1886. The marriage was completely unexpected, and as with
every significant act of Lou's, it had a superhuman aspect—Lou demanded

that the couple's married life not include sexual intimacy, and this condition was upheld for several decades. While biographical sources offer descriptions of Andreas's frustrated passion and Lou's fierce resistance, Lou could not explain her actions, even many years later as she was writing her memoirs.[33]

Lou's decision to enter into a platonic marriage with Andreas, however, was deeply and irrefutably significant. In everything she did, Lou lived out Nietzsche's favorite aphorism, "Become what thou art." Her husband was incapable of drawing her into the intimacy to which he had full right, because she did not wish it; she allowed herself to live according to her own personal interests or fears. When she finally found a desire for intimacy, it was with other men, and she was not prepared to sacrifice that desire for her husband's sake.

It is a dictum of universal logic (otherwise known as common sense) that each person's pleasures are paid for by other people. The superman conceived of by Nietzsche scorns common sense as something that must be mastered; what he gives and takes lies outside the realm of morality, beyond good and evil. Nietzsche said nothing concrete about how superpeople would interact among themselves: Neither he nor his Bolshevik successors were concerned with obvious, commonsensical questions such as how and wherewith the superman was to be created, what he should do to avoid hurting others, and how he was to live and change with the times.

Nietzsche's *Übermensch* exists only in the singular. Zarathustra is not lonely in the same way as people can be, nor in the same way as Nietzsche. He is lonely not because he is sick or at loggerheads with someone or because that's the way his life turned out. He is lonely on principle, and he would not want to be any other way.

But Lou lived within the framework of history and changed along with the people around her. Did she really carry out the Nietzschean myth in practice? She was becoming herself, and other people either got out of her way or tried to fall into step. This attempt ended differently for each of them, but for now we are more concerned with Lou herself. Myths are static, while the world changes. Tomorrow a person will not be the same as he was yesterday; in becoming what he is, a person may well find himself different from what he was. A person's self-realization thus becomes the story of his life. Become what thou art, Nietzsche told Lou, employing the words to get what he wanted from her. With other men did she become what she was—that is, what she couldn't be—with Nietzsche? Biography is almost inexplicable, and a person's development is equally unpredictable, because everyone realizes himself in connection with other people, and with each new partner the ego changes, being practically re-created anew. Thus, in becoming herself under Nietzsche's strong influence, Lou became a totally different person.

Historians disagree about the identity of the man who initiated Lou's sexual experience. According to the most intriguing variant, her deflowerer was a prominent member of the German Social Democratic Party and the founder of the Marxist newspaper *Vorwärts,* Georg Ledebour. Ledebour was for many years a member of the Reichstag. In later decades, his revolutionary activism would bring him into contact with Trotsky in Vienna. What we do know for certain is that when Lou lost her virginity, she was past thirty and the event rocked the Andreas family's life. Fred was ready to kill himself, and Lou was on the verge of doing the same. In the end, the crisis was resolved nonviolently, with a settlement that would define their roles for the rest of their lives: Lou obtained unlimited freedom, while still living under the same roof with her husband and maintaining a close friendship with him.

In several of Lou's publications that were written around this time—works that made her well known to the intellectual elite—she succeeded in establishing her independence from Nietzsche's influence. In one piece, she presents an interpretation of the Gospel story in which Christ is portrayed as a lonely, suffering hero. Another book deals with Nietzsche's philosophy directly. This treatise enjoyed wide success, and relatively quickly, in 1896, a Russian translation appeared in the symbolist journal *Severnyi vestnik* (Northern Messenger), which was published in St. Petersburg under the editorship of Lou's acquaintance Akim Volynsky.

In May 1897, Andreas-Salomé met Rilke, and the two were immediately attracted to each other. René Maria Rilke was twenty-one, fourteen years younger than Lou. He had known many women in his life; he would write them poetry, quickly become entranced by the prospect of happiness, and lose interest just as quickly. His relationship with Lou stands out sharply against this background: Although their romantic intimacy lasted only four years, for the next thirty Lou remained Rilke's foremost authority and possibly his closest friend.

Under her influence Rilke even changed his name, transforming the indefinite, intimate René into the solidly romantic Rainer. ("Your name willed it so, and you chose the name," Marina Tsvetaeva wrote Rilke many years later, infatuated with him from afar.[34]) Rilke's creative periods alternated with chronic episodes of ennui, fear, and helplessness. Lou was at once his lover, his mother, and his therapist: She accepted his emotions even though they often seemed to her overblown; she valued and stimulated the channel of expression that was Rilke's savior—his poetry; and when it became necessary, she could patiently woo him back to reality.

Russia was their common passion. "True Russians are people who say at dusk what other people reject in daylight," Rilke wrote to his mother.[35] "In his poetic imagination, Russia rose up as a nation of prophetic dreams and patriarchal traditions," wrote Rilke's Russian acquaintance, Sophia Shil.[36] All his life, Rilke tried to find his way into just such a Russia: He studied the language, wrote poetry about Russian monks and mythic heroes, and corresponded with Russian poets; at one time, he even intended to emigrate to Russia. During his final days, his Russian secretary never left his side.

Fiction in the Mass of Reality

In 1898, Lou published in the German press an article with the unusual title "Russian Philosophy and the Semitic Spirit," in which she presented a highly original survey of contemporary Russian intellectual life.[37] In her article, Lou professed astonishment at the intense battle raging among Russian intellectuals for the philosophical and spiritual development of their compatriots. For the time being, she asserted, these intellectuals would find it difficult to achieve any philosophical elevation beyond the limits of naive religious metaphysics. Their attempts to do so were mere imitations of German philosophy from Schelling's and Hegel's day; but abstract German philosophy was ill adapted to take root in the Russian mind. Russia needed a more systematic philosophical education, in the interest of its cultural development. Fortunately, Russia already had a group of people "that has developed a talent for abstract theology to the point of genius"—the Jews. Lou believed that Jews could exert a more productive influence on Russia's future philosophy than on any other area, and she cited her friend Akim Volynsky, literary critic and publisher, as an example of such influence.

It was difficult to imagine anything more diametrically opposed, Lou wrote, than the Russian mind with its naive analogies and aesthetic concreteness, and the Jewish Talmudic spirit with its tendency toward extreme abstraction. "The Jewish spirit perceives telescopically what the Russian mind sees through a microscope." And yet, she asserted, unlike Germans, who were at pains to seize any phenomenon in their conceptual "claws," Jews saw phenomena through eyes full of love and enthusiasm. This characteristic brought them closer to the youthful culture of the Russians; but Russian culture was closed to Jews at the time, and for this reason "Jewish dialectic force has set a subtly aggressive course." As soon as Russia's philosophy departments gave Jews the chance to compete freely, Lou predicted, one would see these two nations learning to understand and interact with each other, even though they started out from opposite cultural poles.

Nietzsche had written twelve years earlier that "any thinker who has the future of Europe on his mind will turn to the Jews and the Russians as the most reliable and probable factors in the great game and struggle of forces."[38] The century that followed was indeed marked by the tragic brand of these three ethnic questions—German, Russian, and Jewish. In light of subsequent events, the perceptiveness and at the same time the limited scope of Lou's analysis are striking. She foresaw the great spiritual eruption that would result as soon as the Russian and the Jewish traditions began to "intersect"; but she had no inkling of the social orientation that would characterize the new blend of beliefs born of this collision.

In April 1899, Mr. and Mrs. Andreas-Salomé arrived in Russia with Rilke. Their fairy-tale expectations were confirmed during Easter week in Moscow, where they met artist Leonid Pasternak (father of Boris), sculptor Paolo Trubetsky, and Leo Tolstoy. Their Russian interlocutors were hospitable but disagreed with their guests' perception of Russia, and no particular warmth arose between them. Rilke would only find spiritual acceptance in Russia after the new generation came of age: Boris Pasternak considered him a great poet; and Marina Tsvetaeva, who had never met Rilke but had merely seen him in photographs, was head over heels in love with him. Both Russian poets corresponded with Rilke for many years. The Russia that Rilke worshiped was an equally attractive fairy tale for Russians like these, who survived only by a quirk of fate, huddling in communal living quarters or in emigration.

A year later, Lou and Rainer were in Russia again, this time without Andreas. The impression they left on ten-year-old Boris Pasternak fills the opening pages of his memoirs, written many years later. The pair made a striking image:

> An express train was leaving Kursk station on a hot summer morning in the year 1900. Just before the train started someone in a black Tyrolean cape appeared in the window. A tall woman was with him. Probably she would be his mother or his elder sister. . . . There on a platform thronged with people, between two bells, this stranger struck me as a silhouette in the midst of bodies, a fiction in the mass of reality.[39]

Lou and Rainer were on their way to visit Tolstoy at his home in Yasnaya Polyana. It could be that septuagenarian Tolstoy also found the pair lacking in "non-fictitiousness." In any case, he showed no particular interest in Rainer's poetry or Lou's ideas. These found more resonance at the time with a little-known peasant poet named Spiridon Drozhzhin.

After a two-month stay in Moscow and St. Petersburg, the travelers returned to Berlin. A short time later, one of Lou's friends found her and Rilke so engrossed in the study of Russian language, history, and literature that when she met them at the dinner table they were too tired to maintain a conversation.

For Lou the trips to Russia carried a different meaning than they did for Rilke. For her they were a homecoming—to youth, to her family, to the familiar places she loved in childhood, to reality. The poetic visions that bound Rilke so tightly to Russia now appeared to her overdone and even unhealthy. Love for Russia, which at one time had brought her and Rilke closer, now forced them apart.

Rilke's tragic emotion for Lou was encoded in many of his poems. One of his most famous was first published in *The Book of Pilgrimage*, after his breakup with Lou and marriage to Clara Westhof, but was written, according to Lou, in 1897:

> *Extinguish both my eyes: I can descry you;*
> *Slam my ears to: I can attend to you;*
> *without feet I am able to draw nigh you,*
> *without a mouth I still can conjure you.*
> *Break both my arms away, and with my heart,*
> *as with a hand, I'll capture you again;*
> *arrest my heart's, there'll be my brain's pulsation;*
> *and if you cast a fire into my brain,*
> *I'll carry you on my blood's circulation.*[40]

The correspondence between Rilke and Lou Andreas-Salomé fills a thick volume. Over the decades that followed the end of their romantic relationship, Rilke wrote to Lou about everything he was afraid to express in his poetry. Whenever the anxiety that washed over him seemed too strong, he would beg for a rendezvous, but nearly always her answer was no. Clearly intended to hold an unstable partner at a distance, Lou's letters also fostered Rilke's artistic life. She saw his poems as a spontaneous and irreplaceable form of self-treatment. Later, in 1912, after advising Rilke to begin the course of psychoanalysis that he was seriously but reluctantly considering, she began to doubt the wisdom of her advice. The two subsequently agreed that although psychoanalysis would likely help Rilke rid himself of emotional crises, it probably would also deprive him of the ability to write poetry. Just a month after he broke off negotiations with one analyst, Rilke began composing his Duino Elegies. Thus history has, at the very least, proven the corollary: Without psychoanalysis, Rilke's genius remained intact.

Later, one of Lou's patients in Königsberg recalled a story she had told him in the course of his treatment.

Once I was sitting in a train with Rilke and we amused ourselves by playing the game of free association. You say a word and your partner answers with any word that comes to his mind. We did this for quite a while. And suddenly I understood the reasons why Rilke wanted to write his military school novel and I told him so. I explained to him the nature of the subconscious forces that were urging him to write because they had been repressed while he was at school. He laughed at first, then he looked serious and said that now he did not have to write the novel at all. I had taken it off his soul. This shocked me and I suddenly realized the danger of psychoanalysis for the creative artist. To interfere here means to destroy. That is why I later always advised Rilke against having himself analyzed. For while a successful analysis might free an artist from the devils that beset him, it would also drive away the angels that help him create.[41]

The Erotic

In 1903, Mr. and Mrs. Andreas moved to Göttingen. The area reminded Lou of a Volga landscape. She spent only a short time there, however, as she traveled around Europe with friends, visited her mother each year in Petersburg (until the latter's death in 1913), and lived extensively in Berlin.

In 1910, Lou was befriended by Martin Buber, one of the most important philosophers of the twentieth century. At Buber's request, Lou wrote a book entitled *The Erotic*.[42] The book was successful mostly because of the unabashed ecstasy it expressed concerning the physical aspects of sexuality; but rave reviews from an authority like Buber also reflected the work's high intellectual level. All living things love each other, Lou wrote, but as one moves closer to man, and as man develops, love becomes more individualistic. The more individual a person, the more demanding and subtle his choice, and the more quickly saturation and the demand for change will set in. Love, and more specifically the act of copulation, is experienced differently by men and women. For a man, Lou wrote, the sex act was a moment of satisfaction. For a woman, it was a condition—a normal and self-sufficient phenomenon, the peak of her human essence.

At about the same time, similar ideas were circulating among Russian philosophers such as Solovyov, Rozanov, and Berdyaev, who equated male sainthood with asceticism and asexuality, while female sainthood—as Lou pointed out, referring to the Virgin Mary and to Mary Magdalene—was the realization of woman's erotic essence as a mother and lover. In sex, a woman approached the condition that Lou dubbed "everything." In her definition, "everything" was to a woman what the outside world was to a man. Andreas-Salomé's erotic "everything" is paradoxically reminiscent of the mystic concept of "all-oneness" in Russian philosophy of that time.

Whatever the name one might assign to this experience, it seems to have helped Salomé maintain stable relations with her husband. *The Erotic*, along with Lou's other publications, also seems to have won her a degree of notoriety; her suitors and friends were among Europe's intellectual elite. Yet one crucial element was missing from Lou's intricate internal makeup.

Moses and Magdalene

In September 1911, Lou visited the Psychoanalytic Congress in Weimar, where she met Freud. She had already passed her fiftieth birthday, but this was yet another new beginning for her. To Lou's request to attend the famous "Wednesdays," Freud responded, "When you come to Vienna, we shall all do our best to introduce you to what little of psycho-analysis can be demonstrated and imparted."[43] Arriving in Vienna after the Congress, Lou made a most favorable impression on Freud's close-knit circle of analysts. Freud himself conducted the weekly meetings, which took place without fail on Wednesday evenings, starting in 1902; the meetings eventually metamorphosed into sessions of the Vienna Psychoanalytic Society.

Lou became involved in the psychoanalytic movement at a key juncture in its development. Freud had been successful in reworking the theories and methods of clinical psychoanalysis; at any moment, psychoanalysis would begin its triumphant march across the world. However, one also can detect the first signs of the worrisome phenomena, as yet unclear to Freud, that would soon lead to the dissident activity of Adler and Jung and to a deep schism in the psychoanalytic movement.

It is surprising that after intimate contact with two monumental romantics, Nietzsche and Rilke, Lou was able to accommodate herself to Freud's strict realism; but, as was the case at every significant juncture in her life, Lou immediately sensed in which direction her vital interests lay, and she responded without any particular resistance. Later, she singled out two factors that made her so receptive to Freudian psychology: the fact that she grew up among Russians, who were particularly open to self-analysis; and her lengthy interaction with a man of uncommon inner direction—Rilke.[44]

Freud was nearing fifty-six. This brilliant man, whom many (in Russia, almost everyone) would later consider the overthrower of all moral values, was also a father of six, whose well-ordered life flowed by quietly inside the walls of his apartment in Vienna. He was always immaculately dressed, his speech was commendably correct and well enunciated, and his grandiose manners were something out of the nineteenth century. The intellectual bravado of his adventures in the realm of the mind was balanced by absolute predictability in his private life: Day after day he rose, worked, and went to bed according to the same schedule. His office was a few doors down from his bedroom, so during the short breaks between seeing patients he could only walk back and forth through the rooms of his apartment. His patients were well acquainted with his punctuality and knew how seriously he took their tardiness. His only weaknesses were cigars and a collection of classical and oriental statuettes that swallowed all his extra money, particularly toward the end of his life. Freud's desk was covered with these statuettes, arranged in exemplary order, leaving a perfectly measured space for the sheets of paper he used to write his book. Any patient who showed particular courage in uncovering the depths of his own unconscious was rewarded with a short tour of the collection.

Even knowing so much about human passions, Freud lived a life that was completely subordinated to intellectual control. The assistance that he offered his patients was justified by his greater mission, and he encouraged his patients to think of their treatment the same way: as cooperation toward the common cause of learning more about the unconscious. The struggle with hypocrisy in society, so familiar from his books, was also his struggle with himself. From a modern point of view, his opinions on sex seem puritanical. He discovered sexuality in children, but these discoveries were unpleasant and even repulsive to him. Having laid the foundation for sexual education, Freud sent his sons to a doctor so they could learn the necessary facts about sexuality from someone else. One of his daughters-in-law recalled how he had scolded her, saying that she stroked her infant son too much, arousing his oedipal fixation. He was only forty-one when he wrote to one close friend that sexual arousal no longer interested him.[45] His natural scientist's mind saw sexuality as a powerful natural force, but in showing its power and universality he felt no rapture; he actually felt rather regretful about it. Above all, Freud never sought to harmonize himself with this force in practice based on the new knowledge he had collected. He invariably condemned those of his disciples who violated the rigid moral code of psychoanalysis and entered into sexual relations with their patients, regardless of whether they were succumbing to temptation or experimenting for the advancement of the cause. Freud's official biographer reproduced the words he once used: "The great question, to which there is no response and which I was unable to answer despite my thirty years of research into the female psyche, is the question as to what a woman really wants."[46] He was impressed by heroic figures such as Moses and Leonardo da Vinci, who succeeded in liberating themselves from the overwhelming pressure of their sexuality, thus performing the miracle that was impossible according to the theory of psychoanalysis.

In this sense, Freud's study of Leonardo da Vinci is particularly eloquent. Incidentally, in mentioning da Vinci, Freud was following in the footsteps of Dmitry Merezhkovsky, whom he considered the only poet who ever came close to solving the great artist's riddles. Like Leonardo himself, Freud lived in an era that "was witness to a struggle between sensuality without restraint and gloomy asceticism,"[47] and he saw his own life infused with the same lofty and asexual inspiration that he found in da Vinci, who "converted his passion into a thirst for knowledge."[48] Like Leonardo, he was a model of "the cool repudiation of sexuality—a thing that would scarcely be expected of an artist and a portrayer of feminine beauty."[49] And, like his hero, Freud could hardly have foreseen how grossly misunderstood his example would be.

Freud consciously sought to free himself and his doctrine from the temptations of Nietzsche, whom he saw as the most dangerous competitor in the struggle for intellectual influence. Freud's disciples—Jung, Otto Rank, Ernest Jones, Spielrein, Eduard Hitschmann, and others—frequently and for various reasons demonstrated their dependence on Nietzsche, and this always provoked Freud's displeasure. Lou Andreas was still associated with Nietzsche in her new circle. Jung, for example, saw her appearance at the Vienna Society as a possibility to expand the intellectual influence of psychoanalysis in Germany, "where Frau Lou enjoys a considerable literary reputation because of her relations with Nietzsche."[50] Freud must have found in her a new, attractive battlefield for his old rivalry.

We know that in his youth Freud read the early works of Nietzsche and that he even participated in the German Students' Club of Vienna, which combined political radicalism with adoration for Schopenhauer, Nietzsche, and Wagner. In 1900, Freud wrote Fliess that he was studying Nietzsche's books, hoping to "find the words for what remains mute inside me." One of the meetings of the Vienna Psychoanalytic Society in 1908 was specially dedicated to the discussion of Nietzsche's ideas. The speaker, Paul Federn, said that Nietzsche's views came so close to those of psychoanalysts that it remained only to figure out how, if at all, they differed. Freud replied that Nietzsche had failed to discover displacement mechanisms and infantile fixations. However, Freud then affirmed that the level of introspection attained by Nietzsche was indeed higher than anyone before and probably after; but he concluded that he could not read Nietzsche's works, resorting to a justification that smacked of paradox: Nietzsche's ideas were too rich.[51]

In 1921, Freud was sifting through metaphors that might allow him to understand the nature of the irrational mobs that had begun to define the century's terrifying face and the role played by their leader. Was he a hypnotist? The chieftain of some prehistoric horde? In the end, Freud compared the leader of the mass movement he found so heinous to Nietzsche's *Übermensch*.[52] Later, in 1934, when this theme had acquired unprecedented import, Freud tried to talk Arnold Zweig out of writing a book about Nietzsche, particularly objecting to Zweig's intention to compare him with the creator of the superman.

There was no sexual relationship between Andreas-Salomé and Freud, nor could there have been. But in his own way, in sublimated form, Freud was enchanted by her and had no trouble expressing his feelings. He sent her flowers and walked her back to her hotel after lectures. Once, when she did not come to a Wednesday meeting, he sent her a note, jealously inquiring whether her contact with Adler was the reason for her absence. During his lectures, Freud had the habit of picking out someone from the audience whom he would address directly; in his note, Freud confessed that he had read his last lecture to the empty chair where Lou ordinarily sat.[53]

Ernest Jones, commissioned by Freud's daughter Anna (who, some say, underwent analysis with Lou) to write the official biography of the founder of psychoanalysis, noted that Freud was attracted to women "of a more intellectual and perhaps masculine cast. . . . Freud had a special admiration for Lou Andreas-Salomé's distinguished personality and ethical ideals, which he felt far transcended his own."[54]

After entering the close circle of Freud's disciples, Lou immediately befriended the one who seemed to her the most capable: Viktor Tausk. The handsome, blue-eyed physician was much younger than she: He was thirty-three, while she was fifty-one. Paul Roazen, who wrote a sensational biography of Tausk based on interviews he did in the 1960s with seventy people who knew Freud personally, thought Lou's charm stemmed mostly from her reputation as the girlfriend of brilliant people.[55] Tausk was vain, and perhaps it flattered him to find himself in the same company as Nietzsche and Rilke; but much more important to him was Lou's relationship with Freud. Like Adler and Jung, Tausk was attempting to compete with Freud; but unlike them, he was not strong enough to do it openly and suffer certain rejection by his former teacher. The history of their relationship is full of mutual mistrust: Freud suspected Tausk of plagiarism, although he himself was at times imprudent in using the ideas and words of his students. Tausk tried to overcome the distance between them by asking Freud to take him on as a patient, the only opening that Freud left others as he became increasingly isolated with the passage of years. For a while, Lou—who had no difficulty being Freud's friend and Tausk's lover at the same time—restrained and balanced this precarious situation. Tausk was probably able to reassure himself with the knowledge that he possessed what Freud could not, while Freud discussed his rival with Lou for hours on end, thus keeping him under control. However, Lou's relations with Freud were much more important to her, and soon Tausk found himself alone, with Lou denying him intimacy and Freud refusing him treatment. For several years, Tausk tried unsuccessfully to evoke sympathy from one of the two, and in 1919 his story ended tragically: He took his own life in a meticulously planned fashion, tying a noose around his neck and then shooting himself in the head. Freud dedicated a mournful eulogy to him, and at the same time showed the kind of cruelty of which he was capable, confessing to Lou in a letter that Tausk's death was no loss. "I had long taken him to be useless, indeed a threat to the future."[56]

The Origin of Optimism

Enthusiasm and optimism are characteristic of Andreas-Salomé's psychoanalytic works, clearly differentiating them from the gloomy stoicism of late Freud. Her generally joyous worldview even changes her interpretation of concrete clinical phenomena. For example, narcissism is for her not an infantile condition into which an adult might be drawn by sickness or misfortune, as it is for Freud, but a positive feeling of love for oneself and even an affective identification with existence, with everything. Narcissus, she writes, looked at himself not in a mirror made by the hands of men but in a sylvan spring. Therefore, he saw not the reflection of his own face but his divine oneness with the infinite world of nature.

The unity of subject and object that encompasses the entire universality of nature and culture represents for Lou the very essence of love. It is incorrect, she writes, to see nature and culture as a set of opposites like light and darkness. Those who, like Prometheus, create human culture as a second reality are truly Narcissuses in the extreme. Narcissus loves himself, and consequently he loves the entire world that is embodied in him. For this reason, she continues, the adorer is doomed to disappointment; not because love fades with the passage of time, but because it is beyond the capacity of individuality to fulfill the expectation of universality that the adorer invests in the object of his affection.[57]

The unique pattern of Lou's ideas, it seems, was based on Russian sources with which she was very familiar but which were inaccessible to her European colleagues. The most influential of these sources was the moral philosophy of Vladimir Solovyov. The image of all-oneness as the embodiment of the "universal soul" and a spiritual ideal were central to Solovyov's thinking, and because of him these were extremely popular ideas in Russia at the beginning of the century. For Solovyov, as for Andreas-Salomé, all-oneness has feminine traits; his symbol is Sophia, the mystical image of the Eternal Feminine and, at the same time, of godmanhood.[58] As Russian culture assimilated Solovyov's philosophy, Sophia began to take on more and more sensual characteristics, culminating in Alexander Blok's "beautiful stranger."[59]

The interests of Solovyov and Salomé clearly intersected at least in one area that was important to them both: the interpretation of Nietzsche in a Russian context. Solovyov released a series of articles in 1893 entitled "The Meaning of Love," which achieved notoriety in Russia. The translation of Lou's book on Nietzsche, which became the first systematic analysis of his philosophy in Russian, was published in 1896. Some time later, Solovyov's essay "The Idea of the Superman" was issued, in which he starts from the proposition that "somewhat to his detriment, Nietzsche seems to be becoming a trendy writer in Russia" and moves on to his own interpretation of the superman: Nietzsche is in a way better than Marx and Darwin; Christ was the real *Übermensch*. The most important thing about the superman, said Solovyov, is his immortality, and the impending solution to humanity's problem, the "total and decisive victory over death," will make the *Übermensch* a reality.[60]

Solovyov's shift away from the philosophy of eroticism to the mysticism of all-oneness and the utopia of godmanhood had a profound impact on the development of Russian thought, establishing the limits within which the search for knowledge would take place for nearly a century. The mystical worldview of Vladimir Solovyov was as far as can be from Freud's rationalism and individualism. At the same time, aspects of Solovyov's philosophy of love brought him surprisingly close to psychoanalysis. "The beginning of everything good in this world comes out of our dark sphere of unconscious processes and relations," he wrote, before Freud's first book was ever published. "This force of physico-spiritual creativity in man is merely the transformation or *turning inward* of the same creative force that in nature, being outwardly focused, results in mindless, endless physical reproduction."[61]

In Solovyov's ideal of all-oneness, the differences between man and woman, life and death, were overcome. The human being of the future, who would overcome death and gender, was Solovyov's dream, and it tied him inextricably to the generation of Russian intellectuals that would follow. It was Solovyov in Russia who first considered the interconnection between love and death. This interconnection would be incorporated into psychoanalysis through the writing of Spielrein and subsequently through the latter works of Freud. It would also be assimilated into the philosophy of Berdyaev and other religious thinkers of the Russian diaspora (see chapters 2 and 5). Solovyov cited Heracleitus with deep understanding: "Dionysus and Hades are one and the same." Thanks to him, this vague aphorism was adopted by Russian and European thinkers of the new century, and later was transmogrified into Freud's lesson about Eros and Thanatos. "As long as Man reproduces like an animal, he will die like an animal." The sex act, and even the very division of people into men and women, is a path leading straight to death. The perversions that psychiatrists deal with are merely "more barbaric forms of one, all-penetrating perversion," that is, sex. "A simplistic attitude towards love ends in that final, extreme simplification that we call death."[62]

Solovyov asserted that the only absolute value of human life lies in the establishment of the unity that has been predicted since Plato, in which all opposites are melded together. The human of the future is androgynous, physico-spiritual, and godmanlike; obviously, he/she will have no need of sex. All this is attainable only in the godman's mystical formulation of the future. Ironically, sexual love became Solovyov's metaphor for this ideal world, since all-encompassing divinity is achieved by blending the masculine and the feminine, the physical and the spiritual, the singular and the infinite. It should be noted that the creator of the philosophy of godmanhood was seriously convinced that his ideas were more than mere poetry and could be implemented in actual practice.

Andreas-Salomé most likely viewed Solovyov as an anachronism. She characterized him as "one of the most typical representatives of Byzantine Russia."[63] Unlike the Western scholars who made up Salomé's circle—psychoanalysts, sociologists, and psychologists—Russian philosophers were not concerned with the technical, prescriptive side of their lofty ideas. All the same, the erotic psychology of Lou Andreas-Salomé, while combining such diverse intellectual trends as Nietzsche's romanticism, Solovyov's moral philosophy, and Freudian psychoanalysis, remained continuously linked to the basic current of Russian culture in her day.

Narcissism, Feminism, and Nationalism

Narcissism is not simply admiring oneself in the mirror (a childish theme that Lou carried with her throughout her life). In Freud's understanding, it was also the diversion of the libido from higher goals. Salomé inverted the Freudian concept of narcissism, which for her was a mature rather than an initial stage of development. For her, narcissism was not the cause of psychotic stagnation and abnormal development but the source of love, art, and ethical behavior. As a result, in Lou's view, the most positive thought mechanisms of psychic life were embedded in the concept of narcissism. Narcissism was the most important component in all objective symbolizations of the libido, "the feeling of identification with totality," and even the action of "transsubjective force."[64] It was narcissism that raised sex to the level of love and love to the level of friendship, and finally, that transformed all human feelings into the "masterpiece of narcissism" and the "symbol of symbols of love"—God.[65] In order to understand the meaning of narcissism, one must study cases where the libido has not been too "masculinized" or subjected to the ego's overeager aggression, when it has not yet been totally separated from "everything."[66]

Lou reintegrated the Freudian "id" as another closely analogous image. This concept was originally defined by Freud exclusively in terms that were logically and normatively negative. Salomé invested the id with concrete and even optimistic content. Her revision of psychoanalytic theory went beyond the bounds of any one concept, touching on the entire range of lower and pre-rational psychic forces, in essence covering the entire territory that psychoanalysis had discovered and described. Freud found a formidable new opponent in this landscape, one who could be defeated only with the help of deep, systematic reconnaissance. Salomé radically shifted the telescope's focus: She perceived the Freudian unconscious as a reversible state of personality—a state that was familiar and even pleasant. Her narcissistic "unification with everything" was in fact the stuff of erotic pleasure and cultural creativity. Freud's sublimation of lower forces—their ever incomplete and embattled subjugation to the control of higher forces—in Salomé became a partnership between these opposing forces, a chain of reversible transactions and alliances. Salomé melded the political and often aggressive metaphors of Freudian analysis with a completely different set of mystical and erotic associations.

The national dimension of Salomé's ideas is significant but underappreci-ated. Russia occupied just as privileged a position in her geography as did narcissism in her psychology. The qualities Andreas-Salomé used to define narcissism in her psychoanalytic articles written in the late 1910s are the very same qualities that she attributed to Russians in her earlier and later works: "Childlike directness in interpersonal relations; . . . a breadth of spirit bereft of all routineness; a preference for spending over saving; a lack of understanding of rules, duty, constancy, legality, and responsibility; insuf-ficient strength to take action, except in special conditions of ecstasy or fa-naticism."[67] In her memoirs, these three dimensions—gender-based, na-tional, and structural—are equally and subtly intermingled with one another. One chapter, entitled "Russian Experience" (and squeezed in among such chapters as "Experience of God," "Love Experience," and "Experience of Friendship"), is an astounding attempt to integrate this expe-rience from the time of her childhood with the thoroughly different concepts that were layered over it in adult years. She appreciated the complexity of her ideal, and distinctly contrasted it to the masculine, European, rational world that she encountered daily in her partners; she more than willingly of-fered this construction to her readers—and probably her suitors.

In fact, this triple construction—feminine, Russian, and narcissistic—has little in common with Freudian psychoanalysis and bears a far greater re-semblance to Russian populism. Salomé absorbed the populist attitudes of the Russian intelligentsia through her father, an official during the period of official *narodnost'*, and from the atmosphere of opposition that reigned during her youth, an atmosphere she eloquently described in her memoirs: "I was able to meet people . . . who allowed me to relate to the Russian na-tion in a new way—namely, politically. For the spirit of revolution which found its first political program in the *Narodniki*, the 'people's party,' was already bubbling and fermenting in the schools. It was hardly possible to be young and energetic without being affected by it."[68]

Historians have offered various interpretations of Andreas-Salomé's at-tempt to refashion the psychoanalytic tradition by rehabilitating narcissism, the unconscious, the id, and what she called the "passive instinct." Angela Livingstone saw a similarity to Jung's collective unconscious; Biddy Martin deemed Salomé's approach a feminist revision of psychoanalysis.[69] According to Salomé's own elucidation, she envisioned an analysis that was less individ-ualistic and rational, less hostile to religious practice, and more sensual and feminine. What Freud could not accept in Jung, he forgave in the feminine—and Russian—Salomé. It is understandable that researchers in our day are more inclined to see Salomé as a pioneer of international feminism than to ascertain the sources of her inspiration in nationality and other cultural fac-tors. These factors are quirky, or at least archaic, and perhaps that is why they have as yet aroused little interest among historians outside Russia.

Nevertheless, in Salomé's world, values were different. Ideas that today's historians tend to suppress, Salomé espoused actively and with obvious satisfaction, using them to her apparent advantage as leitmotivs of self-representation. The game she played with national stereotypes was an important part of the charm that has made her so irresistible to Western intellectuals.

"The Russian 'collective' is marked by attachment to the people, to what is fundamental, an intimacy of the heart rather than the principle of civilized behavior, or intelligence, or rationality. All ecstasy finds its expression *there*, in no way diminished, with an emphasis upon the difference between the sexes: for passive submission and receptivity mesh with a sharp, active, revolutionary . . . state of spiritual alertness."[70] These words of Salomé's, penned in 1932 and full of fascination with the Russian *obshchina* [traditional village commune], echoed the populist ideas of more than half a century before. Salomé shared a romantic populism, acquired at home and in school, with the Russian revolutionaries she met in Europe. The memoirs that became the receptacle of these views are naturally peppered with terms related to her theory of positive narcissism: "In fact, revolutionaries of both sexes looked to the Russian idea as children look to their parents. . . . The peasant remained for them the model person. . . . All of the strength of spiritual life was concentrated in this primitivism—the childlike state that no one can fully avoid, even a mature and self-assured adult."[71]

In her memoirs, Lou held Pastor Gillot responsible for her "de-Russification";[72] but the memoirs themselves scream of "re-Russification." Nationality here is visibly a psychic process, and a reversible one (Lou performed exactly the same operation with narcissism in other texts). The reader sees Salomé crossing from Russia into Europe as though undergoing a metamorphosis, and returning again enriched. In her memoirs Salomé paraphrased Russian history in similarly dynamic terms: After Russia converted to Christianity, the religion was transformed by a process of Russification; later, Orthodoxy was de-Russified by Patriarch Nikon; and the resultant schism was an attempt to Russify Orthodoxy once more.[73]

Eros was in constant interaction with nationality in Salomé's life and texts. The heroine of her novella *Fenitschka* asserts that she could never have a non-Russian lover: "Not a Russian? No, I could not imagine that. My whole life rests on his being a Russian, my compatriot, my brother, a piece of my own world."[74] But Lou herself, as far as we know, never had a Russian lover. In general, all the men in her life, beginning with Gillot and ending with Freud, strove to "de-Russify" her; but none was able to do so. In her memoirs, Lou indicted them all in condemning Gillot, whom she contrasted with her "Russian," or more accurately "Russified," father. In the complex and often cruel game that Salomé played with Western men— a game on behalf of another world, at once open and inaccessible—she laid down both of her trump cards, femininity and Russianness. She forced her partners, and her readers after them, to uncover two dimensions of her life at once, two aspects of the "other": gender and nationality.

Salomé's heroine, saddled with the demonstrably Russian name Fenitschka, strolls through St. Petersburg with a random friend (with the demonstrably German name Max Werner). They spot the popular illustrations to Lermontov's *Demon* in a shop window. The pictures show the entire course of history: male seduction, mutual caresses, the death of a woman. "You can find those pictures here in every house," Fenitschka says. Looking at them, Fenitschka translates *Demon* into German out loud, as perhaps Salomé did during her strolls with Nietzsche. "Very appropriate pictures for a young girl," Werner quips. "Did that not make you imagine love to be something very demonic? Fight with an angel, hellish delights—Bengal lights—end of the world." But Fenitschka protests. Love is something "totally different."[75] Not the end of the world, but the opposite state, like recollections of childhood, narcissistic pleasure, returning home; and if love ends in death, then it is in the death of the male partner. Salomé chose her own demons in order to defeat them on the field of battle—in the West, in rationality, and in sex—escaping from them by retreating into her femininity and mysticism, and to Russia when the opportunity presented itself.

In analyzing the sources of Rilke's creative energy, Salomé found a ready analogy in her own experience of returning to Russia: "I felt a simple joy . . . , a happy replenishment I had been denied by my early emigration. . . . For you the creative breakthrough . . . was also a matter of something your whole being had been profoundly anticipating from the very beginning," she wrote to Rilke.[76] This sort of feeling is unlikely to be founded in historical reality and thus the subject is prepared to ignore or discount any change. As Fenitschka said of Russia in 1898: "I have been away for so long. But now I feel at home again, in all the old and familiar surroundings. Russia has an enormous advantage in this respect, because you can be quite sure here that everything is precisely where it was."[77] More interesting yet is that we find the same idea in Salomé's memoirs, written in 1932: "Whenever I returned home . . . , reaching the Russian border . . . [I felt] an unforgettable feeling of happiness. . . . I only know that it remained substantially unchanged through the wonderful years in which . . . I was so preoccupied with other matters, so absorbed by quite un-Russian intellectual endeavors."[78] Andreas-Salomé's worship of the Russian soul and Russian revolutionaries never ceased; but these "wonderful years" had nevertheless so changed the face of Russia that even she was forced to come to terms with the most difficult of problems, that of bringing together the fairy-tale Russian past with the worrisome Russian present.

In Lou's theory, the highest expression of narcissism was the idea of God, and the key to the history of narcissistic Russia was the uniqueness of the nation's religious life. Bolshevik Russia could only be understood as the re-

sult of this fundamental uniqueness of the Russian soul, closer simultane-
ously to God and the flesh, and "less prone to dualism," than the soul of
Western man. A Russian must overcome the opposites of daily life in his
bosom; Russian heaven was less abstract than Western heavens, while
Russian earth was less burdened with a feeling of guilt.[79] Salomé recalled
the Russian schism and sects, following the 1926 release of a book by
Freud's Munich publisher, René Fueloep-Miller, *The Mind and Face of
Bolshevism*.[80] The author, who had just visited Soviet Russia, described
what was happening there as the victory of a militaristic, apocalyptic sect,
using this insight as the framework for a full-length book and illustrating it
with a variety of eloquent, semi-factual, semi-fanciful observations.
Salomé, however, altered the author's assessment significantly in her own
gloss: The victory of the irrational that to Fueloep-Miller and Freud was a
sign of catastrophe seemed to her a rebirth or emancipation, the fulfillment
of a positive, narcissistic regression on a universal scale.

Salomé's psychoanalytic background is perceptible only in the particular
attention she gave to the politics of sex: "It seems to me that all this influenced sexual love in Russia as well, releasing to a certain extent the extremes of tension which in Western Europe had developed over almost a
thousand years."[81] Salomé was referring here to Russian sectarians:
skoptsy, with their "ritual castration," *khlysty* with their "sexual mysteries," and Rasputin with his "monstrous peculiarity."[82] Although the existence of these phenomena might be taken to indicate that sexual tension in
Russia had attained a level unheard of in Europe, Andreas-Salomé, driven
by her childhood populism or by the nationalism that served her so well in
her adult years, came to a different conclusion: "[I]n Russian Bolshevism
we see blood and passion flow into the dry, cold theories inherited from the
West, until it . . . appears . . . as the precondition for a new dawn, to which
Russia invites the universe in terms beyond nation and rationality."[83] Lou
perceived this "new dawn" of civilization, the nightmare of so many brave
men, without fear or condemnation: The predicted end of Europe was not
the end of the world, but a new, fascinating experiment, a source of pleasure and art; and she wrote of this in the same triumphant intonation that
she employed in relating the sexual side of love to her timid readers—just
as a therapist might describe orgasm to a patient who fears it.

Gratitude

Lou worked extensively as a psychoanalyst, although she, like many of
Freud's closest disciples, never underwent analysis herself. We know that
Freud tried to convince her to take on fewer patients, saying that ten to
eleven hours of analysis in a single day was too many. Evidently, she often
fulfilled important requests from Freud, as well. She spent half a year in

Königsberg with local psychiatrists and their patients. One of the doctors in Königsberg recalled:

> I confess that the way Lou analyzed me left a deep impression on me and has been a great help to me all my life. . . . For the rest, I had the impression that Lou was more interested in the psychological than in the medical aspects of psychoanalysis. And after all: every life is a novel. For a writer, such as Lou was originally, nothing can be more interesting than to descend into the lives of others. . . . I suppose that Lou turned to psychoanalysis because it enabled her to penetrate into the deepest secrets of life in her fellow men. . . . She had a very quiet way of speaking and a great gift of inspiring confidence. I am still a little surprised today how much I told her then. But I had always the feeling that she not only understood everything but forgave everything. I have never again experienced such a feeling of conciliatory kindness, or if you like, compassion, as I did with her. We usually sat opposite each other in semi-darkness. Mostly I talked and Lou listened. She was a great listener. But sometimes she would tell me stories of her life.[84]

Lou's dedication to psychoanalysis did not prevent her late blossoming in matters of the heart. From 1911 to 1913, besides her romance with Tausk, she also had a romantic relationship with Swedish psychoanalyst Paul Bjerre, who introduced her to the psychoanalytic world, and, it seems, with another of Freud's young followers, Emil von Gebsattel. Besides this, she kept up constant correspondence with Rilke and saw him occasionally. We can hear the recollections of his girlfriend, a young artist by the name of Loulou Albert-Lazard, who was living with Rilke in Munich when they were visited by Lou Andreas-Salomé and Baron von Gebsattel: "From the moment of her arrival our days were filled with her programmes. In the morning a spiritualist seance, in the afternoon historians or astronomers. . . . Taken separately, each of these gatherings might have been interesting, but this mad pot-pourri made me dizzy."[85] Loulou perceived Lou as a "Russian woman," noting that "despite a strong sensuality, she seemed somewhat too exclusively cerebral."[86] She was surprised that Rilke, who was so different from Lou, could stand her friendship for so long.

Freud's friendship with Andreas-Salomé lasted twenty-five years. They left behind over two hundred letters, packed with mutual intellectual interest and solid amity. Mutual admiration and an equal degree of mutual gratitude are the most common motifs in their correspondence. The letters are completely devoid of the passionate and sometimes persnickety egocentrism that characterized Freud's correspondence with his male students. On the contrary, Freud particularly emphasized and valued Lou's originality, which he referred to as her "synthesis," a word that attained even greater significance in the context of Freud's favorite word, "analysis," its exact opposite.

Every time I read your letters of appraisal, I am amazed at your talent to go beyond what has been said. Naturally I do not always agree with you. I so rarely feel the need for synthesis. The unity of this world seems to me so self-evident as not to need evidence. What interests me is the separation and breaking up into its component parts of what would otherwise revert to an inchoate mass. . . . In short, I am of course an analyst, and believe that synthesis offers no obstacles once analysis has been achieved.[87]

With the passing of years, Freud came to recognize the justification and mutual necessity of both orientations:

I am delighted to observe that nothing has altered in our respective ways of approaching a theme, whatever it may be. I strike up a—mostly very simple—melody; you supply the higher octaves for it; I separate the one from the other, and you blend what has been separated into a higher unity; I silently accept the limits imposed by our subjectivity, whereas you draw express attention to them. Generally speaking we have understood each other and are at one in our opinions. Only, I tend to exclude all opinions except one, whereas you tend to include all opinions together.[88]

Strangely enough, Freud's amicable comparison promised fulfillment of Lou's longtime hope for cooperation between the two inherently opposite types of spirituality, Jewish and Russian.

Exchange of political news was not characteristic of the correspondence between Andreas-Salomé and Freud, concentrated as it was on psychoanalysis and psychoanalysts. But in July 1917, Lou wrote to Freud of the "deep solicitude" she felt on hearing of the events in Russia. She was deeply mired in these concerns, notwithstanding the "glorious early summer for which we have waited so long."[89] Contrary to her usual practice, Lou did not reveal the nature of her worries, but her letter exudes unease. Evidently, the Russian revolution had deprived her of her fortune, and from the 1920s on, psychoanalysis and her books were her only source of income. It is well known that Freud gave her financial assistance several times, something he rarely did for his needy disciples.

But despite the approach of old age and the tragic events in her homeland, Lou was happy. The joy of psychoanalysis was the main theme of her book *Gratitude to Freud*.[90] No other relationship, she wrote, can come close in quality to that between analyst and patient; nothing else provides such deep understanding of humanity and so convincingly asserts the dignity of the individual. Freud appreciated the work, although he was unable to make Lou change the title to the more impersonal *Gratitude to Psychoanalysis*.

Lou spent the last years of her life in solitude. Elisabeth Förster-Nietzsche, who to the very end never forgot her, set the Nazis on her, accusing her of perverting Nietzsche's ideas and alleging that she was "a Finnish

Jewess." In light of the barbaric cult the Nazis had made of Nietzsche and the hatred they bore toward psychoanalysis, which they called a "Jewish science," this presented a real danger to Lou, who nonetheless remained at home in Göttingen. She tried to ignore the monstrous changes taking place in Europe before her very eyes. A colleague who visited her on the eve of her seventieth birthday told of how she "conducted a psychoanalytic practice very quietly in Göttingen and lived the mysterious life of a Sibyl of our own intellectual world."[91] To the last hour she was surrounded by friends, a group that included her patients, students, and suitors.

She died February 5, 1937. Her last words were: "Actually I've spent my whole life working—working hard, and *only* working. . . . What for?"[92]

2

Russian Modernist Culture: Between Oedipus and Dionysus

The Science of Daily Existence

Daily life had always been problematic for marginal groups; but as the nineteenth century gave way to the twentieth, doubts began to move the imagination of entire societies. The deepest foundations of life began to shift, as it appeared to many that basic human notions of love and death, reality, and the spirit could no longer be taken for granted. "There are too many unknown forces at play within each of us," Alexander Blok wrote in 1913. Mankind would get control of these forces someday, but "for now, we live in the unknown."[1] The traditional regulators of daily existence, such as religion, morality, and law, were no longer capable of performing their previous functions; the time had come for a practical application of the sciences and humanities, to replace the norms that had disappeared. Such diverse disciplines as political economy, social psychology, psychotherapy, psychoanalysis, education, and eugenics all began to emerge at this time, in competition with one another for the legitimacy that in nineteenth-century culture had been the exclusive domain of millennia-old ideas.

During times of such rapid and fundamental social change, natural and obvious manifestations of human nature begin to seem of secondary importance and to conceal a deeper, more significant reality. Hence, the main goal of scientists, philosophers, and other intellectuals, more urgent than ever at times like these, is to decipher the reality that lurks behind daily existence and remains beyond the reach of ordinary man even though his happiness and health depend wholly on his grasp of this inner truth. Different thinkers had different opinions about the nature of this underlying reality, about the ways in which it affected daily life, and about how it could be brought out into the open. However, the idea of a second, hidden reality at the core of all human affairs was present in every prominent or popular intellectual system at the beginning of this century. Thus, the efforts of such divergent figures as Freud, Heidegger, Vyacheslav Ivanov, and Rudolf

Steiner were bound together by a common creative impulse—to decipher the second reality and thus improve daily life—even though they would have agreed on little else.

This era, now commonly referred to as the age of modernism, began differently in different countries and in different arenas of human activity. In nineteenth-century Russia it was foreshadowed by the popularity of three European thinkers: Hegel, whose philosophy exerted a decisive influence on the Russian intelligentsia of the middle of the century; Schopenhauer, who attracted the sympathies of the two subsequent generations of populists; and Marx. At the turn of the twentieth century, yet another German philosopher became the symbol of the new era. "Nietzsche was virtually a god for the young people of that decade," Alexander Benois wrote. "That winter, everyone was reading *Thus Spoke Zarathustra*," Liubov' Mendeleeva-Blok recalled of 1901.[2] "Friedrich Nietzsche, the destroyer of idols, stood at the door of the new century," wrote another contemporary. "The recently melancholy Decadents were transformed into admirers of Nietzsche, anarchists, revolutionaries of the spirit."[3] The philosophers and practitioners of modernism were forced to work in Nietzsche's shadow, whether they were aware of it or not; for Nietzsche was the first to articulate a new question facing mankind, and the first to suggest an answer: Man was moved by something unconscious inside him, something bigger and stronger than he. The individual and collective unconscious would replace an outmoded God in the modern world. Only a superman would be able to control this omnipotent force.

Merely conceptualizing the *Übermensch* was not enough; he had to be produced as well. The new man could be created by altering the nature of today's human beings. The philosophy, sociology, and psychology of modernism therefore became practical disciplines, aspiring to influence human life in the most direct sense. From this beginning sprang new social theories that would later inspire not only revolutions but also a new art form—the art of living. Psychoanalysis likewise grew out of this same general cultural foundation, while attempting to surpass it. "Psychology is once more the path to the fundamental problems," wrote Nietzsche.[4]

The eminent scions of the Russian literary tradition, so renowned for its "psychological nature," had always suspected psychology of harboring just such an overweening ambition. As Pushkin's Mephistopheles mockingly declaimed, "I am a psychologist. Now there's a science." Dostoevsky wrote: "I am called a *psychologist*. It is *not true*, I am merely a realist."[5] Meanwhile, his character Stavrogin (in *The Possessed*) says pointedly, "I can't stand spies and psychologists." Bakhtin wrote of Dostoevsky that "in psychology he saw a degrading *materialization* of the human soul."[6] Before relating his heroine's first menstrual cycle in *Liuvers's Childhood*, Boris Pasternak described psychology as the most ostentatious and entertaining of human prejudices. Psychology is designed, he wrote, to distract people's tasteless curiosity away from life so that life can unfold as it pleases. Vyacheslav Ivanov was the first figure in mainstream Russian literature to employ psychological terminology freely and willingly, and he interpreted Pushkin's phrase as indicating his recognition of the uses of psychology, an "ambiguous and dangerous discipline," through Mephistopheles, who was perceptive enough to see its worth.[7]

According to Vasily Rozanov, however, the quality inherent in Russians and their culture was not psychology but "psychologicality"—that is, the natural quality rather than a vague speculation about it. It was a self-evident, natural phenomenon, requiring no substantiation: "'Too little sunshine' is all there is to the explanation of Russian history. 'The nights are so terribly long' is the explanation for Russian psychologicality." Rozanov italicized the word "psychologicality" (*psikhologichnost'*) and subsequently provided a definition: "when a thought is hammered deep into the human soul." The "psychologicality" of the soul was Rozanov's primary object: He had no desire to influence mentality, which did not concern him, or to alter others' convictions; for, he confessed, his own had changed more times than he could count. "My influence would lie in the expansion of the soul . . . So that the soul might become more tender, so that it might have more ear, more nostrils."[8]

In the dominant discourse of the time, man was portrayed as a malleable raw material; he had no inherent properties. He was submerged in culture and formed under the purposive impact of environment, society, and science. As intellectuals' disappointment mounted concerning the possibility that life could be improved, they inevitably focused increasing attention on children. Everything could begin anew through children, who were unencumbered by life's accretions and responsive to new methods. The "science of children," in its philosophical, practical, mythological, and scientific incarnations, hovered near the center of Russian society's aspirations throughout the modernist period, when "pedagogy" first emerged as an ideology and a social science. It would reach its apogee much later, in the heightened transformational enthusiasm of the Soviet period, in the guise of "pedology" (see chapter 8). The underpinnings of this latter form of intellectual pedophilia, however, were laid long before the Soviet era: "Children—those absurd, willful creatures, those semi-conscious passivities . . . children are our grotesques, just as they are sketches of our creation. Such is the world in which our Modernism finds it so pleasant to sing and prattle," wrote the renowned poet (and school principal) Innokenty Annensky in 1909.[9]

Moonlight People

Russian modernist texts abound in direct and indirect quotations from Nietzsche. At the same time, one could easily search in vain for similar references to Freud in the works of such major Russian thinkers of the early

1900s as Vyacheslav Ivanov, Vasily Rozanov, and Andrei Bely. However, these and other philosophers and writers of Russia's Silver Age sought answers to the same questions as Freud; and like Freud, they exposed only one facet of the universal idea of modernism. The most important issue for them was to differentiate between the levels of existence—the superficial and the authentic, the conscious and the unconscious, the trivial and the profound. The name they gave to their movement, symbolism, reflected the very essence of this delineation. Symbolism was not a codified artistic method or philosophical system. Members of the movement liked to say that it was, rather, a particular way of life. In creating their own myths, from Vladimir Solovyov's Sophia to Vyacheslav Ivanov's Dionysus, from Blok's Beautiful Lady to Sologub's ironic *Nedotykomka*, the symbolists hoped to reveal another reality secreted beneath the flotsam of familiar existence. Such intentions were not all that different from the strategic goals laid out by Freud and Jung; at the same time, the Russians completely lacked the constructive drive that prodded European psychoanalysts to spend ten hours a day analyzing symbols drawn from other people's consciousnesses.

Symbolists and psychoanalysts likewise shared an avid interest in sexuality. One modern-day researcher of Vyacheslav Ivanov has claimed that Ivanov sexualized Nietzsche.[10] Berdyaev said the same of Merezhkovsky: "Like many Russians of his time, he linked Nietzschean ideas to orgiastic sexuality." Even Pavel Florensky's theology was essentially erotic, according to Berdyaev, who wrote that in Florensky's work "Platonic ideas acquired a semi-sexual character."[11]

Sex as intellectual subject matter was introduced to the general Russian public by Vasily Rozanov. Rozanov quoted at length from shocking case studies that he had found in popular German psychiatric texts on sexual psychopathology, at the same time deeming it appropriate to expose his own erotic fantasies, which were more than a little racy, but which, due to his literary artistry, astonished rather than aroused his readers. In 1916, Rozanov wrote with pride that the effect of intellectual change during the previous two or three decades had been essentially positive, since many people had begun "getting at the root of things." In Rozanov's peculiar definition, this meant that "people have acquired an interest in their own gender, in their own personal gender."[12]

A man of unusual intuition, Rozanov sensed far more than he could ever know for sure, and his literary talent and easy writing style enabled him to translate nearly unintelligible revelations into a series of successful books. "The body, the ordinary human body, is the most irrational thing in the world," he wrote in 1899.[13] One of his main themes, paralleling Freud, involved the radical expansion of the concept of "gender" (in Russian, *pol*— Rozanov never used the words *seks* and *seksual'nost'*) and the reduction of numerous other aspects of life to gender in this all-embracing sense. For Rozanov, man was "merely a transformation of gender," a creature "that passionately breathes gender and only gender: in battle, in the desert, in self-imposed isolation and asceticism, in trade."[14] Gender was both flesh and spirit, a source of both holiness and sin. "The connection between gender and God was greater than the connection between the mind and God, stronger even than the connection between conscience and God." Only gender was essential to human nature: "Even when we do something or think of something beyond gender, when we have a desire or intend to do something outside of gender, for spiritual reasons, even when we contemplate something *anti*-gender, it is still *gender*-related, only wrapped up and disguised in such a way that it is hard to recognize its face," Rozanov wrote in *Moonlight People: The Metaphysics of Christianity*.[15]

At the same time, the masculine and feminine essences need not be mutually exclusive; they could coexist in each individual in different proportions. Rozanov was quick to inform his readers that women found him unappealing, and that apart from their "mystique," women generally appealed to him only "from the shoulders up."[16] Sexuality, for Rozanov, did not lead people into debauchery, as for Tolstoy; nor into incest, as for Freud; nor did it lead to the mystical union of everything in existence, as for Solovyov. By Rozanov's account, "gender" simply drew people into normal domestic life; but for Rozanov, ironically, marital life was a problem. He had married Dostoevsky's ex-lover, who made him suffer as least as much as she had Dostoevsky; but the Orthodox church would not permit Rozanov to divorce her and remarry. He nonetheless chose to live with another woman, with whom he passed many happy years in common-law union.

According to Rozanov, only in marriage did gender attain its normal, pure, and "most aristocratic" form. People excluded from family life, such as Russian Orthodox monks and nuns, provoked his suspicion: Was their "gender" somehow impaired? In his veneration of the family, Rozanov echoed Orthodox tradition, which unlike Catholicism allows priests to marry; for him, traditional Christian asceticism was anathema. He asserted that Christianity should be reformed in order to embrace all of gender's great power as did the ancient religions of Egypt and Israel.

This revelation of gender's importance to the family might have found its natural outlet in a handbook on family life; but fortunately, Rozanov chose a different path. As happened with Freud in a totally different context, Rozanov felt compelled to explain why his native culture was so hostile toward gender (sexuality), even in marital relations—the better to understand why it was so resistant to his ideas. In seeking an explanation, Rozanov made a contribution of considerable significance, throwing open a subject previously neglected in Russian culture and one that has been problematic for cultures generally.

Dissatisfied with his predecessors' treatment of gender in the fields of philosophy (Solovyov's *The Meaning of Love,* with its idea of bisexuality, was unacceptable to Rozanov) and psychology (he used Otto Weininger's *Sex and Character* extensively but considered its author a "sodomite" and opposed his sudden popularity in Russia), Rozanov launched straight into the most complex area, perversion. He began with an overview of clinical cases of homosexuality, then proceeded with an analysis of the "layers of sodomy" in Tolstoy, Dostoevsky, the Bible, the Talmud, and Russian Orthodoxy.

According to Rozanov, celibacy was unnatural, and those who diverged from their masculine or feminine predestination, whether monks or hypocrites, were doing more than suppressing their sexuality; they were acting on an inborn perversion. That is, the impulse behind the sexual taboo was sexual perversion, albeit perhaps latent. Thus, Chernyshevsky's idea of free marriage as articulated in the novel *What Is to Be Done?* was "mental homosexuality" in Rozanov's view, because it recommended that husbands resign themselves to their wives' "friendship."

Rozanov's "sodomites," "moonlight people," and "effeminates" were all homosexuals under various labels (the unstable terminology of Rozanov's time may partially explain why his ideas about homosexuality have been so thoroughly neglected). To Rozanov, "sodomites" were a different class of people: "The sodomite's eyes are different! The way he shakes hands is different! His smile is completely different!" Sodomites, wasting no energy on sexual activity, had created the lion's share of human culture, Rozanov was certain. Since sexually normal ("sunlight") people generally channeled their strength into family life, the highest of cultural achievements were permeated by a vein of sodomy—a homosexual, antisexual, antifamily spirit. Rozanov illustrated this point with a variety of examples: Plato, Raphael, Tolstoy, and even Christ. Thus, "sodomy gives rise to the idea that copulation is a sin."

Rozanov considered sodomites conservative and hostile to sexuality: A sodomite was just as repulsed by normal marriage and childbirth as was a normal person by homosexual acts. Therefore, Rozanov concluded, "moonlight" and "sunlight" people could never be reconciled. He had no doubt that throughout human history countless anti-sexual ideas like abstention, asceticism, and gender equality were all articulated by sodomites. To today's reader, some of Rozanov's speculations might seem perceptive, others extremely naive (such as, for instance, his recommendation that newlyweds make love once a week).[17]

In Russian literary criticism, Rozanov sometimes has been compared to Freud. Andrei Sinyavsky, however, contrasted the two.[18] As opposed to Freud, who was an atheist, Rozanov attributed paramount significance to sex as a signpost in life, something that might be identified with God; thus, Rozanov deified sex, whereas Freud sexualized religion. Sinyavsky concluded from this that Rozanov was Freud's antithesis insofar as his attitudes toward sex and God were concerned. Although this assertion has some merit, it oversimplifies the situation; Rozanov's interpretation of the relationship between sex and culture was indeed quite close to Freud's. Both men believed that sex and culture were inversely correlated and that this relationship was key to human endeavor: The greater a person's self-realization in sex, the less energy he or she would have to pursue other aspirations; conversely, cultural heroes throughout the ages had had a peculiar, often underdeveloped sexual drive. Freud wrote that Leonardo da Vinci was a man "whose sexual need and activity were exceptionally reduced, as if a higher aspiration had raised him above the common animal need of mankind."[19]

Freud considered such people neurotics, while Rozanov called them sodomites. Freud would not have agreed with Rozanov that homosexuality was a basic means of cultural sublimation, although in certain cases, such as his analyses of Leonardo and Dostoevsky, he attributed great significance to this factor.[20] Rozanov, in turn, was far removed from the sophisticated dynamic models that Freud used to describe the human mind and behavior. The idea that sexual taboos could have positive, culture-forming significance, a concept vitally important to the austere and introverted Freud, was alien to Rozanov, as is clear from the sensationalist, confessional style of his writings on the subject, which practically ooze with primordial sexuality.

Despite these and other differences between the ideas of Rozanov and Freud, their similarity was obvious to those of their contemporaries who read works by both. Mikhail Gershenzon expressed his gratitude for a copy of *Moonlight People* that Rozanov had sent him, writing: "Your intuition has led you in the same direction that science is headed in right now, though your vision is far clearer. You must be aware of the theories put forth by Prof. Freud and his colleagues."[21] Leon Trotsky, who did not hold Rozanov in terribly high regard, also compared him to Freud; and in the early 1920s, Roza Averbukh presented her analysis of Rozanov's work at a meeting of the Psychoanalytic Society of Kazan University. However, as far as we know, Rozanov himself was not familiar with Freud's theories, nor did he ever mention psychoanalysis.

D. H. Lawrence, who recognized Rozanov as his forerunner, offered this unique interpretation: "Tolstoy would be absolutely amazed if he could come back and see Russia of to-day. I believe Rozanov would feel no surprise. He knew the inevitability of it."[22] In one of his more far-fetched essays, Rozanov had earnestly propounded a system by which sex would be absolutely mandatory, something he perceived as beneficial and desirable:

A passer-by stops before an attractive woman and tells her, "Hi, I'm with you." She stands up and enters her home without looking at him. She becomes his wife for the evening. Certain days of the week, month, and year are set aside for this sort of thing. This order should be established for all "free women (those without husbands, who are not 'moonlight people')."[23]

This very idea would later become the subject of the anti-utopian night-mares of Zamyatin, Orwell, and Huxley.

Alchemy of the Soul

Life in the real world, meanwhile, continued in its own equally unique way. As Vladislav Khodasevich recalled: "We were living in a state of frenetic tension, aggravation, and fever. In the end, everyone got tangled up in a net of love and hate, both personal and literary. . . . All you had to do to join the order (in a way, symbolism was an order) was to burn incessantly. It didn't matter what possessed you, as long as it possessed you completely."[24] The "order" of symbolists, infused as it was with Dionysian suffering and mystical spiritualism—fashionable trends in Europe at the time—was also reminiscent of the Russian sect of flagellants (*khlysty*), with their collective eroticism and meditative practice, and their radical dreams of a "new man" who would inherit the future.

In one of Andrei Bely's early articles ("On Theurgy"), considered one of the manifestos of Russian symbolism, Bely proceeded from "divine inspiration" in the vein of Vladimir Solovyov's moral philosophy to a practical approach to the problem of the new man: In order to transform the world, man must be reborn spiritually, psychologically, and physiologically. Solovyov believed that the world would be transformed only in its final hours; Bely, like many of his contemporaries, was not content to wait.[25]

Shortly after his article was published, Bely saw a chance to test his plan to bring art to life. He tried to save one of the multitude of "young ladies of modernism—thin, pale, fragile, mysterious, languorous"—who appeared out of nowhere to fill the auditoriums of the Literary Artistic Circle (the chairman of which was a psychiatrist) and the symbolists' salon-communes. The object of Bely's "theurgic" aspirations was Nina Petrovskaya, wife of the editor-in-chief of the Grif publishing house. "She was completely at loose ends, sickly, tormented by an unhappy life, and clearly psychopathic. . . . [She] would invest herself in the words she heard around her nearly to the point of madness."[26]

Bely wrote out special instructions for Petrovskaya, entitling them "Stages of Development in Normal Spiritual Life." Delighted, she accepted him as her guru. Her obsessive thoughts of suicide and morphine began steadily to recede. Suddenly, catastrophe struck—"heavenly love went up in the flames of earthly love." Bely was completely unprepared for this development, which at the time had been noted only in the field of psychoanalysis. He had imagined himself in the role of Orpheus leading Eurydice out of hell, and what ensued felt to him like a "fall from grace, a betrayal of my calling." Mochulsky wrote that there were passion, repentance, sin, and torture on both sides. Then another would-be therapist entered the fray: Bely's friend and enemy Valery Briusov, who at that time was engaged in occultism and practicing black magic.[27] This ménage à trois continued for about a year. In spring 1905, Nina attempted to shoot Briusov at a public lecture delivered by Bely (a similar episode appears in Boris Pasternak's *Doctor Zhivago*). Her Browning misfired.[28]

In 1911, Petrovskaya left for Italy to seek medical treatment. There she underwent hypnosis, writing to Briusov that her treatment was "not psychotherapy, but a theurgical act."[29] The goals of "theurgy," as understood in their circle, were closely related to the goals of psychotherapy. Freud, evidently, knew of the prevalence of such views in Russia. In 1909, he wrote to Jung that his Russian colleagues wanted to change the world much more quickly than was possible using psychoanalysis.[30] Twenty years later, an enthusiastic Russian reviewer still interpreted Jung as saying that "psychology is truly an alchemy of the soul which teaches us how to transform base, subconscious affects into precious metals, genuine diamonds of the spirit."[31]

Theurgy was conceived of as a momentary, mystical event that could only be brought about by the spiritual efforts of rare individuals. Such an act, however, could irrevocably change human nature. The focus of this dream was the fundamental transformation of each person and of society as a whole. The daydreaming symbolists, like their predecessor Nietzsche, did not give much thought to the mechanisms that would bring about such a mass transformation of men, nor did they conceive of the consequences; but they knew they could not do without psychology. Much later the characters of *The Master and Margarita* found their way to mystical "transfiguration" only after a stint in a psychiatric ward. However, Bulgakov's intent was to parody rather than propagate these ideas,[32] so he invested his "theurgy" in a completely inappropriate host, a typical *homo sovieticus*. Bulgakov's novella *A Dog's Heart* likewise takes the motif of transformation to the level of total absurdity.

In 1928, summarizing the history of symbolism from the dawn of its creation to cooperation between the movement's leaders and the Bolshevik ministry of education (Narkompros), Bely bitterly recalled the "terrifying profanation of the symbolists' intimate experience" and the "degradation of this experience into mysticism and promiscuity, elements introduced by a decadent and corrupt society into the theme of commonality and mystery." Bely lamented that the mystery had been transformed into "an ideological mystification on a theatrical stage," and the communal life reduced to the casual swapping of sexual partners.[33]

Even in view of their involvement with Narkompros, the symbolists can hardly be held responsible for the distorted way in which Nietzsche's dream of a "new man" metamorphosed into the words and deeds of the Marxist god-seekers, and later, into the thinking of Bolsheviks such as Lunacharsky, Bukharin, Yenchman, and others.

The Religion of Dionysus

Russian symbolism was as far as it could be from Freud's orderly scholarly community, built according to the art of scientific organization. Vyacheslav Ivanov, one of the most popular poets and philosophers of the time, made an attempt to introduce a kind of organization into the symbolist movement after he returned to Russia in 1904 from a term of study in Berlin and Paris. Andrei Bely trumpeted the entry of "an outstanding ideologue like Vyacheslav Ivanov" into the world of modernism, pronouncing it a crucial moment in the history of Russian symbolism. Bely regretted, however, that Ivanov had offered up for publication in the popular media material far too elusive and uncontrollable for consumption in such a vulgarized form. Ivanov had gone so far as to rework Nietzsche in order to reduce his obscure profundities to a generally accessible common denominator. From this point of view, Ivanov had "polluted the pure air of the symbolic environment itself." Most of all, Bely resented Ivanov's efforts to consolidate the divergent currents in modernism. By "welding together decadents, neorealists, symbolists, and idealists," Ivanov had clarified and simplified the ideology of symbolism to the point where it seemed accessible to all kinds of "seekers." In his pursuit of a universal myth, Ivanov had "equated Christ with Dionysus, St. Mary with any woman giving birth, the virgin with the maenad, love with eroticism, Plato with Greek love, theurgy with philology, and Vladimir Solovyov with Rozanov."[34]

Ivanov's contemporaries and successors described his contribution in mutually contradictory terms: To Bely, it was "immense, in a good and bad sense"; to Averintsev, "more and more dubious."[35] Anna Akhmatova, in turn, called Vyacheslav Ivanov a great mystifier, a new Count Saint-Germain, and eagerly rehashed stale gossip about him.[36]

After 1905, Vyacheslav Ivanov's apartment in the tower of a building on Tavricheskaya street in St. Petersburg became the construction site for a new myth, one well suited to modern circumstances, as they used to say in those days. An original interpretation of Nietzsche's philosophy served as the foundation on which Ivanov built his syncretic symbolism. It was not the *Übermensch* that Ivanov borrowed from Nietzsche, but Dionysus, dying and resurrected for eternity; the god of wine, the underworld, orgies, and religious ecstasy.

Ivanov described his ideal as the "eros of the impossible." A great many stories have wafted down to us of the erotic experiments sponsored by two St. Petersburg couples: Ivanov and his wife, poetess Lydia Zinovieva-Annibal; and by Dmitry Merezhkovsky and his wife, writer Zinaida Hippius. Many *intelligenty* of the St. Petersburg elite took part in both groups. It is hard to say just how far these experiments went. Homosexuals played a significant role in Ivanov's salon, among them Mikhail Kuzmin, who left detailed descriptions of their activities in his diaries. Berdyaev, who always spoke highly of Ivanov, claimed that the groups had engaged in nothing more shocking than circle dances. "Eroticism always contained a shade of idealism for us," he wrote, adding that Ivanov's primary interest was to win people over, and that in this he excelled. "His penetrating glance had an irresistible effect on many, especially on women."[37]

Although the sexual revolution arrived later in Russia than elsewhere in Europe, the country had its own revolutionary precursor in the *khlysty*, a sect that combined assiduous piety with sexual promiscuity. Interest in the *khlysty* was particularly high among Russians at the beginning of the century. Journalists and historians later described Rasputin as a *khlyst*. Andrei Bely wrote his novel *The Silver Dove* about a similar sect. Berdyaev frequented pubs in order to converse with sect members. In 1908, Blok and Remizov attended a *khlyst* "conference," after which Blok wrote to his mother, with some embarrassment: "We went to the sectarians and spent a few good hours there. It will not be the last time. It is kind of hard to write about it."[38] At one point Ivanov himself produced a "sectarian madonna," a young and beautiful peasant girl whom he brought to his lectures. When asked if she could understand the lecture, which contained a good deal of technical vocabulary, she said: "Course I do! The names and words are different, but the truth is the same."[39]

Ivanov associated the essence of his new religion with the figure of Dionysus, borrowed from Nietzsche. He liked to repeat that while for Nietzsche, Dionysianism was merely an aesthetic phenomenon, he himself saw it as a religious phenomenon; and he rebuked his predecessor for not believing in the god he had created. Ivanov was literal and consistent in achieving his goal as the mouthpiece and propagator of the new religion of Dionysus, the god who suffers and is reborn. He employed all the means he had at his disposal as the leader of a movement, and as a philosopher and poet. One participant in Ivanov's Wednesday gatherings said: "[He] never provoked quarrels or argued vigorously; he always sought ways of bringing different people and different tendencies together. He had a zeal for articulating new platforms."[40] All kinds of people met in Ivanov's tower: poets and revolutionaries, Nietzscheans and Marxists, god-seekers and god-makers. After the Bolshevik revolution, they all went their separate ways; some became government ministers, or "people's commissars," like Lunacharsky; others, like Berdyaev, found fame in emigration; still others, like Khlebnikov and Blok, died early and did not witness the new Russian reality. But back then, on the eve of the upheaval of 1905 and immediately after, they sought their future together. In this search Ivanov aspired to the role of leader and captivator:

> I'd pluck one of my love's bright stars;
> in someone's soul I'd carve a furrow,
> and then to plant my starry seed,
> in living, virgin soil I'd burrow.[41]

This straightforward, aggressive male sexuality, this urge to achieve as much power over the soul as could be had over the body, coexists in Ivanov's work with sophisticated poetic imagery, revealing Russian modernism's quest much more clearly and consistently than many other symbolist works. Ivanov's "soul-hunting" was extremely successful: "Oh, how many frigid, empty souls were penetrated by your cold!" a disillusioned Blok later wrote. According to Nikolai Berdyaev: "A Dionysian wind was blowing across Russia. . . . Orgiastic eros was in fashion. . . . Eros clearly had the upper hand over Logos."[42]

The "religion of the suffering god" combined its own brand of erotica with a peculiar form of collectivism. "Orgy" and "conciliarism" were the most commonly used words in the new lexicon. These two unexpectedly related notions shared one common facet: the mistrust of the ego—or in other words, the refusal to accept physical and mental limits to the human self, combined with an obsessive desire to break down such barriers. "The horrifying descent into chaos summons us with a mighty call, imposing the most imperative of commands: It calls us to lose ourselves."[43] Various means were proposed to allow people to leave their own egos behind and enter other selves, to destroy the borders between themselves and to commingle. The means of exiting the self included "pre-Dionysian sexual ecstasy," "divine intoxication and orgiastic oblivion," the mystical experience of theosophy, and the Orthodox ideal of conciliarism.

These mystical ideas were more than just a projection of the individual desires of the founders of Dionysianism. Berdyaev, who for three years chaired the meetings in the tower, found Ivanov's ideas typical of the Russian intelligentsia, with its "quest for a national, orgiastic, collective and conciliatory culture."[44] This goal, according to Berdyaev, was suicidal for the Russian intelligentsia. Some time later, in his article "The Death of Russian Illusions," Berdyaev identified the Revolution with "Dionysian orgies out of some dark, peasant kingdom . . . that threaten to push Russia, along with all its values and wealth, into nothingness."[45] "Dionysus in Russia is a dangerous thing," Ivanov wrote in 1909, without further comment.[46] "Red Dionysus strolled through Moscow and sprinkled his ruddy intoxicant over the crowd," wrote Sergei Bulgakov, recalling the year 1917.[47]

Although Ivanov borrowed Dionysus from Nietzsche, he was far more critical about another famous character—Zarathustra. Nietzsche's more radical followers, such as Lunacharsky and Gorky, singled out the idea of the superman as the essence of Nietzschean philosophy, deriving from it a license for future amorality and for the total alteration of human nature; but the liberal Ivanov had no need of such excuses. His popularization of Nietzsche in Russian ended up inverting Nietzsche's original intent: Individualism was no longer viable, Ivanov wrote in 1905. Pushkin, he stated, was an individualist, but Dostoevsky's spirit was a spirit of solidarity and conciliarism. In Ivanov's interpretation, the *Übermensch* took on uncharacteristic features such as conciliarism and primitive religious communality; these qualities, combined with the dream of actually producing a new man, paved the way for collectivism, with all its beastly consequences.

"No matter what we might experience, we have nothing to say about ourselves personally," Ivanov once asserted, without any sign of regret. Individualism was blindness, according to the leader of the Silver Age, and enlightenment would lead those it touched to the triumph of conciliarism. "Let those who will not sing the song of conciliarism leave our circle, hiding their faces. They can die, but they will not be able to live apart."[48]

One of those who would later leave the circle, Osip Mandelstam, singled out this same "astonishingly penetrating image" for further comment. This image, Mandelstam wrote, "like the axiom of two parallel geometries," radiated "two broad vistas on the future." Even as early as 1909, this poet of the younger generation knew that he did not agree with the "voices singing in unison" that his teacher seemed so ready to join with nary a backward glance. Mandelstam found Ivanov's book "as charming as Zarathustra," and found the fortitude to admit to his teacher that he himself had different, "strange taste": "I love electric lights at night, . . . courteous lackeys, the quiet ascent of the elevator. . . . I love bourgeois, European comfort." Though it flew in the face of modernism, Mandelstam felt he had a natural right to his "strange taste," and he made no attempt to justify it: "I never ask myself whether it is a good thing."[49]

Did Ivanov ever remember how he had wished death on those who would not chime in with the chorus, later, when he was working in the ministry of education under Lunacharsky and preparing to leave the country? Boris Zaitsev recalled that period of Ivanov's life with irony: "It was as if his dreamy doctrines of 'conciliarism' and the end of individualism had begun to come true, . . . and now he could dream only of escaping from that very 'conciliarism.'"[50] At any rate, in 1919 Ivanov accepted intellectual responsibility for what was happening, admitting that it weighed heavily on his conscience:

> Our own, the match that lit this blaze,
> As conscience has confirmed,
> While prescience, too, proved accurate:
> Our heart will be consumed.[51]

Even as Ivanov admitted that he had foreseen that he would become the first victim of the fire "they" had set, he persisted in using the word "we," to the point of absurdity: "our heart."

Ivanov's poetics has been characterized as a "poetics of equation." According to Sergei Averintsev, Ivanov's predilection for "equating and uniting what can be neither equated nor united" led to deception and a dubious reputation.[52] In other words, Ivanov's anti-individualism went hand in hand with anti-intellectualism. Ivanov wrote: "I am no symbolist if I cannot use some elusive hint or influence to awaken in the heart of my listener some inarticulate feelings. These sentiments can be something akin to a primal reminiscence, sometimes they are like a distant, vague foreboding, while other times they are like the kind of trembling that comes on when someone familiar and well-loved draws near."[53] Ivanov also expressed this idea in verse:

> *Of borders, years, and "you" and "I"*
> *She is divinely unaware;*
> *She draws unfiltered nectar from the midst of life,*
> *And she remembers not a soul,*
> *In her unity "You" and "I" mean nothing.*[54]

"She" was a nymph, dryad, or maenad. The borders in the conventional world were erased between "I" and "you," between personality and universality, when Apollo was equated with Dionysus, masculine with feminine, and life with death. The masculine, Oedipal essence was doomed: "The scarce solar force is insufficient in sons, Jocasta's husbands, and they die again, blind as Oedipus, that is, lacking the sun."[55] Erotic tension in this world was paradoxically linked to asexuality. Plato's idea that love could unite two incomplete parts, masculine and feminine, into a perfect twofold or asexual whole, was extremely popular in Russian culture, where it found increasingly literal expression. "In order to preserve his individuality, man restricts his desire to unite with the beyond"; but the most valuable moments occurred during that "ecstasy of contemplation when there is no frontier between us and the uncovered abyss. . . . This realm has no borders or limits. All forms are destroyed, frontiers are leveled, distorted images disappear; individuality does not exist there. . . . White foam alone covers vigorously falling waters. In the midst of this night impregnated with deep veins of gender there is no distinction of gender. . . . The chaotic sphere is the realm of bisexual, feminine-masculine Dionysus."[56] Ivanov compared the new school of poetry to a somnambulist, and it did indeed contain much that was drawn from altered states of consciousness, be they narcotic, hypnotic, or meditative.

The religion of the asexual, ever renascent god offered its own peculiar solutions to the eternal problem of love and death. In Berdyaev's overview of Russian philosophy, this theme was central; the three greatest thinkers of the epoch, Solovyov, Rozanov, and Fyodorov, likewise focused on the interaction of sexual love, the struggle against death, and the idea of rebirth. For Solovyov, the androgynous integrity of an individual was restored through love; man ceased to be a fragmented, defective creature and thus had a chance to overcome death, which was merely a result of the division of genders. Rozanov viewed childbearing as a means of conquering death, and argued against the Christian moral tradition that blessed childbearing but cursed physical love. Fyodorov, in turn, called for a universal struggle against death and a single act that would resurrect all the deceased, with the help of a brand-new science that was expected to "transform erotic energy into the energy of revivification."

Many decades after Solovyov had founded this tradition, Berdyaev brought it full circle by repeating much the same thing: "The Greeks already knew that Hades and Dionysus were one god; they felt the mystical connection between death and birth." Berdyaev sensed a "mortal anxiety . . . in the very depths of the sexual act."[57] A similar intuition later led Sabina Spielrein to her discovery of the attraction to death as the obverse of the two-sided sexual instinct (see chapter 5). Divining the common nature of love and death, Spielrein, too, found support for her ideas in cultural mythology.

Even Leo Tolstoy, the lonely opponent of Russian modernism, tackled this problem in his famous novellas *The Kreutzer Sonata* and *The Devil*, in which love leads to death and is generally indistinguishable from it, and sexual temptation is thus an attraction to death. It little mattered who the victims were; the results would be the same. Tolstoy emphasized this point by providing various endings to the story: In one version of *The Devil*, the protagonist kills his lover; in an alternate version published in the same volume, he kills himself.

A New Savior

The ancient religion of the dying and renascent god was attracting attention and adherents in a host of European cultures. The famous Scottish ethnographer James Frazer made an attempt to analyze religion by the methods of positivist science in which he interpreted all pagan and biblical narratives as derivatives of one and the same source—the cult of Dionysus. Nietzsche, too, attributed universal significance to the religion of Dionysus; and true to the spirit of German romanticism, he managed to purify it of any trace of nagging reality. He seized on Dionysus and Apollo as universal symbols of chaos and order, emotion and reason, will and tranquillity. Although in Nietzsche's interpretation Dionysus held the upper hand over Apollo, the latter was seen at least as a potential partner for dialogue.

Ivanov considered the cult of Dionysus a current indigenous to the Slavs. "[The Slavs] were the true followers of Dionysus, which is why their predestined Passions were so much like the Hellenic god's sacrificial power, as he gives himself up to be tortured and devoured until the end of time," he said ardently, in a public appearance on the eve of the October revolution.[58] The Slavs' "Germanic and Latin brothers," meanwhile, were governed by an Apollonian "concord and order, secured through strict external and internal self-limitation."

On his deathbed, Blok smashed a bust of Apollo with an iron poker. Ivanov practically never mentioned Apollo, but in his writings Dionysus was transformed into a symbol of infinite depth in which any intellectual, seeker, or sinner might find what he lacked. Dionysus became monological and all-explaining, self-begetting, and therefore, a self-sufficient whole. Dionysus solved all problems and answered all questions through his self-defining act of death and rebirth, a process that embraced and negated every concept ever invented by man to understand and explain the world: birth and death, subject and object, love and hatred.

The influence of Nietzsche's Dionysian ideas was also enormous among Austrian intellectuals at the beginning of this century; and just as in Russia, these ideas were interpreted there in both political and aesthetic terms. The interaction of the same two principles—Dionysian art and populist politics—dominated the work of such diverse Austrian modernists as composer Gustav Mahler, psychiatrist Theodor Meynert, and Social Democratic Party founder Victor Adler.[59] These admirers of Dionysus also were present in Freud's closest circle: Meinert was at one point Freud's friend and employer, and Mahler was his patient (Freud recalled that no one had ever understood him better than Mahler); and Freud viewed Victor Adler, his erstwhile friend and rival, with extraordinary respect. In sum, Dionysianism, the simplest possible vision of the world, was offered up for consumption by the most outstanding intellectuals of the day. Their contribution was to shape the near future of Germany and Russia.

The idea of Dionysus found absolutely no sympathy with Freud. Jung, however, was more responsive. In early 1910, Jung suggested to Freud that they transform psychoanalysis into a new religion centered around the dying and renascent god:

> Only the wise are ethical from sheer intellectual presumption, the rest of us need the eternal truth of myth. . . . The ethical problem of sexual freedom really is enormous and worth the sweat of all noble souls. But 2,000 years of Christianity can only be replaced by something equivalent. An ethical fraternity, with its mythical Nothing, not infused by any archaic-infantile driving force, is a pure vacuum and can never evoke in man the slightest trace of that age-old animal power which drives the migrating birds across the sea and without which no irresistible mass movement can come into being. I imagine a far finer and more comprehensive task for psychoanalysis. . . . I think we must give it time to infiltrate into people from many centers, to revivify among intellectuals a feeling for symbol and myth, ever so gently to transform Christ back into the soothsaying god of the vine, which he was, and in this way absorb those ecstatic instinctual forces of Christianity for the *one* purpose of making the cult and the sacred myth what they once were—a drunken feast of joy where man regained the

ethos and holiness of an animal. . . . A genuine and proper ethical development cannot abandon Christianity but must grow up within it, must bring to fruition its hymn of love, the agony and ecstasy over the dying and resurgent god, the mystic power of the vine, the awesome anthropology of the last Supper—only *this* ethical development can serve the vital forces of religion.[60]

The content, style, and lexicon of this document, so different from the usual sober spirit of correspondence between Jung and Freud, are akin to the ideas and words of Russian symbolists of the time. The issue in this case is not so much mutual influence as common sources. The most important of these sources must have been Nietzsche: Nearly every phrase of this letter can be correlated to his ideas. Jung was then embroiled in a crisis brought on by his relationship with his Russian patient, Sabina Spielrein (see chapter 5), and he informed Freud that he was "sitting so precariously between the Dionysian and the Apollonian."[61] The answer that came back was severe: "Dear friend, yes, in you the tempest rages, it comes to me as distant thunder."[62]

Jung and his disciples tried many times to combine Nietzschean philosophy, Frazer's ethnography, and Freudian psychoanalysis. As a matter of fact, Jung's *Psychology of the Unconscious: A Study of the Transformations and Symbolisms of the Libido* was most of all an attempt to combine Oedipus and Dionysus. It was this work that led to Freud's disappointment in Jung as a theoretician. Freud could accept no synthesis of these two principles, for he knew it would undermine the very foundations of psychoanalysis. Many years later, Jung was still framing the most recent historical experience in the same terms. In 1936, Jung asserted that Nietzsche's Dionysus was merely one of many embodiments of the mighty Wotan, the god of storm, magic, and conquest. Wotan, from his point of view, was the true god of Germany, a nation of spiritual catastrophes.[63]

Dionysus and Oedipus

Dionysus became a key figure in the world of Russian symbolism, just as Oedipus did in Freudian psychoanalysis. What makes a comparison of the two more interesting is that structurally, Dionysus (for Vyacheslav Ivanov) and Oedipus (for Freud) represented the universal images that inhabit the unconscious depths of human nature. Comprehensible only through interpretation, these icons contained the most important human truths, the universal script governing human behavior. However, the two images were as different in essence as they were analogous in function: In his Russian paraphrase, Dionysus became the polar opposite of Freud's Oedipus.

The essence of Oedipus lies in his simultaneous uniqueness and identicalness. He is a human being, a man and a son, belonging to a family, a gender, and a generation. His feelings and actions are intensely individual; he loves only his mother and kills his father. He never confounds his feelings; love is kept separate from hatred. In Oedipus's world, love and the death instinct are just as distant from one another, just as impossible to combine, as the delineation between mother and father, woman and man. In this world, opposites exist in their purest forms; they can find no mediator, nor should they seek one.

In order to apply this conception to female patients—because it was impossible to imagine Oedipus as either asexual or bisexual—Freud was compelled to select another myth, that of Electra. Similarly, in order to use analysis on another generation, on mothers, analysts had to introduce the Jocasta complex. Oedipus could not accommodate opposite feelings, opposite genders, or opposite generations; the whole point of the tragedy would be lost if these opposites were "dialectically" joined in his soul.

Dionysus, in contrast, alleviates through synthesis the opposition between individual and universal, man and woman, parent and child. His essence is cyclical death and rebirth. Since he revives himself, Dionysus has no need of parents, children, or a partner of the opposite sex. He is unfamiliar with the horror that struck Oedipus, Electra, and Jocasta. He is surrounded by poetic nymph-maenads, but these are of use only to the poets who write about Dionysus. The god himself would have no idea what to do with them; his eros is directed toward himself. Yet although Dionysus is Narcissus, he is also Osiris. Because he loves and hates at the same time, because he is born and dies through a single act, Dionysus is at the same time Christ and Zarathustra. Thus were sophisticated philosophical speculations employed in a way contrary to their original purpose—not to analyze and differentiate but to blur the lines between different persons and opposite notions.

An article by Odessa psychoanalyst Yakov Kogan, published in 1932 in the journal of the International Psychoanalytic Association under the title "One Schizophrenic's Experience of the End of the World and Fantasies of Rebirth," provides an excellent illustration of the Nietzsche-inspired Russian variant of the Dionysian cult. The article relates the difficult clinical case of a Russian patient in exhaustive detail, with a host of expressive quotations. The largely uneducated patient had gone to work for a military library after his return from the front at the end of World War I. There he read all the latest fashionable literature. In his delirium, the patient saw himself as an eternally reviving being. The thought that he might have been born of a woman made him indignant. For him the world had already come to an end and he—almighty, feverish, lonely, and eternal—spoke of "ascent" and "descent" in a style eerily reminiscent of certain well-known texts. Kogan interpreted his patient's delirium as a radical solution to the oedipal complex, in which the patient, incapable of accepting or changing his relations with his parents and the world, denied their existence.[64]

Symbolists on the Couch

In one of his early works, *Return: The Third Symphony*, which came out in 1905, Bely described a therapeutic case in terms that eerily foreshadow psychoanalysis. Perhaps this is yet another example of Bely's characteristic premonitions (it is commonly believed that Bely foresaw the atomic bomb and described its operation in fiction written at the beginning of the 1920s). In any case, the protagonist of *The Symphony* comes into dramatic conflict with his fellow chemists, defending the Nietzschean theory of "eternal return" while his colleagues stick to "social issues." These ideological disagreements provoke hallucinations in the protagonist, in the style of a symbolist painting, for which he seeks treatment from Orlov, a wise old psychiatrist who wields great power within the confines of Orlovka, his private sanatorium. In the midst of treatment, however, the psychiatrist takes a trip abroad. "The chuckle of the unsolved and the howl of what has been irrevocably lost poured together into a single melancholic, plaintive wail." *Third Symphony* is perhaps more a prediction of the need for psychoanalysis than a description of psychoanalysis itself; but this work offers a glimpse of Bely's anticipation of his tragic break with Emile Medtner, in which psychiatrists played a telling role.

Blok's wife (and the object of Bely's conflicted love), Liubov' Mendeleeva-Blok, often turned to Freud in her memoirs, which were written much later. The relationships she described in these memoirs are more likely to be encountered in a psychoanalyst's office than on pages penned by a poet. The Bloks' marital life was, to a large degree, a test of Vladimir Solovyov's idea of superhuman love drawing attention away from fleshly love. This experiment yielded depressing results. Based on the philosophical negation of sexual relations in the name of "white love," Alexander Blok's abstinence from sex in the long run mired his marital life in a series of adulteries and produced serious conflict between his mother and his wife. In an effort to understand what had happened, Liubov' turned from Solovyov to Freud (at the beginning of the century, she had been a student of psychology). She had styled her memoirs as a chain of free associations designed to "provide some kind of material, albeit incomplete, for a Freudian analysis of events."[65] She likewise offered up her conflict with her mother-in-law "to Freud's disciples." She wrote that she had come to understand even the discoveries of her father, an outstanding chemist, as an outlet of "subconscious forces" through a restraining sluice.

"Freud's science" was not foreign to Blok's circle, although Blok himself clearly rejected it. In April 1917, psychoanalyst Yury Kannabikh diagnosed Blok as neurasthenic and offered him treatment. Less than a month later, in a letter to his mother, Blok commented on the treatment she was undergoing in Kannabikh's psychotherapeutic sanatorium in Kryukovo (see chapter

4): "You are counting on some psychological effect; as for me, I don't believe in it (and never have). All I see is different combinations of actions taken by another will from afar."[66] Yet in his cycle *Retribution*, the poet announces his "neurosis, anxiety, and spleen" as a consequence of his lamentable past, the "humanistic fog" that enveloped him in "psychosis instead of feats of valor."

At the end of 1911, a young man who by heritage and proclivity was at the center of symbolist culture was admitted to a psychiatric hospital after two suicide attempts. This was poet Sergei Solovyov (1885–1942), Vladimir Solovyov's nephew, Andrei Bely's closest friend, and best man at the wedding of Blok and Mendeleeva. Very little is known of Sergei Solovyov's problems. Several years prior, he had become involved in the Blok family drama, instructing them on how to dethrone the "dark element of astartism" and the "dragon of lasciviousness" (Vladimir Solovyov's terms) in order to arrive at genuine, fleshless love, expecting just this sort of "white love" to arise from the Bloks' marriage.[67] However, Solovyov later asked Blok to inform his wife that the former's "love for her would soon take on sinful overtones." From time to time, he found himself "still drawn to the old life, but death peers out from it and life acquires an astartic form." He even imagined that there might be a posthumous biography of him someday, entitled *The Fornicator of the Twentieth Century*.

This may have been no more than youthful pathos, but then the way in which culture shaped this youth's sensibilities becomes all the more interesting. In 1905, Sergei Solovyov wrote to Blok: "You argued with me when I tried to convince you that Christianity at its very core is beyond gender. Now I think a final understanding of Christianity is attainable only through lust. Only for this reason do bunches of grapes shine through in Christianity—an eternal doctrine, the religion of the future."[68] Sergei Solovyov's interpretation of Christianity as a "religion of holy lust"—what he considered the only correct reading of his uncle's teachings—is curiously evocative of Carl Jung's quest to "turn Christ back into a prophetic god of wine."

After a few months in the city clinic, Solovyov was transferred to the sanatorium at Kryukovo, on the outskirts of Moscow, where most of the capital's psychoanalysts were working at the time. His attending physician was none other than Yury Kannabikh, who by that time had published several articles on the psychoanalysis of paranoia; later he would become president of the Russian Psychoanalytic Society. Psychoanalysis, routinely combined at Kryukovo with various kinds of physiotherapy, soon proved helpful to Solovyov. In 1913, he took a drastically different tack and joined the Russian Orthodox priesthood; in the 1920s, he converted to Catholicism and became a priest of "Greco-Russian rites." In later years, he was repeatedly in and out of Soviet psychiatric clinics.

Another friend of Bely's, Emile Medtner, had a different medical history, one that proved even more fertile for Russian psychoanalysis. Medtner was the brother of a famous composer and the head of the prominent Musaget publishing house. He was at the epicenter of contemporary literary life. Musaget issued a large number of books by symbolists during the years of its operation, among these Bely's works. Medtner supported Bely until the latter became involved in anthroposophy, something Medtner tried in vain to prevent.

According to Fyodor Stepun's colorful recollections: Medtner would arrive at the Musaget editorial office, and "after quickly dropping his elegant fur coat with its immense skunk collar and cuffs in the foyer, . . . full of solitary thoughts about Goethe, Wagner, and Nietzsche, he would burst into his small, olive-painted office and, rubbing his crimson, frostbitten hands, flop down in his editor's chair in a very businesslike manner."[69] When Bely wrote of Medtner, he also alighted on clothing: his wide-brimmed hat, green-gray coat, and red kid gloves. When they were introduced to each other, Bely was struck by Medtner's "tanned, lean face, which radiated ardor and obstinacy."[70]

This persuaded Westernizer, editor, and literary critic, whose contribution to Russian literature is comparable to Sergey Diaghilev's to Russian ballet, was treated by a Moscow psychoanalyst during his time at Musaget. In the 1970s, Marietta Shaginyan recalled that Medtner had shown "pseudo-Ménièrian symptoms of hysteria" and underwent powerful seizures of "psychical pain." According to her, Medtner also participated in the associative experiments conducted in Moscow by Jung's recent students.[71] Further details have been gleaned from the memoirs of Vyacheslav Ivanov's daughter, Lydia. One symptom of Medtner's "psychosomatic illness" was his aversion to music: "Intolerable noise in his ears and splitting headaches were the result whenever Medtner heard musical sounds. Prior to his disease, he lived for music." Family and friends assumed that his illness was "psychic in nature," tied to Emile's concerns about his brother. "After a hard-fought but magnanimous struggle," the love of Emile's life had married his brother Nikolai, a popular composer.[72]

Emile met Vyacheslav and Lydia Ivanov in Davos in the summer of 1929, and as they sat in a café, music began to play. Medtner's friends were concerned, as they remembered his problems in Moscow. There was no reaction from Medtner, though: "It's because of Jung's treatment," he explained. Lydia recalled that Medtner was "aging and completely exhausted" when he asked Jung to treat him in Zurich. Jung cured him: "All signs of illness disappeared, he became a normal human being again and even received Jung's blessing to treat patients using psychoanalysis." After spending the day with him, the Ivanovs learned that Medtner had become "Jung's close friend and occasional assistant." All of this increased

Vyacheslav Ivanov's interest in Jung. According to his daughter, Ivanov followed Jung's publications, and, in fact, Ivanov makes reference in his later works to Jung, as in his 1934 sketch, "Anima."[73] Later (for example, in a 1947 article on Lermon-tov), he not only made use of specifically Jungian terminology, he also brought to bear a broader framework of psychoanalytical understanding. After this meeting with Medtner, Ivanov evidently found some similarity between the stories he had heard about analytical psychology and his own mystical insights of long before. He dedicated his 1917 sonnet "The Threshold of Consciousness" to his friend:

> *Probing mind, a lighthouse shining*
> *Scans out into the desert sea*
> *Of one night soul in harmony,*
> *That sings of parted, fruitless pining.*[74]

Lydia Ivanova perceived the result of Emile's analysis in her own way: "For me personally, Medtner's image left a depressing impression: it was as if he was already partly dead, although he was still walking around and functioning normally. As a result of the treatment, something was killed (music?) in his soul. Something meaningful. His soul was no longer full of life, it was maimed, amputated. Is this what Jung achieved with his psychoanalysis? But at what price!"[75]

Such resistance is typical of Russian intellectuals. We should recall that it was for similar reasons that Lou Andreas-Salomé tried to talk Rilke out of seeing an analyst. In the Moscow intelligentsia there is a legend that continues to circulate today (one that might very well be true) that a certain Moscow psychoanalyst turned Sergey Eisenstein away on the same grounds, saying that after psychoanalysis the filmmaker would have to look for an accounting job in the State Planning Committee.[76] Meanwhile, Anna Akhmatova spoke mockingly of young English intellectuals who flocked to Freud for treatment of their complexes. "So, does it really help them?" Akhmatova asked one of her guests from Oxford (who was probably Isaiah Berlin). "Oh, yes," he replied. "But when they get back, they're so boring you can't talk with them about anything."[77]

Musaget Carries On in Zurich

The outbreak of the war in 1914 found Medtner in Munich, whence he was quickly expelled to Switzerland. He made Jung's acquaintance in Zurich and evidently started taking psychoanalytic treatment from him right away. Jung's unpublished letters, currently kept in the Russian national library's Moscow archives (seventeen of Jung's letters to Medtner, written between 1917 and 1935, arrived in Moscow from Zurich in 1960), shed a good deal of light on their relationship.[78] In his letters, Jung addressed Medtner informally, consistently expressing warm feelings for his correspondent. The letters testify to the fact that theirs was a long and stable friendship, based on Medtner's enthusiasm, Jung's sympathy, and mutually beneficial collaboration. Their correspondence contains more than just invitations to dinner; Jung also noted that Medtner's plans to visit him in France, where Jung was serving in the military, would have to be cancelled, as his hospital was to be transferred. On January 19, 1919, Jung wrote:

Dear friend,

Thank you for your New Year's greetings. The world has yet again turned upside down. We still have no clear understanding of what is going on. . . . You must be in a horrendous position. To know that your colleagues are stuck in that bedlam . . . Surely, the Bolsheviks will be kicked out of the Entente by spring.

A letter of January 31, 1933 provides insight into other interests the two men held in common:

Dear Emile,

I'm sorry to hear that you are so sad. I wish I could send you at least telepathic aid. . . . I spend my time in a terribly old-fashioned way, reading Origen's *Contra Celsum* and tracing the psychological parallels between him and others: from Plotinus and Proclus via Hegel to—last, but not least—Karl Marx.

The archive also contains several friendly notes to Medtner from Jung's wife, Emma. Medtner was also on close terms with Toni Wolf, Jung's former patient, who later became his good friend and a psychiatrist. It was she, evidently, who introduced Medtner to American millionairess and philanthropist Edith Rockefeller McCormick, who was the wife of one of Jung's former patients. This wealthy benefactress had offered to finance the translation and publication of Jung's works in Russian and French, and work on this project had begun at the end of 1916. According to Medtner, Jung's permission for the Russian translation was contingent on one nonnegotiable condition: that the translation be "as literal as possible, even at the expense of lightness and, moreover, grace of language."[79]

It was probably Jung who suggested that Medtner send several translations to Sabina Spielrein for proofreading. She was dissatisfied with their quality, however, and in December 1917 wrote to Jung that after numerous attempts to improve the translations she had sent them back to Medtner. He reproached her for nitpicking. In the end, Spielrein took part in the publication.[80]

According to the original plan, four hefty volumes were to be released simultaneously. Medtner accepted Jung's offer to compose extended forewords to each volume, not only to give a summary of each book but also to "un-

cover the reasons behind the rift between the Zurich and Vienna schools."
This shows Jung's great trust in his new Russian patient and friend.

Later events altered this plan, but amazingly enough the project was fulfilled almost to the last page. In 1928, work was disrupted by financial crisis.
A year later, the project's backer, Rockefeller McCormick, died. Medtner
himself lived only long enough to see the first volume, *Psychological Types*,
in print (it was released in 1929). In all, three volumes of Jung's *Selected
Works in Analytical Psychology* were published in Russian translation in
Zurich, authorized by Jung and edited by Emile Medtner. Medtner imprinted
the Musaget logo on the first volume, emphasizing the continuity between
the new publication and the famed publisher of symbolist writers. "It would
be too bad if Musaget never got the chance to touch upon psychoanalytic issues," Medtner remarked. His foreword was launched with an epigraph selected from Vyacheslav Ivanov. Medtner found various ways to defend the
continuity of the symbolist tradition, which he saw extended in Jung's writing. Clearly, Medtner was forced to deepen the contradictions between Jung
and Freud in order to bring Jung closer to the symbolists. Medtner dismissed
Freud's influence on Jung: Jung "had his own theme, different from that of
Freud." Overall, Jung was "more than a psychoanalyst" to Medtner.[81]

In his foreword, Medtner also offered a compelling discussion of the
polemic in academic journals that surrounded the publication of Jung's
works, a polemic to which he had contributed. From time to time, however,
he substituted symbolist language for psychoanalytic terminology. "The
symbolic product must perform an act of subconscious liberation," proclaimed Medtner, citing Jung alongside Ivanov, who defined the goal of symbolism in similar terms, as liberation of the soul, and as catharsis. The
Russian edition of *Psychological Types* was effusively praised by another author in *Put'*, an émigré journal of religious and philosophical orientation.[82]

The second and third volumes, which contained *Psychology of the
Unconscious: A Study of the Transformations and Symbolisms of the
Libido* and a series of Jung's articles on the theory and practice of analytical
psychology, came out only in 1939. By that time, publication was being
handled by the Psychological Club in Zurich; using the late Medtner's materials, prominent Russian diaspora philosopher Boris Vysheslavtsev assisted in editing the works. In the articles published as introductions to the
two volumes, Medtner further pursued the kinship between psychoanalysis
and symbolism: Dreams were just as symbolic as artistic images or the
highest expressions of religious wisdom. A symbol resolved the inner contradictions of the psyche and thereby possessed liberating power.

In the last of Jung's preserved letters to Medtner (of July 31, 1935), he
ardently expressed his gratitude for close partnership and offered support
to his ailing friend. The occasion for the letter was an anniversary collection that Medtner had compiled for Jung's sixtieth birthday; but he must
have had other Russian translations in mind when he wrote:

Dear Emile,

I am so grateful to you for your contribution to this edition. I was very moved by it. I immediately snatched up your article and read it with great interest. You found an original solution to your task. The article demonstrates that your philosophy matches your temperament and, therefore, you always evaluate personality in the light of ideas. I was charmed by this; your work is extraordinarily engaging to read. . . . The style is genuinely impressionistic. I cannot help but tell you how much I appreciate the fact that you took up your pen on my behalf, let alone all the efforts demanded by the quantity of work you had to do. Rest assured that your work is as interesting as it will be lasting, and it reflects your inner essence.[83]

Resisting Evil by Force

Medtner's friend Ivan Ilyin, a philosopher and junior lecturer at Moscow University, was treated around 1912 in Vienna by psychoanalyst Eduard Hitschmann, who was one of the analysts closest to Freud.[84] From 1911 on, Hitschmann had served as vice-president of the Vienna Psychoanalytic Society (Freud was president at the time). A participant in the Russian revolution of 1905 and a member of the Russian Socialist Democratic Workers Party (RSDWP), Ilyin even attended one of the party's congresses held in Helsinki in 1905. Soon, however, he abandoned his revolutionary activism.

Ilyin's relatives knew of his psychoanalytic treatment, and they had little confidence in it. According to Yevgeniia Gertsyk:[85] "Meeting Freud was crucial for him. He went to Vienna, underwent a series of discussion treatments, and it seemed for a while that something within him improved and expanded. But even the Freudian key cannot unlock a safe sealed with seven locks."[86] The most unpleasant thing about Ilyin was the way he "hated, despised, and insulted his ideological adversaries," among whom Gertsyk listed Vyacheslav Ivanov, Berdyaev, Voloshin, and Bely: "Ilyin meticulously picked out all their weaknesses and triumphantly uncovered 'sexual perversities' in everyone."[87] It seems Ilyin particularly disliked Ivanov. Ivanov's daughter artfully related one scandalous scene that erupted between the two men: "Ilyin appeared suddenly from out of nowhere and began shouting gibberish in Vyacheslav's general direction. He was shaking convulsively, and there was foam on his lips."[88]

His enemies, however, responded with equal cruelty. Bely, for instance, described Ilyin as "young, obsessed, pale as a skeleton . . . I believe he had suffered from mental illness long before there were any obvious symptoms; . . . he was a prime candidate for a mental institution."[89] Even Berdyaev, who was typically even-tempered, lost his composure when speaking about him: "I've hardly ever read a book as nightmarish and horrid as Ilyin's."[90]

According to Gertsyk, Ilyin's personality was scarred by "hatred bordering on neurosis," which she felt was due to the fact that since his youth he had deprived himself of everything, particularly "all manner of lustful-ness," for the sake of an abstract idea. Whatever the origin of this hatred, Ilyin's contemporaries sensed it even in his philosophical writings. One of Ilyin's main ideas was that "resisting evil by force" was justified and neces-sary, and he dedicated reams of passionately written pages to this concep-tion. However, the idea provoked an outcry among the intelligentsia of the day, which had been raised on Tolstoy's sermonizing. History has shown that Ilyin had a point, and they should have heard him out.

Lydia Ivanova remarked with surprise that Ilyin had no obvious reason to hate the symbolists; this observation lends his reasons all the more weight. Ilyin's books and lecture transcripts demonstrate that his aggressive attitude toward Bely's mysticism and anthroposophy was well thought out and well documented. The philosopher articulated his criticism in terms that can be unmistakably identified as psychoanalytic. The anthroposophs, Ilyin wrote in 1914, "like to cover themselves with the word 'science,' but in reality they preach some sort of pseudo-mystical spiritual practice. In this dark spiritual practice . . . the spirit's rationality is dissolved in . . . the most physiological aspects . . . of the soul. Their 'science' is magic, and the message of their 'teachings' is but a vague chimera. The 'anthroposoph' tries to magically capture the mystery of his personal unconscious by means of magic, becoming engaged to this end in direct, living communication, not with an object but with his own subconscious. Such communication plunges the center of his personality into the incomprehensible depths of communal instinct, and this is done not for the sake of knowledge: like any true magus, the anthroposoph seeks not knowledge, but rather possession of and power over the rebellious, dissatisfied element of his essence."[91]

Ilyin asserted that what anthroposophs and other mystics referred to as occult "is nothing other than communal aspects of the unconscious." He had psychoanalysis in mind when he wrote that anthroposophs "are un-aware that scientific experience has penetrated farther and deeper than has their method into the unconscious and . . . that the very 'mystery' of their mysterious practice has already given way to science."

"Purification of the mind and soul" required constant internal effort, and mankind, like individual men, "has been long and painfully seeking the right way to achieve such purification." Describing these means, Ilyin com-piled a long list, starting with the yogi and traversing Pythagoras, Descartes, and Spinoza to "the cautious and perceptive Sigmund Freud." Ilyin characterized psychoanalysis as a "method by which man can not only heal and purify his unconscious but also bring his spirit to a state of organic wholeness, sensitivity, and flexibility." In this psychoanalysis could assist philosophy, which was threatened by the "pressure of the uncon-scious realm, in all its subtlety, passion, and elusiveness," which prevented the philosopher's mind from comprehending its subject matter. "All the spiritual wounds collected since childhood remain untreated throughout one's life, often corroding the mind and subjecting it to various psychoses and neuroses ... that make the mind less suited for objective experience and research," Ilyin wrote.

Ilyin, who at that time considered himself a Hegelian, evidently saw psychoanalysis as an indispensable instrument for philosophy: "One tool for philosophical investigation is the living being of the philosopher himself." "A philosopher, to a greater extent than any other scholar, should maintain control over the forces of his unconscious." A philosopher who had not passed through a long and excruciating mental purge was at best capable of only a "more or less successful compromise between requests from his personal unconscious and from conscious ideology."[92]

In 1921, Ilyin was elected chairman of a respectable Moscow Psychological Society. However, in the fall of 1921, he was expelled from Russia, along with dozens of Russia's most prominent philosophers and writers. As an émigré Ilyin published many books, including the fundamental *Axioms of Religious Experience*. In these works, psychoanalysis is ignored, as is neo-Hegelianism. Only once did Ilyin comment disparagingly about Jung's idea of the collective unconscious, which, from Ilyin's point of view, undermined the sovereignty of the individual.[93] Ilyin's apologetic biography makes no mention at all of psychoanalysis.[94] The environment among Russian émigrés did little to encourage psychoanalysis; but in private conversations, it seems, Ilyin allowed his unusual interests to come through. In 1931, Ivan Bunin wrote of Ilyin in his diary that "he has come to understand even the Russian Revolution according to Freud."[95]

Ilyin exerted an unbelievably strong personal influence on Russian communities abroad. After his death in 1954, émigré newspapers extolled him as the "leading ideologist of the Russian diaspora," "an adamant and talented friend of the White cause," and even as the "spiritual leader of the White movement."[96]

Psychoanalysis Against Anthroposophy

Andrei Bely wrote in his memoirs that Medtner had been his enemy since 1915, and he compared the "ideologies that separated us and disrupted a wonderful friendship" to coffins.[97] Bely's postwar "ideology" is well known as anthroposophy, Rudolf Steiner's innovative doctrine that combined fashionable mysticism with no less fashionable pseudoscience. And in what kind of ideological "coffin" did Bely feel Medtner had buried himself?

Most likely, he felt it was a psychoanalytic coffin. It is quite probable that he saw his discord with Medtner and Ilyin, who were undergoing psychoanalysis at the time, as a consequence of the negative influence of psychoanalysis, evidence of its hostile and alien nature.

In December 1914, Bely wrote in his diary: Medtner "tells me a lot about his friendship with Ilyin; he seems to be threatening me with Ilyin; all this only fans my aggressive pathos, urging me to attack . . . Medtner." In the same entry, Bely noted that "Medtner has changed a lot, he has aged and soured . . . ; he has repeatedly proclaimed himself a devoted admirer of Freud and Jung, and he said that 'psychoanalysis' is inscribed in him; this Freudianism in Medtner repulses me; I perceive Medtner's interests with hostility."[98]

Bely recalled that Medtner's admiration for Nietzsche (he had worked on his biography since 1902) did not prevent him from constantly inveighing against mysticism and the "inevitable transformation of other Romantic tones into the mystical." After visiting the leader of anthroposophy, Rudolf Steiner, in 1909, Medtner passed decisive judgment: "He is some kind of theosophic pastor, spitting out total banalities," he wrote to one of Bely's friends.[99] In 1916, Bely published a book on Steiner and Goethe, directed against one of Medtner's recent works. Fyodor Stepun, who knew both adversaries, called it a "nasty blow" that Medtner, for the remainder of his days, "could not talk about without unbearable agony."[100] Medtner made no attempt to respond to Bely's attack, but Ilyin intervened in his behalf, writing an open letter that in turn insulted Bely.

Evidently, psychoanalysis was an important, although latent, cause of schism in the symbolist movement. Under pressure from opposite cultural influences—rationalistic psychoanalysis on the one hand and mystical anthroposophy on the other—Russian symbolism split into two mutually hostile currents. Former friends such as Medtner and Bely found themselves at opposite poles.

Such an understanding of the conflict's origins is indirectly corroborated by the uproar that erupted around psychoanalysis inside the Anthroposophic Society. In 1911, a certain Mr. Bolt released a brochure about Steiner. According to Bely, Bolt "confounded his views with those of Freud and clung stubbornly to this confusion; one group of members supported Bolt; different factions within anthroposophy were revealed for the first time, precisely in connection with Bolt." Steiner "hotly denounced the 'Boltist' tendency, which found shelter under the banner of anthroposophy." This debate dragged on until the Second Congress of the Anthroposophic Society in January 1914. Bely participated in the congress, and it was with great indignance that he observed the schism, the protests, and the members' gossiping about their leader, Steiner. And it was all because of psychoanalysis.[101]

Psychoanalysis and anthroposophy, so far apart in our modern conception, were perceived then, and even later, as competitors. Valentin Voloshinov (see chapter 10), for instance, believed that the influence of psychoanalysis in Europe could be compared only to that of anthroposophy.[102] Nikolai Osipov also published an article devoted to this subject, in which he attempted to compare and juxtapose psychoanalytic and mystical views of the world.[103] Osipov related that, in 1913, while he and his young wife were traveling by train, he stepped out of the car at a station for a short walk and was late returning; the train left with his wife onboard. This happened in the very same city where a woman with whom Osipov would later become involved, after his divorce, was living. A mystic would explain this occurrence as the result of unknown influences that directed Osipov's actions against his will; a psychoanalyst would deduce an unconscious protest against his wife. One gets the feeling, however, that even for Osipov, a professional analyst, it was no easy matter to choose between these two possibilities.

Bely's contact with anthroposophy brought him catastrophe in his private affairs. His friends in Russia shunned him, and his wife left him in order to be closer to the "Doctor," as Steiner's followers called him. The Doctor himself seems to have seen Bely as just one of his many eccentric admirers, a position to which Bely could not bear to be relegated.

In his "intimate" notes, intended for publication only after the author's death (and published only recently), Bely described the "temptation of St. Anthony" that he experienced after his wife left him and he had become an ascetic. Unlike St. Anthony, he had no spiritual weapon he could wield in the fight against temptation. "A generalized image of woman began to haunt my imagination. . . . In order to avoid a fall and to overcome sensuality, I had to kill the flesh with rigorous exercise; but this had only the effect of temporary anaesthesia; I lashed my flesh, it contorted under the whip but did not submit; I increased the dosage of meditation; I meditated for hours every day for months on end, and meditation brought me ecstasy and delight. . . . But after they subsided, these moments seemed unhealthy to me, and I felt I was doomed to the same sensuality."[104] Here one cannot help recalling Ilyin's words, that an anthroposoph seeks not knowledge but power over some rebellious and unhappy element in his being.[105]

During a visit to Bely in the anthroposophic community in Dornach, Medtner told him of his recent experience with psychoanalysis. Bely, who was going through one of his worst phases, took him for a "spiritual spy." His notes abound in all kinds of astral suspicions. Khodasevich, who knew Bely for many years, described his condition in classic psychoanalytic terms:

> This theme, essentially bordering on paranoia, was always one of his favorites. I deeply believe that it arose in childhood, when he was convinced that some dark force was out to ruin him, pushing him to commit crimes against his father. Bely actually carried the monster . . . within him, but the self-preservation instinct drove him to search for it in the external world, so he could shift the blame for his darkest designs, desires and impulses.[106]

Since then, other strange details have come to light from the somber period that ensued after Bely's break with anthroposophy. For example, he suddenly fell in love with the foxtrot and danced all night long in the cabarets of Berlin, whirling like a Russian *khlyst*—and returned, nonetheless, in despair to Russia.

Russian Oedipus, or Kotik the Fatherkiller

"Here is my sincere answer to the questions *how* I became a symbolist and *when*: I *never became* a symbolist, but I have always *been* one (before I ever encountered the words 'symbol' and 'symbolist')."[107] Bely then proceeds to one of his childhood memories: "The doctor says I am too excitable and that my fairy tales should be taken away, and I feel that the saving grace of this play of images is being taken away from me by external force and that in their absence I will be thrown into the abyss of gibberish; if adults had understood my childish fear of losing fairy tales, they would have expressed it thus: 'He's struggling for the integrity of his ego, so as to avoid a nervous breakdown.'" Bely considered these acts of symbolization his only defense against an "explosion of inner feelings." For him, the symbol was a way to "overcome the early stages of lemur-atlantic chaos and move into something concrete and logical." In other words, the symbol was the "third of two worlds, the intersection of parallel lines, forming a *cross*, with the inner world at its center."[108]

Bely never tired of repeating this structural principle, which he saw as the source of the rift between his closest colleagues and friends: "Any symbolist who repudiates his logical genesis—his experimental gibberish—will degenerate into mental illness if he is sincere (like Blok), or he will become a stylist if he is not thoroughly sincere (like Vyacheslav Ivanov)."

An unbelievably sharp yearning to "wrap words around the very earliest events in life" produced *Kotik Letaev*, an unprecedented experiment in verbal reconstruction of preverbal childhood experiences. "The *symbol* allowed me to emerge from fear," Bely repeated, time and again; and he continued to emerge in his novels. In the course of three hundred pages bereft of plot and characters, Bely describes "how clouds of events puff up at me; how they run back again" exclusively by means of rhythm, semantics, and acoustics: "On the brink of my third year I stand before myself; we—converse with each other; we—understand each other."[109] In the delirious labyrinth of awakening consciousness, where the division into "I" and "not-I" has barely begun and space and time do not yet exist, Bely discerns periods and characteristics that vaguely resemble the Kantian foundation common to all Russian symbolists. In this description, we can pick out the meditative metaphors of anthroposophy that Bely would later adopt: "The world and thought are just scum on the surface of looming cosmic images." Later, Bely even wrote that *Kotik Letaev* was the result of anthroposophic training. But Bely's acquaintance Aaron Steinberg had written with remarkable insight of *Kotik* that "besides anthroposophy, upon which the whole work is built . . . , there is also what modern psychology and psychoanalysis call infantilism."[110]

A psychoanalyst, of course, will immediately recognize this infantile world as his own. Childhood as described by Bely is full of fears, yearnings, and images that would be used repeatedly by future Russian analysts to illustrate their theories. To the professional eye, *Kotik Letaev* remains an extremely expressive source. But Bely's discourse itself is devoid of the psychoanalytic vision.

The first to reveal the psychoanalytical meaning of Bely's novels was not an analyst but one of the most brilliant Russian poets and literary critics of this century, Bely's younger contemporary, Vladislav Khodasevich. In two essays,[111] Khodasevich made an attempt, rare in its clarity, to separate out and describe the content of Bely's novels *Petersburg, Moscow,* and *Kotik Letaev,* correlating them with events in the writer's biography.

Khodasevich observed that Bely's novels were "fragmentary variations on one plot theme, singular in its deepest essence," dramas that were played out in the writer's family long ago. Little Kotik Letaev, "Moscow eccentric" Mitya Korobkin, and the terrorist hero of *Petersburg,* Nikolai Ableukhov, are all reflections of the same person at various stages in life: Letaev as a child, Korobkin as a high-school student, and Ableukhov as a university student. Khodasevich demonstrated the similarity in these characters' outward appearances, their dispositions, and the roles they played in the novels and in life. "Uncontrollable lust is their constant companion, and it is the first, main and exclusive motive of their actions. And these actions are, in fact, crimes." Bely himself said the same of the protagonist in his famous *Petersburg*: "Nikolai Apollonovich became a mix of disgust, fear and lust."

"He despised his own flesh and lusted after others'," Bely wrote in *Petersburg.* Ableukhov's hatred of his own flesh coincided with his hatred for his father. In Bely's novel, "Whenever father and son came into contact with each other, they resembled two ventilators that had been turned on facing each other; and the result was a most unpleasant draft. Their proximity bore little semblance to love; Nikolai Apollonovich regarded love as a humiliating physical act."[112]

In his memoirs, Bely noted that his Oedipal experience of standing before the Sphinx during his trip to Egypt was an important factor in the writing of *Petersburg.* Khodasevich, who knew both Bely and his mother quite well, once described the author and all of his characters at the same stroke: "He was afraid of his father and hated him in the strongest way; . . . he pitied his mommy and admired her to the point of sensual delight." Bely's characters are always inflamed by people they loved in their youth, "but having stoked them, these people push them away at the last minute with equally passionate contempt." According to Khodasevich's scheme, this is why Bely's characters commit their crimes; they are always driven by their suffering sensuality.

Nikolai Ableukhov, the protagonist of *Petersburg*, takes up company with a group of revolutionaries and promises them that he will kill his father, a prominent senator. They give him a time bomb, which ticks through the whole narration. "Nikolai Apollonovich takes revenge on his father for his own impotent desire, for the futile lust which he sees as his inheritance." With the brutal bluntness of a psychoanalyst, Khodasevich emphasizes that this is the only true motivation for Nikolai's crime.

Mitya Korobkin, the protagonist of *Moscow*, is the son of a professor who has invented a substance of enormous destructive power, a fictional prototype of the atomic bomb. Mitya steals and sells off his father's books. He needs the money to seduce the daughter of a German spy, von Mandro, who is living incestuously with her father. Because of Mitya's burglary, von Mandro manages to intercept a sheet covered with enough of the professor's formulas to blow up Europe. This is the kind of crime that a touching Kotik dreams up against his father in particular and his father's world in general.

Khodasevich's sketches about Bely were presumably written under the direct influence of Freud's essay on Dostoevsky. Khodasevich's conclusion is clear: "All political, philosophical, and day-to-day goals in Bely's novels . . . are in fact just a pretext to recall and re-assimilate the impressions that struck him in early childhood." Bely's main motif, like that of Dostoevsky according to Freud, is the drive to commit patricide, guilt over this desire, and yearning for punishment. Both authors transfer these weighty feelings onto other people, the state, and the world at large.

However, Khodasevich mentioned neither Freud nor Oedipus in his essays, and only once did he refer to Bely's novels, beginning with *Petersburg*, as an "oedipal series." Regardless of this omission and whatever its cause, Khodasevich's essay may certainly be regarded as a classic example of psychoanalytic criticism in Russian literature.

Forward to Plato

Russian modernist culture created its own theory of sexuality, closely linked to the ideas of symbolism. This theory arose out of Vladimir Solovyov's quest for Sophia, but Nikolai Berdyaev embellished it with more detail and in 1916, published his thoughts on the matter.[113] A powerful sense of the centrality of gender is characteristic of our times: Sex has emerged from secrecy into the light of day, and sexuality is perceived in every facet of human life. Gender-specific sexual functions are believed to be the result of differentiation in some protosexual life, and there is a great deal of emphasis on these functions.

According to Berdyaev, however, it would be a mistake to equate gender with the sexual act. For although one could achieve control over the sexual act, gender could never be controlled. Sexual energy could be channeled in various directions; such energy could be directed into creative activity, for instance. The division of genders came as a consequence of Adam's fall: Adam was androgynous. Only a girl-boy, a unified, bisexual person, could reflect the image and likeness of God. Christ also was halfway between man and woman. Human sexuality was nothing more than a painful search for lost androgyny; but unification through the sexual act was illusory and entailed retribution, Berdyaev believed. The sexual act was sickly and defective insofar as it was finite and differentiated (whereas it should be eternal and be performed by androgynous beings). Thus, the sexual act was internally contradictory and opposed to the meaning of the world. The sexual act was essentially contrasted with genius, and sexuality hindered a person's creative forces. There was always mortal anxiety buried at the very core of the act, for what gave life could also kill.

Surprisingly, we find in Berdyaev yet another aspect of the drive to transform mankind, squaring off in this case against one of the most basic of human features: masculine and feminine genders. Berdyaev wrote that his contemporaries were living in a transitional period, that a new natural order was on the rise, in which the birth-giving sexual act would be transformed into a liberated act of creation. In this new era, the previously firm boundaries between male and female would fade and blur. At this transitional moment, Berdyaev insisted, one might well ask whether the sex act could be an anomaly.

It should be noted that no matter how we feel about these speculations, they were not just the result of Berdyaev's individual improvisation. This Russian philosopher was expressing the revelations and prejudices, the desires and fears of an entire generation, and perhaps even of the culture as a whole; hence his popularity then and now in Russia. Berdyaev never claimed to be original. On the contrary, he was at pains to emphasize the continuity of his ideas and cited Otto Weininger along with Jakob Böhme, and Vladimir Solovyov in the same breath as Freud. Most astonishing of all is the author's lack of embarrassment in his zeal for androgyny; he made no attempt to soften this key point for readers. According to Berdyaev, those he considered his main authorities, from Plato to Solovyov, shared his belief that the meaning of love lay in the androgynous.

At the same time, a personal component shines through in this philosophy, one that Berdyaev never fully realized. "In unhealthy, tormented half-sleep, something rose out of the depths of my nature, . . . something disgusting and repulsive to the point of terror," the young philosopher wrote his future wife from exile in Vologda. "Since early childhood, the question of sex has seemed to me at once frightening and important, one of the most important in life. This has caused me a lot of emotional anxiety that took on meaning for my very existence. All my life, I have thought that there is something mystical about sex, that it has religious significance." What is more, he confessed to the woman he loved, a "curse of sexual abnormality and degeneration" was hanging over him.[114]

It is easier to get a clear idea of what was tormenting this generation when we take a closer look at this outstanding thinker, whose development passed from Marxism to existentialism and religious personalism, with his rare talent for matching words with feelings. Normal sex caused Berdyaev the same fear and sense of personal guilt as did the calamitous events of his time. "Everyone is soured nowadays, everyone is joyless and unhappy, everyone is dismayed in their heart of hearts," he wrote in November 1917. "The intelligentsia is being used to espouse the most irresponsible ideas and utopias, which have never been put to trial through real life experience," he added, warning that "severe punishment will follow these ecstatic moments of strength and glory."[115]

Boris Zaitsev recalled Berdyaev in 1906 as a "handsome man with dark, curly hair, sitting in an armchair; he expatiates ardently and at times (nervous tic) opens his mouth wide, sticking out his tongue. . . . It's very unusual, I imagine the execution in Dante looked something like that."[116] According to Yevgeniia Gertsyk, who was close to Berdyaev in the 1910s, the philosopher showed clear signs of a "horror of darkness and chaos," as if "hovering over an abyss." The perceptive Gertsyk deduced this from his tic and the jerky movements he made with his hands. She also reported that when Berdyaev once spent the night at her house in the Crimea: "Several times in the course of the night, I heard a terrifying scream coming from the other end of the house. In the morning, he told me with embarrassment that in his sleep he had dreamed that something like a tangled blob of serpents or a giant spider was descending on him from above." Gertsyk remarked that Berdyaev's "many minuscule, insignificant eccentricities" could be traced to the same source, "his disgust and near phobia toward everything soft, caressing, and engulfing."[117] Against the background of these observations, which require little commentary, Berdyaev's claim that he "never discovered anything in himself approaching the oedipal complex"[118] takes on different overtones.

Berdyaev found Freud's works interesting. "Freud does not suffer from the usual psychiatric stagnation; he demonstrates freedom and audacity of thought." Berdyaev appreciated the fact that "Freud provides scientific substantiation of the truth that sexuality suffuses the entire human being and is even inherent in infants." Like many others, however, Berdyaev reproached Freud for pansexualism. He was especially shocked by Freud's interpretation of religion. But even his criticism was original: "The tendency of the Freudian school to explain everything, including religion, as the upshot of unrealized sexuality takes the form of a maniacal idea, typical of psychiatrists. This pansexualism, too, can in fact be explained as the result of unrealized sexuality in those who created it." Later, Berdyaev referred to psychoanalysis as the "shamelessness of the modern epoch, but also a major enrichment of our knowledge about human beings."[119]

Friendship Was Possible . . .

During the mass exile of 1922 and subsequent voluntary departures, a number of important Russian philosophers found their way to the West, where they continued to preserve their rich and particular culture. In the new surroundings, many encountered psychoanalysis—through their personal interests or by happenstance—which they tried to reinterpret in their own fashion.

At the beginning of the 1930s, when the Russian translations of Freud's *Future of an Illusion* and Jung's *Psychology of the Unconscious* came out, psychoanalysis for a time became a favorite theme of Russian moral philosophy. Philosopher Boris Vysheslavtsev, who was close to Berdyaev, devoted his *Ethics of Eros Transformed* to a new interpretation of psychoanalysis in the light of Russian Orthodox philosophy. This new ethical system "combines Christian Platonism with the discoveries of modern psychoanalysis."[120] The "hearts and wombs" of the Old Testament, the apostle Paul's "flesh," and, certainly, Plato's Eros, are all presented as foreshadowing Freud's unconscious. In this work, the philosopher embraced everything, undaunted even by sexuality. Vice was derived from the same material as virtue, Vysheslavtsev insisted, which explained why the soul's sinful intentions could be sublimated. Sublimation was the main principle of his ethics. "All of Christian asceticism is one grandiose project of sublimation," according to Vysheslavtsev, who viewed sanctity as the pinnacle of that project.[121] Only the images of Christ resurrected and of the City of Kitezh could "sublimate the chaos of the Russian subconscious," he wrote, alluding to particular Russian sects.[122] Psychoanalysis also had an impact on Vysheslavtsev; but in his improvisations on the theme of religious ethics, Freudian thought became distorted by a range of completely alien ideas. Certainly Freud's view of religion as "one illusion" must have been totally foreign to Vysheslavtsev. The Russian philosopher rebuked even the mystically inclined Jung for excessive scientism, despite their reputed personal acquaintance and professional collaboration.

Another Russian author of the time, Semyon Frank, also reproached psychoanalysis for pansexualism, nihilism, and even demonism in a little-known article, "Psychoanalysis as a Worldview."[123] "From a philosophical point of view, psychoanalysis is unable to handle the treasure of profound emotional life it has found," Frank wrote. He rejected the Freudian thesis that would have garnered even Vysheslavtsev's support—that the psychoanalytic libido was the same as Plato's Eros. Plato saw the erotic essence of man reflected in his highest achievements, while Freud saw it in his lowest. Frank likened Freud to Marx, whom he despised, rather than to his beloved Plato: both Freud and Marx were materialists; the former was a "sexual materialist," and the latter an economic materialist. According to Frank, who viewed sexuality as an even more dubious foundation for humankind than profit, Freud went even further than Marx down the materialist road to ruin.

Philosopher Nikolai Lossky was a friend of Russian psychoanalyst Nikolai Osipov, who had also emigrated to Prague (see chapter 4). Their relationship was a mix of personal intimacy and surprisingly profound intellectual kinship, as attested by numerous references to Lossky in Osipov's later articles (Osipov considered himself a student of Lossky's even before they met). The closeness of their friendship is also revealed in the article that Lossky contributed to the collection dedicated to Osipov's memory,[124] and in the several pages he dedicated to the analyst in his exhaustive *History of Russian Philosophy*.[125] Overall, he saw Osipov's philosophy as an attempt to "reexamine Freudian psychological theory in the context of Lossky's personalized metaphysics."[126] On the other hand, he noted Osipov's affinity to the classics, primarily to Plato. Lossky cited Osipov approvingly: "The empirical meaning of Freud's research will not change if physiological desire is replaced at its center by love in its eidetic sense, as an absolute value."[127] He believed that only death had prevented Osipov from developing his "doctrine of love as the basic factor in the cosmos." Lossky referred to Osipov's article "Revolution and Dreams," which included some of the most expressive and analytical ruminations about that era (see chapter 6), as "rather original in its conception," but he apparently decided not to paraphrase it in his *History*.

Philosopher Lev Shestov was introduced to psychoanalysis by his sister, Fanya Lovtskaya (1873–1965), who had been studying in Bern since 1898. After defending her doctoral thesis in philosophy (Bern, 1909), Fanya went to Geneva to study psychoanalysis. Her analyst there was most likely Sabina Spielrein. In 1922, Fanya moved to Berlin, where she studied psychoanalysis with Max Eitingon. Shestov received this news from his sister excitedly: "I was terribly glad to get your last letter! Who is this Dr. Eitingon? I have never heard anything about him! Is he Russian or German? Judging by the fact that he has read my books, it seems he must be Russian, but then how was he able to get such a position in Berlin?"[128]

Shestov made friends with Eitingon through his sister and stayed with him in Berlin on numerous occasions. They corresponded: Shestov wrote in Russian, Eitingon responded in German. At the beginning of their acquaintance, in December 1922, Shestov wrote from Paris (he had emigrated in 1920):

I see Eitingon often. I've met his wife, they are both nice people. He lent me some articles by Freud—they have a lot of interesting and important material. I told Eitingon that it's a pity that Freud became a doctor instead of a philosopher: if he had not had specific medical tasks, his audacity and skills of observation might have led him to some interesting discoveries. Eitingon responded that if Freud had known me, he would have thought it a pity that I am not a doctor.

Shestov wrote with understanding to his sister Fanya, who had informed him of some difficulties she was having with a patient: "In future, be always ready for possible friction and approach it with businesslike serenity. You must by all means develop this serenity within yourself, as you have decided to do something as practical as treating patients with psychoanalysis."[129]

Lovtskaya had her own understanding of her brother's works, an interpretation with which he did not agree. "His work on self-improvement foreshadows psychoanalysis. . . . He can't seem to understand that Freudianism will grant him immortality, since he is one of Freud's most exceptional predecessors," she told Aaron Steinberg. Steinberg once pointed out that such an evaluation of Shestov's philosophy was quite common: "In Weimar Germany, there was a group of Russian literary scholars, apart from Shestov's sister, who were involved with the psychoanalytic journal *Imago* and whose decisive verdict was that Shestov's mode of thought was closely related to Freudian doctrine."[130] (However, this fact did not prevent others from referring to Shestov as the Russian Nietzsche.)

Eitingon often came to his impractical friend's aid with advice and money. Meanwhile, his friendship with Shestov made Eitingon's house in Berlin (Steinberg called it a "psychoanalytical salon") a center of gravity for the Russian diaspora (see chapter 7). Steinberg, who closely observed life in this circle, remarked with disapproval that Shestov's friends in Berlin were convinced that the philosopher shared their ideas of "moral revolution."[131]

Eitingon never failed to admire Shestov's books, and he sent one to Freud in 1928.[132] Freud read the book but admitted in his response that he had been unable to follow the author's train of thought. "Probably you cannot imagine how alien all these philosophical convolutions seem to me . . . every time there is a psychological or even a psychopathological problem behind them."[133]

In this case, Freud hit the nail on the head: Shestov was indeed suffering from a serious neurosis, which manifested itself in painful neuralgia, chronic fatigue, and uncanny bursts of creativity. At the age of 19, he had experienced a "time of profound despair and internal catastrophe" that he kept secret from everyone.[134] Despite his considerable later success and personal charm, this great Russian philosopher still came across to his audience as a broken man.

The paths of Freud and Shestov crossed yet one more time: In 1930, Shestov asked Thomas Mann to nominate Ivan Bunin for the Nobel Prize. Mann responded to Shestov that, as much as he may have liked to see Bunin receive the prize, he considered Freud a more worthy candidate: Freud's "research made such a deep impact on psychic science and literature."[135] Bunin nonetheless was awarded the Nobel Prize a short time later, in 1933, and Freud never did receive this honor.

Shestov was known and appreciated by Buber, Heidegger, Berdyaev, Bunin, and Lévy-Bruhl, and he enjoyed a mutual understanding with Eitingon. This understanding was possible despite profound differences in professional interests, political views, and lifestyles. Shestov often asked Eitingon for financial help and, evidently, for medical consultation. Their friendship lasted fifteen years. After his friend's death, Eitingon wrote to his family in Russian: "Few people have had a place in my life as significant as he. I believed that I understood what he taught us and where he was calling us to go. I loved him for his limitless kindness and for the quiet beauty of humanism that he personified."[136]

But the Place Was Occupied

Let us draw some conclusions, then, about the early history of psychoanalysis in regard to its Russian manifestations. Psychoanalysis was well known in Russia in the early twentieth century, and counted among its followers influential figures in medicine (see chapter 4) and in the cultural and artistic community at large. At the same time, the influence of these individuals was quite limited. For instance, there was not a single paper even vaguely related to psychoanalysis presented at the All-Russia Conference on Experimental Pedagogy or at the First All-Russia Conference on Popular Education (although there was a section that combined medicine and education), held at the end of 1913 and the beginning of 1914, respectively. Until Ivan Ilyin was elected its chairman in 1921, the widely respected Moscow Psychological Society did not accept psychoanalysis either.

One can identify a number of reasons for this situation, but one stands out far above the others: Russian symbolism was filling the same roles and performing roughly the same sociocultural and psychological functions that psychoanalysis had come to fill in German- and in English-speaking countries around that time. It is another question altogether how well symbolism performed these tasks and how far its influence extended beyond the world of literature and philosophy.

According to Blok, the only thing that Russian and French symbolism had in common was their Greek name. Russian symbolism was a movement that transcended literature and was "indissolubly connected with issues of religion, philosophy, and community."[137] During the height of symbolism's popularity in Russia, a number of intellectual and biographical threads closely linked it with moral philosophy, the bitter political struggle of the time, and the practical search for a new style and meaning of life. As Khodasevich wrote: "Symbolism did not aspire to be merely an artistic school, a literary trend. All the while it strained to become a life-giving method, and herein lies its deepest, possibly its unattainable, truth."[138] In the opinion of this respectable witness, the symbolists had a more "indivisible connection between life and creative activities than almost anyone, before or since." One cannot "disentangle this web until one reads the lives themselves, in addition to their books."[139] "The history of the symbolists became a history of broken lives. . . . Part of their creative energy . . . was channeled into writing, but another part did not achieve complete incarnation and flowed out into life, as electricity drains away when insufficiently insulated."[140]

Many of these statements are equally applicable to psychoanalysis. Neither movement limited itself to the realm of speech; and each created a different mode of life, an almost inarticulate general atmosphere. What Khodasevich referred to in symbolism as a "life-giving method" could have been described by an analyst in talking about his or her goals and milieu, just as a psychoanalyst might easily have adapted the aphorism that "whoever breathes the air of symbolism is forever marked by something."

The Russian symbolists' aspirations coincided with psychoanalytic aspirations and methods also in several other ways: Both intellectual movements tried to capture the inexpressible, to become conscious of the unconscious. In both, there is a prevailing intuition that a secondary reality exists deep inside each human being, radically different from anything known to reason; advocates of both movements believed that their awareness and description of this reality would effectively change real life.

As ways of life, both movements contained the means of affecting individual human beings. In both cases, these means were concentrated on emotionally charged interpersonal relations.

As intellectual trends, both movements were essentially semiotic. Both functioned in the linguistic sphere and both attempted to transcend language, moved by the belief that another, nonverbal reality had decisive significance in human affairs. Both movements prescribed refined methods of interpretation, correlations between meanings and signs, emotional experiences and symbols, and dreams and words.

As pictures of the world, both movements attempted to answer the same set of questions: What is the composition of the "internal man," whom we can readily sense but never know, and what does he do? How can we come to understand this special reality, and how can it be transformed? Which forms of human existence and culture—dreams, myths, works of art—will open the way to this reality? What is the meaning of religion for the new man, who has discovered his individuality? What is the meaning of gender, why is its significance so consistently underestimated by culture, and how can human sexuality be integrated into civilization? What is homosexuality, and is bisexuality a normal, natural human feature?

At the same time, a number of key traits distinguished symbolism from psychoanalysis: a total absence of the pragmatism, consistency, and discipline so essential to psychoanalysis, without which no real "transformation of man" is possible; an undifferentiated religiosity that led symbolism into sectarian rites, dreams of theurgy, godmanhood, and anthroposophy; and an absence of the passion for scientific analysis that was so characteristic of Freud and his followers. Symbolism created nothing like the systematic practice of therapy ("theurgy," according to a parallel set of terms) that could be applied to people in need, although the demand for this kind of help among Russian symbolists was obviously enormous. Finally, at its deepest roots, Russian symbolism, while tightly bound to parallel trends in western European culture, was in contrast a de-individualizing and to some extent anti-intellectual school of thought. In this respect, it was the polar opposite of psychoanalysis.

The attitude that prevailed among symbolists toward this emerging field is amply demonstrated by the following advertisement, placed by Lydia Berdyaeva, the philosopher's wife, in *Boulevards and Crossroads,* a satirical journal that had become popular with the Moscow intelligentsia since the publication of its first issue in 1915.[141]

Physicians and Hospitals
Berdyaev, private practitioner: Mental illness. Diagnosis of crises. Secularization of illness. X-ray equipment, X-rays.
Ivanov, Vyacheslav, Lecturer: Hypnosis, magnetism. Rhythmic gymnastics. Steam and ether treatment.
Shestov, dentist. Specialty: root extraction.
Florensky, professor, staff physician. Neuropathologist. Specialty: obsession, frenzy.
Gershenzon, surgeon. Specialty: psychic surgery, straightening of twisted personalities.
Bely, psychiatrist. Private hospital for all forms of mental illness. Specialty: violent insanity.
Steiner, president of the First Aid society. Distance makes no difference. Patients can be treated by psychic medium.

Another author, Vladimir Ern, placed a more malicious "advertisement" in the same journal, this time on behalf of Ivan Ilyin.

Authentic quotations from various obscure authors individually crafted according to a new and improved German method. A ruble a dozen and up.

Orally, only! Address: The Freud Club, Suite 666, 1 Ilyin Lane, Ostozhenka. Ask for Ivan Alexandrovich.

Yet despite gibes like these—or according to them—many agents of Russian modernist culture were connected with psychoanalysis in one way or another and altered by its influence.

3

A Case of Neurosis in the Revolutionary Generation: Sergei Pankeev, the Wolf-Man

According to Freud's official biographer, Ernest Jones, most of the patients Freud treated in Vienna came to him from eastern Europe, particularly from Russia. It is therefore only natural that the most famous of Freud's case histories is the story of a Russian. Jones called it "assuredly the best of the series."[1] One contemporary historian has described it as "fascinating and rich."[2] "The most famous case" were the words the patient used in referring to himself.[3]

The Best History of Its Kind

Freud's Russian patient was to retain his connection to psychoanalysis (or his dependence upon it) for the duration of his long life. A few other analysts worked with "Sergei P." after Freud; as a result, there is probably more literature about him than about any other patient in the history of psychoanalysis. Together, these writings provide an interesting body of material that can be used to understand how this Russian patient was perceived by his Western analysts. We can draw upon this information to see how his unusual clinical history may have been linked to the role he played in Europe as the "other," as the bearer of a distinct, exotic culture; and perhaps even to understand why Freud needed a Russian patient, specifically, in order to write his canonical "case history."

Preparing the reader for an exploration of Freud's clinical history of Sergei P., Jones wrote with passionate conviction: "Freud was then at the very height of his powers, a confident master of his method, and the technique he displays in the interpretation and synthesis of the incredibly complex material must win every reader's admiration."[4] It is up to the reader to make his own judgment in this regard. In and of itself, the life of a man who weathered the century's worst storms and managed to conserve his human integrity through it all, thanks to psychoanalysis (and himself), remains interesting not merely as a historical episode. The living material presented us by analysis is also valuable for anyone who believes in analytical interpretation, as well as for anyone who is critical of psychoanalysis. The patient's life story with its overlay of psychoanalysts' views and actions inspires admiration as a remarkable microcosm of human history.

"Personal peculiarities in the patient and a national character that was foreign to ours made the task of feeling one's way into his mind a laborious one," said Freud of Pankeev in "From the History of an Infantile Neurosis," the primary published record of the case. Freud went on to underline "the contrast between the patient's agreeable and affable personality, his acute intelligence, and his nice-mindedness on the one hand and his completely unbridled, instinctual life on the other. . . ."[5] What was the source of the striking disjuncture noted by Freud? we might ask ourselves. Was it the patient's personality, or his ethnic identity?

Sergei Pankeev (1887–1979) was born on his family's estate on the Dnieper and belonged to the same social caste and generation as Nikolai Berdyaev, Mikhail Bulgakov, and Boris Savinkov, the talented writer and terrorist; but in many respects his youth reminds us, most of all, of Alexander Blok's. Did Blok's "music" chime within him? We know that Pankeev was no stranger to art, nor to politics. He painted landscapes, he was interested in literature, and he left behind memoirs, which he seems to have written with great ease. In sum, he was a typical Russian intellectual of the beginning of the century.

Pankeev was a bit younger than the author of *Sexual Confession of an Anonymous Russian*, an erotic manuscript written in 1912 in French and published in English translation by Havelock Ellis in his *Psychology of Sex*;[6] but in many ways, Pankeev and his unknown countryman were similar. In a short introduction, Ellis described the work's author as of Russian background, from a good family, well educated, and gifted, like many of his countrymen, with an aptitude for psychological analysis. Perhaps Freud chose Pankeev as the subject of his most important case study precisely because he was typical of the patients Freud saw during those years. Pankeev's life and experience were in no way exceptional for a person of his generation, a generation that played such a tragic role in Russian history; if this one case deviated from the standard fate of that generation, it was only in that Pankeev was lucky enough to live to old age.

Sergei's father, Konstantin Pankeev, a rich landowner from Kherson, was an activist in the party of Constitutional Democrats (known by the acronym "Kadets"), one of the leaders of the group's influential southern branch, and the publisher of the liberal newspaper *Iuzhnye zapiski* (Southern Notes). During the critical period after the 1905 revolution, the Kadets, a party of professors and industrialists, became the dominant political force in opposition to the czarist regime. The Kadets finally came to power in the revolution of February 1917, and that year, the younger Pankeev also joined the party; but he was never much caught up in politics. Only one all-embracing feeling could breathe life into him and make him act with conviction, and that was love, the kind of love that leaned toward dependence. Freud would call this form of neurotic behavior "breakthrough to a woman." At the height of his passion, Pankeev sometimes bore a resemblance to Yuri Zhivago. But more than anything he would remind the Russian reader of Klim Samgin, the hero of Gorky's unfinished novel, another "typical example" of the contemporary intellectual: honest with everyone else and yet constantly deceiving himself; using his refined upbringing as a defense against any collision with real life; and rebelling against all abstract forms of authority while yearning for personal dependence.[7]

In a well-known essay on Gorky written forty years after Freud's first meeting with Pankeev, Erik Erikson perceived the young writer as more or less the same sort of immature, dependence-prone intellectual. "Neither Luther nor Calvin showed him any new spiritual realms; there were no pioneers or founding fathers who could discover unknown continents before him where he could overcome his internal and external slavery." But from this exceptional American psychoanalyst's point of view, the situation was not hopeless. Erikson found in Gorky's life "the hub stations in the formation of a new Russian world view, Russian individualism." As a whole, Russian history seemed to him "the delayed establishment of Eastern Protestantism" in which the universal values of individual responsibility and initiative would also win out. "We must succeed in convincing the Alyoshas that—from a very long-range point of view—their protestantism is ours and ours, theirs."[8]

A Descendant of the Brothers Karamazov

There were more than a few instances of depression, suicide, and other upper-class forms of mental leave-taking among Sergei Pankeev's relatives. For instance, when Uncle Nikolai decided to get married, it turned out that his father had been no less earnestly courting the same woman. The lady preferred the younger Pankeev, and Sergei's grandfather cut off his son's inheritance, deeply offended. Despite this imbroglio, Uncle Nikolai later became a member of the Duma. The story of Uncle Peter, Sergei's favorite relative, had a less fortunate ending. Peter, a rich man notorious for his eccentricity, lived out his last days in the Crimea as a hermit, allowing only cows, pigs, and other beasts to enter his home. His death was noted in the newspapers under a sensationalistic headline, something like "Millionaire Eaten by Rats." (Blok's father died under similarly shocking, though somewhat different circumstances.) Sergei's mother referred to her in-laws as "the Brothers Karamazov."

Despite this heritage, Sergei grew up a physically healthy, though somewhat tense, child. At age four, he developed a fear of wolves. Later, he began to tease the house pets obsessively, sometimes flying into a rage for no reason. He masturbated in his nanny's presence and carried on sexual games with his older sister. Still later, he would frequently flirt with the servant and peasant girls. He loved to read Lermontov.[9] At eighteen or nineteen, he picked up gonorrhea (Blok also had just such an episode in his youth). Apart from these details, we know very little about Pankeev's childhood and youth, although the work Freud wrote about him is entitled "From the History of an Infantile Neurosis." To proceed further, we will have to reconstruct Freud's chain of reasoning, since it unfolded within his own mental framework and had no direct connection to his patient's biography. For the time being, however, let us examine the few additional facts left at our disposal.

In 1905, Sergei graduated from high school with honors and entered Odessa University. He took a summer trip across Europe with his mother and his sister Anna, who was two years his senior. At the time, Odessa was in an uproar: There were strikes under way that were destined to go down in history as the first Russian revolution.

When they returned from Europe, Anna left for the Caucasus. Like everyone in her family, she had a great love for Lermontov. She wrote poetry herself, which her father often compared to Lermontov's verse. After visiting the spot where the poet had perished, she took poison, and she died in agony two weeks later.

For Sergei, the period that ensued was what he would describe much later as a state of "unconscious grief." When he found out about his sister's suicide, he felt no sadness at all; yet, several months later, he went to Pyatigorsk and soaked Lermontov's death place with tears. He tried to distract himself with his university studies, but things went poorly.

Sergei turned to psychiatrist Vladimir Bekhterev on his father's recommendation and complained to him of "depression." Bekhterev was at that very time involved in a search for funds for his future institute. Sergei's father was about to finance the construction of a psychiatric hospital in Odessa dedicated to his daughter's memory. Bekhterev's waiting room was packed with patients, but he received Sergei immediately. After placing the student in a hypnotic trance, Bekhterev suggested, "Tomorrow you will awake hearty and healthy. You will study with enthusiasm and pass your exam with flying colors. . . . Convince your parents to donate funds to build the Neurological Institute." After he awoke, Sergei remembered Bekhterev's words perfectly, and he was so surprised by the change in subject that he related everything to his father. He never went back to Bekhterev.[10] His parents sent him instead to the renowned Emil Kraepelin, whom textbooks still dub "the father of modern psychiatry." Sergei's father also had gone through treatment with Kraepelin in his youth.

Breakthrough to a Woman

After all the records of this case written by Freud, Jones, and other analysts, we still do not know exactly what was wrong with Sergei Pankeev at that moment. According to his own recollections, Pankeev felt his life was hollow, everything that happened to him seemed unreal, and all the people around him were like wax figures or painted marionettes. Generally, similar feelings can be found in many texts of the period. Blok, who was a few years older than Pankeev, wrote to his fiancée in 1903: "Now is the sort of time when you can sense disquiet everywhere, human relationships are foundering in frustration and pettiness, notions are multiplying . . . ; for example, even marionettes lurching about on strings might come to mind and give rise to morbid anxieties."[11]

On the other hand, we do know what Pankeev was doing in the Bavarian sanatorium to which Kraepelin had sent him. At a carnival on the institution's grounds, Sergei saw a woman dressed in Turkish garb who turned out to be a nurse by the name of Therese. Pankeev's condition changed drastically for the better, as life now seemed wondrous. "But only on condition that Therese would be willing to enter into a love affair with me."[12]

For a patient who has just checked into a sanatorium, getting to know a nurse is not easy. Pankeev found out where Therese lived and burst into her room to set up a rendezvous with her. She accepted the invitation, though not right away. Love alternated with quarreling between the rich patient and his pretty nurse. After each spat, Sergei would try to leave the sanatorium. Kraepelin interpreted his condition as the transition between phases of manic-depressive psychosis and categorically refused to discharge him. Finally, having undergone four months of treatment at the sanatorium, Sergei insisted that he be released. After a stay in Paris, where his uncle took him around to all the night clubs, as he considered this the best way to avoid unpleasant recollection, he returned to one of his father's estates near Odessa. At long last, he felt well.

In the summer of 1908—during the period known in Russian history as the "years of reaction"—Sergei's father died suddenly in Moscow. Konstantin Pankeev was forty-nine years old, perfectly healthy, and, so his son thought, died of an overdose of veronal, which he took to help him sleep. In such a situation, any clinician would have suspected suicide; Freud later concurred with Kraepelin's diagnosis that Konstantin Pankeev had been depressive.[13]

As after the death of his sister, Sergei was restless rather than distressed. He took off for Munich to consult with Kraepelin and to visit Therese. Kraepelin refused outright to continue treating him, confessing (if we are to take Sergei's word for it) that his previous diagnosis of manic-depressive psychosis had been incorrect. While spending the night with Therese, Sergei awoke in a state of unbearable anguish. Kraepelin gave in and sent him back to the sanatorium in Heidelberg. A peculiarity of this establishment was that each male patient was assigned a young lady, all of whom, as Sergei recalled, were from fine families; but the Russian patient had feelings only for Therese. Each new encounter with his lover ended in a stormy breakup, but Sergei always returned to her.

Therese Keller was almost ten years older than Sergei, and she had a daughter. She had a reputation in the sanatorium as a scrupulous nurse; but the strange Russian man—who, it should be said, was successful with ladies throughout his life—broke down the barriers she had raised to protect herself.

For a time, Pankeev returned to Odessa. His mother, concerned about the mésalliance that was taking shape, did her best to cure him of his attachment to Therese. Among the doctors who came to the estate was physician Leonid Droznes, of Odessa. Droznes was fascinated by the new directions in psychiatry that he had plumbed in books by Paul Dubois and Freud, and he tried to apply these theories to his bright, wealthy, young patient. For the first time since he started seeing psychiatrists, Sergei began to take an interest in his own experiences. However, their sessions in Odessa lasted only a short while, as Droznes became fixated on the idea of bringing Sergei to see the great figures of European psychoanalysis. Most of Sergei's wealth, inherited from his father and uncle, was controlled by his mother, who had no qualms about spending money on her son's treatment. So Pankeev, Droznes, and a student (who was needed as a third partner for card games) soon left together for Geneva and Dubois, by way of Vienna.

An Hour a Day for Four Years

The impression that Freud made on Sergei Pankeev was strong enough to remain vivid even some forty years later when he described his first meeting with the famous psychotherapist. He was struck most of all by the "intelligent, dark eyes, which looked at me penetratingly but without causing me the slightest feeling of discomfort." In general, Sergei's perception of Freud fits closely with what we know from a plethora of other sources. Pankeev emphasized Freud's sensitivity, simple and self-assured manners, conventional attire, and emotional equilibrium. "Freud's whole attitude, and the way in which he listened to me, differentiated him strikingly from his famous colleagues whom I had hitherto known."[14]

However, the accuracy of these recollections does not reflect the patient's condition at the beginning of his treatment. Freud characterized this state as unstable and utterly dependent on other people.[15] Jones, conveying the opinion that Sergei's behavior during the first sessions was absolutely unacceptable, gives the example of Pankeev's desire, expressed in shockingly crude terms, for homosexual relations with Freud.[16] At the end of his life, Pankeev himself denied the veracity of this claim. Generally speaking, it also does not mesh with Freud's description of his patient; and it hardly seems likely that Freud would have suppressed such evidence of the disturbed condition of his patient's psyche at the beginning of treatment— especially when that treatment had ended quite successfully, in his estimation.

In any case, doctor and patient spent an unbelievable amount of time with one another. For four years, Freud received Pankeev every day, not counting Sundays and summer holidays. Freud wrote that under less auspicious circumstances, the course of analysis would most likely have been interrupted much earlier and thus would have been ineffective. Freud insisted that such cases demanded that the therapist operate "outside of time," in much the same way as the unconscious.

The first years of analysis effected almost no change in the patient. According to Freud, he "listened, understood, and remained unapproachable." His fear of "an independent existence was so great as to outweigh all the vexations of his illness."[17] Every time the patient made some small modicum of progress, he would immediately stop trying, in order to avoid any further changes. In the end, Freud overcame his patient's resistance by marking a final date by which the analysis would have to end. It was then, nearing the close of four years and in anticipation of the ineluctable deadline, that "in a disproportionally short time, the analysis produced all the material necessary to . . . remove his symptoms."[18] Freud thought the results of analysis extremely satisfactory overall. Many of the details he had uncovered, however, seemed so incredible that he was unsure whether anyone else would believe them. In the course of his "History," Freud would revisit these doubts three times.

Wolves in a Walnut Tree

At the beginning of his analysis, the patient related a dream he remembered from childhood. It took years to produce an interpretation. The dream plays a role of key importance in the entire case history. Freud relied on it in nearly every judgment he made about the patient, and it is from the dream that Sergei Pankeev obtained his otherwise undeserved nickname, which he carried with him into the history of psychoanalysis: the wolf-man. The dream goes like this:

> I dreamt that it was night and that I was lying in my bed. (My bed stood with its foot towards the window; in front of the window there was a row of old walnut trees. I know it was winter when I had the dream, and night-time.)

Suddenly the window opened of its own accord, and I was terrified to see that some white wolves were sitting on the big walnut tree in front of the window. There were six or seven of them. The wolves were quite white, and looked more like foxes or sheep-dogs, for they had big tails like foxes and they had their ears pricked like dogs when they pay attention to something. In great terror, evidently of being eaten up by the wolves, I screamed and woke up.[19]

Sergei associated the dream with the memory that his sister had once shown him a wolf in a book of fairy tales to frighten him. Probably, he thought, it was an illustration of the story "Little Red Riding Hood," taken from the volume by the brothers Grimm that was so popular in Russia. However, he agreed with Freud that it could have been an illustration from another fairy tale—possibly, "The Wolf and the Seven Little Goats." In that case it would be understandable why there were seven wolves in the tree. Freud noted that the two tales had much in common: being eaten by a wolf, cutting open the stomach, the little girl and goats emerging from the wolf's stomach. But the wolves in the tree simply sat there and watched, and it was precisely this passive behavior that so frightened the patient.

Years of daily meetings passed, and the patient gradually filled in various other details of his nightmare. At one point he decided that the window that opened in his dream was his own eyes; Freud submitted that this would mean that it was not the wolves carefully watching Sergei, but the boy intently surveying something terrifying.

Through his work with Sergei, Freud formulated the concept of the "primal scene," a central theme in psychoanalytic theory, which occurs when a child views his parents having sex. Such a scene inspires the fear of castration in the child. In those days, Freud thought that viewing such a primal scene would necessarily have a specific effect on a neurotic's further development.

The wolves were white because the sheets on which the boy's parents lay as they made love were white. The wolf in the picture from the book of fairy tales that Sergei's sister used to frighten him was scary because it stood in the same position as the boy's father had when he was caught in the act: straightened to full height, with one paw stretched forward. Like a detective, the analyst deduced from these highly indirect signs not only the origin of Sergei's fixation on a certain coital position, but also the time when the primal scene took place—Sergei was one and a half years old; and the circumstances that caused the infant to bear witness to his parents' sex life. The conclusion that Freud feared the reader would have a hard time believing was that the four-year-old's dream of wolves in the walnut tree was an unconscious recollection of the scene of his parents making love, which he had witnessed at the age of one and a half. This picture would become even more unbelievable when the reader learned that on that summer night in 1888, the Pankeevs had had sex in front of their little boy three times in a row.

The strange absence of common sense with which this last detail is asserted is a bit disconcerting. The fact that Freud himself believed such a tale and that later researchers also failed to note its strangeness probably has something to do with "the Russian stereotype," a conception held by Westerners that Russia is an exotic place where even the most incredible excesses are possible, be they political or sexual.[20] Freud wrote that "it is perfectly possible" that a small child might witness the sex act of his parents, and he insisted that such occurrences were not confined to "proletarian families."[21] It is easy enough to imagine a husband and wife making love, caught up in the heat of sudden desire, while their one-and-a-half-year-old child sleeps in their bedroom by chance or because of an illness; it is harder to believe that they would indulge in a massive, hours-long sexual feast in the presence of their child, particularly in a huge manor house with all sorts of nannies and servants on hand.

It might be credible that the images Sergei perceived at age one and a half, tucked away in his unconscious, could have come out at age four in a frightening dream and might later have been transformed into the symptoms that haunted him for the rest of his life; but it is impossible to believe that a one-and-a-half-year-old child would have followed the entire endless sex scene through before finally interrupting it with a scream, and that his unconscious would have broken it all down into individual acts, counting all the way to three.

Just in Case

These were not the only noticeable inconsistencies in the story of the wolf-man's infantile neurosis, but they did accentuate the artificiality of other elements. Clearly, Freud was troubled by these discrepancies both while writing "From the History of an Infantile Neurosis" and for a time after its publication. While working on the case history, Freud was totally convinced that one-and-a-half-year-old Sergei really did witness the primal scene and then later "remembered" it in distorted and encoded dream form. But some time afterward, in his equally famous lectures, "An Introduction to Psychoanalysis," Freud confessed that such a strong assumption was far from automatic. Childhood recollections like those of a primal scene "are false most of the time . . . , and occasionally are in total contradiction with the historical truth."

Freud found this amendment, which had to be introduced into his theory of psychoanalysis, both striking and embarrassing. Indeed, it radically twisted a picture that, had it been affirmed in fact, would have seemed as convincing as a law of physics. In reality, "infantile experiences that are reconstructed or revived through recollections during analysis may be in one case unarguably false, in another undoubtedly true, but in most cases they are a mix of truth and falsehood." Sometimes, the primal scene was a memory of a true viewing of the parental sex act, while other times it was the patient's fantasy, stored away in the subconscious and recalled as reality in the peculiar environment provided by analysis.

After this, Freud was forced to make yet another conclusion, one that led him quite far from the picture of the world with which he began his research. He found that fantasy also has the quality of psychic reality. "We are gradually coming to the understanding that in the world of neuroses, psychic reality is decisive, and therefore fantasy must be attributed importance equal to that of real events." Freud's new position was that events such as a child's observation of parental sexual relations, the seduction of a child by an adult, or the threat of castration either actually happen or "are composed out of hints, complemented by the imagination." Regardless of their source, the result was the same: neurosis. The founder of psychoanalysis felt that his science had failed to show any difference in the consequences, whether the childhood event was actual or fantasized. People had an inherent, inborn mechanism for experiencing such events, and if reality did not provide them, people would get by on fantasy.

Returning again to his "History of an Infantile Neurosis," Freud was compelled to make certain additions that strongly contradicted his original thesis. In the new version, he allowed that the image of the sex act between parents (as before, he had no doubt that the meaning of the wolf dream lay in parental coitus) could have emerged from Sergei's witnessing the mating of sheep in his father's flock. Perhaps he saw sheepdogs instead of sheep, which would explain the white wolves. So, as it turned out, Sergei witnessed the copulation of the sheepdogs three times. All this may inspire respect for the author's intellectual fortitude, but it does little to encourage faith in his interpretation. Freud's interpretation had been irrevocably deprived of the classical lucidity and purity that Jones had attributed to it.

In addition, the very idea of sheep shows that Freud was in the end unable to resign himself to the compromise he attempted to make in his "Lectures." In fact, if it made no difference whether the patient witnessed the primal scene in reality or in fantasy, then the whole history of the patient's personality, as reconstructed by the psychoanalyst, loses all means of verification. It becomes impossible to confirm or reject such stories using the "detective" method so dear to Freud's heart, whereby the analyst examines each piece of factual evidence and deduces a consistent whole. It was no accident that, as Pankeev informs us, Freud loved Arthur Conan Doyle so much. Freud explained his collection of classical statuettes to Sergei in much the same way: A psychoanalyst is like an archeologist, restoring something whole out of a single, minuscule detail. But this detail must be fact, not fiction. Therein lies the difference between fantasy and reality: It is impossible to be sure of the former's authenticity. When Freud spoke of sheep, he meticulously proved that in those years Sergei did in fact see the flocks of sheep that belonged to his father; but it is impossible to verify assertions that in his early childhood Sergei simply imagined his parents making love. There is no one to ask, apart from Sergei himself. There is nothing with which to corroborate these fantasies and thus there is no way to determine their veracity, nor at what time or age they appeared.

You're Gonna Get It!

With his interest in Dostoevsky, Freud may have known of the Russian writer's childhood fear of wolves, a phobia that flowed through his pen into the common domain. In one of his works, the nightmarish vision of a wolf is chased away when Marei the peasant speaks the words of Christ and places his finger to a frightened child's lips.

In a similar vein, Osip Mandelstam wrote in 1908:[22]

> *In the wood there are Christmas trees*
> *With golden tinsel blazing*
> *In the thickets toy wolves are gazing*
> *With terrifying eyes.*

There is a certain resemblance between these lines and Pankeev's dream. In the visions of both Mandelstam and Pankeev, the wolves peer menacingly out of the woods at the child (and do nothing else). Why were wolves and fir trees so important to the nineteen-year-old poet that he would describe them in the opening lines of his first book of poetry? As with the dream, the verse contains no inherent interpretation. "We envision death coming like the wolf in a fairy tale," wrote a youthful Mandelstam. But many years later, he would tell death, "I am no wolf by blood." Evidently, the same images may be borne by the rhymed couplets of poets and the free associations of patients undergoing psychotherapy.

The Christmas tree is an unusual point of intersection between nature and culture, and its symbolic meaning is understood by any Russian child: The tree is transported from the woods into the house, it hides gifts, and it almost ceases to be threatening. The transport of the Christmas tree indoors, like Santa Claus, signifies dressing up, the carnival-like atmosphere of the most important holiday of the year. Disturbed children, who grow up to be patients and poets, do not accept the metaphor offered by grown-ups, seizing instead on literal meaning: A forest is still a forest, and wolves in a fir tree are still scary wolves, even if they are just ornaments. This infantile refusal to accept the juxtaposition of nature and culture, forest and home is particularly clear in Mandelstam's short poem.

But Pankeev did not see his wolves in a fir tree, nor did he see them in just any tree. He saw them "in a walnut tree." This seems to be the only detail in the dream that Freud refrained from interpreting, contrary to his own methodological principle by which the most important elements in dream interpretation are those that seem meaningless and unrelated to the subject matter and the dreamer's libidinal experience. The fact that the tree in Pankeev's dream was a walnut is just such a detail; but nevertheless, Freud only mentioned it in passing.

It is difficult to reinterpret a dream that took place a century ago. It is even more unthinkable to attempt to complement or correct Freud's analysis, which has significance only as a unified whole. However, one such attempt was made, and it attained a degree of notoriety. In 1926, immediately after a clash with Freud, Otto Rank offered his own interpretation of Pankeev's dream. The wolves in the tree, he said, were a reflection of the photographs of Freud's six closest disciples, the members of the so-called Committee (including Rank himself). The patient had seen them in Freud's office, then dreamed about the wolves—a dream in no way drawn from his childhood. Freud was forced to go back to Pankeev for more confirmation that his former patient did indeed have the dream as a child.[23]

There is still one point that I would like to bring out, particularly since it may have been inaccessible to Freud, for obvious technical reasons. We know that Sergei learned German from a certain Herr Riedel, who passed several successive summers at the Pankeevs' southern estate. The lessons ended when the teacher fell in love with Sergei's sister, who was fifteen or sixteen years old, and was turned away. This means that Sergei began studying German when he was ten years old. Even sixty-odd years after he met Freud, years that he spent almost entirely in Vienna, Pankeev still spoke German with a slight Russian accent.[24]

Opinions vary among psychoanalysts as to whether analysis can be carried out in a language other than the patient's mother tongue. Theoretically, the answer should be negative. One might amend Lacan's famous formula, which states that the unconscious is structured like a language, and assert that it is structured like a person's *native* language. All of the symbolic material related to childhood events is preserved within the protective covering of the native tongue. Whether these symbols are extracted from memory, as the psychologist would claim, or from the subconscious, as the psychoanalyst would maintain, anyone can see that this difficult process of rediscovering events from early childhood is made even more difficult when the patient is forced to translate the material from his "childhood" language into one of his "adult" ones, a language acquired much later. Each language has its own rules, idioms, sayings, and phonetic associations that are crucial to any analysis and yet often simply untranslatable from one language to another. This process is at least as difficult as the translation of poetry, which is feasible only for professionals—and even then often with great difficulty and inevitable losses in meaning. It would be strange to expect a patient to be capable of more.

But psychoanalysis is a practical discipline, and if Freud had really believed in such a principle, his doctrine never would have gotten beyond the bounds of the German language. In fact, Freud's solution to this question was purely pragmatic: Pankeev was left to cope as best he could with his linguistic difficulties, and Freud was free to interpret his patient's German as he saw fit. At the same time, the possibility can never be denied that material presented by the patient in translation from his native tongue into the analyst's language might have been interpreted quite differently in the original.

There is a common Russian idiom, one that any child would know: "Poluchish' na orekhi!" This expression—the equivalent of the English phrase "You're going to get it!"—might be used by a mother, father, grandmother, or nanny if they are angry with a child and want to threaten him or her with punishment. The origin of this popular expression is unclear; but the expression is the more peculiar in that it is usually used with very young children. Its meaning might well be ambiguous to such children and thus all the more disconcerting: The phrase could be misunderstood as "I'll give you something to buy nuts with!"; or in a more threatening idiomatic vein, "I'll give you one on the nuts!" But what nuts? the hearer might well wonder; for the Russian word "orekhi" does not carry the same figurative meaning as the modern English slang word. In addition, because "orekhi" can mean "nut trees" as well as "nuts," a child might misunderstand this expression as "You're gonna get some in the nut trees!" In this connection, remember that according to Sergei Pankeev's story, a row of walnut trees stood just outside his bedroom window.

Freud wrote that it was approximately at the age of two or three years that Sergei began playing with his penis in front of his nanny, "which, as with many cases when children do not conceal their masturbation, should be viewed as an attempt at seduction." In response, as far as Freud knew, the nanny declared to the boy that children who did that got a "sore" on their private parts. However, a somewhat different scene, truer to life, might have unfolded, a scene in which the nanny, seeing the boy amusing himself with his sexual organ, threatened to give it to him, as he thought, "in the nut trees." In his rising fear and guilt, the boy would have wondered what terrible thing went on in the nut trees; and so, a little later, he had a dream in which he supplied the most comprehensible answer.

Pankeev's dream becomes understandable in light of this idiom, and it can be interpreted as the realization of his fear of punishment, extrapolating simple visual imagery from the usual threat "You're going to get it!" Wolves, the most horrible thing he knew both from life and from fairy tales, were sitting in a nut tree. Considering everything we know from Freud about Sergei's childhood, the dream can be understood as a reflection of the boy's fear of castration, a terror that came from his nanny—the focal point of his libido.

Childhood with a Nanny

Russian culture has always been full of nannies and grannies, at least since Pushkin's famous nanny, Arina Rodionovna. Her absurd image as the great poet's true muse, his inspiration and tutor, deeply infiltrated the mass consciousness of generations of Russian and Soviet schoolchildren. The institution of the nanny is firmly rooted in Russian national tradition, along with a particular affection for ancestors. The psychological structure that lies behind this tradition is markedly different from the general European mindset and stands in even sharper contrast to the American psyche.

This phenomenon immediately attracted the attention of psychoanalysts as soon as they began thinking about Russia. Two classic papers written by psychoanalysts about Russians—Freud's monograph on Pankeev and Erikson's essay on Gorky—treat this theme as a key point. The protagonists in Sergei's early childhood recollections are his Russian nanny and a series of French and English governesses. To Freud, the nanny was the central object of little Sergei's sexual attraction. The nanny was not only the focal point of his libido, she also had power over its expression: After she threatened Sergei, he immediately stopped masturbating. This, according to Freud's system, knocked him back in development to an earlier, anal-sadistic phase.

In Erikson's view, the grandmother was the dominant image in little Alexei Peshkov's surroundings.[25] Erikson saw her as the image of paradise lost, of a timeless existence that he considered characteristic of Russians. The grandmother was the symbol of Russian political apathy, the essence of Russia's inertia, and the reason for the Russian people's childlike gullibility.[26] Perhaps she was the very asset "that makes a people endure and permits it to wait," as Erikson noted sarcastically in 1950.[27] According to him, agrarian Russia was characterized by diffused motherhood, so children were protected from "exclusive maternal fixation" and instead received "a whole repertoire of giving and frustrating maternal images." This meant grandmothers, nannies, aunts, neighbor ladies, and so forth. This made the world "a more reliable home, since mothering was not dependent on one frail relationship, but was a matter of homogeneous atmosphere."[28]

The nanny is a professional in child rearing, something like a prostitute in the field of sex; she should be skilled, but love is by no means necessary.[29] Her monopolistic control is far more effective than the control of the parents, who are busy with their own affairs and rarely coordinate their efforts in child rearing. Matronly and asexual, she is devoid of both the mother's erotic attraction and the father's libido, which stimulates growth and challenges the child to compete. The nanny can do only one thing for the child, but it is something she does faithfully and effectively: She draws him or her into the value system of traditional peasant culture. This is ex-

actly the nanny's function—to transmit traditional culture between generations. Smoothing and muffling intellectual parents' cultural deviations, the
nanny forces each generation to begin its search anew, from the node of
frozen peasant tradition.

"It is not universities that raise the true Russian, but kind, illiterate nannies," Rozanov concluded approvingly. When a different mood struck the
philosopher, it was to the nannies that he turned for salvation: "Old, sweet
grannies, keep the Russian truth. Keep it safe; there is no one else who
will."[30] It was with horror that Andrei Bely recalled being left for a time
without his nanny at age four: "I was totally defenseless: no nanny, no
bonne; my parents were there, but they were tearing me in two; I over-
flowed with fear and anguish."[31] As one last bit of documentary evidence,
we will refer to Leon Bakst's portrait of Sergey Diaghilev, a marvelous specimen of his generation.[32] Surprisingly enough, the famed impresario, cosmopolitan and homosexual, is not portrayed against the background of an
applauding concert hall or fluttering ballet dancers; instead, sitting near
him, in the corner, is his wrinkled nanny.

Logically speaking, if motherhood is not individualized, then fatherhood
simply ceases to exist; if motherhood is diffused in the atmosphere, then fatherhood is no more than a mere symbol. According to Freud's description,
Sergei's libido was transferred from his nanny to his father at a time when
the latter had long since left home.[33] Elsewhere, Freud related the story of
Pankeev at age six: He had not seen his father for many months, when his
mother one day promised the children she would take them to the city and
show them something they would like. She took the children to the sanatorium, where they saw their father; "he looked ill, and the boy felt very sorry
for him."[34]

Oedipus would hardly have felt at home in such a situation, with the maternal element distributed among grannies and nannies, while the paternal
element just looks on pitifully from the sidelines. Whom is the little boy to
want, from whom is he to liberate himself, for whom and with whom is he
to fight, when he is confronted only by his nanny's relentlessly persistent
control and aged flesh? Dionysus would have felt much more comfortable
in Alexei's or Sergei's shoes. Strange as it may seem, it was exactly in the
world of Dionysus that the two men lived, a world of grandmotherly fairy
tales about eternal resurrection and sexless love. The multifarious rejec-
tions of maleness in the works of Pankeev's contemporaries such as Andrei
Bely, Vyacheslav Ivanov, and Nikolai Berdyaev are more easily understood
when viewed as the result of an attraction to paradise lost; not the paradise
of feminine, maternal sexuality, but that of grandmotherly asexuality. Their
childhood stories, embodied and justified through the work of Dionysian
Russian symbolists and the androgyny of Russian neoplatonists, were not
all that different from "From the History of an Infantile Neurosis."

Russia Is a Sphinx!

Freud considered ambivalence his Russian patient's most identifiable characteristic, and he had no shortage of strong epithets to describe this feature. Pankeev's ambivalence seemed to Freud "extraordinarily clear, intense and protracted" and even "unbelievable."[35] Freud also deemed his Russian colleague Sabina Spielrein "abnormally ambivalent."[36] There is no doubt that Freud was in this case influenced by cultural stereotypes. In October of 1920, Freud confided to Zweig, "Even Russians who are not neurotic are also very noticeably ambivalent."[37] In the same letter, he wrote that "ambivalence is a legacy from the psychic life of primitive races; with the Russian people, however, it is far better preserved and has remained more accessible to consciousness than elsewhere, as I was able to point out only a few years ago in the detailed case history of a typical Russian."[38] In his work on Dostoevsky, Freud repeats more or less the same idea: "A man who alternately sins and then in his remorse sets high moral standards . . . reminds one of the barbarians. . . . Ivan the Terrible behaved in exactly this way; indeed, this compromise with morality is a characteristic Russian trait."[39]

Another of Pankeev's characteristics was narcissism of a breathtaking intensity. Freud noted yet a third feature common to Pankeev and Dostoevsky: bisexuality. Freud found in the latter "a clearly expressed bisexual tendency," while the former's "homosexual attitude . . . persisted in him as an unconscious force with . . . very great tenacity."[40] Moreover, Freud reminded his reader, from the very start of Pankeev's analysis "all work was centered on the effort to open up his unconscious relations to men." Sergei's suppression of his homosexuality explained in part his inability to remain faithful to any woman for long, a tendency that disturbed him greatly.[41]

Freud drew a connection between Pankeev's latent homosexuality and his fantasies of rebirth. Around this time, Jung began to speak of rebirth fantasies as the most basic content of a neurotic's unconscious life. Freud used the Pankeev case to take up the theoretical debate, insisting that fantasies of rebirth also derive from the "primal scene." But anyone obsessed by such fantasies identifies with the passive actor in the scene rather than the active one: with the mother, not the father. In much the same way, Pankeev's fantasy indicates his desire to step into a woman's shoes; to replace his own mother, make love with his father, and give birth to his child. "Here, therefore, the phantasy of re-birth was simply a mutilated and censored version of the homosexual wish-phantasy."[42]

Freud dedicated a good deal of space in his case history to four-year-old Pankeev's earliest religious impressions. He begins this analysis with the caveat that he had found it hard to believe at first Sergei's insistence that certain conclusions subtle enough to be the product of an adult mind originated in his early childhood. Nevertheless, Freud takes this placement in time at face value. When the boy learned about the passion of Christ, he was indignant at the behavior of God-the-Father. "If he were almighty," the boy reasoned, "then it was his fault that men were wicked and tormented others and were sent to Hell for it. He ought to have made them good; he was responsible himself for all wickedness and all torments."[43] Around the same time, Sergei's sadistic streak began to show through in his treatment of animals. His sadism made him feel like God-the-Father; his masochism made him feel like Christ himself. He would blaspheme and then make the sign of the cross to atone for his sin. Whenever he did this, he would breathe in or out deeply, bringing the Holy Spirit into his game as well. However, all this ended at the age of ten in a feeling of total indifference to God, when a young German tutor was invited to take over his daily care and education. "His piety sank away with his dependence upon his father, who was replaced by a new and more sociable father."[44]

Freud noted that Pankeev's piety had generally developed under feminine influences (his mother's and nanny's), while the masculine influence would have facilitated his emancipation from religion.[45] He drew the conclusion that Sergei's struggle against religion was directly linked to his suppressed and improperly sublimated homosexuality. The suppression of forceful homosexual feelings relegated this indispensable part of his spiritual life to a place too deeply buried in the unconscious. "For this reason, the patient was without all those social interests which give a content to life," Freud concludes this section with unexpected pathos. "It was only when, during the analytic treatment, it became possible to liberate his shackled homosexuality that . . . each piece of the homosexual libido . . . sought out some application in life and some attachment to the great common concerns of mankind."[46]

This text was written as a dry, clinical description. Here and there, however, it contains some glimpses of emotional timbre. Here we have a case that Freud chose from among a myriad of similar cases, all of which must have been interesting and important in some way. Why did the founder of psychoanalysis choose the case of Sergei P. for his monograph? Was it mere chance that his favorite patient, like his favorite author, was Russian? It seems that the mention of "characteristically Russian traits," scattered throughout Freud's texts, bears witness to the fact that, just as Pankeev "preferred the German element" (and this, according to Freud, "created a great advantage for transference during treatment"), Freud felt drawn to the "Russian element" and felt that Russian material would give him a certain advantage in comprehension and exposition.

In the end, the characteristically Russian traits pointed out here by Freud—ambivalence, bargaining with the conscience, and bisexuality—are characteristic of many neurotics. Could it be that Freud was drawn to Pankeev and Dostoevsky because, due to some Russian peculiarities of which he was aware, their conscious minds had more direct access to the universal mechanisms of the unconscious? This image of Russians as creatures closely engaged with the subconscious was widespread in both external and internal perceptions of Russian culture at the time. In 1911, Alexander Blok, whose poetry dealt with dreams no less often than did Freud's analysis, wrote to Andrei Bely, "We are living these deep and disturbing dreams, and we have to constantly jump up in the middle of the night to chase them away."[47]

As Freud began his second analysis of Pankeev, in 1918, Blok was writing his poem, "The Scythians," a work as inspired as it is bizarre. In this famous poem, Blok compared Russia to a sphinx, while he likened the European West to Oedipus. Unlike other sphinxes, this particular beast was most terrifying in its love. Addressing the West in the guise of Oedipus, Blok wrote:

> *That Sphinx is Russia, grieving and exulting,*
> *And weeping black and bloody tears enough,*
> *She stares at you, adoring and insulting,*
> *With love that turns to hate, and hate—to love.*
> *Yes, love! For you of Western lands and birth*
> *No longer know the love our blood enjoys.*
> *You have forgotten there's a love on Earth*
> *That burns like fire and, like all fire, destroys.*[48]

This metaphor was the inverse of Freud's, in that Oedipus is active and ambivalent. In this case, oedipal qualities are attributed to the sphinx. The image of the sphinx was popular, and Russians tended to identify more with the sphinx than with Oedipus. Vyacheslav Ivanov wrote of this tendency: "We see ourselves together in the Sphinx." Blok, however, went much further.

Blok's Russia correlated with the West as Freud's unconscious correlated with the conscious: It had no sense of time ("For you centuries pass, for us a single hour"); it had no qualms about contradiction ("grieving and exulting"); it had no measure or boundary ("there are millions of you, but uncounted hordes of us"); it did not discriminate, forget, or sublimate ("We love everything. . . . We remember everything. . . . We love the flesh"); and it narcissistically blended "I" with "we." In Blok's poem, moreover, emotional ambivalence is emphasized several times in a row: Hate and love, rejoicing and gloom meld into one. This kind of love, long since forgotten in the West, leads to death:

> *We love raw flesh, its colour and its stench.*
> *We love to taste it in our hungry maws.*
> *Are we to blame then, if your ribs should crunch,*
> *Fragile between our massive, gentle paws?*[49]

And so, the Russian sphinx's central riddle is the ambivalence of love, innate in the barbarous Scythians but incomprehensible to Western men. As surprising as it may seem, in essence Blok had in mind here the same idea that Freud expressed in a letter to Zweig—that emotional ambivalence was a primitive trait, preserved more in Russians than in other nations.

On the other hand, Freud's assertion that ambivalence was characteristic even of Russians who were not neurotic is difficult to prove with this example. "The Scythians" was ripening in Blok's mind just around the time when Yury Kannabikh diagnosed him as neurasthenic and he began taking bromine treatment. Fifteen years earlier, during the first rosy days of his relationship with his future wife—a relationship that probably came no more easily to him than it did to Pankeev—Blok already felt that "when the duality that lies in *every* human soul awakes, it shows its sharp and merciless features—this duality must be defeated." Here Blok emphasized the word "every," implying that this unsettling duality was a universal, not pathological, trait. But at that time Blok was still far from taking pride in this duplicity, in contrast to his attitude during the late revolutionary period. On the contrary, it was a flaw that "must be defeated," and "there is no solution, other than a constant struggle," for happiness could only be "achieved consciously, one way or another."[50]

During the same years, actor Mikhail Chekhov was suffering from a serious nervous disorder. He was treated by psychiatrists, hypnotists, and psychoanalysts, but in the end the extraordinary actor was able to cure himself (see chapter 4). He later described the sensation that he believed had helped him to weather his crisis: "I perceived good and evil, right and wrong, beautiful and ugly, strong and weak, healthy and sickly, great and small as a kind of oneness. . . . I did not believe in straightforward, simple psychological systems. . . . They did not take into account that to be human means to reconcile opposites."[51]

Chekhov believed that he had been taught this truly "Scythian" definition of man by Russian life itself, with all its contrasts. For example, when he was a schoolboy, his family had controlled his every move, but his father, an alcoholic (who had written books on the harmful effects of drinking), once gave him three rubles to hire a prostitute. Reading Dostoevsky also served him well in living with the paradoxes of life. In much the same way, Bely drew his "dialectic" out of a childhood need to bridge the gulf between himself and his parents, between his father and mother, and between various authorities.[52] Such a "dialectic," reconciling and intertwining the opposite forces in life as if contradictions do not exist, is another way to describe the ambivalence that so surprised Freud in Russians. It would be only a short time before the "dialectic" became the logical basis and justification for the intellectual authoritarianism that was to take shape in the Soviet state.

In general, the particular themes that Freud injected into his description of Pankeev's case resonate deeply with the basic themes in the "Russian idea," themes that ring clear in the novels, poems, and philosophical treatises written by Pankeev's countrymen throughout the years of his childhood and youth (see chapter 2). We see this in a rationalistic critique of religion coexisting peacefully with a vague sort of mysticism; in an obsession with death and rebirth; in an unusual focus on issues of homosexuality, sodomy, and androgyny; and in a strikingly intense inner life combined with complaints of a lack of real social concern.

We do not know, nor will we ever know, what was really going on in Pankeev's mind as described by Freud, or in the Russian soul in general as described by the philosophers and poets of the Silver Age. All that we have is portraits and self-portraits; but when a variety of images overlap, we can begin to guess at the reality underneath. It is difficult to say on which level these coincidences exist: whether they are the product of stereotyped perception, and in part self-perception by a certain culture; or evidence of a deep commonality, observed equally on many levels. Could the images of man proposed by Freud's psychoanalysis of an infantile neurosis, by Russian symbolist poetry, and by Russian religious philosophy truly be various facets of a single, credible syndrome? Were particular features of this syndrome inherent in people of that time, in a sociological and statistical sense?

Here the relationship between Sergei Pankeev and Alexander Blok is useful, both in their parallels and differences. Pankeev offers us the image of a Russian Oedipus, resigned to the position that the Western sphinx has put him in, and throughout his long life never quite solving the sphinx's rationalistic riddle. Blok represents the Russian sphinx, mysterious and two-faced, shining and absurd, threatening, but more frightening to itself than to anyone else. Soon after he had issued a call to revolution "with all your body, with all your heart, with all your consciousness," after he had written the gospel of the revolution and accepted a job in the Ministry of Education, Blok died in a psychotic crisis comparable only to Nietzsche's horrid end.

We know from psychoanalysis and from cultural history that there is no such thing as coincidence. These themes were very familiar and important to Russian intellectuals of that time, and Freud knew this circle of people: It was the pool from which he drew his patients, and later, from which he selected a sufficiently representative character for his case history. His judgment was perfect. The analysis of the infantile neurosis revealed the very same key problems and characteristic features that became clear as the most developed cultural class reached the apogee of its development. Little Sergei Pankeev's subconscious exhibited the same motifs as the highest, professionally sublimated levels of his native culture.

Russian philosophers never shied away from such correlations, which might seem to today's readers a bit too direct. According to Fyodor Stepun, "our personal feelings unexpectedly brought us to ask the ultimate moral and even theological questions."[53] It could be that Freud's notions about Russians' psychological features were no more than illusions of perception and self-perception, born of historical circumstances and ethnocultural stereotypes, both of which inevitably influence the thinking of even the most sophisticated observers. In any case, as far as is known, Freud's ideas—whether accurate or not—had no consequences outside the intellectual realm. Meanwhile, Blok's "Scythians" played a role in the popularization of Eurasianness, a concept that in the 1930s thrust the Russian diaspora into the "massive, gentle paws" of the KGB.

A verse by Tyutchev suggests yet another explanation for the sphinx's power. Although Tyutchev's words were applied to evoke an image of nature, they could equally well be applied to Russia (indeed, they may well have served as a springboard for Blok's poem):

> *Nature is a Sphinx. Her inquisition*
> *Can, thus, more surely break the man she tries;*
> *For fear may put an edge on her perdition,*
> *That in her timeless bulk no riddle lies.*[54]

This verse carries the same Russian ambiguity, dialectic, and ambivalence as Blok's "Scythians"; but what ruse or ploy could the Russian sphinx use to lure and destroy human beings, if it had no riddle to recite? And if it held no riddle, then what did Freud find so interesting in Russians? Nevertheless, the end of our century, so different from its beginning, hints at just such an interpretation of the "Russian idea": "That in her timeless bulk no riddle lies." If we find this convincing, then yet another, more pragmatic explanation of Freud's gravitation toward the Russian "element" suggests itself. Complex and dubious constructions are easier to accept (even for their author) in an exotic context, even more so in a context that is buttressed by preexisting stereotypes. Russian material was particularly valuable to Freud because it provided certain advantages. Pankeev's story was written by and large in refutation of the criticism that had been leveled at the "primal scene" theory by Freud's disciples as they distanced themselves from him. Many a radical intellectual has endowed his story with some modicum of verisimilitude by setting the scene in an exotic country about which little is known and therefore in which anything seems possible. Thus, Russian romantics sent their heroes off to run with the gypsies or to the Caucasus; Montesquieu portrayed his ideas as they would be implemented in Persia; Nietzsche placed his *Übermensch* in more or less the same area; Bogdanov was forced to launch his social ideal even further afield, on

Mars; and Lévi-Strauss discovered his ideas among the savage Indians. When Charles Fourier, a century before Freud, had need of material for his ideas about a new world of love where all passions—even the most unusual—would find guaranteed satisfaction, his favorite example turned out to be of Russian descent as well: a certain Muscovite princess Stroganoff so bothered her serving girl, that by her example Fourier discovered "unconscious lesbian" passion.[55] Freud was interested in psychological theories and the specific human lives that could confirm them, rather than some social utopia, but the function of exotic material in his work remained the same. Exoticism became necessary when it seemed that his doctrine might expand beyond the bounds of credibility.

Recollections of Psychoanalysis

Later, the "wolf-man" became a celebrity. More and more psychoanalysts of the Old and New Worlds sought to meet with him, as he was one of the few patients of Freud's who were accessible to the public. Two parts of Pankeev's memoirs, along with essays about him written by his other two psychoanalysts, were released in the same volume as a republication of Freud's "From the History of an Infantile Neurosis." A Viennese journalist interviewed Pankeev toward the end of his life, in the middle of the 1970s, and after his death she put out a book drawing on her conversations with the "wolf-man." In the interview, Pankeev spoke of Freud one moment, and described his latest lover the next. We hear the voice of a man whose life was strange and broken, but in his cultural milieu this was nothing remarkable. Having lived the larger part of his life as an émigré, he tells the young, curious Viennese woman of Kerensky and Lenin, of Pasternak and Solzhenitsyn. Some of his musings are interesting in their own right: For example, he notes the similarity between Tolstoy's departure from home and his subsequent death and the circumstances surrounding Verkhovensky's flight and death in Dostoevsky's *The Demons.* For us, of course, Pankeev's most interesting statements relate to how, at the end of his life, he viewed the influence that psychoanalysis had on him.

Generally speaking, he was skeptical. "What is less good about psychoanalysis is that one gets used to living according to another person's guidance. I would say that psychoanalysis weakens the ego. It may perhaps relieve the id somewhat, but the ego suffers because it submits to an authority."[56] Elsewhere he formulated his dissatisfaction in a different way: Psychoanalysts were "always the same."

They only go by what Freud discovered. By those principles and symbols, and they aren't getting beyond that. I read about Lenin, that his success was due to the fact that he was always in tune with the times. He said, for example, "All power to the Soviets." Two months later he said, "That's no longer relevant, times have changed. We will accomplish nothing if we keep doing the same thing." But the psychoanalysts forever do the same thing. They make no progress. Today, I am more critical of psychoanalysis.[57]

This quote might be amusing, were it not coming from a man who had spent a huge amount of time with Freud himself, from a man to whom Freud jokingly referred as "a piece of psychoanalysis" and of whose recovery Freud seemed to have no doubt.

Pankeev did identify two elements that he had found useful: Freud's positive attitude toward Therese, and the "paternal transference" that immediately took place, with Freud generating in him feelings that were similar to those he had toward his father.

We learn from Pankeev's memoirs that the first question he asked Freud concerned his relationship with Therese: Should I marry her or not? "Had Professor Freud, like the other doctors whom I had seen previously, said 'No,' I would certainly not have stayed with him."[58] But Freud gave a different answer: Maybe, but let us wait a few months, till the analysis is complete, and then we shall see. The analysis was completed, as we already know, four years later. All this time, Sergei corresponded with and periodically visited Therese. "I would have married Therese then and there, had this not been contrary to the rule Professor Freud had laid down."[59] In the end, the Professor made an unusual move, and agreed to see Therese. He liked her very much. A good deal later, in 1970, Pankeev would say that it was this promised and tensely awaited denouement that served as the primary catalyst of his cure.

However, Sergei's father and his relationship with his son were much more central, to Freud's way of thinking, than was Therese. In his memoirs, Pankeev repeated Freud's words several times, words that are truly difficult to forget: "You are lucky your father died. Otherwise, you would have had no chance to get well."[60] Pankeev only superficially understood what Freud was suggesting. "What he had in mind was that if my father had not died, I would have been unable to create a transference." The transference was intense, and the Russian patient was forced to work through the positive and negative facets of the psychoanalytically induced phenomenon. Until the end of his days, he felt a deep gratitude to Freud, and at the same time blamed him for many of his misfortunes.

From Analysis to Analysis

As the deadline that Freud had set for the completion of Pankeev's analysis approached, the patient began to produce more recollections of early childhood trauma. In turn, the analyst became acquainted with his patient's lover and gave his blessing to their marriage. The two men were satisfied; both had what they wanted.

Their last session took place on July 29, 1914. The day before, Crown Prince Ferdinand of Austria and his wife had been killed in Sarajevo. As he parted ways with his patient, Freud noted that if Ferdinand had come to power, Austria would have been drawn into war with Russia.[61] As we know, this event nonetheless did come about, even absent Ferdinand; the powers of comprehension are limited, even in the most intelligent of men.

In the short epilogue to "From the History of an Infantile Neurosis," Freud wrote about the conclusion of Sergei's analysis: "I parted from him, regarding him as cured, a few weeks before the unexpected outbreak of the Great War; and I did not see him again until the shifting chances of war had given the Central European powers access to South Russia."[62]

The war began a few hours after Sergei crossed the Russian border. Therese Keller and her daughter Elsa remained for the time being in Munich. When Pankeev arrived home, his mother ordered a church service to celebrate her son's cure. Their parish priest intoned a prayer in honor of Sergei and his doctor, "Sigismund." Sergei felt splendid on his estate near Odessa, where he succeeded in evading the draft, as he was his mother's only son. Despite his mother's objections, he began preparations to obtain a Russian visa for Therese, who was now the national of a belligerent state. Sergei was successful in this as well. Therese left her daughter in Munich and traversed Romania. They were married. Around the same time, Sergei passed his exams at the law department of the University of Odessa by correspondence. Everything was going well, apart from the conflicts between Therese and her new mother-in-law.

In 1918, Austro-German forces entered Odessa and renamed occupied Ukraine the "Hetman Republic." Meanwhile, news arrived that Elsa had contracted tuberculosis, and Therese left as soon as she was able to obtain a visa, traveling to Munich by way of Kiev. In November, the Central Powers suffered utter defeat. Odessa was soon occupied by the English, French, and Poles. The ruble underwent a catastrophic devaluation. The Odessa branch of the Russian Bank burned to the ground, sending all of the Pankeevs' capital up in smoke. What was left was spent on acquiring visas and emigrating.

On May 29, 1918, Freud wrote to Lou Andreas-Salomé that he had received a letter from Odessa. "The young man . . . whom after three and a half years' treatment I had discharged as cured, as I thought, on 14 July 1914 . . . has become my enemy, who might, for all I know, have fired on my eldest son."[63] The war was still raging, and this young man, nonetheless, was asking for another meeting. Without confiding his motives in Lou, Freud asked her to come to Vienna, for the sake of "your six big brothers, who were all so nice to you," and take up his old patient's case in his stead. Lou, however, did not come.

This sort of situation, in which an analyst perceives his patient in the context of the former's own intense personal struggle (in this case, also a situation of political battle) and projects his unfounded fears on that patient, is a fairly characteristic, though not classic, case of countertransference. It must have had a certain therapeutic effect, but Freud never again mentioned his worries that the Russian he had cured would become fatally connected with his son while fighting on the Russian front. Then again, he did pen a metaphorical passage in "From the History of an Infantile Neurosis," likening Pankeev's difficult and plodding treatment to "the situation . . . when . . . an enemy army needs weeks and months to make its way across a stretch of country which in times of peace was traversed by an express train in a few hours and which only a short time before had been passed over by the defending army in a few days."[64] Drawing on what we know of this case, the only external manifestation of Freud's own unanalyzed emotions appears in his persistent attempts to send his patient to another analyst. In such a context, it is also curious that these appeals were made to women, that is to people without military responsibilities, and that these analysts were all "belligerent" nationals—Lou Andreas-Salomé, a Russian, and Ruth Mack Brunswick, an American.

In April 1919 Pankeev nevertheless made his way to Vienna. Freud presented him with a copy of "From the History of an Infantile Neurosis" with a friendly inscription. He noticed that Pankeev evidenced a small remainder of unanalyzed emotion, and took up his treatment again himself. These sessions lasted from September 1919 until Easter of 1920. Under the circumstances, Freud felt compelled to give his patient money from time to time. Sergei then found a job as a humble clerk in an insurance company, where he would work until his retirement, at the point at which he became eligible for an Austrian pension.

The impetus for this new round of analysis was a digestive problem. Sergei explained this problem as the result of an unsuccessful previous treatment he had received from Doctor Droznes in Odessa, whereby the physician had prescribed medicines designed for animals. Freud interpreted these symptoms differently: "He then came to Vienna and reported that immediately after the end of the treatment he had been seized with a longing to tear himself free from my influence. After a few months' work a piece of the transference which had not hitherto been overcome was successfully dealt with. Since then the patient has felt normal and has behaved unexceptionably, in spite of the war having robbed him of his home, his possessions, and all his family relationships. It may be that his very misery, by gratifying his sense of guilt, contributed to the consolidation of his recovery."[65]

Later, Pankeev concluded that if he had gone home while Odessa was occupied by the English, he could have saved the remainder of his fortune; but Freud would not let him go, explaining his desire to return home as a form of neurotic resistance. By the time Sergei's problems with transference and abnormal peristalsis had been solved to Freud's satisfaction, the Reds had arrived in Odessa.

In 1926, a nearly insolvent Pankeev came to Freud for the third time with hypochondriacal complaints that bordered on paranoid delusions. After a minor nasal cavity operation, he had begun to fear that his nose was on the verge of falling apart from scars, cracks, or something of the sort. Dermatologists had been unable to help him; they had insisted that everything was fine.

This time, Freud ended up sending Pankeev to his colleague Ruth Mack Brunswick, who was living in Vienna at the time. It is difficult to say what played a more important role in this decision—countertransference and a guilt complex linked to the patient, Freud's disappointment at the failure of what he thought had been successful therapy, the fact that he was busy with other patients, or financial difficulties. The septuagenarian professor had just reduced the number of his patients in 1926 from six to five, at the same time raising his fee from 20 to 25 U.S. dollars per session. On the other hand, Pankeev recalled, Freud demanded that his followers receive at least one patient for free. These are clearly the terms under which Brunswick took him on. Although he had been severely hurt himself by the inflation of the Austrian kronen, Freud helped his former patient for many years, slipping him the few dollars or pounds sterling he received from foreign clients.

Pankeev's sessions with Brunswick lasted five months. She was certain of the diagnosis: hypochondriacal, paranoid delirium. It should be said that her clinical report on this case evinces much less respect for the patient than did Freud's "From the History of an Infantile Neurosis." In it, Brunswick confesses that at first she had trouble believing that the man before her was the same as the intelligent and honest wolf-man of Freud's descriptions. She saw a psychotic whose primary characteristics were hypocrisy, narcissism, and avarice. Was this a personality change or an illusion induced by countertransference? Paul Roazen, who closely examined Brunswick's own clinical history, was inclined to suspect the latter. Brunswick, who had been a longtime patient of Freud's, perceived his former favorite as a competitor.[66]

Pankeev recalled that he was so indignant at the diagnosis of paranoia, as well as at the fact that this time he had not been treated by Freud himself, that he decided to get well as quickly as possible. In 1927, he met Muriel Gardiner, another psychoanalyst, who would have occasion to see Pankeev regularly and to assist him over the course of the next few decades. He gave her Russian lessons. She found him an excellent conversationalist and wrote that he impressed her as a healthy and perfectly reasonable person.

The Riddle of Therese Keller

Therese had always been proud of her Spanish roots. In the anti-German atmosphere of Russia in 1914, she had a difficult time, as she knew neither Russian nor French. Pankeev recalled that she was aided only by the fact that she looked more like a Spaniard or an Italian than a German. Freud found her beautiful and described her as a "real Tsarina."

However, after the death of her daughter, Pankeev said, Therese changed. She took on eccentricities, becoming stingy and antisocial. Sergei never did learn how much older she was than he; she had lost her documents before moving to Russia. She complained of accelerated aging, although she remained attractive to Pankeev. Nevertheless, he was constantly unfaithful to her.

After the *Anschluss* in 1938, when the Germans annexed Austria, the Viennese reacted in various ways. The Jews got the worst of it. As always, a few managed to emigrate, while an epidemic of suicides swept through the ranks of those that remained. Pankeev was under suspicion. One day, a Nazi appeared at his door and began asking questions about his life and his family. Sergei showed him a photograph of his father. The Nazi said he was satisfied—Sergei's father looked like one of the tsars. He confessed that he had come to find out whether the Russian immigrant was a Jew. Soon after this incident, Pankeev suggested to his wife that she send to her native Würzburg for documents proving her Aryan blood. Therese responded "with a strange look" that he would remember always.

It was around that time that Therese suggested to Sergei that they commit suicide together. "You're crazy," he snapped. "We're not Jews." On March 31, 1938, Sergei Pankeev found his wife dead. She had killed herself by inhaling gas.

For some reason, neither Pankeev nor the analysts who worked with him ever expressed an inkling of what seems, in retrospect, self-evident: that Therese Keller was probably Jewish. She hid this fact her entire life, with good reason. Perhaps this explains why Sergei's mother and Kraepelin were so set against Sergei marrying Therese, considering their union a mésalliance. If so, it might also explain the legend of Therese's Spanish origins that she fed Sergei, knowing it would appeal to his romantic nature. In his memoirs, Pankeev described his love for Therese in a chapter entitled "Spanish Castles."

A year after Therese's suicide, Sergei sought out her brother in Munich, driven by his unrealized grief, as was always the case with him after a loss. "Your grandmother was Spanish," he remarked for some reason. "Spanish? That's news to me," the brother responded, and then added, "but our Grandmother is said to have had an affair with an officer of the Bavarian nobility."[67]

Psychosis and Reality

After the loss of his wife, Pankeev turned once more to psychoanalysts for sustenance and survival. He ran straight to Gardiner, who armed him with a fake passport and sent him out of occupied Vienna to London and Ruth Brunswick. More hours and months of analysis followed, during which he asked endlessly, "Why has this happened to me?" Finally, he returned to Vienna. Until his death in 1979, he led a quiet and apparently healthy life as a clerk, and then a pensioner, periodically becoming mired in laborious relationships with women. He also earned some money from his memoirs and sketches, which he sold through the American Psychoanalytic Society as Freud's most famous patient.

His only relapse into supposed "paranoia" occurred in 1951. That summer, Pankeev wandered into the Soviet-occupied zone of Vienna with his easel. He was immediately arrested by Soviet soldiers and thrown into a holding cell. An hours-long interrogation followed, and Sergei was accused of drawing a military base and of generally being a White émigré and a traitor to the motherland. He tried to justify his emigration by explaining that his wife was German, but felt the senselessness of any attempt at justification. Like millions of his perfectly normal countrymen who have found themselves in such circumstances, Pankeev struggled in vain against a paralyzing sense of guilt and fear. After three days he was released, on the condition that he return in three weeks with all of his drawings. It was then that he began to experience a psychosis "just like when I was seeing Dr. Brunswick, only then I felt a physical defect, and in this case the flaw was moral."

Understanding that he could never again return home, he presented himself at the entrance to the Soviet zone exactly twenty-one days later. The officer who had interrogated him was no longer on the base, and no one else had any use for Pankeev.

When he related all this to Gardiner, he concluded with the question, so characteristic of this case: "What do you think, Frau Doktor? Do you think it was my mental illness that made me take this incident so seriously?"[68]

4

Psychoanalytic Activity
Before World War I

Russian Connections

Freud's interest in Russia dated from his childhood, and his connections to Russian culture went back even further. His mother, to whom he was very close, was born in the little town of Brody, in northeastern Galicia, near the Russian border. She spent part of her youth in Odessa, where two of her brothers had settled. In 1883, when Sigmund was twenty-seven, his father decided to straighten out the family's ramshackle financial situation by starting a business in Odessa. One biographer characterized septuagenarian Jacob Freud's trip to Russia as a "ray of hope" that, nevertheless, ended in failure.[1]

Freud's teacher Charcot treated many Russian patients, including members of the czar's family. For a long time, Russians were for Freud a symbol of wealth and a reliable source of prosperity. In 1898, when Nicholas II issued his Peace Manifesto, Freud announced that he had long suspected that the czar suffered from an obsessional neurosis, expressed in his characteristic indecisiveness and perfectionism. "We could help each other. I would go to Russia for a year and would cure his neurosis just to the point of alleviating his suffering but I would leave just enough to prevent him from starting a war. After that we would have congresses three times a year, and exclusively in Italy, and I would treat all my other patients for free."[2]

Years passed, and Freud became popular—if not with the czar, then at least with other wealthy Russians who did become his patients. When the Russian student and son of a millionaire landowner whom we met in the last chapter introduced his lover to Freud, the latter reacted ebulliently: "She is a real Tsarina!" There were many others like Pankeev. In his early years as well as later on, Viennese and Germans in general constituted only a portion of Freud's clientele. According to Jones, "most patients came from Eastern Europe: Russia, Hungary, Poland, Rumania."[3]

Even in Paris, Freud managed to find Russian company. During his internship with Charcot in 1885–1886, he befriended neuropathologist

Leopold Darshkevich (1858–1925). Together they visited Notre Dame, which Freud claimed to have loved even more than neuropathology; together they worshiped Sarah Bernhardt; together they wrote an article on the anatomy of the aural nerve. Freud once described Darshkevich in a letter to his fiancée: "[he] attracted my attention by his melancholy disposition, typical of . . . Little Russians. . . . I discovered in him a quite profound fanatic. He was averse to all distractions and his soul was absorbed in the motherland, religion, and brain anatomy. His ambition was to write the first book on brain anatomy in the Russian language."[4] Darshkevich a little later fulfilled his dream: In 1904 he published the first volume of a textbook on neuropathology in Kazan, which would become a classic and be reprinted many times throughout the Soviet period.[5] In 1889, Darshkevich returned to Moscow, and five years later he became a professor at Kazan University, where he organized one clinic for the treatment of mental diseases and another for alcoholics—the first of its kind in Russia. In his *Course on Mental Diseases,* he recommended the application of "Freudian psychoanalysis" in certain cases of hysteria.[6] Later, however, Darshkevich spoke out vehemently against the Freudian approach to the pathogenesis of neuroses. But it is hardly accidental that the most powerful center of psychoanalysis in provincial Russia arose in Kazan. Darshkevich's other claim to fame is that he was "one of the first to point out the syphilitic origin of dorsal tabes," as the *Bol'shaia meditsinskaia entsiklopediia* (Great Medical Encyclopedia) informs us. He treated Lenin, and was the founder and first rector of the Superior Medical School in Moscow, where he inaugurated the department of psychology.

But for Freud, Dostoevsky was the veritable personification of Russia, and his contacts with Russians were full of associations with the great writer. He read Dostoevsky over and over for decades. Pankeev recalled that one of his analytic sessions with Freud before World War I was devoted to interpreting Raskolnikov's dream. Freud referred to *The Brothers Karamazov* as the greatest novel ever written. In 1928, Freud published his famous sketch "Dostoevsky and Patricide," which he wrote at Max Eitingon's request, as the introduction to the German edition of this novel. The essay demonstrates that Freud was not only familiar with Dostoevsky's novels but also knew the literature about him and a good deal of Russian history and politics as well.[7] However, Freud's attitude toward Dostoevsky was no less complex than the relations between the writer's characters— "ambivalent," as Freud used to say, or "dialogic," in Bakhtin's words. In a letter to Theodor Reik, Freud confessed: "In spite of all my admiration of Dostoevsky, of his intensity and perfection, I do not like him. That is because my tolerance for pathological cases is drained by psychoanalysis."[8] Besides Dostoevsky, Freud spoke often of Dmitry Merezhkovsky, whom he considered worthy of praise, and of Leo Tolstoy.

When Freud discovered the psychic mechanism that selectively prevents the conscious realization of unacceptable content, he called it censorship. In an 1897 letter, he explained that he had borrowed the word from Russian life and that it implied an "imperfect instrument of the czarist regime for preventing penetration of alien Western influences."[9]

Freud wrote the major theoretical work of his later period, *Beyond the Pleasure Principle*, under a strong and variegated Russian influence. In this work, he suggested that the death wish be considered a motivating force behind human behavior, just as fundamental as the drives for life, love, and procreation. The idea of the death wish had been expressed long before the publication of Freud's study, by Russian psychoanalyst Sabina Spielrein. Naturally, it was impossible for Freud to ignore her contribution, but he referred to it with understandable ambivalence. It is quite possible that he closely associated this theory with Spielrein's unusual personage (see chapter 5), which must have created additional difficulties for him in elaborating the new doctrine. During his work on the text of *Beyond the Pleasure Principle*, Freud reread Dostoevsky and wrote a new epilogue to his "History of an Infantile Neurosis." Finally, it is significant that the tragic and inescapable idea of the duality of human attraction is more closely tied to notions that were dominant in early twentieth-century Russian culture than to the ideas reigning in the world of early Freud, a world accessible to therapy and at least potentially rational (in the same sense that Freud's beloved detective novels were rational, where the horror and chaos of life were subordinated to a cold logic that could and must find a solution).

Freud's two sons fought on the Russian front, and he worried about them for years. Many of his students and friends served in the medical corps of the Austro-Hungarian army. An interpretation of the terrifying spectacle of Europe straining toward self-destruction required new terminology. It could be that Freud's idea of the death wish was inspired by his observations of the Russian revolution and occasional contacts with Russians in Vienna, refugees and Bolsheviks alike. At any rate, American historian James Rice is justified in characterizing this idea of the death wish as Russia's contribution to psychoanalysis.[10] Freud's interest in Russia had a variety of roots: biographical, ethnic, historical, economic, and most interestingly, intellectual.

The intellectual affinity that Freud and his circle felt toward Russia seems only natural in light of biography and history. The military borders of the two belligerent empires had only recently divided the continent, which had been a single, organic whole for its Yiddish-speaking inhabitants. Only one generation separated the Jewish intellectuals of the Austro-Hungarian and Russian empires from their common ancestors, whose cultural territory once covered all of central and eastern Europe. In Freud's books we run across the same old jokes that are still told in Petersburg, New York, Jerusalem, and points in between. The fathers of Freud, Kafka, and Trotsky shared the same cultural frame of reference; and their sons built new structures on a common foundation.

In a more universal sense, the crux of what Freud wrote about Russia boils down to a few discernible points. Russians were closer to their unconscious essence than were "Western" people. Therefore, psychoanalysis met with less resistance among Russians; this is why Russians were such apt patients and students; therefore, Russians preempted the discovery of some of the deepest mysteries of the unconscious, above all its attraction to death. But by the same token, the forces of ego, consciousness, and discipline were less developed among Russians than among European nations. For this reason, their desires were untamable, in sharp contrast to their noble thought patterns.

It is not all that surprising that these views of Freud's, being intuitive rather than rational in their origin, were close to the stereotypes about Russians common in the West. Sexual freedom was ascribed to Russians, along with a mystical sort of concentration; their inherent desire to turn the world upside down was balanced by an inability to do meticulous work; an ability to achieve facelessness among the masses was imputed, along with some innate knowledge of love and death. It would seem that all these contradictory features couldn't possibly be amalgamated in a single image; it is this gap between the nation's various characteristics that lies at the center of the enigmatic Russian soul. Everything that Freud and the people of his culture knew of Russians—Lermontov's poems and Dostoevsky's novels, Pankeev's dreams and Spielrein's ideas—generally supported such a notion, but offered no solution.

Russia was perceived as the "other," and a great deal could be projected onto its great, unexplored, spiritual space—hopes and dreams, most of all. For Freud early in his career, intent on uncovering the mysteries of unconscious human existence, these hopes were more than anything an aspiration to come to know the unconscious. "Russian material" offered certain advantages in this regard.

If there were ever a nation that lived exclusively through the unconscious, it would undoubtedly have been a great find for any psychoanalyst, or for any intellectual, for that matter. But if this people were to differ too much from Europeans, if they were dwarf-sized or had the heads of dogs, for instance, interest would be merely academic: The unconscious among such people would be too different to support comparison. Russians, on the other hand, were in many ways just like Europeans. This was why it was so interesting to see them as people who, as Rilke said, "say at dusk what other people reject in daylight," or, as Freud claimed, who have better preserved the "legacy from the psychic life of primitive races," making it "more accessible to consciousness than elsewhere."[11] As Europeans, they probably have a European unconscious, but as Russians they are more aware of their unconscious. In other words, the transitive, intermediary position the Russians occupied between Europe and the rest of the world—a place they so willingly claimed for themselves—became for the psychoanalyst a transitive, intermediary position between the conscious mind and the unconscious. Russians naturally enjoyed a privileged status in Freud's world, as they served to lower the most basic barrier to psychoanalysis.

First Contacts

Russian psychiatrist Nikolai Osipov (1877–1934) began his medical education at the University of Moscow. After being expelled in 1899 for participating in a student strike, he began to "wander from one foreign university to another," continuing his studies in Freiburg, Zurich, Bonn, and Bern, and he completed a doctoral thesis on histology in Basel. However, on returning to Russia in 1904, he lost his fascination with this particular field of specialization, which for him had become a symbol of materialism and nihilism. "I deeply believe it was the unresolved mystery of the soul, and of man in general, that drew me to psychiatry. In any case, it was the philosophical, not the medical side that attracted me." Osipov worked in Moscow psychiatric hospitals, and was soon transferred to the clinic at the University of Moscow, which was under the direction of Vladimir Serbsky. "I was particularly interested in neurotics, from a psychological point of view. Studying this particular group of patients, I was confronted with questions of hypnosis and suggestion," Osipov wrote later. There was no shortage of specialists in the field to teach him in Moscow. For a long time thereafter, Osipov remained a psychiatrist who "had mastered the techniques of psychoanalysis and the techniques of suggestion in equal measure."[12]

"I first became acquainted with Freud's works in 1907. Freud was not at all well known in Russia at that time. . . . I can safely claim to have been the first to popularize Freud in Russia," Osipov remembered. In Moscow, he published several overview articles on psychoanalysis, and gathered admirers of Freud around him. His colleagues from the Serbsky clinic, Yevgeny Dovbnya and Mikhail Asatiani, were also interested in psychoanalytic treatment. Together with Nikolai Vyrubov, in 1910 Osipov founded the journal *Psychotherapy,* which offered its readers both Russian and translated works on psychoanalysis.

On January 2, 1910, Freud wrote to Jung: "Dr. Osipov, assistant at the psychiatric clinic in Moscow, has written to me; his credentials are two thick offprints, in one of which the tangle of Cyrillic signs is interrupted every two lines by the name Freud (also Freudy and Freuda) in European print, while the other makes the same use of the name Jung. The man has two other, original works at the printer's." Further, Freud informs Jung of the address of the Moscow psychiatric clinic in Devich'e Pole, translating the curious place-name as "Virgin's Field."[13] Osipov wrote: "In 1910, I visited Freud in Vienna, Bleuler and Jung in Zurich, Dubois in Bern." A copy of the Russian edition of *Three Essays on the Theory of Sexuality*, published by the Psychotherapeutic Library and edited by Osipov and Osip Feltsman in 1911, is still kept in Freud's house in London. The book was autographed by Osipov, with the inscription: "To the Brilliant Professor Mr. Freud."

Fyodor Stepun once reminisced about the "mystical, erotic, revolutionary chord" reverberating in Russia at that time, a chord that only later degenerated into the awful cacophony of Rasputin's prerevolutionary era: "In Moscow of the early twentieth century, among the mercantile patrons of arts, bombastic barristers, actors spoiled on the adoration of audiences, connoisseurs of enigmatic feminine souls, and women who dreamed of being deciphered . . . psychology lorded over elemental spontaneity, emotional experience over passion, melancholy over debauchery."[14] Philosophy, psychology, and literature were treated as personal issues, and people looked for the solution to their own problems in these disciplines. Seventeen-year-old adolescents sought answers to the questions of flesh and death that tormented them either in Tolstoy's *The Kreutzer Sonata*, or, at the other extreme, in the works of Nietzsche. In the end, like Stepun, they would often come to the desperate conclusion that "there's no choice but to study, you can't get through life without philosophy," and leave for Heidelberg. The majority sought and found the structure that was missing in their lives by turning to religious philosophy; but the rising interest in psychoanalysis, with its direct but difficult practical applications, is quite understandable in this atmosphere.

The Moscow psychiatrists' interests were more practical in nature. After the death of Sergei Korsakov, the founder of Russian psychiatry, a schism arose in the community, centered around conflicting attitudes toward Kraepelin's German school of psychiatry. One group, headed by Pyotr Gannushkin, followed in Kraepelin's footsteps to pursue the classification of mental diseases and personalities susceptible to such ailments. During the Soviet period, Rosenstein, a key player in these events, wrote that the other group, "led by Serbsky, became the first to proliferate the ideas of Freud, Jung, and Bleuler in Russia."[15]

Vladimir Serbsky, who replaced Korsakov as the director of the psychiatric clinic at Moscow University, never practiced analysis himself but urged his students to do so. Young doctors from Moscow usually interned at the Burghölzli clinic under the supervision of Eugen Bleuler and Jung. When they returned, they no longer thought of therapy in terms of bromide preparations, hypnosis, and dietary restrictions, but as a series of psychoanalytic sessions. As for the scientific method, Kraepelin's intricate classifications were replaced by dynamic hypotheses, bolstered by Jung's associative experiments and references to Freud's classic cases.

Serbsky was familiar with Freud's books, and like many psychiatrists of the time, he believed that psychoanalysis overstated the significance of the sexual etiology of neuroses. French researcher Jean Marti cited from Osipov's unpublished memoirs: "Serbsky, who had a good command of foreign languages, nevertheless mispronounced Freud's name, saying 'Freud,' with the accent on the last syllable," evoking an archaic Russian word for "sexual organs," *udy.* "Then I decided to pronounce Freud's name like 'Freund' (friend)," Osipov continued, "thus expressing my attitude toward Freud's theory."[16] Meanwhile, Serbsky tolerated and even encouraged young, enthusiastic, and evidently inexperienced psychoanalysts in his clinic. "Serbsky has given his blessing to this young clinic where new ideas in the psychotherapeutic trend will be studied," wrote Rosenstein.[17]

Osipov described Serbsky's political views as close to the leftist Constitutional Democrat faction. In Rosenstein's opinion, Serbsky was "almost the only psychiatrist who accepted the revolution as a healthy undertaking." In 1911, the government limited university autonomy. Many professors at Moscow University resigned in protest, including Professor Serbsky and his assistants. Private practice gave them independence. As Osipov recalled: "Thanks to private practice, my resignation from the clinic . . . had no impact on my financial situation. During my last years at the clinic, as well as in later years (before the Bolsheviks came to power), my financial situation was brilliant: I made about 2,000 rubles per month."[18] However, after his conflict with the administration, Osipov pinned down a position as junior lecturer at the Moscow Women's High School (Vysshie Zhenskie Kursy), with Bazhenov's patronage. This implied a kind of independence from the government that was hard to attain during the Soviet period.

Serbsky remained a patron of Moscow analysts until his sudden passing in 1917. "The death of outstanding Russians is always tragic and absurd: they die just when they are needed most," lamented the future leader of Soviet psychoanalysis, Ivan Yermakov, in an obituary dedicated to Serbsky.[19]

In 1914, Freud wrote in his *On the History of the Psycho-Analytic Movement*: "In Russia, psycho-analysis has become generally known and has spread widely; almost all my writings, as well as those of other adherents of analysis, have been translated into Russian. But a really penetrating comprehension of analytic theories has not yet been evinced in Russia; so that the contributions of Russian physicians are at present not very notable."[20]

Taking into account Freud's usual, skeptically reserved tone, his evaluation of the state of psychoanalysis in Russia does not seem all that low. On the previous page he noted "the absence of any deep-rooted scientific tradition in America," and that France offered less fertile ground for psychoanalysis than other European countries. Speaking of Russia, Freud pinpointed the main problem of budding psychoanalysis there, a problem that he expected to become more acute in future: the contradiction between the widespread popularity of psychoanalysis and the lack of productivity and depth in therapeutic practice.

Freud continued: "The only trained analyst there is M. Wulff who practices in Odessa." In 1909, Moisei Wulff (1878–1971), a Russian psychiatrist, was fired from the Berlin clinic where he worked because he espoused psychoanalytic views. In August of the same year, Wulff left for Russia, which, as Jones wrote much later, "was then a freer country than Germany in such matters."[21] On November 10, 1909, Abraham wrote to Freud: "A Russian doctor by the name of Wulff, who has been Juliusburger's assistant in a private mental hospital for some time, is now going to settle in Odessa. He is very interested in psycho-analysis and, because of this, lost his last job in Berlin after only a few weeks. I know him to be a hard-working and reliable man who is unfortunately in very difficult financial circumstances. Perhaps you or one of your colleagues in Vienna might be able to send him some patients. I expect he will write to you personally as he has asked me for your address. Juliusburger also tells me that Wulff would like to do translations into Russian."[22] After his arrival in Odessa, Wulff corresponded with Freud and Ferenczi, published articles in Moscow journals, and soon put out several excellent translations of Freud.

Some time later, a young man from Odessa, Leonid Droznes, introduced himself to Freud. He was the author of a radical brochure about "the struggle with modern neuroticism," in which he wrote, "the prevention of physical and psychological degeneration of the population depends upon the fundamental political and economic reform of Russian life."[23] Nevertheless, Droznes did not wait for those fundamental reforms to occur before sending his rich patient to Freud (see chapter 3).

In 1912, Freud wrote to Jung: "In Russia (Odessa) there seems to be a local epidemic of psychoanalysis."[24] The fun-loving, cosmopolitan microcosm of Odessa would have a warm place in Russian and later Soviet culture for generations. Due to its special status as a *porto franco,* Odessa was then a flourishing commercial and cultural mediator between Russia and Europe. Not only was the ruble convertible back then, it was valued as one of the strongest currencies in the world. A growing sector of Russian and Jewish merchants from this region in southern Russia, highly receptive to European innovation, was sending its children to study in Germany and Switzerland.

Psychiatry in St. Petersburg was at that time developing under the powerful and in many ways restrictive influence of Vladimir Bekhterev (1857–1927). An army general and academician who had made himself indispensable at court while at the same time enjoying a reputation as a liberal, Bekhterev was an outstanding administrator. In psychoneurology (as he called his science) he had faith only in anatomical and physiological explanations for mental illness. His psychotherapeutic interests were focused on hypnosis. His propagandistic and organizational talents were fully unleashed during the Soviet era, his crowning achievement being the creation of the Second Petrograd University out of the Psychoneurological Institute he had earlier founded. Bekhterev proved useful to the new government: For instance, he wrote an appeal to the nations of the Triple Entente, urging them to ship provisions to Russia during the famine that the Bolsheviks had induced after the end of the Civil War. When Bekhterev was invited to give Stalin a consultation, he dared to diagnose paranoia in the Great Leader. He lived only one day after this event. Kremlin physicians determined that the cause of his death was intestinal poisoning from canned food.[25] The year was 1927.[26]

Other analysts in St. Petersburg, Petrograd, and Leningrad tended to pale next to Bekhterev. There was private practice, as everywhere. For some time Aron Zalkind worked there; Elias Perepel conducted analysis from the 1910s until his emigration at the end of the 1920s; Tatiana Rosenthal succeeded in adapting psychoanalysis even to the conditions of the Bekhterev Institute. However, active propaganda and organization in the Muscovite style was never undertaken in Petersburg.

Not a Society, but a Journal

In the second decade of this century, psychoanalysis stepped out onto the international stage. The discipline gradually sprouted out of a single man's hobby, blossomed into a cluster of apostles, and matured into an ever expanding international movement. Immediately after the Second International Psychoanalytic Congress in Nuremberg, national psychoanalytic societies were founded in Berlin, Vienna, and Zurich. Ferenczi's attempt at the time to organize a similar society in Budapest ended in failure. Nor was a psychoanalytic society formed in the United States, although Freud's lectures had caused a sensation there; American psychoanalysts were subsumed under the newly founded American Psychopathological Association. Psychoanalysis was practically unknown in those days in France and Italy.

The First Congress of the Russian Union of Neuropathologists and Psychiatrists was held in Moscow on September 4–11, 1911. Along with preliminary materials for the meeting, the editorial board of *Psychotherapy* published an announcement sent from the Nuremberg Congress on the foundation of the International Psychoanalytic Association and its regional affiliates. But the psychoanalysts of Moscow were channeling their organizational skills in a different direction. The institutionalization of psychoanalysis in Russia would follow its own, original path.

The newly elected governing body of the Russian Union of Neuropathologists and Psychiatrists chose Nikolai Bazhenov (1857–1923) as its chairman. Bazhenov sympathized with psychoanalysis and psychoanalysts, backed Osipov, and, at least in one case in 1909, referred a problematic patient to Freud. Bazhenov was also the chairman of the Moscow Literary and Artistic Club, an elite group of writers, professors, lawyers, doctors, and merchant philanthropists. Khodasevich described him in the following way: "Bazhenov the psychiatrist is obese, bald, rubicund, and snub-nosed, resembling a teapot with a broken spout. He is a wine connoisseur, a connoisseur of ladies' hearts, and the author of a psychiatric portrait of Baudelaire."[27] In addition, Bazhenov was a prominent Mason. In 1908, as Master of "Liberation Lodge," he traveled to Paris, where he obtained the legalization of the Moscow and St. Petersburg lodges from the French Masons of the "Great Orient."[28]

Nikolai Vyrubov, a psychiatrist with analytic interests and the editor of *Psychotherapy*, was elected secretary of the Russian Union of Neuropathologists and Psychiatrists. Osipov was chosen to serve as one of the secretary's assistants. Hence, psychoanalysts were well represented, and perhaps even dominant in the elective body of the union that covered all Russian specialists in mental illness. Instead of creating an isolated psychoanalytic "sect," as happened after the Nuremberg Congress in other European countries, the Russian analysts preferred to preside over more broadly based medical circles. That they succeeded in doing so proves that psychoanalysis met with less resistance in prerevolutionary Russia than in the West.

This could be why the Russian Psychoanalytic Society was not formally established in the 1910s. Evidence to this effect in Western histories of psychoanalysis is based on Jones's words, which were drawn, in turn, from Freud's report. On May 2, 1911, wrote Jones, Dr. Droznes called Freud in Vienna to inform him that, together with Osipov and Vyrubov, he had decided to establish a Russian Psychoanalytic Society.[29] Freud, and later Jones, considered this decision enough to warrant recognition of the Russian Society. However, I have found no official dispatch on the foundation of such a society in Russia (the journal *Psychotherapy*, published by the prospective organizers of the Society, would certainly not have ignored such an event). Clearly, Osipov and Vyrubov chose to form a coalition with such sympathetic psychiatrists as Serbsky and Bazhenov and, rather than creating a separate Psychoanalytic Society, they acted within and on behalf of the Russian Union of Neuropathologists and Psychiatrists. Translating this peaceful atmosphere from an organizational level to the level of intellect, Nikolai Osipov asserted in 1911 that there was no contradiction between psychoanalysis and the academic tradition. Osipov's article, published in the main Russian psychiatric journal, is subtly paradoxical: The author justifies Freud by referring to Rickert, and he buttresses psychoanalysis with neo-Kantian theory. Neo-Kantians taught that the world is endlessly variegated, and that scientific cognition of the world could be achieved through simplification and "stylizations" of various sorts. Osipov transferred this speculation to what he called "Freud's stylization." Reduction of "all emotions to a single one, namely sexual, is a legitimate way to simplify real life," proclaimed the young doctor, who had also studied in Freiburg.[30]

In 1912, the psychoanalysts organized a seminar called "Lesser Fridays" (as opposed to the Russian Union's "Greater Fridays"), chaired by Serbsky. Osipov "managed" the seminar. The Lesser Fridays were held regularly until the outbreak of the World War I. Their psychoanalytic orientation was well known and was recognized later even by Soviet officialdom: "Most speeches were not clinical in nature but sociopsychological, with a strong Freudian tendency."[31]

Psychotherapy, a journal of psychoanalytic leanings, was established in Russia around the same time that the Viennese school was setting up its first journal. Most likely, *Psychotherapy* was only the second journal in history dedicated to the psychoanalytic movement. Its analytic tendency became more and more pronounced with each passing year. According to the estimation of one modern researcher, in 1910, 42 percent of all articles took a psychoanalytic stance; by 1911 the proportion had climbed to 62 percent; in 1912, to 71 percent, and in 1913, to 87 percent.[32]

The general direction of the journal's work was set by the very first issue. At that time, psychoanalysis was competing freely and successfully with other trends in psychotherapy, hypnosis in particular. The journal opened with Yury Kannabikh's survey article describing the evolution of nineteenth-century psychiatric ideas and the school of hypnotherapy, and pointing to psychoanalysis as the cutting edge of science. Osipov contributed an overview of Freudian analysis, which was continued in subsequent issues (these were the texts about which Freud wrote to Jung). Vyrubov presented an article on a "combined hypno-analytic method" to treat neurotic anxiety, which was just one of many attempts made by Russian psychotherapists to combine psychoanalysis with hypnosis.[33]

Hypnosis and the Will to Power

Hypnosis achieved significantly more popularity in Russia and, subsequently, in the Soviet Union, than in the West. This rift between Russia and the West steadily deepened with the passing decades. In the West, Freud's criticism of Hyppolite Bernheim ("this was an evident injustice and an act of violence," Freud wrote of Bernheim's "astonishing arts"[34]) and Freud's own rejection of hypnosis ("the history of psychoanalysis proper begins with the new technique that dispenses with hypnosis"[35]) proved destructive for hypnosis in the long run. Only in the 1970s was there a kind of revival of the forgotten art. In the USSR, on the other hand, hypnosis remained the only legal method of psychotherapy, widely practiced even during the darkest years (see chapter 9). This is understandable: Hypnosis is obviously akin to the psychological mechanisms used to implement totalitarian power. It was not without reason that Freud compared a leader's power over the mob to a hypnotist's sway over his patient. In the late 1980s, one of the best Soviet historians, Nathan Eidelman, made an effort to define the essence of Stalinism as a case of mass hypnosis. Many memoirs of that time are saturated with hypnotic metaphors, in particular those of Nadezhda Mandelstam. The focus of psychotherapy on hypnosis was also characteristic of Nazi Germany. Hypnosis again became disturbingly popular in the USSR at the beginning and middle of the 1980s, an unstable time of apocalyptic expectations. The more paranoiac a society, it seems, the more significance it attributes to hypnosis.

However, the unusual popularity of hypnosis in Russia had its origin much earlier, as was the case with many other Soviet traditions. As early as 1910, Muscovite Osip Feltsman, who had just returned from Bernheim and Dubois, wrote, "At present, we are living through a psychic epidemic, one of the most dangerous symptoms of which is an overblown attraction to hypnosis."[36]

We know about the life of early Russian psychiatrist-hypnotists from Osip Mandelstam's *The Noise of Time*,[37] a source that provides a wealth of interesting details. Around 1905, the poet frequented the house of the "famous Petersburg doctor who cured by suggestion," Boris Sinani (1851–1920), whose son was Mandelstam's friend. "It was a family of powerful intellectual character bordering on expressive primitivism," wrote Mandelstam. Sinani was Gleb Uspensky's doctor and Nikolai Mikhailovsky's friend. He was immersed in politics and acted as an "advisor and confidant to members of the Social Revolutionary party central committee." As for medicine, he "had very few patients, and he kept them intimidated, especially the women."

Mandelstam sensed Sinani's duality no less perceptively than would an analyst: "He was a vehement rationalist, and due to this fatal contradiction he felt the need for an authority figure—he involuntarily worshipped authority, and suffered because of this." The doctor's eyes were always glued to "harmful, worthless books full of mysticism, hysteria, and pathology of all sorts; he struggled with them, put them aside, but he could not help coming back to them." His enemies were the eternal Russian "mysticism, stupidity, hysteria, and boorishness." Meanwhile, the "reason was simultaneously joy, health, sport, and almost religion." At the same time, as

Mandelstam would recall much later, in 1925, his "greedy mind was swallowing every possible source of scarce nourishment: the endless debates between Social Revolutionaries and Social Democrats, the role of personality in history, the figure of Mikhailovsky, famed for his harmonious nature.
. . ." This striking portrait embodies much of what was to characterize Russian psychiatry (especially as practiced in St. Petersburg) during the decades to come: rationalism in theory, hypnosis in practice, and dependence on the current political authorities.

Russian psychoanalysts tried to oppose this influence. According to Pevnitsky:[38] "We used to treat patients with hypnosis. . . . The main peculiarity of this method—and this also applies to treatment through suggestion—is that the doctor does not understand why the patient submits to him."[39] Pevnitsky was fascinated by Freud, and compared his discoveries in psychotherapy to Paul Ehrlich's contribution to pharmacology, salvarsan. Salvarsan, the first effective medication in treating syphilis, was a new sensation that symbolized the power of knowledge. To Pevnitsky, hypnosis was for witch doctors, as its primitive curative mechanisms were impenetrable to science. In the years that followed, Moscow analysts took an even more critical attitude toward hypnosis. The methods of Bernheim, Charcot, and Dubois seemed archaic compared to the profound intellectual exploration being pursued by analysts in Zurich and Vienna.

The Moscow psychotherapists moved further and further away from the primitive solution that hypnosis offered for the problem of power and submission, turning more and more to Adler, who interpreted the "will to power" with a psychoanalytic slant. Over the years of its publication, *Psychotherapy* exhibited a clear and increasing bias toward Adler, which first became obvious in 1913. At the very least, two of the journal's regular contributors, Bernstein and Zalkind, demonstrated a conscious preference for "individual-based psychological analysis." Kannabikh and Vyrubov also sympathized with Adler, as indicated by their references and terminology. Personal relations were probably also involved in this appreciation. The journal regularly published reports by Adler's Russian wife, Raisa Timofeevna, on the proceedings of the "Verein of Free Psychoanalytic Research," a group that broke off from the mainstream of Freudian analysis in 1911.

Evidently, Adler's own "will to power" struck more of a chord with Russian analysts, connected as they were with political and Masonic circles, than did Freud's ideas, which were farther removed from the issues of the day. Jung's influence is almost imperceptible, despite his personal connections to a number of the journal's contributors. The only trace of it is in Yevgeny Dovbnya's articles on the associative experiment, but the author follows a purely scientific path of exploration, eschewing Jung's mystical models. One article published in 1913 in *Novyi zhurnal dlia vsekh* (The

New Journal for Everybody), popular among leftist readers, demonstrates the dangerously exaggerated expectations that went hand in hand with early attempts to popularize psychoanalysis in Russia. From the author's point of view, psychoanalysis not only solves all the riddles of psychotherapy, it can be applied to criminal investigation as well. Laying out some of the results from associative experiments, a certain Vavulin concludes by interjecting his own opinion: "We can only hope that further research in this field will allow legal practitioners to abandon, with a clean conscience, the use of material evidence against criminals. If this should happen, the trial will be reduced to an involuntary confession . . . , which would be the inevitable result of the perfection of psychoanalytic technique. . . . Hence, that which hypnosis could not achieve will be achieved by the new psychoanalytic method."[40]

However, the best of the Moscow psychoanalysts' works were guided by common sense and clinical experience, influences not confined to any therapeutic school. A. Pevnitsky, for instance, was one of the first therapists to apply analysis to the treatment of alcoholism. His article on the subject,[41] published in 1912, could be incorporated without amendment into any Russian psychological journal eighty years later. Moreover, it would inspire the same reaction as it did all those years ago, the same enthusiasm and the same objections. Pevnitsky wrote that alcoholics are people of the masses: That is, psychoanalysis is effective in a number of situations, illustrated by the author through case histories; but even after treatment, an alcoholic needs a "society that will take him in hand." Temperance societies are essential; without them, the patient runs the risk of resuming his drinking habits. The article, which deserved to be included in anthology after anthology, was instead completely forgotten, as was its author.

A Story of Sadism

In Russian practice, psychoanalytic concepts often were applied in a general cultural context—art, politics, and so on—before finding their direct application on the analyst's couch. For example, in one of his articles published in *Psychotherapy*, Vyrubov attempted to psychoanalyze the speeches of State Duma deputies, pointing out their characteristic slips of the tongue. In this way, psychoanalytic paradigms gradually infiltrated the thought processes of Russian psychiatrists and educated people in general. One piece of indirect evidence of this process is a case where psychoanalytic evaluation led to a very serious conclusion, even though no reference was ever made to Freud—as if the connection was taken for granted. In 1912, Dr. Nikolai Krainsky published an article entitled "Pedagogical Sadism," without any special commentary.[42] The article related the case history of K., a 48-year-old school inspector who had earned a reputation as an extraordinarily strict and cruel examiner. Every spring, K. traveled the countryside, supervising the administration of final examinations. "This agent soaked his district with blood," Krainsky wrote, referring to the suicides of eighteen students, which Krainsky felt had been provoked by K.'s senseless cruelty. At the same time, K. was so intelligent and extremely polite in his professional dealings with his peers that even teachers who hated him found it impossible to oppose him.

Three years before the publication of the article, K. came to Dr. Krainsky complaining of nervousness, insomnia, attacks of apathy, and ennui. An examination yielded some intriguing results. Krainsky noted that K. constantly entertained not only thoughts of suicide but also a strong urge to kill himself. The patient led a reserved married life and had never known another woman. His erotic fantasies, on the other hand, were rich and cynical. "K. experienced concupiscence, excitement, and pleasure in mentally tormenting his students during tests. With time, torturing examinees became an unbridled need. He would experience sexual arousal only when a student failed his exam. . . . During these moments, he would experience erection and sometimes ejaculation. K. achieved supreme pleasure when students committed suicide."[43]

Krainsky failed as a doctor. When K. realized that his physician saw through to the root of his problem, he stopped making appointments. Krainsky wrote that he couldn't bring himself to reveal a medical secret in order to stop K., but his presence on occasion did serve to restrain the sadistic inspector. Once Krainsky attended an exam along with K., and the fact of his presence, the doctor maintained, saved two students.

Suddenly, K. came down with sarcoma. When his disease was fairly advanced, he went to Gomel to give an exam, induced one last student to commit suicide, and died himself shortly thereafter.

Krainsky waited a year before publishing his report on the case. Whether purposefully or not, he left a sufficiently clear trail in the text to identify the murderous examiner: Kosakovsky, the inspector of the Vilnius Educational District. The article provoked a scandal. The son of the deceased official, an army second lieutenant, challenged Krainsky to a duel. Krainsky explained himself on the pages of the *Stock Exchange News*, expressing his readiness to "give satisfaction in the traditional manner" if the young Kosakovsky did not find his explanation convincing. The young man still insisted on a duel. Negotiations between the men's seconds yielded contradictory results. After a five-hour session, the officers' Honor Tribunal "recognized the challenge as proper according to the dueling code."

Kosakovsky set January 26, 1913, as the date for the duel. At this point, the trail of information turns cold.[44] Clearly, Krainsky came through this trial alive and with his dignity intact, for at the end of the same year he was appointed to the position of professor extraordinary at the University of Warsaw.

Behind the Backdrop of the Soul

Psychoanalysis found unexpected popularity in the Russian theater, which was developing rapidly at this time. The outstanding actor Mikhail Chekhov, a nephew of famous author Anton Chekhov, named Freud as one of the idols of his youth. In his younger years, Mikhail Chekhov had suffered from a severe mental disorder and, distrusting psychiatrists, treated himself through acting, reading, alcohol, and anthroposophy. In his own words, during his most unbearable moments, one of the "three elders"—Schopenhauer, Darwin, or Freud—would always appear on his desk. During the brighter intervals, he would read Tolstoy or Solovyov. Chekhov recalled being tormented by feelings approaching paranoia. He was able to conceal his emotions in public, but in fact they brought him to the verge of suicide. One day, for instance, he came to the realization that the "world is a potential catastrophe that originated in infinity." However, this realization came in 1917, so such thoughts cannot be automatically written off as pure delirium. "People did not wish to think, and I pitied them; I was indignant and I secretly thought they were crazy."[45]

Chekhov was treated by several hypnotists, and he consulted with well-known psychologist G. Chelpanov (who advised him to pay more attention to religion and to abandon philosophy and psychology), but neither effort proved helpful. Just when his illness was at the most critical stage, his beautiful wife of four years ran off with a visiting hypnotist.

Konstantin Stanislavsky, with whom Chekhov worked onstage, sent him to a consultative group of famous Moscow psychiatrists for a thorough examination. As long as the doctors asked routine questions, Chekhov was eager to answer, and they "established a subtle, delicate relationship." But when one of the luminaries, evidently intending to provoke the patient, asked him to crawl between the back of the sofa and the wall, while another suggested they go out for a walk together, Chekhov was outraged: "What sort of plot are they hatching?" In the end, he agreed to go for a stroll with one thin, short doctor; while walking he observed every move his companion made. The consultation dragged on for a long time. "The meeting with celebrated scholars (whom I had until then respected) further contributed to my disillusionment with people," Chekhov recalled. As the doctors were leaving, they told Chekhov that they would inform Stanislavsky of their diagnosis.[46]

Stanislavsky had his own method for treating actors. One day, Chekhov began to stutter, and came to Stanislavsky to let him know that he would be unable to work. Stanislavsky announced that Chekhov would stop stuttering as soon as he opened the window. This is exactly what happened. There is a hint of hypnosis in this story; but in the end, Chekhov sought treatment at the sanatorium in Kryukovo, where psychoanalysts held the upper hand.

According to Chekhov, he spent hours arguing with Stanislavsky as to whether an actor should "use or dismiss his personal, incomplete feelings while working on his role." Stanislavsky was convinced that "memories from the actor's personal, affective life could yield the vivid, creative feelings needed onstage, if the actor would only concentrate on them." Chekhov considered this approach counterproductive and believed that the actor should instead create his image while remaining completely oblivious to his personal emotions. He argued that the passionate memories in Stanislavsky's method often provoked "nervous and even hysterical fits in actors (primarily actresses)." Chekhov's stance is psychologically understandable: For a psychotic who was intent on controlling his delirium, immersion in his own affective sphere could hardly be helpful.

Stanislavsky saw no particular need to control feelings, whether his own feelings or his actors': "Our subconscious is our best friend," he wrote in his famous work *An Actor Prepares*.[47] 'Subconscious' was one of his favorite terms. He used it even in his publications of the 1930s. His method had as its primary aim to "bring an actor to the point where the subconscious creative process ignites within him." "How can one take a conscious approach to something that is not subject to consciousness, something subconscious?" Stanislavsky's system included a number of techniques to activate the subconscious: identification, immersion in personal memories, physical workouts, and so on. "Fortunately for us, there is no sharp delineation between conscious and subconscious experience."

Stanislavsky never referred to Freud, although he must have been familiar with his books and seems to have been susceptible to Freud's influence, if only indirectly. The conceptual relationship between "Freud's science," as psychoanalysis was then called in Russia, and "The Stanislavsky Method" deserves someday to be the subject of a more in-depth analysis. For now, I will simply note that the two shared common features, and that Freud was popular in Stanislavsky's circle.

In the 1910s, one of the most outstanding playwrights and theatrical figures of the era, Nikolai Yevreinov (1879–1953), presented a new philosophical system: "the theatricalization of life" and "intimization of theater." Yevreinov's theory was based on the expansion of his professional experience into all spheres of life, on Nietzschean stylistics, and on a strong and relentlessly increasing infusion of psychoanalysis. A man of the modernist era, "he developed pronounced theatrical mannerisms, dressed extravagantly, displayed striking wit, and always praised his favorite author, Oscar Wilde."[48] His erotic staging of *Salomé* was banned by the authorities in 1908; this did not keep Yevreinov from publishing his bold book, *Nudity on Stage*. The body interested him as an image and as the focus of a variety of human interactions. It was during these years before the revolution that Yevreinov wrote his monumental *History of Corporal Punishment in Russia*.

Raised on Russian symbolism, Yevreinov sought new ways of substantiating and applying the symbolist approach, but in the end he lowered symbolism to the final depths of absurdity. Two books came out of his research: *The Origins of Drama: Primitive Tragedy and the Role of the Goat in Its Origination* and *Azazel and Dionysus*. Both works treat the myth of the dying and regenerating god that is central to symbolism. Considered in light of Yevreinov's "comparative folklore studies," tragedy appears akin to phallic fertility cults; the Nietzschean "spirit of music" is derived from "a tipsy peasant chorus at the festival altar"; and finally, Dionysus is actually a goat. "The goat is a zoomorphic emblem for Dionysus," who is also reflected in the Semitic god Azazel. In general, all ancient orgiastic cults prescribed the ritual offering of a goat, the most lustful of animals.[49] This is just one step away from Konstantin Vaginov's *Goat Song*—the intelligentsia's bitter farewell to once-dear illusions. However, unlike Vaginov's texts, Yevreinov's are devoid of irony. Could this man of the theater really have been completely unaware of the denigrating and distorting effect of his discourse? How right he was when he wrote, in a different work, that "laughter is the orgasm's worst enemy."[50]

The basic idea behind Yevreinov's creative approach was that "man is a theatrical beast." Theatricality was an inherent biological feature of man, although not only of man (one of his books is entitled *Theater Among Animals*). Whatever a man might do in the presence of others, be it court proceedings, sex, religion, or war, he did it with his audience in mind. What man did in solitude, most of all in his meditations, was actually *Theater for Oneself* (the title of Yevreinov's primary, three-volume book). An apologia of theatricality and the attraction of theater, the instinct to transform the world, and the identification of theatricality with erotica are the main elements of Yevreinov's conception.

Some time later, Yevreinov devised the term "theater therapy." People heal, he asserted, when their lives are transformed. And what can transform life more deeply than the theater, an art form based entirely on the "transformational instinct" and on catharsis, known since the days of Aristotle? As early as 1920 in Petrograd, he "proposed this method of treatment to the doctors and theatrical figures who control (as strange as it may sound at first) one of the means by which humanity can be healed, and a very powerful means at that."[51] Both in articulating and in ardently advocating his conceptions, Yevreinov was far ahead of the main streams in Western social psychology and psychotherapy, which would eventually also be based to a great extent on the "theatrical metaphor."[52]

But more than anything, the maestro was interested in *Theater as It Is* (as another of his books was entitled). Here, Yevreinov invented his own genre, "monodrama," a theatrical analogue to "stream of consciousness," a "dramatic performance with the aim of conveying the character's state of mind to the spectator in its most complete form and, therefore, of presenting the surrounding world on stage as it is perceived by the character." In 1912, Yevreinov staged his play *Behind the Backdrop of the Soul* at the Carnival Mirror Theater of Parody and Grotesquerie in St. Petersburg. The play provided a visual image of man reinterpreted anew, in whom tragedy and irony, mysticism, and analysis are intertwined. In the prologue, a professor draws graphs on a blackboard, explaining that they represent "strictly scientific work corresponding to the latest psycho-physiological data," and referring to Freud, among others. Yury Annenkov's scenery depicted the backdrop of the soul: heart, nerves, and lungs. The Soul was played by three actors: One personified the rational self, the second, the emotional self, and the third, the subconscious self. The rational self argued comically with the emotional self about its relationships with the subject's wife and mistress, and, pulling on strings representing nerves, both urged their master to suicide. The subconscious self slept almost until the final gunshot.[53] Sergey Eisenstein saw the performance and recalled:

> The subconscious self is waiting in Yevreinov. It is waiting for the emotional self to finish pulling at the nerves . . . and strangle its rational adversary. . . . A shot rings out. Strips of scarlet silk, a stage prop symbolizing blood, hang from the torn-open heart. A trolley conductor in mournful attire approaches the sleeping subconscious. He holds a lantern in his hands, since it has become dark on the stage. "Citizen, you have to change trolleys here."[54]

In 1920, Yevreinov revived the performance, changing only the names of the three "selves." They became the Accounting Self, the Motivating Self, and the Slumbering Self.

Yevreinov refers to Freud practically in every theoretical work: "All our dreams are nothing but theater—we know this for sure from Freud's marvelous work *Interpretation of Dreams.*"[55] His detailed analysis of erotica and all sorts of perversity as theatrical acting is based primarily on illustrations from Krafft-Ebing, but clearly points also to his knowledge of analytic literature. Two interesting works published in the 1920s evidence Yevreinov's orientation toward psychoanalysis: *The Underground of Genius: Sexual Sources of Dostoevsky's Oeuvre,* by Anna Kashina-Yevreinova (1923), and *The Mystery of Rasputin,* by Yevreinov himself (1924).

The book on Dostoevsky was written by the young actress whom Yevreinov recently had married, and it opens with the dedication "To my 'old' husband, from his 'young' wife." It seems likely that the author's elder spouse participated in the project or at least gave it his stamp of approval. In the book, Freud is praised in superlative tones as "famous for discoveries" that unraveled the "deepest mysteries of the soul" and "infinite horizons." He is described as "the greatest genius" and "the most remarkable man."[56] However, the author appears truly to have understood and assimilated only one of Freud's discoveries—the sexual origin of neurosis and of the psyche as a whole. Nonetheless, the book does demonstrate that psychoanalytic interests were in no way considered shameful at that time.

Yevreinov's book about Grigory Rasputin was completely different.[57] Written clearly and splendidly, full of details that seem scandalous even half a century later (in 1990, nine publishing houses in Ukraine and Russia were issuing new editions of the book), this work belongs to the class of sources that offer history to later generations in ready-made form. According to the laws of drama, Yevreinov begins with an exposition of Rasputin's incredible strength and influence, describing him as a Siberian peasant who became the undeclared monarch of Russia. Therein lies the mystery of Rasputin. Yevreinov examines possible solutions. The first and the most obvious for him and his readers is hypnosis. There is documentary evidence that Rasputin took private lessons in hypnosis from one of the numerous practitioners in St. Petersburg. Even the czar's minister of internal affairs, Khvostov, referred to Rasputin as "one of the most powerful hypnotists I have ever met" in his official deposition to the Extraordinary Investigatory Committee in 1917. Yevreinov introduces his own opinion that Rasputin was a born actor who turned everything that came his way into a performance. In addition, Yevreinov pieces together evidence to prove that Rasputin was a *khlyst*.

However, Yevreinov is not entirely satisfied with these explanations. Referring to manuals on hypnosis, he cites Bekhterev, who proposed in his musings on Rasputin a focus not only on "ordinary" hypnosis, but also on "sexual hypnosis." Sexual hypnosis, according to Bekhterev, accounted for the special impact Rasputin made on high-society ladies. Seeking a deeper understanding, Yevreinov looked to the works of Vyacheslav Ivanov, Nietzsche, and Freud. From the first two thinkers he borrowed the "mask," a cover in which each person invests himself, forcing others to believe in the mask to the same extent that the bearer identifies himself with it. Rasputin, like the sectarian *khlysty*, thought of himself as Christ and made others believe it, as well. At this point the author refers to the "extensive Freudian literature" and most of all to *Totem and Taboo,* which had already been released in Russian translation. Yevreinov comes close to suggesting that Rasputin's relationship with "the cantankerous and hysterical Czarina" and the generally unhappy and sickly royal family was actually transference: "One does not have to be a psychologist to understand how easily and simply a man who instills a thought of his mission of salvation in another person . . . with time becomes not only that person's closest advisor but also his supreme leader, not only a 'friend' but also a 'master.'" Yevreinov's final diagnosis was unequivocal: Rasputin was a "hysterical epileptic who suffered from an obviously erotic, religious mania."

In 1920, Yevreinov wrote his famous play *The Most Important Thing.*[58]
The protagonist, Paracletus (which means "advisor, assistant, comforter"—
ironically, these are also names used in the Bible to refer to the Holy Spirit),
introduces himself as an "entrepreneur in the theater called life." One of
Paracletus's masks is referred to in the course of the plot as "Dr. Fregoli."
But, unlike his famous Viennese colleague who bore a similar name, this
doctor tries to use specific, theatrical means to help people in real life: He
hires actors and dictates skits to them in which they play at love with
wretches who take them seriously: a timid young woman, neurotic young
men, and an old spinster. The awful consequences of such uninvited intervention in other people's lives are not played out and, seemingly, not thoroughly thought through. On the other hand, Yevreinov succeeded in establishing an ideological foundation that—judging by the play's history and
many other signs (see chapter 7)—was acceptable to the Bolshevik elite and
reflected its own quest. Dr. Fregoli reasons: "Socialism promises a great
deal, starting with a more just distribution of roles. . . . But there are millions of people in the world who cannot enjoy intimacy due to their infirmity. Socialist equality will seem a bitter mockery to these millions of people. Of course this is not to argue against socialism, but merely to state that
we have more to do."

Theater therapy in this context is not an outdated form of catharsis, but
an amateur blueprint of totalitarianism and, even more, a technical foundation for possible psychological manipulation. It was devised, however, by a
brilliant intellectual, portrayed with admiration by his acquaintance
Mikhail Bulgakov in his *Notes on Cuffs.* Moreover, *The Master and
Margarita* to a large extent continues the ideas laid out in *The Most
Important Thing.*[59] In both cases, outside intervention results in people getting something they could not have achieved on their own; in both cases a
continuous theatrical play unfolds, with the action carefully choreographed. But the differences are also immense. The author of the play and
his audience, the authors of the revolution, did not identify with the poor,
deceived wretches in the streets but with the wise men who manipulated
them. In Bulgakov everything is reversed: The author and the reader identify with the Master and Margarita in all their hopes and disasters. In contrast, there is not the least hint of magic in Yevreinov. His doctor performs
using exclusively theatrical means: costumes, money, the actors' play. The
almighty Woland, on the other hand, gives his protégés free choice and
does not know their answer until the choice is actually made. Conversely,
Yevreinov's earthly doctor makes decisions for living people like a playwright making decisions about his characters. Yevreinov appears to have
wanted to prove that it was still technically possible to "do something,"
and he demonstrated how he would do it with his own means, which harmonized in all respects with the totalitarian idea.

The play *The Most Important Thing* was immediately performed in revolutionary Petersburg, and it enjoyed success even beyond that city: Later, it would be performed in more than twenty countries around the world. On November 7, 1920, Yevreinov also staged the monumental show "Assault on the Winter Palace," a reenactment of the Bolshevik coup in Palace Square, involving 7,000 participants. So it is understandable why, when Yevreinov emigrated in 1925, Dmitry Filosofov made things difficult for him, accusing him of being a Bolshevik agent. Nevertheless, he would lead a long and productive life abroad.

Yevreinov's "theatricalized" idea developed organically throughout the long years of war and revolution, and it clearly shows the continuity between the elite intelligentsia's mission before and after the October coup. Yevreinov's sincere solidarity with Trotsky, imbued with hidden meaning, is expressed in one of the former's books, written at the same time as *The Most Important Thing*: "I am deeply indebted to Leon Trotsky, as are all who share my views (whether willingly or not) for the invaluable support for the idea of theatricalization expressed in his recent literary works."[60]

In Marietta Shaginyan's novel, *One's Own Fate*, written in 1916 (but published only after the Bolsheviks came to power, in 1923), psychiatric problems take a leading role.[61] At the time, Shaginyan was close to symbolist circles. The action in the novel unfolds in a sanatorium in the Caucasus, which may have been inspired by the Kryukovo sanatorium near Moscow. Psychiatric treatment and the figure of Förster, the head physician, are depicted in such an idealistic light that one gets the impression that the author has just come out of successful treatment. The personnel at the sanatorium subscribe to the concept of "organic treatment," a system adversarial to both psychoanalysis and Yevreinov's theater therapy. Förster says, for instance: "Shakespeare knew that one has to reject magic in order not to lose one's humanity. Everything theatrical is in fact magic. . . . Under no circumstances would I allow a mentally ill patient to partake of the pleasures of theater." Yevreinov himself cuts a nasty figure in the novel as Yastrebtsov, a maniacal patient, the source of all evils in the sanatorium. Expounding in typical symbolist terminology, he "enhances every temptation in each person," stages a symbolist performance in the sanatorium, called "My Dream," drives one patient to suicide, and at the end denounces the remarkable Förster.

Psychoanalysis is also distorted through caricature. A high-society lady of "advanced ideas" writes to the sanatorium from the capital: "All this psychopathology is twaddle, except for psychic analysis. The thing is, you have to lie down on a couch and associate, . . . and the doctor has to sit nearby with a pencil and write everything down. That is all there is to the treatment. The results have been so impressive that all of medicine is in awe." One psychiatrist tells the other about a neurasthenic patient who "clung to the couch with all his heart. He kept every little note, and was sure that he would use them to write another *Zarathustra.*" The other psychiatrist is even more radically inclined: "Associations made lying down are moral depravity!" Nevertheless, Förster himself "uses psychoanalysis, but awfully seldom and with caution."

Much later, in 1954, while reworking the novel for a new Soviet edition, Shaginyan took the opportunity to insert a long and rather flat anti-Freudian passage in Förster's words.

Before the War

In one of his 1913 articles, Moscow analyst Aron Zalkind (see chapter 8) wrote of the indignation and contempt that had greeted Freud's and Adler's concepts in the West, adding confidently: "fortunately, the situation in Russia is incomparably better."[62]

Indeed, work was moving along, and the future looked bright. Contacts between the psychoanalysts of Moscow and Vienna were well in hand, operating efficiently. Detailed summaries of the main publications of the International Psychoanalytic Association were published in almost every issue of *Psychotherapy*. Russian translations of these works were released within a year of their original publication. Translations of Freud's most recent works were published on a regular basis. For example, his famous article "The Question of Lay Psychoanalysis," published in German in 1910, appeared in the third issue of *Psychotherapy* for 1911. Later, in 1919, Freud admitted to Sabina Spielrein, who wanted to translate his works into Russian, that there was nothing left to translate, everything had already been translated, even though he had given formal permission only twice: for *Psychopathology of Daily Life*, which was published in 1910 by a certain Dr. Medem (an unknown pseudonym) and *Five Lectures on Psychoanalysis,* published in 1911 by Osipov.[63] To the best of our knowledge, Freud never lodged an official protest against the unauthorized Russian translations.

At the same time, works by Russian analysts were welcomed in Europe. In just one 1911 issue of the Vienna analysts' journal, there were four articles by Russian authors (one by Tatiana Rosenthal of St. Petersburg, one by Epstein of Kiev, and two by Odessan Moisei Wulff; and one of these works included a detailed survey of Russian publications about psychoanalysis). For the sake of comparison it is interesting to note that psychoanalysis took root in England only after Jones's return in 1913, and in France of the 1910s it attracted only ridicule.

At the beginning of the 1910s, the Russian journal *Modern Psychiatry* regularly advertised a psychotherapeutic sanatorium run by a certain Mr. Khrushchev in Kryukovo, in the vicinity of Moscow, which provided patients with exemplary living conditions. Freud's psychoanalysis was first among the methods of psychotherapy practiced there. Yury Kannabikh was in charge of the sanatorium's medical affairs, and Aron Zalkind and Nikolai Vyrubov were among the physicians. The sanatorium charter reserved preferential treatment for doctors, writers, and relatives of Anton Chekhov. Obviously, the late Chekhov was somehow involved in founding the Kryukovo sanatorium.[64] The sanatorium operated at least until the Bolshevik takeover. Sergei Solovyov, Yevgeny Vakhtangov, Alexander Blok, and Mikhail Chekhov were among the patients treated there.

In 1914, because of the war, the journal *Psychotherapy*, which was printed in the General Staff publishing house, ceased to exist. Psychoanalysts, however, continued to publish. In the March 1914 issue of *Modern Psychiatry*, for example, a long article by Moisei Wulff appeared.[65] It consisted of a meticulous case study about the successful psychoanalytic treatment of a young man who had been unable to enjoy life and sex.

The war, however, did eventually disrupt the fruitful work of Russian analysts. Many doctors went to the front; patients could no longer pay for services rendered. The rapid growth of anti-German and anti-Semitic sentiment during the war also hindered the development of psychoanalysis. The next act of the psychoanalytic drama, which was to begin in Russia after 1917, would unfold amidst different scenery, and the actors' speech would be different. Nevertheless, the cast would not change all that drastically.

5

Back to Russia: Sabina Spielrein

More than a century has passed since Sabina Spielrein was born, and a half-century since she died. Her grandchildren and great-grandchildren, the descendants of her patients, and her students' students might have been living and working in Russia today; but they are not.

The Soviet regime sought to eliminate her profession. If she continued to practice under the regime, it was in deep secrecy, and we do not know who her patients and her students were or whether they are still living.

The Nazi regime strove to annihilate her people. Along with two of her daughters and a host of other Jews, she was shot to death against the wall of a Rostov synagogue.

Everything Is Linked

Everything is linked. Yesterday, too, for instance, when the landlady pressed me to her heart, kissed me, told me she liked me so much, I was such a good person, etc., I was deeply moved. Do I deserve this? Can anyone really love me this way? It stirred me deeply that this woman, who has so many worries of her own, can enter into my feelings, can share my sorrows, without my even mentioning anything to her. I should have liked to tell her a great, great deal, but I could not bring out a word. I just hugged her and then commented on the curiously eerie lighting in the hallway. I was glad to be by myself again; even today I cannot quite face her; I feel somehow inhibited. I would like to do such nice things for this woman and cannot find a single kind word! Inwardly so deeply moved—outwardly so dry in manner! I am tired.[1]

Sabina Spielrein was born in 1885 to the family of a wealthy Jewish merchant in Rostov-on-the-Don. She had three younger brothers: Isaac, Jan, and Emile. All of the Spielrein children received formidable educations in Europe and became professors during the Soviet period. Isaac's life will be examined in greater detail later in this chapter, as he became the founder and leader of Soviet industrial psychology.

Practically nothing is known about Sabina's youth, which she spent in Rostov-on-the-Don. However, Chaim Weizmann, the founder and first president of Israel, who was born and raised in the Belorussian town of Pinsk, studied in Geneva at the same time as Sabina Spielrein, and he left behind fascinating recollections of her circle:

> In Geneva ... in 1900, I met my future wife, who arrived with several other Jewish girls, schoolmates from her native Rostov-on-the-Don. Like many others, she came to Geneva to study medicine because she had no access to education in Russia. This group of girls from Rostov ... differed significantly from ordinary Jewish university girls in Switzerland at that time in their appearance, manners, and views. They were much more attractive than girls of their age from the Pale of Settlement; they were less absorbed by Russian revolutionary ideas. Not that they were indifferent to them, they simply allocated more time to studies and less to endless meetings and debates. ... Many of the students were against the Rostov girls but they paid no attention to hostility.[2]

Weizmann described the small Jewish community in Rostov as relatively wealthy: His wife's father, like Sabina's father, belonged to a merchant guild and could afford to support and educate his children abroad. This is one reason why the Rostov girls "were such a contrast to the majority of Jewish female students in Geneva, who, for the most part, looked nervous, disillusioned, exhausted, and hungry."[3]

Spielrein, however, was unwell in Switzerland. It is unclear exactly what her illness was. Only the dates of her admittance and discharge are documented at the famous hospital Burghölzli, near Zurich: August 17, 1904, and June 1, 1905.[4] The director of the clinic there was Eugen Bleuler, one of the founders of modern psychiatry; and Sabina's attending physician was a young intern named Carl Jung. We know virtually nothing about the circumstances of her hospitalization, the kind of treatment she received, or for how long she was treated after her discharge from the hospital. Much later, when Freud was writing his *History of the Psycho-Analytic Movement*, he requested information from Abraham concerning the beginning of psychoanalytic work at Burghölzli. Abraham responded that as early as December 1904, Jung had been analyzing a hysterical female patient there. This could only have been Sabina. The young woman was Jung's first psychoanalytic patient.

The letter that Jung sent to Freud later, on October 23, 1906, further illuminates Spielrein's condition.

> At the risk of boring you, I must abreact my most recent experience. I am currently treating an hysteric with your method. Difficult case, a 20-year-old Russian girl student, ill for 6 years.
>
> First trauma between the 3rd and 4th year. Saw her father spanking her older brother on the bare bottom. Powerful impression. Couldn't help thinking afterwards that she had defecated on her father's hand. From the 4th–7th

year convulsive attempts to defecate on her own feet, in the following manner: She sat on the floor with one foot beneath her, pressed her heel against her anus, and tried to defecate and at the same time to prevent defecation. Often retained the stool for 2 weeks in this way! Has no idea how she hit upon this peculiar business; says it was completely instinctive, and accompanied by blissfully shuddersome feelings. Later this phenomenon was superseded by vigorous masturbation.

I should be extremely grateful if you would tell me in a few words what you think of this story.[5]

The Freud-Jung correspondence had just begun; this was only Jung's second letter to his future teacher. Freud, who was twenty years older than Jung, was excited to find a professional psychiatrist working in a prestigious clinic who was interested in his work. Freud responded to Jung's first letter as cordially as possible. While developing the relationship and telling his elder colleague of Sabina's case, Jung did his best to make himself out to be a practicing analyst deserving of professional confidence.

Freud replied in detail, utilizing in his letter all the information available to him:

I am glad to hear that your Russian girl is a student; uneducated persons are at present too inaccessible for our purposes. The defecation story is nice and suggests numerous analogies. . . . It must be possible, by the symptoms and even by the character, to recognize anal excitation as a motivation. Such people often show typical combinations of character traits. They are extremely neat, stingy, and obstinate, traits which are in a manner of speaking the sublimations of anal erotism. Cases like this based on repressed perversion can be analyzed very satisfactorily.

You see that you have not bored me in the least. I am delighted with your letters.[6]

Freud came up with a saying that later became popular: Life can be understood only in retrospect, but the trick is that it must be lived forward. Seven years later, after his final break with Jung, Freud would write to Sabina Spielrein, "When I had to take sides at the beginning of our correspondence, it looked as if it would work out."[7]

To Give a Little Bird Its Freedom

I could never stand by the window that way on purpose. The conscious has to be circumvented in some subtle manner, and then . . . one can indulge oneself a little. When I was fully dressed, except for my belt, I noticed that a nice young gentleman was gazing into my room; I felt myself blushing deeply, and this mild manifestation of the unconscious, which I noted quite objectively, pleased me very much. For a moment I hesitated. Modesty won out, and I hid behind the curtain. A little later an older gentleman looked out of the upper building.[8]

Twenty-four-year-old medical student Sabina Spielrein considered it another indulgence to write down these lines, evidently for her analyst's benefit. Although he might well have found them trivial, for us they are full of veiled meaning and anticipation of what lay ahead of her.

It was just as Jung was administering therapy to Spielrein, his first analytic patient, that Freud informed him of his latest discovery, one that had yet to be made public. On December 6, 1906, he wrote to Jung that he would have to keep certain elements of the treatment of neuroses under wraps for the time being, since "it is not possible to explain anything to a hostile public." Perhaps such volatile topics should be cloaked in esoteric language, intelligible only to the initiated. The most important of these as yet hidden psychoanalytic discoveries was transference:

> You are probably aware that our cures are brought about through the fixation of the libido prevailing in the unconscious (transference), and that this transference is most readily obtained in hysteria. Transference provides the impulse necessary for understanding and translating the language of the [unconscious]; where it is lacking, the patient does not make an effort or does not listen when we submit our translation to him. Essentially, one might say, the cure is effected by love. And actually transference provides the most cogent, indeed, the only unassailable proof that neuroses are determined by the individual's love life.[9]

So it was stated: A cure is achieved through love. Today, this is an obvious truth to any psychoanalyst, but Freud articulated the essence of transference a long time ago. According to Freud's controversial theory, the patient's feelings, which until transference remained unconscious and caused illness, resurfaced and could be experienced anew through love for the doctor. Adult love, into which forgotten but no less heartrending childhood fears and passions were transferred (and it was through this transfer that adults became conscious of these old feelings), was the only path that led one safely through the world. It was a path toward a cure, but not necessarily to happiness, as the satisfaction of desire in this situation would be as impossible as it had been in childhood.

During the fourth year of Sabina's treatment, Jung related the following story to Freud:

> An hysterical patient told me that a verse from a poem by Lermontov was continually going round in her head. The poem is about a prisoner whose sole companion is a bird in a cage. The prisoner is animated only by *one* wish: sometime in life, as his noblest deed, to give some creature its freedom. He opens the cage and lets his beloved bird fly out. What is the patient's greatest wish? "Once in my life I would like to help someone to perfect freedom through psychoanalytic treatment." In her dreams she is condensed with me. She admits that actually her greatest wish is to have a child by me who would fulfil all her unfulfillable wishes. For that purpose I would naturally have to let "the bird out" first.[10]

Vladimir Nabokov commented on this letter in 1974.[11] He explained to his Western readers that the poem in question was written by Pushkin, not Lermontov, and was entitled "A Little Bird." Moreover, the poem was "absurdly paraphrased." Pushkin wrote the poem during his exile in Kishinev. The protagonist in the poem releases a bird each spring, carrying on his native custom in a foreign land. This consoles him:

> *Why should I mutter against God,*
> *When even to one creature*
> *I was able to give freedom!*[12]

However, there is neither prisoner nor cage in this poem. Both are included in Pushkin's well-known poem "The Captive" ("A captive, alone in a dungeon I dwell. . . .").[13] In this poem, however, no one sets the eagle free, and the sad "comrade" simply dreams of flying away with the captive and calls to him. In essence, the bird is in a cage with the prisoner in one poem, and is released in another. Which poem was on the Russian patient's mind?

Perhaps the young woman recited and translated so much Russian poetry to her young doctor that one or the other of them confused the two poems. Regardless of the origins of this confusion, Jung considered the poems that were on Sabina's mind a kind of symptom, and her psychoanalytic treatment would necessarily be based on his interpretation of these symptoms. The patient offered her own interpretation: She dreamt of becoming a psychoanalyst, and therefore recited poems about liberating living things. For Jung, however, such an interpretation appeared to be just another, more profound symptom: In her dreams, the patient was confusing herself with her analyst. In his understanding, the patient saw herself as a prisoner and dreamt that her doctor, like the eagle out of the poem, would call her "where turbulent seas rush to merge with sky."[14] Her dream of liberating a living creature was a reflection of her desire to give birth to his child. This could happen only if, switching from the lofty genre of romantic Russian verse to a sleazy Swiss idiom, "he let his bird out." Thus, Sabina (who is undoubtedly the person in question) interpreted the poetry as indicative of her desire to become an analyst, while Jung interpreted it as a hint at her desire for sexual intimacy with him. Who was right: Spielrein, Jung, both, or neither? Only the future would tell.

Meanwhile, Jung found himself more and more in Freud's confidence. Jung was chosen to represent psychoanalysis at the International Congress of Psychiatry and Neurology in Amsterdam, which was held in September 1907. This was the first time a psychoanalyst would publicly address an official gathering of psychiatrists, and Freud was extremely serious about it. He wrote to Jung in Amsterdam:

Now of all times I wish I were with you, . . . telling you about my long years of honourable but painful solitude, . . . about the serene certainty which finally took possession of me and bade me wait until a voice from the unknown multitude should answer mine. That voice was yours. . . . Thank you for that, and don't let anything shake your confidence, you will witness our triumph and share in it.[15]

In his address, Jung spoke of a case that he knew well, that of Sabina Spielrein, but he was nevertheless doomed to experience the bitterness of defeat. Both sides were too aggressively set against one another. One of the experts in attendance declared that Freud's method could not be taken seriously, since every word was interpreted in sexual terms—which was extremely harmful for the patient. The speaker himself never allowed his patients to mention anything related to sex. Meanwhile, Jung's address went over the time limit, and he refused to obey the chairman's request that he finish up. When he was finally forced to abandon the podium, he stormed out of the hall in indignation.[16]

The Practice That Deters from Theory

Mother says it is impossible for my friend and me to remain friends once we have given each other our love. A man cannot sustain pure friendship in the long run. If I am nice to him—he will want love. If I am always cold—then the [illegible] hurt his feelings. That depressed me so, so much! Oh dear, what should I hope for? If I could move Fate, if I could be sure that a plea spoken before witnesses would be fulfilled, I would pray here: dear Fate, allow us, my friend and me, to be exceptions. Allow us to meet each other always radiant with pleasure, to support each other in joy and sorrow, to form one soul, even *à distance*, to reach out our hands to each other in the search for the "higher, farther, wider," or, as my friend says, "the good and the beautiful," that we may be a support to many who are weak.[17]

Four of Sabina Spielrein's fellow Russians were also learning psychoanalysis in Burghölzli at the same time. These were Fanya Shalevskaya, Max Eitingon, Esther Aptekman, and Tatiana Rosenthal. All were Jewish and had come from southwestern Russia, and each played a distinctive role in the history of psychoanalysis. The most significant figure, but also the most controversial, was Max Yefimovich Eitingon, who became acquainted with Freud just shortly after Jung. The long walks that Freud and Eitingon took together through the Vienna streets in early 1907 were later taken by historians as the first attempt at a training, didactic form of psychoanalysis. In September of the same year, Freud informed Jung from Rome: "Eitingon, whom I met in Florence, is now here and will probably visit me soon to give me detailed impressions of Amsterdam. He seems to have taken up with some woman again. Such practice is a deterrent from theory. When I have totally overcome my libido (in the common sense), I shall undertake to write a 'Love-life of Mankind.'"[18]

Jung was irritated, for reasons that will become clear: "I consider Eitingon a totally impotent gasbag—scarcely has this uncharitable judgment left my lips than it occurs to me that I envy him his uninhibited abreaction of the polygamous instinct. I therefore retract 'impotent' as too compromising. He will certainly never amount to anything; one day he may become a member of the Duma."[19]

Jung's attitude toward Eitingon was a mixture of mockery and suspicion, concealing the envy that lay beneath: Eitingon was rich, whereas Jung confessed to Freud that his solvency was dependent on his wife's wealth. What was worse, Jung saw in Eitingon the freedom of polygamy. The son of a pastor, Jung condemned such behavior in others, but felt an ever increasing urge to succumb to it himself.

James Rice, an American scholar who analyzed this part of the correspondence between Freud and Jung, discovered in this letter Jung's "Russian stereotype," an intuitive conception of Russians, dominant in European culture of the early twentieth century and shared by both Freud and Jung. Rice indicated that a component of this stereotype was sexual freedom, ascribed to Russians and perceived with a full measure of natural ambivalence.[20] On the other hand, however, it is difficult to overlook the desire to humiliate a rival in Jung's association of polygamy and impotence, as well as in the suggestion that the windbag Eitingon would one day become a member of the politically impotent Russian parliament. Here, Russian exoticism is merely a convenient form.

There was more at work here than just stereotypes, however. In the same letter, Jung hopped by free association from Eitingon to Otto Gross, an early German psychoanalyst and a drug addict: "Dr. Gross tells me that he puts a quick stop to the transference by turning people into sexual immoralists. He says the transference to the analyst and its persistent fixation are mere monogamy symbols and as such symptomatic of repression. The truly healthy state for the neurotic is sexual immorality. Hence he associates you with Nietzsche."[21]

It does not take a psychoanalyst to find something suspicious in Jung's repetition of the same motifs when describing two different people. Jung was interested in individuals who displayed "uninhibited abreaction of polygamous instincts," and moreover, those who did so with their patients. Jung wrote about them as if only to debunk them: He discarded Eitingon by way of the "Russian stereotype," which combined sexual freedom with pompous twaddle. Gross was taken out by way of the Nietzschean stereotype, which had no less meaning for Freud, in which amoralism was linked with the quest for power. However, Jung was not just struggling with his competitors; even more importantly, he was struggling with himself. His theoretical views were still orthodox at that time, and he employed them to convince himself of his own rectitude: "What is civilization but the fruit of adversity? I feel Gross is going along too far with the vogue for the sexual short-circuit, which is neither intelligent, nor in good taste, but merely convenient, and therefore anything but a civilizing factor."[22]

Occasionally, Jung attempted to analyze his own feelings, but he invariably encountered insurmountable obstacles. As he had never undergone psychoanalysis—even the primitive form of it that Freud administered to his early students—for Jung, correspondence with his teacher replaced analysis and took on all its aspects. Most of all this meant resistance and transference. Jung sometimes went weeks without responding to Freud's letters, and he often avoided discussing his "intimate affairs." Freud pointed this out, mildly at first, and then gradually more insistently. In one of his letters (of October 28, 1907), Jung explained his delays in correspondence as a patient might justify tardiness or skipping sessions, or insincerity. The first reason he offered was his "work load." The other "is to be found in the realm of affect, in what you have termed my 'self-preservation complex.'"[23]

However, Jung presented a different explanation a few lines later. "So the self-preservation complex does not come from there; it is rather that my veneration for you has something of the character of a religious crush. Though it does not really bother me, I still feel it is disgusting and ridiculous because of its undeniable erotic undertone. . . . *I therefore fear your confidence.* I also fear the same reaction from you when I speak of my intimate affairs."[24]

This explanation did not change the situation because Jung still had not even begun to plumb its depths. The pauses in correspondence became longer and longer. In another attempt to justify himself (in his letter of March 7, 1909), Jung again complained of his busy schedule and of overwork:

The last and worst straw is that a complex is playing Old Harry with me: A woman patient, whom years ago I pulled out of a very sticky neurosis with unstinting effort, has violated my confidence and my friendship in the most mortifying way imaginable. She has kicked up a vile scandal solely because I denied myself the pleasure of giving her a child. I have always acted a gentleman towards her, but before the bar of my rather sensitive conscience I nevertheless don't feel clean, and that is what hurts the most because my intentions were always honourable. But you know how it is—the devil can use even the best of things for the fabrication of filth. Meanwhile I have learnt an unspeakable amount of marital wisdom, for until now I had a totally inadequate idea of my polygamous components despite all self-analysis. Now I know where and how the devil can be laid by the heels. These painful yet extremely salutary insights have churned me up hellishly inside, but for that very reason, I hope, have secured me moral qualities which will be of the greatest advantage to me in later life. The relationship with my wife has gained enormously in assurance and depth.[25]

A Deal with the Devil

And yet I always felt so heavyhearted when I submerged myself in the atmosphere of the solitary cottage surrounded by that green carpet. I could never surrender completely to a peaceful life in the bosom of my family. Perfect stillness makes me anxious. I have to have people with passionate strivings around me, I have to experience the life of many individuals, I must be inspired by mighty and profound feelings, I must have music. . . . In truth, I could never be satisfied. And what about my old ideal of wandering through the world like the ancient Greek philosophers, surrounded by a crowd of disciples, teaching them outdoors, in harmony with nature?[26]

Love between a psychiatrist and his patient is an oft-described phenomenon. It is frightening to love a person you do not understand. To call such a person "ill" is to take bearings, to anticipate that the condition is hopeless, and thereby to relieve one's own fear. "Schizophrenia" is a word used to define people whose feelings are incomprehensible; incomprehensible at least to those who use the word. When an author composes a novel about how a doctor becomes a drunk or a broken man after falling in love with a schizophrenic patient, he provides his readers with an image of their own fear, helping them to get well. The entranced reader will know what he has to fear from the dark recesses of human relations. In many novels on this subject (from those of F. Scott Fitzgerald to those by Mikhail Chulaki, a Russian writer of the 1980s), the doctor is drawn by a fateful force that sets the sick woman apart. Unable to resist his emotions and consequently her disease, the doctor loses his own mental health, or at least his self-respect.

The psychoanalyst relies on another side of this interaction: Love must not bring disease to the doctor, it must grant healing to the patient. The feelings of sick people are at the very least immature, and they can establish fresh contact with the world of the healthy only through strong emotion. The psychoanalyst's duty is to uncover these emotions, to tolerate, analyze, and discuss them with the patient for years on end. The patient's passions are an inevitable and even desirable reality, an indispensable element of the analyst's work. However, according to the spirit and letter of the psychoanalytic method, a sexual relationship between analyst and patient is impermissible. Such affairs are prohibited by professional custom. Psychoanalysis should not be used in order to satisfy either party sexually. Formulated by Freud, this rule may have been violated in practice, but it has rarely been questioned as one of the cornerstone principles of psychoanalysis.

On March 9, 1909, Freud informed Jung that "I too have had news of the woman patient through whom you became acquainted with the neurotic gratitude of the spurned." Arthur Muthmann, a Vienna psychiatrist, had come to Freud to tell him of a woman who had introduced herself to him as Jung's lover. "But we both presumed that the situation was quite different and that the only possible explanation was a neurosis of his informant."[27]

Freud was expansive in his attempt to console his protégé, who had found himself in a precarious position, but one not unusual in "our trade." "To be slandered and scorched by the love with which we operate—such are the perils of our trade, which we are certainly not going to abandon on their account." Freud quoted from Goethe, referring to the great poet as Jung's grandfather:[28] "In league with the Devil and yet fear fire?" Freud also soothed his student by inviting his "dear wife" for dinner.

This time, Jung responded promptly: "Dear Professor Freud, I must answer you at once. Your kind words have relieved and comforted me. You may rest assured, not only now but for the future, that nothing Fliess-like is going to happen. . . . But I shall not be unfaithful to psychoanalysis on that account," he swore, although Freud did not yet suspect anything of the kind. Jung added, for some reason using his teacher's imagery, "It's just that for the past fortnight the devil has been tormenting me in the shape of neurotic ingratitude."[29]

The teacher wrote of the "neurotic gratitude of the spurned," whereas the student wrote of the devil's "neurotic ingratitude." Jung's expression is somewhat clumsy: Why should the devil be grateful to Jung, and can the devil be a neurotic at all? This substitution revealed Jung's genuine feelings for the woman whom he came to identify with the devil. However, he insisted there was no woman at all: "The story hawked round by Muthmann is Chinese to me. I've never really had a mistress and am the most innocent of spouses. Hence my terrific moral reaction! I simply cannot imagine who it might have been. I don't think it is the same lady. Such stories give me horrors."[30]

Something rings false in Jung's words. He knew that the gossip concerned his relationship with the very same woman about whom he has just rushed to tell his teacher. It was to his advantage that he managed to tell him in time: He probably would not have offered the information if he had not sensed danger. He had reason to be scared, which is why, without any obvious connection, he brought up Freud's painful break with Fliess, the friend of his youth, and naïvely promised that nothing of the sort would ever happen to him. Freud could not have ignored the mistakes in style and emotion made by the heir to his throne.

It had been quite awhile, about two months, since Freud first heard about Jung's scandalous affair with his patient, when he received a letter dated May 30, 1909.

Dear Professor Freud:

I would be most grateful to you if you would grant me a brief audience! It has to do with something of greatest importance to me which you would probably be interested to hear about.

If it were possible, I should like to ask that you inform me of a convenient time somewhat in advance, since I am an intern at the hospital here and therefore would have to arrange for someone to substitute for me during my absence.

Perhaps you expect me to be a brazen seeker after fame who plans to bring you some wretched "earth-shaking" scholarly paper or something of the sort.

No, that is not what leads me to you. You, too, have made me feel awkward.

With expressions of my esteem,
Looking forward to your kind reply,

S. Spielrein[31]

Spielrein must have come across Russian stereotypes often enough during her years abroad—in particular Westerners' expectation that all Russians want to change the world—that she found it necessary to let Freud know from the very start that she had other interests. This, however, did not help her.

At that very time, a young psychiatrist from Moscow, Mikhail Asatiani, paid Jung a visit. Asatiani was fascinated by psychoanalysis but complained that it yielded few therapeutic results. Jung wrote Freud that Asatiani's lack of effectiveness was connected with the imperfection of his healing skills as well as with "the Russian material, where the individual is as ill-differentiated as a fish in a shoal." Jung continued, "The problems of the masses are the first things that need solving there."[32] Since Asatiani did not know German, the conversation was made possible only with the help of a translator. This was particularly wearisome for Jung.

Was it Sabina who served as translator? There were other Russians living in Burghölzli. But Jung's condition—weariness because of the translation and irritation with Russians in general—was caused, undoubtedly, by the situation at hand. It is interesting to note that Jung's view of Russia corresponded closely with the ideas of those who, like the Bolsheviks, believed that the most pressing problems in Russia were related to the masses.

At that time, however, Jung and his wife took up residence in a new house on a quiet Swiss lake, where they would live for the rest of their lives. Freud's congratulations probably did little to cheer Jung.

Dear friend,

Hurrah for your new house! I would say it louder and longer if I didn't know how you Swiss dislike emotional effusions. . . . Of course I understand your silence and even now I would leave you more time if another letter—which I enclose—had not reached me at the same time as yours. Weird! What is she? A busybody, a chatterbox, or a paranoiac? If you know anything about the writer or have some opinion in the matter, would you kindly send me a short wire, but otherwise you must *not* go to any trouble. If I don't hear from you, I shall assume that you know nothing. . . . Your Russian (and I must tell you again how I admire your patience, or rather your resignation) probably has some utopian dream of a world-saving therapy and feels that the work isn't getting on fast enough. The Russians, I believe, are especially deficient in the art of painstaking work. . . . With very special regards to you, your wife and children in your new house.

Yours,

Freud.[33]

There are several interesting aspects to this letter. First, Freud found no allusions to Jung in the letter he had just received from Spielrein, besides its return address in Zurich. Nevertheless, he forwarded the letter to Jung with precise comments that leave no doubt as to how much he knew. Second, Freud switched promptly to the subject of Russians, admiring Jung's humility in his contacts with them, and ascribing to the Russian nation certain utopian ideas and an inability to do painstaking work. At that moment he was undoubtedly thinking of Spielrein's letter, wherein she declared that she did not intend to turn the world upside down, at the same time that she was interfering with Jung's work and doing none of her own. At this time, too, Freud was reorienting his business toward America, so perhaps his derogatory remarks about Russians were a signal of his new financial freedom. In any case, he sent a curt letter to Fräulein Spielrein in which he refused to receive her and suggested that she present her request in written form.

The Discovery of Countertransference

> Life is so hemmed in by the stupidest formalities, which one must honor, no matter how petty, if one does not wish to be stamped out. Well, all this is well known. Enough for today, I think. I could not express the main thing, and that is that my friend loves me. More about that later.[34]

On June 4, 1909, Jung sent Freud a cable in response to the latter's request and mailed him a long letter. In a desperate attempt to at once safeguard Freud's confidence and prevent Spielrein from spreading the information any further, he told Freud much, but as will soon become clear, not everything. In his letter, he accused Spielrein of trying to seduce him, interpreted her actions as revenge for his rejection of her usual hysterical demands, and compared her to Gross, whom Freud regarded as a traitor. Nevertheless, he called Spielrein his "psychoanalytic test case," and admitted that he maintained friendly relations with her for years, "until I saw that an unintended wheel had started turning."[35] He wrote that of all his patients, only Spielrein and Gross enjoyed so much of his friendship and that they were also the ones who had brought him the most grief.

Freud responded that Jung's explanations had confirmed his supposition.

Such experiences, though painful, are necessary and hard to avoid. Without them we cannot really know life and what we are dealing with. I myself have never been taken in quite so badly, but I have come very close to it a number of times and had a *narrow escape*. I believe that only grim necessities weighing on my work, and the fact that I was ten years older than yourself when I came to psychoanalysis, have saved me from similar experiences. But no lasting harm is done. They help us to develop the thick skin we need to dominate "counter-transference," which is after all a permanent problem for us; they teach us to displace our own affects to best advantage.[36]

In this letter, Freud remained what he had always been—a sober, ironic, and rigid moralist. "The way these women manage to charm us with every conceivable psychic perfection until they have attained their purpose is one of nature's greatest spectacles. Once that has been done or the contrary has become a certainty, the constellation changes amazingly."[37] He advised his student to draw useful lessons from the affair, consoled him, and lent him the support of a trusting handshake. For Freud, however, whether the seductress had succeeded or failed made all the difference: He had never been caught "like that."

A most important point that this letter illustrated was that Freud learned from the mistakes of others: The letter brings out something new, a concept still enclosed in quotation marks, the notion of countertransference. This idea describes the analyst's feelings for his patient, which naturally reflect the analyst's own personal problems. An analyst's competence and the course of his analysis depend on the extent to which he is conscious of his own problems. One can assume (as does the French historian of psycho-analysis A. de Mijolla[38]) that Freud realized the significance of counter-transference precisely when he was trying to make sense of the difficulties that Jung encountered as he treated his Russian patient. Freud publicly un-veiled his theory of countertransference at his earliest opportunity, at the Nuremberg Congress of April 1910.

Freud sent another letter to Sabina in which, without accusing Jung, he urged her to "suppress and eradicate" "the feelings that have outlived this close relationship."[39] He avoided personal involvement and interference, although the tone of his letter left Sabina some hope that the intrigue might continue. She was quick to take advantage of this ambiguity.

Jung continued to regret in his "theological" style, as Freud ironically dubbed it: "[f]or actually it is too stupid that I of all people, your 'son and heir,' should squander your heritage so heedlessly."[40] In his response, Freud begged him not to "go too far in the direction of contrition and re-action," and he employed the following metaphor to present the moral of the story:

Remember Lassalle's fine sentence about the chemist whose test tube had cracked: "With a slight frown over the resistance of matter, he gets on with his work." In view of the kind of matter we work with, it will never be possible to avoid little laboratory explosions. Maybe we didn't slant the test tube enough, or we heated it too quickly. In this way we learn what part of the danger lies in the matter and what part in our way of handling it.[41]

It was during this period that Freud developed his habit of conveying his regards to Jung's spouse in all of his letters.

Meanwhile, a messy situation was about to erupt, involving Sabina's parents, Jung's wife, and of course Freud himself. Sabina continued to share new details with Freud, supposedly trying to make him demonstrate to her that Jung was worthy of love and no villain. She rejected Freud's advice to suppress her feelings, not because it was impossible, but because she considered such a move useless: If she were to eradicate Jung from her heart, she would never be able to love again; she felt that by leaving the door open, someone else might someday enter.[42] Sabina's mother received an anonymous letter. Sabina suspected that Jung's wife, Emma, had written it. Finally, Jung himself wrote to Sabina's mother.

In his cold letter, Jung differentiated the roles of doctor and lover in the following way: The doctor was paid for his work and, therefore, he knew his limits well. A man and a woman, on the other hand, cannot maintain purely Platonic relations forever. Therefore, Jung earnestly suggested that Mrs. Spielrein start paying "suitable recompense," which would enable him to confine himself to his role as a doctor. At the end he even named the price. If he were to remain Sabina's friend, her mother would have to take her chances. "For no one can prevent two friends from doing as they wish."

All this would have been normal if it had occurred at a different stage in the relationship; but at that moment it was much too late to make such proposals. Everything had already happened, as Jung was the first to recognize: "I moved from being her doctor to being her friend when I ceased to push my own feelings into the background. I could drop my role as doctor the more easily because I did not feel professionally obligated, for I never charged a fee. This latter clearly establishes the limits imposed upon a doctor."[43] Under the circumstances, it was impossible for Jung to go back to his role as a doctor, and his request for fees amounting to ten francs per hour therefore seems obtuse revenge.

Sabina's parents were of an exceptionally sober sort. On June 13, 1909, Sabina wrote to Freud: "I am really lucky that my parents have reacted so reasonably to these events. I described the manner of our parting to my mother, and she passed it along to my father, who said only, 'People have made a god out of him, and he is nothing but an ordinary human being. I am so glad she boxed his ears! I would have done it myself. Just let her do what she thinks necessary: she can take care of herself.'"[44] Later, Freud would meet Sabina's father, Naftul Spielrein, and he would remember him with respect many years afterward.

In 1915, Freud wrote in his article "Observations on Transference-Love" that when the analyst and his female patient fell in love with each other in the process of analysis, "there is a complete change of scene; it is as though some piece of make-believe has been stopped by the sudden irruption of re-ality—as when, for instance, a cry of fire is raised during a theatrical per-formance."[45] Successful analysis is impossible without transference, but love should not be equated with transference; love is only one of its most intensive and acute forms, facilitating effective treatment, provided the therapist is skillful enough. Clearly, not all patients and their relatives would agree. "Any relative who adopts Tolstoy's attitude to this problem can remain in undisturbed possession of his wife or daughter; but he will have to try to put up with the fact that she, for her part, retains her neuro-sis and the interference with her capacity for love which it involves."[46] Love brought on by analysis, according to Freud, must never be consum-mated. "The treatment must be carried out in abstinence,"[47] and this is not so much an ethical principle as it is a therapeutic necessity: "I shall state it as a fundamental principle that the patient's need and longing should be al-lowed to persist in her, in order that they may serve as forces impelling her to work and to make changes."[48] Suppression of the patient's craving for love was no less perilous than its gratification, and therefore the doctor's task was to achieve a complex balance between these two simple extremes. The only possible way to do this, Freud insisted, was to treat the craving for love as something symbolic, emphasizing the role of resistance in this love but not questioning its authenticity.

What would happen, Freud asked himself and generations of his follow-ers, if the doctor satisfied his patient's desire, liberating his own feelings of transference? "The patient would achieve *her* aim, but he would never achieve *his*."[49] Freud illustrated this point with an old Jewish joke about the pastor who came to visit an insurance agent on his deathbed. Their conver-sation went on for so long that a relative waiting impatiently outside began to hope that the dying agent would be converted to the true faith before his passing. At last, the door opened and the pastor came out, fully insured.[50]

Perfect Honesty

Yes, those were two bad nights. My love for my friend overwhelmed me with a mad glow. At some moments I resisted violently, at others I let him kiss every one of my little fingers and clung to his lips, swooning with love. How foolish to talk about it! So this is I, usually the soul of pure, clear reason, allowing myself such fantasies. How am I supposed to withstand this savage force? Here I sit, weary from all the tempests I have endured, and repeat to myself: not this! Better an ab-solutely pure friendship, even *à distance*. That he loves me is certain, but "there is a but," as our old natural-history teacher used to say, and that is that . . . my friend is already married.[51]

On June 21, 1909, Jung wrote to Freud,

> I have good news to report of my Spielrein affair. I took too black a view of things. After breaking with her I was almost certain of her revenge and was deeply disappointed only by the banality of the form it took. The day before yesterday she turned up at my house and had a *very decent* talk with me, during which it transpired that the rumour buzzing about me does not emanate from her at all. My ideas of reference, understandable enough in the circumstances, attributed the rumour to her, but I wish to retract this forthwith.[52]

It is hard to imagine how difficult it must have been for Jung to write this letter. He was forced to admit the total falsity of his clinical vision. He even admitted that Sabina's sexual contrivances were an illusion: "[I was] imagining that I was talking theoretically, but naturally Eros was lurking in the background." Moreover, now he claimed that the patient had freed herself from transference "in the best and nicest way and has suffered no relapse (apart from a paroxysm of weeping after the separation)." He no longer accused her of hysteria and blackmail, totally accepting and repeating her motives: "Her intention to come to you was not aimed at any intrigue but only at paving the way for a talk with me." At this point he confessed, although not quite straight out, that he had committed a sin, and repentance was evident in everything that followed: "Although not succumbing to helpless remorse, I nevertheless deplore the sins I have committed, for I am largely to blame for the high-flying hopes of my former patient."

However, admitting that his letter to Sabina's mother had been an attempt at deception, he provided the following explanation, which would also have appeared patently deceptive not just to Freud, but to any reasonable adult:

> When the situation had become so tense that the continued preservation of the relationship could be rounded out only by sexual acts, I defended myself in a manner that cannot be justified morally. . . . I wrote to her mother that I was not the gratifier of her daughter's sexual desires but merely her doctor, and that she should free me from her. In view of the fact that the patient had shortly before been my friend and enjoyed my full confidence, my action was a piece of knavery which I very reluctantly confess to you as my father.[53]

Finally, he asks his teacher, father figure, and most serious competitor for help, and most likely for collaboration: Freud was to provide Sabina with documented confirmation of his student's "perfect honesty," and by so doing fulfill one of the conditions for capitulation:

> I would now like to ask you a great favour: would you please write a note to Frl. Spielrein, telling her that I have fully informed you of the matter, and especially of the letter to her parents, which is what I regret most. I would like to give my patient at least this satisfaction: that you and she know of my "perfect

honesty." I ask your pardon many times, for it was my stupidity that drew you into this imbroglio.

The long letter ends with an unsuccessful attempt to follow Freud's advice and to extract a modicum of benefit from the situation: "But now I am extremely glad that I was not mistaken, after all, about the character of my patient, otherwise I should have been left with a gnawing doubt as to the soundness of my judgment, and this would have been a considerable hindrance to me in my work."[54]

Jung, a psychiatrist, the author of superb academic works, Freud's closest heir and protégé, lost the battle and had to admit his failure in a humiliating confession. And to whom did he lose? To his former patient, one diagnosed by his boss as a schizophrenic. And where did he lose? In his own professional field, the business of relations, in a reworking of transference, in coordinating feelings with reality. And what did he lose?

Three days later, fulfilling his student's almost unmanageable request that he testify to Jung's "perfect honesty," Freud wrote to Sabina Spielrein:

Dear colleague,

I have today learnt something from Dr. Jung himself about the subject of your proposed visit to me, and now see that I had divined some matters correctly but that I had construed others wrongly and to your disadvantage. I must ask your forgiveness on this latter count. However, the fact that I was wrong and that the lapse has to be blamed on the man and not the woman, as my young friend himself admits, satisfies my need to hold women in high regard. Please accept this expression of my entire sympathy for the dignified way in which you have resolved the conflict. Yours faithfully, Freud.[55]

While consoling Jung again later, Freud remarked in passing, "perhaps I am already too biased in your favour." His curiosity was piqued; he wanted to know more about this Fräulein Spielrein. "Amazingly awkward—is she a foreigner by any chance?"[56] he asked Jung. This time Jung took his time with an answer: "First of all I want to thank you very much for your kind help in the Spielrein matter, which has now settled itself so satisfactorily. Once again I took too black a view. Frl. S. is a Russian, hence her awkwardness."[57]

This is how Freud first learned that Spielrein was Russian. Only at this point could he have understood that the heroine of Jung's love affair was the same Russian patient whose "defecation story" Jung had related to him so long before. Although it would have been difficult, Freud could have found that early letter in his archives: It was Jung's second letter and by this time there were about a hundred. The letter is fascinating when reexamined in light of these later events: Jung was seeking an opinion about a twenty-year-old female patient who had been ill for the past six years, yet he wrote only about her anal games at the age of 3 or 4. Jung requested a consultation in this difficult case without explaining why it was so difficult. He was seeking advice, but did not indicate what he was doing or planning to do. The letter was a symptom in itself: Jung could have used an analysis in the struggle with his unfamiliar feelings, trying to comprehend his own turbulent unconscious. This is why he appealed to Freud. But, like any other patient, he was unable to articulate his problem, concealed what was really worrying him, and presented his letter as an expression of his professional interest. Freud, nevertheless, took it at face value and began to discuss anal character. Later, Jung repeatedly asked Freud's advice regarding the same young woman, concealing his feelings and withholding even her name. Sabina's name was not a matter of chance; Freud taught that there is nothing random in psychoanalysis, and that every detail contains meaning. In German, Spielrein contains two words, "pure" and "game."

Later, Jung wrote: "The cause of the pathogenic conflict lies mainly in the present moment. In constructing a theory which derives the neurosis from causes in the distant past, we are first and foremost following the tendency of our patients to lure us as far as possible from the critical present."[58] This is just what Jung did in his attempt to impart to Freud his deepest concerns, worries that were unclear even to himself. He did not provide Freud with any key to understand his real anxieties, and he distracted attention away from himself in the present by focusing on past events in the life of his patient. Jung's behavior in this case corresponded perfectly to the stereotype of neurotic behavior at the beginning of therapy: He was ambivalent, sought the psychoanalyst's help, and desired intimacy with him, but was at the same time stricken with fear that the analyst might understand the true character of his problems. He therefore substituted various lies for his true problems.

Between Jung and Ivanov

He wanted to show me we were complete strangers to each other, and it is humiliating if I now go to see him. I decided to go the following Friday, but to act completely professional. The devil whispered other things to me, but I no longer believed them. I sat there waiting in deep depression. Now he arrives, beaming with pleasure, and tells me without strong emotion about Gross, about the great insight he has just received (i.e., about polygamy); he no longer wants to suppress his feeling for me, he admitted that I was his first, dearest woman friend, etc., etc. (his wife of course excepted), and that he wanted to tell me everything about himself. So once more this most curious coincidence that the devil so unexpectedly turned out to be right. Should one praise him or damn him? This immortal saying: "Part of power that would/Alone work evil, but engenders good." This demonic force, whose very essence is destruction (evil) and at the same time is the creative force, since out of the destruction (of two individuals) a new one arises. That is in fact

the sexual drive, which is by nature a destructive drive, an exterminating drive for
the individual, and for that reason, in my opinion, must overcome such great resistance in everyone; but to prove this here would take too much of your time.
    Time for bed![59]

In the process of freeing herself from her feelings for Jung, Spielrein made
the discovery that the sex drive is not the only force at work in mankind, an
idea contrary to Freud's opinion on the subject. Coexisting with the sex
drive but directly opposite, she found another attraction—to destruction
and the annihilation of life. Freud at first did not accept this idea, which
distorted his theory of libido and required a reevaluation of many postulates inherent in the psychoanalytic method. However, toward the end of
his long life, Freud incorporated this very idea—that Eros and Thanatos are
two equally powerful forces in human nature—into the foundation of the
final edifice of his doctrine. Thirty years later, the quotation from Faust
that had given rise to Sabina's musings on the subject (as yet, only in her diary) would serve also as a starting point for works by Freud (in the introduction to the psychological biography of President Wilson) and Bulgakov
(in the epigraph to *The Master and Margarita* [see chapter 9]).
    During those intervening years, Sabina Spielrein achieved professional
recognition. Her relations with Jung were obviously fixed at some mutually
acceptable level. She still dreamed of having a child, and she confided in
Freud that she entertained fantasies about her future son, Siegfried, who
would be sired by Jung and who might become the second savior of
mankind, as he would embody the best qualities of the Jewish and Aryan
races. In 1911, Sabina successfully defended her doctoral thesis and set herself to writing the article "Destruction as the Reason for Becoming,"[60]
which was to become famous. She wrote to Jung about the article:

Dear One,

Receive now the product of our love, the project which is your little son
Siegfried. It caused me tremendous difficulty, but nothing was too hard if it was
done for Siegfried. If you decide to print this, I shall feel I have fulfilled my duty
toward you. Only then shall I be free. This study means more to me than my life,
and that is why I am so fearful. . . . Siegfried has an enormous creative thrust,
even if he was temporarily consigned to a shadowy existence in the realm of
Proserpina. . . . I do not want to disturb your peace and quiet: on the contrary,
the dissertation is supposed to add as much as possible to your well-being.[61]

Spielrein's work begins with the question of why the mighty sexual instinct gives rise not just to pleasure but also to negative feelings: anxiety,
disgust, and squeamishness. Her voluminous essay alternates between quotations from Jung and a paraphrase of Gogol's *Inspector General*, inte-
grates Otto Gross with Oleg the Wise,[62] and seats Shakespeare next to

Zarathustra. Spielrein also wrote of her patients, but mythology and cultural history provided her with more fertile material. Nietzsche and Freud dominate in the footnotes. The context reflects the equally powerful influence of Vladimir Solovyov and Vyacheslav Ivanov.

For something to be constructed, Spielrein argued, what came before has to be torn down. Therefore, every act of creation implies a process of destruction. The instinct of self-reproduction contains two components: the life instinct and the death instinct. The attraction to death and destruction is not external to life and art, something that might defile them, or something that can be purged from them. On the contrary, the attraction to death is an inseparable element of the attraction to life and life's continuation in a new human being. After offering a number of biological examples, Spielrein proceeded with an exploration of the phenomenon in mythological and literary sources. She found proof of her theory in many cases where love was born of hatred, when it arose out of death or engendered death, as in masochism and sadism. The most obvious illustration was suicidal lovers, like Romeo and Juliet. Oleg the Wise, in the Russian legend, met his end in the skull of his favorite horse, which embodied his sexuality and his death. The flip side of love was the desire to destroy the object of desire; every birth was a death and every death a birth.

The theoretical conclusion was that "a species' self-preservation instinct requires that the past be destroyed to the same extent that something new is created, and ... is essentially ambivalent.... The instinct of self-preservation protects Man, while the dualistic instinct of self-reproduction changes him and resurrects him in a new aspect."[63]

Spielrein presented this paper at a session of the Vienna Psychoanalytic Society on November 25, 1911. Eighteen people were present, including Freud, Federn, Rank, Sacks, Steckel, and Tausk. The talk was followed by a lively discussion. Tausk criticized Spielrein's approach as deductive, as opposed to the inductive, concrete spirit of psychoanalysis. Several years later, his horrible death would become an illustration of Sabina's abstract ideas (see chapter 1).

Freud expressed a similarly mixed attitude toward Sabina and her paper: "She is very bright; there is meaning in everything she says; her destructive drive is not much to my liking, because I believe it is personally conditioned. She seems abnormally ambivalent."[64]

Eighteen years later, however, Freud would admit, "I remember my own defensive attitude when the idea of an instinct of destruction first emerged in psychoanalytic literature, and how long it took before I became receptive to it."[65] Time had passed, however, and in his famous work, *Beyond the Pleasure Principle*, written, it is often assumed, under the influence of the experience of the war and a succession of personal losses, Freud had repeated Spielrein's basic conclusions. He paid tribute to her in his typical style: "A considerable portion of these speculations have been anticipated by Sabina Spielrein (1912) in an instructive and interesting paper which, however, is unfortunately not entirely clear to me."[66] Jung, however, considered such a reference insufficient: He wrote that the idea of the death wish was developed by his student and simply taken up by Freud.[67]

Freud's characterization of Spielrein's work is strangely ambivalent: How can something that is obscure to one also be "instructive and interesting"? Perhaps Freud was acknowledging Sabina's formal precedence, while indicating he did not understand the Russian context that was so meaningful for her and that to a large extent motivated her work. This might well have been what made Spielrein's article "not entirely clear" to him.

The composition and content of Spielrein's article were reminiscent of Vladimir Solovyov's famous essay, "The Meaning of Love." Solovyov also began with the means of procreation among insects and fish; he also stated that the god of life and the god of death were one and the same. At the same time, he drew completely different conclusions from all of this, underlining the need to transform sex and fight against death. Spielrein based her argument more on the contemporary symbolist tradition, which had been popular during her youth and was based, in turn, on Nietzschean philosophy (see chapter 2). In her article, Spielrein referred extensively to Nietzsche's dreams of eternal resurrection and lent new, psychological meaning to the superman's physical resurrection, a teaching that already had many Russian adepts, from Fyodorov to Merezhkovsky. Spielrein interpreted "eternal resurrection" and the idea of the *Übermensch* as the result of Nietzsche's identification with his mother: His loving union with his mother was such that he could only conceive of himself as his mother, and of his mother as himself. He was pregnant with himself, and so was truly prepared for constant, eternal rebirth.[68] For Nietzsche, he himself, man in general, and humanity in its entirety were like a mother carrying a wondrous child in her womb. Man was what would have to be overcome, because only man could give birth to the superman.

Spielrein offered no biographical evidence to support her conception, instead analyzing Nietzsche as ready-made mythological material. Spielrein's approach probably harmonized well with Jung's methodology, which was summarized around that time in *Psychology of the Unconscious: A Study of the Transformations and Symbolisms of the Libido*, though it was a purer form of that methodology. This book, one of Jung's major works, appeared at almost the same time as Spielrein's article.[69] Later, Jung indicated that Spielrein's ideas were linked to one of the chapters in his book, one in which he discussed the double meaning of maternal symbolism. This is probably true, but it is more likely that both drew upon Nietzsche as their primary source; around this time, Nietzschean motifs began to multiply in Jung's correspondence. As for Spielrein's long article, Nietzsche was by far the most oft-cited author in it, with significantly more references to him than to Freud or Jung. Spielrein stressed that one of her achievements was a more profound understanding of Nietzsche. Paul Federn felt more or less the same way about her work: It was a "contribution to the analysis of the mystical modality of the mind."[70]

In 1909, Vyacheslav Ivanov, the spiritual father of the Russian cult of Nietzsche, who centered his quest around the "religion of Dionysus, the suffering god" (an idea, as we have seen, that was also at one time espoused by Jung), published his manifesto *Following the Stars*. In this treatise, Ivanov wrote of the relationship between Passion and Death, "Eros' feet rest on both, out of both arises Love, something at once akin and alien to both."[71] Ivanov's sources were the same as Spielrein's: Nietzsche, world philosophy, and Russian literature of the nineteenth century. "The fatal charm of the mystically attractive and horrifying truth that emanates from Pushkin's *Egyptian Nights* lies in the unconscious, primordial memory of the preordained death of the masculine and of the need to exchange life for the possession of a woman."[72] Just as in Sabina's article, in Ivanov's work lofty mythology intertwines with examples from biological life (in this case, bees). Ivanov wrote that "the highest truth is reflected in the biological fact that the male of the species dies after copulation." The very essence of Dionysus implies the unification of love and death in the cyclical acts of birth and death. If Dionysus had any passion, it would undoubtedly be a double-edged attraction to life and death.

We do not know whether Sabina read Vyacheslav Ivanov or how she felt about him. We know only that he was read extensively by her whole generation, from high-school students to the philosophers and poets of the elite. Later, the philosopher Berdyaev, the painter Bakst, the novelist Merezhkovsky, and the literary scholar Bakhtin all developed and popularized Ivanov's ideas in various forms. Ivanov's obscure symbols became the common denominators of Russian modernist culture, "driving decadents, neorealists, Symbolists, and idealists into a single herd."[73]

This culture was for the most part alien to Freud. He had crossed paths with it only through some of his sources, primarily Nietzsche and Wagner, or through his Russian students and patients. Spielrein, on the other hand, grew up immersed in it.[74] In a symbolic sense, she made her dream come true: She gave birth to an article that, like Siegfried, was spawned by two intellectual traditions, Jewish and Aryan.

Referring to Spielrein, Freud continued his speculations in *Beyond the Pleasure Principle* in a very unusual way. Under the sway of a new kind of logic, he moved slowly, wordily—as he put it, "limping"—from the idea of the death wish to the directly related idea of gender mix (see chapter 2). As one might expect, Freud cited Plato's mythic androgyny, recalling along the way a similar tale from the Upanishads. It was precisely at this point that

Freud felt himself the closest he had ever come in all of his writings to the role of devil's advocate. One sees the striking image of a normally bold and self-assured thinker coming up against an alien tradition: "But here, I think, the moment has come for breaking off. . . . I do not know how far I believe in [my own hypotheses]."[75]

The idea of attraction to death switches psychoanalytic discourse from Oedipal logic to a completely different way of thinking, the logic of Dionysus. Freud's clear, rational, and heterosexual thoughts were unfolding before the reader's eyes with the help of discordant ideas found in Plato, Nietzsche, and the Russian symbolists—a contradiction that might have necessitated a fundamental reevaluation of the basic values of psychoanalysis, had Freud not stopped just in time. He admitted that his difficulties were moral in nature and that he submitted to self-imposed censorship: "Unfortunately, however, people are seldom impartial where ultimate things, the great problems of science and life, are concerned. Each of us is governed in such cases by deep-rooted internal prejudices, into whose hands our speculation unwittingly plays."[76]

Next to Freud

Sabina Spielrein was admitted to membership in the Vienna Psychoanalytic Society on December 11, 1911. This happened during the same meeting at which Freud expelled Adler and five of the latter's supporters. It was the start of a period of schisms and exhausting battles within the psychoanalytic movement. While the "old master," as Freud called himself, kicked out one "son" and heir after another, he became more and more dependent on his adopted daughters. Paul Roazen counted about a dozen such female psychoanalysts who, each in her turn, took a place next to Freud.[77] They included Eugenie Sokolnicka, who committed suicide in 1934 despite the treatment rendered her by Freud; Princess Marie Bonaparte; and several of Anna Freud's girlfriends. Sabina Spielrein is entitled to top, or near-top billing on this list. The words that Freud wrote to her on October 27, 1911, relating the noisy confrontation with Adler and his followers, reveal the significance this female company had for him at that time, as well as much later:

> As a woman you have the prerogative of observing things more accurately and of assessing emotions more closely than others. It is therefore most pleasant that you should wish to smooth out wrinkles and folds with a soft hand, as it were. True, I am often hurt by my inability to raise the level of personal conduct and mutual understanding among our members to that which I would like to foster among psychoanalysts. Our last evening was not exactly a glorious one. But I am not always as humorless as I must have appeared on that particular occasion. For the rest, I fully approve your attitude and look confidently to the future.[78]

He informed Jung of the initiation of Spielrein, "who turned up unexpectedly," and wrote with obvious pride that "she said I didn't look malicious, as she had imagined I would."[79]

So far, Freud was still sharing his impressions with Jung. On November 30 he wrote about Spielrein's article, playing with the pronouns "her" and "your":

> Fräulein Spielrein read a chapter from her paper yesterday (I almost wrote the *ihrer* [her] with a capital "i"), and it was followed by an illuminating discussion. I have hit on a few objections to your [*Ihrer*] (this time I mean it) method of dealing with mythology, and I brought them up in the discussion with the little girl. I must say she is rather nice and I am beginning to understand.[80]

Jung responded with masculine emotion: "I'll gladly take Spielrein's new paper. . . . It demands a great deal of revision, but then the little girl has always been very demanding with me. However, she's worth it. I am glad you don't think badly of her."[81] When Jung received the article, however, he subjected it to devastating criticism, proving that the idea of the death wish was not their common brainchild, but Spielrein's alone.[82]

It doesn't take a psychoanalyst to see that such idyllic unity could not last long. Freud wrote to Jung on March 21, 1912: "Zurich is beginning to withhold its support at a time when foreign developments are so gratifying. In Russia (Odessa) there seems to be a local epidemic of psychoanalysis."[83] Now we are in a position to interpret Freud's remark: For him, Zurich represented Jung. Russia at that time was personified for the most part by Spielrein. Freud was making a choice, but he was still unready to admit it.

Who's Got the Neurosis?

Sabina Spielrein played a vital role in the history of the Jung-Freud relationship. As Jung's first psychoanalytic patient, she became the focus of her therapist's unmediated, unanalyzed attraction; but her "hysterical psychosis" and "anal character" metamorphosed into an incredible receptiveness, feminine intuition, and the ability to creatively exploit everything that Jung gave her during their long relationship. "The neurotic gratitude of the spurned"[84] had turned into the creative gratitude of a talented colleague who has made her own way and, regardless of personal differences, continues to serve the common cause.

The correspondence between Freud and Jung is an astonishingly powerful historical and human testament. It is the most dramatic document of psychoanalytic history and, undoubtedly, one of the outstanding monuments to those bygone days when people actually wrote letters to each other. This correspondence has various aspects, and it has been and will continue to be interpreted from various points of view. One of the most important angles is to examine the letters within the context of Freud's and Jung's relations with Sabina Spielrein.

The correspondence began with the meeting of the two analysts, immediately followed by Jung's introduction of his "difficult case," the Russian student. The correspondence continued with Jung's veiled and open abreactions concerning the developing relationship with his patient, and with Freud's attempts to reveal and work through his correspondent's unconscious feelings. The correspondence reached its culmination after Jung's immature and ill-prepared breakup with Sabina, to which she responded with unusual alacrity. In the end, nevertheless, Freud was compelled to recognize Sabina's behavior as the most honorable resolution to the situation. The correspondence ended with the correspondents' mutual disillusionment with their competition for a large number of common values, including relations with Sabina.

Freud fully understood and was not inclined to intensify the anxiety and guilt that Jung experienced as a professional who had failed in his first test case, flubbed it to the point of scandal. But Freud was probably also amazed to find that his favorite student was unfamiliar with the simplest, most basic principles of psychoanalysis. This thirty-four-year-old man, who thought of himself as a spouse beyond reproach, turned out to be completely unaware of his own lust. Since he had not undergone analysis, he was unprepared for the trials of his trade. His first encounter with the "greatest spectacle of nature," as Freud referred to the charms of his female patients, ended in total disaster. Acquaintance with Sabina helped Jung to discover completely new spaces in his own eros, a realm that he sincerely believed was confined to his happy marriage. His ethical principles seemed so contradictory to his inner reality that, at the peak of his crisis, he was horrified even by a trivial invitation to give a lecture on ethics: "I am so thoroughly convinced that I would have to read myself the longest ethical lectures that I cannot muster a grain of courage to promote ethics in public, let alone from the psychoanalytic standpoint." At this time he was "sitting so precariously on the fence between the Dionysian and the Apollonian" that he began to investigate various spiritual systems, as often happens in youth. Vacillating between these ideas and trying to apply them to himself, he strove to bring his internal chaos into some kind of order by using the formulas of others. At one point he wondered "whether it might not be worthwhile to reintroduce a few of the older cultural idiocies, such as monasteries."[85] Almost at the same time, he began a lengthy paraphrase of Nietzsche, devoid of references, which he subsequently mailed to Freud. At the next moment, he suddenly started prodding his teacher with speculations about the value of homosexual communities.

> All sorts of things are cooking in me, mythology in particular, that is to say mythology should gain by it, for what is cooking is the nuptial complex as is

evidently fit and proper at my time of life. My dreams revel in symbols that speak volumes, for instance my wife had her right arm chopped off.[86]

The crisis in his relationship with Sabina did indeed bring Jung to the insights that he articulated for the first time in his *Psychology of the Unconscious*—thoughts that he would rework many times. He was dissatisfied with Freudian psychoanalysis, the mode in which his mind had been operating during the crisis and that, after all, was expressly designed to deal with such crises.

> What I have done and still am doing to promote the spread of psychoanalysis must surely be of far greater importance to you than my personal awkwardness and nastiness. . . . Of course I have opinions which are not yours about the ultimate truths of psychoanalysis. . . . Let Zarathustra speak for me: "One repays a teacher badly if one remains only a pupil." This is what you have taught me through psychoanalysis. As one who is truly your follower, I must be stout-hearted, not least towards you.[87]

As had often happened before in the history of psychoanalysis, the student joined forces with Nietzsche in order to distance himself from Freud.

Freud never did forgive his student for the intellectual quest reflected in the unexpectedly vigorous inspiration of Jung's 1909 letters. It was not Jung's moral failure or professional mistakes that pushed Freud away from his former favorite; Jung's heterodoxy was far more important in this regard. Freud perceived this heterodoxy in familiar terms, as a neurosis. Rejecting his student as an intellectual partner, he demoted him to the position of patient.

> You speak of the need for intellectual independence and quote Nietzsche in support of your view. I am in full agreement. But if a third party were to read this passage, he would ask me when I had tried to tyrannize you intellectually, and I should have to say: I don't know. I don't believe I ever did. Adler, it is true, made similar complaints, but I am convinced that his neurosis was speaking for him.[88]

Adler had already been dismissed as a neurotic in denial—the worst possible vice for a psychoanalyst. Jung was still being offered the opportunity to admit his neurosis: "Still, if you think you want greater freedom from me, what can I do but give up my feeling of urgency about our relationship, occupy my unemployed libido elsewhere, and bide my time until you discover that you can tolerate greater intimacy?"[89]

At the height of their row, Jung and Freud once again realized bitterly the problems that would yet shake the psychoanalytic community many times:

> One thing I beg of you: take these statements as *an effort to be honest* and do not apply the depreciatory Viennese criterion of egoistic striving for power or

heaven knows what other insinuations from the world of the father complex. This is just what I have been hearing on all sides these days, with the result that I am forced to the painful conclusion that the majority of psychoanalysts misuse psychoanalysis for the purpose of devaluing others and their progress by insinuations about complexes. . . . The pity of it is that psychoanalysts are just as supinely dependent on psychoanalysis as our opponents are on their belief in authority. Anything that might make them think is written off as a complex. This protective function of psychoanalysis badly needed unmasking.[90]

Freud reluctantly agreed: "I too have been disturbed for some time by the abuse of psychoanalysis to which I refer, that is, in polemics, especially against new ideas. I do not know if there is any way of preventing this entirely; for the present I can only suggest a household remedy: let us each of us pay more attention to his own than to his neighbour's neurosis."[91]

Freud must have known that this kind of admonishment would be no more helpful than advice to a neurotic that he control his emotions:

Dear Professor Freud,

May I say a few words to you in earnest? I admit the ambivalence of my feelings towards you, but am inclined to take an honest and absolutely straightforward view of the situation. If you doubt my word, so much the worse for you. I would, however, point out that your technique of treating your pupils like patients is a *blunder*. In that way you produce either slavish sons or impudent puppies (Adler-Stekel and the whole insolent gang now throwing their weight about in Vienna). . . . Meanwhile you remain on top as the father, sitting pretty. For sheer obsequiousness nobody dares to pluck the prophet by the beard and inquire for once what you would say to a patient with a tendency to analyse the analyst instead of himself. You would certainly ask him: "*Who's got the neurosis?*"[92]

"Why should I mutter against God, when even to one creature I was able to give freedom!" Sabina had quoted from Pushkin for Jung's benefit, in both Russian and German. But there was indeed something to mutter about: A person who acquires freedom also liberates himself from his emancipator. Success in psychoanalysis implies the patient's ability to finally break ties with the analyst, ties they have been building together through prolonged, intensive labor. Tragedy could be lurking just behind this kind of success. Is it really possible to reconcile freedom and intimate relations, maturity and dependence, honesty and ambivalence? Although he had insulted his teacher, Jung still did not consider schism with Freud inevitable, and entertained hopes that their relationship could be transformed:

You see, my dear Professor, so long as you hand out this stuff I don't give a damn for my symptomatic actions; they shrink to nothing in comparison with the formidable beam in my brother Freud's eye. . . . Do you *love neurotics* enough to be always at one with yourself? But perhaps you *hate* neurotics. . . . Adler and Stekel were taken in by your little tricks and reacted with childish insolence. I shall continue to stand by you publicly while maintaining my own views, but privately shall start telling you in my letters what I really think of you.[93]

However, their relationship was drawing to its tragic dénouement. It is not for us to judge who was right and who wrong: the great teacher who fell short of perfection only in his fondness for his own greatness, or the brilliant student who turned out to be too impatient an heir. Perhaps the fault lay in their method, which allowed both to understand the situation but did not help them to change it. Could it be that the fateful breakup was brought about by forces inherent to human nature that are most clearly demonstrated at the highest echelons of the human spirit? Or is the source revealed by the old adage—*chercher la femme*—was it Sabina Spielrein, who maintained the best possible relations with both of the male characters in the story?

In January 1913, Freud informed Sabina: "My personal relationship with your Germanic hero has definitely been shattered. His behavior was too bad. Since I received that first letter from you, my opinion of him has greatly altered."[94] In May, he conveyed nearly the same feelings. "I am sorry to hear that you are consumed with longing for J., and this at a time when I am on such bad terms with him. . . . I imagine that you love Dr. J. so deeply still because you have not brought to light the hatred he merits. . . . I am glad that I am now as little responsible for his personal achievements as I am for his scientific ones."[95]

Freud's remark is striking. Nine years of correspondence between the two men—359 letters—testify to a multitude of shared interests, supported by genuine respect and mutual affection; but clearly, there is a suggestion in Freud's letter that their relationship was as much defined by Jung's behavior toward Sabina ("his personal achievements") as by his behavior toward Freud. It is worth comparing this statement of Freud's with one made by Jung in a letter to Sabina: "*The love of S. for J.* made the latter aware of something he had previously only vaguely suspected, that is, of a power in the unconscious that shapes one's destiny, a power which later led him to things of the greatest importance."[96] The two realms of Jung's "achievement"—personal and professional—were in this respect closely connected.

There can, of course, be no certain and perfect interpretation of Spielrein's role in the history of the extremely complex relationship between the two men. Their parting of ways was caused by a variety of factors—intellectual, social, ethnic, and personal. Jung's mystical interests were foreign to Freud; and the latter must have been even more repulsed by the collectivization of the unconscious that Jung would soon embrace, in welcoming the new concept of the German race. Their conflict can also be seen as the result of an unwinnable competition between two male egos that by its nature precluded any truly peaceful resolution. Spielrein's middle ground in the clash, first provoking it and later as a mediator, fits well with such an analysis.

One can also find evidence that their conflict was the result of personal incompatibility, temporarily smoothed over by mutual professional interests and by emotions in transference. In one of his first letters to Jung, Freud pointed out the difference between their characters, describing himself as psychasthenic and Jung as hysteric. If this was truly the case, then Sabina's role is particularly remarkable, as she managed to maintain friendships with both.

No matter what the interpretations, the fact remains that between 1909 and 1923, Sabina was in constant correspondence with both Freud and Jung: Twenty of Freud's and thirty-four of Jung's letters to her are still extant. Most of these were written after the two great analysts finally broke off correspondence with one another in 1913. To some extent, Sabina was the intermediary who carried on some contact between the two men; she was also a witness who had seen and who remembered the errors of both, a judge from whom each demanded confirmation of his own rectitude, and an attractive woman whose affections were prized by both.

Remnants

Meanwhile, Sabina married a doctor from Rostov, Pavel Scheftel. Freud learned of their union in 1912 in Karlsbad. He congratulated Sabina and suggested that her marriage was a sign that she was cured of her neurotic dependence on Jung, or at least half cured. "The other half still remains; the question is what is to be done about it." There had been an agreement between Freud and Spielrein that she would undergo analysis with him, in order to "drive out the tyrant," as he put it. After Sabina's marriage, Freud found it necessary to inquire whether she had changed her mind. He recognized that her husband "has rights as well." "Only what remnant he fails to clear up belongs properly to psychoanalysis."[97]

Sabina was expecting a child. Once, Freud had interpreted one of her dreams as indicative of her wish to have Jung's child, a desire she often mentioned in her diary. Freud noted, "You could have the child, you know, if you wanted it, but what a waste of your talents."[98] It was then that she realized with surprise to what extent Freud encouraged sublimation in his patients. Now that she was married, Freud hoped for her "complete cure" from her old fantasies of giving birth to a new savior in a mixed Aryan-Semitic union with Jung. Freud added that her fantasy did not appeal to him at all. "In that other anti-Semitic period, the Lord arranged for him to be born of the superior Jewish race. But I know these are my prejudices."[99]

In his letters to Spielrein, Freud reiterated this new motif, inspired both by his disappointment in Jung and by his anticipation of future events:

> I can hardly bear to listen when you continue to enthuse about your old love and past dreams, and count on an ally in the marvelous little stranger. I am, as you know, cured of the last shred of my predilection for the Aryan cause, and would like to take it that if the child turns out to be a boy he will develop into a stalwart Zionist. He or it must be dark in any case, no more towheads. Let us banish all these will-o'-the-wisps! . . . We are and remain Jews. The others will only exploit us and will never understand or appreciate us.[100]

Jung was Freud's only close follower who was not Jewish, and Jung's interest in "will-o'-the-wisps" and the essence of the race was pulling him toward the Nazi movement. Did Sabina know about this, and did she think of it as she and a crowd of Rostov Jews were being driven forward by machine-gun butts?

Apparently, it was at least as hard for Freud to rid himself of his feelings for his former student and heir as it was for Sabina to get rid of her feelings for her former therapist and lover. Freud's persistent reminders to Sabina of her past and his offers to psychoanalyze her reveal a personal interest: Freud often used his female disciples for his own abreaction during the drama that resulted from fallings-out with his male followers. Analysis by Freud could hardly have proven useful for Spielrein, nor is it clear that she really needed psychoanalysis at all. At any rate, she did not go to Vienna.

Sabina's letters to Freud and Jung are distinguished by a subtle understanding of the situation and a level of reserve that appear to have been lacking in her correspondents.

Dear Dr. Jung,

> It is very possible that Freud will never understand you when you propose innovative theories. In his lifetime Freud has accomplished such extraordinary things, and he has enough to keep himself occupied for the rest of his days, simply working out the details of his vast edifice. You, on the other hand, are still capable of growth. You can understand Freud perfectly well when you wish to, i.e., if your personal affect does not get in the way. The Freudian theories were, are, and will remain extraordinarily fruitful. To reproach Freud with one-sidedness seems very unfair to me, since each of us, and particularly one who constructs a mighty world-edifice, at first appears a king; then, when people have had enough and want to free themselves from his sphere of influence, he is denounced as one-sided and distasteful. You should have the courage to recognize Freud in all his grandeur, even if you do not agree with him on every point, even if in the process you might have to credit Freud with many of your own accomplishments. Only then will you be completely free, and only then will you be the greater one. You will be amazed to see how markedly your entire personality and your new theory will gain in objectivity through this process.[101]

She wrote to Freud in the same well-defined and appeasing tone: "In spite of all his wavering, I like J. and would like to lead him back into the fold. You, Professor Freud, and he have not the faintest idea that you belong together far more than anyone might suspect." Anticipating Freud's indignation, she added, "This pious hope is certainly no treachery to our Society! Everyone knows that I declare myself an adherent to the Freudian Society, and J. cannot forgive me for this."[102]

We know that in 1912 Sabina Spielrein lectured on psychoanalysis in Russia. Later, she lived in Berlin, where she had problems finding patients and solicited help from Freud. But Freud had a hard time abandoning his former perception. He replied in the same vein, interpreting her professional request within the triangle that still held meaning for him:

Dear Frau Doctor,

Now you are going crazy yourself, and, what is more, with the same symptoms as your predecessor! One day I, all unsuspecting, received a letter from Frau Jung saying that her husband was convinced I had something against him. That was the beginning; you know the ending.

And your argument that I have not yet sent you any patients? Exactly the same thing happened with Adler, who pronounced himself persecuted because I had sent him no patients. Do you not recognize the well-known mechanism of unduly magnifying a man in order to hold him responsible? . . . What in the world could I possibly have against you after the relationship we have had up till now? Isn't it nothing more than your own bad conscience due to your failure to free yourself from your idol?[103]

Freud had no patients in Berlin, and he advised Sabina to appeal to Abraham. Sabina's wealthy countryman Max Eitingon was also in Berlin, but they evidently did not get along. Later, the Scheftels moved to Switzerland, to Lausanne, and then on to Geneva. In Geneva, yet another extraordinary event took place.

Jean Piaget's Psychoanalyst

The year 1921 was crucial for twenty-five-year-old Jean Piaget. His cognitive energy, which had until then raced back and forth from the classification of mollusks to philosophical epistemology, finally found its focus. It was in 1921 that Piaget published his first article, devoted to children's speech and thought development, and in the same year he discovered egocentric speech. Also in 1921, Piaget underwent psychoanalysis with Sabina Spielrein. The analysis lasted eight months, with sessions held every morning. The treatment, according to Piaget, was neither therapeutic nor educational, and was merely a "question of propaganda."[104] Piaget recalled that Spielrein had been sent to Geneva by the International Psychoanalytic

Association. Her goal was the proliferation of psychoanalysis, and he admitted later in life that he had been happy to "be the guinea pig." Piaget was deeply interested but had some reservations about certain theoretical issues. In the end, it was Spielrein who broke off the analysis because she was unwilling, as Piaget put it, "to waste an hour a day with a fellow who refused to swallow the theory."[105] Besides, he was not planning to become a psychoanalyst, although he joined Spielrein at the Berlin Congress in 1922. Around the same time, Piaget's name began to appear in the membership lists of the Swiss Psychoanalytic Association. In his autobiography, Piaget does not mention the psychoanalytic treatment he received. But in his interview with James Rice in 1976, Piaget confirmed once more that Spielrein had been his analyst, and he described her as a very intelligent person, full of original ideas.[106] He told Rice that he had tried to contact her after her return to Russia, but failed.

A year before she met Piaget, in 1920, Sabina Spielrein "of Lausanne" presented a paper at the Sixth International Psychoanalytic Congress in The Hague. An abridged version was published in the official journal of the International Association under the title "On the Origin and Development of Speech."[107] Spielrein explained to her colleagues that there were two types of speech: autistic speech, which was not designed for communication, and social speech. Autistic speech was primal and served as the basis of social speech. In a 1923 article entitled "A Few Analogies between Infantile, Aphasic, and Unconscious Thought,"[108] Spielrein continued her argument, setting up the system of analogies (a child's autistic speech, aphasic thought, and the Freudian unconscious) that would play a key role in psychology during the century to come. Spielrein reinforced her ideas with observations of and small experiments performed on her elder daughter Renata. In another presentation, given at the 1922 Berlin Psychoanalytic Congress and therefore chronologically coincidental with Piaget's earliest experiments, Spielrein mused about the genesis of concepts of space, time, and causation in children's consciousness.[109]

For our purposes, it is important to note that the list of Piaget's works on psychology opens with a survey article entitled, "Psychoanalysis and Its Relations to Child Psychology," published in Paris in 1920.[110] A year later, he launched a series of research projects that marked the beginning of a new era in the study of developmental psychology. In these early works, Piaget contrasted egocentric speech with socialized speech, which gradually replaces the earlier form, allowing the child to communicate with its parents and friends. These ideas, articulated by Piaget in a bevy of experimental works published over the course of more than half a century, gained him global recognition.

Spielrein traced the first words in social speech, "mama" and "papa," to the sounds made by a suckling infant. The child produced the sound "mo-

mo" when it wanted to eat and suck on its mother's breast; the sound "po-po" was produced when the child was sated and playing with the breast. During the autistic phase, the child received pleasure from smacking its lips, even when the mother's breast was nowhere nearby. Then the child linked these two types of sounds with the parents; this was how the first words in social speech arose. When a hungry child satisfied itself by slurping "mo-mo," its mother appeared; linking its movement with the appearance of mother's breast, the child became aware of the magical properties of the sound it had produced. Later, the "po-po" sound of sated pleasure became tied to the father. In mastering social speech, a two-year-old child retained many qualities of autistic thought. For instance, he or she was insensitive to contradictions, easily switching from one idea to another and just as easily back again. A child showed many signs of the mental peculiarities that distinguished those stricken with aphasia. A small child, like someone who was dreaming, knew only the present. The first phase in the formation of the concept of time was the idea that something—the mother, for example—continued to exist, even when she could not be directly observed.

In all of this, Spielrein's ideas were remarkably close to those of young Piaget. Positing the very same problems, Spielrein and her Swiss patient began from a common point but set off in different directions: on the one hand, the logic of formal thought operations that Piaget was to discover; on the other, an analysis of the interconnection between speech, mental processes, and the emotionally charged parent-child relationship. Spielrein's approach was psychoanalytic, attributing the greatest importance to the content of the child's interaction with its parents; Piaget gradually came to reject this attitude, forming his own, structural approach. Of course, Piaget and Spielrein discussed the similarities and differences of their opinions more than once, as the patient questioned the theoretical basis of analysis and the therapist presented her counterarguments. The famous Swiss psychologist's work continued for many decades to be stimulated by an interest in the key issues set before him by Sabina Spielrein in 1921.

In 1923, Spielrein published an experimental work entitled "The Three Questions."[111] Students at the Rousseau Institute in Geneva were asked to think of the three most important questions they could ask God, fate, or some other higher power. A week later the experiment was repeated, but this time the students sat with their eyes closed for two minutes before beginning. During the second experiment, the students' questions were more concrete and, as Spielrein described them, "egocentric." Finally, in 1931, Spielrein used a different experimental procedure in Rostov-on-the-Don to pursue the same key issue of the relationship between conscious, social, adaptive thought and unconscious, egocentric, autistic thought.[112] Several groups of children and adults were told to draw with their eyes open and closed. The drawings made with eyes closed were not only technically primitive, they were also more closely tied to kinesthetic experience, more projective, and in many ways reminiscent of children's sketches.

Given all this, can it be said that Spielrein's ideas dominated the thoughts of young Piaget (as might be said of the aging Freud's)? Whatever the power relations between the two, one cannot fail to recognize Spielrein's obvious contribution to the trajectory of Piaget's scholarly development, a contribution both emotional and intellectual.

The Word "Love" on a Poster

At the beginning of World War I, Pavel Scheftel had left Sabina behind in Geneva and returned to Russia. He settled in Rostov-on-the-Don, and lived there in common-law marriage with a Russian woman, a physician, who bore him a child in 1924. From a letter written by Freud in 1913, we know that Sabina was still "consumed with longing" for Jung.[113] This might have been reason enough for Scheftel to leave. However, Freud might have slightly exaggerated the problem, so significant was it to him.

In 1917, Emile Metner sent Spielrein several translations of Jung's works for proofreading and checking of terminology. After reviewing some pages and becoming convinced that the translation was poor, she told Jung that she would not take part in the project; a familiarity with Russian was not necessarily the same as a familiarity with current Russian psychoanalytic terminology. Spielrein was particularly concerned that it was impossible to find previously published Russian translations of Freud in Geneva, or any texts that could be used to make the technical terms uniform. The problem was that "neither of us [Spielrein nor Metner] can lay hands on any book on analysis translated into Russian." Spielrein advised Jung to withhold permission for the Russian version, as she felt that inaccurate terminology would cause additional problems for the Russian reader, especially considering that "because of political events in Russia the ground is not ready for scientific matters." Fortunately, Jung did not follow her advice, and later Spielrein herself participated in translating Jung's works into Russian—eliciting further jealous remarks from Freud.[114]

In 1922, as mentioned earlier, Spielrein attended the International Psychoanalytic Congress in Berlin. Her presentation there played an important role in getting the Congress to recognize the Russian Psychoanalytic Society, which was no simple matter (see chapter 6). The following year, she herself returned to Russia to live and work. There are few clues suggesting why she made this move at the time. However, that same year, a French journal published two short articles she had written on several clinical cases—works that, as was almost always the case, reflected her personal interests and concerns.[115] The first article was entitled "The Automobile as a Symbol of Masculine Power." A woman patient had a dream in which she saw herself riding in an automobile, felt afraid of bumping into a wall, but always managed to get to where she wanted to be. According to Spielrein's interpretation, the wall was an obstacle preventing union with her beloved, while the automobile symbolized virility, which could overcome that obstacle in the young woman's perception. The other article also dealt with the dreams of two young women, one of them sane and the other a schizophrenic. In their dreams, stars fell in a golden rain and the word "love" was written in gigantic letters on a poster in the sky. Could Sabina's choice of subject in these articles have been prompted by latent feelings for Jung or by a longing to return to her husband? Or did it perhaps spring from a subconscious desire for new love? The available evidence suggests that Spielrein's career had stalled. In 1915, Sabina had paid her membership dues to the Vienna Psychoanalytic Society; in 1919, she was unable to do so, and Freud persuaded the journal to continue delivering her subscription on credit. In 1922, she had come into conflict with other psychoanalysts from Geneva and asked Freud to intervene. Freud was on her side in the theoretical matters that caused the conflict, but he refused to come in person, ostensibly for fear that he would "produce nothing but national-patriotic resentment against the old leader who feels entitled to play the psychoanalytic pope."[116]

The History of the Question

Sabina Spielrein was an outstanding player in the history of psychoanalysis. She was a pioneer in many of the discipline's most important aspects: She was Jung's first psychoanalytic patient, and her case was key to the elaboration and confirmation of basic methodological concepts in psychoanalysis, such as transference and countertransference—especially the latter. Most importantly, Spielrein herself first articulated the primary discovery of Freud's latter years, one that he considered the *coup de grâce* of psychoanalytic knowledge: the death wish.

In spite of all this, or rather as a result of it, Spielrein's life and work were shrouded in mystery. Psychoanalysts, following in Freud's footsteps, often referred to her article on the destructive instinct; Jung did the same; but nothing further was heard of Spielrein in the West after 1931, when her last work was published.

Historians of psychoanalysis first turned their attention to Spielrein after the publication of the Freud-Jung correspondence. The letters were published fairly recently, in 1974, as the heirs had long refused to give permission for publication. Spielrein's name and work are mentioned in forty of these letters. Her central role in the relationship between Freud and Jung is unmistakable.

In 1977, Jungian analyst Aldo Carotenuto was given a voluminous stack of papers left by Sabina Spielrein in the basement of a building in Geneva where the Institute of Psychology was located. Among the papers were forty-six of Jung's letters to Spielrein, twelve from Spielrein to Jung, twelve letters from Freud to Spielrein, and two from Spielrein to Freud, as well as her diary covering the years 1909 to 1912. Carotenuto wrote a book based on this find, which was immediately translated into most of the European languages.

Few paper traces remain of Spielrein's life in Russia after her return in 1923, although the membership roll of the Russian Psychoanalytic Society, which was published periodically by the International Association, listed her as a member until 1934 and recorded her address in Rostov-on-the-Don.

In 1983, Swedish journalist Magnus Ljunggren, who was working at the time in the USSR (composing a book on Andrei Bely), found Sabina's niece in Moscow. Ljunggren promptly published her brief story, and it was incorporated into subsequent editions of Carotenuto's book.

While writing this book, I too was able to meet with M. I. Spielrein and other relatives of Sabina's in Moscow. They told me they had not known her well because she practically never visited Moscow in the 1930s. I also managed to locate several documents in the State Archives of Russia that contained bits of information about the work Sabina did in Russia after her return. Among the documents was her personnel record from the State Psychoanalytic Institute. It was a great stroke of luck that I also found Sabina's stepdaughter, the child of her husband Pavel Scheftel, living in St. Petersburg. A professional translator working for a publishing company, Nina Scheftel had always remembered her strange stepmother with respect; but she was astonished to see books about her in foreign languages. The family knew that Sabina and her husband had visited Freud, but they knew nothing of her life in the West. Instead, they talked a great deal about the Soviet half of Spielrein's life—a story no less amazing in its own right.

It Was Not to Her Husband That She Returned . . .

In January 1917, Sabina Spielrein had a dream. The vision and its interpretation, which she conveyed to Jung, give us a sense of her feelings about living in Switzerland rather than Russia. In the dream, the wife of famous psychiatrist Vladimir Bekhterev, who lived nearby, was leaving for Russia. Her little daughter was with her. Spielrein asked Mrs. Bekhterev to carry a card to her parents. Spielrein interpreted this dream as the embodiment of her desires: to be an "important figure in psychiatry," like Bekhterev, and to go home. "I could be as useful to my . . . parents in Switzerland as at home," Sabina commented—apparently, help from abroad was vital even before the revolution. But her parents were not the point. The main question, "which I often consciously ask myself," was "Will I be able to establish contact with my countrymen?"[117]

It took five years for Sabina to make up her mind to return to Russia. We do not know to what extent personal and family circumstances influenced her plans; but we do know that she did not immediately rejoin her husband. We also know that Spielrein made her decision during the winter of 1922–1923 and wrote to Freud about it, prompting him to respond in his letter of February 9, 1923:

> Dear Frau Doctor,
>
> I am in receipt of your letter and really believe that you are right. Your plan to go to Russia seems to me much better than my advice to try out Berlin. In Moscow you will be able to accomplish important work at the side of Wulff and Yermakov. Lastly, you will be on home ground. These are difficult times for us all.
>
> I hope to hear from you soon, but would earnestly request that you write your address on the inside of your letter, which so few women are wont to do.
>
> Cordially yours,
>
> Freud[118]

It is difficult to interpret the contents of this letter, beyond the fact that Freud previously had advised her to go to Berlin, where Max Eitingon had already established his psychoanalytic clinic and was providing employment for a number of analysts. Fanya Lovtskaya, who was probably Spielrein's student (see chapter 2), was one of the many who left Geneva for Berlin in order to work with Eitingon. For some reason, possibly because of her attitude toward Eitingon, Spielrein decided to go to Moscow instead. Freud knew about the situation in Russia: He was in correspondence with Osipov, who had escaped from the Bolsheviks and had been living in Prague for some time; the journal of the Psychoanalytic Society had published Tatiana Rosenthal's obituary; and the Bolsheviks had deprived Andreas-Salomé of her fortune, forcing her to seek charity. Freud likewise knew of Sabina's marital tribulations, we can assume, as the usual polite regards to her husband are missing from his letter. While he approved of her decision to go back to Russia, he supposed she would be going to see her colleagues, not her husband. He knew all of this, and yet he advised her to go back.

Sergei Pankeev once recalled that when he had asked Freud whether he should remain in Russia if there were a revolution, Freud answered in the affirmative. When Pankeev told this to one of Freud's distant relatives who had studied in Russia, the latter responded, "You know, Freud knows human intelligence very well, but he doesn't seem to know the Bolshevist intelligence."[119]

Nor to Her Brother

Isaac Spielrein, recognized as the founder of industrial psychology in the USSR, was a man of European schooling and unusual productivity. He received his training in philosophy from Hermann Cohen in Germany (at about the same time, another prominent Soviet psychologist, Sergei Rubinstein, also was studying with Cohen, as was Boris Pasternak). Isaac had been in a POW camp during World War I, and he returned to Russia only after the revolution and by a long route—via Constantinople and Tbilisi. On his way home, during the summer of 1919, he also had visited Freud. Isaac worked for a time at the Soviet embassy in what was then independent Georgia, which was headed by Sergei Kirov. By 1921, two years before his sister, he had made his way to Moscow.[120]

In Moscow, Isaac worked in the press bureau at the ministry of foreign affairs, and later at the Central Labor Institute. The director of the Labor Institute at the time, Alexei Gastev, espoused radical leftist views, a tendency illustrated by the following anecdote: When Isaac Spielrein's mother died in 1921 and he approached the director to ask for a short leave to attend her funeral, Gastev refused, saying that funerals were just bourgeois superstition. "What do you need leave for? She's dead anyway." Gastev's personal convictions about the "scientific organization of labor" also governed his institute.

Soon enough, Spielrein and Gastev parted company. In 1923, Isaac Spielrein became the head of the industrial psychology division of the Institute of Philosophy, as well as of the Laboratory of Industrial Psychology under the ministry of labor. At that time, he held numerous commissions for research projects in applied fields. He conducted professional evaluations, consulted with enterprises on rescheduling their hours of operation (in particular, on the changeover to a seven-hour workday), proposed methods for selecting Red Army personnel, and the like. In the theoretical realm, Spielrein was a follower of William Stern, and he was not afraid to speak openly about this connection—even at the Congress on the Study of Human Behavior, held in 1930.

Spielrein's interests stretched beyond the limits of even such a seemingly limitless field as industrial psychology. His book *The Language of a Red Army Soldier* was a meticulous sociolinguistic study that probably remains unsurpassed methodologically in the Russian literature even today. It brings together grammatical analysis and frequency lexicons, painstakingly developed psychological tests, and a statistical breakdown of linguistic errors, which together describe the language of the typical Red Army soldier in 1924.[121]

Spielrein's 1929 sociopsychological sketch "On Change in First and Last Names" leaves the same impression of sensibility and rare precision. In this study, he analyzed cases of unmotivated change in last names, a frequent occurrence in a Russia that was losing its identity. According to his calculations, Russian names were changed to Jewish ones more frequently than the other way around: A Jewish last name was almost chic in the 1920s.[122] Spielrein also wrote a Yiddish textbook.

In 1928, Spielrein became editor in chief of the new journal *Industrial Psychology and the Psychophysiology of Labor* and chairman of the All-Russian Society for Industrial Psychology. In Bulgakov's Moscow of 1931, he initiated an international conference on industrial psychology. It was through this new applied branch of the field that Soviet psychology began to approach international standards; and Spielrein, along with Stern and Henri Pieron, was a member of the presidium of the International Society for Industrial Psychology.

Isaac Spielrein's daughter recalled that in 1931 Sabina came to Moscow to attend the international conference. But overall, there is no evidence of professional collaboration between Sabina and Isaac. There were no joint publications, nor did Sabina speak at any of the conferences that her brother organized or publish any articles in *Industrial Psychology*, the journal that he edited. Sabina completely lacked the breadth of interests and the flexibility of people like Luria or Zalkind, qualities that made a relatively long life in Soviet science possible. Unlike them, she also had obtained enough experience elsewhere to enable her to make comparisons.

Meanwhile, the ranks of industrial psychologists were expanding exponentially. The ideology of the "new man of the masses," an idea alien to Spielrein, began to dominate in this field as well. In 1930, there were five hundred "organized industrial psychologists" in the USSR. The Congress proposed a plan to involve three million people in the labor ministry's professional consultation network in 1932. On July 25, 1931, the ministry of education adopted a resolution based on Isaac Spielrein's report, calling for the foundation of a college of industrial psychology.

In October 1934, the entire vast web of industrial psychology establishments was blasted to pieces: By order of the Council of Ministers, twenty-nine research institutes were shut down and Spielrein's journal was liquidated. On January 25, 1935, Isaac Spielrein was arrested and charged with participating in the Trotskyist opposition. His daughter remembered: "On that day I turned nineteen. . . . Only in 1939 was I told that my father had been sentenced to ten years in prison without the right to correspond."[123] In actuality, such a sentence meant death by firing squad.

She Returned to Enjoy Her Work

According to an official report of the International Psychoanalytic Association, Dr. Sabina Spielrein, former member of the Swiss Psychoanalytic Society, joined the recently organized Russian Society in the fall of 1923.[124] Alexander Luria and two other Kazan analysts became members at the same time. Spielrein's authority and scholarly connections were recognized from the start. In 1923, she was included in the five-member committee that was to oversee the State Psychoanalytic Institute and the

Russian Psychoanalytic Society. Judging by a January 1924 document sent to the Ministry of Education for signature by the director of the State Psychoanalytic Institute, Ivan Yermakov, Sabina Spielrein also was then a member of the institute's staff.[125]

At the institute, Spielrein gave a course on the psychology of unconscious thought and a seminar on child psychoanalysis, and worked in the outpatient clinic. At a meeting of the Russian Psychoanalytic Society in November 1923, she read a paper entitled "Aphasic and Infantile Thought," in which she asserted that the disruption of thought processes in cases of aphasia was similar to children's thoughts, and that both of these types of thought shed light on the processes of speech formation. Spielrein was by that time the author of thirty published works. In a staff questionnaire, she wrote that she was planning to complete two new works on symbolic thought and publish them in Russia (this never happened). In that year, seven of Spielrein's articles were released in Western psychoanalytic journals.[126] We do not know exactly when she left for Rostov-on-the-Don, but it was probably at the end of 1924 or 1925. The institute was liquidated in August 1925.[127]

According to a ministry of education employee questionnaire,[128] Spielrein was holding down three jobs from September 1923 on: as a researcher at the State Psychoanalytic Institute, as a doctor and pedologist in a village called Third International, and as chair of the child psychology division at the First Moscow University. She defined her profession as "psychiatrist and physician-pedologist." Spielrein filled out her questionnaire very scrupulously. Similar questionnaires filled out by Yermakov, Luria, and other employees of the institute are more cursory; many seemingly pointless bureaucratic questions were deemed undeserving of answers and left blank. Spielrein answered all of the questions sincerely and with respect for the procedure, just as anyone who had come to a country to help would answer questions asked by the government.

Of her qualifications Spielrein wrote, "I began to do independent research very early on, partly on topics which I chose myself, partly on the topics proposed by Profs. Bleuler and Jung." Further, beyond the "private practice" that Spielrein characterized as her primary source of income before the revolution, she had worked in "Prof. Bleuler's psychiatric clinic, at a psychoneurological clinic with Prof. Bonhoeffer in Berlin, and in psychoanalysis with Dr. Jung in Zurich and Prof. Freud in Vienna. In Munich, I worked in the field of mythology and the history of art; I served as a pedologist at the Rousseau Institute in Geneva, and I practiced psychology in the laboratory at Prof. Claparède's Psychological Institute in Geneva."

In the block of questions eliciting suggestions to the administration, Spielrein wrote that she felt it necessary that her workload be lightened, that she be given more independence and be allowed to have students. In addition, she was dissatisfied that the State Psychoanalytic Institute was not providing her the opportunity to observe children in person. This turned her work with teachers into "purely theoretical speculations" and "platonic advice *in absentia*." To the question "Do you have any scientific or artistic activities at home?" Spielrein responded that she considered her work as a doctor both scientific and artistic.

To the question on general job satisfaction, Spielrein responded: "I enjoy my work and think that I was born for this job, that it is my calling. My life would have no meaning without it."

Spielrein's article "The Problem of the Unconscious in Contemporary Psychology and Marxism" was listed in Luria's draft of the table of contents for the second volume of *Psychology and Marxism* (which was never released).[129] In his draft, Luria penciled in another possible author, Militza Nechkina, who later became a member of the Academy of Sciences and an expert on the history of the Decembrist movement. One can imagine with what disdain Spielrein, whose social circle had so recently included Freud, Jung, Claparède, and Piaget, must have regarded the academic contributions of her junior colleague, Boris Friedmann, who had filled dozens of pages in the first volume of *Psychology and Marxism* with a mishmash of quotations from Freud, Engels, Plekhanov, and Kautsky.

In the small and extremely active circle of Moscow psychoanalysts of that time, Spielrein could have become by rights a very powerful figure. On the one hand, she was more closely connected with the world leaders of psychoanalysis than were any of her Muscovite colleagues. She knew their latest theoretical discussions firsthand, was personally acquainted with every significant participant in the European psychoanalytic movement—the presidents of national societies, the editors of journals, and so on—not to mention her relations with Freud, which became more and more valuable as time passed. Given the other connection, to her influential brother, she could have penetrated at will to the very epicenter of the most rapidly developing sector of Soviet psychology. She did not take advantage of either opportunity.

Sabina was lonely in Moscow. The interests of the local analysts, who could argue about the correlation between "Freudism" and "reflexology" and "scientific materialism" for years on end, were thoroughly alien to her. Her connection to Freud was of no use to her there. Spielrein's withdrawal from the Moscow Psychoanalytic Society can be interpreted as indirect proof that as early as the 1920s (during its heyday), the activities and relationships within the society were far from the atmosphere that reigned in European centers of psychoanalysis.

The Missing Link

Returning from her extended stay abroad and finding her bearings in Moscow's confusing atmosphere, Spielrein emphasized medical and psychological work with children. At the same time or a short time later, Lev

Vygotsky did much the same thing, returning from provincial Gomel. In his career and his theoretical interests, Vygotsky followed in Spielrein's footsteps. The difference was that Spielrein at that time was already a scholar of worldwide repute, and Vygotsky was a precocious debutant. It could also be added that Sabina's brother Isaac Spielrein was and would long remain Vygotsky's dear and respected colleague (for example, in 1933 Vygotsky served as Spielrein's deputy when the latter was chairman of the International Society for Industrial Psychology[130]).

Researchers of Vygotsky's life have noted the peculiarity of his biography.[131] He gave his first professional oral presentation in Petrograd at the beginning of 1924 and entered immediately into the world of Moscow science and politics. That same year, six of his works on psychology and abnormal development were released. "The Mozart of psychology," as later apologists liked to call him, was not all that young—that year, he turned twenty-eight—and he had not published a single psychological work prior to 1924.[132] This last fact might be explained by the fact that life in revolutionary-era Gomel was not especially conducive to scientific work. However, in view of Vygotsky's unusually high level of productivity following his presentation in Petersburg, it seems necessary to seek another explanation for his sudden psychological "conversion."

A parallel to this phenomenon may be found in the psychological "conversion" of Piaget, which took place two years earlier and in another world, but, one might suppose, under the influence of the same person. Spielrein possessed not only exceptional creativity but also a talent for influencing other people. We know from her relations with Freud that she was able gradually to overtake even the most powerful of minds. We also know of her feminine tact and ability to "smooth out our folds and wrinkles with a gentle hand," so important in those stormy years. Her relations with Jung bespeak her feminine charm, boldness, and ability to extricate herself from difficult situations. From her relations with Piaget we know of the role that direct communication with her could play in stimulating intellectual activity and growth.

Spielrein was working in the State Psychoanalytic Institute at just the time when Vygotsky was cutting a swath for himself in a field that was new to him. Young Luria, the secretary of the institute, and young Vygotsky, who was soon to become a member of the Russian Psychoanalytic Society (he is listed as a member as of the 1929 roll[133]), might well have attended her course, perceiving her lectures as the last word in international science. They were provincial enthusiasts who believed science would solve their country's problems, and Spielrein would have seemed to them the embodiment of advanced European thought: She knew Freud and Jung, Bleuler, Claparède, and Piaget; and she didn't just *know* them. . . .

The foreword to Freud's *Beyond the Pleasure Principle*, written jointly with Luria, was Vygotsky's first theoretical publication. *Beyond the Pleasure*

Principle was the very same Freudian work that Spielrein had so deeply influenced earlier. In their foreword, Vygotsky and Luria wrote of their Freudomarxist problems; but in reading the work that followed their ecstatic introduction, they must have noticed that Freud—Freud himself!—referred to Sabina Spielrein, saying that she had "anticipated . . . a considerable portion of these speculations."[134] Vygotsky and Luria, however, made no reference to Spielrein. Whatever their reasons for this omission, it seems clear that Sabina did not create around her person the aura of prestige and power that normally accompanies successful people. Perhaps she never mastered the philosophical newspeak that was surging around her with stunning speed, flowing from the pens of psychologists close to her—her brother Isaac, her assistant Boris Friedmann, and the secretary of her institute, Alexander Luria—among countless others eager to please the new powers.

The intellectual interests and development of talented people can be set for a long time to come by impressions gleaned at the very beginnings of their careers from contact with a bright, famous, productive figure. Vygotsky's acquaintance with Spielrein could have played just such a role in the formation of his psychological interests. It seems likely that Spielrein served as a mediator between the two schools of world psychology, Jean Piaget's genetic psychology and Lev Vygotsky's cultural-historical psychology. Piaget later credited Vygotsky with originating the idea of internal speech and the hypothesis that it was derived from egocentric speech.[135] Once again, we sense the presence of Spielrein in Vygotsky's innovations. Piaget refrained from commenting on the historical roots of the strange concurrence between his and Vygotsky's views and interests, which is even more surprising considering the two men's markedly different circumstances in Moscow and in Geneva of the 1920s.

For Spielrein, in contrast to Piaget, Vygotsky was a man of the same culture to which she herself belonged. His intellectual heritage and problems were well known and easily understandable to Spielrein. In her experiments with words, with what lies behind words, and with what can be done without them, one senses the same interest, widespread in post-symbolist culture, that led Vygotsky into psychology, Mandelstam into poetry, and Shklovsky into literary theory.

This set of problems remains important today. Try to imagine what "theoretical differences of opinion" stalled Piaget's analysis long ago in Geneva, and how Spielrein might have answered his objections: More than likely, your internal speech is re-creating Vygotsky's arguments in *Thought and Speech*. Like Spielrein, Vygotsky attributed importance to those emotional factors in a child's communication with his parents that Piaget was inclined to ignore. Vygotsky's approach, which integrated Piaget's structural models with Vygotsky's own intuition about the role of the "other," in essence continued the approach outlined by Spielrein. Vygotsky underlined his own contribution as "Marxist"; but in the end, his ideas came much closer to psychoanalysis than to Marxism.[136] Genetically, Vygotskian theory is more deeply connected to a Freudian understanding of parental roles than to the infinitely politicized concepts that were referred to as the Marxist study of environment—in contrast to the theory of Aron Zalkind, who began from the same psychoanalytic foundation as Vygotsky but evolved in a different direction. Did Piaget recall his long-ago disputes with Spielrein, as he defended himself against Vygotsky's critique? In any case, late in his career Piaget acceded, in the face of rather harsh criticism, to the perceptiveness of his Russian colleagues. This brought him one step closer to the psychoanalytic interests of Spielrein and the early Vygotsky, but of course, not to the Marxism of the late Vygotsky and Zalkind.

A detailed analysis of the continuity between Spielrein's works and the early works of Piaget, Vygotsky, and Luria has yet to be written. For the time being, we must content ourselves with observing the striking temporal coincidence in the change of interests in young people so far apart from each other, in Moscow and Geneva, after meeting this extraordinary woman. The two, Piaget and Vygotsky, began studying the same issues: egocentric speech in children, its relationship to social speech and the genesis of internal speech; the attempt to analyze the bonds between infantile cognitive development and the child's affective relations with others; the analogy between aphasia, neurosis, and the Freudian unconscious; and finally, the search for an experimental approach to nonverbal thought components. There is also a striking similarity among the clinical procedures that Spielrein, Piaget, and Vygotsky used in their work with children, particularly in their experimental research from 1920 on.

The Last Choice

Each of Spielrein's steps is a riddle that demands a solution: Why did she really return to Russia, and why did she not go back to the West in the mid-1920s, when it was still possible and when some of her closest colleagues were doing so?

About a year after Sabina's return to Russia, her private life took another strange turn: She went back to her husband, moving from Moscow to Rostov-on-the-Don. In 1926, a second daughter, Eva, was born to Sabina and Pavel. She was only two years younger than Nina, Pavel Scheftel's daughter from his second marriage. Old Naftul Spielrein was also living in Rostov. Not long before, he had owned income property and a trading company in the center of town. Even during the years of the New Economic Policy, he had managed to preserve a part of his earlier fortune; but then history turned the tables yet again. Thus, in the 1930s, the Scheftels and their two daughters were living in three rooms allocated to them in the stables that stood in the yard of an old house in Rostov. In one room, homemade shelves supported rows of German and French books—several multivolume series. Nina described them as "something like what is called 'scholarly papers.'" It is not difficult to identify them as the published studies of the various psychoanalytic societies.

There is, however, at least one curious point in my interview with Nina Scheftel, Sabina's stepdaughter.[137] I mentioned that the places where psychoanalysts live and work are usually furnished with a couch. "Oh, yes," Nina said animatedly. "In that old stable, there was a room that was totally empty except for a huge, lonely sofa." Nina was not sure whether Sabina Spielrein received patients there, but it is more than likely that she did. Nina did remember that a mysterious aura surrounded Sabina: One day, she cured a little girl's headache simply by holding a hand above her head, without making physical contact. She never talked about her work. Her niece recalled that Aunt Sabina was in correspondence with a poet or writer from Leningrad whose nickname was Crocodile. She interpreted his dreams and gave him advice in her letters.

Western scholars believed that she taught at the University of Rostov, while others thought she was the force behind the Psychoanalytic Orphanage there. Neither of these theories can be substantiated. According to Nina, Sabina worked as a school pedologist, and after the elimination of pedology in 1936, as a part-time school physician. In 1935, Sabina's father and brother were arrested. Her father was subsequently released, after he had been fleeced of all he owned.

Nina met Sabina in the fall of 1937. As she told me: "She was, in everyone's opinion, terribly impractical. She only wore clothes that were given to her. She looked like a little old woman, although she wasn't that old. She was bent, wearing some old, black skirt that reached the ground. She wore boots with clasps that people now call 'farewell, youth' boots. I think she had brought them from Berlin. That's how my grandmother used to dress. It was obvious, she was a broken woman." But another time, Nina Pavlovna said that Sabina looked like Lydia Ginzburg, a highly regarded woman of letters who was hunched and gray, but nonetheless a person of remarkable clarity and intellectual capacity.

In 1937, Pavel Scheftel died of a heart attack. It seems his family did not understand him. There are still family legends about his hot temper and eccentricity, features that relatives attributed to mental illness. His reunion with Sabina after ten years of separation was perceived in much the same way. However, Sabina and her husband were bound by deep and clearly enduring feelings. One of Nina's memories from her childhood reflects her stepmother's attitude toward her deceased husband. Once, while visiting Sabina some time after Scheftel's death, the order-loving Nina decided to gather up the greeting cards that were strewn over his desk. Sabina got very upset: Her husband's papers deliberately had been kept in exactly the same place where he left them.

Half a year after her husband's death, Sabina Spielrein performed an act reminiscent of her youth. She went to Scheftel's former wife and suggested that they share responsibility for his little daughters. "If something happens to you, I'll take care of Nina; if something happens to me, you'll take care of Eva." The two women came to an agreement. Preparing for the worst, they decided to introduce the daughters to each other. Sabina invited Nina for New Year's Eve. A Christmas tree stood in the empty room with the massive couch.[138] Renata had come back home from Moscow for the New Year. She was beautiful and looked like an actress in her evening gown.

Then the war broke out. Sabina Spielrein could have been evacuated from Rostov, but chose not to go. The other wife of her deceased husband, who was ethnically Russian, managed to leave the city and save her daughter, Nina. Spielrein made a conscious decision to remain with her daughters in the occupied city. (Shortly before the city was occupied, Renata had come to visit again from Moscow.) So there they were, waiting for the Nazis in Rostov—an old Jewish woman with her two daughters.

Did Sabina recall her own discovery of the unconscious death wish during those months between the two holocausts, Communist and Nazi, that she was fated to experience? Perhaps it was the death wish that guided her actions back then, although she had been the first to recognize its existence. We will never know the role that Thanatos played in her mind: Did her concept of death help her to comprehend the bloody, absurd events that shook her destitute, lonely life in Rostov? Did it help her to understand the execution of her brother as a Trotskyist agent, or the concentrated activity of the people around her who were creating death and death alone, no matter what it might be called in Soviet terminology?

In any case, the means of understanding life that had guided her through the fantastically complex fabric of relations with Jung and Freud could no longer help her. Spielrein, who had so skillfully manipulated her own affections and given them such an original philosophical interpretation, was tragically unprepared for her collision with history.

Her stepdaughter, Nina, is probably right in her understanding of Spielrein's choice as a reasonable conclusion, drawn from the knowledge she had accumulated earlier about the world in which she lived. Her view of life was completely different from that of her husband's other wife, and from ours: Having lived among Germans during the best part of her life, she could not believe they were dangerous. Freud likewise put off his departure to the last minute, saying that evil could never come out of the nation of Goethe—and this despite the fact that he lived so close to the center of nascent madness, had many famous friends who had already escaped, and was coauthoring a book, with the U.S. ambassador to Paris, about an American president.

Spielrein, like those around her, received information about the outside world exclusively from Soviet newspapers and radio. She knew too well how distorted the information was—at least, the part she was in a position to check; she believed nothing that originated with the Soviet government. Thus, she might well have considered information about the extermination of Jews by the Nazis just another lie cooked up by Bolshevik propaganda. And she had already paid dearly for trusting the Bolsheviks. Perhaps she believed that the German invasion would mean a return to a normal life.

Such is Sabina Spielrein's life story. It is an uncommon tale, in which flights of the human spirit are tragically intertwined with mistakes of the all too human mind.

6

Psychoanalysis in the Land of the Bolsheviks

Psychoanalysis became truly fashionable in Russia after the revolution of 1917, as many writers of the time have attested. Let us begin, in the spirit of bygone days, by citing Lenin: "Freud's theory is a kind of popular fad, nowadays."[1] With a healthy dose of irony, Mikhail Bulgakov's friend Sergei Yermolinsky wrote of the Moscow intelligentsia in the 1920s that "Freud and Spengler have come into fashion."[2] According to the reminiscences of Nadezhda Mandelstam, a neutral observer in this regard, in 1922 Freud was an interesting novelty in Kharkov. He was "the subject of everyone's discussions, but information was just too vague and formless."[3]

Bolshevik writer Alexei Voronsky deduced the popularity of psychoanalysis among the newly politicized elite, and participated in organizing a psychoanalytic society in Moscow. He noted that "Marxist-agitating and Marxist-leaning segments of the non-Party intelligentsia were particularly susceptible" to the temptations of Freudian doctrine.[4] Fyodor Stepun, an émigré philosopher who held exactly opposite political views, used a surprising phrase to convey his impressions of postrevolutionary Moscow: "We walked into every office as if it was an institute of psychoanalysis."[5] What he had in mind was more or less banal—how one had to decode hints and gestures in order to distinguish friend from foe; but at the same time, the very combination of words—institute of psychoanalysis—was so familiar that Stepun could use it metaphorically.

It is as telling to trace the influence of psychoanalysis through those who showed no outward interest toward the doctrine as through those who passionately supported it. Not long before he was executed by the Bolsheviks, poet Nikolai Gumilev wrote a novella entitled *Cheerful Brothers*. The traveling protagonist, whose baggage consisted of a pack of smokes and a little volume of Nietzsche, was a student of psychoanalysis. He encountered a Russian sect that was determined to return the world to its medieval order. Mystical temptation got the better of the hero, and he set off with the sectarians to find the utopian "city that isn't on the map but will be more important to the world than Moscow."[6] Viktor Shklovsky, the founder of the formalist school of literary theory, took a more serious approach: "I am no Socialist, I am a Freudian. . . . Russia has invented the Bolsheviks like a dream, . . . the Bolsheviks themselves are not to blame for appearing in the dream."[7] In June 1924, poet and critic Kornei Chukovsky wrote in his diary, "I am reading Freud—without much enjoyment"; but in the same breath he interpreted his feelings during bouts of insomnia as a "death wish."[8] Poet Mikhail Kuzmin likewise read Freud in 1926, not long before he wrote his long poem "The Trout Breaks the Ice," a composition full of dreams and animated corpses. "I lay down and took up dreams and interpretations by Freud. Of course, he's a dirty Yid and a speculator, but he talks about interesting things."[9]

This is what enthusiastic Freudians Lev Vygotsky and Alexander Luria wrote in 1925: "Here in Russia, Freudianism commands exceptional attention not only in scholarly circles, but among the reading public at large. At present, nearly all of Freud's works have been translated into Russian and published. Before our very eyes a new, original psychoanalytic trend is unfolding in Russia, in an attempt to achieve a synthesis of Freudianism and Marxism with the help of conditioned reflex theory."[10]

"We were all under Freud's influence," said Natalya Traugott, one of the most important Soviet physiologists, speaking of her generation. Traugott recalled the ditty that was circulating among Freud-fixated students during her studies in the department of pedology at a Leningrad institute in 1926–1927: "Affects suppressed and complexes to spare/Without Freud, without Freud, you'll get nowhere."[11] Psychoanalysis was not taught systematically as part of the curriculum, however.

Practicing analyst Sara Naidich, who left Petrograd in 1920 for Berlin, wrote a reserved, and probably objective comment in the official journal of the International Psychoanalytic Association: "Representative men of science show but little interest for the theory of psycho-analysis and none whatever for the practice thereof. At their meetings mention is occasionally made of the Freudian dynamic conception of mental processes. Freud's sexual theory, a priori, meets with little sympathy. In spite of this aloofness the position is not unfavourable."[12]

Around this time, concepts borrowed from psychoanalysis began appearing in literary discourse. Galina Belaya, a researcher of Pereval,[13] a movement that was influential at the beginning of the 1920s, noted that the school turned its "constant, unwavering attention on the unconscious."[14] Belaya insisted that the question of the unconscious "was for 1920s literature an expression of a general interest in the motive forces of revolution." This can hardly be the only explanation. It is no less important to consider the way in which literary figures viewed and described the people of the revolution, and this is explained more by intellectual trends and fashions than by historical events as such. Osip Mandelstam noted with surprise the rejuvenation of interest in psychology and daily life among prose writers. "The ulcer of psychological experimentation has penetrated into the literary consciousness; the prose writer has become a surgeon, and prose—a clinical disaster,"[15] he wrote in 1922.

Indeed, literary figures of the 1920s often reasoned in simplified psychoanalytic terms. According to Alexei Voronsky, the leader of the Pereval movement, "The revolution pushed to the fore new heroes with a particular mindset, with particular conscious and unconscious emotions."[16] He even found that Babel, Pilnyak, and Pasternak put too much emphasis on "the unconscious sources in life," while his primary literary adversaries suffered, in his opinion, from excessive rationality. Dmitry Gorbov, one of Voronsky's close associates, wrote that for these opponents the "world of subconscious *attractions* is forcibly torn from the world of conscious *convictions*." However, Pereval's opponents from Proletkult[17] employed basically the same language: The journal *Na postu* (On Guard) formulated the goal of any writer as the "illumination, the electrification of the huge, damp cellar of the subconscious."[18] The *Concise Literary Encyclopedia* informs us that "following in Trotsky's footsteps, Voronsky reduced the role of the *Weltanschauung* in literary works and set up the 'unconscious' in opposition to it. . . . This practice was dubbed 'Voronskyism' by his contemporaries."[19]

Some of the brightest writers of the age were accused of Voronskyism at the height of the cultural war that ensued. Aptly labeling the first anti-utopian work of the twentieth century, Yevgeny Zamyatin's novel *We*, "counterrevolutionary," the new government's ideologues detected in Zamyatin, Pilnyak, and Voronsky a proclivity for language in which primitive Freudianism was jumbled together with equally primitive Marxism: "The essence [of these authors'] statements is clear. Art is a dream, and like a dream, it is unconscious. . . . These essentially bourgeois authors cannot help but struggle against consciousness and chase it away, because every single conscious perception of social reality is proof to them of their impending and inevitable destruction."[20]

Meanwhile, Zamyatin wrote clearly and with no trace of fear: "[I]n railway sleeping-cars and in every compartment there is this little handle inlaid with ivory: If you turn it to the right, the light comes on. If you turn it left, it's dark. If you turn it to the middle, a blue lamp comes on, and you can see everything, but the blue light doesn't keep you awake, nor does it wake you up. When I am asleep and dreaming, the handle of consciousness is switched to the left; when I write, the handle is set in the middle, and my consciousness shines with a blue light. I dream on paper, my imagination works as in a dream, moving along the same path of associations, but the dream is carefully (in a blue light) directed by the consciousness. As in a dream, one need only think for a moment that it is just a dream, one need only completely turn on the consciousness, and the dream disappears."[21] Thus begins Zamyatin's essay "Backstage," which was published in 1930 in a collection he initiated himself, entitled *How We Write*. The collection was preceded by a questionnaire that Zamyatin had sent to Maxim Gorky, Andrei Bely, and the other writers he invited to participate in the project. Among the sixteen questions on various aspects of literary technique were others of a different nature, such as: "What quantity of drugs do you take during working hours?" and "Which of the senses most often serve as the basis for images (visual, auditory, tactile, and so forth)?" But despite his considerable boldness, Zamyatin could no longer reveal the source of his approach to the psychology of art, and the textual fragment that did so was left "backstage," not included in the final draft:

> The room where my desk stands is swept every day, and nevertheless, if you move the bookshelves to one side, in some nook or cranny you will find a dusty spot—with grey, shaggy, and perhaps even living clumps, from which a spider will scurry out and along the wall.
>
> These nooks and crannies can be found in the soul of each of us. I (unconsciously) pull almost unnoticeable spiders out of there and feed them, and they gradually grow into my [heroes]. This is something like Freud's method of treatment, when the doctor makes his patient confess, expelling all his "suppressed emotions."[22]

Vsevolod Ivanov, one of the Serapion Brothers (see chapter 10),[23] wrote: "Man usually has two lives. He doesn't like to touch the second, latent life (nowadays it is called unconscious). And why would he? It is only rarely that the second life rises to the surface to disrupt the first."[24] The novel *U*, written by Ivanov in the middle and late 1920s and published only at the end of the 1980s, is infused with psychoanalysis—in its terminology, plot, and meaning. Freud's doctrine is at times expounded, at times parodied, at other times simply implicit.

The story is told from the point of view of the accountant at the "Kraepelin Psychiatric Hospital, located an hour and a half from Moscow." The situation in the hospital is described knowledgeably: One bloc of doctors, including the director, promotes the theory of "nosological units," or, as Ivanov defined it, "roughly speaking, the possibility that human mental diseases can be subsumed under concrete and unfailing classifications." Other doctors were "fighting for the detailed exploration of the psyche" and practiced "intensified psychotherapy," using to this end Adleresque terminology such as "will to power" and "escape into illness." When the accountant decided to quit smoking, the insane psychoanalyst, Doctor Andreishin, who had been assigned to the hospital's "Semi-Calm Patients Division," forced him to "recall that when I was two years old I was prone, if not toward murder, at least toward violence against my nanny." We might well ask whether Ivanov had read Freud's "From the History of an Infantile Neurosis." Throughout the strange, often absurd plot are interspersed exclamations like "call it psychoanalysis if you will, but I felt as if I had been doused with slops!"

The protagonists of the novel, in a complex way undergoing the same metamorphosis as was Soviet psychoanalysis at that time, want to move from the Moscow psychiatric hospital to a construction facility in the Ural Mountains, where they will direct the "mental division," working on the "mental refabrication of people" according to a four-year plan.[25] Only the narrating accountant guesses that "there is a unique psychological experiment going on here, more real and more tangible than all the efforts of Doctor Andreishin."[26]

The Horror of the Void

The political elite became more and more acutely aware of a sense of impasse, which compelled them to search for new ideas. Of the many problems with Russian literature in 1923, Yevgeny Zamyatin considered the most important the absence of a "philosophical synthesis, which is exactly what is needed most right now; there is a thirst for it, a hunger. Everything we depended on has been destroyed—along with everything that might have been." Switching to Latin, he described the new man's world as *horror vacui*—the horror of the void.[27]

The entire range of radical leftist prescriptions was well known by then, and they had been debated many times, even before the revolution. Now that these proposals had been implemented and had failed, any repetition could have only ritual significance; but a move to the right, toward economic liberalization—which was the direction Lenin headed in, in fits and starts and without much consistency—would mean losing the power so treasured by the Bolsheviks. In this situation, the desire to break out of the accustomed political-economic decisionmaking spectrum (from left to right, from radical nationalization to emancipation of private initiative) was only natural, and to many it seemed feasible. The "alteration of man" appeared to be a new facet of the revolutionary process, implying a deep-rooted transformation of human nature within the socialist mold. As Nikolai Yevreinov wrote in 1920, stating the case for his "theater therapy," "This is not to argue against socialism, but merely to state that we have more to do" (see chapter 4).

Later, in the mid-1930s, Andrei Platonov wrote with remarkable expressiveness about the same phenomenon in his novel *Happy Moscow*, then still in manuscript form.[28] "You get sick of being the same old natural man: The tedium is impossible to shake." "Man is still such a jerry-rigged, feebly constructed creature, no more than a vague embryo, an unrealized blue-print; there is so much more work to be done to turn this embryo into the aerial, lofty image that is buried in our dreams." Such are the feelings expressed by Platonov's characters, who most likely never read Nietzsche. Human sexuality had the hardest going in this new world. "Either socialism will penetrate man's innermost recesses to the very last cache, releasing all the pus that has accumulated there drop by drop over the centuries, or nothing new will happen, and every inhabitant will go off to live alone, jealously hoarding within himself the frightening hiding place of the soul." Without referring to Freud, the novel's protagonist discovers that the "passion of life" is centered not in the stomach but in another place, one that is "worse, more hidden and shameful." It was essential to realize this right away, since "he had long feared for Communism, that it would be defiled by the frenzied shudder rising constantly from the dregs of the human organism."

And so, everything that political and economic structural changes had failed to achieve was sought, contrary to Marxism, with the help of psychological and educational experimentation. The political leader of this new trend in Bolshevism was unquestionably Leon Trotsky. Anatoly Lunacharsky, the minister of education, became the main executor of plans for the alteration of man. The members of Proletkult were the immoderate propagators of these ideas. Vacillating and ignoring common sense, many intellectual Bolsheviks also supported this course, including Nikolai Bukharin and Nadezhda Krupskaya, who acted as the political supervisor of the ministry of education at the beginning of the 1920s.

It was neither Marx nor Freud but Nietzsche who laid the philosophical foundation for the idea that man could be altered. His romantic dream of the *Übermensch*, which logically gave rise to contempt for run-of-the-mill, philistine, living people; his radical call for the reexamination of all values; and his neglect of all evidence of reality were actualized by the ministry of education. Nietzsche's influence on the Bolshevist consciousness is a fascinating question. Researchers already have demonstrated the adaptation of Nietzsche's ideas in works by Bogdanov, Lunacharsky, Gorky, and many others.[29] But there was no way that Nietzsche could become a legitimate source for the new policy. He had already played on the Russian stage, when Trotsky and his comrades were still young, and he had been compromised by those earlier discussions. Simply put, he was no longer new. Such arguments, however, did not prevent the other transformers of human nature, the German Nazis, from adopting Nietzsche as their political oracle.

In contrast to the Nazis, the Bolsheviks found Freud far more attractive. Science was one of the highest values in their consciousness. Even Stalin cloaked his insanity in pseudoscience, although in the end he eliminated anyone who reminded him of the naïve aspiration to alter the vicious, cunning, and selfish nature of man, which could be disciplined only by force. Those who inspired the efforts of the ministry of education and Proletkult, unlike Stalin, were gifted intellectuals. Trotsky was a truly brilliant commentator, Lunacharsky a great rhetorician, Bogdanov excelled in philosophy, and Blonsky in psychology. These people knew the ins and outs of science and could precisely evaluate to what extent it was applied. Unlike their political successors, they reacted unequivocally when faced with intellectual fraud. The Marxist schooling of these intellectuals, complemented first by their experience of émigré life in Europe and later by their bureaucratic administration of huge, chaotic organizations, created a penchant for analyzing everything that happened in generalized, scientific terms and attributing decisive significance to this understanding. Critical philosophy of the second half of this century, which has striven to eliminate such extreme expressions of rationalism, dubs this frame of mind "logocracy"—the belief that knowledge of the truth is enough to change the world. This cult of consciousness had a strong advocate in Trotsky, who found it acceptable to promote the idea even in his political oration (see chapter 7).

Nietzsche's irrational dreams, therefore, made him seem naïve and unsuited to inclusion in the Bolshevist canon. In contrast, the importance that Freud attributed to the conscious in changing human behavior seemed more attuned to the new tasks at hand. These elements of Freud's teaching indubitably came to dominate the simplified version of it that was presented in the works of Soviet analysts such as Ivan Yermakov. "Freudism," as the Bolsheviks labeled psychoanalytic study, by analogy to the accustomed word "Marxism," was perceived as a scientifically based promise of the real, not the hypothetical, alteration of man, achieved through the reformation of his consciousness. The scale, of course, would be different, but Bukharin's intentions were clear when he mused about the Lilliputians of bourgeois science and the Gullivers of proletarian science. The Bolsheviks most likely saw Freud, with his examining couch and individual patients with whom he would have to work for years, as the forerunner of psychoanalytic factories of the future—something akin to how Saint-Simon's dingy commune gave rise to the Gulliverian constructs of communism. After a time, former psychoanalyst Aron Zalkind would announce the resounding success of his pedological experiments in scientifically constructing a "new man of the masses."

Observers of those years note the gradual rehabilitation of private life, which came as a surprise to many. Men began returning from the front after a war that had dragged on for almost a decade. City dwellers again took up their daily routines, which had been disrupted by war communism; bureaucrats, intellectuals, and Nepmen (small entrepreneurs) all abruptly returned to their personal lives. Christian morality had been discredited, but its communist counterpart was not yet firmly established. Even Lenin-style

Bolsheviks postponed its implementation to the indeterminate future, while setting an example of completely traditional behavior in their private lives. The lives of millions of people were to be redesigned from scratch. Young people, refugees, and newly minted Communist Party cadres experienced a moral vacuum, an absence of understandable and somehow justified standards of action in interpersonal relations, family life, and even in the professional realm. The modern study of science has correlated the flourishing of such fields as psychoanalysis, social psychology, and sexology with periods of social breakdown, when the place once occupied by traditional norms and behavioral regulators (i.e., religion, law, and tradition) is left vacant and science is hastily drafted to fill the vacancy.

Sexuality unexpectedly became a topic for public discussion. Alexandra Kollontay, the heroine of revolutionary sailors and at that time ambassador to Sweden, published a letter to proletarian youth in *Krasnaia nov'*, in which she affirmed that Party members could love, too, and moreover, had a right to love. Voronsky felt compelled to publish a reply by one indignant Bolshevik woman, who compared Kollontay's opportunistic position to the "petty bourgeois verse" by Akhmatova.[30] Lunacharsky spoke out authoritatively at the end of this discussion, attempting to explain that the government was in no position to start regulating people's sexual lives.[31]

Such liberal views notwithstanding, a number of pseudoscientific publications were released in the 1920s containing various recommendations on limiting sexuality and channeling it toward a "conscious" level. The culmination of these works was the oft-reprinted "precepts" of Aron Zalkind, which stated that a class has the right to interfere in the sex life of its members for the sake of revolutionary expediency (see chapter 8 for details). The anticipated results were described by Yevgeny Zamyatin in *We* and Andrei Platonov in *Antisexus*, which remained unpublished in Russia until the 1980s. Panteleimon Romanov elaborated on the difficulties encountered by the ordinary "new man" when, for example, he experienced love for the first time and felt shame at his bourgeois emotion, or experienced jealousy and therefore felt like a counterrevolutionary. In 1925, Lydia Ginzburg wrote, "Erotica has become the cornerstone of literature, most of all as an unfavorable motif."[32] Osip Mandelstam, probably unaware at the time of the literal meaning of his metaphor, referred in 1922 to contemporary literary figures' preoccupation with psychology and daily life as akin to "a convict's love affair with his cart."[33]

The life of that day has come down to us also through the data collected in several sociological surveys on sexual behavior among young people.[34] All in all, these data bear witness to untraditional and inconsistent sexual habits among college students at the beginning of the 1920s. A high rate of early marriage, frequent divorce, and an abortion rate twice as high as the birth rate were accompanied by unrealistic attitudes, general dissatisfaction, and common complaints of sexual problems. Three-quarters of

Odessa's students in 1927 said they felt a need for a more intensive sex life, and forty-one percent complained of a lack of sexual stamina. "Classes, intellectual work, and massive waste of intellectual energy, together with an incorrect diet, seriously aggravate sexual problems," wrote one contemporary scholar.[35] According to data collected by Aron Zalkind, eighty-five percent suffered from "nervous or bronchial disorders." The wave of suicides that swept through Russia's large cities after poet Sergei Yesenin took his own life in 1925 reflected the extent of disorientation among urban youth. Answering questions on the topic "The Social Hygiene of Sex," students expressed radical demands, such as state-secured, equal distribution of women and the opening of free bordellos. At the same time, they nearly unanimously spoke out against the harm caused by masturbation and the unacceptability of homosexual tendencies.

The professed goals of this culture were also reflected in an unbelievably high level of sexual repression uncovered by surveys—if one can believe the data collected in a series of research projects by the universities of Moscow, Odessa, and Omsk. More than half of the female students surveyed said that they had remained virgins until the age of 30, while eighty percent of male students in Odessa said they had at least once in their lives attempted to swear off sex forever. Zalkind announced with satisfaction that more than a third of the Moscow college students in his study were not sexually active, since "they were channeling their sexual energy into creative social activity." Less than half of the Odessan students believed in the existence of love, although sixty-three percent replied that they had experienced love in their own lives. Less than half of the female students dreamed of marriage; on the other hand, only a quarter of the girls were in favor of "free love."

This total lack of concurrence between actual sexual behavior and perceptions of sex gave rise to a high demand for an intellectual system that could explain human relations and at the same time would not come into stark conflict with the Bolshevik ideology that these same young people so enthusiastically supported. On the other hand, unfulfilled needs can distort any intellectual system, twisting ideas to suit them.

In this context, it is easy to understand why the two-volume edition of Freud's *Introductory Lectures on Psychoanalysis*, released by the Gosudarstvennoe (State) Publishing House in 1922 with a circulation of 2,000 copies (a quantity that Jones considered fantastic enough to write about thirty years later) was snatched up in a single month.

Turning to Children

These aspects of Russian culture in the 1920s were also closely linked with a characteristic interest in children. This fixation did not appear suddenly, but it was perceived as something new, even though it entered the minds of the most diverse figures simultaneously.

Recalling the 1920s, Lydia Ginzburg had her own take on the literary process: "We turned to children." According to her, Kornei Chukovsky "invented children's literature." Before 1917, he had been a popular journalist and literary critic who "was sort of like a newborn himself after the revolution." After Bely's *Kotik Letaev* was published, Pasternak's "Liuvers's Childhood" and Mandelstam's autobiographical essays about his own childhood were released almost simultaneously. In her journal entries from 1925–1926, Ginzburg wrote with irony: "Everyone is terribly excited: 'Is Ivan Ivan'ich going on about psychology again?' I say, let it be Vanechka."[36]

Gorky followed with *My Universities*, while in painting, Petrov-Vodkin's little boys become the symbol of the new era. Nikolai Rybnikov created a huge collection of journal entries describing child development and tried to push a large-scale project through the ministry of education to found a biographical institute that would be charged with maintaining such collections. One point on the political agenda was the organization of a new, "Gulliverian" science in the vein of Bukharin, dealing with children and the transformation of man: pedology.

A plethora of associations and institutes began to spring up with unprecedented speed, dealing with a smattering of medicine, psychology, and pedagogy, within a more or less psychoanalytic framework. In Moscow, in spring 1918, the Child Institute was founded with two subdivisions, somatic and psychological, along with a related experimental kindergarten. During the same year, V. P. Kashchenko's private sanatorium was transformed into the Educational Medical Clinic by order of the ministry of education, and on October 1, 1923, it became a Medical and Educational Research Center with a widely conceived research mandate. In August 1919, the Clinical Psychotherapeutic Institute was founded in Petrograd. Our old friend Aron Zalkind became the director; the small staff of three also included another psychoanalyst, Ilya Perepel. During the first postrevolutionary years, Bekhterev's massive clinical and scholarly organization, the Psychoneurological Academy, was taking shape in Petrograd, growing out of the Second Petrograd University. One part of the academy was the Pediatric Examination Institute, under the direction of A. S. Griboedov, which became the venue for Tatiana Rosenthal's 1918 psychoanalytic research on children.

The First Suicide, the First Emigration

Rosenthal was a figure typical of Russia's psychoanalytic movement. As her friend Sara Naidich wrote in her obituary, "If psychoanalysis took root in Petersburg, it was thanks only to the activity of Tatiana Rosenthal."[37] In her youth, she was an activist in the Social Democratic Party, and she took part in the revolution of 1905 as a member of a Jewish workers' movement. For a time, she was the chairperson of the Moscow Women Students'

Association. In 1906, she appeared in Zurich, "tired and upset," trying to choose between medicine and law, attempting to ascertain which profession would be more useful for her activism. It was then that she happened across a book by Freud. We can still read her subsequent exclamation: "What harmony results when one brings together the ideas of Freud and Marx!" After she received her doctorate in psychiatry (almost at the same time as her colleague Sabina Spielrein), Rosenthal returned to St. Petersburg and dedicated all of her energy to the practice and spread of psychoanalysis.

We know little about her career. In 1919, she participated in the research that was going on in the newly formed Bekhterev Brain Institute, heading up the Department of Pediatric Neuropathology and Psychopathology. During the winter of 1919–1920, Rosenthal gave a series of lectures on psychoanalysis at the institute. At the All-Russian Conference on Caring for Mentally Handicapped Children, which took place in Moscow in 1920, Rosenthal forwarded a resolution demanding that anyone involved in children's education be trained in psychoanalysis. For reasons unknown, Naidich tells us, the resolution was never published.

In 1919, her essay entitled "Dostoevsky's Suffering and Art" was published in a journal edited by Bekhterev.[38] Rosenthal called her method "psychogenetic" and credited Freud with its development, but she objected to the latter's psychosexual monism. In her clinical interpretation of Dostoevsky, Rosenthal was ahead of Freud, who would later repeat a bevy of her theses in his own writings, without a single footnote. Both Freud and Rosenthal spoke of Dostoevsky's ambivalence, of the role played by his childhood trauma, and of the nature of his epilepsy. The similarity between their reasoning on the last point is particularly striking. Just as Freud asserted later, Rosenthal maintained that Dostoevsky's epilepsy was not genuine (or, in Freud's terms, organic), but affected. Her clinical argumentation and even several of her examples are identical to those employed by Freud: that attacks were brought on by emotional disturbances; that there was no weakening of personality; that the great author's emotional life was unusually ambivalent; and that his condition improved while he was interned in a labor camp, and the attacks stopped.[39] As if illustrating Freud's idea, she wrote that "[Dostoevsky's] attacks were his punishment. He had no more need of them when he was being punished in another way." Rosenthal cited the writer's own words: "O, it was a great joy to me, Siberia and prison. Ah, if only you were sent there!"[40]

She was not about to wait to experience this joy for herself. In 1921, Tatiana Rosenthal killed herself.

Dr. Naidich wrote in her obituary,

She was an unusually complex creature: very active, very productive, but filled with deep internal dissatisfaction. Under her cold exterior, her confident manner, her sharpness of speech and clarity of thought were hidden ceaseless, profound alarm and a gentle, romantic, and mystical soul. Her poetry, published in 1917 in Petrograd, shows this distinctly. She was young (36 years old), gifted, active in her field. She was the mother of a wonderful child whom she loved dearly. She greeted her own death as the victim of a fate she chose for herself.[41]

Alas, this is all we know. The year that brought the Kronstadt and Tambov uprisings, mass famine, and the first signs of the New Economic Policy provided plenty of reasons for the suicide of a former activist of the workers' movement. An analyst's work, as is clear from the history of psychoanalysis, does not protect the practitioner from suicide. Nevertheless, it seems that we are still guessing at solutions to the riddles of Tatiana Rosenthal: Who analyzed her in Zurich? What was she doing in Petrograd from 1911 to 1919? What was the nature of her relationship to Bekhterev? Did Freud know of her work on Dostoevsky? Why does her poetry not appear in bibliographies? What happened to her child?

The same year that Tatiana Rosenthal committed suicide, another pioneer of Russian psychoanalysis, Nikolai Osipov, emigrated to Prague. Until his death in 1934, he practiced analysis there and taught at Charles University. Along with his student Fyodor Dosuzhkov, Osipov became the founder of Czech psychoanalysis. It is only there that one can still find the heirs of Russian psychoanalysts.

The sixth congress of the International Psychoanalytic Association, at The Hague in 1920, was held under direct pressure from the Russians, who demanded attention and recognition. Their representative at the congress was Sabina Spielrein, who had arrived from Lausanne. At the first organizational meeting, Spielrein took the floor and suggested that the *International Journal of Psychoanalysis*, the German- and English-language official publication of the international association, systematically publish articles in Russian, and that summaries of Russian research be published in the journal's languages. Theodor Reik objected that it would be too expensive to print articles in Cyrillic. Freud stood up, and recognizing the seriousness of the issue, promised to do something about it in the future.[42]

Spielrein's suggestion was soon carried out, at least in part: Overviews of Russian work, as well as official reports on the activity of the Russian Psychoanalytic Society, began to be published regularly.

Letters from Kazan

At the jubilee meeting of the Moscow section of the Soviet Psychological Society in 1974, famous neuropsychologist Alexander Luria related: "I remember the years 1918, 1919, and 1920, when, as a very young man, I began to work on everything at once. I was interested in social science and I actively investigated issues in the development of social sciences and utopian socialism."[43] Luria had just matriculated in the department of law at the University of Kazan when it was renamed the department of social sciences, with a former professor of ecclesiastical law lecturing on sociology. "I was a person of absolutely average capabilities, and like all young men I came up with a whole run of projects that were practically impossible, but which served as motivation."

Luria was a remarkable capable man, and his most important plan of those days was actually accomplished. The nineteen-year-old student, stuck in a faraway corner of a huge country turned topsy-turvy by the Bolsheviks, formed a psychoanalytic group, entered into correspondence with Freud himself, and managed to get his Kazan group recognized by the International Psychoanalytic Association.[44] The members of the group, which included seven physicians, two teachers, five psychologists, and a historian (M. V. Nechkina, who later became a member of the Academy of Sciences), met regularly to discuss translations of Freud and the works of Dostoevsky and Rozanov. Transcripts and other documents related to the group were kept in perfect order by Luria, a fact that distinguishes his group from other psychoanalytic undertakings in Russia.

Kazan, despite its provincial location, was in no way cut off from the outside world intellectually. The membership of Luria's group was typified by Roza Averbukh, a native of Russia who spent the years from 1901 to 1909 as a student at the universities of Bern and Zurich. She returned to Russia in 1912, participated in the local civil service, and from 1917 on worked in the hospital at the University of Kazan.[45] In 1921, she translated and published "Group Psychology and the Analysis of the Ego" in Kazan, a work considered by local Freudians (for good reason) the most appropriate to the historical moment.

It is possible that the Kazan group's remarkable activity and its recognition by the International Psychoanalytic Association were in some way aided by the longtime acquaintance between Freud and the founder of the Kazan School of Neuropathology, L. Darshkevich (see chapter 4). The doctors in Luria's group were Darshkevich's students. Although we do not know for certain that any of the group members actually practiced psychoanalysis systematically, the very existence of the Kazan group took on important organizational implications later on.

Psychoanalysis and the Ministry of Education

In May–June 1922, the Russian Psychoanalytic Society (RPSAS) was forming in Moscow. The organization's charter is still kept in the files of the Main Scientific Directorate of the ministry of education.[46] Psychoanalysis, according to the charter, "by its nature is one of the methods of teaching and training man in his social surroundings; it aids in the struggle against the primitive, antisocial aspirations of an underdeveloped personality and can be very useful both in the field of pure science and in the applied sciences." After this follows a long list of "applied fields," in which psychiatry is named last. The registration form is signed by fourteen people; among them are four teachers (all of whom were highly placed in the ministry of education), four doctors, two professors of art history, two physics professors, and two authors.[47] The signatures at the end of the application were gathered in September 1922. The first names listed are those of Otto Schmidt and Ivan Yermakov.

The ministry of education was a highly unusual institution.[48] The huge and still growing bureaucratic structure was managed by a motley cast of characters. Bolshevik commissars who had just returned from the front sat at the same desks as Bohemian theatrical types accustomed to the adoration of audiences; wizened ministerial officials mixed with radically inclined enthusiasts of unheard-of educational techniques; university professors worked alongside the wives of the new power elite.

"I recall our work at the ministry of education as a joyful oasis, a place where you get together with your friends, you develop some glowing utopia on a global scale, and forget for a while about the nightmare that's all around you," wrote the daughter of Vyacheslav Ivanov, who worked in the School Division from 1918 to 1920 under Nadezhda Briusova, the famous poet's sister. Ivanov himself ran one of the sections of the Theater Division. His boss was Olga Kameneva, Trotsky's sister and the wife of another Bolshevik leader, Lev Kamenev. Trotsky's own wife headed up the Museum Division, next door.[49]

Plans for a glowing utopia—in the most incredible combinations—were considered and adopted through a highly developed bureaucratic system inherited from the Russian empire. For example, on December 24, 1924, the presidium of the State Academic Council (SAC) of the ministry of education, chaired by Mikhail Pokrovsky, examined the following issues: approval of a plan proposed by the scientific-artistic section of the SAC to sponsor a talk by the famous avant-garde artist David Shterenberg; what to do about "the Divisions of Popular Education forcing people to purchase books that have been banned by the SAC from their warehouses"; and an expository note by Professor Ilya Ivanov, "On the artificial crossbreeding of humans and monkeys." Reporting on this last item was Otto Schmidt, who had also been charged with organizing a commission to "develop" the proposal.[50]

As far as we know, only three of the founding members of the Russian Psychoanalytic Society actually practiced psychoanalysis: Yermakov, Kannabikh, and Wulff. Only the latter enjoyed the recognition of his colleagues abroad. The membership of Stanislav Shatsky and Pavel Blonsky, the leading theoreticians of educational reform, as well as that of the director of the education ministry's Main Directorate for Social Training, G. P. Weisberg, guaranteed the psychoanalysts official support. At the same time, there had to be a price, and it was a price to be paid on a scale and in a form acceptable to the young government. One professor who became associated with the group and contributed to its reinforcement, Otto Schmidt, launched his political career at precisely this time.[51]

The Cast and Characters

Schmidt's strange name and unmistakable appearance were to become familiar to everyone in the Soviet Union. A famed polar explorer, Otto Schmidt (1891–1956) had previously headed expeditions aboard the *Sedov* and *Cheliuskin*. He was the chief of the Main Directorate of the Northern Sea Route (MDNSR), and vice president of the Soviet Academy of Sciences (1939–1942). He was one of those drafters of Stalin's five-year plans whose image inevitably became the stuff of legend. What were the expeditions for? Who was the MDNSR transporting? No matter who might have asked such questions, within the country or without, the scholarly authority of the eccentric mathematician with his huge black beard could arouse no suspicions. Before the revolution, he was just a junior lecturer at the University of Kiev, but during his tenure as a high official of the Soviet regime he elaborated a theory worthy of a prestigious appointment—a theory on the formation of the solar system. After joining the Communist Party of Bolsheviks in 1919, Schmidt immediately began to play a noticeable role in the young government's undertakings. In the 1920s, he was simultaneously or sequentially a member of the collegiums of the ministries of food, education, and finance, the State Planning Committee, and the Main Statistical Directorate. In 1921–1924, Schmidt headed the Gosudarstvennoe (State) publishing house, and during those years the State Planning Committee released a series of exceptional books, including most of the "Psychological and Psychoanalytic Library" series. Then Schmidt switched to a less logical post as the head of the natural science section of the Communist Academy, where, as the Soviet Encyclopedia informs us, "he allowed a number of incorrect, nondialectical attitudes to develop." Clearly, it was only the speed of his reflexes that saved him from the fate met by many of his colleagues at the Academy, who were sent nearly as far north in the 1930s as the icebreaker *Cheliuskin* had been. The heroic polar explorer and talented scientific organizer was so perfectly fitted for his role that although he found himself always at the heart of the storm, he was able to weather each wave of repression. The high level of influence and trust Schmidt enjoyed in scientific and ideological affairs is indicated by the fact that during the worst decade and a half of Stalin's rule, between 1924 and 1941, Schmidt was never replaced in his duties as editor in chief of the

Great Soviet Encyclopedia, which gave the official Bolshevik rating to every phenomenon in the universe, including leaders living and dead.

The first president of the Russian Psychoanalytic Society was Ivan Dmitrievich Yermakov (1875–1942). A psychiatrist and a former student of V. P. Serbsky's, Yermakov dedicated his first scholarly works to the observation of mental illnesses at the front during the Russo-Japanese war.[52] In 1911, Yermakov remained in the psychiatric clinic of Moscow University after the scandalous departure of Serbsky and Osipov, who quit in protest against government decisions that proscribed traditional academic freedoms. From that time forth, intense enmity reigned between Yermakov and Osipov. Indeed, their paths would diverge even further later on—which goes to show the breadth of possibilities for free choice that the entire Russian intelligentsia still possessed.

Yermakov's publications began to touch on psychoanalysis in 1913. He was a prolific writer, and his interest in literature and art, unusual for a physician, became more pronounced as the years passed. As a result of his enthusiasm, in 1929 the magazine *Under the Banner of Marxism,* in uncovering the ideological errors made by the most important Russian philosophers, declaimed, "Everyone knows that if you read Husserl in Russian you get Shpet, Freud becomes Yermakov, and Bergson sounds like Losev."[53]

On the eve of the revolution, Yermakov published an article entitled "On Delirium Tremens" in the January 1917 issue of *Psychoneurological News.* The first words of the text had the ring of a slogan: "We are living at the dawn of a new era in the development of our society. We have been called upon not to turn away from reality, nor to deceive ourselves, but to expand our perception, to attempt to understand and make sense of our surroundings, and to give all our strength for the bright future that (we believe) awaits our country."[54]

In the years directly following the revolution, Yermakov was a professor at the State Psychoneurological Institute, where he founded the psychology department. In 1921, he organized the Psychoanalytic Orphanage-Laboratory, which was transformed in 1923 into the State Psychoanalytic Institute, which Yermakov headed until the place was shut down. In 1921 he also formed the Moscow Psychoanalytic Club for the Study of Artistic Creativity.

Stanislav Teofilovich Shatsky (1878–1934) would play a subtle and unexpectedly important role in the history of the Russian Psychoanalytic Society. Shatsky was a member of the State Academic Council and one of the most active figures in the ministry of education. He was particularly close to Lenin's wife, Nadezhda Krupskaya, who had a great deal of influence in humanitarian fields while her husband was alive. Shatsky's frantic organizational career began long before the revolution, however.[55] In 1906, he organized a society in Moscow called "Settlement," a colony for the medical care and education of children. The organization operated on funds donated by Moscow businessmen, particularly the famed philanthropist Ivan Sytin. Settlement was composed of a network of children's clubs ("English Club," "American Club," "Austrian Club," and so forth), with fifteen children in each, operating as compact, self-governing republics, with the children themselves serving as elected officials. The monarchist newspaper *Old Moscow* wrote of Shatsky's brainchild: "Whose diabolical mind invented this means of making children into future fanatical revolutionaries, injecting them from the earliest age with parliamentarian habits?" According to the audit that led to the closing of Settlement in 1908, the society's facilities were "thoroughly comfortable, all the furniture well-made, electrical lighting connected everywhere, with marvelous bathrooms." According to the government report, however, children were being educated incorrectly: They addressed their elders informally, they shook hands in greeting, and at the drop of a hat they would call a meeting, during which they would choose a chairman and secretary and hold a secret ballot.

In 1919, Shatsky organized the First Experimental Educational Research Center, also based on self-governance. When Lenin learned of the institution from Krupskaya, he reacted enthusiastically: "Now that's some real work, not empty babble." In 1928, the clinic was visited by John Dewey, one of America's most prominent philosophers. According to his impressions, the Experimental Research Center's work was unprecedented. He enthused that the revolution had assisted contemporary educational reformers, and that reformers in other countries had never been in a better position.[56] The center was located in Maloyaroslavets, in Kaluga province, which did not keep Shatsky from fulfilling his chairmanship obligations in Moscow, holding meetings of the educational section of the Russian Psychoanalytic Society twice a month. Shatsky died quietly in 1934 at his post as director of the Moscow Conservatory, having been squeezed out of all his more influential positions due to his unfashionable views. Krupskaya wrote him a touching eulogy.

The twists and turns in the life of yet another theorist and organizer of Soviet education, Pavel Petrovich Blonsky (1884–1941), who made a notable contribution to the development of psychoanalysis in Russia, provides more food for thought. As with the other characters in this story, Blonsky's professional life took shape before the revolution, and when it came, he was a mere junior lecturer, a historian of classical philosophy. He had also been an underground member of the Socialist Revolutionary movement. The great neoplatonist philosopher Alexei Losev wrote that Blonsky's work *The Philosophy of Plotinus* had, in equal measure with the works of Pavel Florensky, opened a new era in the understanding of Platonism.[57] In his own autobiography, Blonsky emphasized his indifference to traditional teaching. As a teenager he loved to mock the absurdity of high school education, and later he decided that it was "not funny, it was horrid." According to him, prerevolutionary pedagogy boiled down to a "very, very well-developed system to bring up stupid and unscrupulous people." With revolutionary fervor Blonsky set about "destroying this cursed training." He saw trade schools as an important means toward this end. Later he would confess that he wrote his blueprints for trade schools in 1918 "as if the classless society were already built."[58]

From 1922 onward, Blonsky worked in the ministry of education. He participated in the drafting of new curricula, which the ministry would be at pains to implement over the coming decades. It seems this work was not to Blonsky's satisfaction. He turned to pedology as "the vital source," becoming one of the new discipline's leading theorists. Entering retirement in 1935, Blonsky wrote *Outlines of Infantile Sexuality*, a curious book constructed as a dialogue with psychoanalysis.[59]

A less remarkable figure among the founding members of the Russian Psychoanalytic Society was V. I. Nevsky (1876–1937). After the revolution, Nevsky became rector of the Sverdlov Party University, head of the Party commission for auditing the ministry of education, director of the Lenin Library, and the man in charge of the Central House of Enlightenment (Tsentral'nyi dom prosveshcheniia). In the words of one modern historian who made a special study of Nevsky's work, "the posts he held were so diverse that it is hard to pinpoint where he was based in formal terms. . . . It is more important to realize that Nevsky was part of a tiny group of trusted party leaders who supervised activities in many areas."[60]

One founding member whom we have already met is Alexei Voronsky (1884–1943), who belonged to an even narrower circle of first-generation Bolsheviks of the former underground. At the time the Psychoanalytic Society was being chartered, he was the head of the Main Directorate for Political Education in the ministry of education and was editor in chief of the political literary journal *Krasnaia nov'*. He "was truly in the victors' camp," as Nadezhda Mandelstam recalled. "The irony is that everyone met the same fate."[61]

In addition to these individuals, a number of other names in the membership roster also enjoyed the respect of the intelligentsia. These people were tastefully chosen to symbolize the connection that the Russian Psychoanalytic Society would have with the intellectual elite at large. Among them was art critic Alexander Gabrichevsky, one of the best Soviet cultural historians. His wife, Natalya Severtsova, the daughter of a famous Russian zoologist, spoke of their circle of friends, which included Gustav Shpet, Mikhail Bulgakov, Vasily Kandinsky, and Robert Falk:

New people were joining us all the time, people who fed on each other's minds, although they were often total and irreconcilable opposites. . . .

Evenings we would go to visit people, drink vodka, stop into basement cafés on Arbat street to sip beer. We ate little, had a lot of fun, and nobody ever grumbled about the way things were. We did our jobs, got paid next to nothing, and two weeks later we were sitting there without a penny to our names, waiting for the next paycheck.[62]

The Gabrichevskys' apartment, which was one of the centers of this lifestyle, was on Nikitskaya street, right near the building that housed the State Psychoanalytic Institute.

A short time after the society was founded, it was joined by Aron Zalkind, a neuropathologist and the future leader of the pedological movement (see chapters 4 and 8). Then came Mikhail Reisner (1869–1929), a professor of law and one of the authors of the first Soviet constitution (as the father of Larissa Reisner, the romantic heroine of the Russian revolution, he was the father-in-law first of Fyodor Raskolnikov and then of Karl Radek). Hungarian immigrant and communist N. Vargyas followed soon after, at that time a philosopher at the Institute of Red Professorship specializing in Freudomarxism. Also joining the group was Bolshevik diplomat Viktor Kopp, who would soon be sent off to Tokyo as ambassador. By 1923, the thirty members of the Russian Society composed a full eighth of the total membership of the International Psychoanalytic Association.

As we have seen, doctors played a relatively inconspicuous role in the group, to say nothing of practicing analysts. At the same time, many of the members were prominent Bolsheviks, extremely close to the highest echelons of power in the country. Far-reaching political intent seems to have been at least as important in the organization of the Russian Psychoanalytic Society as was the natural desire of people like Yermakov, Wulff, and Gabrichevsky to gather others of like mind around them. Who, then, was their protector on high?

Jean Marti, an expert in the field, thought the Schmidts were relatives of the old Bolshevik and labor minister V. V. Schmidt, who could have assisted them actively as part of his policy supporting specialists whose honest labor might be useful to the new government.[63] Luria himself recalled that the Russian Psychoanalytic Society's organizers were supported by "Karl Radek and a slew of others." He made this statement at the beginning of the 1970s, however, when it was still impossible to mention the names of those "others."[64] It seems to me that the most serious figure behind the scenes was probably Leon Trotsky, who had his own reasons for supporting psychoanalysis (see chapter 7).

Thanks to benefactors in high places, the Psychoanalytic Institute was allocated a beautiful building—the Ryabushinsky house on Malaya Nikitskaya street. Twenty-one-year-old Alexander Luria, the institute's secretary, was given, in his own words, "a marvelous office with silk wallpaper, where once every two weeks the meetings of the Psychoanalytic Society were held in a frightfully solemn atmosphere."[65] Later, the house was given over to Maxim Gorky; today it houses a museum in his honor.

The Kazan Incident

In 1923, the *International Journal of Psychoanalysis*, under the editorship of Ernest Jones, published information on the work of the Kazan Psychoanalytic Society. The text was given equal space with news on the activity of the Vienna, British, Berlin, and other well-known societies. The information from Kazan included a list of the fourteen members of the Society (corresponding roughly with an earlier list found in Luria's archives), an additional list of seven honorary members (all of them physicians in Kazan), and the minutes of the organization's 1922–1923 meetings. In the same issue, under the rubric "The Psychoanalytic Movement," which generally provided information about events in countries where psychoanalytic societies had yet to be officially organized, such as France, Switzerland, and so forth, Jones included a report on Russia. In fact, this article concerned only Moscow.[66]

The application of the Russian Psychoanalytic Society for admittance to the international association, submitted at the seventh congress of the association, in Berlin (September 24–27, 1922), was very controversial.[67] Ernest Jones, the president of the association and organizer of the congress, proposed that consideration of the Russian society's application be postponed—immediately after he had admitted the newly formed Indian Psychoanalytic Society to the international association. Freud himself intervened (this was the last congress he would attend). Insisting that he was abreast of the situation, he suggested that the Russian society be admitted. Next to take the floor, however, was Jones's onetime deputy president in the British society, Douglas Bryan. He declared that it was impossible to admit the Russian society, for exclusively technical reasons (the Russian society had failed to submit its charter to the Central Executive before the deadline). Freud was forced to agree, but he announced that he "proposed that the Central Executive be empowered to admit the Moscow Society as soon as the formal conditions of admission should be satisfied."[68] This suggestion was followed.

Subsequently, Jones raised a different issue: He suggested an amendment to the charter of the International Psychoanalytic Association, giving the organization the right to directly unite local groups operating in member-states. Freud moved that this procedure be applied only to small local groups, on which motion the amendment was passed unanimously. Vienna and Swiss society member Sabina Spielrein spoke during the discussion, expressing her thoughts on the application of this amendment to groups in

Russia. The exact words of her statement, unfortunately, have been lost. She could only have been speaking of the competition between the group of Muscovite psychoanalysts supported by Freud and the Kazan group, which was assisted by Jones. A compromise, from the point of view of the highest echelons of leadership, was to be reached by offering Kazan a kind of sovereignty.

This situation also was one of the main problems that drew Otto and Vera Schmidt to visit Freud and Abraham in the autumn of 1923.[69] Abraham was then the secretary of the international association, and support from him and Freud could have countervailed against the opposition of the president, Jones. Indeed, after their discussion, the journal of the international association informed the public of Jones's decision to temporarily admit the "Moscow Society," pending confirmation at the following congress. (The Salzburg congress in April 1924 later affirmed the decision.)

Before the Schmidts departed, negotiations were held between the leaders of the Moscow and Kazan groups. As a result, the following resolution was adopted in Kazan on September 4: "In order to concentrate the psychoanalytic movement in Russia, it seems desirable that the members of the Kazan Psychoanalytic Society join the All-Russian Psychoanalytic Union, based in Moscow. At present, it has been agreed upon that A. R. Luria, Dr. B. D. Friedmann, and R. A. Averbukh should move to Moscow."[70] Luria was immediately elected secretary of the Russian society.

It should be noted that even in 1957, as he compiled the index to his three-volume biography of Freud, Jones continued to view the Kazan society as an independent subdivision of the international association. It seems that Jones's actions, aimed at postponing the admission of the Russian society, and his veiled disagreements with Freud in this regard, can be explained by his deep bias in favor of the Kazan society. Understanding that it would eventually become necessary to give in to Russia's demands, Jones invented the right of "local groups" to be admitted as well, putting the Kazan group on equal footing with the all-Russian society. Although the political game that Jones was playing seems strange in retrospect, he received Freud's consent for this solution.

The beleaguered Muscovite initiators, who nevertheless wielded immense capabilities within their country, decided it was preferable to solve the international situation by simply transferring Luria and his people to Moscow. The problem ceased to exist, along with the Kazan group itself. One might even suspect that twenty-year-old Luria was pushing for just such a result. It is curious to note that in his subsequent official reports as secretary of the Russian Psychoanalytic Society, Luria seemed reluctant to reveal the details of the affair and asserted that the all-Russian society had been immediately recognized by the international psychoanalytic movement.

Three Organizations of Soviet Analysts

One of the psychoneurologists of the Bekhterev school who was an uncompromising opponent of psychoanalysis, M. I. Astvatsaturov, wrote in 1924 that "the followers of Freudian doctrine form a particular caste, with their own journals and conferences."[71] This may well have been the case in Russia, as it was just about everywhere else.

Member lists of the Russian Psychoanalytic Society were published several times in the journal of the international association. The list that was published in 1924 included the founding members, with whom we are already familiar, with the addition in autumn 1923 of Sabina Spielrein and three Kazan psychoanalysts, led by Alexander Luria.[72] Most of the previous art historians and writers were missing from the list that was released to the international association six years later, but there were new names that would later play a prominent role in Soviet science: Lev Vygotsky, who gained world recognition through his works on the theory of thought; and Nikolai Bernstein, the future author of *The Physiology of Activity*.[73]

The work of the Russian Psychoanalytic Society overlapped significantly with that of two other organizations of analysts, the State Psychoanalytic Institute and the Orphanage-Laboratory. It is clear that all three organizations existed thanks to the intense activity of a single set of people. The director of the institute and president of the society in 1924 was Ivan Yermakov. Moisei Wulff also played a major role in both, as head of the society's medical section (and later as Yermakov's replacement at the post of president) and director of clinical admissions at the institute. Alexander Luria was at once secretary of the society and secretary of the institute. Yermakov was also in charge of the Orphanage-Laboratory, but in fact Vera Schmidt was responsible for its scholarly and practical work. Her husband published a multivolume series, the "Psychological and Psychoanalytic Library," out of the State Publishing House, which he controlled, and the compilation and editing of the series was Ivan Yermakov's dearest project.

This group formed rather early on—at the latest, in 1921—and held together in its compact form for about five or six years. The elite circle had a wide network of intellectual and political contacts, but no new members were ever initiated into its ranks. An astonishing example of the exclusivity of the clique was the entry into the group and sudden disappearance of Sabina Spielrein. After returning to Moscow in 1923 with Freud's blessing, Sabina set about enthusiastically to find a project in which she could participate. The institute's course catalog[74] lists her lectures and seminars on child psychoanalysis, a practicum with elementary pupils (that is, student practice in psychoanalyzing schoolchildren), and a walk-in clinic conducted by Spielrein in tandem with her new assistant, Dr. Friedmann. If any of this actually came to fruition, it didn't last long. Spielrein soon left Moscow for Rostov-on-the-Don, where a sad fate awaited her (see chapter 5). All three psychoanalytic organizations proved unable to hold this person, whose qualifications were unequaled in all of Russia.

In 1923, according to the *International Journal of Psychoanalysis*,[75] a committee was formed in Russia that was to coordinate the activities of the institute and the society. Ivan Yermakov became president of the committee, Otto Schmidt vice president, and Luria secretary. Among the committee members were Spielrein and Wulff. This body was comprised of truly able analysts (with the exception of Schmidt), but unfortunately it was never again mentioned in official documents.

There are two versions of the 1923 course catalog of the State Psychoanalytic Institute in the Ivan Yermakov archives. These two different study plans provide answers to a range of puzzling questions. The Psychoanalytic Institute is described as the residence of the Psychoanalytic Society, the location for its "organizational and informational" meetings. "The Society retains its right to manage itself ideologically." There were to be five subsections within the institute: the Orphanage-Laboratory, an outpatient department, a clinic, psychological laboratory, and a library. Yermakov and Wulff were prepared to give a course together on general principles of psychoanalysis; Yermakov planned an additional special class on the application of psychoanalysis in education.

Of the eleven seminars included in the institute's course offerings, ten were to be in the arts and education. Several of the same figures were called upon to take charge of many of these classes, but there were new faces as well. Nadezhda Briusova was to give a course on "Music and Children." The head of the Main Directorate for Social Training, G. Weisberg, taught a seminar on "Organizing a Children's Collective." The only exception in terms of subject matter, listed first in the course catalog, was Wulff's seminar on the therapeutic applications of psychoanalysis. Apart from these seminars, the pedagogical section of the society held its meetings in the institute, jointly with the Shatsky Experimental Pediatric Clinic and Voronsky's literary section of the society.

In the truncated version of the course catalog we find a somewhat different assortment of figures. Topping the list was Sabina Spielrein: Her duties were to include consultations, child psychoanalysis, outpatient consultation, and a lecture series. Next came Wulff, Yermakov, and Alexander Luria, who seems to have been assigned courses in both literature and science ("The Psychological System of Psychoanalysis: Literary Overview" and "Psychological Laboratory"). They were followed by two lesser-known scholars from Kazan, Boris Friedmann and Roza Averbukh. A totally unfamiliar name closes out the list, A. Belousov, next to which was the modest designation "Medical Psychoanalysis."

Between Leon Trotsky and Vasily Stalin

One unique aspect of the situation in Russia was the unusual closeness of Soviet psychoanalysts to the highest echelons of power. This intimacy is evident in the broad overlap between the composition of the Russian Psychoanalytic Society and upper government bodies and in the harmony between the scholars' most characteristic statements and the dominant ideological line. This kind of proximity to power can be found nowhere else and at no other time, and may well be the most distinguishing feature of Russian psychoanalysis in the 1920s. This closeness became obvious even in the Psychoanalytic Orphanage-Laboratory, which was for all intents and purposes run by Vera Schmidt, and which was perhaps the furthest of all the Moscow analysts' undertakings from the gravitational pull of politics.

A teacher by profession, Schmidt never had any professional analytical education. Nevertheless, her publications in international psychoanalytic journals received high praise from her foreign colleagues. Her works were dedicated to the methodology and the experimental work of the Orphanage-Laboratory, plus a monograph describing the development of the Schmidts' son, Alik. It is said that Anna Freud and Marie Bonaparte were fascinated by these works. Wilhelm Reich, incidentally, has noted that the International Psychoanalytic Association took a half skeptical, half hostile attitude toward Vera Schmidt's experiments.[76]

Besides Vera Schmidt's book and Alexander Luria's regular reports published by the International Psychoanalytic Association, we have a stream of archival documents at our disposal that shed light on the work of the State Psychoanalytic Orphanage. There is a handwritten rough draft of Yermakov's detailed report, capped by the title "The International Solidarity Psychoanalytic Institute and Laboratory." It covers the history of its founding, sources of financing, details of its pedagogical approach, and plans for further scholarly work. The text is undated, but it can be tentatively identified as having been written in 1923.[77] We also have the institute's founding documents, employee records, reports of the commission of the ministry of education that was investigating the orphanage's activity, orders from the ministry's scientific-educational section and state academic council concerning these audits, and the ensuing correspondence.[78] Additional details are contained in the unpublished memoirs of Alexander Luria and in an article by Jean Marti, who most likely received his information from Moisei Wulff.

The orphanage-laboratory opened in August 1921 in the mansion on Malaya Nikitskaya street, on the second floor of the same building that housed the State Psychoanalytic Institute. The orphanage's place in the tangled organizational structure of the ministry of education posed a problem from the very beginning. According to Yermakov's report, it was originally opened under the auspices of the Academic Center, which shared control of scientific institutes with the Main Scientific Directorate. The orphanage was then given over to the main directorate for social training, which oversaw all other orphanages. "Finally, at a special meeting, the minister of education ordered that the institute be left under the auspices of the Academic Center, where it remains today." Thus, the orphanage was seen in point of fact as a scientific research institute. Formally speaking, and most likely in practice as well, the institute and orphanage were one and the same organization. Yermakov occasionally referred to it as the "Psychoanalytic Institute-Laboratory."

However, the institute did not receive funding from the Academic Center. It was financed, according to Yermakov's report, "partially" by three different sponsoring organizations: the directorate for social training, the ministry of food production, and the Gosudarstvennoe [State] publishing house. The publishing house, in fact, allocated a certain percentage of the profits from the sale of books in its Psychological and Psychoanalytic Library series. However, the institute was constantly mired in financial and food supply difficulties. In March 1922, the institute was visited by Comrade Witt, a representative of the Union Coalition of German Manual and Intellectual Laborers. According to Yermakov's report, Witt was "intrigued ideologically by the work of the institute," and after negotiating with the Comintern, the academic council of the ministry of education, and the Russian miners' union, he agreed to sponsor the orphanage. It was then that the psychoanalytic institution was assigned the name International Solidarity.[79]

The institute's personnel consisted of a director, eight officers with pedagogical experience, and "various workers who could not be included in the regular staff, as a result of cutbacks." This last classification included Moisei Wulff.

In a more philosophical section of his report, Yermakov accentuated the "success of the new trend in psychology, which has broken all connection with previous, idealistic currents." He defined its primary scientific objective as "methodical observation in a special institution for children" the likes of which had never been conducted "anywhere, neither in the West, nor here in Russia." The practical intent of this scientific activity was to develop prophylactic methods of fighting certain abnormal phenomena in mental development. Psychoanalysis was touted as "a powerful means of liberating a deficient person from social constraints." Yermakov established as his goal "educating the socially useful individual within the collective."

In describing his charges, Yermakov made a remark that sheds new light on the nature of the institution he directed. "The children: most of them are the children of Party officials who spend most of their time doing important Party work, and are therefore unable to raise children."[80] Luria underlined the same idea; according to his recollections, the "psychoanalytic kindergarten" took care of the children of the politically powerful, including the Schmidts' son (the very Alik whom his mother described so voluminously) and Stalin's son. Luria was probably referring to Vasily Stalin, who was born in 1921.[81]

Apparently, the experimental psychoanalytic orphanage was quite an elitist institution, where Party functionaries "unable" or unwilling to raise their own children could hand them over for safekeeping. Of course, these important people provided the institution with everything it needed, whatever the circumstances. Psychoanalysis, scientific observation, management by the Academic Center, and other such subtleties were in part a good cover for privilege, in part fashionable practice that for the time being elicited no objections.

Nevertheless, the educational principles presented by Yermakov sound convincing. At least in theory, he truly laid out a plan for psychoanalytic research. He wrote that the period before age four was the most important for later development and also the least explored. Erogenous zones and instinctive attractions were given enormous significance in Yermakov's plans. "What adults consider negative and improper is not seen the same way by children. Each aspect of the child is valuable, since it allows us to acquaint ourselves more deeply with his internal world. But in order that the child might reveal himself fully, we must create an atmosphere of total trust and respect on the part of the adult toward the child, as well as vice versa." There is one last principle here, which corresponds with the main pathos of Yermakov's own theoretical works: "A child grows up by limiting the importance of the 'pleasure principle' over the 'reality principle.' However, this limitation must be carried out by the child himself and must lead him not to a feeling of weakness but to a sense of control, of conscious achievement."

Personnel at the institute-laboratory were required to observe certain rules:

> It is possible to study the child only by establishing contact and rapport with him.
>
> Contact can be made only if employees work on the unknown processes that are buried in the unconscious and prevent us from seeing, understanding, and maintaining contact with children, as these processes cause a reaction in children in the form of incomprehensible caprices or similar behavior.
>
> Through contact (transference) with his teacher, the child finds it possible to make a connection with reality and reject corporal pleasures (e.g. anal) that stunt his development and make him antisocial.
>
> To this end, the child must not only trust the teacher in terms of everyday relations but also in those areas that are usually considered improper to adults but not to children. Much of what serves to cure a patient's neurosis becomes humanly possible only from the moment when he finds the courage within him to open up to himself and to someone else.[82]

There was also a research plan that called for studying the children, keeping daily journal entries and individual dossiers, exploring the different types of erogenous zones, and analyzing the children's games, fears, dreams, and art projects—their drawings and other constructions.

At the same time, there was no reference in Yermakov's papers to the principle that from the start was considered key to the success of the entire operation: All of the employees and teachers of the psychoanalytic pediatric facility were themselves to undergo analysis. As the journal of the International Psychoanalytic Association described the Moscow orphanage's intentions, "All those persons who look after the children will be analysed, in order to nullify the injurious effects of their own complexes on the work."[83] Given the conditions of the time, this idea was probably so unrealistic that Yermakov never even promised to do anything about it. He would pay for his neglect, in the end.

Inspections and a Dissenting Opinion

Inspection documents found in the archives of the ministry of education allow us to get a sense of the atmosphere that surrounded the Moscow analysts as they worked (Jean Marti also mentions five inspections).[84]

In April 1923, the psychoanalytic orphanage on Malaya Nikitskaya street was visited by an inspection team composed of State Academic Council member I. L. Tsvetkov and two education ministry inspectors, R. V. Larikova and P. V. Karpov. The detailed report of this audit[85] was proffered to the next organization up the chain of command from the orphanage-laboratory, the Academic Center. According to the report, the orphanage had been opened in August 1921. The staff included fifty-one people when work began, but by the time the inspection was carried out, only eighteen were left after a series of layoffs. The inspection team recognized Yermakov as the orphanage director. When the institution opened in 1921, there were twenty-four children in his charge, and at the time of the inspection only twelve remained. Of these, five were four-year-olds, four were three-year-olds, and three were two-year-olds. The children were tidy and communicative. The kitchen, according to the inspectors, was good. The business office, on the other hand, was chaotic at best. "The so-called archives are in total disorder." Finances were drawn from three sources. During the first three months of 1923, the orphanage-laboratory had received 30,000 rubles from the Moscow Finance Division, 3,600 from the State Publishing House, and 1,545 from the children's parents. In addition, the first delivery of food had arrived from the German trade union in June 1922: 320 kilograms of flour, 200 cans of condensed milk, and much more. Food deliveries from Germany continued to arrive later on. The inspection commission found stores of unused food in the larder.

Little was written about the scientific part of the work at the orphanage. The children were observed with the assistance of teachers, who kept journals, maintained personal dossiers and schedules, and so on. Children were offered drawing, paper collage cutting, and various games. All the results were meticulously noted, and a great deal of unique data had been collected. All of the data were being studied under the watchful eye of Professor Yermakov, and the work was mainly of a descriptive nature. There was no laboratory on the premises—not even an ordinary scale on which the children could have been weighed—nor were the children subjected to regular medical examinations.

The commission's conclusion included the following:

> Externally, the orphanage is well kept, and the same can be said of the children living there. But a pleasant exterior should not be a value and a goal that justifies such an expensive orphanage; and as for its scientific work, ... the research plan and methods are slapdash and amateurish, since it is concerned mainly with mere description; there is no laboratory work at all, and those here who are interested in an accurate approach to the scientific study of children know little about it themselves, to say the least.
>
> Appearance and observation, of course, are easily achieved, which is why this first stage of work has been completed. Not only has serious laboratory work not yet begun, there has not been the slightest effort in this direction, although the orphanage has pretensions to the title of laboratory and institute. In view of the fact that its scientific work is wanting, the commission is opposed to considering this orphanage a scientific institution.

On April 26, 1923, the case was reviewed by the presidium of the scientific-educational section of the State Academic Council. Chairing the session was Mikhail Pokrovsky. Among those present were some figures we already know: Tsvetkov, Blonsky, and Shatsky, along with three other presidium members. Yermakov was also invited to attend. The minutes of the meeting speak not of an orphanage-laboratory but of the International Solidarity Psychoanalytic Institute and Laboratory. After hearing presentations by the inspectors and Yermakov, the presidium resolved

> a) that the research performed in the orphanage in its present form expends a disproportionately large quantity of government funds, when compared with the results produced;
> b) that there is no basis to assume that the activity of the International Solidarity Psychoanalytic Laboratory can be utilized for the immediate tasks set before the State Academic Council.[86]

Shatsky, however, registered a dissenting opinion that deserves some attention.[87]

> Assuming that the presidium's decision raises the immediate question of whether to close the orphanage, I find it impossible to agree with its reasoning.

The issues explored by the institution in question are so important that any attempt in this direction must be supported. In the case at hand, it has been established incontrovertibly that educational affairs are well conducted; the children are treated with attention, care, and fondness. The teachers are working hard to improve observation methods and notation of pedagogical phenomena. The data collected are extremely interesting. From a scientific point of view, it would be desirable to invest a great deal of energy, but this is obviously not so straightforward, and the institution in question can hardly be blamed in this regard. As a result, measures can be taken only to improve, and perhaps to reorganize (administratively) certain aspects of the institution's work. There should be more economy, some anatomical and physiological observation should be done, but work should not be halted entirely. A great deal of scientific energy all over the world is being expended to explore problems of psychoanalysis in education. We have at our disposal a whole series of fascinating foreign publications (*Psychoanalysis in the Primary School*, for example), and there is only one place in Russia where such issues can be applied. This is the Psychoanalytic Society and its base: the institution in question.
S. Shatsky.

Two days later, the case was presented to the next highest instance, the presidium of the State Academic Council. The council refrained from making its own comments about such a complex situation, and ordered the materials to be handed up even higher, to the collegium of the ministry of education. Perhaps the council presidium had been seeking informed advice on the orphanage when it had invited Lenin's wife Nadezhda Krupskaya to its meeting, ostensibly to "discuss questions involving the scientific-educational section." Shatsky's close relations with her were well known.

Two Meetings in a Single Day

On May 16, the presidium of the ministry of education, chaired by Mikhail Pokrovsky (described colorfully by one historian as "the third whale of the ministry," after Lunacharsky and Krupskaya[88]) accepted Schmidt's proposal to keep the International Solidarity Institute-Laboratory open "for a probation period of one year" and to create yet another commission, in the interest of improving the institution's operations.[89] This time, the commission was composed not of semi-literate inspectors but of the best specialists who had a connection to psychoanalysis or showed a clear affinity for the discipline. O. L. Bem, an influential bureaucrat from the ministry of education, was appointed chairman of the commission, while its members were Schmidt, Blonsky, Kornilov, and Glivenko. Thus, of a five-man commission, three were founding members of the Russian Psychoanalytic Society; two—Blonsky and Kornilov—were prominent and well-qualified psychologists.

As the commission worked, bureaucratic clouds continued to thicken around the Psychoanalytic Institute and Orphanage-Laboratory. On July 9, the Council of Ministers itself demanded an investigation of International Solidarity.[90] The archives have preserved the long correspondence between the ministry of education and the Council of Ministers, in which the superior body demanded a report on the results of the inspection, while the subordinate body answered evasively. Judging by the fact that the institution in question was referred to in the correspondence as the "International Solidarity Orphanage-Laboratory," it seems it was the work of the orphanage that alarmed authorities, not the activity of the Psychoanalytic Institute.

One can still read the minutes of those commission meetings, and they provide a general impression of the style in which they were conducted.[91] The commission met for the first time on September 17, 1923; in attendance were Bem, Schmidt, Kornilov, and a secretary. The matter at hand was treated with all due seriousness, judging by the minutes. A report was made on the composition of the commission, and then it was resolved to bring in the missing Blonsky and to invite Spielrein and Luria in as consultants. It was also decided to begin with an inspection of the premises, with departure for the institute and laboratory set for September 20.

This creative plan of attack, however, was not to be fulfilled. On the same day, September 17, the commission met again, this time in the presence of the head of the Main Scientific Directorate, N. F. Petrov. Without any further inspection, expert testimony, or postponement, five resolutions were immediately passed. One was an affirmation of the "great pedagogical value of this institution, unique not only in Russia but in Europe as well, which is truly capable of studying phenomena in the mental activity of children under conditions that guarantee objectivity." According to the commission, the institution sought "methods of forming a personality that is socially valuable within the collective, based upon the data of psychoanalysis." To this end, it was necessary to expand the orphanage's mandate to include "the study of social principles governing child development." The commission recommended that the orphanage be subordinated to the leadership of the Psychoanalytic Institute "on the condition that Marxists have a guiding influence in its work." As for the children, it was advised that the orphanage strengthen the "proletarian contingent" and increase their number beyond the present twelve, thus reducing the maintenance cost for each child. The commission expressed the highest possible regard for both the scientific and educational work performed at the orphanage.

Who wrote these resolutions? Clearly not the experts, Spielrein and Luria, who were never hired. Nor could it have been Schmidt or Kornilov, who apparently later found themselves facing similar *faits accomplis*. Neither could it have been Petrov, who had no connection whatsoever to psychoanalysis.

These minutes were appended in full to the resolution of the committee that was subsequently submitted to the ministry of education. Only one point from the original text disappeared from the resolution. The missing lines are telling, even striking: "c) To have the Main Scientific Directorate include in its agenda the creation of a psychoanalytic institute and define its relationship to the orphanage."

The individual who dictated these ideas to the commission seems to have forgotten that the Psychoanalytic Institute already existed within the Science Directorate's system. He was a man who clearly had his own political invest-ment in Russian psychoanalysis. He was clearly literate in the discourse of both psychoanalysis and ideology. He was more powerful than both Schmidt and Shatsky, so when he told Petrov what to do in his own office, his orders were carried out the very same day. Finally, he was a man who, even knowing whose children were being cared for at the orphanage, not only was not afraid to point it out, but even proposed diluting them with children from the working class. This man could only have been Trotsky.

It was around this time, just ten days after the events at hand, that Trotsky sent a letter to Ivan Pavlov, telling him of his acquaintance with Freudianism, asserting the doctrine's relative value, and, getting to the heart of the matter, offering his sponsorship for a project that would synthesize Pavlov's theory of conditioned reflex with Freudian psychoanalysis. This could not have been a mere coincidence of dates. Trotsky attributed great importance to the letter, a fact borne out by its inclusion in his *Collected Works*, one of his last publications in the USSR, released in 1927 (the letter is cited and discussed in more detail in chapter 7). Be that as it may, a formi-dable intervention decided the future of this one small institution within the system of the Main Scientific Directorate, and it was immediately recognized as "the only one of its kind, not only in Russia, but in Europe as well."

In October, the collegium of the ministry of education, under Anatoly Lunacharsky's chairmanship, approved the commission's report, extolling its conclusions as "absolutely right."[92] In a decree passed by the ministry of education, the first point dictated that "it is essential to preserve the or-phanage, as it is carrying on extremely valuable work, observing and study-ing children in general and child sexuality in particular." The commission's conclusions were then duplicated to serve as guiding directives. Of particu-lar interest here is the mention of child sexuality, which had never before attracted the attention of the ministry of education leadership. The decree was sent upward, and "considered" at a meeting of the Lesser Council of Ministers on January 25, 1924. It was finally approved on behalf of the Greater Council of Ministers by Alexei Rykov on February 6.[93]

Transference Within the Collective

Immediately after receiving support from on high, the Schmidts set out for Vienna, where they were to report to Freud himself on their achievements.

In the archives of the ministry of education there is a record of the "business trip abroad taken by Psychoanalytic Institute employee V. F. Schmidt and Institute Curator O. Y. Schmidt in September 1923 in order to inform the International Psychoanalytic Association of the progress made in Moscow."[94]

On October 18, 1923, Otto and Vera Schmidt reported to the Moscow Psychoanalytic Society on their trip to Berlin and Vienna, "intended to form direct contacts between psychoanalytic groups." According to the report, published by Jean Marti:

> Particular interest had been expressed in the Moscow Orphanage and State Psychoanalytic Institute. Professor Freud, Dr. Otto Rank, and Dr. Karl Abraham made a series of interesting comments concerning the Orphanage's work. One issue that was discussed was the relationship between collective training and psychoanalysis (and what happens to the oedipal complex within the collective).[95]

This discussion, during which the Muscovite organizers of psychoanalysis conversed on an equal footing with the movement's world leaders, was probably the apogee of the development of the Russian psychoanalytic movement. As history would have it, the Schmidts gained backing simultaneously from Freud and Trotsky, from the leadership of the International Psychoanalytic Association and the presidium of the ministry of education. Right after their visit, the international association admitted the Russian Psychoanalytic Society as a full-fledged member. But the triumph, if it was one, did not last long. A new court intrigue immediately began around the Moscow psychoanalytic movement.

In July 1924, seven teachers from the orphanage-laboratory wrote a voluminous appeal to the curator of the Psychoanalytic Institute.[96] After three years of experience, this group of educators had come to the conclusion that it was impossible to continue working under current conditions. In other countries, wrote the teachers, the most important prerequisite for the practice of psychoanalysis was extensive training in the field. Such training protected teachers—those who worked with children, educated them, and, in particular, taught sex education—from "internal conflicts that slow things down terribly and have an effect on the nervous system." The authors of the letter emphasized that they had received no such training. As a result, a strange situation had arisen in the orphanage-laboratory. "The unbelievably difficult atmosphere is based on the so-called 'transference effect,' which Freud describes in depth in his works. A certain portion of the child's feelings for his father or mother are transferred onto another person. . . . This results in an immense degree of dependence on this person."

Further on, this theoretical introduction was decoded into clearer terms. The heart of the matter was actually a conflict between the teachers and Ivan Yermakov, the director of the Psychoanalytic Institute. The teachers continued: "The moment of transference is a powerful means of training people, but with conditions as they are in our orphanage, with so little respect for the personality of teachers on the part of the director, it . . . changes into negative transference. . . . Due to the fact that the institution is run by a single person, he has become the only object of transference for the whole collective. The resulting sense of massive dependence was impossible to overcome, since we had never undergone analysis." However, the educators were more than favorably disposed toward the results of their work, and had no desire to close up shop. "The orphanage-laboratory is truly important, as the only institution in the world where the basic suppositions of psychoanalysis are applied to pedagogy." The orphanage, they insisted, had collected "material that is one-of-a-kind, with data on the uncontrolled sexual development of children." This material, however, remained unutilized, due to many shortcomings in research management. There was no plan or method, hypotheses were chosen as if at random, there was a total lack of initiative. "The upshot is a high level of dissatisfaction in our work and a total inability to rectify it by ourselves." Moreover, the data collected remained inaccessible; even employees of the psychoanalytic institute and members of the Psychoanalytic Society could not get access to the orphanage's studies, and "there is a thoroughly abnormal situation unfolding, in that this huge store of material has been collected and is still being collected for use by a single person." (As the reader may recall, Sabina Spielrein was also displeased that she could not observe the children personally, nor put the teachers through analysis, which is why her work with them was "purely theoretical speculation" and "platonic advice.")

Again, the teachers' "massive dissatisfaction" was accompanied by the "extraordinary social importance of the institution." Total disorganization, a total lack of continuity in long-term research, and the turnover of fifty teachers during the previous three years had induced the desperate teaching staff, who still believed their mission could be accomplished, to write this exposé.

The teachers' suggested solutions were as diverse and well thought out as was their exposition of the problems. The orphanage should be run by "someone with more social and educational experience." "Several members of the Russian Psychoanalytic Society" should be brought in as consultants. There should also be continuing education courses arranged at the Psychoanalytic Institute to retrain the orphanage staff, courses which should last from one to two years. Temporary employees should be hired for the duration of retraining to fill in for permanent personnel, since it would be impossible to combine work with psychoanalytical study.

This unique document allows for several different interpretations. On the one hand, it might be viewed as a "ladies' revolt," which in the Soviet system was a common outgrowth of a female staff working under the direction of a man. On the other hand, the obvious root of the dispute was a certain divergence of interests between the Schmidts (one of whom was the addressee, and the other undoubtedly one of the authors of the appeal) and Yermakov. Taking into account the fact that the Schmidts had just returned from Vienna and Berlin, it is likely that the object of debate was influence or representation in the International Psychoanalytic Association. Perhaps Otto Schmidt saw himself as the new head of Russian psychoanalysis. It is impossible, of course, to deny the validity of the teachers' remarks, as they really did lack the qualifications to work as psychoanalysts; there is also no reason to doubt their evaluation of Yermakov's managerial abilities. Finally, it could be that the beginnings of change in the political situation were reflected in this private conflict. To appreciate the subtle game of historical realities that was being played out in the text, it is essential to reread the key complaint in this document, written just after Lenin's death and during Stalin's rise to power: One person was the single object of transference for the entire collective. The resultant sense of dependence was impossible to overcome, since they had never undergone psychoanalysis.

The letter from the teaching staff addressed to the curator is kept in the archives of the ministry of education. Whatever Schmidt's motives, he was the person designated in the official roll as curator of the Psychoanalytic Institute, and he passed the letter on. The Main Scientific Directorate, naturally, set up a new commission. On July 3, the Psychoanalytic Society held a hearing on the matter. In the resulting resolution, the society recognized that "the orphanage-laboratory can work in full harmony with the demands of psychoanalysis only if it has at its disposal teachers who are well acquainted with the theory and practice of psychoanalysis and have undergone analysis themselves." It was recommended that the Psychoanalytic Institute immediately set out to train such a staff, and until this task was accomplished "the institute may not take responsibility for the orphanage's educational work." For the time being, it was considered expedient to completely separate the administration of the two institutions. However, they would both remain in the same building on Malaya Nikitskaya street, "to allow the psychoanalytic institute to make observations and set up experiments in the orphanage." The orphanage was to independently choose its own administrators, "but only from among those people who accept the basic values of psychoanalysis."[97]

The Curator Washes His Hands

"In the 1920s, not only was it not dangerous to practice psychoanalysis, it was prestigious," recalls Natalya Traugott.[98] But ever so slowly, the storm clouds were gathering. On April 24, 1924, the head of the Science Division of the Main Scientific Directorate, A. P. Pinkevich, demanded that there be "fundamental reorganization designed to widen the scope of the institute's mandate in the field of educational research." Yet again, the powers that be were trying to meld psychoanalysis with the new science of the transformation of mankind. The latest commission resolved that although Pinkevich's suggestion was desirable, it was unattainable.[99]

At the end of 1924, the Psychoanalytic Institute and the International Solidarity Orphanage-Laboratory were administratively separated after the institute's budget was split in half. In addition, all of the teachers working there were fired, and four new educators were hired in their place. Was this the implementation of Vera Schmidt's idea to hire a temporary staff during the main teaching corps' year or two of psychoanalytic training? Unfortunately, this was something else altogether.

In November 1924, Otto Schmidt sent a letter to the deputy minister of education, V. N. Yakovlev, and the head of the Main Scientific Directorate, N. F. Petrov.

Respected Comrades:

Three years ago, the orphanage-laboratory was founded under the aegis of the Psychoanalytic Institute with my assistance. Since I am quite familiar with psychoanalysis, am a member of the presidium of the Russian Psychoanalytic Society, and because I have more than once defended the orphanage in the face of attempts to close it, an attitude has formed that I carry some responsibility before the ministry of education and the Party for the orphanage-laboratory's work.

The work has been fascinating, and the results of research have been published abroad and inspired the intensive attention of Freud and his followers, as well as of international medical and educational circles.

As the children grew older, however, the lack of teachers with psychoanalytic training began to have a more marked effect. Not wishing to use insufficient means to carry on experiments that attract the scrutiny of psychoanalysts the world over, we decided to leave the orphanage administration until such time as the cadre of pedagogues is fully trained.

The Main Scientific Directorate, as you know, has concurred with this decision and has moved to utilize the well-situated Orphanage as a laboratory not only for psychoanalytic experiments but for all kinds of scientific and educational institutions.

Psychoanalysts have practically no influence left in the orphanage.

I wish the Main Scientific Directorate the best of luck in its multifaceted utilization of our inheritance, but I feel it is my duty to inform my dear comrades to whom this letter is addressed that in future I will have nothing to do with this orphanage and I will take no responsibility, direct, indirect, or even moral, for its work.[100]

Two instructions are inscribed on this letter of November 20, 1924. The first is "to be forwarded to the Scientific Division, 11/28, attention Petrov," and the second "to be filed, 06/24/25." Schmidt's letter was later used as evidence in behalf of the closure of the Psychoanalytic Institute; but the letter contained no criticism directed at the institute or its leadership and not the slightest hint that Schmidt condemned psychoanalysis—only a tinge of pique, masked by sarcasm, at the "dear comrades" to which it was addressed.

Jean Marti mentioned several bits of gossip that were circulating about the orphanage—for instance, that the children there were subjected to experiments in order to stimulate premature sexuality.[101] Yermakov's daughter also spoke of rumors about sex experiments; according to her, the rumors caused her father a great deal of trouble.[102] Vera Schmidt also mentioned them. It seems probable that this sort of gossip, although it was likely groundless, provided the impetus for the endless commissions convened to decide the institute's future. The latest of these commissions, which gathered on January 2, 1925 (consisting of Petrov, Pinkevich, the new director of the orphanage, Zhukova, and parent representatives), had practically confirmed the rumors. The minutes reported that "sexual phenomena such as masturbation have been observed in most of the children living at the orphanage, while masturbation has not been observed in children just entering the orphanage from families."[103]

This was bound to lead to scandal, particularly keeping in mind who the parents were. On February 24, Pinkevich piled on yet another resolution: The orphanage was to be cut off from the Psychoanalytic Institute once and for all. The institute itself could remain in Moscow "only if it joins up with someone (with the Psychological Institute, for instance)." Then someone came up with the idea of moving the Institute to Leningrad. Since Pavlov lived in Leningrad, this may well have been another expression of the idea "of creating a synthesis of Freudianism and Marxism through the study of conditioned reflexes." Yermakov countered that the Psychoanalytic Institute bore a resemblance to the Psychological Institute only in name; that the Psychoanalytic Institute was the only place of its kind not only in the USSR, but in Europe, and for this reason it had to be left in the capital; and that all of the institute's employees lived in Moscow, a fact that would equate its move to Leningrad with closure.[104] But now all of these protests were in vain.

In January 1925, the presidium of the ministry of education, chaired by Lunacharsky, adopted a curious resolution: "Concerning the relocation of the Institute for the Study of Arid and Desert Areas to Leningrad and the Psychoanalytic Institute to someplace outside Moscow—No objections." A separate decision recommended that "Comrade Schmidt be used full time in the ministry of education."[105]

On August 14, 1925, the Greater Council of Ministers, chaired by Minister of Health Nikolai Semashko, adopted the following resolution based on Pinkevich's report: "The Psychoanalytic Institute and International Solidarity Laboratory are to be liquidated."[106]

The End

We still have the institute's "work plan" for its last season of operation, from September 1924 to July 1925.[107] Lectures were given each day in the institute. The Russian Psychoanalytic Society met there twice a month, and in addition, the society's pedagogical section held its own meetings there twice a month. Yermakov combined his clinical work with lectures on the psychoanalysis of literary works and also with research on hypnosis, in which he had become deeply involved by this time. In addition, together with Vera Schmidt he planned to speak about the research done by the already closed orphanage. Roza Averbukh was to continue the work she began in Kazan on the psychoanalysis of Vasily Rozanov's writings. Boris Friedmann was preparing a paper on the psychoanalysis of idealism (using Turgenev's character Rudin as the prime example). The only new face was a political immigrant from Germany named Wilhelm Rohr, who was to give lectures in German on "The Psychoanalysis of Collective Thinking."

In November 1924, elections were held in the Psychoanalytic Society. Moisei Wulff was elected president, as he was truly the most prominent authority among the candidates, as well as a close acquaintance of Freud and a great benefactor of Russian psychoanalysis. Yermakov and diplomat Viktor Kopp became vice presidents. Kopp (more about him in chapter 7) was now a member of the Trotskyist opposition. Luria was elected secretary, and Kannabikh became a member of the bureau.[108]

At the tenth congress of the International Psychoanalytic Association in Innsbruck, in 1927, President Max Eitingon said in his opening speech that "in Russia, one of the older countries to interest itself in analysis, the circle which has really gone further in the subject has grown. We shall all understand that our colleagues there are working under very difficult conditions, and I should like in the name of us all to express our deep sympathy with them."[109] Annual dues (two dollars per person), Eitingon added, had been collected in Russia, but had not yet been received due to technical difficulties. Freud, however, who either had a better grasp of the situation or, unlike Eitingon, had no reason to be hypocritical (see chapter 7), wrote to longtime émigré Osipov on February 27, 1927: "The [psycho-] analysts in Soviet Russia are, by the way, having a bad time. From somewhere the Bolsheviks have caught the opinion that psychoanalysis is hostile to their system. You know the truth that our science is not able to be put into the service of any party, but that it needs a certain liberal-mindedness in turn for its own development."[110]

The work of Soviet psychoanalysts continued lethargically but uninterruptedly until the beginning of the 1930s. The center of activity was Moscow, although some work also was taking place in Leningrad, Odessa, Kharkov, and Rostov. Around 1930, an Odessa psychiatrist who had served as Freud's interpreter, Yakov Kogan, acquired a double-sided portrait for his office; on the front was Pavlov, on the back Freud.[111] During the day, Dr. Kogan saw patients and conversed with his superiors under the portrait of Pavlov; then he would flip the painting over and consult with his secret analytical patients all evening under Freud's likeness. Leningrad doctor Ilya Perepel put out a few psychoanalytic books using his own money; the last of these works, released in 1928, contains a preface written by Alexei Ukhtomsky, an outstanding physiologist, which is full of kind words for both the author and his method.[112]

Psychoanalysts were truly trying to make themselves useful. Wulff, for example, did some fascinating applied research, although the results came out only after he had emigrated.[113] Based on a massive study of Moscow bus drivers and trolley conductors, data were collected on the extent of sexual disorders prevalent in that particular profession, most of all impotence. Deeper analysis revealed that while they were on the job, many drivers experienced sexual arousal. During coitus, on the other hand, they tended to recall their place behind the wheel. Wulff suggested a psychodynamic explanation for this strange case—an explanation that, in keeping with Freud's observation, could hardly have served the interests of the proletariat. Boris Pilnyak knew about similar studies done in the printing industry, mentioning in his novel *Ripening Fruit* "the psychic alteration brought about by lead, a theory promoted by several Moscow psychoanalysts."[114]

The Russian Psychoanalytic Society continued to operate, and held fifteen to twenty meetings a year between 1925 and 1927, judging by its reports to the international association. In 1926 the society spent some time conducting hearings on pedology, the novel science that was then taking shape in the womb of the movement. In April 1927, Luria left his post as secretary of the society. A great future in science awaited him, and in the 1960s he would become one of the most important neuropsychologists in the world.[115] Meanwhile, at the end of the 1920s, judging from his unpublished memoirs, he was already seeking his fortune in applied fields. He had constructed a primitive lie detector that he had used in an associative experiment, with pneumatic gauges that measured finger tremors (the connection is obvious between the idea behind his detector and the associative experiments conducted by a youthful Jung). Vera Schmidt filled in for him at the society, and it was she who traveled to Innsbruck in 1927 to speak before the annual congress of psychoanalysts.

On November 3, 1927, Wulff left for Berlin on a business trip, leaving Kannabikh to perform his duties for him. He never returned. In his presidential speech at the eleventh congress of psychoanalysts, in Oxford in 1928, Eitingon would make oblique mention of this desertion:

> Owing to the circumstances in which the Russian Society carries on its work, it has, of course, been impossible to effect a change in the situation there, espe-

cially since their valued leader, who for many years had directed the society, has gone to live elsewhere. Our colleagues in the Moscow Society, together with individual members in Kiev and Odessa, continue, with a courage which must excite our admiration, the struggle to preserve and consolidate what they already possess.[116]

Until 1933, Wulff worked in Germany, publishing extensively in the journals of the International Psychoanalytic Association. After the Nazis came to power, he emigrated once again, this time to Palestine, where together with Eitingon he helped to organize the local Psychoanalytic Society. After Eitingon's death, Wulff became the president of the Palestinian Psychoanalytic Society, and he remained in that post for ten years. In many ways repeating in his new homeland what he had already done in Russia, he organized a series of Hebrew translations of Freud. Wulff lived a long life, and died in 1971.

The Russian Society was flickering out. Still, as late as 1930 it held a few meetings, one of which was dedicated to "planning work for 1931." Later, another émigré, Leningrad native Ilya (Elias) Perepel, wrote in an American journal that "the psychoanalytic movement slowed down, and about the year 1930 came to a standstill. From this date it officially ceased to exist."[117]

In 1936, a Dr. Lerman of New York met with Vera Schmidt, who told him that the psychoanalysts' meetings continued and that there were fifteen people participating.[118] Two years later, Perepel wrote an article about the "death sentence" that had supposedly been meted out to psychoanalysis by the regime, and called on his colleagues in the West to intervene.[119] On the whole, these and several other similar accounts are more than likely just legends. Psychoanalytic medical practice continued underground, and probably unpaid, carried on by a few remaining loners. One example of this might be the examination of Mikhail Zoshchenko that was performed in 1937 by the Leningrad physician I. Margolis (see chapter 10). The horrible fate of Sabina Spielrein, unhappy and unemployed in provincial Rostov, is the best illustration of how the psychoanalytic profession was perceived in the inhuman conditions of the 1930s. Any systematic activity, particularly out in the open, such as the gathering of a psychoanalytic club, was dangerous for all involved.

In 1948, professor of psychiatry A. S. Chistovich was fired from the Military Medical Academy in Leningrad because he used "the building blocks of psychoanalysis" in his lectures on dreams and did not deny it when he was called to task at a Party meeting.[120] Aron Belkin, however, has related how in 1952 he underwent psychoanalysis in Siberia; the analyst was Professor I. S. Sumbayev.[121] Soviet political prisoners turned to various systems for spiritual comfort—some to Marxism, others to Orthodoxy, still others to Buddhism. Yevgeny Gnedin, for example (the son of Leonid Parvus, who allegedly financed Lenin's efforts in Russia in 1917), recalled

how after monstrous torture he adopted a new faith while sitting in the isolation chamber, a belief reminiscent of Buddhism and practical yoga.[122]

The Yermakov Library

One practical accomplishment of the Moscow psychoanalysts that cannot
be overlooked is the publication of the "Psychological and Psychoanalytic
Library" series. Over a very short period of time, from 1922 to 1928, a
colossal amount of translation and editing was poured into these books.
Among the works translated were *Introductory Lectures in Psychoanalysis*
and *Psychoanalysis of Infantile Neuroses*. The *Outline of the Psychology of
Sexuality* was reissued, and wonderfully chosen collections of essays by
Freud (*Basic Psychological Theories in Psychoanalysis* and *Methods and
Techniques of Psychoanalysis*) and his followers (*Childhood Psychoanalysis*
and *Psychoanalysis and the Doctrine of Character*) were translated, as was
Jung's *Psychological Types* and books by Klein and Jones.[123]

Russian translations of the basic theoretical canon—*Introduction to
Psychoanalysis*, *Totem and Taboo*, and others—were done by Moisei
Wulff. He is also credited, along with Nikolai Osipov, with the development of Russian psychoanalytic terminology. But on the whole this project
was a large-scale success due to the efforts of Ivan Yermakov.

Thirty-two books were slated for publication in the series, including new
editions of older translations of works such as *Interpretation of Dreams*, a
few collections of new translations, the psychological works of Bleuler and
the American psychologist William McDougall, *Foundations of Psychiatry*
by William Alanson White, and, finally, a collection of essays from the
International Solidarity Orphanage. It is surprising only that Yermakov
was able to carry out such a large portion of this plan.

The reissue of Freud created a sensation in the Soviet Union in the 1980s,
but few people know that almost all of those editions were reprints of old
books from the 1920s, mostly edited by Yermakov (the translators' names
are often not even indicated in the new editions, as if Freud wrote in
Russian!). There has been much criticism of these translations, but so far
no one has done any better.

Many of the books published in the Library were prefaced by Yermakov.
Reading these introductions, it becomes clear that most of all their author
appreciated the ethical aspects of psychoanalysis and its educational purpose: He repeatedly emphasized the "bright" mechanisms of the conscious
in their hard-fought struggle with the recalcitrant unconscious. Yermakov
devoted much less space to Freud's other ideas, such as transference, infantile sexuality, bisexuality, and the death wish. It is difficult to say whether
his understanding of psychoanalysis was really so simplified, or if this was
just the result of many years spent adapting his analysis to the limited capabilities of his audience.

Yermakov's personal archives hold the transcript of an interesting meeting of the psychoanalytic club, held when he was acting as chairman.[124] There were seven people present, all of them, it seems, amateur psychoanalysts. Yermakov conducted the meeting as a group session, discussing classic themes such as the relationship between the unconscious and intuition. One of the female participants quipped that she had often observed patients who had been treated with psychoanalysis, but that she herself had a definite dislike for it. In response, Yermakov laid out his credo: "Healthy people restrain themselves, while psychoneurotics are unable to do so. ...Any adult's goal is to take account of his surroundings. A psychopath considers only himself. We lead the patient back to reality by having him learn about himself and his own unconscious. There you have a diagram of what's going on."

Within the same series, Yermakov released two of his own books on the psychoanalysis of Russian literature: one on Gogol, the other on Pushkin.[125] These works have practically disappeared from scholarly circulation, and it is unlikely that they will return (the book on Pushkin, however, has been reissued by an émigré publishing company). In reading these unstructured, wordy "Outlines" and "Sketches," the reader senses the author's personality. Yermakov noted that Gogol, "with his suppressed aggression," had a tendency to use other people's themes in his work in a way that was "contrived and forced." "I have followed this kind of phenomenon, characteristic of neurotics, in a very large number of cases subjected to psychoanalysis," he wrote.[126] As we know, a psychoanalyst's pet discovery is often a feature of his own character.

"All our expectations and excitement, important events in life and everyday experience, all lead to something that is somehow hopeless and vain," Yermakov began his analysis of Gogol's stories. Yermakov's texts often transmit his own fear to the reader, his internal inhibition and self-censure. The author seems afraid to relate the entire idea he wants to describe, and he ceases to see it in its entirety. Sometimes this self-limitation comes out in the text. For example, in the middle of his musings about Gogol's character Chichikov, Yermakov suddenly interrupts himself: "Perhaps there is quite a bit of symbolism in all this which I am unfortunately unable to uncover." Pointing to the incestuous motif in the story "A Terrible Vengeance" (a motif that is totally obvious, as Gogol openly describes the magician's lust for his daughter), Yermakov suddenly writes, "even if everything I say here is dubious, I still consider it necessary at least to mention it." There are a slew of medical legends tied to Gogol—that he was stricken with syphilis or schizophrenia, that he died of excessive masturbation. In Yermakov's texts we find plenty of hints, but few clearly formulated and well-documented hypotheses. Rozanov, who knew nothing of psychoanalysis and wrote twenty years earlier, had no qualms about saying that Gogol's sexual secret was necrophilia. Berdyaev, who wrote about Gogol at the same time as

Yermakov, also posited "some kind of unguessed-at secret." He interpreted this secret, however, in a different context. Yermakov could not have helped but see this context, but nowhere did he let on that he noticed: "There is something Gogolian in all this revolutionary tastelessness. . . . Perhaps the gloomiest and most hopeless thing about the Russian revolution is its Gogolian aspect."[127]

In his analysis of Pushkin's *Little Tragedies,* an important and endlessly layered work, Yermakov's perception was distorted by his own feelings to the extent that he could see only one thing: "In these four tragedies, fear is the unifying emotion." The stingy knight is afraid of losing his wealth; even Mozart is afraid because he failed to hand over his requiem. Don Juan is a criminal who has shoved his guilt back into his subconscious, which is why he is forced to repeat his crime. According to Yermakov, fear is his basic emotion, as it is for all the rest of Pushkin's dramatic protagonists. In the final scene with the Stone Guest, he attributes absent-mindedness, helplessness, and meekness to Don Juan (as opposed to Akhmatova, who saw Don Juan as "a mix of cold cruelty and childlike carelessness"[128]). The statue's visit is merely a hypnosis-induced hallucination. "The outward strength of Juan's passion hides his internal inferiority." These statements contain far more moralizing than they do real analysis. Yermakov manages to reach a new vision of the text when he reads "The Little House in Kolomna," which he unexpectedly interprets as an ironic inversion of Pushkin's own "Prophet." Thus Pushkin, Russia's revered genius, is turned into a poet of fear, while his most romantic hero is obsessed with fear and meek servility. "Fear brings out the vilest facets of the human soul."

The same was said even more strongly in Yermakov's book on Gogol, which came out a year later. "Dead men look on, they look on and wait for the end, they wait—and the weak and pitiful get scared." Yermakov wrote these words about Gogol's "Viy," but they described real life as well: Although the Civil War was past, ahead stretched the Great Terror. At the time these lines were written, the omnipotent power that decided the fate of so many people was busy deciding the fate of the State Psychoanalytic Institute and its director.

Ilya Ehrenburg recalled how he visited the Kremlin with his make-believe superman Julio Jurenito, and he conveyed his impression of Lenin, Trotsky, and their ilk:

> Not that I believed all the charming legends that portrayed the Bolshevik bosses as something halfway between Jack-the-Giantkiller and an apocalyptic locust swarm. No, I was just afraid of these people who could not only do something to me, but to other people as well. I have always felt this fear of power, even as a boy. . . . In recent years, seeing my acquaintances, drinking buddies and classmates become ministers, commissars, and other "high and mighty" types, I have realized that my fear is churned up by the Cap of Monomakh, by a brief-

case, by a teeny little warrant. God knows what they'll want next, but in any case (and this is for sure), whatever they want, they can get.[129]

Everything had changed, and now for a Russian intellectual like Ehrenburg the *Übermensch* was simply anyone unafraid of having a word with the authorities.

Yermakov was deprived of his positions relatively swiftly: After the State Psychoanalytic Institute was closed in 1924, he ceased to be its director, and in 1925, Wulff replaced him as president of the Russian Psychoanalytic Society. In 1928, the State Publishing House shut down Yermakov's Library, although a great deal of energy and money had already been spent on the series. Yermakov did not publish after this (however, he did manage to print Freud's *History of an Illusion* as late as 1930), but he continued to write. His archives include a hefty tome on Dostoevsky, executed in the same style, as well as a variety of essays and articles on literary criticism. His passion was collecting ornamental Tatar embroidery, and he wrote extensively about this art also. It seems he wrote nothing on the practice or theory of psychoanalysis in the 1930s. His compositions gradually lost their analytical flavor as the years passed.

In 1940, Ivan Yermakov was arrested on a typical charge, and he died two years later in a labor camp.

Revolution and Dreams

Nikolai Osipov was the same age as Yermakov and knew him from their Lesser Friday Society meetings. He later became a Russian refugee and lecturer at Charles University in Prague, living and working far away from the storm of the century.[130] In his memoirs, written just before his death, he repeated often that he "never got involved in politics." But as Bismarck said, if you don't get involved with politics, politics gets involved with you. Political problems followed Osipov around throughout his life. In 1899, he was expelled from Moscow University in his second year for organizing the first general student strike. "I was far removed from politics of any ilk. . . . I danced a lot and worked little. Somehow, I've no idea how, I was elected by my classmates to the executive committee. . . . Before I even learned that I'd been elected, I was arrested."[131] He was an assistant professor in 1911, when he and Serbsky once again abandoned Moscow University, this time in protest over the policies of the erstwhile minister of popular education (Yermakov was brought in to replace them). In 1921, Osipov fled the new government. "The pre-Bolshevik period of the revolution made me feel totally repulsed by any socialist movement. For me, the Bolsheviks were absolutely unacceptable."[132]

Osipov worked extensively as a psychotherapist (he collected data from 1,030 cases for his planned book *Psychology of Neurotics,* which he never had time to write), he corresponded with Freud, and in Prague he wrote some important theoretical works. The histological leanings of his youth were left far behind, and he remained unmoved by the "materialist" ideas about the link between psychodynamic processes and brain substrata that so excited his Soviet colleagues—ideas that had their roots in the early works of Freud and culminated in Luria's works. As a curiosity, Osipov collected quotations from the works of Russian psychiatrists that began with the claim that no organic changes had been found in patients with a given psychological disorder but ended with the dogmatic assertion that the disease in question was based on physiological, anatomical changes.[133] Osipov, like Jung, likened those who studied psychic life by analyzing the brain to a person who wants to understand what a house is and thus goes about analyzing the chemical makeup of bricks.[134] But unlike Jung and many of his Russian contemporaries, Osipov also put no stock in the flaccid mysticism of the Dionysians. His political and psychoanalytic experience both contributed in equal measure to his clarity of thought, which differentiated what he knew from what he hoped to learn, as well as from what he had no hope of ever understanding.

The irrational exists. Most of all, it exists in ourselves. A brave adult does not feel fear in the face of irrationality, according to Osipov's definition, as he might at the prospect of some real danger. He feels mystical horror, as does a person who perceives something uncanny, fantastic, and irreal. Mystical horror and evil spirits are just temporary pseudo-irrationality, incomprehensible only as long as they remain outside the realm of comprehension. Rationalism saves us from fear, but not from mystical horror; horror has to be experienced, interpreted, and evaluated.

To a certain degree, Osipov's interests developed in parallel to Yermakov's. Osipov also became involved in the analytical interpretation of Russian classics. Moreover, he was fascinated by the same aspect of these works as was Yermakov: "The Frightful in Gogol and Dostoevsky" was the title of one of his most important articles. The tone, however, is completely different: While Yermakov stubbornly insisted that Gogol, Pushkin, and Dostoevsky, along with their characters, were all in constant fear of something, Osipov was more concerned with the ways in which they overcame their fear. "How to make a fool of the devil" was the phrase that struck Osipov as Gogol's main idea.

Osipov analyzed the erotic nightmares of "Viy," the incestuous plot in "A Frightful Vengeance," and the gory episodes from "Taras Bulba" as resurrected childhood fears, "the inheritance of our own childhood or the childhood of humanity."[135] Infantile fears in adult life, Osipov insisted, were the primary symptom of neurosis. "The fear of a father figure is the resurrection of our childhood fear," he wrote, referring to Gogol's protagonists, to his Czech patients, and most likely, to the countrymen he left behind.

The mass of horrid occurrences in Gogol, and in life in general, were all interwoven around sex; but sex was not the only source of fear. The intersection of love and death was the primary target of analysis. "The mistake made by many Freudians, including Yermakov, is that they falsely attribute pansexualism to Freud, and, lovingly engrossing themselves in sexual issues, distort his entire doctrine. Freud asserts, along with basic sexual attraction, still another basic attraction, the obsession with death."[136] The Freudian death wish, which is normally perceived as something tragic, presents the possibility of bravery for Osipov. If attraction to death is just as natural and fundamental as attraction to life, then fear of death is just as much a symptom as fear of sex. "Fear of death is a neurotic symptom," Osipov wrote not long before the end of his life.[137] "Gogol and Dostoevsky, although they themselves suffered from infantile, archaic fears, can teach us to overcome these fears, to overcome timidity (the word 'timidity' [*robost'*] comes from the word 'child' [*rebenok*]), and to be brave."[138]

In 1931, Osipov published his article "Revolution and Dreams."[139] (It is clear from one of his letters that Osipov planned to send the text to Freud in translation.[140]) His idea was simple and paradoxical: The equilibrium of a healthy person is disrupted in his sleep so that it can be rejuvenated during his waking hours. Perhaps, Osipov suggested, we observe the same thing in society as a whole during revolution.

Osipov tried systematically to compare these two phenomena in his article, both of which he knew well. A dream, according to Freud, was the fulfillment of suppressed desires, the revolt of certain "sub-egos" against others that usually have a firm grip on power. Revolution was the realization of the suppressed, subjugated desires of one social class. The ambivalence, instability, narcissism, and archaic symbolism that were characteristic of dreams could also be found in revolution: "Soldiers who once would have given their lives for their officers were ready to flay the skin off their backs. At the same time, these soldiers were transformed into the unwavering slaves of their new bosses."

Osipov also suggested that the "class-based, narcissistic self-affirmation" of revolutionary masses led to the same profound disruption of the principle of reality as did a dreamer's quirky visions. The author took this argument to great lengths:

Revolution and dreams have the same content: the revelation of infantile, archaic "desires," primarily narcissistic, sublimated and unsublimated. The form of these revelations is also the same. . . . This form is downright incomprehensible, confusing, senseless, like a word puzzle. Both revolution and dreams require interpretation. Interpretation shows that the slogans of the revolution are actually lightly covered, false weld, just like the disguised symbols in dreams.

Thus, one could "compare a nation in conditions of law and order with an individual in a state of alert wakefulness, or a nation in conditions of revolution with an individual in the process of dreaming." Osipov sensed the intellectual precariousness of such an analogy, but remained firm: "Revolution and dreams are one and the same phenomenon; they are both the expression of narcissism, just on different levels of daily life."[141]

All of this was written clearly, analytically, and with no sign of fear. Indeed, "neurotics and psychotics experience fear when a healthy person feels mystical horror at most."[142]

After Osipov's death of heart disease in 1934, his friends—literary scholar A. Bem, psychoanalyst Fyodor Dosuzhkov, and philosopher Nikolai Lossky—published two volumes dedicated to his memory, entitled *Life and Death*. Two hundred copies of the first volume were released on the first anniversary of Osipov's death, and two hundred copies of the second volume were printed exactly one year later.[143]

On the cross over his grave in Prague, there is an inscription: "Doctor of Medicine N. E. Osipov, Docent at Moscow University."

7

Between Power and Death:
The Psychoanalytic Passions
of Trotsky and His Comrades

Western literature on the history of Soviet psychoanalysis tends to attribute disproportionate significance to the ideological debates that took place at the end of 1920s.[1] In an oblique way, Western scholars are in agreement with the Soviet debaters they study, many of whom really believed that the force and ideological purity of their arguments could shape something tangible in the future. The future, however, was decided in the end by people who had trouble understanding not only Freud but even Marx; thus, the course of debate was in many ways predetermined. The lives of the people involved, in contrast, are much more telling.

Fire and Water

Some time after the end of World War I, Freud told Jones that a Bolshevik had paid him a visit and had half converted him to communism. Jones was amazed. Freud explained: The Bolsheviks believed that their victory would be followed by several years of suffering and chaos, which eventually would be replaced by general prosperity. Freud quipped that he believed the first half of this prognosis.[2] As Hanns Sachs recalled: "After the Revolution, when Freud's works had begun to be published by the Russian government (the State Publishing House), I spoke optimistically about the influence that psychoanalysis could have in creating a new Russia. Freud, retaining his skepticism toward the Russian soul, retorted: 'These Russians are like water; they fill any container, but do not retain the form of any.'"

The ambivalent interest in Russia that was characteristic of Freud's circle was and remains extremely common among left-leaning Western intellectuals. This same attitude was evidenced by Marx, who through most of his life viewed Russia as a terrifying threat to civilization and hoped the creation of the First International would serve to block Russian influence in

Europe. At the end of his life, Marx suddenly came to believe that socialism was possible in Russia. He was thrilled by the Russian translation of *Das Kapital*, he began studying Russian himself, and after his death two cubic meters of papers on Russia were found in his office.[3]

According to James Rice, who interviewed Freud's niece, the founder of psychoanalysis had dozens of relatives in the Russian empire.[4] They often sent patients to young Dr. Freud from Zhitomir, a center of Jewish habitation in the Ukraine that suffered horribly from pogroms. Freud also had personal contact with revolutionary struggle, as his uncle Joseph Freud, who became the hero of one memorable episode in *Interpretation of Dreams*, spent the 1860s in an Austrian prison. Not long ago, this case turned up in the Austrian police archives. As it turned out, Uncle Joseph was holding a huge sum of counterfeit rubles printed by Jews in London to support the uprising in Lithuania.[5]

Freud's own political views were not radical. Many times he expressed his distrust of utopian ideas about rebuilding society, and his skepticism grew with the years. In February 1918, Freud wrote to Lou Andreas-Salomé:

> I am sorry to hear of the state of your fatherland and that its radical policies have been so discredited. Revolutions, I believe, are acceptable only when they are over; and therefore they ought to be over very quickly. What the human beast needs above all is restraint. In short, one grows reactionary, just as incidentally did the rebel Schiller in the face of the French Revolution.[6]

Despite his sober evaluation of events, Freud continued to entertain hope for quite a while, and he spoke of this hope many years later. In November 1930, Zweig sent him a sort of manifesto that he or his friends had written in support of Soviet Russia, hoping for Freud's signature. Freud refused, confessing both his former leftist sympathies and his present disillusionment with socialism: "Any hope that I may have cherished has disappeared in this decade of Soviet rule. I remain a liberal of the old school. In my last book, I criticized uncompromisingly this mixture of despotism and communism."[7] Freud wrote in that book that the communist economic program had gone beyond the government's capacity, and that Soviet ideological postulates were no more than unfounded illusions. In June 1933, Freud wrote to Marie Bonaparte that the world was turning into one big prison, and he predicted an "amazing paradox": Nazi Germany "started out by declaring that Bolshevism was its worst enemy; it will end up totally indistinguishable from it." All the same, if he had to choose between these two hopeless alternatives, Freud preferred the Russians: "Bolshevism, any way you look at it, has borrowed revolutionary ideas, while Hitlerism is totally medieval and reactionary."

Some of Freud's close disciples were active Social Democrats.[8] Even Jung, who was further to the right on the political spectrum than most of his colleagues, characterized the Bolshevik revolution in Russia as an "expansion of consciousness." At a seminar on March 13, 1929, Jung said: "Fire puts an end to everything, even an end to the world. Fire that is the sap of culture can burst forth and destroy everything. This happens from time to time, as for instance in the Bolshevist revolution, when the cultural form could not hold the tension of energy any more, and the fire broke forth and destroyed the Russian civilization."[9] It is curious to note how Freud and Jung, each searching for his own metaphor to encapsulate the mysterious Russian soul, came up with totally opposite images: Freud compared it to water, while Jung likened it to fire.

Psychoanalysis of the Proletariat

The intersection of psychoanalysis and socialism has often been cited as a phenomenon of intellectual history that gave rise to such exceptional thinkers as Herbert Marcuse and Erich Fromm. These same common ideas brought many of their followers to the barricades during the "student revolutions" in Europe and the United States. Disillusionment with Stalin's version of socialism in the USSR and shock at the victory of national socialism in Germany were two equally important factors that pushed a great many liberal intellectuals into psychoanalysis. If socialism was so hard to achieve, if the masses were ready to support the most inhuman political regimes, then politics could not be the only factor involved; there had to be something built into the nature of man that also required attention. At the same time, professional analysts both before and after the war were clearly drawn to radical ideas.[10] Jacques Lacan, for instance, once declared that his teaching was to Freud's doctrine what Lenin's ideas were to Marx. As recently as the 1990s, French leftist psychoanalysts held a conference on this very topic, and a prestigious publishing house released the papers read there, subsumed under the title *Marx and Lenin, Freud and Lacan.*[11]

The discussion of the relationship between Freud and Marx began at a meeting of the Vienna Psychoanalytic Society in 1909. The keynote speech was given by Alfred Adler and entitled "The Psychology of Marxism." For Adler, this was no theory. He was married to a Russian socialist, he knew Trotsky well, and the Russian Adolf Ioffe was one of his patients. Lou Andreas-Salomé, who had many dealings with Adler, referred to him as an heir to Marx and noted in 1912: "For the proletariat, social utopia is based on the motives of envy and hate, and Adler sees in children a similar ideal that forms a personal utopia based on social comparison."[12]

Ferens Eros, who delved into the materials left behind by the Vienna Society, found that the discussion of Adler's speech brought out three points of view.[13] According to Adler and his supporter Paul Federn, the same aggressive instincts that were suppressed in neurotics were transformed in the proletariat into the class consciousness addressed by Marx. The opposite opinion held that socialism was nothing but a substitute for religion, and perhaps was even a particular type of neurosis. Freud tried to find a liberal compromise, as he always did in matters of politics.

Ten years later, after revolutions had shaken eastern and central Europe, Federn argued a different point of view in his book *On the Psychology of Revolution*, based on new information. He asserted that Bolshevism was nothing other than the replacement of patriarchal power, the power of the father, with matriarchal principles of brotherhood. The Soviets, he claimed, signaled a return to prepatriarchal forms of fraternal cooperation, but there persisted a constant danger of "psychological Thermidor," the restoration of the patriarchal principle. Federn warned that brothers who are deprived of their father will always seek a replacement, and in this same way the dictatorship of the proletariat could be transformed into tyranny.[14]

Early revolutionary regimes, nonetheless, were well disposed toward psychoanalysis—and not only in Russia. During a short period of success after the Hungarian revolution of 1919, one of Freud's closest colleagues, Sandor Ferenczi, was appointed director of the Psychoanalytic Institute at the University of Budapest. Even Ernesto "Che" Guevara considered himself a connoisseur and lover of psychoanalysis. Then, too, the German social democrats, like Karl Kautsky, liked to refer to Freud and Adler in their musings on mass psychology. Of course, psychoanalysis to them seemed closer to reformist socialism than to Bolshevik-style communism. Their Russian counterparts, led by Trotsky, felt otherwise.

Freudomarxism in Russia

In Russia, the problem was first articulated by the Kazan club. The minutes of one 1922 meeting state that there was a similarity between the methods of Marx and Freud: "1) both are analytical through and through; 2) both are concerned with the human unconscious; 3) the object of both methods is the personality in its social and historical context; 4) both study dynamics."[15] At the meeting, Luria, Averbukh, Friedmann, and Nechkina were assigned the task of preparing a special discussion of this topic. The first three later shifted the discussion onto the pages of the Party press after their move to Moscow.

From 1923 onward, the topic was continually on the agenda at meetings of the Moscow analysts and in the journals they published. They had accepted a commission from the government, which allowed them to live in relatively tolerable and even privileged conditions: to seek a new ideological face for Bolshevism. At the same time, the analysts had to respond to crude attacks from their numerous opponents, who posited the incompatibility of psychoanalysis with Soviet Marxism, attempting to dislodge

Freudianism from the politically advantageous position it occupied. Many theories were vying for the title of "the only materialist conception of man": Bekhterev's reflexology, Pavlov's physiology of conditioned reflexes, and the set of ideas that were developing within the framework of pedology, which would later come to dominate the Soviet scene under the cumbersome rubric, "The Cultural and Historical Theory of Activity of L. S. Vygotksy, A. N. Leontiev, and A. R. Luria."

In this struggle, which was more political than scientific, Soviet psychoanalysts had two strategies from which to choose. One tactic, which we will call the "idea of particularity," sought to prove that psychoanalysis was a particular case within one of the other "materialist conceptions of man." Since it was a particular case, psychoanalysis did not contradict Marxism, and it could even strengthen Soviet science with its empirical observations. This particular case idea was first expressed by a philosopher who later achieved notoriety, Bernard Bykhovsky. Quoting Freud extensively in the journal *Under the Banner of Marxism*, Bykhovsky attempted to demonstrate that psychoanalytic theory was monistic, materialist, and dialectical. Bykhovsky's model was the reflexology of Bekhterev, under which he felt psychoanalysis was subsumed.[16] Later, Aron Zalkind followed in his footsteps for a time.[17] The pursuit of this strategy, of course, brought up certain unsolvable logical problems. Even setting aside these inconsistencies, psychoanalysis would still end up subordinate to other conceptions. This position might have pleased many, but it certainly was not to the psychoanalysts' liking.

The other, more profound approach would today be dubbed the "idea of complementarity." Psychoanalysis and the conception chosen by materialist science complement each other, so goes the argument, since they are different points of view on the very same phenomena. If this was so, then psychoanalysis and reflexology or Pavlovian physiology were equal spheres that, in essence, need not logically be linked by any interrelations. Clearly this idea of complementarity allowed psychoanalysis far more freedom than the idea of particularity. The complementarity strategy was articulated first by Leon Trotsky; in his oft-repeated metaphor, he likened Freud to a man who looked down a well and saw the bottom only murkily but in its entirety, while Pavlov was like a diver who painstakingly examined every grain of silt from below.[18]

Mikhail Reisner, who had close connections to the authorities, continued this motif in his essays of 1923 and 1924.[19] He particularly appreciated the psychoanalytic concept of sublimation, anticipating later Western attempts at Freudomarxist synthesis, such as those associated with Reich and Marcuse. Then again, the pathos of sexual revolution typical of Western Freudomarxists was completely absent from Reisner's articles.

Psychoanalytic (or more accurately, Freudomarxist) ideas dominated other approaches in *Psychology and Marxism*,[20] a collection released in

1925 and edited by the new director of the Institute of Psychology, K. Kornilov. In their contributions to this volume, Alexander Luria interpreted psychoanalysis as a "system of monistic psychology," Reisner explored the relationship between Freudian social psychology and Marxism, and Boris Friedmann wrote on "Freud's Basic Psychological Views and Historical Materialism." In these early attempts to coordinate two attractive world-views, there is no sense of the fear that would become clear in texts published only a few years later. These works remain fully in line with the academic tradition of the time, which might in part explain why they seem so hopelessly out of date today. For serious psychoanalysts, however, this kind of approach likely would have seemed unacceptable even back then.

The most famous Soviet psychologist, Lev Vygotsky, made his own contribution to the Marxist critique of psychoanalysis. This contribution remained unappreciated for many decades. Vygotsky was a skilled methodologist, and his attention was drawn to the immense breach between Freud's ideas and the way they were elaborated by Soviet supporters as they adapted them to the present moment. "Not a single psychoanalytic journal, of course, would ever publish articles by Luria and Friedmann," he pointed out reasonably in an essay composed in 1927 but published only half a century later.[21] The genuine ideas of psychoanalysis, Vygotsky wrote, were profoundly different from the way Soviet theoreticians made them out to be, and these scholars were misleading their readers when they declared that Freudianism and Marxism were close. "A strange situation results: Freud and his school never call themselves monists, nor materialists, nor dialecticians, nor supporters of historical materialism. But they are told: 'You are all of them, and you don't know yourselves who you are.'" Vygotsky was absolutely correct, but if this text had been published at the end of the 1920s it would have had the effect of a political denunciation. Vygotsky, who had once been (according to the 1929 roll) a member of the Russian Psychoanalytic Society and had friends and coauthors from among the group's ranks, refrained from publicizing his position.

Adolf Ioffe, Patient

Although Soviet Freudomarxism of the 1920s was a bizarre, unforeseen phenomenon that seemed to have neither roots nor consequences, it did have a sort of history.

Adolf Abramovich Ioffe (1883–1927) was one of the central figures of the Russian revolution. He was a professional guerrilla and the organizer of the October uprising, and he later became an important diplomat. After joining the Central Committee in July 1917, he became the chairman of the Military-Revolutionary Committee in October. He was also the chairman of the Russian delegation to the Brest peace conference, participated in the

Genoa negotiations, and served as ambassador to Germany, China, Japan, and Austria. Ioffe was one of the leaders of the Trotskyist opposition, and after the group's purge he committed suicide.

Such was Ioffe's life. His autobiography yields more detailed information.[22] In 1908, when he met Trotsky in Vienna, where they were founding the newspaper *Pravda* together, Ioffe was a fugitive from justice for the fifth time. He had done much in his twenty-five years: He had spread propaganda in many Russian cities, masterminded an unbelievable jailbreak out of the Sevastopol military prison, delivered illegal literature to Baku, and been expelled from Germany by special order of the imperial chancellor. He had also been a university student in two different fields: medicine (in Berlin) and law (in Zurich).

Leaving Ioffe's autobiography behind and lending an ear to Trotsky's memoirs, we learn something quite astonishing. The younger man's revolutionary feats of valor seemed to Trotsky a "meager political past." In Vienna, Ioffe lived the life of a student of medicine and a patient. To quote: "Despite his extremely impressive appearance, too impressive for his young age, the remarkably calm tone of his voice, his patient gentility in conversation and exceptional politesse and other signs of internal stability, Ioffe had been a neurotic since his early childhood." Trotsky's clinical observations were derived from "his eyes, as if distracted and at the same time deeply concentrated. One could read in them the tense and agitated work going on inside." More surprising still, but nonetheless true, was that "even the necessity of explaining himself to certain people, even to converse over the telephone, made him nervous, frightened, and exhausted."[23]

Vienna at that time was the world capital of psychoanalysis, and the matching of neurotics with their analysts must have been decided in the heavens: Alfred Adler became Ioffe's analyst.[24] Adler was Freud's closest student, and it was just at the time in question that he was putting forward his own version of psychoanalysis, which rested on the primary importance of one particular motive. This motive, the will to power, was as fundamental to Adler as eros was to Freud. It stands to reason that Adler's interaction with young Russian Marxists would have aided him in formulating his ideas.

Freud did not accept Adler's innovation, and the latter was soon forced to leave the Vienna Psychoanalytic Society along with his followers. Trotsky was aware of Adler's problems but understood them in his own way: Ioffe "was treated by Alfred Adler, who later became famous as an 'individualist psychologist.' Adler emerged from Sigmund Freud's school, but by that time had broken with his teacher and formed his own faction." This event took place at the end of 1911. Trotsky met "from time to time" with Adler later on as well, and in 1923 he described these meetings in this way: "Over the course of the several years I spent in Vienna, I came into relatively close contact with Freudians; I read their works and even went to their meetings."[25] Trotsky also wrote of Adler in his memoirs:

My first introduction, and a very summary one at that, to the secrets of psychoanalysis was given me by the heretic who became the founding teacher of a new sect. But my true guide through this new and largely unknown field of heresy was Ioffe. As a young doctor, he was a follower of the psychoanalytic school, but as a patient he invariably put up resistance, and therefore a slight note of skepticism could be detected in his psychoanalytic propaganda.[26]

Trotsky himself harbored ambivalent feelings for the Freudian movement: "I have always been struck by their approach, combining physiological realism with an almost belletristic analysis of mental phenomena."[27]

It is clear that Trotsky spoke with some knowledge of psychoanalysis, knowledge he owed not only to Ioffe. Isaac Deutscher, the author of a three-volume biography of Trotsky, asserted that he "studied psychoanalytic issues deeply and systematically, and therefore knew the method's shortcomings."[28] But back then in Vienna, Trotsky naturally was not about to be left in debt to the younger Ioffe: "In exchange for lessons in psychoanalysis, I preached to Ioffe the theory of permanent revolution and the necessity of breaking with the Mensheviks."[29]

Ioffe's own psychoanalytic treatment was intensive: During those years he visited his analyst five or six times a week. It was expensive, too. The Party coffers most likely did not cover Adler's fees. Ioffe would have had to get by on his personal funds; luckily, his father was a wealthy Crimean merchant. We do not know how long the treatment lasted. In any case, in 1912 Ioffe was arrested again, and he was interned in a Siberian prison until the February revolution. There he performed amateur psychoanalysis on the other inmates, and he published the results from prison in the journal *Psychotherapy*.[30] This was a downright weak piece of work, more likely than not published by the journal as a political prank. It described the case of an exiled medic whom Ioffe had attempted to cure. After a number of false alarms, the medic committed suicide as his wife and friends looked on; it seems a few sessions with Ioffe did little to help him. The article concluded with an eery epilogue, given how Ioffe's own life would end: "Such was the tragic end of one of the many 'healthy' people of our time. Life is such a riddle! But if there is some key to solving this mystery, it can lie only in making the secret clear, in becoming conscious of the 'unconscious.' Someday this problem will be totally solved, and many, many people will be saved from the same tragic fate."

Ioffe, however, was not saved.

The Revolution Dealt with It Better

After a seven-year hiatus, Ioffe met Trotsky again. Trotsky related the circumstances:

Ioffe had been elected to the St. Petersburg City Duma, and he became the head of the Bolshevik faction there. This came as a surprise to me, but in the chaos of the era I had no time to enjoy the progress made by my old friend and student from Vienna. After I had become chairman of the Petrograd soviet, Ioffe appeared one day at Smolny to report on behalf of the Bolshevik faction in the Duma. I must confess, I was concerned about him, as I remembered him from before. But he began his speech in such a calm and assured tone that all my reservations vanished immediately. The large audience in the White Hall at Smolny beheld an impressive figure at the podium, brunette, with a wide, thick beard streaked with grey; this figure must have seemed the very embodiment of positive attitude and self-confidence.[31]

Ioffe had a deep, velvety voice, spoke in well-structured sentences and with measured gestures, and was surrounded by an aura of calmness. He had the ability to rise from colloquial tone to the level of true pathos. Trotsky was a good judge of charisma, and he gave the thirty-four-year-old Ioffe high marks for potential. "In the glamorous attire of a diplomat, with a soft smile on his peaceful face, . . . Ioffe watched with curiosity as shells exploded nearby, without speeding or slowing his step."[32]

Recalling all this from far-off Mexico, Trotsky cherished the memory of his friend, and at the same time never missed a chance to underline the striking metamorphosis that he felt had come over the man. "It came as a pleasant surprise to me: The Revolution had dealt with his nerves far better than psychoanalysis. . . . The Revolution lifted him, straightened him out, concentrated the stronger sides of his intellect and character. Only occasionally in the depths of his pupils did I encounter an excessive, almost frightening concentration."[33]

For a clearer understanding of Ioffe's neurosis and personality, it is illuminating to turn to part of his correspondence with Lenin. In a letter to Ioffe composed March 17, 1921, Lenin wrote:

> It was with great sadness that I read your deeply disturbed letter of March 15. I see that you have the most understandable reasons to be displeased and even indignant, but I assure you that you are mistaken in seeking such a reason.
>
> In the first place, you are mistaken in repeating (more than once) that I am the Tseka. This could be written only in a state of great nervous irritation and overexhaustion. Why get so upset as to *write a completely impossible, a completely impossible phrase*, like "the Tseka—that's you." It must be overexhaustion.
>
> In the second place, I am not in the least displeased with you, nor do I distrust you.[34]

The specific source of the spat is not particularly interesting: Ioffe, offended that Lenin and the Central Committee had ignored his opinion, was reprimanding Lenin for, shall we say, undemocratic tendencies. Of course, Ioffe had to be absolutely confident of his own position as a public figure, and a very brave person in general, to declare to Lenin, "the Tseka is *you*." In his response, Lenin was highly agitated, twice repeating the same words and underscoring them with a thick line. More than that, he brought up Stalin as an example to convince Ioffe: "How can this whole affair be explained? Fate has dealt you a poor hand. I have seen it in many officials. Stalin, for instance. Of course, *he* would stand up for himself." Counseling Ioffe to take a vacation, "maybe it would be best to go abroad, to a health resort," Lenin ended his letter with a stream of compliments in his typical style: "You have been and remain one of the most prominent and best of our diplomats and politicians. . . ."

In November 1924, Ioffe was appointed ambassador to Vienna, and Austrian diplomats guessed at possible underlying reasons for the appointment—either Ioffe's illness and need for treatment by the best Vienna doctors, or the decline of his influence in Moscow. In November of the following year, Ioffe arrived in Vienna for treatment once again, this time outside of his official capacity.[35] He was accompanied by his family and his personal physician, Yury Kannabikh—psychotherapist and the last president of the Russian Psychoanalytic Society.

In 1925–1927, Ioffe served as deputy chairman of the Main Committee on Concessions of the USSR, under Trotsky. He was treated in Russia by Kannabikh and Sergei Davidenkov, physicians who were at least sympathetic to psychoanalysis and who probably practiced it as well.

Not One Day Without Meaning

What happened next we know from the letter that Ioffe sent to Trotsky just before his death, on November 16, 1927. The letter was meant to be distributed among their comrades, and so three hundred copies had been made.[36]

Ioffe pinpointed the primary means used to destroy the Trotskyist opposition intellectually and organizationally as "the Party policy denying work to opposition members." After Ioffe was removed from all Party and Soviet posts by decree of the Politburo, his health went quickly downhill. Kremlin doctors diagnosed tuberculosis, myocarditis, colitis with appendicitis, and a gall bladder infection. Most of all, Ioffe was tormented by polyneuritis, which confined him to bed or a stretcher. "Prof. Davidenkov supposes that the reason for the relapse of my serious case of polyneuritis is that I have been so worried lately."[37] Ioffe's doctors informed him that he must not work, that Russian health spas would do him no good, and that he had to go abroad for treatment, for at least half a year. As we know, this was common practice at one time. But at this time, the Central Committee repeatedly delayed deciding on the question. Meanwhile, the Kremlin pharmacy stopped giving Ioffe his medicine. It was then that Ioffe recalled that he had "given several thousand rubles to our Party, in any case more than I was worth, since the Revolution deprived me of my fortune."[38] He realized that he was no longer able to pay for his own treatment.

He wrote in a letter to Trotsky that more than thirty years earlier he had "adopted the philosophy that human life is meaningful only to the extent and as long as it serves the eternity that we call humanity; after all, since everything else is finite, work in the service of anything else is without meaning." Adolf Ioffe had been only ten years old "thirty years before." "It seems to me," he wrote, "I have the right to say that my entire conscious life I have been faithful to my philosophy. . . . It seems I have the right to say that there was not a single day of my life, in this sense, that I lived without meaning."[39]

It is difficult to judge to what extent this philosophy was related to Adler's. Ioffe's psychoanalyst probably had tried to reveal all the most vital implications of this philosophy of the infinite, then striven to introduce his patient to the transitory and finite nature of human reality. If Adler interpreted Ioffe's philosophy as a symptom of his neurosis, he more than likely concluded that the illness was incurable.

In any case, Ioffe had come to the conclusion that "death now can be of more use than continuation of life." Along with Trotsky's recent expulsion from the Party, Ioffe hoped that his suicide would become "just the push needed to rouse the Party." Near the end, he decided to tell Trotsky what he had never said before. "You lack Lenin's inflexibility, his unwillingness to give in. . . . You were always right politically, but you often denied your own rectitude. . . . Now you are more right than ever . . . so do not fear, now."[40]

In His Own Hands

There is a particular motif in Trotsky's words, as they stray far from the familiar intonations of Lenin and Stalin. It is probably due to this motif that he has retained his attraction for his followers at opposite ends of the planet.

> Man at last will begin to harmonize himself in earnest. He will make it his business to achieve beauty by giving the movement of his own limbs the utmost precision, purposefulness, and economy, in his work, his walk, and his play. He will try to master first the semiconscious and then the subconscious processes in his own organism, such as breathing, the circulation of the blood, digestion, reproduction, and, within necessary limits, he will try to subordinate them to the control of reason and will. Even purely physiologic life will become subject to collective experiments. The human species, the coagulated *homo sapiens,* will once more enter into a state of radical transformation, and, in his own hands, will become an object of the most complicated methods of artificial selection and psycho-physical training. This is entirely in accord with evolution.[41]

This dreamer, a minister of defense and of the navy, was prepared to go further than his colleagues: He aimed to seize upon and consciously regulate not only what went on in the factory, the marketplace, and the family, but also what went on in the conjugal bed and even within the human body. Exactitude and expediency, Trotsky's highest values, were attainable only one way: through awareness. For him, beauty was equated with consciousness. The opposite held true as well; everything unconscious, random, and spontaneous was ugly and repulsive. Nothing should happen by itself, he felt, as it had in the accursed past. Only what was thought through, conscious, and systematic deserved to exist.

"As he rises, Man purges from the top down: first he rids himself of God, then the foundation of government starting with the Czar, then he purges his economy of chaos and competition, then he moves on to his internal world, driving out the dark and the unconscious."[42] Trotsky's pen slips ever so smoothly, almost unnoticeably, from atheism and socialism into psychoanalysis, from Bolshevik banality to ideas that are completely extraordinary, ideas more utopian than the communist utopia itself! All this fits together into a cogent and familiar pattern: a purge from the top down.

Throughout this passage, layers of youthful romanticism and revolutionary pragmatism alternate: The old life is hateful, but the new one must be kept under control. "Communist life will not be formed blindly, like coral islands, but will be built consciously, will be tested by thought, will be directed and corrected. Life will cease to be elemental, and for this reason stagnant."[43]

What's wrong with coral islands, one might ask? For Trotsky, there was no such thing as a nature where beautiful things came into being of their own accord. Man could and should alter nature. He was already altering it. When he had remade the nature of things, was it not inevitable that he would set about changing his own nature? "We may be able to drive a railway across the whole Sahara, build the Eiffel Tower, and talk with New York by radio, but can we really not improve man? Yes; we will be able to! To issue a new 'improved edition' of man—that is the further task of communism."[44]

All this was well and good, but Marxism never went quite that far. Marx had provided instructions on how to transform the relations of production, but he seemed to think man would change automatically. This never came to be, however, and moreover nothing should happen "automatically" for a revolutionary. Therefore, many people at that time were casting about in all directions, seeking a superstructure that would adequately update and equip Marxism for new tasks. Later, throughout the 1930s, many leftist intellectuals, including such serious thinkers as Karl Mannheim, wrote of the possibility of "transforming mankind" with the help of psychoanalysis.[45] Against this background, Trotsky's approach doesn't look all that out of place. Within the bounds of his logic, Freudianism emerged as the direct continuation and even the perfection of Marxism, just as Marxism was the continuation and perfection of science in general. If Marxism drove the natural element out of the base, Freudianism would eliminate it from the superstructure.

> This is entirely in accord with evolution. Man first drove the dark element out of industry and ideology, by displacing barbaric routine by scientific technique and religion by science. Afterwards he drove the unconscious out of politics, by overthrowing monarchy and class with democracy and rationalist parliamentarianism, and then with the clear and open Soviet dictatorship. The blind elements have settled most heavily in economic relations, but man is driving them out from there also, by means of the Socialist organization of economic life. This makes it possible to reconstruct fundamentally the traditional family life. Finally, the nature of man himself is hidden in the deepest and darkest corner of the unconscious, of the elemental, of the sub-soil. Is it not self-evident that the greatest efforts of investigative thought and of creative initiative will be in that direction?[46]

It is indeed clear that they were already headed in that direction; and only the crass and uncouth could have had any second thoughts in this regard. According to Trotsky, the old Nietzschean task of reconstructing man presented no particular difficulties. He found only two problems: First, there had to be boldness and concentration on this important goal. This task was perfectly clear to the man who had been chairman of the Revolutionary Military Council. It had to be emphasized again and again, sparing no eloquence, with total confidence: "Man will look for the first time at himself as if at raw material, or at best, as at a half-finished product, and say, 'I've finally got you, my dear *homo sapiens;* now I can get to work on you, friend!'"[47] Secondly, science was of the utmost importance. Trotsky understood this and formulated the problem in a politically correct, materialistic way: "We must first know Man from every angle, we must know his anatomy, his physiology and the part of his physiology that is called psychology."

Much later, in 1932, as an unwanted emigrant but still a powerful orator, Trotsky would repeat in Copenhagen:

> Anthropology, biology, physiology, and psychology have accumulated mountains of material to raise up before mankind in their full scope the tasks of perfecting and developing the body and spirit. Psychoanalysis, with the inspired hand of Sigmund Freud, has lifted the cover of the well which is poetically called the "soul." And what has been revealed? Our conscious thought is only a small part of the work of the dark, psychic forces. . . . Human thought, descending to the bottom of its own psychic sources, must shed light on the most mysterious driving forces of the soul and subject them to reason and to will.
> Once he has done with the anarchic forces of his own society, man will set to work on himself, in the pestle and the retort of the chemist. For the first time mankind will see itself as raw material, or at best as a physical and psy-

chic semi-finished product. . . . [T]he man of today, with all his contradictions and lack of harmony, will open the road for a new and happier race.[48]

The Well Metaphor

Ivan Pavlov was an awkward man for the authorities, as he did many things for which no one else would have been forgiven. In 1920, he applied for emigration. The question was mulled over at the highest levels of government by Lenin, Gorky, Lunacharsky, and others. The great scientist was persuaded to stay after he was promised firewood and meat for his laboratory, after certain confiscated property was returned, and probably after some threats.

At about the same time, a large-scale expulsion of scholars was in the works, a campaign that affected many of the famous people who disagreed with the new government: Berdyaev, Ilyin, and many others. Pavlov was treated differently. It could be that his specialty was seen by the Bolsheviks as strategically important, directly related to their plans to remake and reforge mankind. We might recall that it was about this time that Otto Schmidt—a Bolshevik, astronomer, and the "curator" of Soviet psychoanalysis—gave a speech before the ministry of education supporting the plan to crossbreed man and monkey.

After negotiations between Lenin and the Cheka,[49] Pavlov was allowed to tour the West on a lecture circuit. He returned from his trip even more independently inclined. The lecture he gave on September 25, 1923, is particularly well known for its sharp criticism of the Bolsheviks.[50] There were immediate and totally opposite reactions from two key players in Russian history of that time: Trotsky and Bukharin. The latter rebuked Pavlov in a series of long, crude, and perfectly typical articles (see chapter 8): "As for our governing circles, we venture to assure Professor Pavlov that they understand a good deal more of biology and physiology than Prof. Pavlov does in the social sciences."[51] Meanwhile, just after Pavlov's lecture, Trotsky sent him a personal letter.[52] Although it was quite personal, the letter was published in Trotsky's collection of works, prepared by him just before his expulsion, one of the only epistles that was included. It is clear, therefore, that the letter's theme and addressee were of importance to him.

The subject of Trotsky's communication is surprising. The letter proposes that Pavlov's physiology of conditioned reflexes be united with Freudian psychoanalysis. Trotsky wrote respectfully, admitting that he was but a dilettante in these issues, but he did not neglect to mention his personal acquaintance with the Freudians of Vienna, a connection he hoped would justify his initiative. Trotsky wrote, "Your doctrine of conditioned reflexes, it seems to me, embraces Freud's theory as an individual case." If Pavlov had agreed with this, psychoanalysis in Russia would have had the support of his authority. Arguing for the compatibility and complementary nature of the two greatest scientific schools of the century, Trotsky found a powerful image: "Both Pavlov and Freud assert that the 'bottom' of the soul is its physiology. But Pavlov, like a diver, plunges to the bottom and painstakingly examines the well from the bottom up. Meanwhile, Freud stands above the well and tries to see or divine the outlines of the bottom, staring penetratingly through the depths of the ever rippling, murky water." The same logic was also applied to the connection between Marxism and Freudianism. "The attempt to declare psychoanalysis 'incompatible' with Marxism and turn our backs on Freudianism is simpleminded, or at least a bit simplistic. But we are in no way obliged to adopt Freudianism."

In 1923, Trotsky was the second in command of the Bolshevik government. Pavlov, a Nobel laureate and quite nearly the Bolsheviks' most treasured intellectual asset, was also an influential figure. In addition, the letter was published not by archivists but by Trotsky himself, while he was still in the USSR. Trotsky felt no need to hide this strategic idea, even after he had suffered defeat.

Since then, Pavlov and Freud have been compared and contrasted any number of times, and decades of dogmatic discourse have wiped out any interest in Russia in the question that Trotsky raised. At the same time, Pavlov and Freud each recognized each other's scientific accomplishments. An American mathematician who visited Moscow in the 1930s met with Pavlov, who told him that the idea of inhibition came to him as he was reading a book by Freud and Breuer on hysteria. Passing through Vienna on his way back, the American related this to Freud, who commented dolefully that if Pavlov had said something about it earlier, this affinity might have been of use.[53] Other early psychoanalysts also looked favorably on Pavlov's experiments and even on his theories. Jones, for example, in the 1920s published a positive review of the English translation of Pavlov's book on higher nervous system activity.

Even during the darkest years, there were intelligent, thinking people working within the framework of the Pavlovian school, people who respected the ideas of psychoanalysis. In 1947, Sergei Davidenkov's book was released in Leningrad, in which he attempted a theoretical synthesis between Pavlovian physiology and evolutionary genetics and the ethnography of Sir J. G. Frazer and L. Sternberg. In his book, Davidenkov displayed unexpected erudition and intellectual daring. He named Freud, whom he referred to as a "subtle observer" and "a talented clinician," the direct forerunner of his ideas.[54]

Davidenkov was an eminent neuropathologist who had worked with Vyacheslav Ivanov as the rector of the University of Baku at the beginning of the 1920s. He had served as a physician in the Kremlin for a time and later headed the Leningrad Neurosis Clinic, where Pavlov held his

Wednesday meetings. According to Natalya Traugott, who attended these sessions at the beginning of the 1930s, clinical talks on psychoanalytic treatment were quite common. At these seminars, which were conducted as a form of clinical investigation, Pavlov often digressed into theoretical tangents. He showed no irritation when speaking of Freud, and said that "Freud digs from above, while we dig from below." This formula, in fact a paraphrase of Trotsky's well metaphor, carries on the same idea: that psychoanalysis and "materialist physiology" are compatible.

But as far as is known, seventy-four-year-old Pavlov never responded to Trotsky's call to action. Bukharin, however, did manage to gain the scientist's confidence. Pavlov once gave his opinion of him: "Nikolai Ivanovich is a man with a fine mind, a real intellectual. But how can he be a revolutionary at the same time? After all, he's a true Russian intellectual sniveler!"[55]

A Chance for Power
Is a Chance for Psychoanalysis

"What is one to say about the psycho-analytic theory of Freud? Can it be reconciled with materialism, as, for instance, Karl Radek thinks (and I also) . . . ?"[56] Such were Trotsky's words, inscribed in the platform of the Trotskyist movement, the book *Literature and Revolution.* Trotsky was then the mighty leader of a totalitarian state, and the texts he published, the letters he sent, even mere rumors about their contents, were taken as guidelines for action—although not by everyone, naturally. Around this time, several articles were released in central Bolshevik magazines sharply attacking Freudianism and, in the same stroke, indirectly deriding the movement's instigator in Russia. Nonetheless, the thinking of Moscow's Freudo-marxists such as Alexander Luria and Boris Friedmann was very close to Trotsky's position in both theoretical and political terms.

Georgii Malis, the author of a book called *Psychoanalysis of Communism,* published in Kharkov in 1924, cited Trotsky liberally, enthusiastically putting forward ideas and completing thoughts that the great leader either never intended to express or that simply had never occurred to him. The book begins with an assertion in boldface that is indeed very important: "It is not by chance that psychoanalysis has been given such an opportunity to develop in our country." Psychoanalysis, according to Malis, was a fundamental tool in the great reexamination of values, in conjunction with Marxism. This reevaluation would soon transform the whole of human intellectual life. The current scale was not large enough to satisfy the author: "Human thought has to bring about the same revolution in ideology as has already begun in economics." As culture became more complex, Malis argued, man was forced to sublimate his desires more and more, which was why the number of mentally ill was on the rise. In the harmonious society of tomorrow, as was the case in prehistoric societal groupings, there would be nothing to sublimate, nor any reason to do so. "We have the good fortune to bear witness to the painful birth of a new society, one that will reveal to each human being all forms of gratification." Malis insisted that "in communist society there will be no neuroses, no religion, no philosophy, no art." What would there be, then? The response sounds a bit abstract: "Social structure will be the social implementation of the human unconscious." The year was 1924, a communist government was in power, and it needed more concrete prescriptions. Here, Malis naturally hung all his hopes on the children and their education in a new spirit: "Children must be united into monolithic social groups with elected leaders"; these "communist battalions" would be able to "swallow the child whole." The primary enemies of this golden age, unexpectedly, would be the teachers; Malis's childish hatred toward them is perhaps the most surprising feature of his essay. "Because soon in the diversity of communist society each unit will be able to find a true place for itself, there will be no 'teachers,' people unable to find that place now." School reformers, whom Malis acridly called "instant pedologists," would not be up to the task. Teachers were the "most broken-down element of society." Psychoanalysis, however, was presented as a communist alternative to all teaching methods, a path even more radical than the policy adopted by the ministry of education.[57]

The political link between Trotsky and Russian psychoanalysts has been underestimated in Western literature on the history of psychoanalysis. Trotsky's own public statements, as well as references to him made by communist supporters of psychoanalysis, are not the only evidence in support of the hypothesis that the early Soviet psychoanalytic movement was highly dependent on him. The movement's historical window of opportunity unmistakably shadowed the zigzag of Trotsky's political career. The apogee of the movement's strength in the beginning of the 1920s was the time when Trotsky was exerting maximal influence; 1927—the year of his downfall—was the year when Moisei Wulff defected and the Russian Psychoanalytic Society fell into stagnation. By the beginning of the 1930s, a time of violence against everything that bore any resemblance to Trotsky, all memory of the recently frantic activity of Russian psychoanalysts had vanished. In the ideological polemics of the end of the 1920s, psychoanalysts (and later pedologists as well) were often accused of Trotskyism. And indeed, some of the members of the Russian Psychoanalytic Society, like writer Alexei Voronsky and diplomat and society vice president Viktor Kopp, were conspicuous figures in the Trotskyist opposition.

The Moscow-based analysts participated willingly and actively in the construction of communism. These people were enchanted by the perspectives thrown open for the scientific transformation of life; they were equally enchanted by their newfound intimacy with the government and fascinated by political intrigue. They sincerely believed that their psychoanalytic knowledge would make a great, even a decisive contribution to the victory of the new ideas of which their knowledge was a part. Meanwhile, the unparalleled privileges that psychoanalysts enjoyed at the beginning of the 1920s, such as the supply of foodstuffs from German labor unions, could probably not have been arranged without the direct support of the highest authorities. In the Soviet system, assistance from political elites was given anonymously, and as a result, without responsibility. We have noted certain signs that the activity of the Moscow Psychoanalytic Society and its orphanage was supported by a variety of people—Krupskaya, Radek, and even Stalin. But this indirect evidence cannot compare with Trotsky's direct speech.

In popularizing and defending Freud's ideas in the Marxist press, the group of Moscow analysts and the philosophers who shared an affinity with them were at the same time developing and defending Trotsky's theses, which were well known to their readers. On the one hand, they were standing up for their right to do what they loved to do, something they were sure was useful to society; on the other hand, they were participating in a dangerous political game, the outcome and stakes of which remained a mystery to all.

This political aspect of the Russian society's activity is extremely important. It would be inaccurate to imagine the organization's leaders as dissidents bravely opposing the system, or as autistic intellectuals who paid the political process no heed and occupied themselves exclusively with their patients and books. Both images merely confound these people of the 1920s with those who gained their political and clinical experience in Russia half a century later. Nor was the situation reminiscent of the moment when psychoanalysis was quashed in Nazi Germany, which Jones characterized as "one of Hitler's few successful achievements."[58] The situation was certainly nothing like the peaceful but alienated coexistence of analysts and the state so familiar in the West.

The people who created the revolution were then facing one vital, all-encompassing problem: The new society had been formed, but there was no way people could live in it; they didn't know how, and more importantly, they didn't want to. This has been proven, and it was common knowledge. Let us, then, examine the choices faced by those who came to grips with this dilemma for the first time, and the paths they might have taken to overcome this situation.

One possibility was retreat. Let people live the way they want, the way they know, and as they are able—or at least something approximating that. This choice was generally associated with Lenin and his New Economic Policy. There was another possibility: to use artificial selection to pick out those prepared to live in the new society, and get rid of everyone else. This path is also familiar, and it is associated with Stalin and the gulag. It seems that Trotsky, whom political opponents endlessly criticized for haughtiness, was looking for a third possibility, the most ambitious and romantic of all, and the most unrealistic. If people were incapable of living in the new society, then people had to be remade. To transform human nature! But how? Marxism couldn't help there, as Marx hadn't foreseen the situation at hand. Risky incursions into unfamiliar territory had to be made.

Reading Trotsky's works from the 1920s, it begins to seem as if the Kremlin dreamer sincerely believed that at any moment he would find the Philosopher's Stone among the latest scientific advances, some device that would make people happy in the society that he and his comrades had created. He seems to have been confident that once he found it, he would be able to justify everything. This is probably why he appeared to be so passive during the years that proved so decisive for him and for history—there was more at stake for him than just power. To bring together Pavlov and Freud; to conclude a union with them on behalf of the victorious Party, and to put old *homo sapiens* to practical work at long last—with goals like these, who wouldn't have their minds on higher matters!

Reich in the Communist Academy

In 1929, Wilhelm Reich, a psychoanalyst and communist who tried his whole life to achieve a Freudomarxist synthesis, made a two-month pilgrimage to Moscow. In Reich's opinion, "sexuality became aware of itself in the person of Sigmund Freud, just as economy began to be aware of itself in the person of Karl Marx."[59]

His special interest was the sexual revolution, and at the beginning of the 1930s he applied unbelievable energy trying to involve the German Communist Party and the Fourth (Trotskyist) International in his "sexpolitik." In 1931, Reich organized the German Association for the Sexual Politics of the Proletariat, known by the acronym Sexpol. He wrote to Trotsky in October 1933, generalizing his impressions of Russia: The onset of reaction there, he concluded, was due to the fact that the sexual revolution had been halted in 1923. As their correspondence bears witness, Trotsky politely declined Reich's invitation to participate in the global sexual revolution.[60] A year later, Reich tried to get Sergey Eisenstein on his side, but failed on that count as well.[61]

While plugging his ideas in Moscow in 1929, Reich gave several lectures at the Communist Academy and published an article in the journal *Under the Banner of Marxism.* His visit had no further effect, as he was unable to convince the Academy of the need for sexual revolution. Later he would accuse "those scoundrels" in Moscow of organizing a campaign against him in the German Communist Party.[62]

When he returned to Vienna, Reich published a report on his travels in a psychoanalytic journal.[63] According to him, the Russians did not decry psychoanalysis as an empirical method, they were only against "Freudism," which they saw as a false social doctrine. Young people, he said, were very interested in psychoanalysis; but the ruling party was condemning it because debates on psychoanalysis were distracting them from political work. Aron Zalkind, he held, was his most aggressive critic in Moscow: Zalkind had scolded him for being diplomatic and accused him of trying to hide the real substance of Freudianism from the Communist Academy. In Berlin, the recently emigrated Moisei Wulff wrote a rebuttal to Reich's article for the same journal, saying that Reich was "trying to prove that psychoanalysis can be acceptable to Marxists," but that this would not happen to psychoanalysis, "because what would be left if it should happen would hardly deserve the name of psychoanalysis." According to Wulff, "in a country where Party censorship rules, where there is no freedom of speech nor freedom of thought," psychoanalysis was doomed. Wulff concluded, however, that there was "a strong interest in psychoanalysis outside the Communist Party—among scholars, teachers, lawyers, and even doctors."[64]

In his book *Mass Psychology and Fascism,* first published several months after the Nazis came to power, Reich asserted that fascism enjoyed the mass support of the working class. He explained that this phenomenon, never recognized by orthodox Marxism, was the realization of the authoritarian character structures that form in sexually repressed people within patriarchal systems.[65]

Reich's views passed through a curious evolution with time, one reminiscent of the Soviet Freudomarxists', who gradually retrained themselves as pedologists (see chapter 8). Beginning with traditional psychoanalytic work, he eventually came to a conclusion incredible for an analyst: that therapy was pointless. "There is no use in individual therapy! Of course, you can make money and help here and there. But from the point of view of social problems, problems of mental hygiene, there is no use." Like his Soviet opponent Aron Zalkind, Reich switched over to working with children. It seemed to him then that only this kind of work would provide the means to transform human nature in the desired direction. "There is no use in anything except working with children. You should go back to the unspoiled protoplasm."[66]

In 1934, Reich was expelled from the International Psychoanalytic Association. According to Jones, "Freud had thought highly of him in his early days, but Reich's political fanaticism had led to both personal and scientific estrangement."[67] Almost simultaneously, but probably for other reasons, Reich was kicked out of the German Communist Party as well.

A Man of High Integrity

The life and career of Max Eitingon (1881–1943), one of the leaders of the early psychoanalytic movement, is also strangely intertwined with Soviet

Russian history, the applied policy of the Bolsheviks, and Trotsky's fate. Born in Mogilev, Eitingon lived in Germany from early childhood, studied at one of the centers of Russian student life in the West—the department of philosophy at Marburg—and then took up medicine. As an assistant at the Burghölzli clinic with Jung, Eitingon was the first foreigner to visit Freud and express admiration for his works, and also the first to consult with him on a difficult case. In 1909 (at the same time as Tatiana Rosenthal and a bit earlier than Sabina Spielrein), he defended his doctoral dissertation at the University of Zurich. His topic was the associative experiment under conditions of epilepsy.[68]

Jung, who was Eitingon's doctoral advisor in Zurich, treated him with a measure of irony. We have already read Jung's words to Freud about how Eitingon would someday become a deputy to the Duma.[69] Jones had a hard time believing that Freud could take Eitingon's intellectual capacity seriously. On the other hand, Eitingon remained ever faithful to Freud, whose "lightest wish or opinion was decisive for him." For the rest, Jones added, Eitingon was very susceptible to influence, "one could not always be sure of what his own opinion was."[70]

Sandor Rado, who worked closely with Eitingon, told much about the man in his memoirs. "He was philosophically excellently trained, cultured, enormously inhibited, but extremely good as a man who could build an organization; and he idolized Freud. . . . He never in his life wrote a clinical article or ever delivered anything but a general speech. He was an organizer, which meant that his name was put on paper while other people did the work. But do not get me wrong. He was a man of high integrity."[71] A certain duality, or perhaps incompleteness, marks almost all recollections of Eitingon. Analysts like Ferenczi and Binswanger thought very highly of him, however. Lev Shestov, an important Russian émigré philosopher and a man of immaculate scruples, also harbored deep respect for Eitingon (see chapter 2).

Freud trusted Eitingon immeasurably, and this trust only grew with the years. In 1920, Eitingon became a member of the committee, the secret group made up of Freud's six closest students, a panel that exerted decisive influence on the policy of the International Psychoanalytic Association. Eitingon was one of Freud's closest protégés; he was given the authority to speak for the teacher, and he headed a variety of psychoanalytic enterprises. He is credited with the opening of the Berlin Psychoanalytic Institute and Clinic in 1920, which saw the first systematic examination of patients and elaboration of procedures for psychoanalytic training. The Berlin Institute was doubtless the model for the State Psychoanalytic Institute in Moscow. In 1926, Eitingon was elected president of the International Psychoanalytic Association, and he fulfilled his responsibilities in that capacity for many years.

Eitingon practically never missed Freud's birthday, and Freud's door was always open to Eitingon, although for others he became more and more inaccessible. For example, in 1929 only Lou Andreas-Salomé and Eitingon attended the ailing Freud's birthday.[72] Unlike those in his professional circle, however, he was an unproductive scientist and author.

Eitingon was rich, and this rare quality was unfailingly mentioned by all who wrote of him. Jones, for example, referred to him as the only psychoanalyst in the world at that time who owned private capital.[73] It is well known that he used his own funds to finance the opening of a psychoanalytic publishing house in Vienna that put out Freud's works, journals of the Association, and so forth; the founding of the Berlin Institute, of which he was the director; the famous sculpted portrait of Freud; and many other efforts. Eitingon was also responsible for the modest sums of cash that were given periodically on Freud's behalf to Lou Andreas-Salomé, who had lost her money to the Bolsheviks but still managed to help her relatives, who remained in Russia until the 1930s. Finally, Eitingon often lent money to Freud himself during the lean, postwar years, a practice that met with displeasure in Freud's family.

Freud himself deeply appreciated this assistance. An impression of their relations can be gleaned from a letter addressed to Eitingon in honor of the fifteenth anniversary of their meeting (in 1922):

> For many years I was aware of your efforts to come closer to me, and I kept you at bay. Only after you had expressed in such affectionate terms the desire to belong to my family—in the closest sense—did I surrender to the easy trusting ways of my earlier years, accepted you and ever since have allowed you to render me every kind of service, imposed on you every kind of task. . . . So I suggest that we continue our relationship which has developed from friendship to sonship until the end of my days.[74]

Ten years later, Freud wished Eitingon a happy fiftieth birthday, writing: "I rarely said this to you, but I never forget what you have done for us over the years." Official congratulations from the International Psychoanalytic Association to its "Dear President" were composed by Ferenczi. The note stressed Eitingon's "high merits," his "boundless and productive activity," and "unfailing manners and readiness to help."[75]

When historians note Eitingon's exceptional contribution to the development of the international psychoanalytic movement, they usually speak of his great entrepreneurial spirit and energy as an organizer and his ability to extract some benefit for his cause from any circumstances.[76] Elisabeth Roudinesco, whose study came out before any compromising material on Eitingon was uncovered, held him up as a hero of the diaspora, a wanderer in eternal search of a homeland and an identity. "In Zurich he was from Vienna, in Vienna he was a Berliner, and in Berlin he dreamed of Jerusalem. Everywhere he was Russian, . . . and most of all he was a Jew."[77]

It was thought that Eitingon had inherited his fortune. On the other hand, Jones said the family business that yielded Eitingon's income was based in America. The crisis of 1929 put Eitingon in a difficult position, according to Jones, and he was forced to take up a collection among his colleagues for the maintenance of the Berlin Institute, and a year later for the psychoanalytic publishing house.[78]

Immediately following Hitler's rise to power, Eitingon traveled to Vienna to discuss the situation with Freud. The Nazis were demanding that Jews be fired from administrative positions in scientific institutes and societies. Freud called on Eitingon to stand firm: "Just like you I shall leave my place only at the very last moment and probably not even then."[79] Nevertheless, both were lucky enough to escape, each in his own way. Freud left five years after Eitingon (see chapter 9), who resigned from his posts in Berlin as early as August 1933.

The new chairman of the German Society of Psychotherapy, M. H. Göring (Hermann Göring's cousin), purged the ranks of psychoanalysis on ethnic grounds. Jung cooperated with Göring, in the interest of constructing a new, Aryan psychology. True, Jung was far away in Switzerland, and his contribution was mainly theoretical. But he remained active in his position as editor of the Nazi psychotherapeutic journal as late as 1940, when he finally resigned.

Eitingon left for Jerusalem, where he organized a local section of the International Psychoanalytic Association (recognized by the parent group as early as 1934) and the Psychoanalytic Institute.[80]

Soviet Furs for International Psychoanalysis

Max Eitingon (Soviet and Israeli sources call him Mark) was the co-owner of an enterprise that traded furs from the Soviet Union. This was the source of his fortune, as well as the primary source of financing for the undertakings of the Berlin psychoanalysts. From the memoirs of Sandor Rado we learn:

> His personal income did not come from his medical practice, which he did not have; but it flowed from a fur enterprise his family ran in five countries. The Eitingons were one of the biggest fur traders. They had an establishment in Russia, one in Poland, one in England, two in Germany, and one here [in the United States]. The old man had died, and Max Eitingon's brother-in-law ran the whole enterprise, and then came the years of the depression, during which all this began to collapse. For a while, even under the communist regime, they had the biggest contract with the Russians for furs.[81]

The monopoly on foreign trade was one of Lenin's main ideas, and more importantly, one of his government's few attainable goals. The Eitingons' large-scale export of Russian pelts to the West could have been conducted only with approval from the highest echelon, as hard-currency earnings did not come in through the usual state export-import channels. Ironically, whatever else the money earned by the Eitingon brothers' fur imports was spent on, we know for certain that some of it was used to finance the psychoanalytic movement.

He Never Became a Duma Deputy, but Was He an NKVD Agent?

Max's relative Naum Eitingon (or Ettingon; there are different records of his first name, as well: Western sources refer to him as Leonid[82]) was one of the most powerful commanders of Stalin's NKVD,[83] an organizer and participant in many of its secret operations. In the words of Russian historians of the era, "In the 1930s Naum Eitingon stood behind the scenes of many (and perhaps all) of the NKVD's sabotage operations abroad."[84] General Eitingon orchestrated the most famous of these adventures personally, including the murder of a Soviet defector and former NKVD agent named Ignaz Reiss in Switzerland in 1937, the abduction of General Yevgeny Miller in Paris the same year, the assassination of Trotsky's son, Lev Sedov, in a Paris hospital in 1938, and finally the liquidation of Trotsky himself in Mexico in 1940. Naum Eitingon was Caridad Mercader's lover, and it was he who hired and paid her son Ramon to break into Trotsky's home and plant an icepick in his brain.

After Naum Eitingon returned from Mexico, he was received by a grateful Stalin, who awarded him the Order of Lenin, embraced him, and swore that as long as he, Stalin, was alive, not a hair would be touched on Eitingon's head. As the deputy head of the GRU,[85] Naum Eitingon directed Soviet espionage in the West until 1952. Only a short time before Stalin's death was he removed from that post, which he had occupied longer than any of his colleagues. At the end of 1953, after Stalin's death, Eitingon was sentenced to twelve years in prison for supporting Beria. Nevertheless, the master's promise was kept even after his death. After waiting out his sentence, Eitingon returned to Moscow and lived out his days peacefully and inconspicuously, working as an editor at the Mezhdunarodnaia Kniga publishing house.

Psychoanalyst Max Eitingon was implicated in at least one of General Naum Eitingon's illegal schemes, the scandalous kidnapping of General Miller, by subsequent testimony in criminal court proceedings. At the time of his murder, Yevgeny Miller headed the Russian Inter-Army Union (ROVS), an émigré organization of the White (anti-Bolshevik) movement. Soviet propaganda, beginning in about 1925, accused the ROVS and Trotskyists of joining forces to carry out sabotage within the Soviet Union.[86] Soviet intelligence agents gradually infiltrated the organization's leadership until it was peppered with them. Emigré politicians Boris Savinkov and Vasily Shulgin were forcibly returned to the USSR, and Generals Alexander Kutepov and Yevgeny Miller disappeared. Miller's abduction was part of a larger and more ominous conspiracy. The plan was carried out by Naum Eitingon, along with a White general named Nikolai Skoblin—a double agent for the Soviet NKVD and its Nazi German counterpart, the SD—who became the next head of the ROVS. Fake documents prepared under Skoblin's direction, alleging that Marshal Mikhail Tukhachevsky harbored pro-German sentiments, were handed over to Stalin through the president of Czechoslovakia. We know that Hitler was aware of the operation and approved of it. It is unclear whether Stalin knew that the documents he received were forgeries. In any case, the result was the annihilation of the entire Soviet military command on the eve of the German invasion.

When Naum Eitingon kidnapped General Miller in September 1937, the way was opened for Skoblin to take over the White émigré movement. By other accounts, Miller was taken out because he knew too much about Skoblin's interests. The case was taken up, however, by the French police, which usually did its best to turn a blind eye to such happenings in the émigré community. Skoblin disappeared forever, and the trial focused on his wife, popular émigré singer Nadezhda Plevitskaya.

Czar Nicholas II once told Plevitskaya during an encounter at Livadia, his summer palace in the Crimea: "I once thought it would be impossible to be more Russian than me. Your singing has proven otherwise."[87] During her wild youth, the singer toured Russia with Nikolai Kliuyev, a poet and self-proclaimed *khlyst*. In Berlin, one of Plevitskaya's admirers was Max Eitingon (we recall the words Freud wrote long ago of young Eitingon's romantic fancies, that "such practice is a deterrent from theory"[88]). Later, Plevitskaya spilled the beans in court, admitting that Max "dressed her from head to toe" and financed the publication of her two-volume memoirs. In the records of the police investigation, which have not yet been fully declassified by the French, Max Eitingon's name is mentioned several times, according to historian J. Dziak. Dziak followed the trail of this case at the request of U.S. military intelligence, and he went so far as to presume that Max Eitingon recruited both Plevitskaya and Skoblin.[89] Plevitskaya testified that Max saw her off at the train station two days after Miller's kidnapping, where she got on a train for Florence with the intention of fleeing from there to Palestine. Dziak's hypothesis was corroborated by the singer's prison diary, which recently turned up in the archives of Columbia University.[90] The journal included allusions to the fact that Skoblin met "with the Bolsheviks" in the 1920s in Max Eitingon's Berlin home. The latter subsequently sent them a Bible from Jerusalem that contained cipher codes. The book was seized during a search and became one of the key pieces of evidence against Plevitskaya. The singer and her friends knew about the "Eitingons' dealings with the Bolsheviks, how they buy up furs in

Siberia and send them off to London." In addition, it was established during the trial that Plevitskaya and Skoblin spent ten times more than they earned.

The singer was convicted by a French court for her part in Miller's abduction. Nina Berberova was at the trial and included the story in her memoirs, relating how Plevitskaya denied everything.[91] Later, however, she confessed to her lawyer that the accusations against her were correct. She died in a French prison in 1940.

Plevitskaya's testimony and Rado's recollections indicate that Max Eitingon could well have been an accomplice in a subtle political game that was being played on a pan-European scale, in which the leader of international psychoanalysis carried out the commands of Stalin's secret service. However, most of the evidence to that effect is circumstantial. A definitive judgment will have to wait until the opening of the Soviet and French archives. Nonetheless, Rado's claims about Eitingon's financial affairs and about the Soviet sources of his capital seem extremely important. It would appear that today there are sufficient data to link Max Eitingon in one degree or another with his brother-in-law's schemes. In any case, we can conclude from what Sandor Rado revealed that at the beginning and even the middle of the 1920s, during the reign of Trotsky and the height of Soviet psychoanalysis, the international psychoanalytic movement was financed indirectly by Soviet money.

In this light, the psychoanalytic interests of another political figure, Viktor Kopp, begin to make more sense. This diplomat of the Bolshevik school, the first official Soviet representative in Berlin (1919–1921), showed up at the Russian Psychoanalytic Society soon after a series of speeches by Trotsky in which the latter attempted to enlist psychoanalysis in the service of communism, declaring himself a defender of the discipline. Kopp, who was three years older than Ioffe, was also in Vienna in 1909 and worked alongside Ioffe under Trotsky's direction at *Pravda*. Later, in 1918, it was Ioffe who laid the groundwork for Kopp's diplomatic career.[92] Of course, he also became involved with the psychoanalytic interests and acquaintances that his *Pravda* colleagues maintained in the Vienna émigré community. Beyond these specifics, we know nothing about the psychoanalytic career of the man who became vice president of the Russian society. We do know that Kopp later became the Soviet ambassador to Japan and Sweden; and in 1927 he joined the Trotskyist opposition.

During his term as vice president of the Russian Psychoanalytic Society, Kopp also occupied a post as the representative of the foreign ministry to the Council of Ministers, and he was a member of the collegium of the foreign ministry. This probably meant that he was responsible for coordinating the Bolshevik government's foreign economic, diplomatic, and hard-currency operations.

One might suppose from these facts that Viktor Kopp's participation in the management of the Psychoanalytic Society was not so much scientific or organizational as it was operational. This supposition is indirectly supported by the unusual ties between psychoanalytic Moscow and psychoanalytic Berlin in 1923–1924. The State Psychoanalytic Institute in Moscow was financed by a German trade union, Otto and Vera Schmidt traveled to Berlin, and Kopp was elected vice president of the society shortly after he arrived from Berlin. One might suppose that Kopp was linked to the Eitingons' fur business. As vice president of the Russian Psychoanalytic Society, Kopp became Max Eitingon's official partner, creating a channel of communication that was legal from a Western point of view and could serve as a cover for joint activity of a totally different sort.

The Suicide of the Intelligentsia

If Max Eitingon took part in the crimes committed abroad by the Stalin regime, he was certainly not the only intellectual to have done so; even more famous people participated in these events, including some who had absolutely no connection to Russia. Under Naum Eitingon's direction, the armed attack on Trotsky was carried out by Mexican artist David Siquieros, while Chilean poet Pablo Neruda was fired from the diplomatic corps for issuing Siquieros the visa that allowed him to escape from the Mexican authorities after the assassination. Lev Sedov and Ignaz Reiss were killed through the direct collaboration of Mark Zborovsky, an anthropologist who worked with Margaret Mead and later leaked to the Americans the whereabouts of a network of KGB agents—information that bought him a pardon.[93]

Sergei Efron, author and husband of Marina Tsvetaeva, a Eurasianist by conviction, also took part in the plots cooked up by Naum Eitingon's group. Reiss's murder was on his conscience, and he participated in the Miller affair. Efron managed to escape back to the USSR, something he had dreamt of for decades in emigration. In his homeland he was arrested a short time later and executed. Tsvetaeva, who probably learned of her husband's involvement only after his departure, found herself ostracized by émigré circles in Paris. Nobody wanted to talk to the wife of a Bolshevik agent. Only Eitingon's cousin, who was living in Paris at the time, came to her aid.[94] In the end Tsvetaeva herself, though a brilliant poet and a woman of unimpeachable respectability, returned voluntarily to the USSR, to her murderous husband and the control of murderers.

Tsvetaeva's fate, giving up her freedom and returning to inevitable suicide, was symbolic of that entire generation of Russian intellectuals. Pavlov once wrote: "It can be said without exaggeration that the former intelligentsia is now partly destroying itself and partly decaying."[95] But the Russian intelligentsia sealed its own fate; and it was responsible for its own destruction, not some outside force. This fact was affirmed by people whose political reputation remained impeccable. Berdyaev called the Russian revolution the suicide of the Russian intelligentsia.[96] Nina Berberova wrote with her characteristic precision: "Now . . . I see that annihilation came not by the direct route, but subtly, through a kind of blossoming; it was not so simple to make it through this 'heyday,' some people did indeed thrive, and some perished, and some destroyed other people without even knowing it." In presenting several examples of this, Berberova chose three of our story's characters from among hundreds of possible names: Trotsky, Voronsky, and Pilnyak.[97]

We do not know how Eitingon felt about Soviet Russia (although by one account he tried to convince Freud to reject a text that he considered anti-Soviet[98]). Aaron Steinberg recalled that ideas of "spiritual revolution" were popular in Eitingon's "psychoanalytic salon" in Berlin; Eurasianists were common guests there, including the movement's ideologue, P. P. Suvchinsky.[99] In contrast, Jones informs us that in the mid-1920s Eitingon was a true Germanophile. Thus, he would have had all the more reason to hate Nazi Germany, which had forced him to emigrate to Israel.

Was Max Eitingon motivated by a desire to wreak vengeance on Germany, the country he had once loved but that had so viciously and senselessly ruined him and his career? He might well have collaborated with his brother-in-law Naum out of the conviction that espionage was necessary in order for the new, progressive Russia to oppose the new, regressive Germany. There were, to be sure, other possible motives for such a collaboration. At the beginning of the 1920s, Max Eitingon received money through Naum Eitingon and Viktor Kopp. This was either Bolshevik "assistance" offered to progressive fields of Western science or payment for representation and business services—perhaps even for keeping tabs on émigré circles. Trotsky's fall from grace and the regime's about-face must have liquidated these sources of income for Eitingon, forcing him to close not only his fur business but the Berlin psychoanalytic clinic as well. The Great Depression in the United States would have provided Eitingon a convenient explanation for his new financial troubles. But history pressed forward: Hitler seized power, presenting a direct threat to Max Eitingon, to psychoanalysis, and to all German Jews. It is believable that at this point Eitingon might have begun to pull old strings. In hopes of counteracting fascism, perhaps he joined a risky game where the means and ends were out of his control. Or perhaps he was confronted by demands to return the money that had already been spent, in part on the earlier undertakings of analysts in Vienna and Berlin, and more recently in Palestine. Naum Eitingon, the head of Soviet counterintelligence, certainly had at his disposal the means to force his relative, the head of international psychoanalysis, to cooperate in covert operations.[100]

A Scene from Real Life

As we know, at the end of the 1920s and the beginning of the 1930s Lev Shestov, a Russian philosopher and then political refugee in Paris, often visited his friend, psychoanalyst Max Eitingon, at his villa in the stylish Berlin district of Tiergarten. One day he encountered there his old acquaintance Aaron Steinberg, another Russian Jewish philosopher who once organized the Free Philosophical Association in postrevolutionary Petrograd. Steinberg would soon become a prominent figure in the World Jewish Congress.[101]

A practicing Jew, Steinberg viewed what was going on in Eitingon's "psychoanalytic salon" with irony and instinctual alarm. "Shestov's trips to Berlin gave Dr. Eitingon the desired excuse to invite people over. . . . Along with people of his own school, he invited émigré intellectuals from various countries," Steinberg wrote in his memoirs. Corroboration of this report can be found in another source. In June 1924, Vyacheslav Ivanov was sent on an open-ended "business trip" by the ministry of education. One of Shestov's friends, in telling him about this, asked him to "force" Ivanov to read his poetry "at Dr. Eitingon's, like Remizov read his *Petka* last year."[102]

It seems that many of the heroes of our story found their way to the villa at Tiergarten. Vyacheslav Ivanov might well have conversed there with Lou Andreas-Salomé; Moisei Wulff might have sat with colleagues fondly remembering Sabina Spielrein; and of course, Otto and Vera Schmidt could not have passed by Eitingon's salon during their trips to Berlin. . . . Freud had occasion to visit, as well. Naum Eitingon also might have dropped in, under one of his professional aliases. It is highly likely that Viktor Kopp was a frequent guest. Might Trotsky also have visited? Ioffe? Metner? Yermakov? Bullitt? Bely? Zalkind? Pankeev? Eisenstein? Nabokov?

We leave these suppositions behind for the moment. During the evening that Steinberg recalled, the usual visitors were gathered at the villa: Shestov, who came to stay with Eitingon and see his sister the psychoanalyst; "a variety of Russian émigré literary scholars connected with the journal *Imago*"; "other guests, specialists in psychoanalysis and believers in all sorts of syntheses"; and, finally, "one totally unexpected guest"—the famed Russian singer Nadezhda Vasilievna Plevitskaya, accompanied by General Skoblin and the rest of her entourage.

Steinberg's memoirs have preserved snippets of the conversation. "Both of them, Freud and Shestov, have yanked the same mask from the face of our civilization, the mask of lies and hypocrisy," one of the young partygoers parroted. The salon's hostess, Nadezhda Eitingon, was trying to persuade Shestov to read "something of his own." Meanwhile Suvchinsky, who was one of the singer's biggest fans, exclaimed: "Just think! Shestov and Plevitskaya—it's got to go down in history!"

"We'll get ourselves into history yet," Steinberg punned angrily, clearly smelling a rat. As per the custom of southern Russia, Plevitskaya sang "Honor and Glory" to Shestov, but mispronounced his Jewish name and patronymic. Steinberg saw it all as "intolerable mockery," clowning "to pander to God knows how low-caliber an audience." With uncanny perceptiveness, he inquired of Suvchinsky: "Say, who is the director of this tacky scene? Could it be Plevitskaya?" But in the end, Shestov was persuaded to read from his philosophical writings at the dinner table.

Shestov read a fable entitled "The Philosopher of Miletus and the Phrygian Shepherdess."[103] Thales of Miletus was so engrossed in his lofty thoughts one day that he didn't notice a cistern of water that lay in his path. He stumbled and fell in with a splash. The quiet evening was suddenly shattered by resounding laughter. It was a young Phrygian shepherdess, who was driving her goats from the pasture to the city. The question arises, who was right? Philosophy teaches that the wise man was right in not watching where his feet landed, if in doing so he uncovered the primal essence of things. But it is more than possible, Shestov concluded his tale, that the giggly shepherdess was wiser than the wise man.

"Oh, how marvelous! That's just gr-r-eat!" Plevitskaya drawled in a singsong voice, clapping her hands ecstatically and bowing to Shestov.[104]

All-Powerful, Because It Was True

The Enlightenment began with the breakdown of the old, once meaningful picture of the world—a world that had been built on a higher reason, which was nevertheless analogous to human reason and therefore theoretically accessible to human understanding. The Newtonian-Darwinian world offered reason an entirely new place. Man could understand how the planets moved and how monkeys developed; but the meaning of it all remained a mystery. Nor could man understand the meaning behind Braun's movement of people, goods, and ideas in the new society. Human beings had their place in society, life taught them to value this place and fight for it; but the spiritual system that defined views, opinions, and tastes did not define man's role or purpose. Man's place in life was no longer a logical extrapolation of the meaning of life. Meaning disappeared, and all that remained was space and man, lost in that space.

Marxism fundamentally changed all this. Unlike Darwinian evolution, Marxist history had coherent meaning. More than that, on the basis of this new understanding, man could change the world! Changing the world was the primary task set before science, the most prestigious institution in the new society. Along with the new system of meanings, a new system of places was built.

Man regained his faith in the supremacy of reason, in the ultimate rationality of existence. Natural or traditional life was seen as intolerably squalid and sluggish, with no more reason than a can of worms. Life, therefore, could and should be rebuilt on a new and conscious foundation. Reason would no longer be set in motion by a God separated from mankind, nor by some abstract and isolated absolute; reason would be implemented directly by the hands of man and his comrades. For Trotsky and his comrades, this was key: "Socialist construction is in essence a consciously planned construction, . . . striving to rationalize human relations, . . . to subordinate them to reason, armed with science." The conditions for this process were ripe all over the world: "The forces of production have long been ready for Socialism. . . . There is only one last subjective factor missing: consciousness is missing from life."[105]

The belated Russian Enlightenment found its best expression and highest fulfillment in Trotsky's words and deeds. Trotsky's favorite tactic, the "purge from the top down"—of God and czar, of chaos and competition, of unconsciousness and darkness—was the last word of the Enlightenment. No longer dramatic, this word today sounds both tragic and ludicrous. Violence was inevitable along this path; violence invariably accompanied the Enlightenment, and not only in Russia. The defeat of Trotsky put an end to an entire period of history, perhaps the best period for intellectuals. Stalin's political victory meant the victory of dark force for its own sake over bright, abstract dreams, the victory of will over reason, earth over culture, charisma over utopia, Nietzsche over Hegel. It meant the defeat of the Enlightenment, empirical proof that the epoch's great project was unviable, or at least insufficient.

Lenin's words were taken up and repeated many times by Stalin: "Marx's doctrine is all-powerful because it is true." Usually this phrase is perceived as empty tautology; but it is in fact a profound, truly philosophical formula. All one had to do in order to change the world was to find the truth. Things would then be transformed magically, in a revolutionary way, in the twinkling of an eye. Revolution was conceived in just this way: as a one-time act of universal understanding and illumination. There is a similar concept in psychoanalysis: insight, the instantaneous act of understanding and restructuring accumulated memory.

However, not even the most dedicated psychoanalyst can set his sights on a conscious understanding of the processes that occur in every cell of the human body. The true art of psychoanalysis is the search for a delicate balance between what needs to be brought out into the conscious for arbitrary regulation and what can and should remain in the unconscious. A great multitude of processes take place in human beings that we cannot realize and that cannot therefore be regulated consciously. There are other processes that are accessible to the conscious, but that work much better without its interference. Any actor or rhetorician, anyone who can dance, knows that all it takes is one little thought about what you're doing, and you're sure to screw up. Consciousness is engaged during certain stages and disengages itself during others, when emotional or intuitive factors are more important—curiosity, arousal, inspiration, or fear. These other factors go beyond the limits of consciousness, and there is no way to replace them by conscious thought. The amazing idiosyncrasy of communist theoreticians was the persistence with which they rejected the significance of such unconscious factors in every realm: in economics, in the organization of labor, in education, in philosophical ponderings about thought processes, and in psychotherapy. "They wanted to organize everything, so the sun would come up according to schedule and the weather would be determined in an administrative office. They could not understand the anarchy of life, its unconsciousness, the fact that a tree knows best how it should grow." Viktor Shklovsky was right on the mark when he wrote these words in 1923.[106]

Psychoanalysis combined the elaboration of practical ways to translate the unconscious to the conscious with an extremely detailed study of the unconscious itself. An instantaneous act of realization could follow extended, years-long analysis of the subconscious. Bolshevism began from the other end. The elemental unconscious was completely devalued. Only what was self-conscious, according to the only true scientific theory, deserved to exist.

These conclusions seem consistent with the primary idea of Bolshevism: the statization of property. In point of fact, private property could be controlled "unconsciously" as well as consciously—based on traditions, practical experience, or intuition. Collective property, like stocks, could be controlled based on democracy; but state property could be controlled based on science alone, or at least in its name.

In this worldview, ideas were more real than reality itself. Bolshevik science in every way resembled the real thing, but in fact it was the exact inverse, the mirror image: In place of facts there were plans, in place of hypotheses—reality. If reality did not correspond to the plan's ideal, then it had to be remade or eliminated, just as a scientist might amend or reject an unconvincing hypothesis. Then again, scientists could create without compunction whatever they pleased within the ethereal world of ideas: Rejected hypotheses won't rot with dystrophy and scurvy, they don't fill mass graves to overflowing, and their bones won't protrude from foundation ditches on construction sites half a century later.

So-called war communism, introduced under Trotsky's direction during the years after the revolution, meant total control by the state not only of material and intellectual production but also of distribution and consumption. From then on, the reins of this massive control network were to be put in the hands of reason, not subjected to pitiful, individualistic demands. To each person his ration; less would be illogical, more would also be illogical.

Of course, it is easier to weigh a ration of bread—provided there is bread—than to determine a reasonable measure in culture or sexuality.

This was the purpose of the various fields of Soviet science. From the beginning of the 1920s, there were heroic attempts to create scientific norms in the organization of labor, daily life, recreation, nutrition, education, and everything else that accompanied human life. The dramatic part was that scientifically these attempts were not at all without merit; on the contrary, they gave rise to the greatest accomplishments of Soviet science, recognized the world over. For example, work aimed at culling scientifically tested instructions for performing maximally efficient basic actions (how to hold a hammer, how to walk, and so forth) was the starting point of Nikolai Bernstein's concept, which later became famous around the world in the field of physiology. Research on labor organization was run by Alexei Gastev, a poet of the radical avant-garde; but even there, serious work was done in industrial psychology, in many ways ahead of its time. The work of pedologists, dedicated to introducing scientific principles into the education of the new generation, was carried out on a grand scale.

There were some truly important scholars scattered among the semi-educated masses that took part in the activity of the steadily expanding planning bodies. One was theologian and mathematician, Father Pavel Florensky; God knows if he was any good at his new job. Even the Main Political Directorate and the Procuracy had their share of serious researchers: Andrey Vyshinsky, for instance, included the associative experiment in interrogation and investigation. Here, however, as in other areas of government, methods of physical persuasion were deemed far more practical.

To Recast Dreams as Reality

It is interesting to compare the ideas of Trotsky and the Moscow analysts of the 1920s with the vision that has formed today on the basis of this century's difficult experience. We cite the English poet W. H. Auden, whose pithy formulation is an excellent substitute for a more long-winded discussion:

> Both Marx and Freud start from the failures of civilization, one from the poor, one from the ill. Both see human behavior determined, not consciously, but by instinctive needs, hunger and love. Both desire a world where rational choice and self-determination are possible. The difference between them is the inevitable difference between the man who studies crowds in the street, and the man who sees the patient, or at most the family, in the consulting room. . . . The socialist accuses the psychologist of caving in to the status quo, trying to adapt the neurotic to the system, thus depriving him of a potential revolutionary: the psychologist retorts that the socialist is trying to lift himself by his own boot tags . . . so that after he has won his power by revolution he will

recreate the same conditions. Both are right. As long as civilization remains as it is, the number of patients the psychologist can cure are very few, and as soon as socialism attains power, it must learn to direct its own interior energy and will need the psychologist.[107]

Freud, too, voiced his judgments on this question. In 1913, he told the son of Theodor Herzl, the socialist founder of Zionism: "Your father is one of those people who have turned dreams into reality. This is a very rare and dangerous breed. . . . I would simply call them the sharpest opponents of my scientific work. It is my modest profession to simplify dreams, to make them clear and ordinary. They, on the contrary, confuse the issue, turn it upside down, command the world. . . . I deal in psychoanalysis, they deal in psychosynthesis."[108]

And Freud admonished young Hans: "Stay away from them, young man, . . . stay away, even though one of them was your father; . . . perhaps because of that."[109]

8

Pedological Perversions

Dneprostroi and the Science of Man

Relating the successes of the pedological movement during the 1920s, Aron Zalkind was hard pressed to favorably compare the level achieved under the Soviet regime with progress made before the revolution, since pedology had been practically nonexistent before the revolution.[1] Zalkind was an extremely active participant in almost all of the important events in the history of Soviet pedology, and as such he was doubtless a biased observer.

The founder of the interdisciplinary science of the child and the man who coined the very word "pedology" was G. Stanley Hall, one of the giants of American psychology. He also became part of the history of psychoanalysis, for it was he who arranged Freud's famous trip to America in 1909. Later, in 1911, Stanley Hall became one of the founding members of the American Psychoanalytic Society. That same year, the First Pedological Congress was held in Brussels.

Pedology and psychoanalysis crossed paths frequently both in Russia and in the West. This was only natural: Both disciplines shared an interest in childhood and a practical orientation. In western Europe and America, however, psychoanalysis continued its triumphant expansion into the humanities, social service, and daily life, while pedology quickly lost in importance. Twenty years later, Vygotsky informed readers of the newly founded Soviet journal *Pedology* that in the West, as opposed to the Soviet Union, this progressive science had long since died out or at least had become a walking corpse.[2]

In the Soviet Union, the picture looked completely different. By the end of the 1920s, psychoanalysis had been all but stamped out, while pedology was undergoing an unprecedented boom. Nevertheless, several of the leading figures in pedology, the foremost of whom was Aron Zalkind, had received psychoanalytic training. The best conceptual achievements made in pedology, generally associated with the late works of Vygotsky and Blonsky, bear the incontrovertible mark of a dialogue with psychoanalysis. In 1923, Polina Efrussi, who was not at all sympathetic to psychoanalysis, noted that

"Freud's method has managed to penetrate over the last few years from psychiatry and psychopathology into Russian pedology as well."[3]

Besides psychoanalysis, Vladimir Bekhterev's school of psychoneurology served as an important source for the post-revolutionary pedological movement. The first pedological institution in Russia was founded quite early on—in 1909 in St. Petersburg—as part of the Psychoneurological Academy, funded with money donated by businessman and philanthropist V. T. Zimin.[4] The small building that housed the pedological facility still stands today next to the fence surrounding the Psychoneurological Institute. Today it is occupied by government offices.

Several typically bureaucratic attempts were made to implement Bekhterev's research program, which called for an all-encompassing study of mankind. A few years after Bekhterev's demise and the collapse of the Psychoneurological Academy, which he had founded, "at a meeting chaired by Comrades Stalin, Molotov, and Voroshilov and attended by Maxim Gorky, . . . the decision was made to reorganize the Institute of Experimental Medicine in Leningrad into the All-Union Scientific Research Institute for the Comprehensive Study of Mankind." This decision, according to one eyewitness, "was met with general approval, . . . and due to the exceptional importance and grand scale of the Institute's proposed goals, it was nicknamed the 'Dneprostroi' of Natural and Medical Science."[5] The idea of undertaking a comprehensive study of man through an interdisciplinary synthesis, first proposed by Bekhterev on the eve of the first Russian revolution, turned out to be remarkably popular in a totalitarian atmosphere and outlived more than one generation of scholars and administrators.

In the first decade after the Bolshevik revolution, pedology ripened and consolidated its strength in the shelter of Bekhterev's looming authority. His tragic death, the story of which is today common knowledge (see chapter 4), is also symbolic, in that it occurred after the close of the First Conference of Neurologists and Psychiatrists and on the eve of the opening of the First Pedological Conference. Bekhterev was supposed to chair both conferences. The Pedological Conference began with a memorial service at which Vyshinsky and Kalinin paid their respects. The death of the great leader of psychoneurology was followed by a series of conflicts between his closest disciples. In the end, pedology emerged as the leader of the new sciences that had reached maturity within the confines of psychoneurology. The role of ideologue and leader would pass to Aron Zalkind, a pedologist and former psychoanalyst.

Border Conflicts

Pedology was a scientific discipline characteristic of the beginning of the twentieth century. The new concepts that were competing for status as fields of knowledge or even as sciences at that time emerged not as a result of the continuous, gradually accumulating labor of generations of scientists but through the revolutionary work of brilliant individuals who were establishing new ways of looking at phenomena. Such was the genesis of psychoanalysis. The result of this process generally was a school that might be more or less productive but that would always remain only one of many subfields within a given science. In the atmosphere of intolerance that accompanied the struggle for survival and power under Bolshevik rule, any new school tended to squeeze out its competitors, pushing for a monopoly of understanding in its field. Each school declared its point of view the only true approach, while other points of view were dismissed as unscientific. This situation, as a rule, was recognized not as a dispute within the science itself, but as a "border conflict" between distinct disciplines with claims on a single subject matter—for example, between biology and sociology, psychology and physiology, pedology and industrial psychology, and pedology and education. Endless discussions about "lines of demarcation" to divide the sciences and prescribe the permissible field of endeavor for each discipline were typical of scientific development in the totalitarian society—in part, perhaps, because the level of abstraction that characterized these disputes made them understandable to political leaders. Interdisciplinary discussions differed from other scientific disputes in that they allowed for simple, administrative solutions: The losing side of the debate could simply be closed down, as was done later with pedology, while the winning side—education, for instance—was declared the only revealer of truth. Another way such disputes were solved was by interdisciplinary synthesis, which involved the creation of new organizational structures: After the synthesis of structures had been accomplished, the representatives of distinct sciences were obliged to communicate with one another, which was supposed to induce intellectual cross-fertilization. Pedology was constructed precisely in this latter way, as a comprehensive science of the child rather than a range of "partial" sciences that studied various aspects of infantile life—psychology, sociology, anatomy, physiology, and so forth—in isolation from one another. However, the integration of information gathered by different scientific disciplines remains to this day extremely problematic because of the divergence of methods used in the various disciplines.

The leaders of pedology wrote voluminously about their new field, insisting that it was not just a casserole thrown together from the leftovers of other disciplines. Pavel Blonsky was stricter than most in defining pedology's field of study: "Pedology is the study of the entire set of symptoms of the various eras, phases, and stages of childhood, their temporary consequences, and their dependence on a range of conditions." It was not simply the "study of children," it was the "study of childhood."[6] Blonsky conceived of pedology as a scientific, theoretical basis for applied education. In the effort to get his point across, he expressed this thought with a metaphor that might shock readers today: "As an animal breeder relies on zoology in his work, so must a teacher rely on pedology." However, the course on pedology that Blonsky wrote was roughly equivalent in its scope to today's courses in developmental psychology, with descriptions given consistently by age groups. Psychological data were correlated with the results of physiological, anatomical, and genetic research.

Vygotsky, who made a special attempt to clarify the relationship between pedology and industrial psychology, went through quite a bit of paper trying to reinforce the special status of both sciences. At the same time, he noted that differences between two disciplines do not necessarily prevent them from intersecting in a certain object—in this case, the child. Each science, he said, could continue on its merry way, minding its own affairs.[7] Isaac Spielrein made the same claim from a position in industrial psychology, insisting that there had to be "a decline in artificial delineations, that is, those not inherent in the objects under study, delineations of the sort that exist between such related sciences as pedology, psychology, experimental education, and industrial psychology."[8] On the other hand, Vygotsky saw that "we fear intermingling like the plague," since it "would seem to mean the end of existence for separate sciences."

The political leaders of the scientific community worried more than anyone about the demarcation and subordination of various disciplines, since for them the importance and universality of the discipline they headed were always direct indicators of their personal political weight. Bukharin hinted at this when he described the situation of pedologists: "The relationship between pedology and education . . . is such that from a certain point of view pedology is the servant of education. But . . . the position of servant here is [different], in that the servant is giving the orders."[9] Zalkind, who was a contender for leadership in the field of psychoneurological science, tended to exaggerate the importance of pedology to the point where it became a universal science of human development. In much the same way, Vygotsky occasionally likened his quest for interdisciplinary synthesis to pedology, asserting that a pedology of adults was possible and necessary.

The theoretical views of pedologists were expressed in the form of "principles." The principle of unity and the principle of development seem to have been shared by all pedological theoreticians. To these Zalkind added the principle of activity: "Personality is studied as an active, rather than a contemplative, phenomenon." Apart from these concepts, pedologists also emphasized the concept of plasticity, in other words the principle that environment exerts a formative influence on children's development. Environment itself, Zalkind insisted, must be studied not "like an inventory, but within its active, dynamic purpose." These principles, codified by pedological publications of the late 1920s, would later be incorporated indelibly and without significant alteration into the methodological canon of Soviet psychology.[10]

But the most profound pedological principle may have been formulated by Nikolai Rybnikov. In his book *The Language of the Child* [11] (which is still unique, along with its appendix *The Russian Child's Dictionary*), Rybnikov wrote: "Pedology tends to see childhood not only as the preparatory stage leading to adulthood, but considers the childhood period to have significance in and of itself." The language of the child, for instance, is not simply a primitive form of adult speech; it has its own rules, its own lexicon, its own logic. Today, even in Russia, the "discovery of childhood" in science is attributed to American ethnography of the 1920s and 1930s, and particularly to the works of Margaret Mead.[12] The work of Nikolai Rybnikov, who led the first large-scale study of the language, ideals, and political conceptions of the Russian child, was forgotten in Russia and remained unknown in the West, despite its originality and potential usefulness.

The Organized Simplification of Culture

It would be impossible to comprehend the metamorphosis that transformed Russian psychoanalysis into pedology without at least partially understanding the political atmosphere during the early years of the Bolshevik regime, an atmosphere that suffused the life and work of the movement's leaders and many of its practitioners. While society's mood swings have little to do with science, they can determine the direction, values, and global methodology that scientists adopt. This influence becomes particularly marked when the dominant mood in society acquires the unusually extremist character that it did in Russia during the 1920s.

"Listen to the Revolution" was Alexander Blok's 1918 call to the intelligentsia. The cause and duty of the intelligentsia, he wrote, was "to see what has been thought up. . . . What has been thought up? To remake everything. To make everything anew; to make our false, tedious, horrid life into one that is just, pure, happy, and beautiful."[13] This jubilant embrace of the new government was typical in the social groups that formed the cadre base for pedology. Bekhterev, who did much to cause this turnaround in the mood of the intelligentsia, announced at the end of 1923 at the All-Union Conference of Scientific Workers: "Back in 1920, after my public speeches in favor of Soviet rule, my colleagues wouldn't leave me alone; they called me a turncoat and a traitor. Now in scientific circles it would be considered strange not to recognize the huge advances and historic wisdom of the October revolution."[14]

Ivan Pavlov at that time took a different attitude toward events. In 1923, Pavlov wrote that it was impossible to understand from any angle how the Bolsheviks could be so certain that global revolution would win a speedy victory. "A lot of money is being spent on things, like on Japan, with an eye to the global revolution, while our academic laboratory gets only three rubles in gold per month." He added, "Certain people have imagined that they can entirely remake today's educational system, despite their own admission of ignorance." The great scientist had a hard time understanding how the Bolsheviks' lofty goals could be attained by workers whose ignorance was obvious even to the Bolsheviks themselves. Much later, on October 19, 1928, Pavlov wrote to the government:

> Educated people have been transformed into mute observers and executors. They see how mercilessly and for the most part unsuccessfully everything in life is being changed to the foundations, how mistakes are being piled one atop the other. . . . You have simplified man too much in your work, in hopes of making him truly common property, for instance by locking him up in all sorts of endless meetings to hear the same doctrine repeated over and over.[15]

Bukharin replied hotly, coming right to the point: "And we *will change it*, just as we need it to be, there is no doubt we will change it! We will change it just as we have changed ourselves, as we changed the government, as we changed the army, as we are changing the economy, as we changed [the peasants of Russia] into an active, strong-willed, quickly growing, popular mass that is greedy for life." Everything can be changed, and what's more changed in just the way we would like. Bukharin's condescending attitude (shared by Pavlov as well) toward the ignorant masses in no way dampened his faith in the feasibility of change (it did Pavlov's), and, on the contrary, only fanned his enthusiasm. "A common mistake among important people (and particularly among scientists) of the 'old world' is that when they evaluate the catastrophe of the entire old regime they vainly console themselves by applying the standard measures [to which they are accustomed] of peaceful, 'normal' capitalist life. This is like Gulliver trying to put on a baby Lilliputian's pants."

There was a dichotomy between the new science of Gullivers and Pavlov's Lilliputian science.[16] The new science of man was the science of his transformation. The question, "What is it?" from then on would be replaced by the question "How can it be transformed?" Everything intrinsic, stable, and inaccessible to external influence was declared insignificant or outdated, unimportant, and Lilliputian. The process of development under the influence of outside forces was declared the only important factor. In his speech to the First Pedological Conference, Bukharin said: "The question of social environment and its influence must be solved, in the sense that the influence of social environment is greater than usually supposed. Changes can take place much more quickly, and the profound reorganization that we call the cultural revolution has a sociobiological equivalent that reaches down to the very physiological nature of the [human] organism."[17] There is nothing specific here concerning methodology, and Bukharin's announcement is simply an adaptation of the general principle that "there is no fortress that Bolsheviks cannot take." In nature and society, in the child and his development, there was nothing that could not be influenced; everything could be changed, including the physiological nature of the human being.

There was consensus regarding this point of principle: Minister of Health Nikolai Semashko parroted the Party leader at the same pedological conference: "The development of pedological science, which includes medicine, is distinguished today by the attention paid to the influence of environment."[18] Nadezhda Krupskaya, who was slipping from her position, still managed a relatively aggressive statement to this regard: "Some see underestimating the influence of environment as an antidote against the Marxist elements that are penetrating the school ever more deeply."[19] When the spread of Marxism depends upon a recognition of the influence of environment, to underestimate the influence of environment is to speak out against Marxism. In these statements we find the origins of the barrier that Lysenko later raised in genetics, economics, and the whole of Soviet science. Scholars found themselves faced with a choice: to be swept under the carpet, or to promise to storm any fortress and change any principle.

But the minister of education, Anatoly Lunacharsky, was most expressive of all, declaring that "when pedology has learned the nature of the child and the laws by which children develop, . . . it will have illuminated the most important question: . . . How to produce a new man that will parallel the production of new equipment in the economic sphere."[20] Not only is it striking that a cultured, intelligent person could say such a thing; it is also shocking that in this new world such statements had become so commonplace.

A few years earlier, Blonsky, who had been a junior lecturer and neoplatonist but at that time was serving in the ministry of education, had written: "Along with botany and animal husbandry, there should be another, analogous science: human husbandry, and education . . . should take its place along with veterinary medicine and phytoculture, borrowing methods and principles from them as from more developed, related disciplines."[21] This passage, written in all earnestness, formed the core of a run-of-the-mill textbook on education, a book on which more than one generation of teachers probably cut their teeth. Bukharin was expressing the same idea more directly when he wrote: "We need to direct our strength not into abstract chatter, but into an effort to produce a certain number of living workers in the shortest possible time frame; qualified, specially schooled machines that we can start up right away and set into motion."[22]

Old-school psychoanalysts clearly perceived a threat to their position. In 1926, Moisei Wulff wrote: "The ideal teaching method should be absolutely free of any ulterior motives, of all principles and interests outside of the child. . . . I can repeat this triumphant truth because lately under the influence of a misinterpreted doctrine of reflexes, there has arisen a renewed form of the old, naive conception of the child as a tabula rasa on which anything can be written. There have been some assertions put forward that with the help of the appropriate catalysts, the teacher can develop whatever 'conditioned reflexes' in the child that he wishes and thus mold the 'right kind' of person."[23]

Freud himself responded respectfully but skeptically to the idea of a new reconstruction of human relations in his work *The Future of an Illusion,* which was originally published in the 1920s and republished in Russian translation by Ivan Yermakov in the 1930s.[24] "That would be a golden age," he wrote. "The grand nature of the plan and its importance for the future of human civilization cannot be disputed." At the same time, he expressed doubts that the idea was attainable: "It may be alarming to think of the enormous amount of coercion that will inevitably be required before these intentions can be carried out," he wrote, with amazing foresight.[25]

Old revolutionaries found their own ways of processing and expressing the spiritual and political dead end in which they found themselves. In 1923, Krupskaya published a sympathetic description of Taylor's system (the division of labor into its simplest elements and the institution of an exact definition of each worker's function), proposing it as a means to fight against the rampant bureaucratism of Soviet institutions.[26] Emmanuel Yenchman, who had served as a military commander during the civil war that followed the Bolshevik revolution, declared in his *Theory of the New Biology* that any discussion of knowledge, reason, or worldviews was just an exploitative ruse. He asserted that after the overthrow of the exploiters, everyone would let down their guard, after which all the "reactions of knowledge" would be annihilated, giving rise to a "single system of organized movements."[27] Yenchman explained that by "producing an organic cataclysm" within himself, he had "gained a few years head start on the revolting mass of laborers." For this reason, he seriously put forward his own candidacy for the position of head of the "Revolutionary Scientific Council of the Republic" or even of a "world commune with corresponding subordinate bodies all over the republic or even the globe" (incidentally, the brilliant poet Velimir Khlebnikov also had designs on that position).

Despite the absurdity of these ideas, they bear the imprint of a Russian culture that not long before had entertained seemingly well-founded claims to greatness. As Moisei Altman, a student of Vyacheslav Ivanov's and later a prominent scholar of literature in his own right, wrote:

> Perhaps besides all these eugenics,
> I, though a bookworm Pharisee,
> Am more of a decadent and neurasthenic.

"All these eugenics" was Altman's poetic way of denoting the various sciences that were in fashion at the time, disciplines that stylish people were involved in, either simultaneously or in series. Altman recalled how he wrote his "terribly long and terribly revolutionary" articles using a new orthography, while he wrote his diary using the old. Ivanov sensed this dualism in him, a feature characteristic of the entire generation, but chose to ignore it. "I heard two songs, but chose to listen only to one."[28]

Meanwhile, Bukharin devoted dozens of pages of newsprint to denouncing Yenchman's delirium.[29] He and other opponents agreed that they would never have reacted to Yenchman's far-fetched writings if the "theory of new biology" had not found support among young Communists. All of this, however, was merely a discussion among soft-spoken, cultured people. In contrast, the tone of Mikhail Levidov's manifesto, published in 1923 by the journal *Krasnaia nov'*, was probably much more understandable and gratifying to Party members who had just finished fighting a war: "The repugnant word 'intellectual' has already disappeared from circulation among the younger generation; that spineless, flabby, morose, damp-chicken word, the likes of which you'll not find in any human tongue. . . . In twenty or thirty years, the tribe of intellectuals will disappear from Russian lands." The only honorable thing for an intellectual to do, Levidov wrote bluntly, was to kill himself; or if he wanted to dishonor himself, an intellectual could emigrate; but the most despicable intellectual for Levidov was the one who remained alive in Soviet Russia.[30]

Levidov's poetic sentiments were fully compatible with the tone of his day, dominated as it was by the ill educated and the illiterate. In 1923, eight to ten times less was spent on each college student's education than had been spent in 1914. The average salary for rural teachers was only seventeen percent of what they had earned in 1914. Overall, spending on education per capita was four times lower. "But the pre-war situation is really not our educational ideal," wrote the ministry of education bureaucrat who presented these figures, and there was a touch of melancholy in his words.[31] Fifty-two percent of school-age children were not in school in 1923, which meant that about four million children were receiving no education at all. Only thirty-two percent of the population could read. The ministry of education was saddled with the colossal task of universal education and literacy.

A series of decrees from the ministry of education had radically changed teaching in the Soviet Union. Grades and exams were abolished, and homework was eliminated. The State Academic Council, under the leadership of Krupskaya, Blonsky, and Shatsky, introduced new school curricula. Gargantuan efforts were undertaken in order to set in motion a system of vocational training. Teachers opposed these measures, as they were unprepared to implement them and felt that they were losing control over the children. "The teachers didn't exactly sabotage the process, they were simply . . . incapable of accepting and assimilating a mass of new ideas." The ministry of education logically concluded that this was "not the teacher's fault, it is his problem and his misfortune."[32]

But Lunacharsky and his colleagues were unable to slow down the pace of the cultural revolution. Bukharin's "reconstruction of man as he should be" and Levidov's "organized simplification of culture" had to proceed as planned by the Marxist intellectuals in the ministry of education. New times were at hand, and they promised changes that even Levidov had never imagined in his wildest dreams.

The Infrastructure of Utopia

At the First All-Russian Conference of Psychoneurology, which took place in Moscow in January 1923, Polina Efrussi professed astonishment at the volume and popularity of the work done by practicing psychologists. In particular, she singled out pedologists and industrial psychologists. "Before our very eyes, there has been an incredibly swift reevaluation of psychology's importance in daily life."[33] This amazing productivity is no less puzzling today: Where did the money come from to support such frenetic intellectual activity in poverty-stricken, postrevolutionary Russia, which could barely find the funds with which to provide its citizens even a rudimentary education?

It is difficult for us now to understand the hopes that the new government had invested in pedology. The science was generally viewed as a powerful, magical force that would swiftly solve any problem. Lunacharsky, whose ministry for decades to come would struggle to accomplish even a small portion of the tasks it had been assigned, announced at the First Pedological Conference: "Our school network can approach the standards of a truly normal school network . . . only when it is penetrated clean through by a network of pedologists with sufficient scientific training. . . . Also, there must be a strong little pedologist living in the brain of each teacher."[34] It wasn't firewood, or school buildings, or teachers that Lunacharsky needed more than anything to build a new educational network—he needed pedologists.

In order to construct a kingdom of reason in a country where seventy percent of the population could neither read nor understand the words pronounced from the podium, naturally a new intellectual elite had to be created. At the very least, nothing was to be done that might interfere with the thousands of young people who were gripped by abstract ideas and wanted to make their own immediate contribution to the construction of utopia. The number of teacher training colleges in the country increased by fifty percent over the course of the 1919–1920 school year, but the colleges were still overflowing with teachers in training: In 1921, there were six times as many students enrolled as there had been in 1914.[35]

Lydia Ginzburg recalled with a touch of irony the frantic activity of young intellectuals: "During the war communism years, when once prestigious, inherited professions were extremely insecure and often inapplicable, the youth of the intelligentsia flocked in droves to become musicians, actors, writers, and journalists, turning their household talents and hobbies into professions." It is simple enough to add educational reformer, pedologist, and industrial psychologist to this list of new professions. "There was a kind of ease and momentary applicability, something akin to the pressure and transitory nature of the time, something that suited the vision of an old world forever in ruins. Everyone had to put bread on the table, besides, and nobody imagined then how difficult it could be to get bread."[36]

In 1922, several new institutions of higher learning opened their doors in Moscow: the Superior Courses in Pedology, Psychological Research Courses, Superior Courses in Scientific Education, the Central Institute for Organizers of Popular Education, the Academy of Social Training, and the Teachers' Institute for the Study of Defects in Children. Educators were also being trained in four other teachers' colleges and nine vocational schools. There was also a wide range of scientific research centers operating in the field: the Psychological Institute of the First Moscow State University (directed by G. I. Chelpanov), the Central Pedological Institute (whose administrator was N. A. Rybnikov), the Moscow State Psychoneurological Institute (A. P. Nechaev), the State Medical Pedological Institute of the Ministry of Health (M. O. Gurevich), the Laboratory for Experimental Psychology and Pediatric Psychoneurology under the auspices of the Neurological Institute at the First Moscow State University (G. I. Rossolimo), the Medical-Pedagogical Clinic (V. P. Kashchenko), the Central Psychological Laboratory of Auxiliary Schools (P. P. Sokolov), the Experimental Psychological Laboratory of the General Staff Academy (T. E. Segalov), the Soviet Labor Unions' Central Labor Institute (A. P. Gastev), the Ministry of Labor's Laboratory of Industrial Psychology (I. N. Spielrein), the Central Educational Institute for the Humanities (V. N. Shulgin), the Museum of Preschool Education (E. A. Arkin), and even the Institute of Social Psychology (R. Y. Wipper).[37] At first, only the ministries of education and health were involved in pedology. Soon, the ministry of transportation opened its own pedological office, followed by the industrial ministries. The labor union and the ministry of labor were actively engaged in applied, industrial psychology.

Natalya Traugott, who in 1927 was studying at the department of pedology at the Leningrad Teachers' Institute, recalled the "exceptional" education she received there. Lectures were given by Bekhterev, celebrated pedologist M. Y. Basov, prominent animal psychologist V. A. Wagner, and by Vygotsky and Blonsky, who came up from Moscow regularly.

Pedological work went on in the provinces as well as in Moscow and Petrograd. In 1923, the first issue of the *Pedological Journal* was published in the town of Orel, edited by Basov; Bekhterev became coeditor after the first issue. This mouthpiece of the Orel Pedological Society did not last long—just long enough to acquaint its readership with a passable explanation of the Rohrschach ink-blot test, an overview of Anglo-American IQ tests, a few articles by Riga's psychoanalysts, and finally a marvelous bit of empirical research on the children of Orel, done in 1918 (see below).

A community of professionals was gradually taking shape. By the mid-1920s, a number of collective actors—scientific societies and associations—had evolved: In 1923 in Moscow, there were a Psychological Society (chaired by Ivan Ilyin), a Psychoanalytic Society (headed by Yermakov), and a Society of Experimental Psychology (chaired by A. P. Nechaev). May 1927 saw the founding of the Moscow Association for Psychological Testing, under Blonsky's chairmanship. In November of the same year, the All-Russian Society of Industrial Psychology was registered (with I. Spielrein as chairman). By the end of 1927, the Pedological Society was ready to hold its first conference.

The pedological movement was developing to a large degree from the bottom up, rather than from the top down. In preparation for the conference, the director of the Central Pedological Institute, Nikolai Rybnikov, attempted to survey sister institutions across the country. He was taken aback by the scale of the pedological movement, and most of all by the fact that it was mainly the result of grass-roots activity. "The network of pedological institutions has proven incredibly expansive—significantly larger than we thought when we began our research." The network of "grass-roots cells" was particularly huge. Rybnikov mentioned specialized pedological institutions in Ryazan, Tashkent, Orel, and the town of Sarapul in the Ural region. The laboratory at the Uglich Teachers' Vocational School, for example, was working on typical pedological problems: the concepts held by local schoolchildren, their interests and ideals; knowledge tests; anthropometry; the study of environment. Unfortunately, however, Rybnikov found that these pedological institutions were linked together in a haphazard manner.[38]

It was only in 1931, after a change in management (Alexei Bubnov replaced Lunacharsky), that the ministry of education brought a measure of order to the work of the nation's practicing pedologists. Directives were issued concerning "regional pedological laboratories" and "local pedological offices." The roll of personnel in each regional pedological laboratory was to include a minimum of thirteen employees—pedologists, psychologists, industrial psychologists, physicians, and technicians:

Laboratory Director	1
Research Fellows (one of whom is the director of the psychometric lab, and the other, a specialist in industrial psychology)	5
Researcher in Pedology and Abnormal Development (also director of the "difficult childhood" section)	1
Pedologist-educators	4
Physician-pedologists	1
Physician-neuropathologists	1
Technicians	5

There is nothing to indicate how many such laboratories and offices were set up across the country. In Moscow, however, according to a report given by R. G. Vilenkina at a conference of Muscovite pedologists in 1931, there was not a single district in town where pedological research was not under way (there were eighteen pedologists in the Lenin district, nineteen in Krasnopresnensky district, and so on). In addition, there were pedological offices in a great many schools. Nevertheless, to Vilenkina's mind there were still too few pedologists; in some districts there were 1,500 children to a single specialist. Vilenkina characterized this situation as deplorable. Funds had been allocated, but there were too few professional pedologists. Vilenkina's analysis indicated several practical functions currently being performed by pedologists in schools and clinics: composing pupil groups according to individualized testing methods; selecting students for admission to remedial educational facilities; studying deviants; evaluating student performance (however, Vilenkina added, pedologists should not replace teachers in this task); working with parents; and analyzing the environment. There was also a certain amount of experimentation taking place with pedological consultation in the workplace and with pedological clubs for teachers.[39]

Anna Lipkina, who worked as a pedologist in a Moscow school, recalled that pedologists for the most part were engaged in IQ measurement. The slower children were examined first of all. If children fell behind in class and gave low indicators on standardized tests, they were to be transferred into remedial schools. There primary education lasted seven years, and the teachers were experts in abnormal psychology. On average, five pupils were singled out for transfer from each class of thirty-five.

Students managing at least a C were not transferred to remedial schools. Pedologists sat in on lessons, systematically observing the children. If tests showed that a child had a low IQ, he was to be observed in class in order to evaluate the extent of his involvement and memory. There was work to be done with parents, as well, gathering information about family life and examining the environment at home. Besides mentally handicapped children, there were others who were difficult to educate, and these were often passed over by the system. This category was not transferred to remedial schools but was provided with special teachers in a normal school setting. If there was drinking or physical abuse in a child's family, the pedologist was obliged to work with the parents. The pedologist was not required, however, to educate or train children—this was left to the teacher.[40] Gradually, individualized work with children and their families came to replace the psychological testing that had been so fashionable in the beginning. (As S. S. Molozhavy had written in 1927: "Standardized testing is threatening to become a daily phenomenon of our school life. Some schools order tests by the bundle from Moscow, and then with striking single-mindedness use them to test their children. Other schools take it upon themselves to develop their own 'local' tests."[41])

Pedologists were held in high regard in their schools, and administrators were reluctant to part with them. In 1932 in Leningrad, the government came up with the idea to ship pedologists off to collective farms; at that time 100 pedologists were working in Leningrad's school system, one in each school. Not one school in the city was willing to give up its pedologist.[42]

The Zalkind Trajectory

Sabina Spielrein's life and work naturally paralleled the trajectory of Soviet psychoanalysis, and according to her adopted daughter, she worked as a pedologist in a school in Rostov-on-the-Don from the end of the 1920s through the early 1930s. Other former analysts complemented the personnel of quite a few pedological offices and laboratories. The work offered them a useful niche that they could fill and enabled them to survive in what might otherwise have been intolerable conditions.

But Aron Zalkind (1888–1936) was a totally different sort of figure, one thoroughly typical of his time. The trajectory of his life, from psychoanalytic practice to his role as organizer of "the new science of childhood" and the builder of a "new man of the masses," is at once unbelievable and possessed of an unmistakable logic.

During the 1910s, the young doctor—like most of the other psychoanalysts working in Moscow—attended the Little Friday seminars run by Vladimir Serbsky (see chapter 4). Zalkind's breed of analysis leaned toward Adler, and he was interested in issues unfamiliar to many psychoanalysts, such as somnambulism. Even before World War I his work had already been published in the primary journal of Russian psychoanalysis, *Psychotherapy,* where his articles were assigned a place of honor, conveying their author's reputation as an engaged and highly successful psychotherapist.[43]

The definition Zalkind gave of creativity sheds some light on his views and, most likely, his intentions at that time: "Whatever field it might involve, creativity is the process of maximally efficient utilization of spiritual force in order to achieve the highest possible goals within the limits of a given situation."[44] It is doubtful that the author foresaw the direction his life would take, or what kind of creativity would be demanded of him in order to achieve the highest imaginable goals given the limits under which he was to work. Rarely does history provide examples of such exact implementation of theoretical mistakes.

Zalkind embraced the revolution ecstatically. Having offered his services to Party members (the 1925 *Directory of Medical Physicians* described his specialty as "psychopathology"[45]), he soon became convinced that the analytical approach was ineffective in treating members of this group. He quickly worked out a new, absurdly ideologized view of mental health issues: "The great French Revolution, as a massive therapeutic measure, was healthier for humanity than a million hot baths, running water, or a thousand new medicines."[46]

However, in his book *Outlines of the Culture of Revolutionary Times* and other articles published in the middle of the 1920s, Zalkind described a fascinating situation that he alone seems to have noticed. The core of Party activists, which was carrying the heaviest burden in the construction of revolution, was burning out fast, he insisted. Thirty-year-olds were presenting symptoms of diseases normally experienced at age 45; forty-year-olds were practically old men. Zalkind pinpointed the cause as constant nervous excitement and overload, neglect of normal hygiene, cultural backwardness, and even a lack of appropriate qualifications among certain workers. Up to ninety percent of Zalkind's Bolshevik patients suffered from neurological disorders, while nearly all had high blood pressure and poor metabolism. Zalkind even went so far as to assign a specific name to this set of symptoms: "the Party triad." In his essay "On Ulcers in the Russian Communist Party,"[47] he complemented this clinical portrait with skillful sociopolitical analysis, demonstrating his understanding of the situation within the Party. Zalkind had uncovered a high incidence of neuroses in members of the opposition. Opposition leaders were stricken with excessive emotionality, which was the essence of neurosis, as Zalkind asserted back in his Adlerian period. For all such cases, he recommended one treatment: "redoubling the Party's reeducation efforts."

Among the Communist student body (which, it should be noted, for the most part supported the Trotskyist opposition), the incidence of nervous disorders as Zalkind understood them was between forty and fifty percent; there was also no shortage of clinical illness, averaging out at ten to fifteen percent. Several of the cases Zalkind examined are interesting in their own right. One twenty-two-year-old college student who had been a unit commander during the civil war was suffering from depression—life during the NEP was "nasty." Another Red commander experienced hysterical somnambulism, his sleep haunted by visions of "cheering *Nepmen*, fat and well-dressed." Zalkind interpreted this hallucination as a "switch into an alternate world, where his desires come true, where he finds himself in battle again, a commander serving the revolution in his own way." One female commissar who had been raped by czarist forces suffered from neuralgia; Zalkind observed ten such cases, but said that usually "these comrades dealt with it like revolutionaries," and did not experience any "ideological crisis" after being raped.

Whether because of his psychoanalytic past or his experience working specifically with Party members, Zalkind put particular emphasis on sexuality in discussing the proper hygiene of Party activity. Modern men suffered from sexual fetishism, he claimed, and it was the task of science to put sex in its proper place. "It is essential that the collective have a stronger pull than the sex partner." To this end, Zalkind developed a detailed system: the twelve commandments of sexuality.[48] The general idea was that the energy of the proletariat should not be distracted by sexual ties that serve no purpose in its historic mission.

"Sex should be subordinated to class," he declared, "in no way interfering with class interests, and serving them in any way possible." Therefore abstinence should be practiced before marriage, until 20 or 25 years of age; the sex act should not be repeated too often; there should be less sexual experimentation; sexual selection should be arranged according to class interests and revolutionary, proletarian expediency; there should be no jealousy. The last and most important of the twelve commandments held that a class had the right to interfere in the sex lives of its members in the interest of revolutionary expediency.

At the Second Psychoneurological Conference that took place in Leningrad at the beginning of 1924, Zalkind's talks attracted everyone's attention. Only 429 of the 906 delegates to the conference were physicians; many of the participants considered themselves Marxist educators. One observer concluded that among teachers, the "move toward revolutionary ideology is taking place much more quickly than among other sectors of the intelligentsia, where people are shut up in a narrow circle of isolated practice."[49] Zalkind addressed this audience, which would soon form the nucleus of pedology, presenting a remarkably eclectic program. The reception he received was highly animated. The magazine *Krasnaia nov'* summarized Zalkind's speech as "sociogenetic biology combined with the doctrine of reflexes, with a cautious use of a variety of very useful Freudian concepts and his own separate experimental methods." The journal concluded that this mix would "surely enrich Marxist theory and practice." Zalkind's speech was lauded by a special resolution of the conference as "a consistent sociological analysis of a variety of neurological, psychopathological, and pedological problems in the light of revolutionary public-spiritedness."

The First Pedological Conference was held at the end of 1927. In his address, Zalkind proposed a platform that could unite all 2,500 conference-goers, who represented several different scientific fields and countless theoretical orientations. Among the throng there were certainly some psychoanalysts who, given the unprecedented tightening of social control and the elimination of anything resembling private practice, had found employment with the government in schools and other ministry of education structures.

In April 1928, the Planning Commission for Pedological Research in Russia began work under the auspices of the Main Science Directorate of the ministry of education; Zalkind was appointed chairman. That same year, the journal *Pedology* began publication under his editorship. In 1930, Zalkind held a Conference on the Study of Human Behavior, as his aspiration to lead expanded to embrace the entire science of man. His address at that conference, entitled "The Psychoneurological Sciences and the Building of Socialism," deserves particular attention; this speech signaled a great turning point in pedology.[50]

Over the course of twelve years of Soviet rule, Zalkind concluded, the nation had seen the birth of a new man of the masses. It saw him in the economy, where he showed indefatigable creative initiative. He could be found in the military, in child care, in art, and even in science. It was with great difficulty that this new man pushed his way through the educational establishment, because he had been set to work without a scientific system. The revolutionary era threw him together in slapdash form, but he was winning battles left and right nevertheless. It was a shame, however, that the psychoneurological sciences had offered no assistance to the new masses. A rift had formed between the cultural revolution and psychoneurology. Psychoneurological literature had to be written for the masses, widespread consultation should be given, as well as mass instruction in the discipline. There was none of this, and there were ominous augurs running through psychoneurology; this science was not yet prepared for work with the masses. The governing bodies of the Party had their work cut out for them with cadres and education, and science had nothing constructive to say on these matters. On the contrary, one even heard negative exhortations, threats directed at the new man of the masses. It was more than obvious, Zalkind concluded, that most of psychoneurology was not doing what it should for the revolution.

It is difficult to judge today to what extent Zalkind's campaign was forced on him by circumstances. An ideological war had been declared, but it was still far from its climax, and the politically aggressive tone of Zalkind's speech seems remarkable for that time. Whatever the case, at the end of 1930, the Psychological Institute in Moscow was reformed into the Institute of Psychology, Pedology, and Industrial Psychology. Zalkind replaced M. K. Kornilov as director of the institute.[51]

A Pine Stake Through
the Heart of Soviet Freudianism

Unlike the "new man of the masses," Zalkind had a past, and now he had a chance to get rid of it. People of his status were never allowed to forget their biographies, nor to force others to forget. The stature of those in relatively high places allowed them only to reinterpret their past mistakes in a new light; they could never be free from fear of others who had the power to apply their own view of the past.

The most damaging stain on the pages of Zalkind's life story was his Freudianism. His own take on this shameful episode is unusual and psychologically curious. Zalkind admitted: "[I] objectively aided the popularization of Freud in the USSR between 1923 and 1925, but later did so only by inertia. In any case, I contributed my own particular understanding to 'Freudism,' which in fact was a total perversion of Freud's doctrine. However, I continued to call my views Freudian, and this drew in the 'little people.'"[52]

Zalkind recalled that he had always tried to reinforce "an extreme sociogenic conditionality, the plasticity of man and human behavior." He claimed that he had constantly defended the conception of personality as an "active, aggressive, creative essence." But Zalkind did not find this in old, reactionary psychoneurology and psychology. "I encountered Freud in 1910–1911, and it seemed to me I had finally struck gold. In fact, personality in Freud burns and struggles; it is dynamic and takes from others, adopts a stubborn strategy, changes the direction of its aspirations, its energy reserves, and so forth. In short, it seemed to me then that Freud had finally tossed the empty, sluggish ego of old psychoneurology out of science once and for all." Clearly, on this particular point Zalkind can be taken at his word: This is just how Freud was perceived by romantically inclined young people during the years of his greatest popularity in Russia, and even twenty years later, such feelings would not have been foreign to Zalkind. "I took the new, fresh, active part of personality from Freud, and made it the leading part."

Of course, Zalkind was even then far from Freudianism, and he moved even farther away later in his career. One need only recall his twelve commandments of sexuality to be convinced that he was subjectively honest in this regard as well. But the further development of their predecessors' ideas along the lines of their own personal interests—a normal phenomenon among scientists—was inadmissible for Zalkind and his cohorts. Thus, Zalkind's "self-criticism" bears little resemblance to the typical recollections of scientists about how they used to think and to whom they owed the evolution of their views; But neither is it a mere show of repentance. The sincerity of Zalkind's tone is a hint at his attitude toward the words as an action of all-consuming importance for himself: His future depended on whether others believed his story.

I drew in the little people, Zalkind confessed: "This is the worst damage done by my 'connection' with Freudianism, and I bear some of the blame for Freud's persisting popularity here. . . . The reinforcement of the dictatorship of the proletariat hammers—once and for all—a pine stake through the heart of Soviet Freudianism."

People of the old school did not agree with this vampiric metaphor and in general did not understand the magical meaning of Zalkind's actions. Krupskaya, for instance, rushed to Freud's defense: There's no sense in overcompensating, she said, the unconscious has some role to play in life.[53] But the damage had been done, and Zalkind had pretty much said it all. His new methodology declared: "We have been transformed from the slaves of scientific methods into their masters. . . . The vast majority (if not all) of scientific research today should be short-term, giving quick, definite conclusions applicable to the near term." This, he exulted, "sounds like a coup d'état in the so-called ethics of science."[54]

It was all for naught. In 1932, Zalkind was removed from his posts as director of the Institute of Psychology, Pedology, and Industrial Psychology (after less than a year in office, he was replaced by V. N. Kolbanovsky) and as editor in chief of the journal *Pedology*. The journal itself had only one more year to live.

In 1936, Zalkind died of a heart attack after reading the Central Committee decree "On Pedological Perversions. . . ."[55]

The Children Revisited

"Meanwhile, these children have no idea what's written on their faces, and only their blue, astonished, inquisitive eyes shine from their very depths with unknown secrets, calmly and sadly fixed on the scroll of life." These were the words that Andrei Bely used in reference to the generation born in the 1910s.[56] Hardly anyone during Bely's time would have supposed that surveys taken of schoolchildren in Orel, Odessa, and Samara would retain more value for future generations than public ideological debates held by the leaders of pedology; however, this was exactly how things turned out. If not for the research of a humble group of provincial pedologist practitioners, we would have known practically nothing about the children of the revolutionary era, apart from occasional belletristic impressions.

The Russian tradition of empirical research on children was established long before the revolution, but was most actively pursued in the Soviet period by the Central Pedological Institute under the leadership of Nikolai Rybnikov. In 1916, Rybnikov compiled a collection of research on the "ideals of children in the countryside," containing a statistical analysis of replies to the classic question "Who do you want to be when you grow up?" Also gathered were children's conceptions about morals, religion, and more.

The first survey-based research on children after the revolution was published in the journal of the Orel Pedological Society. D. Azbukin had performed a study of schoolchildren in Orel in 1918.[57] The historic tremors that shook the city of Orel, in Azbukin's poetic words, did not prevent him from collecting 1,000 questionnaires, filled out by children between the ages of ten and eighteen. The forms contained twenty-three questions each, and the children wrote in their answers themselves.

Eighty percent of those surveyed wrote that they had been to the theater at least once in their lives; somewhat fewer had been to the cinema. The most preferred art form was music, favorite writers were Pushkin and Gogol (although children also revered Dumas, Shakespeare, and Thomas Mayne Reid). Most children wanted to be like their parents when they grew up, and then, in descending order, Lenin, Trotsky, Lunacharsky, and Kerensky. A few responded that they would like to be like animals: Animals, they explained, were usually well fed. Most children wanted to be government officials, teachers, doctors, or actors.

Many of the children preferred school to home. Forty-eight percent liked to do physical labor at home, and thirty-eight percent preferred mentally demanding work. Homework had already been abolished, but half of the children surveyed continued to study lessons on their own time, by habit. The least favorite subject, as among children of other times, was mathematics. Most of the children—sixty percent—felt that they were behind in their studies. However, the new school system had gained the children's favor, since the teachers were closer to their students, breakfasts were free, pupils were more independent, and grades had been eliminated. Four percent of the children had already "gone to work," but Azbukin commented that "they had not yet become primary breadwinners, as would be the case with almost all of them later on."

According to data collected in Moscow in 1925–1926 by L. S. Geshelina,[58] only three percent of children in working-class families and twenty-eight percent of officials' children received "good nutrition at home" before they entered kindergarten. Half of working-class children slept in a common bedroom. Psychoanalyst Ilya Perepel wrote around this time that "[j]ust introducing the idea that common bedrooms are colossally harmful could give the population a thousand times more benefit than a thousand educational treatises."[59]

According to the research of Y. I. Kazhdanskaya,[60] in 1924 only nine percent of the schoolchildren in Odessa between the ages of seven and twelve knew who Lenin was. A scattered few could explain who the communists were and what they stood for. On average, the children surveyed were able satisfactorily to answer only eight percent of the survey questions on sociopolitical subjects. After two and a half years of study under a new curriculum, fifty-two percent of answers were characterized as "vague," "absurd," or just wrong, complemented by thirty-four percent that were "hackneyed"—answers that were outwardly correct, but only memorized and formulaic, with no meaning for the child. Two hundred compositions on the revolution were collected for examination. The essays were a "casserole . . . , in which the events of both revolutions were mixed together with the 'ninth of January,'" a date that for some reason stood out most clearly in the children's minds.[61]

"The children are tragically illiterate," Kazhdanskaya concluded. "There is a limit beyond which the popularization of complex concepts leads only to distortion bordering on profanation." On the other hand, the Odessan teacher and pedologist wrote suspiciously in 1928 that "the abundance of bloody episodes in courses on politics over the first two years of education . . . is dangerous, in that it might dull children's sensitivity." The editor of the journal *Pedology* discounted this conclusion in a note as "too categorical and pessimistic."

However, these conclusions echoed the findings of other researchers. Rybnikov,[62] who had by then gathered 120,000 questionnaires from provincial Russian schoolchildren, asserted that only a negligible proportion knew the meaning and history of the most recent revolution. However, all the children, according to Rybnikov's figures, were sure that the Soviet government was better than any other. Meanwhile, the scientist noted an interesting phenomenon where children "underestimated the economic advances made by their own class and overestimated the achievements of other classes." Working-class children pointed to the land that they felt the revolution had given to the peasants; at the same time, peasant children pointed to the eight-hour workday and to the belief that factories had been handed over to the workers.

Half of the peasant children surveyed in the Samara region at the end of the 1930s preferred mental work to manual labor. Only eleven percent preferred various sorts of peasant labor (children in Orel had given totally different responses only ten years earlier). One-third of peasant boys expressed a clear dislike for agricultural labor, and eighty-five percent said that they did not like to do chores around the home: Anti-peasant policies had done their work.[63]

The pedologists' surveys give perhaps the only source of reliable statistical information about children's feelings during that transitional time when collectivization was just beginning, opposition in the party was being crushed, and the country was sliding into mass terror. The press had already been cowed into uniformity and hatred of independent thought. What were people thinking back then?

In 1928, R. G. Vilenkina conducted a survey of working teens by collecting anonymous statements that they wrote on cards and dropped into a box. She repeated the vital and extremely diverse words of a generation that would soon be dragged through repression and war: "Why is it that in the eleventh year after the revolution, there's no bread, no butter, no flour, and no sugar? How long is this going to continue?" "Why are peasants who have only two cows denounced as *kulaks?*" "The land should be taken away from the peasants, so they become rural workers, so they live off a salary like workers." "Why is everyone leaving the countryside for the city? Things must be really bad there." "Why didn't they take Trotsky out and shoot him?" "Opposition leaders should have been converted, not exiled." "What kind of freedom is it, if you can't organize your own party?" And finally, a characteristic judgment that reflected a mood that may have presaged the fate of the entire country: "Young people will eventually abandon revolutionary work, because it's boring. I hope there's a war soon."[64]

A series of pedological expeditions at the end of the 1920s pushed deep into the most remote areas of the countryside. A new field of research was created—the pedology of ethnic minorities, the exact equivalent of today's ethnic child psychology. Research was conducted on the children and adolescents of Buryatia, Altai, and Uzbekistan, and on Tatar schoolchildren in Moscow. This was important work, but to this day its merits remain unrecognized.

The history of science is most of all the history of its internal composition and the people that created it, the history of categories and methods, of leaders and institutions. But there is yet another layer in the history of social science, which has much to do with changing reality: the unique picture captured by science at a certain historical moment. This layer can turn out to be the most important for posterity.

Trouble at the Top

Pedology came under fire immediately after the so-called ideological war on two fronts (both left and right) was declared. At the very start of 1931, a resolution was adopted at a meeting of the presidium of the Communist Academy, which underlined a great turning point in science. The resolution was drafted in response to a report by Otto Schmidt (the very same Otto Schmidt who had recently served as the "curator" of Soviet psychoanalysis). It stated that "it is of momentous import that we unmask all breeds of pseudo-Marxism," and went on to list a number of such deviations from the Party line, among them pedology. On January 25, 1931, the Central Committee of the Communist Party passed an order removing the editor of the journal *Under the Banner of Marxism*. Toward the end of the year, the journal crystallized the political climate: "Within the psychoneurological sciences, there has not been enough open criticism of the mechanical and idealist theories of Kornilov in psychology, Gannushkin in psychiatry and neuropathology, and Blonsky in pedology ... nor of Comrade Spielrein's system of idealist errors, Comrade Zalkind's Menshevik, idealist eclecticism, and so forth."[65]

Zalkind's journal *Pedology* also leaped into this campaign of mutual self-destruction. Zalkind called on his colleagues to unmask themselves voluntarily before events caught up with them. "If these dispassionate pedologists (who have managed to totally avoid publication in our journal—could this be a symptom?) would think a bit harder about the ideological debates on pedology and psychology, they would understand that their isolation from today's practice is organically linked to their Marxist virginity." Such was the tone of editorials in *Pedology* at the beginning of 1931.[66] It is unlikely that Blonsky, Basov, Vygotsky, and Luria were dispassionate during this alarming period, and there is no way any of them could be accused of virginity of any sort. However, they declined Zalkind's offer to help them criticize themselves. What followed immediately thereafter proved this a wise choice.

The journal's pages became crammed with ideological tirades. One example was P. Leventuyev's article entitled "Political Perversions in Pedology." Pedology was digging its own grave, even through its terminology. It spared neither Zalkind nor his journal. On the contrary, Zalkind was removed from his post as editor as early as the end of 1931, and a year later the journal was shut down. Isaac Spielrein, who had remained uninvolved in the debate for the most part and who was very reserved in his response to criticism, continued as editor of *Industrial Psychology and Psychophysiology of Labor* for three more years. He continued to work until the day of his arrest, which coincided almost exactly with the closing of the journal.

Nevertheless, apart from these few cases of leadership turnover, there was no warning of the blow that would finish off pedology suddenly in 1936. Textbooks on pedology were reprinted as before, people continued to be trained, more and more pedologists were working in schools. Moreover, their competence had increased: A ministry of education decree of January 15, 1935, entrusted to pedologists the selection of children for admission to school, in addition to their previous responsibilities. However, the Deputy Minister of Education, M. S. Epstein, who had supervised pedology, was soon removed from his office. B. M. Volin was then appointed first deputy to Minister Bubnov. Both Volin and Epstein, as well as Bubnov, were later arrested, during the terror.

On July 4, 1936, the Central Committee of the Communist Party passed a resolution entitled "On the Pedological Perversions of the Ministry of Education System."[67] The pedological movement was reviled in terms that would have signaled disaster to any Soviet citizen involved: The movement had allegedly created dangerous organizations in the schools, with its own regulatory centers. The Central Committee saw the damage wrought by pedologists in their pseudoscientific experiments, countless examinations, and their senseless and harmful questionnaires and tests. All of these efforts, the Central Committee asserted, were designed to find as much negative or pathologically perverse information as possible to describe the Soviet schoolchild, his parents, his family, and his social environment. Explorations into mental development and talent in children, the Committee declared, were merely formalized mockery of the pupils. Particular attention was paid in the resolution to specialized and remedial schools. The document's anonymous author asserted that the majority of students in such places were perfectly normal. More than that, there were even gifted children stuck in remedial institutions; they all should be sent back to ordinary schools. The Central Committee also held that as a result of the activity of pedologists, the rights of regular schoolteachers had been abridged. Also included was a philosophical analysis of pedological doctrine. The view that child development was fatalistically conditioned by biological and social factors was declared "the primary directive of pedology." This "deeply reactionary idea" was denounced, it being in flagrant opposition to the extensively successful Marxist practice of reeducation in the drive to build socialism.

Exactly why pedology was eliminated remained a mystery to contemporary observers, who sought the reason in secret, random events. A legend formed that pedologists had been studying the son of a certain very powerful government official (as rumor had it, A. A. Zhdanov). The son had allegedly been given an unfavorable diagnosis, which brought the official's wrath down on pedology.

Reading the text of the resolution, one does indeed sense the presence of greater knowledge and personal interest, albeit one-sided, than was usual in such matters. The tone of the document does not wholly correspond with the accepted ideological style of that time, which would have been full of vague delineations and abstract labels that only in the secret world behind closed doors would take on the power of a denunciation. This decree, moreover, touches on common motifs that characterized professional debate in the field.

No other pseudoscience in Soviet history ever rated a special Central Committee decree. The uncommonly high level at which pedology's record was reviewed demands an explanation. Did it really involve a personal grudge on the part of one of the nation's political leaders? Or was the resolution an interim result of some unknown game within the *nomenklatura*, part of some unfinished political scheme in preparation for a larger, later-aborted process?

The decree contains an astonishing array of peculiarities that do not fit well together. There were of course plenty of shortcomings in the quickly expanding activity of pedologists and their new network of special schools.

But the total liquidation of the pedological service, including the closing of special schools, appears to have been unjustified by real circumstances; fatalism, the "primary directive," and other anti-Marxist perversions unjustly attributed to pedology had nothing to do with the problems of specialized schooling.[68] But most surprising of all was that although the resolution contained very strong accusations, including the charge that pedology created an anti-Marxist organization that performed mass experiments on children, it had relatively meager consequences. In the context of 1936, these kinds of accusations, particularly when they were handed down by the highest governmental bodies, were more than enough to warrant execution. No executions followed, however. The word "sabotage," which would probably have been deadly, was absent from the resolution. Pedology was eliminated as a science; but its leaders were not repressed, as were the leaders of industrial psychology, for example. Only later, in 1937–1938, were the employees of the Russian ministry of education and parallel ministries in other republics subjected to near-total purges, and even then it was on different grounds. Nor did the decree on pedology lead to any widespread ideological campaign such as followed on the heels of the Central Committee's interference in philosophy in 1931.

Perhaps the action was intended to discredit the popular Bukharin once and for all (children were at stake!), as he had publicly supported pedology for many years; but Bukharin had already bared his Achilles' heel, and he was taken out of the picture by much simpler means. This time, the heaviest guns in the imposing ideological arsenal were filled with blanks, resulting in no evident sacrifice of human lives.

However, the Central Committee resolution did have decisive importance for Soviet pedology and education. The series of decrees that flowed out of the ministry of education liquidated all pedological institutions and offices, snatched books and textbooks out of libraries, created unified departments of pedagogy in all teachers' colleges, opened courses for retraining pedologists, and restructured specialized schools of all kinds. Only children with the most serious mental illnesses remained in the ministry of education's restyled sanatoriums; even oligophrenics did not qualify. A separate article required that all pedological observations be removed from pupils' files. Another special resolution forbade surveys based on questionnaires.[69]

A few months later, Volin issued a decree "On the Verification of Execution of the Resolution of the Central Committee of the Communist Party."[70] The orders to eliminate pedology, as it turned out, were being executed poorly. There were still forty specialized schools in Moscow, teaching seven thousand children. There were still schools for "mentally handicapped" and "hard-to-educate" children. The large-scale transfer of children had naturally caused huge problems. The system was disorganized, teachers were at a loss, pupils were out of control. The ministry of education decree included the story of how one schoolgirl by the name of Stepanikova stopped going to class after being transferred out of remedial school, complaining that her studies were too difficult. After skipping school for a while, she appealed personally to the ministry of education, asking to be returned to a remedial school.

Bubnov held a series of meetings, trying to explain the motivation behind the Central Committee resolution and to avoid personal responsibility for the organization of pedological science. In his speeches to educators, rather than emphasizing the remedial schools (the transfer of sick and difficult children into regular schools was probably not terribly popular among education professionals), he stressed the lack of control over pedologists, their independence from school administrators, and the subordinate position of teachers. Bubnov concentrated his attack on the recently deceased Zalkind, whom he characterized as the single leader of pedology whose views were "a Menshevik apologia on spontaneity, objectivism, and the Socialist Revolutionary doctrine of interacting factors, combined most of all with Freudianism." Bubnov criticized Vygotsky, also deceased, as another "pillar of today's pedology." He spoke more softly about Blonsky, who was present in the room, chastising him for immediately resigning rather than engaging in self-criticism (Blonsky later came forward with a repentant confession).[71] To all appearances, this was but another attempt to cushion the fist that was poised above all those present, including Bubnov himself.

Based on what we know today of this particular case, we can aspire to explain only the most general mechanisms operating in the functioning, adaptation, and destruction of knowledge in a totalitarian atmosphere.[72] In its struggle to survive, pedology succumbed to the same fate as other, related fields—the hypertrophic development of applied areas without sufficient underlying support in scientific knowledge. In the place of science, designed to describe and understand reality, there appeared a doctrine, a phenomenon specific to Soviet intellectual life, in which remnants of true science were intermingled with irrelevant promises to reconstruct an unyielding reality. This metamorphosis was marked by the appearance on the scene of charismatic scientific leaders, who ran their sciences in the same way as other leaders ran the Party or the railway transport system. In the science of man, this led inevitably to the depersonalization of scholarship, erasing all distinctions between schools, authors, and movements, and also to the de-individualization of its content, which was more and more oriented toward the "new man of the masses."

Soviet pedology, psychoanalysis, industrial psychology, and pedagogy all shared this common fate. A few of the best scholars attempted to resist, allowing the marvelous political centrifuge occasionally to squeeze out extraordinary products of intellect along with the usual streams of worthless tripe. Despite ideological pressure and direct threats of violence that would soon be carried out, the human sciences of the 1920s and 1930s left behind a unique and invaluable record of the people of that time. Pedology can only be properly understood as a historical reality that suffered from the horrendous mistakes of its era, paid a price for those mistakes, and in its occasional valid contributions to science, rose above the limits of that era, preserving it forever.

9

The Ambassador and Satan: William Bullitt in Bulgakov's Moscow

William C. Bullitt, the U.S. ambassador to Soviet Russia in 1933–1936 and later to France (1936–1941), was also one of Freud's patients. It was Bullitt who arranged Freud's escape from occupied Vienna. Psychoanalysts perhaps know Bullitt best for his success in convincing Freud to coauthor with him a biography of President Woodrow Wilson, most of which Bullitt wrote himself.[1] Diplomats know him as a key player in American foreign policy before World War II. Finally, to Slavicists he is remembered for his friendship with renowned writer Mikhail Bulgakov.

Quite a bit is known about Bullitt; but more can still be deduced from the evidence available.

From Wilson and Lenin to Roosevelt and Freud

Bill Bullitt was born to an aristocratic Philadelphia family. His paternal ancestors were French Huguenots and his maternal forebears Polish Jews; both branches of the family were among the first immigrants to America. Bullitt studied at Yale and Harvard, then became a war correspondent and traveled throughout Europe, and in 1917, during Wilson's presidency, he began working for the U.S. State Department.[2] Bullitt's unique life story took its first odd turn in Russia. In April 1919 Bullitt, who had been a participant at the Versailles peace talks that defined Europe's sad state between the two world wars, was sent by Wilson to Russia at the head of a semi-official mission. The situation Bullitt found in the Kremlin seemed to him no less important than events at Versailles.

Lenin had made an offer to the American delegation, which consisted of one diplomat with only two years of experience, one journalist, and one military intelligence officer. Soviet Russia was ready to relinquish control over sixteen territories that formerly belonged to the czarist empire. These lands included Poland, Rumania, Finland, and the three Baltic republics, half of Ukraine and western Belorussia, the entire Caucasus and the Crimea, and all of the Urals and Siberia, with Murmansk to boot. "Lenin had offered to confine communist rule to Moscow and a small adjacent area, plus the city now known as Leningrad."[3] It is not quite clear what Lenin asked for in exchange. He probably asked that his country be included in the Versailles negotiations and that the Bolshevik state be recognized by the former allies of the Russian empire. Bullitt was thrilled with Lenin: "Think, if I only had a father like that."[4] He would find his surrogate father only later; but Lenin did reciprocate the American's warm feelings, even calling him a friend.

The personalities and intentions of the Russian communist leaders so struck Bullitt that upon his return to Paris he did everything he could to attract Wilson's attention to Russia. But the president, notorious for his one-track mind, was much more concerned at the time with demands for reparations issuing from England and France, and he never even considered the Russian offer.

Any signs of interest in the Russian experiment exhibited by Americans irritated the strongly anticommunist president. The first and most telling sign of this interest was John Reed's book, *Ten Days That Shook the World*. Reed died of typhus in a Moscow hospital shortly after the revolution that he described so glowingly in his book. He died in the arms of his companion, Louisa Bryant, who a few years later would become William Bullitt's wife.

Bullitt resigned in protest over the U.S. president's failure to take note of the important diplomatic information he had delivered, and he sent a severe letter to Wilson. The long list of accusations addressed to the president opened with the following statement: "Russia, 'the acid test of good will,' for me as for you, has not even been understood."[5] According to the view that Bullitt elaborated in this letter, America's neglect of Russia and overly intimate relations with France would render the conditions of the Versailles peace agreement unjust. Germany would be subjected to unnecessary humiliation and the League of Nations would be incapacitated in its attempts to prevent war in the future.

After his resignation, Bullitt worked as a film editor for Paramount. For a while he lived in Europe, which at the time was a fashionable mecca for many Americans who were fleeing Prohibition and boredom. Bullitt made friends with F. Scott Fitzgerald and also met Hemingway in Paris. Together with his compatriots, he fell straight into *The Moveable Feast*, leading a carefree, merry life in inexpensive postwar Europe. When the epoch subsided, it left in its wake not only a handful of famous American novels but also a number of more ordinary stories—such as the medical case history of alcoholic Louisa Bryant.

In 1926, Bullitt's novel *It's Not Done* was released.[6] The setting was his home city of Philadelphia. The protagonist struggles with the conservatism of his environment, marries the woman he loves in the face of resistance, and in the end must rescue his son from accusations of involvement with communists. The novel seems to have met with little success. But shortly after its publication, Bullitt's life took another turn—one that inspired him to write a second book, which would preserve his name for posterity.

Beginning in 1925, Bullitt underwent analysis with Sigmund Freud. Nothing is known about the motives that drove this successful man of American high society to Vienna. His wife's alcoholism might have been part of the problem. He told a friend that after slipping from his saddle while horseback riding he had become aware of an unconscious desire to commit suicide.[7] Unfortunately, very little is known about what went on during the analysis. Gradually, as sometimes happened, Freud's patient became his student and friend.

Over the course of ten years, Bullitt visited Vienna regularly to discuss various personal and political problems with Freud. Freud was ill at the end of 1930 when he wrote, in response to Zweig's suggestion that he write a book on Nietzsche and the will to power: "I cannot write the yellow book you wish me to. I know too little about the human drive for power, for I have lived my life as a theorist. . . . Indeed I would like to write nothing more, and yet I am once again writing an Introduction for something someone else is doing. I must not say what it is. . . . You will never guess what."[8] It was an introduction to the book *Thomas Woodrow Wilson*, which Bullitt finally published under two names, Freud's and his own. Freud, of course, received top billing. Freud rarely collaborated, and almost never in his latter years; this work was most likely Freud's only study dedicated to a political figure. Historians and psychoanalysts still argue about the quality of the book and the extent of Freud's contribution.

According to Bullitt, the collaboration was born when he visited Freud in 1930 in Berlin. Freud was sick and gloomy; he said he wasn't long for this world, and that nobody would care when he died, anyway, since he had already written everything he ever wanted to and his brain was empty. Bullitt told Freud about his idea for a book that would include his psychological sketches of Clemenceau, Orlando, Lloyd George, Lenin, and Wilson. Freud shocked Bullitt by proposing that they write the book together. "He had been interested in Wilson ever since he had discovered that they were both born in 1856."[9] A chapter grew into a book. The first draft was completed in 1932, and later was revised several times. The final version was approved and signed (each chapter by both authors) in 1938, but it could not be published as long as Wilson's widow was alive.[10]

It is clear from the book and the history of its writing that Bullitt, although not a professional psychoanalyst, shared Freud's analytical views and understood his philosophical beliefs well enough to be capable of carrying on a dialogue with the doctor. "He was a Jew who had become an agnostic. I have always been a believing Christian. We often disagreed but we never quarreled,"[11] Bullitt wrote in his introduction to the book. Meanwhile, their political allegiances were almost identical in the interwar period. Freud and Bullitt wrote, in particular, that "Wilson's refusal to burden his 'one track mind' with Russia may well, in the end, turn out to be the most important single decision that he made in Paris."[12] Bullitt was for many years one of Freud's most important and reliable sources of information on Russia.

In 1933, after the election of a new president, Bullitt began working for Roosevelt's administration, accepting an appointment as U.S. ambassador to the USSR. George F. Kennan, his subordinate at the time and destined later to become one of the best known of American diplomats, described him in the following way:

> We took pride in him and never had occasion to be ashamed of him. . . . Bullitt, as we knew him at that time in Moscow, was charming, brilliant, well-educated, imaginative, a man of the world capable of holding his own intellectually with anyone. . . . He resolutely refused to permit the life around him to degenerate into dullness and dreariness. All of us who lived in his entourage were the beneficiaries of this blitheness of spirit, this insistence that life be at all times animated and interesting and moving ahead.[13]

At the same time, Kennan characterized the embassy as a "lonely and exposed bastion of American governmental life, surrounded by a veritable ocean of official Soviet ill will."[14]

Henry Wallace, future vice president of the United States, was on close terms with Bullitt and described him as a very attractive personality. According to Wallace's unpublished memoirs, which reside in the Office of Oral History at Columbia University, Bullitt was a world traveler, a connoisseur of sophisticated entertainment and witty conversation, and at the same time a man distinguished by his deep convictions and rare sincerity. He had at his disposal a wide array of anecdotes about his prominent contacts abroad.[15]

In 1933, American financier J. P. Warburg joined Bullitt in organizing a conference on economic issues in Europe. Warburg left behind the following impressions: "He's a naughty boy; he loves to create a scene and he can put on an act of indignation such as I've rarely seen and come out roaring with laughter over it. He had little concern over the success of the conference; he had no concern about anything economic. He's one of these curious people to whom the drama was more exciting than the results."[16] At the same time, Warburg supported Bullitt, because he was "the only person on the horizon a) who knows Europe thoroughly, and b) who has real talent as a negotiator."[17] Warburg also called Bullitt a maverick in all senses of the word. A Soviet historian evaluated Bullitt as an "unusual figure among diplomats, . . . a man of extremes who easily changed his mind, ambitious and suspicious."[18] A recent American biography of Bullitt describes him as "a man of mystery and paradox."[19]

Satan's Ball at Spaso House: Three Literary Variations

On April 23, 1935, a reception was held at Spaso House, the gorgeous mansion on Arbat street which to this day serves as the U.S. ambassador's private residence. Five hundred people were invited to the reception—everyone who was anyone in Moscow, apart from Stalin.[20] The Americans were ready to have some honest fun, and they wanted very much to entertain their guests. For them it would be harder to relax. The fall of the intellectual Bolsheviks (Bukharin, Bubnov, and Radek were among the guests) was only a few months away, and the highest-ranking military commanders (Tukhachevsky, Yegorov, and Budenny) had already become mere pawns in a two-faced game between Soviet and German intelligence. The theatrical elite (Meyerhold, Tairov, Nemirovich-Danchenko, and Bulgakov) expected groundless reprisal at any moment; the wait would be short for some and painfully long for others.

The guests arrived at midnight. They danced in the hall of columns. Multicolored spotlights shone down on them from the balconies. Live birds fluttered behind a net. Baby goats, sheep, and bears roamed in pens in the corners of the dining room. Roosters in cages hung on the walls. The roosters all began to crow at three in the morning. "Russian style," Mikhail Bulgakov's wife ironically concluded the description of the ball in her diary.[21] It was the costumes that attracted her attention most of all. Everyone, except the military officers, wore tailcoats. Bulgakov did not own a tailcoat, so he came in a black suit; his wife was in a black ball gown with pale pink flowers. The Bolsheviks' apparel stuck out like a sore thumb: Bukharin was dressed in an old-fashioned frock coat, Radek wore a hiking outfit, and Bubnov was in a khaki suit. One stoolie notorious in Moscow diplomatic circles attended the ball as well, a certain Baron Steiger, whom Bubnov's wife referred to as "our resident secret policeman." He was dressed, of course, in a tailcoat. The conductor's tailcoat was especially long, reaching all the way to his heels.

Judging by her remarks, the scene was amusing but not particularly remarkable. However, there was a touch of mystery in Elena Bulgakova's perception of the reception: With impressions of the party still fresh in his mind, her husband supposedly wrote a new version of chapter 23 of his new novel, entitled "Satan's Ball." It was this version that was incorporated into *The Master and Margarita*, the most widely read Russian novel of the twentieth century.

The writer's wife claimed that this final draft of the ball scene was written much later, during Bulgakov's final illness, and that it "reflected the reception held by Bullitt, American ambassador to the USSR."[22] She confessed that she was "terribly fond" of the other, former version (where what she referred to as a "small ball" was held in Woland's bedroom, or in other words, in Stepa Likhodeev's room). Elena was so aggressive in her insistence that the "small ball" was better than the "big ball" that the ailing Bulgakov destroyed the old version while his wife was away in order to "avoid mistakes," as Elena Bulgakova later recalled.[23]

This embassy party, called the Spring Festival, was a celebrated event. Ambassador Bullitt wrote to President Roosevelt on May 1, 1935: "It was an astonishingly successful party, thoroughly dignified yet gay. . . . It was the best party in Moscow since the revolution. We got a thousand tulips from Helsingfors and forced a lot of birch trees into premature leafage and arranged one end of the dining room as a collective farm with peasant accordion players, dancers, and all sorts of baby things, such as birds, goats, and a couple of infant bears."[24]

Serious preparations went into building a collective farm in the dining room. The ambassador was fond of extravagant entertainment, and the embassy was known in the Moscow diplomatic corps as "Bill Bullitt's circus." When Bullitt arrived in Moscow, he found nothing livelier than a tenor in the repertoire of local diplomatic entertainment. According to instructions given by the ambassador, the ball was to outdo anything Moscow had ever seen, before or after the revolution. "The sky's the limit," he told his employees as he was leaving to spend the winter of 1934–1935 in Washington.[25] Preparations for the ball, which was to coincide with his return, were entrusted to Charles Thayer, a secretary at the embassy, and Irena Wiley, an advisor's wife. The ambassador covered all of the expenses personally.

Thayer had already had painful experience organizing American parties in Moscow: The previous reception had featured an animal trainer named Durov, whose seals juggled obediently until Durov got drunk, when the seals went for a dip in the salad bowl. The animals for this ball were borrowed from the Moscow zoo. Thayer had become more cautious and refused to trust Soviet trainers. He found out for himself that goats and sheep could not be put in the dining room: No matter how well washed, they still stink. As it turned out, mountain goats were the least aromatic breed, so they were selected for the ball. Tulips also posed a problem. After a fruitless search all over the Soviet Union, the flowers were ordered from Finland. A Czech jazz band that was performing in Moscow at the time was hired, along with a troupe of gypsy musicians and dancers. When the guests arrived, the light in the hall went out, and the moon and stars were projected on the high ceiling. The director of the Kamernyi theater (possibly Tairov) was in charge of the projector. Twelve roosters sat in covered cages. On

Thayer's command, the cages were uncovered, but only one rooster began to crow, albeit loudly. Another rooster escaped and landed on the dish of duck-liver pâté that had been delivered from Strasbourg.[26]

When Bullitt was staffing the embassy in Moscow, he had hired only single men in order to avoid the extreme openness that diplomats' wives might engender. However, "the romantic attachments and resulting complications of the bachelors soon outmatched any indiscretions wives might have committed and today the recruiting policy for the Moscow Embassy is quite the reverse—preferably no bachelors."[27] At the time of the ball, those Americans in attendance were for the most part single men.

The ball ended at 9 a.m. with a *lezginka* performed by Tukhachevsky and Lelya Lepeshinskaya, a famous dancer from the Bolshoi, who was Bullitt's frequent guest. The ambassador at the time was accompanied by his daughter Anna; Louisa Bryant had stayed at home in the United States. Bullitt had a long affair with Roosevelt's personal secretary, who once arrived at the embassy in Moscow to find Bullitt in the company of Lelya Lepeshinskaya. No one at the embassy had any doubt that the ballet dancer, who had the closest connections among the political elite, routinely collaborated with the NKVD.

Despite the romantic atmosphere that was typical of these American bachelors' gatherings in Moscow, the party guests were most impressed by the Russian bears. Thayer's memoirs show just how impressed they were: The book is entitled *Bears in the Caviar*. Russian bears and Soviet people staged a poetic *mise-en-scène* without the assistance of any animal trainer. The symbolism of the act went unappreciated, even by an American connoisseur of Russian realities. Karl Radek, who was known for his sharp wit, found a bear cub lying on its back with a bottle of milk in its paws, and switched the bear's nipple to a champagne bottle. The cub took several swallows of Cordon Rouge before he noticed he'd been fooled. Meanwhile, the malicious Radek had disappeared, and Marshal Yegorov, who happened to be standing nearby, had to console the crying bear in his arms. As the general rocked the bear, it vomited on his medal-encrusted uniform. Thayer soon appeared at the scene of the crime. Half a dozen waiters were fussing with Yegorov, doing their best to clean his suit, as he bellowed: "Tell your ambassador that Soviet generals are not accustomed to being treated like clowns!"[28]

Elena Bulgakova's description of the embassy ball pales against the background of these marvelous details, which could have been the work of a satirist or a historiographer. Satan's ball in *The Master and Margarita,* meanwhile, does not seem to have any connection to the American "Spring Festival," conceived more in the style of F. Scott Fitzgerald's *The Great Gatsby.*

For Muscovites, however, the opulent ball took on other nuances in retrospect—it had been a place where victims enjoyed themselves alongside their executioners, as nearly all the guests were to perish over the next few months, to the astonishment of their hosts. At the time that Bulgakov described the scene, he was probably one of the few people still alive who had been at the ball that the Americans honestly considered "the best party in Moscow since the revolution."[29] Nevertheless, it was not the frightening Abadonna but naked, gorgeous Margarita who became the main figure of Bulgakov's ball.

It is enough to reread this chapter from the novel to become convinced of a fact that will sound surprising to modern readers: It was not political intrigues, grief over the dead, or desire for revenge that reigned at Satan's ball. Of all the "kings, dukes, knights, suicides, poisoners, gallows birds, procuresses, jailers, card sharpers, hangmen, informers, traitors, madmen, detectives, and seducers,"[30] the author shows only one category—sex-related criminals.[31] Monsieur Jacques, who poisoned his king's mistress and the "reverse case"—the queen's lover, who poisoned his wife; a Russian noblewoman who liked to burn her maid's face with a curling iron; a Neapolitan lady who helped five hundred of her female compatriots get rid of their tiresome husbands; Frieda, who was raped by her employer and later suffocated her child; the owner of some peculiar brothel in Strasbourg; a Moscow dressmaker who had made two peepholes in her fitting room, a fact of which every last one of her female clients was fully aware; and a young man who had sold his beloved to a whorehouse. This stream of stories ended, understandably, with Messalina; after that, Margarita could no longer tell one face or sin from another.

It is impossible to ignore the erotic tension in the slowly moving procession, where beautiful, naked sinners appear at the ball with their seducers and rapists. Practically the whole scene was cut out by Soviet censors when the novel was first published in the 1960s. Of course, Margarita was not the first *nue* in Russian literature, but she was appearing naked in an unbelievably public place and, what was even more shocking, she was not the least bit ashamed. Moreover, she was not alone. "The naked women mounting the staircase between the tail-coated and white-tied men floated up in a spectrum of colored bodies that ranged from white through olive, copper, and coffee to quite black. . . . Diamond-studded orders glittered on the jackets and shirt fronts of the men."[32] Sex was not individualized here. As opposed to Nabokov, Bulgakov was not interested in how his character fell into sin. "Satan's Ball" was not twentieth-century psychological erotica but rather an erotic epic, a static picture of the monotonous and insurmountable might of sex: The force of lust knew no boundaries in time or space; it ruled all nations and all epochs.

But it seemed there were exceptions. One such exception was the country and time Woland visited. Although there were only a few political criminals at Satan's ball this time, they all walked straight in off the streets of Moscow.

The "newcomers," as Satan's assistant Koroviev designated them, were all political criminals. Koroviev introduces the last two arrivals nebulously and without much emotion—these two poisoners are the only visitors from the outside world whose sin was not the fruit of love. The last guest, Baron Maigel, whose spilled blood closes out the ball scene, has a clearly political vice, however—he is an "eavesdropper and spy." His prototype was Boris Steiger, who according to Russian scholar Leonid Parshin was the representative of the Collegium for External Relations of the ministry of education who invariably accompanied foreign ambassadors, including Bullitt, on outings to the Moscow Art Theater.[33]

The "newcomers'" sins were not related to sex, and yet the great sinners of the past went to hell exclusively for their sexual adventures. Did this mean that for past generations morals lay largely in the sexual realm, while modern sinners would be judged for their political misdeeds?

As far as we know, this idea has no roots in the works of Mikhail Bulgakov. It could, however, have sprung from the mind of William C. Bullitt.

What Margarita Didn't Know

Very little in the accounts of Elena Bulgakova and Charles Thayer is reminiscent of the famous chapter in *The Master and Margarita*. Only a few curious details coincide. Several times during the evening, Margarita is disturbed by the sound of flapping wings. Thayer's memoirs include a colorful explanation: A flock of birds was borrowed from the Moscow zoo for decoration. Over the course of the ball, the birds slipped out of their cages and flitted all over the building. The next morning, the entire embassy staff was engaged to catch them, with the ambassador at the head of the operation. Another addition to the fund of common details was the expedition undertaken by the Soviet pilot who was dispatched by the Americans to find flowers: He flew first to the Crimea, then the Caucasus, and finally, to Helsinki. This trajectory resembles Likhodeev's fantastic voyage. Finally, there was the conductor's tailcoat, which, according to Elena Bulgakova, "mesmerized [Bulgakov] more than anything else." This tailcoat can be correlated to the "unusually long tailcoat of an unbelievable cut/style" worn by Woland (at a different occasion, however—at the show in the Variety Theater).[34]

There is some incongruity in the story of the tailcoat, however: Bulgakova did not mention it in the journal entry written directly after the event. She wrote about it only as she was editing her diary at the beginning of the 1960s. Bulgakov scholars provide their own perspective: "When [Elena] entered her story about the ball at the American embassy, she had no idea that Bulgakov would make use of his impressions in *The Master and Margarita*. But when she was editing the second draft, she was fully aware of it and, naturally, drew out of her memory some half-forgotten images that had never attracted her attention before."[35] It seems that the edition of Elena Bulgakova's diaries that is available to the public is not so much an eyewitness account as it is the recollections of a memoirist in which facts are mixed in with half-forgotten images. Rather than recording events as they were, the diarist tried to explain in retrospect a fact that she knew from her husband's book but never understood, a fact which therefore stuck in her memory when she was reworking her journal. This fact, clearly expressed by Bulgakov (and probably reiterated during his debates with his wife over which version of chapter 23 to keep), was the association between Satan's ball and the real party at the embassy. What Elena Bulgakova did not understand was the basis for the association. Why couldn't she understand, even though she was present at the ambassador's reception, had served as a prototype for the character of Margarita, and edited her husband's novel? The writer's widow never answered this question, and instead returned decades later to the same theme, introducing new, minute details into her diary that still fail to solve the problem.

We can deduce from all this that there was some connection or similarity between the receptions held by Bullitt and Woland, a commonality of which Bulgakov's wife was aware. But as to exactly what sort of connection it was, Elena was most likely left guessing. At any rate, the link was not based in all the details of Russian-style exoticism, in all the roosters, bears, birch trees, and informers that she saw at Spaso House. The similarity must have been something else, something more important, that even she didn't know about.

He Bedeviled the Russians

Kalinin accepted the Americans' credentials on December 19, 1933. The long-awaited diplomatic recognition of the Soviet Union by the United States was considered a great achievement. The first U.S. ambassador, who was Lenin's friend besides, was welcomed with "effusive Slavic emotion," as American newspapers described the event. Bullitt was quite animated himself. At a Kremlin banquet, he successfully withstood his first test of endurance: an endless stream of toasts during which to eat or sit would have been a breach of decorum. Bullitt even received a personal offer of assistance from Stalin, in the form of land on which to build the new embassy compound in the Lenin Hills. Reporting this encounter in a letter to Roosevelt, the ambassador referred to his own tactics in words reminiscent of Woland's notorious advice: "Never ask for anything! Never, especially of those who are stronger than you. They will offer everything themselves, and they will give everything themselves."[36] His subtle experience in psychobiography was not enough to allow him to see past Stalin's image as a "wiry Gypsy with roots and emotions beyond my experience."[37] Voroshilov struck him as "one of the most charming persons that I have ever met."[38]

According to Wallace, Bullitt was very enthusiastic about the Bolsheviks during his first years as ambassador. He even tried to convince Wallace, then secretary of agriculture, to pay closer attention to the Russians' achievements in this field, for some reason particularly emphasizing the progress they had made in artificial insemination. Stalin received Bullitt regularly; once they talked one-on-one all night. Bullitt recognized the Soviet leader as an exceptional personage, but could not mask his disgust when recalling how Stalin had kissed him with an open mouth. Nor did he enjoy the copious drinking bouts and feasting rituals so common behind the Kremlin walls. Wallace saw Bullitt as a liberal man of unconfined spirit who was used to going wherever he pleased and could not tolerate being restricted or spied on. As a result, Wallace explained, Bullitt's attitude toward Soviet Russia changed drastically over the course of his tenure in Moscow. In 1946, Bullitt compared the Soviet Communist Party to the Spanish inquisition. At the same time, he professed a deep love of Russians and maintained admiration for the women of Moscow—they were more involved than men in the construction of the subway system. In the end Wallace, who after the war became a moderate supporter of rapprochement with the Soviets, began to criticize Bullitt for his instability and extreme anti-Soviet views. People like him brought on the Cold War, he wrote. Wallace added that Bullitt was a wonderful man, but given to sudden mood swings.[39]

Meanwhile, Stalin was in no hurry to keep his promises; the construction of Moscow University had begun in the Lenin Hills, and the people whom Bullitt had won over to his side and whom he loved were disappearing one after another before his very eyes. On May 1, 1935, immediately after the Spring Festival, Bullitt wrote to Roosevelt: "I can, of course, do nothing to save anyone." After the arrest of Georgy Andreichin, former ministry of foreign affairs liaison to the U.S. embassy, Bullitt received a note from prison, written on toilet paper (!), in which Andreichin begged him "for God's sake to do nothing to try to save him, . . . [as] he would certainly be shot."[40] Whether or not Bullitt believed in the authenticity of such messages (and he most likely did, otherwise he would never have conveyed them to Roosevelt), he was virtually powerless. Boris Steiger replaced Andreichin as official liaison but he was soon arrested as well. The ambassador also reported this event to the president.

Later, Bullitt would describe his actions toward the end of his tour in terms fairly unusual for a diplomat: "I bedeviled the Russians. I did all I could to make things unpleasant."[41]

Supernatural Intervention

Bulgakov was living then under the relentless strain of a horrible threat, a danger beyond human capacity to counter. "So, are you really that sick of us?" Stalin asked him during their telephone conversation.[42] Bulgakov wrote later to a friend: "Trust my taste: His manner during the conversation was strong, clear, stately, and elegant." The writer confided in Stalin that since the end of 1930, he had "suffered from a severe form of neurasthenia accompanied by attacks of fear and anxiety"[43] and insisted that only a trip abroad in the company of his wife would help him. After his request was denied, Bulgakov received treatment by hypnosis from Doctor Sergei Berg.

The treatment helped him from the very first session. According to Bulgakova's diary, her husband began seeing Berg on November 21, 1934.[44] The doctor left his patient with the suggestion that the next day he would be able to go out to a party alone. The writer did indeed set out alone the following evening, something he had not done for six months. Two months later, a fascinated Bulgakov began using hypnosis on others. His patient was an artist, Dmitriev, who suffered from "gloomy thoughts." After the first session, Dmitriev called Bulgakov in "ecstatic delight," asking for another session: "He says his gloomy thoughts are gone and that he doesn't even recognize himself."[45]

In February 1935, Berg administered three more sessions to Bulgakov. One round of treatment, in the patient's words as recorded by Elena Bulgakova, was "just marvelous." After another session, the Bergs, the Bulgakovs, and other guests dined together. "As he was leaving, Berg said that he was happy that he had managed to cure Mikhail."

Then Berg fell ill himself. Apologizing that he would be unable to hold the next session, he wrote: "I am truly glad to know that you are in good health. It could not have been otherwise, you know: you have the perfect reserves, the perfect background for absolute and lasting health!" He returned the payment he had received from his patient: "There's no way I can accept money for visiting close acquaintances."[46]

In an odd way, Bulgakov employed a hypnotic tone in his response to the sick hypnotist. It is worth reproducing the unpublished letter from March 30, 1935 in full:

Dear Sergei Mironovich,

I was chagrined to hear that those pains are still dragging on. I hope, believe, and wish that this nasty ailment will unhand you as soon as possible. And so it will be. You will rise again with the springtime sun. I think of you, and don't feel like writing my [illegible fragment].

In short, I feel very well. You have made it so that damned fear no longer torments me. It's far off and muted. I will visit you. I often recall our friendly conversations. It goes without saying that Elena Sergeevna sends her best regards. Best wishes to Sofia Borisovna from both of us.

Yours,

M. Bulgakov.[47]

The Ambassador and Satan

In Bulgakov's work, the childlike state of a hypnotized patient, dependent on the will of another and thus capable of expecting magical assistance from outside without a second thought, took the form of a sparkling, ironic fantasy where every dream comes true. Let the philistines and agents of the secret police take the fantasy as sleight of hand or hypnosis. As in the epilogue of *The Master and Margarita,* "educated people took the viewpoint of the police: a gang of brilliantly skillful hypnotists and ventriloquists had been at work."[48] Naturally, the reader does not trust this conclusion. The reader trusts the author and his tragic credo: Supernatural intervention is not only possible, it is the only way out of the absurdity of Soviet life.

Bulgakov's novel and plays of the 1930s carry the image of an omnipotent helper with absolute secular power and limitless magical might, willing to step in and use them to help a sick and destitute artist. At the beginning of the decade, Bulgakov had expected much the same from Stalin. Apparently, by the mid-1930s his hopes had been reoriented, coming to rest on the U.S. ambassador to Moscow.

For some reason, in December 1933 Elena Bulgakova copied down in her journal the official announcement about the arrival of the "new American ambassador" in Moscow.[49] Something, we are not sure exactly what, attracted the Bulgakovs' attention. Elena was slightly off the mark in her appreciation of the event: Bullitt was the first ambassador, but he was in no way "new." However, the author of the diary was drawn by something other than the event's political implications. The easiest assumption to make is that the couple was concerned about the American copyright for *The Days of the Turbins,* on which negotiations had intermittently taken place. Indeed, Bullitt went straight out to see a performance of *The Turbins* and afterward requested a manuscript of the play through Intourist[50]—he kept the text on his desk. In March 1934, *The Days of the Turbins* was staged at Yale, Bullitt's alma mater.[51] Charles Thayer recalled in his memoirs[52] that his first meeting with the ambassador after his arrival was also connected to *The Days of the Turbins.* Thayer, who had recently taken up Russian lessons, was looking for a job at the new American embassy in Moscow. Bullitt was then housed in the Metropol hotel, and it was only with great difficulty that Thayer managed to push his way past the severe Muscovite doormen to introduce himself to the ambassador. Bullitt asked him to read a page from the manuscript on his desk. It was *The Days of the Turbins.* Thayer could not yet read Russian, but he knew the play and began paraphrasing the plot. His cheating did not escape the perceptive ambassador, but Bullitt appreciated the skills of the young man who was eventually to become his interpreter and a career diplomat.

Bullitt and Bulgakov first met on September 6, 1934, at a regular performance of *The Days of the Turbins* at the Moscow Art Theater. Bullitt approached the playwright and told him that he "had already seen the play four times, and he went out of his way to praise it," according to Bulgakova's diary. "He followed along with an English translation of the script. He said the first few times he had to glance down at the text fairly often, but now he rarely had to."[53]

According to Elena Bulgakova, she and her husband often attended official and informal receptions at the embassy. At first, this relationship seemed sensational to the Bulgakovs' friends: "The curiosity was killing them—friendship with Americans!" Later on, Elena Bulgakova's entries about these contacts become more reserved, even monotonous. On February 16, 1936, she penned: "Bullitt was very courteous as usual"; on February 18, "the Americans are very nice," and on March 28, "At 4:30 we were at the Bullitts'. All the Americans, including him, were even sweeter than usual." Two weeks later she wrote: "As usual, the Americans are extremely nice to us. Bullitt begged us to stay longer."[54] The ambassador was showing off his friendship with the Russian writer, introducing Bulgakov to European ambassadors and lauding his plays.

The relationship between the Bulgakovs and Bullitt and his entourage was like that of close friends: At times they saw each other very often, almost every day, while at other times they did not get together for long periods of time, particularly when Bullitt left for Washington. On April 11, 1935, the Bulgakovs received the Americans in their own home. "Caviar, salmon, homemade pâté, radishes, fresh cucumbers, fried mushrooms, vodka, and white wine." On April 19, they had lunch at the home of embassy secretary Charles Bohlen. On April 23, the Spring Festival was held at the embassy. On April 29, the Bulgakovs once again hosted Bohlen, Thayer, Irena Wiley, and several other Americans. "Ms. Wiley invited us to go to Turkey with her." The next day, the Bulgakovs were at the embassy again. "Bullitt brought many people over to meet us, including the French ambassador and his wife and the Turkish ambassador, a very fat and jolly fellow."[55] The next evening, the third in a row, the Bulgakovs spent again with the U.S. diplomats.

It was around that time that Bullitt wrote to Roosevelt: "I can, of course, do nothing to save anyone."[56]

But help was needed desperately. All this time, the Bulgakovs were trying to obtain exit visas. On April 11, 1935, the Bulgakovs received Bohlen and Thayer. "M[ikhail] A[fanasievich] mentioned that he had requested passports for foreign travel. . . . The Americans thought this was good, and that it was about time we left," Elena Bulgakova wrote.[57] Their documents were accepted by the appropriate office in June 1935. In August, the Bulgakovs received yet another refusal. On October 16, Bulgakov visited Thayer at his summer cottage. On October 18, the Bulgakovs went to dine at the ambassador's residence: "Bullitt came up to us and talked for a long time, first about *The Days of the Turbins*, which he adored, and then he inquired as to when *Molière* would be staged."[58] *The Life of Monsieur de Molière* was performed for the first time in February 1936. Thayer and his colleagues attended the dress rehearsal: "The Americans were delighted and thanked us." On February 21, Bullitt came to see *Molière*: "During the tea break, . . . Bullitt spoke unusually highly of the play and of Mikhail in general, referring to him as a master"[59] (clearly, this word was of great significance for Bulgakov). On February 19, 1936, Bullitt showed his guests a film. The Bulgakovs were among the guests, and the movie was selected with clear intent—it was about "an English servant who remained in America, fascinated with its people and their way of life." Meanwhile, *Molière* was banned from the stage. On March 14, the ambassador once again invited the Bulgakovs for dinner. "We decided not to go, as we didn't want to hear all his questions and expressions of sympathy."[60] Two weeks later, however, they did go back to Bullitt's house. "The Americans, including him, were even nicer than ever."[61] As far as we know from Elena Bulgakova's diary, Bulgakov paid two more visits to the embassy in November.

What did he talk about there? Some of these discussions Elena Bulgakova did not hear, and some she heard but preferred not to record. At any rate, plans for the Bulgakovs' departure must have been discussed with the employees of the American embassy, who in turn supported these intentions through word and film. It is hard to imagine that Bulgakov would not have vested his dearest hopes in them, and particularly in the ambassador himself.

After Bullitt left Moscow, Bulgakov never again visited the embassy. In April 1937, he was again invited to a costume ball, this time organized by the new ambassador's daughter. He did not attend, excusing himself for lack of a costume.

The Order Has Come to Take You Away

William Bullitt was Freud's patient, coauthor, and savior; diplomatic interlocutor of Lenin and Stalin; Roosevelt's colleague; and Bulgakov's patron. He would make a fine fictional hero. But perhaps his novel, a great novel, has already been penned.

Let us go over the sequence of events once more: The Bulgakovs' emigration papers were filed with the appropriate official bureau. In June 1934, Bulgakov's request to leave the country was refused yet again. He appealed this decision in another letter to Stalin, but received no reply. All summer long, "Mikhail has felt horrid"; "can't do anything right, because of all the uncertainty"; "his condition is very bad—again this fear of death, loneliness, and space."[62] On September 6, Bulgakov met Bullitt at the performance of his play at the Moscow Art Theater. On September 21, Bulgakov resumed work on *The Master and Margarita*. On October 13, his wife wrote in her diary: "His nerves are in bad shape. Fear of space and loneliness. He is thinking about turning to hypnosis."[63] In October 1934, Bulgakov wrote a rough draft of the last chapter of the novel: Woland is chatting with the Master: "I have received an order about you. A very favorable one. In general, I should congratulate you. You were a big success. So anyway, I received an order," Woland says. "Someone can give you orders?" the Master replies in astonishment. "Oh, yes. The order has come to take you away."[64]

Neither Woland nor the Master appeared in early drafts of the novel, written before Bullitt's arrival in Moscow. The devil figured in the plot from the very start, but he was at first only an abstract, magical force.[65] With each reworking of the novel, the Devil became more and more earthly and concrete, acquiring more and more human features, albeit unusual ones. With this image, it was only natural that he be a foreigner, even before Bulgakov met Bullitt. Among possible titles were "Consultant with a Hoof" and "The Foreigner's Horseshoe."

Although Bulgakov scholars have found hundreds of allusions to other texts in *The Master and Margarita*, from the encyclopedia and Faust to ancient tomes on demonology and freemasonry, there is general agreement that Woland, despite the fact that he is referred to many times as Satan, cannot be considered wholly diabolical. "Bulgakov's Woland has a long pedigree as a literary character," Yanovskaya writes, "but in fact he bears little resemblance to any of his predecessors."[66] Kreps goes even further in summarizing the reader's usual perception: "Bulgakov's Woland is not just an unusual devil, he is many ways the Satan's antithesis. . . . Woland's role in the novel is not to sow evil but rather to unmask it."[67]

Bullitt's tenure in Moscow coincided very closely with Bulgakov's work on the third draft of his novel.[68] It was in this version that the formerly operatic Devil acquired particular human qualities that can be traced, in my opinion, to the person of the American ambassador. In Bulgakov's eyes, Bullitt personified might and mischief, humor and taste, love of opulence and circus tricks, solitude and stage presence, a derisive but affectionate attitude toward his retinue (it is, indeed, tempting to seek prototypes of the Devil's groupies in the guise of embassy employees). Woland and Bullitt had similar physical traits: Bullitt was bald, his photographs convey a magnetic gaze, and he also suffered from a streptococcal infection that made his joints hurt. It is also known that Bullitt loved Schubert, whose music reminded him of happy days spent with his first wife. And of course Bullitt had a globe at the embassy, a device that allowed him to visualize geopolitical ideas so vividly that to him the seas seemed filled with blood. In any case, one of Bullitt's postwar works is entitled *The Great Globe Itself*.

Wallace made brief mention of the smashing parties Bullitt threw in Paris in the 1920s, at which a butler served guests in the nude.[69] Bullitt probably repeated this trick later as well, or at least talked about it. His sensitive Russian interlocutor was much more interested than Wallace in such tales, thirsting for impressions and details about an inconceivable life abroad. "He would listen eagerly to those who had been abroad, his jaw hanging wide open," Bulgakov's first wife remembered him.[70]

Bullitt's stories and actions would have seemed even more incredible in the Moscow of the 1930s than they had in the Paris of the 1920s. In the real lives of people who were deathly afraid of one another, in the lives of the unreal witnesses and defendants at the Moscow trials, in the lives of Mandelstam, Zoshchenko, Bukharin, and Beria, things like the love affair between the Master and Margarita, or group bathing in cognac, could really happen. But the erotic opulence of Satan's ball is more reminiscent of the literary reality of Bullitt's friend F. Scott Fitzgerald, his novels about millionaires who drank themselves silly out of boredom and threw grand balls every spring. Thence, too, perhaps, the image of the naked maid, Gella, the mere sight of whom drove Muscovites crazy, as well as naked ladies of all kinds walking arm in arm with their partners in tailcoats, and group dives into a swimming pool full of champagne.

Sociopsychological Experiments at the Variety Theater

Bullitt and Bulgakov were both born in 1891, just as Freud and Wilson were born in the same year. Despite all the differences between their lives and positions, in their personalities and interests they had much in common. Bullitt, a patient of Freud's, who had a tendency to interpret everything, including names, and Bulgakov, who dreamed up a great number of curious names, must have surely noticed and discussed the similarity between their last names (one of Bulgakov's pen names was M. Bull).

What stories did Bullitt tell Bulgakov? Did he speak of Parisian beauties and Hollywood receptions in swimming pools? Or did he explain Freud's theory that everything in man, good and bad, can be explained as a manifestation of his sexuality? But the political atmosphere of the day would have been difficult to explain away with sex alone—take Steiger, for example, spying to his own detriment. Perhaps Bullitt told his friend how naive he had been himself in thinking that the Great Experiment had wrought internal change in the populace of Moscow, when in fact an outing to the Variety Theater would be enough to show that the people hadn't changed at all.

Or did Bullitt insist that Goethe had been right, predicting that after passing through Satan's trials the world would change for the better? Mephistopheles' lines "That power I serve/Which wills forever evil/Yet does forever good" serve as the epigraph to *The Master and Margarita,* and are also mentioned in the foreword to the book on Wilson (although the meaning was subverted in the latter case: Wilson eternally willed good but without fail worked evil). Even if the appearance of this quotation from Faust in both books was sheer coincidence, it still testifies to an unexpected connection between the two works.

The ambassador's friend was a man who lived his life under conditions that went beyond the bounds of comprehension, like the person of Stalin himself. Bulgakov was a former physician, and had treated many syphilitic patients and performed a few dozen abortions. He enjoyed politics and filled entire pages in his diary with malicious jokes about Bolshevik leaders and detailed reports of the Soviet government's international negotiations.[71] In his country, he was a popular writer who had invented a whole cast of eccentric characters who seemed nevertheless completely natural to millions of his readers. Bullitt must have been curious to know what his Russian companion would agree with and what he would dispute. But the ambassador could have never imagined the power and grace of the associations that would come to the mind of this handsome man who tried never to ask for anything. Bullitt could not have imagined how Bulgakov would improvise on the theme of his slightest gestures and most careless words, his extraordinary personality and the observations he made in Moscow. Bullitt did not know how integral a part of history he would become, with Bulgakov's help.

The hero of Bulgakov's novel, a "consultant" from abroad, has returned to Moscow in the 1930s after a long absence, and has set himself a very precise goal. His intention is to observe "Muscovites en masse" and "evaluate the psychological changes" in the populace of Moscow. The means he uses appear diabolical to unaccustomed Muscovites, but the associations that his goals evoke are in no way mythological. Although he is endowed with magical abilities to carry out his experiment, Woland uses perfectly ordinary experimental logic. "The Muscovites have changed considerably—outwardly, I mean—as has the city itself. . . . But naturally I am . . . interested . . . in the much more important question: have the Muscovites changed inwardly?"[72] Woland asks a professional question of himself, his companions, and his audience. Incidentally, Freud posed the same question many times, notably in his *Dissatisfaction with Culture.* "A vital question, indeed, sir,"[73] Woland's retinue agreed. In fact, this is the issue of the transformation of man which was so central to Russian culture from the symbolists of the Silver Age to the time of the pedologists, Woland's contemporaries. Modern amateurs and professionals alike are still fascinated by this problem, which is nowadays framed in terms of *homo sovieticus.* Naturally, almost all of the scene at the Variety Theater, as well as the chapter on Satan's ball, was cut from the 1960s edition of the *The Master and Margarita.*

The Devil does not simply torment and torture, he tempts men and puts them to the test. One of Bulgakov's contemporaries, Vyacheslav Ivanov, elaborated on this question at length. According to Ivanov, Goethe's Mephistopheles tempts Faust in the same way that Satan tempts Job in the Old Testament, and, as in the older text, the Devil finds only one weak point: "the sphere of desires." Naturally, Faust's first excursion with his new, omnipotent guide led straight into the witches' kitchen.[74] As opposed to Goethe, Freud, and Ivanov, Bulgakov did not consider desire the most frightful and mysterious aspect of mankind. Margarita and the Master, people of a new age, boldly surrender themselves to their love, making it superfluous for Woland to tempt them or interfere in the erotic side of their life in any way. Woland and Bulgakov see the mystery of mankind in something else altogether: in cruelty and mercy, in dependence and the ability to resist, power over the mob and the ability to fuse with it.

"I'm not really an actor at all," Woland insists after the experiment, trying to explain his epistemological goals and methods. "I simply wanted to see some Muscovites en masse and the easiest way to do so was in a theater."[75] Indeed, he conducts a series of logical, superbly arranged tests at the Moscow Variety Theater. The reaction of the audience to uncertainty and silence is tension and anxiety. They react to the rain of banknotes with general happiness, amazement, and excitement. The reaction to death, to the severed head, is mass hysteria, with a female voice pleading for mercy. All these reactions are quite satisfactory, one might even say universal. Woland muses: "They are people like any others. . . . They're fond of money, but then they always were. . . . They are thoughtless . . . but they sometimes feel compassion too."[76] Woland was in fact putting to the test the Nietzschean-Bolshevik hypothesis that man can be transformed. It was only a mental exercise for Bulgakov and Bullitt, but Woland brought it into the realm of action. The same experiment would be concluded in real life only half a century later. As a result, Woland diagnoses the Soviet people, and his diagnosis has proven correct until this very day: "They're ordinary people—in fact, they remind me of their predecessors, except that the housing shortage has soured them."[77]

The idea that man can be transformed concerned Bulgakov as the quintessential problem of his time. He presented one aspect of the issue in *The Heart of a Dog*, and another in *The Master and Margarita*. Ivan Bezdomny undergoes a complete cycle of transformation after his meeting with Woland. An encounter with the Devil, severe delirium, and the psychiatric treatment that followed transform the proletarian lush of a poet into a respectable Soviet professor. This typical *homo sovieticus,* whose last name is yet another reminder of his nation's "housing shortage,"[78] perceives all that befalls him without much astonishment.

Mikhail Zoshchenko's characters (see chapter 10) speak of their incredible daily adventures in a similar way, with an even more astonishingly jaded tone. The Soviet man is totally immersed in Soviet routine, he ceases to think about his actions, and is delivered of his doubts, surprise, and worries. It takes a foreigner to defamiliarize Soviet life for those who live it. In 1922, Osip Mandelstam wrote: "Everyday routine is foreignness, it is full of false exoticism; it is invisible to the homebound, native eye. . . . A foreign tourist (a fiction writer) is a different story altogether: he stares at everything and his comments are always inopportune."[79] Ilya Ehrenburg's *Julio Jurenito* came out the same year. The plot is structured around the contrast between two visions of Soviet life, seen through the eyes of a foreign *Übermensch* and a local simpleton. A decade and a half later, Woland, the Master, and Bezdomny would demonstrate how exponentially that bifurcated approach had branched out in complexity.

Bulgakov went to a professional psychiatrist to see what he would say about Ivan Bezdomny's "case." The psychiatrist did not think Ivan should be indifferent to his own fate, particularly when he seemed to be stricken with chronic paranoiac aggressivity: "In accordance with the rules of psychopathology, Ivan Nikolaevich [Bezdomny] should be experiencing anxious fear. A man who sees such deviltry cannot help but feel uncomfortable. You have brought this fact out very skillfully in the character of the deceased Berlioz. As for Ivan Nikolaevich, he seems to channel his energy into persecuting his enemies and undermining their designs, but he does not in the least react to things that happen right in front of him or to him."[80]

But only for Woland, Bullitt, and, to some extent, the psychiatrist and the author was Bezdomny's life unbelievable. Ivan saw his own life as completely normal, and Soviet writers can understand this better than any psychiatrist. Stories of "psychic transformation" related by Vsevolod Ivanov in *U* (see chapter 6) also might strike the reader as incredible, while the characters themselves aren't shocked in the least. Generally speaking, Soviet life was stunning only to the external observer.

The Master and Dependence

Thus, we have the foreign ambassador, as much a theater lover as Woland, meeting the Master, Bulgakov, who has fallen into a trap from which he cannot extricate himself without help. However, not even Bullitt's assistance could improve his situation. The Master's omnipotent helper left Moscow and regretfully abandoned the writer and his wife, who would now have to find their way into eternity by themselves. Since all his unlimited abilities had failed to help the Master in his earthly existence, the "foreign consultant" must have thought he had simply distracted the Master for a moment and shared his dream of the peace and quiet no one would let him have. He had no idea the Master would remember him as he traversed the last leg of his earthly journey.

Dependence motivated Bulgakov throughout the last part of his life, supplying him with material for constant creative reworking. But this dependence did not entirely define the content of his writing. Significant aspects of Bulgakov's novel, such as the Gospel theme, had nothing to do with Bullitt. Similarly, the image of Woland integrated a variety of traits that the author commandeered from other sources.

Bulgakov's dependence on Bullitt and the Master's dependence on Woland are similar in some respects to the author's dependence on hypnotist Sergei Berg, although the doctor-patient relationship is different in other ways. Berg was an important figure for Bulgakov at that time. He visited the writer frequently at home, and over the course of several sessions cured him of a serious neurotic reaction. Bulgakov was fascinated by hypnosis and began to work miracles himself: It took him only one session to relieve a friend of the kind of "gloomy thoughts" that were running rampant in 1935.[81] It has long been recognized that Woland and the Master can be superimposed to produce an astonishing effect: The two characters, so outwardly divergent, convey a single history in the novel, each building on the words of the other. One of the psychological mechanisms of dependence is identification with the object of dependence. In much the same way, amidst all his suffering, Bulgakov began practicing hypnosis on his friend, and as a result managed to identify with his own hypnotist. Later he would employ suggestive language in the aforementioned letter to Berg.

Effective hypnosis is a marvelous apotheosis of one man's dependence on another. Not everyone can be a hypnotist, just as not everyone can be hypnotized. But Bulgakov had the ability, and the theme of hypnosis is one of the few that runs through the entire novel: Stravinsky uses hypnosis in treatment, Yeshua treats Pilate in the same fashion, and the "educated and cultured people" of Moscow interpret the tricks performed by Woland and Company as hypnosis (as do a few contemporary literary historians). In April 1938, S. L. Tseitlin, who had advised Bulgakov on the "psychiatric" side of his novel, sent him a "classic book on hypnosis." Rationally inexplicable, miraculous in the literal sense of the word, the art of hypnosis presupposes absolute passivity in one person and absolute power in another. It requires that the subject accept this control willingly and gratefully. This whole setup was well suited to the spirit of the Soviet era, particularly its Stalinist period. Hypnosis died out in the West in the face of Freud's vehement opposition, but it was in fact the only psychotherapeutic method that survived and even flourished under communist rule. The survival of hypnosis in Russia encouraged many popular practitioners, from Wolf Messing in the 1930s to Anatoly Kashpirovsky in the 1980s.

It is highly unlikely that Bulgakov, the patient of a hypnotist, and Bullitt, the patient of a psychoanalyst, discussed their clinical experience. Something else is more important, however: Only a miracle could save a person from the horrible, inexplicable, unpredictable world of Stalin's Moscow. When all that is left is the hope of a miracle, even miracles seem possible and attainable. Stalin was perfectly capable of working miracles. The ambassador of a remote and powerful country could work miracles; a hypnotist could, too; even the patient of a hypnotist could do it. The only condition was that the victim believe in miracles at the moment when he was most frightened and confused.

On October 30, 1935, Akhmatova came to see the Bulgakovs: "She looks dreadful. Her husband and son were both arrested on the same night. She came to submit an appeal to Stalin. She is clearly very upset. Muttering something to herself."[82] Bulgakov helped Akhmatova write the letter of appeal. Then he suggested that she handwrite the typewritten text; it would be more convincing, he contended. The letter was delivered to Stalin. Four days later, Akhmatova received a cable from her husband and son: They had been freed. It was truly a miracle. The events dearest to the human heart depended on the performance of certain mystical rites. Bulgakov's letters to Stalin were precisely such magical acts, and the absence of the desired result would have meant that they had been performed improperly. Thus Zamyatin explained why he had received permission to emigrate and Bulgakov had not: Zamyatin's letter was written "distinctly and clearly," whereas Bulgakov's letter was written "incorrectly."[83]

Dependence, like love, comes in all colors. Bulgakov's dependence on Stalin—one-sided, absolute, totally pure, and deeper even than Molière's dependence on the Sun King—was different from his relations with Bullitt. Regardless of all the contrast in their respective social positions and future plans, theirs was an authentic, amicable, and evidently mutually gratifying affinity. As a result, Woland looks much more like Bullitt physically, emotionally, and personally, than the Louis from *Molière* resembles the real-life Stalin.

This is not to say that Bullitt's personality had a major impact on the artistic side of *The Master and Margarita*. The ambassador was an unusually bright man, but an unexceptional writer. There is none of Bulgakov's magic in his only novel, *It's Not Done*.[84] And yet it is the voice of Bullitt, an admirer of women, Schubert, Goethe, and opulence, that resounds in Woland's admonition: "What good is your little basement now? Oh, thrice romantic master, wouldn't you like to stroll under the cherry blossom with your love in the daytime and listen to Schubert in the evening?"[85] As a sign of their ironic interest in breeding a new species of man, the Devil adds: "Don't you want, like Faust, to sit over a retort in the hope of fashioning a new homunculus?"[86] Bullitt said much the same thing to another thrice romantic master, Freud, who referred to himself as an "old master," hesitant to leave the slaughterhouse his homeland had become.

The difference was that Bullitt could not do for Bulgakov what he did for Freud in a similar situation—help him escape.

The Saga of Foreign Aid

The plot of Bulgakov's novel develops simultaneously in several directions, as do all the main characters.[87] Margarita, for instance, is the Master's affectionate companion, a witch, and a lightly disguised portrait of the author's wife. Her witch persona fulfills the wishes of her wife-companion self, who is incapable of achieving them by earthly means. Woland is at once the Devil and Bullitt. The mythological Woland does well against the backdrop of historical Moscow, a place more terrifying than the Devil himself. He takes the Master and Margarita out of a Soviet life they can no longer bear. Woland's historical prototype was unable to do the same for the author, despite his tremendous influence; but in Bulgakov's novel, what the author's powerful friend could not do for him, the Devil the author created did for the Master.

One can only speculate about the otherworldly "peace" Woland offers to the Master and Margarita, but its earthly analogue is clear: emigration and life abroad. One need only reread the farewell scene to find confirmation of this connection: a "tremor of sadness," "delicious excitement, the gypsy's thrill of the open road," a "profound and grievous sense of hurt," "proud indifference," and a "presentiment of eternal peace."[88] These words could only be the poignant expression of a man forced to quit the city and culture he loves, abandoning them for life as an immigrant, where he will have peace but no light. Light can shine on him only at home.[89]

This is the price the Master has to pay. After this experience, he can look Woland boldly in the eye. "Forever . . . I must think what that means."[90] Bulgakov must have whispered these words to himself as he submitted his papers for an exit visa. Or perhaps he had in mind the last, hurried words and gestures of Yevgeny Zamyatin, one of the luckier Masters who managed to escape. Later, Zamyatin would correspond with Bulgakov, who had never been abroad. Not all his letters found their way to their addressee. In any case, Zamyatin's decision to leave was perceived by both as an infernal act: In a letter Zamyatin sent on the eve of his departure, he referred to himself as Ahasuerus, and this was the name by which Bulgakov would later allude to him.[91]

It is senseless to argue about how the novel really ends, whether the Master and Margarita die or emigrate. It is just as pointless to argue about Woland's true identity. But the reader should certainly mystify the novel no more than the author did himself. Likewise, we cannot ignore the fact that the book's mythological framework circumscribes a real-life drama, and that the Master's farewell is a difficult decision that nonetheless many were prepared to make, including Bulgakov himself.

As we know, the real Bullitt was far from omnipotent. Nevertheless, it is possible that the ambassador's demonstrative attention helped the writer. International acclaim was taken into account even in those days, at least by those who issued the paychecks. At a performance of one overly aggressive play, Stanislavsky exclaimed: "What will America think?" with the same intonation he sometimes used when concerned about Stalin's opinion. During rehearsals for *Molière*, he frightened Bulgakov: "What if the French ambassador walks out after the second act?"[92]

Bulgakov found little peace even during Bullitt's stay in Moscow, but after his departure at the end of 1936 the writer's life took a sharp turn for the worse. In an attempt to save himself and to justify his dependence at the same time, Bulgakov wrote a play about Stalin, *Batum*, and it was expected that the protagonist himself would read it. A psychoanalyst would characterize this process of switching from one powerful figure to another (Stalin–hypnotist–Bullitt–Stalin) as an obsessive search for an object of transference. A neurotic transfers his expectations of supernatural help to a suitable figure, and all his mental energies are concentrated on this object. When a writer is a neurotic who finds himself in a dangerous, humiliating, and nearly untenable situation, his text becomes a message to the object of his transference, conveying love, dependence, and fear. This text resembles the associations directed at the analyst during a psychoanalytic session. In the beginning, while Bulgakov was still strong, while he sustained hope and had a choice of different objects for transference (Stalin and Bullitt), his creative work expressed dependence only in shrouded form, and it did not overlap with his mystically flavored letters to the Great Leader. But the writer's strength ran out, and he was left with only one powerful figure to whom he could appeal. It was then that these two divergent genres were fused in a single text. This text conveys love for the patron, cowering fear before his power, a desire to share unclear feelings, instinctive magic, self-conscious flattery, beseeching, hope, and prematurely expressed gratitude. Such a text becomes the focus of all of life's aspirations. Its acceptance by the patron can save the author and lift him to dizzying heights, whereas denial can lead only to suicide. Bulgakov fell mortally ill on learning that his play about Stalin had been rejected by its subject. It was then that he returned to his novel about Woland, the Master, and Margarita.

If Bulgakov had consciously encoded Bullitt in the image of Woland, it was a carefully guarded secret.[93] He told one of his friends: "Woland has no prototype, please keep this in mind."[94] He invented quizzes for his house guests: "Who is Woland, in your opinion?" "Satan," the guests would respond, much to the host's satisfaction.[95] Bulgakov plainly had said as much in his text, so the purpose of this question was unclear.

However, we would offer a different answer: Woland is Bullitt, the Master's insane dream is emigration, and the whole novel is a desperate cry for help. It is irrelevant whether the help was expected to be supernatural or foreign, hypnotic, magical, or real. *The Master and Margarita* was Bulgakov's "prayer over the cup," in mingled pride and dependency: "You should never ask anyone for anything. Never—and especially from those who are more powerful than yourself. They will make the offer and they will give of their own accord."[96]

Shuffling the Deck

"The result can be amazing when you shuffle the pack!" Woland exclaimed when he realized that a Moscow girl who had been brought to his ball was also the great-great-great-granddaughter of a sinful French queen. "There are some matters in which even class barriers and frontiers are powerless."[97]

In June 1935, several months after Margarita listened to Woland while preparing for Satan's ball, Bullitt made a speech in Virginia: "The noblest words that can issue from the mouth of man have been prostituted, and the noblest sentiments in the heart of man have been played upon by propaganda to conceal a simple truth: that those dictatorships are tyrannies imposing their dogmas on the enslaved people."[98] In November, Bullitt met with his colleague, the U.S. ambassador to Nazi Germany in Berlin. The ambassador to Germany later wrote: "His remarks about Russia were directly contrary to the attitude he held when he passed this way last year."[99] It was around that time that Bullitt asked Roosevelt to transfer him to Paris.

Bullitt's role in France was of tremendous importance.[100] During the two years directly preceding the war, Bullitt coordinated all U.S. policy in Europe. After life in Moscow, his anti-Soviet sentiments welled up to equal his anti-German fervor. As a close friend of Blum's and Daladier's, he insisted on the rapid arming of France and played an important role in the preparation of the Munich Accords. For some time before the German invasion, Bullitt acted as a surrogate mayor of Paris. After the French capitulated, Bullitt, contrary to Roosevelt's order, refused to evacuate the embassy, an act that would have meant recognizing France's defeat. Bullitt wrote to the U.S. state department after he had been caught in an air raid: "I have for years had the feeling that I have had so much more in life than any human being has a right to have, that the idea of death does not excite me."[101]

Bullitt's career as a diplomat ended dramatically.[102] He had discovered that one of Roosevelt's advisors was a homosexual, and informed the president of this. Roosevelt felt that this tale-telling was more immoral than the sin itself. It might well have been due to this mistake that Bullitt was forced to resign for the second time in his career. He then enlisted as an infantry-man in de Gaulle's army. In August 1944, Roosevelt mentioned him in connection with Russia, asserting that Bullitt had acted horribly and that he would burn in hell for his intrigues; and furthermore, he, Roosevelt, had no idea what Bullitt was doing at the moment, whether he had been killed at the front or had survived to become a future French prime minister.[103]

William Bullitt died in his sleep in Paris, twenty-seven years after the death of Mikhail Bulgakov. That same year, two books were published simultaneously in different corners of the globe: the psychoanalytic study of U.S. President Woodrow Wilson and the novel about Woland, *The Master and Margarita*.

10

The Intelligentsia in Search of Resistance

Heirs to the Silver Age

The Russian intelligentsia, which always laid claim to a particular destiny, suffered unimaginably from what happened to the country during the hard decades of Soviet rule; but intellectuals themselves bore a considerable share of responsibility for these events. Anton Chekhov wrote in 1899, a time when such strong words could only have been aroused by remarkable perspicacity: "I do not believe in our intelligentsia—hypocritical, false, hysterical, ill-mannered, and lazy. I do not even believe them when they suffer and complain, since their persecutors emerge from their own ranks." Ten years later his words would be quoted by the authors of the famous essay collection *Landmarks,* in order to reinforce their own equally damning accusations against the intelligentsia that had carried out the first Russian revolution.[1] After the third revolution, in his book *The Apocalypse of Our Time,* Vasily Rozanov chose even harsher words: "Actually, there is no doubt that Russia was killed by literature."[2] Another twenty years further down the road, the bitter truth about the intelligentsia's helplessness and responsibility would emerge clearly even in far-off Kolyma,[3] where prisoner Varlam Shalamov wrote: "The experiment of humanistic Russian literature led to the bloody violence of the twentieth century I see before me. . . . There is no rational basis to life—that is what our time has proven."[4]

Soviet cultural figures were not simply innocent victims of the regime. Many Party leaders, including those who were directly culpable for the destruction of culture and the persecution of the intelligentsia, were undoubtedly the latter's children and grandchildren. More importantly, the most renowned writers, musicians, and scholars collaborated closely with the authorities from the late 1920s on, and with few exceptions maintained these contacts until their arrest or death. This was true not only of talentless pretenders like Trofim Lysenko but also of such masters of their trades as

Stanislavsky and Meyerhold, Maxim Gorky and Alexei Tolstoy, and Vladimir Bekhterev and Pyotr Kapitsa.

The 1930s brought much that the world had never before seen, among which was the development of Soviet high society—a monstrous mélange of personal talent, corruption, and unheard-of cruelty. Salons where generals and Politburo members were constant guests were hosted by beautiful actresses like Zinaida Reich, Yesenin's widow and Meyerhold's wife, who was brutally murdered in her own apartment after Meyerhold's arrest, and Natalya Satz, who was close to both Lunacharsky and Tukhachevsky. Famous writers and poets of the 1930s—Babel, Pilnyak, Ehrenburg, Pasternak, and even a loner like Mandelstam—each had his own patron on high. Conversing over tea or vodka, poets like Mayakovsky and Chukovsky (judging by the latter's memoirs) would often discuss the rich and powerful, knowing whereof they spoke. Trotsky, Stalin, Kamenev, Yenukidze, and even Voroshilov held receptions where poetry was read and opera singers would perform. The children of Party officials most often took up intellectual professions when they grew up: In the 1930s, the intelligentsia was becoming a privileged sector of society, and it enjoyed benefits that approached those of the bureaucratic and military upper crust.

Fear was not the only common motivating factor in the intelligentsia's collaboration with the new leadership. A fuller explanation can be found in the history of ideas, in the events and the beliefs that cast many Western intellectuals into the same sort of political embrace. Westerners felt no threat; nevertheless, many different individuals (including a number with the most impeccable reputations) at various times leaned toward collaboration with the Bolsheviks, from André Gide to Jean-Paul Sartre, from Leon Feuchtwanger to Bertolt Brecht, from Pablo Neruda to Pablo Picasso. Some made an honest mistake, while others were choosing the lesser of two evils; still others were misguided by their belief in utopia, the eternal lure for intellectuals. If one respects these people's conscious and, as a rule, guileless choice, then one must also understand their Soviet counterparts, whose moral convictions were formed under much less sanguine conditions and whose decisions were made under the duress of vitally important threats and rewards. In these circumstances, even unspoken resistance to the regime brought not only conflict with a seemingly almighty power, it also brought rejection from the majority of one's peers.

Two Meanings of Resistance

"Until the waves of this Dionysian tide wash away the last edges of individuality, with the mysteries of death submerging it in the limitless ocean of the universal whole . . ." This challenge to the elements was issued by the leader of Russian symbolism, Vyacheslav Ivanov.[5] Washing away the last edges of individuality would lead to the mysteries of death, just as would historical materialism. We already know of one madman who returned from war to preach the superman in its most absurdly literal form (see chapter 2). Lunacharsky, future head of the ministry of education, also wrote "Dithyrambs to Dionysus." And Ivanov himself later spent some time serving in the ministry of education.

Resistance to the regime became not only deadly, it became intellectually difficult. In that culture, undermined as it was by the efforts of several generations, there was no tradition, philosophy, or language of opposition. It was not by chance that of all the concepts of psychoanalysis, resistance attracted the least attention among professional Russian analysts; for resistance was most pronounced in the attitude of Soviet intellectuals toward psychoanalysis.

The resistance of Freud's Soviet readers was far more political than the resistance that Freud had detected and interpreted in his Viennese patients. For some Soviets, psychoanalysis was associated with the regime's most ambitious claims; for others, it seemed an encroachment on what little was left them that was still uncontrolled and uncensored—their dreams, emotions, and aspirations. Others found comfort and hope in psychoanalysis precisely because of its dissimilarity to the all-penetrating Soviet ideology. Thus, Russians held many different views of psychoanalysis; but the Russians who were familiar with it by more than just hearsay were few and steadily dwindling. By the 1930s, an interest in psychoanalysis was almost invariably accompanied by resistance in both senses of the word, political and psychoanalytic; and in the Soviet context, these two meanings were much closer than the canon would place them.

In contrast to Freudian constructs, for the Soviet intelligentsia of the 1920s and 1930s, the issue of sex was incomparably less troublesome than was the issue of power. The aspects of psychoanalysis that were linked with issues of power and subordination—for example, the asymmetrical relationship between analyst and patient—were subjected to systematic criticism. Having had such a traumatic recent experience with power, Soviet intellectuals suspected that the application of psychoanalysis under prevailing conditions could only lead to a new form of totalitarianism. In light of what we now know about those times, one must admit that those individuals who had heard Trotsky's speeches and read Zalkind had good reason to be suspicious. Even Vladimir Nabokov, who being an émigré was distanced from events, saw in psychoanalysis "the threat of a totalitarian state based on the gender myth."[6]

Psychoanalysis had begun to conflict with the spirit of the times. Outward life was now far too terrifying to attribute any importance to internal fears. Osip Mandelstam's wife once related the nightmares she had during the couple's exile to Voronezh, not long before her husband's second arrest and agonizing death. She exclaimed, "No Freud would dare explain away these dreams with sublimated complexes, suppressed sexual feelings, oedipal nonsense, and other such well-meaning atrocities!"[7] (It should be pointed out, however, that Freud interrupted his work during the occupation of Vienna, explaining that when the conscious was shaken, it was impossible to be interested in the unconscious.) "The conscious is much more terrifying than any unconscious complexes," wrote Mikhail Bakhtin, whose experiences of that time were similar.[8]

The intelligentsia's attraction to psychoanalysis, which had flared so brightly in the early 1920s, quickly dwindled and died in the period of Stalin's rule. History has recorded no firsthand accounts of interest in psychoanalysis among the next wave of philosophers and writers, such as Andrei Platonov and Boris Pasternak. Anna Akhmatova, who knew "in what kind of garbage poems can grow shamelessly," nevertheless told her close friends that she hated Freud. Of the great Russian writers of this century, Nabokov seems to have written the most about psychoanalysis. He called Freud a "Viennese charlatan," and devoted long feuilletons to him.

However, a psychoanalytic approach was still adopted from time to time in the Soviet humanities, even in some of the most ideologically charged fields. One example of this was the research of renowned philologist V. Adrianova-Perets into Russian folklore, the results of which were published in 1935 by the prestigious Academy of Sciences press.[9] Psychoanalysis also continued to play a vital role in the lives and work of several other first-rate creative minds—as we will see, for different reasons and with diverse consequences in each case.

Sergey Eisenstein in the Goosefoot Jungles

For much of his productive life, Sergey Mikhaylovich Eisenstein (1898–1948), the great film director and creator of *Potemkin* and many other films, was an observer and critic of the developing field of psychoanalysis. The theoretical writings he left behind have been partially published by V. V. Ivanov.[10]

Eisenstein's intellectual engagement with psychoanalysis periodically waxed and waned according to his level of interest and the intensity of his resistance; but he continued to be involved with it throughout his life. Pavlov, Freud, and Meyerhold are the first three individuals mentioned in his huge autobiography; through the works of these writers, he undertook his youthful "joust with the windmills of mysticism." Eisenstein first read Freud in spring 1918, while serving as a volunteer in the newly created Red Army. With cinematographic accuracy he recalled, "In the frenzied crush of people I was so engrossed in Freud's little book that I didn't notice that I had long since squashed my pint of milk."[11] F. M. Ermler, a young actor

who was close to Eisenstein in the 1920s and who would later become a famous director, remembered that Eisenstein knew Freud "with the usual systematic thoroughness that characterized his intellect"; according to him,
scenes from the film *New and Old* leave no doubt that Eisenstein used psychoanalysis in his work. Ermler himself was also interested in psychoanalysis, but one day Eisenstein declared to him: "If you don't stop messing
around with Freud, our friendship will be over. You're a jerk. Read Pavlov,
and you'll see that Freud's not the only thing in the world."[12] This charming brutality was a substantive feature of Eisenstein's style at that time.
Another friend related that he had called Eisenstein the "Devil's agent,"
and the nickname had been to the filmmaker's liking.

Eisenstein was friends with Stefan Zweig, who was in Russia not long before he wrote the book *Healing and the Psyche*, which contains a long,
adoring anecdote about Freud. Zweig described Freud to the director as the
"great Viennese," the "patriarch of the new Athenian school." Eisenstein
wryly recalled how these stories "melded Plato and Aristotle into the overwhelming personality of the man with the Wagnerian first name." Zweig
could not resist introducing Eisenstein to Freud, and in 1929 the latter
agreed to a meeting in Vienna. The meeting never took place. Later, in
1946, Eisenstein described his analytic experience as "my raids into the
fantastic jungles of psychoanalysis, jungles penetrated by the powerful
breath of the *lebeda*."[13] *Lebeda*, Russian for goosefoot, was Eisenstein's
pun on Freud's concept of the libido.

In his unfinished memoirs, Eisenstein related how Freud had helped him
understand his relations with his own teacher, Vsevolod Meyerhold. "It
was an oedipal complex like the play of passions within Freud's own
school. The 'sons' were attacking their father more in response to his
'regime of tyranny.' And the father in this case was more like Saturn, who
devoured his own children, than like Oedipus's harmless father. . . . Isn't
this the source of the image of the horde that eats the eldest of its kind?"[14]
Why do I get so excited when I talk about psychoanalysis, Eisenstein asked
himself. There was a ready answer: The whole situation within the
Freudian school unfolded in a way similar to the relations between
Meyerhold and his students. "The same sort of grand old man, infinitely
charming as a master and foully malicious as a person; the same discord, a
rupture in initial harmony; . . . the same energetic growth of individualities
around him. The same intolerance for any sign of independence."
Eisenstein went even further in his introspection. Just as Freud represented
Meyerhold, so Meyerhold symbolized Eisenstein's own father. Little
Sergey's father never told him where children came from, and his later men-
tor was even more evasive in questions of art. "God willed that in questions
of 'secrecy,' my spiritual papa should be just like my biological one."[15]
"How can I tell that to the child?" appears four times in his memoirs, in
German, and moreover, these words were tentatively chosen as the title.

We can easily extrapolate Eisenstein's further thoughts from these general statements: While his father never gave him an answer about sex, Meyerhold demurred when asked to explain professional issues, and likewise Freud's answers failed to satisfy his search for the final truths of the psyche. He saw in both Freud and Meyerhold (and of course, in his father) "the union of creative genius and personal vileness," and suspected Freud of knowing something he wasn't telling.

Otto Rank's famous book *The Trauma of Birth* had an important impact on Eisenstein. A passionate admirer of Nietzsche and at the same time one of Freud's favorite students, Rank sought a psychologically sound compromise between Oedipus and Dionysus. In his book, he introduced the new concepts of embryonic and birth experiences in an analytical context, contending that such early experiences would prove useful in psychotherapy. Bakhtin, who knew the book, perceived it as psychoanalysis taken to absurd extremes. Eisenstein was enthralled by the idea that people were constantly trying to get back into their mothers' wombs, an idea that gave an extremely concrete outline to the myth of rebirth. According to Ivanov, who had conducted research in the Eisenstein archives, the filmmaker tried to use Rank's theory to explain a variety of cultural manifestations, including mystery novels. Like the Minotaur myth or the biblical story of Jonah, mystery novels were focused on the primal quest to find the supreme truth within some secret and inaccessible space, the archetype of which was the maternal womb.[16]

A true Renaissance man, Eisenstein identified with Leonardo da Vinci. His friends in America called him Leonardo, and comparisons between Eisenstein and the Renaissance artist were popular in Western surveys of the director's life. What is known of his personal life does suggest at least one parallel with Leonardo, as Freud described him: Rozanov would have been pleased to include Eisenstein in his list of "Moonlight People." Eisenstein himself, however, told his biographer Mary Seton: "A lot of people say I'm a homosexual. I never have been, and I'd tell you if it were true, . . . though I think I must in some way have a bisexual tendency."[17]

Along with Solovyov, Ivanov, Berdyaev, Bakhtin, and other utterers of the "Russian idea," Eisenstein seriously espoused the Platonist idea of androgyny as the ideal of the whole person. Eisenstein felt that the superman was "originally an androgynous being, only later divided into two distinct cores—male and female—that in matrimonial integration celebrate a new restoration of that initial primary, unitary, bisexual essence." "Everywhere and always the achievement of these features of primal divinity has been linked to the power to attain a superhuman condition. . . . In Nietzsche, this element exists in the image of Zarathustra as well as in those moments . . . when the creator becomes one with the image of superhumanity he has created. . . . [Here] we take a great stride toward the ideal of an original, primal, prehuman state." In another place, however, Eisenstein asserted that he became interested in the problem of androgyny not after reading Nietzsche's *Zarathustra* but rather Freud's "Leonardo."[18] But in all of his statements, Eisenstein clearly made a connection "between the conception of superhumanity and the androgynous complex."[19]

Eisenstein struggled mightily with his own perception, due to deeply ingrained Russian tradition, of Freud as a pansexualist (a feeling possibly underpinned by irritation with Freud's individualism). Eisenstein recalled in his memoirs that as the years passed, he came to understand that the "pool of primal impulses is more than just narrowly sexual, as Freud sees it." The unconscious was the reflection of the earliest levels of undifferentiated social existence. In Eisenstein's view, the unconscious included sex but was not dominated by it. Sex was merely the "biological adventure of human individuals." The author was "drawn to cosmic forms of total union inaccessible to the limited individual." Ethnographic prehistory, which was so fashionable during that decade, when Frazer began jumbling Freud and Marx in the brains of intellectuals, was most interesting to Eisenstein as a clue in the search for syncretic unity. "I would say of myself: this author seems stuck on one idea once and for all, one idea, one topic: . . . the ultimate idea of achieving unity."[20]

The reader should have no trouble recognizing this new incarnation of the familiar ideas of Nietzsche and Vyacheslav Ivanov. And indeed, Ivanov held that "the personification of my 'principles' . . . is of course Dionysus and Apollo." For both Ivanov and Rilke, the synthesis of the two gods could be found in Orpheus. Art, like alcohol, returned man to a former state, to the underworld of the pre-logical, to Dionysus. But there was a difference between their perspectives and Eisenstein's. Unlike Ivanov, Eisenstein had experienced firsthand the magnetic pull of the masses, and for him the return to a former state was not merely a topic for cocktail-party conversation, but a real possibility in life: All one had to do was step out into the street, into the heart of a seething crowd.

Or make a film about it.

Orpheus and the Mob

"Intermediary conditions are the most interesting: not sleep, not wakefulness."[21] For Eisenstein the "royal road" to the unconscious lay not in dreams but in altered states of consciousness. The alterations in consciousness that he had in mind were at once elementary and ideal, both superhuman and subhuman, and governed by their own rules. Eisenstein investigated the options with the practicality of a producer preparing to use the information gleaned in his work: He researched "rhythmic drumming" as a means to "temporarily turn off the upper layers of the conscious mind and become totally engulfed in sensuous thought." Comparing Asian shamans with Russian *khlysty,* he pondered the mechanisms of cultic ecstasy based on "psychic drumming," "when a single image is made to ceaselessly repeat in the conscious, veiled in various forms." He also researched similar occurrences elsewhere in the world—religious ecstasy, in old Jesuit books, and narcotic ecstasy, in the mescaline-induced intoxication of Mexican Indian tribes.

In the final analysis, Soviet life proved an even richer source of such phenomena. Eisenstein's observations of these events emerged from his mind in a series of free associations, and they never appeared in his writing, subject as it was to government- and self-imposed censorship. A much more important and at the same time less controlled medium for Eisenstein was film: *Strike, October,* and *Potemkin* are full of scenes of mass panic and violence, scenes that could have been used as illustrations in Freud's "Group Psychology and the Analysis of the Ego" (with which Eisenstein must have been familiar), if not for the opposite emotional timbre in which they were shot. Unlike Freud, Eisenstein felt no aversion to mass hypnosis; on the contrary, he felt drawn to melt into the crowd, and he invited his mass audience to join him.

And the audience went along; it is no coincidence that scenes such as that on the massive concrete staircase in *Potemkin* became the most celebrated of all. These scenes and the true heroes of Eisenstein's films, his unbelievably expressive masses, attracted hundreds of thousands of revolution-minded viewers all over the world to see *Potemkin.* After Goebbels saw the film, he ordered his cinematographers to make a Nazi version. These people felt the erotic attraction of the mob's unitary, undiscriminating, sexless, and constantly regenerating body, wherein each individual could experience again the soothing security of his mother's womb. The eroticism of the crowd, that final stage of development for Plato's divine Eros, brought to life all of Nietzsche's and Ivanov's imprecise dreams. The "Age of the Mob" found in Eisenstein its most exceptional artist.

When Eisenstein moves on to portray the individual person, his hero becomes the Great Leader—the crowd's omnipotent, cruel, and inscrutable hero. "In my films, crowds of people are mowed down, hooves trample the skulls of farm laborers buried up to their necks, . . . children are crushed on an Odessa staircase, thrown from rooftops, and left to die by their own parents." The list of horrors takes up half a page and closes with a logical segue: "It seems not at all coincidental that for a number of years the ruler of my thoughts and my favorite hero was Ivan the Terrible."[22]

In *Ivan the Terrible,* filmed by Stalin's direct order, Eisenstein found a distanced, beautiful way to paint the monstrous cruelty of Russia's first dictator. He once explained that his fondness for showing violent scenes emerged out of childhood experience, and that he was under the impression that Ivan's cruelty derived from a similar origin. But the czar's cruelty also seemed to Eisenstein fitting for the demands of the time: An iron fist allowed Ivan to promulgate "progressive government initiatives." The director clearly associated himself with his hero (who represented Stalin), as he explained that childhood trauma was the secret of their (all three) historic successes: "When a series of childhood traumas coincides in emotional timbre with the tasks that stand before an adult—it's a fine thing." Adult affairs demanded brutality, and anyone who had been prepared by childhood trauma had a head start. This was psychoanalysis turned on its head. "This was the case with Ivan," but it was also the case with Eisenstein himself: "I think that in this sense I was lucky with my biography. I turned out to be useful to my time, and on my own turf I ended up exactly the way my individuality dictated."[23]

In his latter years, Eisenstein was dissatisfied with Freudian analysis, which lacked the concrete somatic and motivic models that would have brought it closer to his own syncretistic gift: "The curse of a cognition that is incapable of mastering action hangs over all of psychoanalysis," he wrote in 1946.[24] Eisenstein found his gold mine of metaphors in the more activist Marxism. He often likened ecstatic, undifferentiated states of consciousness (the "proto-psyche") to the classless society. For him, the proto-psyche offered a psychological ideal, much as Engels saw his social ideal in the classless, promiscuous social grouping. In such primitivistic ideas, the past and the future, progress and regress are confounded, just as male and female, subject and object, individual and mass are commingled. Nonetheless, a perfect commingling proved unattainable.

For Eisenstein this impossibility of a total union of all opposites was "as painful as Golgotha." A refined intellectual, Eisenstein recognized his own deviation from universality, and it tore him apart. Even the opposition of sensual and symbolic thought was for him a "central trauma." Orpheus remained elusive, and in his place was merely a new incarnation of Dionysus, who had come out onto the square to perish in the ecstatic masses so as to come to life again in their irrational Leader.

It is known that Eisenstein more than once turned to psychoanalysts in Moscow concerning his personal problems; but as far as we know, he pursued no sustained course of analysis. During his short-lived stint in Hollywood in the mid-1930s, he did again seek the aid of an analyst, a Dr. Reynolds whom he had met through Charlie Chaplin, in an effort to surmount difficulties that had arisen during the filming of *The Glass House.* His producer, Ivor Montegu, was disturbed when Eisenstein "began to spend hours—and cash—sitting with Dr. Reynolds on our balcony being analyzed to find out the obstruction that prevented him . . . from thinking of a 'Glass House' story."[25] Fortunately, added Montegu, nothing came of these sessions. Incidentally, Montegu considered Eisenstein's production of *The Glass House* an idée fixe, even a kind of addiction.

However, the idea behind the movie is extremely interesting, and the internal quandaries that induced the director to turn to a psychoanalyst are just as revealing. Having declined the screenplay offered him by the distributor, Eisenstein intended to create a Hollywood version of Zamyatin's novel *We*, a great satire of the socialist paradise, which depicted a man's vociferous resistance to the mass society that had deprived him of his individuality and of love. The creator of *October* and *Potemkin* clearly wanted to take advantage of his stay abroad to express a new, more highly nuanced attitude toward the regime in his homeland. The ambivalence that arose was so intense that it brought on artistic deadlock. "Life abroad is the final test for an artist, the test of whether he is capable of creating outside the revolution."[26] But Eisenstein's choice of Zamyatin's *We* indicated that the acid test lay not so much in combating homesickness as in embracing a hard-won, fresh understanding of himself and his society.

Montegu knew that Zamyatin's novel served as a prototype for *The Glass House*,[27] but he was most likely unaware of what was going on in the utopia from which his boss had so recently extricated himself. We, in contrast, can easily imagine the daunting mixture of creative energy, fear of the regime, garbled ideas, and devotion to ideals that confronted Dr. Reynolds on that balcony in California.

The First Russian Postmodernist

Mikhail Bakhtin's interest in psychoanalysis appears to have been purely theoretical. He was not involved in the practice of psychoanalysis either as patient or analyst. His fundamental field of interest was literature and man, or otherwise stated, how man was revealed through literature. His heroes, naturally, were Dostoevsky and Rabelais. His book on Dostoevsky (the first edition was released in 1929, the second in 1963) became very popular and may well be the most cited Soviet-era work in the humanities.

Bakhtin was a younger contemporary of the majority of the characters in this book. He was born in Orel in 1895. We can imagine the atmosphere in which he grew up and studied, judging by the sociological research carried out in Orel in 1918 by D. Azbukin (see chapter 8). Eighty percent of adolescents had been to the theater at least once. Most of the children of Orel wanted to be officials, teachers, doctors, or actors. Many felt that school was better than home. (Published in 1923, these research findings sounded then—and still sound today—like a history of paradise lost. The provincial centers of the Russian empire gave Bakhtin the impressive education in the humanities that would enable him to astonish Soviet readers in the 1970s.) When Mikhail was nine years old, his family moved to Vilnius, and from there to Odessa. In 1914, Bakhtin moved from Odessa to Petrograd to attend the university there.

The most unique aspect of Bakhtin's biography is his connection to his elder brother Nikolai. Born the same year, the two brothers were unusually close to one another in their studies and, evidently, somewhat divergent in character and habits. Both possessed a keen interest in the humanities; both chose to study in the classics department of St. Petersburg University, under the same professor, a follower of Nietzsche by the name of Faddei Zelinsky. For Bakhtin, interaction with his brother probably took on the same questioning, provocative, and protesting tone that would later become his ideal definition of true dialogue.

By definition, a dialogue is never ending. But the brothers were separated by history: Nikolai joined the anti-Bolshevik White Guard, and after their defeat, he sailed the Mediterranean as a deck hand and served a few years in the Foreign Legion in Africa. After he was wounded, he continued his philological investigations at the Sorbonne, and finally, in 1932, he began a quiet teaching career at one of the colleges in Cambridge.[28] Despite his exotic experiences and marvelous working conditions, Nikolai went down in history only as the "other" Bakhtin. Mikhail, on the other hand, remained in Russia and worked his way through Soviet hell—whether by force of habit, conviction, or infirmity (he had suffered from osteomyelitis since his youth and had lost a leg to it)—succeeding, despite totally adverse circumstances, in proving true what he and his brother had intuited as young men.

The problem with which Bakhtin grappled throughout his creative lifetime was the relationship between the self and the other. For Russian and European thought, this problem was nothing new. Martin Buber and Alexei Ukhtomsky, for example, had suggested their own Judaic and Orthodox solutions. The issue would become vital to Western humanists of the last third of the century; it would be one of the basic themes of the school of thought now known as postmodernism. Bakhtin grasped these themes early on, and developed them with considerable nuance in his work.

The key concept in Bakhtin's texts is dialogue. Bakhtin attributed special status to dialogue and dialogism as cross-disciplinary, humanistic ideas that simultaneously describe human reality and prescribe a particular approach to that reality. His discourse was developed in direct counterpoint to the monologism of traditional science.

"Acting upon a dead thing, on voiceless material that can be sculpted and formed as one pleases is one thing; it is something else altogether to act on an outside, equally viable and vital consciousness." "Not analysis of consciousness in the form of a uniform and solitary ego, but analysis of the interaction between many consciousnesses—not of many people in the light of a single consciousness, but many equal and fully functional consciousnesses." "Not what happens inside, but what happens on the border of one's own consciousness and on the threshold of another's." "Not another person, who remains the object of my consciousness, but another, equal consciousness that stands next to mine, without relation to which my own consciousness cannot exist."[29]

Bakhtin's concept of dialogism meant that any statement about a person made by someone else was bound to be insufficient and defective. Any analysis, interpretation, or evaluation was merely an "externalizing, unconnected definition." The free act of self-realization expressed in words seemed to Bakhtin the most reliable, and probably even the only permissible, form of statement. "The truth about a person heard from someone else's lips . . . becomes for him only denigrating and deadening lies."

It is likely that Bakhtin was the first to formulate this position with such persistence. His stance is exactly the opposite of the analytic position, more widespread in our age and so clearly expressed by Freud: that the truth about a person is inaccessible to him, because he is unable to control his own desire to become the victim of self-deception. Only someone else can learn this truth, the analyst insists, and only if he observes a variety of strict conditions.

As viewed by psychoanalysis, the truth about a person is an objective description of his unconscious that defrocks the illusion of self-understanding. The unconscious cannot be translated into the conscious within the individual; to accomplish this, another person must be included in the equation. This second, external person can also push the conscious and the unconscious further apart, as bad parents do. In the history of psychoanalysis there is a long tradition of evidence indicating that self-analysis is impossible. When Freud analyzed his own dreams, the only justification for his doing so was the absence of colleagues with whom he could have consulted. For his followers, Freud was the "other" who noted the errors in their self-awareness and had every right to correct them.

For Bakhtin, on the contrary, the internal point of view had significant advantages over the external: "There is always something in any person that only he can uncover through the free act of self-awareness and the word." A man and his self-awareness were never alone: "Looking inside himself, he looks another in the eyes or looks with the eyes of another." In Bakhtin's world, a person could only be a subject; he would actively and firmly reject any attempt to consider him an object. "The genuine life of the personality can be penetrated only *dialogically*, and then only when it mutually and voluntarily opens itself."[30] In such a dialogue, "Man is never coincident with himself. The equation of identity A = A is inapplicable to him."[31]

Many years ago, Vyacheslav Ivanov wrote much the same thing: "I am not a symbolist, if my words are equal to themselves."[32] Taken further, this position rejects the utility, reliability, and ethical permissibility of any constructions designed to explain humans from the outside, as well as any logic by which A must equal A. If the only valid data are those perceived through self-awareness, then what is to be done with the unconscious, which by definition does not yield to self-awareness? Many, beginning with Freud, inferred that Bakhtin's favorite author, Dostoevsky, was particularly interested in the unconscious. Bakhtin, on the contrary, was not inclined to attribute any importance at all to the unconscious. For him, any description of the unconscious was a monologic "foreign word," while each person would "always strive to smash the completing or deadening framework of other people's words about him."

Here the idea of resistance will come naturally to the psychoanalyst's mind. It might even seem that Bakhtin's entire construction is, so to speak, a poetics of resistance, a system set up to justify and ennoble resistance.

Authorship and Dialogue

After the October revolution, Mikhail Bakhtin left Petrograd for a part of the hinterland he knew well: Nevel, then Vitebsk. His scholarly reputation and personal magnetism were such that in every city where he lived, a "circle" would gather about him, composed of a few intellectually kindred spirits. Bakhtin's circles had no structure and left behind no charters or minutes. The final results of all the hours of discussion over tea were only ideas without a single master, and in this they fully accorded with the spirit of Bakhtin's theories. "No verbal statement can ever be attributed only to the person who spoke it: The statement is a product of interaction among speakers."[33] Ideas, as Bakhtin understood them, were born of dialogue and perished in dialogue. Books, of course, had some significance—otherwise, why would he have written so many? But in general, books were something like notes to jog the memory, strewn along the path of dialogue, either purely at random or to point out particularly sharp turns in the road. Such indifference to authorship is an unusual trait for a scholar; many, and this applies to some of the most talented, have been eager to sacrifice their relations with others in order to enjoy undisputed mastery over their (but often not entirely their own) intellectual products. Freud might again be taken here as an example diametrically opposed to Bakhtin. Unhappily, as it turned out, Bakhtin's partners in these conversational circles were so inferior to him in authority and talent that no dialogue ever came out of their interactions with the great scholar. Today, historians are inclined to attribute nearly everything that relates to those circles, personally to Bakhtin.[34]

The only one of his published works to treat a contemporary author was his lecture on Vyacheslav Ivanov. The lecture began with the words: "Speaking of Vyacheslav Ivanov as a poet, it must be first of all concluded that he is lonely."[35] The same, strangely enough, could be said about Bakhtin (although both men had typically close circles). Further, Bakhtin compared Ivanov with other contemporary poets: "He is less modernized, there are fewer echoes of the present in him, and that is why he is so little known and so poorly understood." This is likely just how Bakhtin was perceived in Vitebsk in 1920, where he must have encountered Chagall and Malevich—or for that matter in Petrograd/Leningrad, where his potential partners in dialogue might have included Bely and Blok, Florensky and Berdyaev, Merezhkovsky and Zamyatin. But Bakhtin wrote nothing about them or in coauthorship with them. It seems that his life long, he was carrying on a conversation with absent friends: Dostoevsky, Rabelais, and. . . . In third place on this list—and if we put the names in chronological order, in first place—the name of Freud would appear.

Valentin Voloshinov's book *Freudianism: A Marxist Critique* appeared in the "Psychological and Psychoanalytic Library," printed at the State Publishing House by Ivan Yermakov (the book includes an advertisement for the series). The book, which came out in 1927, put an end to Yermakov's publications at the State Publishing House. It is possible that against the background of intensifying ideological debate and the approaching defeat of the Trotskyites, Schmidt and perhaps even Yermakov tried to get out from under enemy fire, releasing a well-documented critique of psychoanalysis and setting a certain level of discourse beneath which, they hoped, the discussion would not sink.

UCLA professor Vyacheslav V. Ivanov (the son of writer Vsevolod) was the first to make a public announcement about the authorship of the work. In the opening essay in a volume published in Tartu in honor of Bakhtin's seventy-fifth birthday, Ivanov asserted with confidence that the "base text" in the book on Freudianism belonged to Bakhtin, while Voloshinov made "only small additions and changes in a few places."[36] However, another book commemorating Bakhtin's birthday was released that same year, in Saransk. In the introductory article, V. V. Kozhinov named the book, *Freudianism,* as one of those written by Bakhtin's friends.[37] The difference in attribution of the book on Freudianism was due to the different roles the two scholars conceded to psychoanalysis in Bakhtin's creative life. Ivanov asserted that psychoanalysis was the starting point for Bakhtin's evolution, and he described Bakhtin's entire theory as "overcoming psychoanalysis from a semiotic point of view." Kozhinov, on the other hand, considered psychoanalysis insignificant to Bakhtin's work.

This is all the more strange because both articles were written by people who knew Bakhtin quite well and both were published simultaneously while the subject was still alive. American biographers of Bakhtin have informed us that not long before his death, Mikhail Mikhailovich categorically refused to sign a document affirming his authorship of the work. This refusal did not stop the All-Union Copyright Agency from issuing an official demand that Bakhtin be mentioned on the title page of all foreign editions of *Freudianism*.[38] Nevertheless, the editor of the translation published in the United States is convinced that the book's author was Voloshinov.

There is also a running debate about the identity of the author of another of Voloshinov's books, *Marxism and the Philosophy of Language,* and several of his articles; and also about the book by Pavel Medvedev, *The Formal Method in Literary Study: A Critical Introduction to Sociological Aesthetics.* All of these works were published at almost the same time, between 1928 and 1929. They differ from Bakhtin's accepted bibliography in their demonstrative Marxist slant, strangely combined with originality in many places in the text. In general, a reading leaves the impression that the works were composed according to the agenda of the day, adapting a naturally evolving, powerful idea to the demands of political power. It also seems significant that Bakhtin, who often returned enthusiastically to his texts, made no attempt, as far as is known, to rework or even reissue these disputed books. While he confessed that he had contributed in some way to these works, he made it clear that he would have written them differently.[39]

The reason why Bakhtin could not or would not publish the books under his own name, if he was their author, remains a mystery. Before his arrest in 1929, he had not been persecuted. The most radical explanation for the ambiguous authorship of at least one of these books was put forth by Viktor Shklovsky: In an interview with Bakhtin's American biographers in March 1978, he asserted that the author had simply sold his manuscript of *The Formal Method* to Medvedev.

Bakhtin had extremely effective connections, and they helped him in situations that were almost beyond help. After Bakhtin's arrest, Gorky and Alexei Tolstoy sent telegrams to the government in his support. The book on Dostoevsky came out in May 1929, a few months after the author's arrest—a fact that is surprising in its own right. Lunacharsky immediately responded with a glowing review in *Novyi mir,* published in the tenth issue of the same year—while Bakhtin was still being held in preliminary confinement! During the investigation, he was accused of political crimes reminiscent of the legendary accusations against Socrates. It was alleged that Bakhtin was a member of the monarchist Brotherhood of St. Seraphim, that he had corrupted young people during public lectures, and that he was named in a list of members of a hypothetical, future, noncommunist Russian government. Bakhtin was sentenced to ten years in prison and sent to a labor camp in Kustanai.

Bakhtin probably chose a strategy that would be most likely to ensure his physical and spiritual survival. If all four books, including the monograph on Dostoevsky, were signed by a single author, and those books struck the central nerve of fierce ideological polemicism, then it stood to reason that the measures taken to undermine his fame would most likely be harsh. An intellectual living in Leningrad in the 1920s would have understood what he had to fear in the near future. On the other hand, even in those classic texts that Bakhtin signed himself, one often senses his desire to imbue the creations of his heroes—Dostoevsky and Rabelais—with his own, completely original philosophical thought. His writing style was unique in that he clearly preferred to find his own thought in someone else's text than to write it down as coming from himself.

This oddity brings Yermakov to mind by way of comparison (see chapter 6). But Bakhtin's gift was of another sort altogether. His talent is better compared with the "surprising process" in Soviet history, noted by Yefim Etkind, whereby "a number of the most important poets became professional translators. . . . Deprived of the chance to have their say in original creative work, Russian poets . . . spoke with their readers through the mouth of Goethe" and other great colleagues.[40] This secondariness is a characteristic trait of an artist accustomed to self-censorship. But it is also typically found, and for different reasons, in the aesthetics of postmodernism. Perhaps because of the intrinsic peculiarities of Bakhtin's tastes and methods, censorship and self-censorship not only did not bother him, they might well have helped him proceed down his chosen path, along which philosophical and ethical doctrine unfolded as literary history.

At the same time as *Freudianism*, in 1927, another book was released, also remarkable in its own fashion: Konstantin Vaginov's *Goat Song*. This novel maliciously but probably accurately depicts the life led by the narrow circle of intellectuals to which Bakhtin, Voloshinov, and their friend Vaginov belonged. We see a repulsive, totally alienated existence, full of as yet incomprehensible fear and a sense that any spiritual efforts were doomed from the start. Some of the novel's characters could be identified as real people in Bakhtin's entourage. Bakhtin himself is portrayed respectfully, as an anonymous philosopher who takes his own life at the end of the novel. In the context of *Goat Song,* the problem of authorship seems relatively unimportant. In any case, as befits Bakhtin's logic of dialogue, we have found no definitive answer to the riddle here.

Freudianism

If the supposition is correct that either Schmidt or Yermakov initiated this critique of psychoanalysis, then it seems strange that either of them would turn to Valentin Voloshinov with the proposal that he write it. In 1927, Voloshinov had just graduated from the department of philology at the University of Leningrad, and in the same year, as his wife recalled, had become an ardent Marxist. Although the idea's execution was technically successful, the project was a political failure. The hammer of ideological debate was falling hard and fast, and instead of restraining it or at least mitigating the force of the blows, this publication in Yermakov's series served a different purpose altogether. The book was like a blacksmith's hammer, indicating the spot where ideological "apprentices" should direct their crude blows. Its serious intellectual pages were soon forgotten, but its anti-psychoanalytic accusations would be repeated a great number of times and in the most primitive formulations imaginable. Even without Bakhtin's hypothetical authorship, *Freudianism* would remain the only serious work among Soviet publications on psychoanalysis for the half-century that began in the late 1920s. It is perfectly natural that this work became a source and model for those that made their living at critiquing "bourgeois philosophy."

Freudianism begins with an acknowledgment of the growing influence of psychoanalysis: "Anyone wishing to fathom the spiritual physiognomy of modern Europe can hardly bypass psychoanalysis."[41] By breadth of influence, the author attested, only anthroposophy can compete. Even during the apogee of their success, the followers of Bergson and Nietzsche were never so numerous as were Freudians at that moment. The basic ideological motif of Freudianism was that "a human being's fate, the whole content of his life and creative activity . . . are wholly and exclusively determined by the vicissitudes of his sexual instinct."[42] This motif, the author continued, was as old as the hills. "It is the leitmotif of crisis and decline." "A fear of history, a shift in orientation toward the values of personal, private life, the primacy of the biological and the sexual in man"—such are the features common to a host of epochs: the fall of Rome and the Greek states, the time before the French revolution, and the contemporary "degradation" of the West.[43] The author, however, failed to make clear exactly how these historical analogies were related to the popularity of Freudianism in his country.

He did introduce a new factor into the equation, a new concept: "The content of our consciousness and of our psyche" was purely ideological, Voloshinov wrote.[44] Even the vaguest thoughts and most indistinct desires were ideological phenomena. Freudian censorship, for example, demonstrated remarkable ideological subtlety; it carried out a purely logical, ethical, and aesthetic selection. None of the other psychic mechanisms described by Freud were natural, either; they all derived from culture and ideology. Freud's conscious and unconscious "are ever at odds; between them prevail mutual hostility and incomprehension and the endeavor to deceive one another."[45] There is nothing of the kind to be found elsewhere in the elemental forces of nature. The conscious mind of a given human being is nothing but the ideology of his behavior. "No ideology, whether of person or class, can be taken at its face value or at its word"; every ideology demands interpretation.[46]

Here Bakhtin and Voloshinov are of one mind, and their view was shared also by Vygotsky. Theoreticians educated in the humanities who found themselves in a postrevolutionary academic vacuum, these men cast their direct personal experience into new fields of study, hoping to understand the psyche, language, and art by analogy with familiar realities of Soviet political and scholarly life. For instance, the author of *Freudianism* defined "consciousness" as the commentary that every adult human being applies to each of his actions. These authors' main supply of analogies, as befits those who had witnessed the final victory of Marxism, was found in the mechanisms of social reality, which exerted a hypnotic effect on them. The psyche was ideology; psychic mechanisms were ideological tools transplanted inside human beings. Ideology could be official or unofficial; any Soviet person understood the difference between the two. The Freudian unconscious was easier to understand if it carried the title "unofficial conscious"; it occupied more or less the same position inside the person—an existing but unrecognized reality—as did unofficial poets, philosophers, and artists (recalling *Goat Song*!) within Stalin's realm. The analogy is interesting and comprehensible, a new take on the key Soviet problem of doublethink. But either the author failed to follow this train of thought through to the end or he understood too well the possible consequences, for he took an extremely rigid and one-sided approach in exploring the problem: "Thought outside the bounds of possible expression does not exist." "Experience . . . exists only in symbolic material." "Symbolic material of the psyche in essence is discourse—internal speech." "Social environment gave man discourse . . . the same social environment never ceases to define and control verbal reactions as long as he lives"; "everything verbal in man's behavior . . . belongs not to him, but to his social surroundings," wrote the author of *Marxism and the Philosophy of Language*.[47] In *Freudianism*, the basic problem of analysis—the relationship between the conscious and the unconscious—was interpreted with much more nuance than is found in the simple formula of "a conflict between internal and external speech and between different layers of internal speech."

In this regard, Voloshinov's book *Marxism and the Philosophy of Language* directly presaged the book *Marxism and Issues in the Science of Language*, by Josef Stalin, with its characteristic speculations: "They say that thoughts arise in a person's head before they are expressed in speech, that they arise without linguistic material, without a linguistic wrapping, in naked form, so to speak. But this is totally wrong. Whatever thoughts might arise in a person's head and whenever they might arise, they can only exist on the basis of linguistic material, on the basis of linguistic terms and phrases. Naked thoughts, free of linguistic material . . . do not exist."[48]

The idea is consistent and completely totalitarian. There is nothing in man that cannot be read. Society, which is identified with social power, acts as a programmer, in total control of the computer's processes. To suspect that there might be some important information inside people's heads that cannot be read is to doubt the omnipotence of the powers that be. What a person hides from himself, he hides from society as well. There is no room for such doubts: Everything important must be under control; only what can be read can be controlled; only what can be expressed in words can be read; and for this reason, there was nothing in Soviet man that was inexpressible in words. "Naked thoughts do not exist," to say nothing of emotions. Nothing at all exists besides words. This is why a confession of guilt was so important to Soviet investigators during the Stalinist era, as there was no such thing as another, nonverbal reality.

The author of *Freudianism*, it seems, also believed that extrapersonal factors were much more important in human life than individual elements. Freudianism was inferior to Marxism to the same degree that man was fully controlled by society. The goal of social control was to create a "healthy collective" and a "socially healthy personality." In such collectives and such people there was no distinction between conscious and unconscious; in the authors' terms, "there is no difference between official and unofficial consciousness." That is, there is no unconscious at all. If the layers that correspond to the Freudian unconscious remain distant from the "reigning ideology," and by the same token distant from the deeply ideologized individual consciousness, it is merely proof of a person's loss of class identity. The unconscious is evidence of the decomposition of the class to which its bearer belongs.

Generally speaking, there is no particular difference between the clearly expressed social ideal in this book and the ideas that were just as clearly depicted in Zamyatin's *We*, published a short time earlier. Zamyatin constructed an anti-utopia; the book *Freudianism* contains the beginnings of a perfectly serious, well-meaning, totalitarian utopia. It is difficult to imagine that it was written by one of the heroes of Vaginov's *Goat Song*—a work built on the total opposition between a fictional society and a degraded private life that nonetheless offered a flicker of hope. "I don't like Petersburg, my dream is over," Vaginov wrote, in despair.

As Bakhtin would later write: "At any moment in the development of dialogue, there are huge, limitless masses of forgotten meaning."[49] But it was during those years that either he or one of his friends transferred to psychology the somber ideal of a state in which there is no discrepancy permitted between official and personal ideology, because the latter must be infiltrated and swallowed by the former.

The unconscious as Freud saw it was by definition inaccessible to social control, if we do not consider psychoanalysis itself to be a form of social control. The existence of such an opaque nucleus within man appears to be an antidote for any social utopia, or for any totalitarian state. This is why the Soviet critique of psychoanalysis following the publication of this book became focused on proving that the unconscious did not exist. If there was no unconscious, then everything important in man could be controlled by his conscious, and consequently, by society and state.

The unparalleled irony of real life is that even the name of the book's au-thor remained unknown, such was the onerous weight of "official ideol-ogy." The mechanism that could be employed to push any reality back into the bottomless depths of historical unconsciousness in this case operated extremely effectively.

Freud, Lacan, and Bakhtin

At the same time, this attempt to overcome psychoanalysis, which contin-ued in other works that did carry Bakhtin's name, contained a foreshadow-ing of one of the main branches that would sprout from psychoanalysis in the second half of the twentieth century. A number of elements in Bakhtin's critique brought him paradoxically close to the conception of Jacques Lacan and his interpretation of psychoanalysis.[50] In contrast to Bakhtin, Lacan is sure both of the existence of the unconscious and of the right that others have to interpret its substance; but like Bakhtin, Lacan strives to pic-ture the unconscious by analogy to a reality that humans can find more comprehensible. For Lacan, this reality is language. The unconscious is structured like a language, according to Lacan's axiom. Psychoanalysis wields only one tool: discourse. Each word is calculated with a response in mind, even if that response is silence.

Bakhtin and Voloshinov wrote more or less the same thing. In general, "Discourse is like a *scenario* of the immediate act of communication in the process of which it is engendered," and "all verbal utterances of the patient . . . are also just such *scenarios*, scenarios, first and foremost, of the immedi-ate, small social event in which they were engendered—the *psychoanalyti-cal session*."[51] The Freudian "unconscious," they sensed, stood in opposi-tion not to the patient's conscious but to the doctor's, as "resistance." The approach adopted by Bakhtin and his circle to discourse—which emerged (another point of commonality with Lacan) in their assimilation and tran-scendence of early Russian structuralism (of the formalist school)—was predicated on an understanding of the entire verbal utterance addressed from the self to the other as the minimal communicative unit. Although in this approach Bakhtin and Voloshinov drew quite near to Lacan's semantic formulas, they veered off again in the opposite direction: Their own social situation, the "scenario" that had also become their discourse, was com-pletely different from Lacan's.

Both psychoanalysis and formalism recognized the incapacity of man to be cognizant of the laws governing his own feelings and affairs, and in this regard both set limitations on the very possibility of transforming man. To achieve utopia, these limitations had to be overcome. A new theory of con-sciousness was needed—if something that recognizes no laws can be called a theory. Bakhtin provided one option, the theory of ideology. Later, Alexei Leontiev offered another option, one that would become established in Soviet psychology for decades to come—the theory of activity.

Paraphrasing Lacan, one might say that for Bakhtin and his circle, the conscious was structured as an ideology. Picturing the conscious and the unconscious as ideology handed them over into the purview of ideological control. Since "self-awareness is always verbal, always a matter of finding some specifically suitable verbal complex," it stood to reason that "any instance of self-awareness . . . is an act of gauging oneself against some social norm—[that] is, . . . the socialization of oneself and one's behavior."[52] However, Lacan showed that the stated precondition did not necessarily give rise to the stated consequence: The semantic interpretation of the ego was compatible with individualism, it raised the issue of the "other" and the "big other" (society) but did not necessarily drown the individual ego in them.

Voloshinov attributed more radical meaning to the socialization of the conscious than just a correlation between the self and the other: "In becoming aware of myself, I attempt to look at myself, as it were, through the eyes of another person, another representative of my social group, my class."[53] The gradual slide of this verbal transition (other–group–class) reflects the attempt to smoothly switch from speculations that are perfectly acceptable to civilized European individualism over to speculations in the spirit of radical Marxism. With the flow of the decades, Bakhtin himself moved in the opposite direction.

The Philosopher Looks in the Mirror

The simple, "ideological" solution to the problem of the relationship between the ego and the greater society—a problem to which post-Freudian thinkers, including Lacan, would return incessantly—may seem dated today; but the analysis of a second problem, the relationship between the self and the other, remains fresh and substantive.

According to Bakhtin, "the most important acts constituting self-consciousness are defined by the relations with another consciousness," but at the same time, the mechanisms that drive self-awareness and consciousness of the other are fundamentally different. The consciousness exists in two forms: "self" and "other," and the switch from one form to the other involves sharp changes in content. Bakhtin credited Dostoevsky with the discovery of the "other": It was in Dostoevsky that "the role of the other was revealed, and it is only in light of this role that any discourse about the self can be built."[54]

Bakhtin's intent was to use Dostoevsky's works as material showing the depth of the transformations through which the human image passes as one moves from an external point of view to an internal point of view or vice versa—transformations that are not so much structural as substantive, psychological, and even ideological. "Dostoevsky had an exceptionally sharp eye and sensitive ear for seeing and hearing the tense struggle between the self and the other in every external expression of man (in every face, gesture, and word)."[55]

If for Lacan the relationship between the analyst and his patient was the prototype for the universal human relation between the self and the other, for Bakhtin this prototype, the dynamic of which he found more comprehensible than anything else, was the relationship between the author of a work of literature and his characters. The author (Dostoevsky, for example) was the self; the character (Raskolnikov, for instance) was the author's other. The author's world is populated by characters, and through them, albeit not exclusively through them, he expresses everything he wants to say. At the same time, literary characters enter into unliterary relations with one another, by the author's will or their own: Raskolnikov and his elderly victim, Raskolnikov and the prostitute, Raskolnikov and the investigator. Conveying all this, the author shows his characters in the same way that others see the self. Meanwhile, in a range of cases the author implants an ego in his character, and then one of them becomes the "self," while another becomes the "other"—not in counterpoint to the author this time but to the character.

Bakhtin commenced this analysis in a philosophical work evidently written at the beginning of the 1920s but published only recently,[56] and he returned to it many times. In this essay, Bakhtin primarily argued for the dialogism of the self and the other, the disparity between the mechanisms of their existence, and the ineluctability of their positions within the framework of human life. Other conceptions of man were monologic, giving priority to one or another position, a position that was passed off as that of man in general: They were either theories of the self or theories of the other. According to Bakhtin, all of psychology, which pretended to be scientific, fell into this latter category. He would, of course, have been reluctant to agree with Freud's well-known formula, according to which parts of the self can be unconscious, even the highest layers. Any speculation about the unconscious for Bakhtin was the embodiment of the other's point of view, describing the self monologically from the outside. "Under the monologic approach, . . . the 'other' remains wholly the object of consciousness, rather than another consciousness."

The ego for Bakhtin was everything through which man discovered and sensed himself and everything for which he was responsible. The ego begins to diverge from the other when there is the perception of appearance. The ego does not see its own aspect, this is something only the other can do. Here, Bakhtin turned to the image of a mirror, an image he employed many times, like Lacan, but with a different end: The mirror was for Bakhtin a mechanical and illusory means to eliminate the opposition of the ego and the other. He categorically refused to believe that such a mechanism could work. The unnatural face of a person looking at himself in the mirror was for Bakhtin proof that there was no middle ground between the opposite poles of the ego and the other. And in point of fact, a philosopher for whom "'to be' means to be for the other, and through him—for oneself"[57] had no problem with Narcissus because Narcissus did not exist. For Lacan, the mirror is the symbol of self-awareness, and the meeting with the mirror is the most important moment in the life of man.

For both Lacan and Bakhtin, the mirror is a reality, understood factually as a mediator of opposition between the self and the other: Looking in the mirror, man can come to know his identity, to see himself as someone else, or to see himself as others see him. But Lacan and Bakhtin each viewed the mirror in his own fashion: For Lacan, the "mirror stage," when a child begins to recognize himself in his reflection and call himself "I," was the culminating moment and the turning point in his development. For Bakhtin, the mirror was an attempt to artificially overcome the opposition between the self and the other, but it failed to do so and merely blurred the distinction. The only true mediator between the ego and the other, for Bakhtin, was the living process of dialogue.

Nowhere did Bakhtin make a distinction between thought and emotion or thought and action; he relied on a unitary category of experience. Experience was "the imprint of meaning in existence," and it existed only on the threshold of transition from ego to other that occurs within man. Narcissus, who persistently plays the role of the other in relation to himself, was for Bakhtin just as anti-natural, just as disruptive of the natural course of things as a psychologist who tried to make the other into an object. "Dostoevsky categorically denies that he is a psychologist. In psychology he saw a degrading *materialization* of the human soul," Bakhtin wrote, as always linking his own ideas and feelings to Dostoevsky.[58] But any experience (in the sense in which a person might say, "I feel . . .") included a moment of self-observation. For this reason, Bakhtin asserted, experience included the other's point of view: It was as if the person were looking into the mirror at his own internal state of being. "I experience the source of my fear as frightening, the object of my love as beloved; in order to experience fear or love as such, I have to become the other in relation to myself." Experience could only be analyzed on the boundary between self and other, as the interaction between self and other.

The "other" here is not Lacan's other, nor the generalized other of George Herbert Mead, but a reflexive position defined by its external point of view in relation to the subject. Bakhtin's analysis constantly emphasized the systematic distinctions between phenomenological pictures of the ego and the other. "The other always opposes me as an object: its external image in space, and its internal existence in time." But the active self existed, in Bakhtin's opinion, outside of space and time; its unity was supported by the categories of meaning and responsibility.

Toward the end of his life, Bakhtin repeatedly applied his early concepts to an analysis of death. Death was tied to the other. Pronouncement of death was always "the other's prerogative." "Death cannot be a fact of the conscious itself. . . . Beginning and end, birth and death are all part of man, life, and fate, but not of consciousness. . . . Beginning and end lie in the objective world for others, not for the conscious itself. . . . No one dies from the inside, that is, no one is aware of his own death." There were very few deaths in Dostoevsky's novels, he remarked; there were only "murders, suicides, and madness," for which man must answer himself. "Man left, having said his piece, but the words he said remain in incomplete dialogue."[59]

And so, "foreign consciousnesses cannot be contemplated, analyzed, or defined as objects, as things—one can only converse with them dialogically." Dialogue was life, it was potentially endless, it was a perpetual motion machine, it was self-valuing and self-sufficient. "Everything is a means to one end: dialogue. One voice finishes nothing and solves nothing. Two voices are the minimum for life, the minimum for existence." And "when dialogue ends, everything ends."

The Circle Is Broken

These ideas, by their very nature and by design, were not meant for practical application—a feature that distinguishes them most clearly from psychoanalysis. Bakhtin's (and if one is to believe him, Dostoevsky's) dialogism can serve as subject matter for a novel or essay, but there is no method in it that might help a specific person move from monologue to dialogue, nor could there be. In a philosophical sense, any such method of education or treatment must combine elements of monologue and dialogue; it must include the privileged point of view of the other and at the same time, the possibility of open and relatively equitable communication with the ego.

In psychoanalysis, the "privileges of the other" are tied quite firmly to the analyst; to understand just how firmly, one need only recall Freud's conflicts with his students. Jung's pretensions toward Freud, for example, evoke Bakhtin's demand for dialogue: "You go around sniffing out all the symptomatic actions in your vicinity, thus reducing everyone to the level of sons and daughters who blushingly admit the existence of their faults. . . . If ever you should rid yourself entirely of your complexes and . . . took a good look at your own [weak spots] for a change, then I will mend my ways and at one stroke uproot the vice of being in two minds about you."[60] In response, Freud broke off their correspondence. He probably would have interpreted Bakhtin's philosophy of dialogue as yet another expression of the characteristic Russian ambivalence (see chapter 3).

With his patient, a psychoanalyst will begin to interpret these sorts of ideas, complaints, and demands for equality as resistance, and step by step he will disentangle the unfolding contradiction, which engenders material for analysis. The procedures of psychoanalysis are conditional and asymmetrical; the rare moments of dialogue, when the analyst and patient communicate as free and equal subjects, are strictly circumscribed by the algorithm of role behavior. For example, the analyst may not discuss his own problems or mistakes with the patient; for this he has his own analyst, whose actions are limited in turn. And so on, through generations of analysts back to Freud himself. The dialogue breaks, changing from a ring into a chain, or perhaps a spiral of mutually reproducing monologues. These limitations are givens, and only by working through and beyond them can the patient become ready for a new dialogue.

But Jung was never Freud's patient. Generally speaking, his request was relatively simple and reasonable: the right to independent commentary, equality in mutual respect, "to stand by you publicly while maintaining my own views."[61] It is striking, however, that in justifying his rights, Jung found himself in such a vacuum that he was forced to accept Nietzsche as his ally. The ideas of Bakhtin and other dialogical philosophers of that time, most of all Buber, were completely new and, as we have seen, in step with the times.[62] Western philosophy—particularly on the European continent—would remain focused on the problem of the "other" for decades to come. Sartre, one of Bakhtin's younger contemporaries, and Emmanuel Levinas in our own era, were among those who followed paths parallel to Bakhtin's, although they started out from different points of origin.

If psychoanalysis had developed in Russia under more normal conditions, Bakhtin's conception might have been assimilated in it and lent Russian psychoanalysis its own national flavor, as Lacan's did in France. Along with an awareness of the role of language and linguistic structures, this variant probably would have employed less restrictive therapeutic relations, allowing the analyst more freedom of action and less leeway for manipulation in therapy. Bakhtin's dialogism would have articulated a conceptual framework for these technical details. Through Bakhtin, the Orthodox philosophical tradition would have had an opportunity for contact with the primary currents in twentieth-century European thought—psychoanalysis and structuralism.

But the real Bakhtin lived in a genuinely Nietzschean world, awash in social experimentation. Ideas were directly implemented in this world, freed of all complications and paradoxes, while resistance was overcome by force. Under such conditions, Bakhtin's dialogism was perceived most of all as a philosophical reaction to that world, as resistance—or more accurately, opposition—to it. Bakhtin saw very clearly that "[t]he unity of consciousness, which replaces the unity of existence, is inevitably transformed into the unity of a *single* consciousness." It was irrelevant, the author added, "what metaphysical form it takes: 'consciousness in general,' 'the absolute I,' 'the absolute spirit,' 'the normative consciousness.'" In practice, it was the consciousness of a single person, who had transformed his monologue into a cult. "Alongside this unified and inevitably *single* consciousness is to be found a multitude of empirical human consciousnesses. From the point of view of 'consciousness in general' this plurality of consciousnesses is accidental and, so to speak, superfluous." Anything individual was seen as deviant, erroneous. Error was the only principle of individuality recognized by such a consciousness. And errors were to be punished. "A single consciousness and a single mouth are completely sufficient for total fullness of cognition; there is no need and no basis for a multitude of consciousnesses."[63]

Bakhtin's particular "clinical" experience—the experience of life in totalitarian conditions—showed him plainly that in the realm of consciousness, any privilege leads to monopoly. "Consciousness is far more frightening than any unconscious complexes." And indeed, what the "ideology" of the day was saying, to his mind, was probably no less frightening than what it was doing. The roots of what was going on around him could be traced back to the rationalism of the Enlightenment. European utopianism, he wrote, was based on the monologic principle of conscious conviction. Moreover, faith in the self-sufficiency of a single consciousness was a structural peculiarity of the entire "ideological creation of the new times." Dostoevsky, in contrast, often interrupted his characters, but "never drowns out a foreign voice." His activity toward his characters is "the activity of God to man, that allows man to discover himself to the final degree."[64]

His whole life, Bakhtin conversed with Dostoevsky and Rabelais, but his lonely dialogue with world culture implicitly included a third partner—the dead monologue, by which many of his contemporaries kept consciousness alive. It is only in contraposition to this monologue that one can fully understand the origins and the originality of Bakhtin's dialogism, and the exaggerated pointedness with which he expressed it.

"At any moment in the development of dialogue there are huge, unlimited masses of forgotten meaning, but . . . there is nothing absolutely dead: every meaning will have its day of rebirth."[65]

The Rebirth of Dionysus

In Bakhtin, the religion of Dionysus took on a new cultural and historical form, at the same time preserving its main features, as befits an eternally self-renewing god. Ivanov's Dionysianism, which existed outside historical time and space, for Bakhtin found concrete and expressive embodiment in culture. In his famous work on François Rabelais, Bakhtin revealed the universal play of "life–death–birth" in European cultural tradition as a carnival in which all roles were inverted and all opposites were blended together.[66] Bakhtin was attracted by the "great, common, popular body," in which individual births and deaths "are mere moments in its ceaseless growth and rejuvenation." The dichotomized, basic categories of human consciousness were united by the mighty force of communal, popular experience. The prime force in this world was laughter, "the world's cheery matter—something that is born, dies, and gives birth to itself; something that consumes and is consumed, but which in the end always grows and multiplies." The carnival was a drama of laughter in which a new world was born as the old world died, and for this reason any image within this space was ambivalent. For example, "images of urine and excrement are ambivalent, as are all images of the low, bodily stratum: they die and are reborn simultaneously, they are at once blessed and debased, death and birth are intertwined within them, labor pains and death throes."[67] In the same sense, ritual sacrifice, ridicule, and beatings were also ambivalent.

Bakhtin tried to further clarify the definition of this complex of images that he found so attractive, describing it at one point as a carnivalesque whole, elsewhere as a grotesque body, in another place as an unofficial canon: "This body is fertilizing–fertilized, birthing–born, consuming–consumed." In contrast, modern man's self-awareness—Bakhtin called it the "new bodily canon"—had brought man to the brink of despair: It was "totally rehearsed, completed, strictly cordoned off, locked, externalized, compartmentalized, and individualized." The body of the new canon was an individual body, and everything that happened to it had unambiguous meaning: Birth was birth, death was death. The grotesque or "popular" body was bisexual: It could not conceive of itself in isolation; death was birth, fertilization was conception, defecation was assimilation of the frightening cosmos. "It should be emphasized that the motif of the 'androgynous' in this particular understanding was extremely popular in Rabelais' time."[68]

We find all the basic motifs of Russian modernist culture in Bakhtin's discussion of Rabelais: the idea of eternal rebirth, the romanticism of deindividualization, the blending or effacing of basic rational categories, and androgyny. These elements form the same kind of unitary "Dionysian" complex in Bakhtin's philosophy as in that of Vladimir Solovyov, Vyacheslav Ivanov, Sabina Spielrein, and Nikolai Berdyaev: If birth is equated with death, then love becomes one with the attraction to death, while the male gender is indistinguishable from the female.

Bakhtin probably borrowed these ideas from Ivanov. In the 1920s, long before his book about the culture of laughter, Bakhtin said that "as a thinker and a figure, Vyacheslav Ivanov had colossal influence. . . . All of his contemporaries were mere poets, while he was a teacher as well."[69] According to Bakhtin, "the unification of love and death" was the fundamental theme in many of Ivanov's poems. Bakhtin looked with approval upon what he saw as a melding of love and death, aimed against individuality: "The ecstasy of love inspires melancholy and a desire to break down the borders of individualization, but it is death that destroys individualization. Therefore, love invokes death."[70]

Bakhtin, today the most influential representative of this line of development in Russian thought, found just the subject matter to give his school real significance. By skillfully applying Russian ideas to European examples, he won worldwide acclaim. Bakhtin's reputation and ideas still enjoy undisputed authority both among Russian philologists and among Western Slavicists. Only in recent years did his most famous student, Sergei Averintsev, subject Bakhtin's ideas of carnival to critical attention, analyzing their literal sense and their possible application to the Russian case. Just how humane were medieval rituals of beating and ridicule? Did laughter always carry with it a deep truth about the world, about man; does it always defeat fear and negate suffering? "The problem is that totalitarianism knows very well how to make use of anything unrehearsed, unlocked, or malleable; it has its own reasons for exaggerating these aspects of existence, for stretching them and surrounding them with an emotional halo of ambivalent laughter and oblivious boldness."[71]

Averintsev demonstrated a surprising and ambiguous link between Bakhtin's concept of natural or medieval man—unrehearsed, unlocked, and unfinished, like everything in life—and Soviet totalitarianism. This view of man, Averintsev wrote, was a weapon against those who sought to commandeer life and history. But in the same image there was something else that Averintsev defined with remarkable accuracy: "The sense of oneself as corpse and child at the same time." As a child, because you are unfinished and always ready to be remade; as a corpse, because you are frozen in mortal fear, knowing that any transformation of man is nothing other than a transformation of children into corpses. This dual sensation is the psychological substratum of the totalitarian regime. "The regime considers only itself complete. . . . Reality has to be plastic, so it can be sculpted and transformed."[72]

The regime in which Bakhtin lived, with all its terror, doublethink, and pretensions to reshaping man, created in its citizens—even in people like Bakhtin—characteristic distortions of self-perception that were projected into their theory to the same degree as their poetry and love. "People should be unprepared, unfinished, in the process of becoming, so they can be trained and retrained, 'reforged'; they shouldn't be taken into consideration, there's no sense in taking them seriously, but they shouldn't despair; they have their whole life ahead of them, like children." Averintsev asked a rhetorical question: How was "a sense of yourself as corpse and child at the same time" different from Bakhtin's "ambivalence in death that gives birth?"[73]

The epitome of the carnival master in Russian history was Ivan the Terrible, who was adept at dethroning–crowning (as was equally adeptly illustrated by Eisenstein, for our benefit and Stalin's, in his film about the bloody tsar). Despite his gloomy seriousness, Stalin also knew the meaning of carnival laughter in his use of personal torture. The ethnography of the Soviet Army and Soviet labor camps was composed of ridicule and beatings, parodies of social hierarchy, and frightful grotesquerie performed on the bodies of people, who were transformed into androgynes by force. Bakhtin left no obvious trace in his books of his contact with this reality, although he could hardly have remained unaware of it after all his wanderings. It remains unclear whether his admiration for the "popular body" was the result of ignorance of Soviet reality, the likes of which one might find only in the most eccentric intellectual; complete alienation from that reality, when events around him ceased to bear any resemblance to culture (which was probably the case with many people); or the upshot of a new, intellectual romanticism.

Ivanov understood that "Dionysus in Russia is dangerous." Rabelais was also dangerous, although Bakhtin said nothing of the sort. Nevertheless, in some of his ideas, most of all in the concept of dialogue, Bakhtin overcame his heritage. At the end of his life, he found his own answers to his own questions in Dostoevsky, much as Lacan found such solutions in Freud. Bakhtin wrote of "Dostoevsky's hostility toward the kind of worldview that attributes a primary role to melding and dissolving consciousnesses in a single consciousness, to the removal of individuality." In essence, consciousness was plural and incomplete. This was the key to overcoming the symbolist ideal of a lonely, eternal, self-engendering consciousness with no need of individuality, development, or love. It was also the point of entry into the contemporary philosophical, cultural, and political problems of postmodernism—a school that accepts the eclectic plurality and unblendedness of consciousnesses as a basic principle of modern life, turning away from systems and isms and back to common sense.

A Soviet Man with a Soviet Analyst

After the rude reality of war and three revolutions, symbolism and Dionysianism lost their attractiveness for both the general public and the Russian intelligentsia. "Respected professional mystics and representatives of science are shunning this girlish nonsense with equal suspicion," Osip Mandelstam wrote in 1922. He predicted that "Russian prose will move forward only when it finally finds a prose writer who is independent of Andrei Bely."[74]

It is hardly by chance that one of the strongest images of the unbelievable changes in Russian life was left us by a writer who emerged from the culture of the Silver Age having demonstratively rejected its basic components. This author's work reflected a peculiar blend of psychoanalytic vision and common sense—an impossible, or at least officially unsanctioned, but fertile mixture that infuriated the literary bosses of the time and enchanted readers. For many decades Mihkail Zoshchenko was one of the most widely read Soviet authors, and he retains his popularity to this day. After all the ideological, futurist babble of Silver Age writers, Zoshchenko's short, primitive sketches produced and continue to produce a reaction of shock. Their heroes entertained simple worries about things the Bolsheviks had nearly forgotten: health and well-being most of all. They understood the strangeness of their worries, as Zoshchenko wrote in his typical manner, that of the apologetic clown: "I admit that in our days of instability, I am really ashamed, downright uncomfortable coming out with such insignificant ideas, with such routine conversations about an individual person." Amazed by the wonders of the new life but never losing sight of common sense, adopting the style of newspaper headlines but believing nothing and accustomed to taking nothing on faith, Zoshchenko's hero is infinitely distant from the Nietzschean "new man." However, he is no closer to the confused man of European existentialism, alone in the world with his dark thoughts.

Zoshchenko's hero is none other than *homo sovieticus,* far from the worst specimen of the human race. People like any other, as Bulgakov's superman Woland remarked. The burdens of life have annoyed them to the point of permanent irritation, and so they feel no loneliness. Trained to practice doublethink and deprived of any tradition of morality, these people can the more easily permit themselves to be totally honest in their own thoughts. Their predicament is unusual, and it calls for uncommon measures.

By illustration, let us paraphrase the following story by Zoshchenko.[75] One day, a man is walking down the street when he suddenly notices that women aren't looking at him. That's too bad, he thinks. Especially since a bourgeois scholar once said that everything we do, we do for women. I've got to eat better, the hero thinks to himself. He eats nonstop; then he does calisthenics; finally, he decides to dress fashionably. Lo and behold, a woman pays attention to him: He bought her stolen overcoat at the market. Walking out of the police station, the hero thinks, "I'll get along without the ladies. My personal life will be labor. I'm going to work. And the bourgeois scholar's words are just so much Western trash." He spits on the ground and turns his back on women passing by.

Here is yet another example, a story about psychoanalysis, which was written in 1933—showing that psychoanalytic treatment was still practiced at the time, although in extremely primitive form. The story so vividly depicts both the environment in which psychoanalysis struggled to survive and the real patients of psychoanalysis that it deserves a short paraphrase here.

The story's protagonist goes for treatment to an outpatient clinic. The place is packed with people, almost as full as the trolley. Most of the people—thirty of them—are lined up to see the neurologist. Only one is waiting to see the surgeon. Two women and one man have come to visit the gynecologist. The nervous patients are talking among themselves. The main character says to them, "I'm surprised at how many nervous disorders there are. Such a disproportionate number!" One of the patients shoots back, "What's surprising about that! People have a natural impulse to trade, but here . . ." Another says to the first: "Well, don't get too carried away with your ideas, or I'll call the cops. They'll show you 'natural impulse.'" He doesn't get the chance to call, though, because his turn comes next. His words are audible from behind the screen: "Actually, I'm healthy, but I can't sleep. Give me some drops or pills." The doctor responds that pills will do him only harm, and that he subscribes to the latest method of treatment. "I find the reason for the illness, and I fight it." The patient doesn't understand what the physician is talking about. "Try to remember," the doctor tells him. "We'll find the reason, we'll overthrow it, and maybe you'll be healthy again. You've suffered for ten years, and now you have to tell me all about your suffering." The patient recalls how he returned from the Civil War and saw his nephew embracing his wife. "Sadness flares up inside me when I see that he's wearing my service jacket." "All right," the doctor interjects. "I'll give you the pills." The other patient, the one with trade on his mind, hurries behind the screen—but medicine isn't going to help him, either.

Leaves Are Falling

The author of these stories, a cavalry officer in World War I who was decorated with five medals for valor, was also seriously neurotic. His hypochondria was deepened by periodic depression. Only his closest friends knew of his disease; his acquaintances recalled him as a reserved, elegant gentleman, always surrounded by women, upon whom he gazed with the fond attention of a "good neuropathologist."[76]

Among a variety of conclusions made about him by army medics (field hospital of the Mingrelian Grenadiers Regiment, toxic gas poisoning, June 1916; First Petrograd Medical Commission, September 1916, moderate neurasthenia; senior physician of the Caucasus Division, February 1917, cardiopathic neurosis and neurasthenia; Medical Commission, Petrograd, February 1919, organic heart disease), he preserved in his archives the diagnosis he received on April 19, 1937, from Leningrad physician I. Margolis.[77] Below I have quoted in full the two pages of hurried medical handwriting:

> The castration complex is corroborated by a series of valuable facts from the patient's early childhood. The patient has mentioned the persistent affect of fear that he experienced during a surgical operation to correct an insignificant ailment near the genitalia. This experience was completely forgotten (amnesia) and covered over with a layer of less valuable affects. The interconnected symptoms and their sources are so infused with *pansexualism* that they can be overlooked only by someone who does not wish to see them. The patient finds it unpleasant to return to this truly tragic theme, and discussion of the episode always exacerbates his symptoms and his fear at the prospect of some deadly chasm, terror that his "libido might stop." The patient's perception of libido has crossed the boundary of healthy defense, and he reacts even to simple physiological arousal with a pronounced indignation that is always visible in a variety of symptoms (torturing himself and variegated symptomatic suffering). The patient sublimates his libido and all pleasure along with it.
>
> The patient honestly seeks some minimal understanding of his suffering in the facts of his past. Resistance often keeps him from learning and seeing everything. The extent of resistance is often incomprehensible to the patient. The castration that has impoverished the libido has deprived his personality of its renowned might, and this keeps him from pushing the attack to the last stronghold of neurosis.
>
> The patient is frightened by action (the gift of life)—particularly libidinal action. He retreats and becomes passive and introverted. This cycle can be broken only through absolutely free penetration into all corners of the libido, though the patient might have to see the strangest and most frightful things there.
>
> The patient's constant fetish, the female bust, which so attracts and tortures him, indicates an involvement of the oedipal complex.

This is not so much a diagnosis as a written continuation of the doctor's debate with a patient whose defensive concepts have to be overcome. There is something unfair and superficial about the diagnosis; the use of the word *pansexualism,* which Margolis underlined, having lifted it from Marxist works on psychoanalysis, is malapropos. Not only does Dr. Margolis not mask his analytic orientation, he enthusiastically underlines it and clearly invites his famed patient to begin psychoanalytic treatment.

We do not know how Zoshchenko felt about this diagnosis or whether he actually began analysis at that time. In any case, several years later he commented respectfully about Freudians (see below), and he kept Margolis's diagnosis among his papers. After experimenting with different types of treatment, Zoshchenko chose self-analysis, which he practiced for decades. It stabilized his condition, allowing him to live a long, productive life that would have been extremely difficult even for a healthy person. He described the process and results of his self-analysis in three books.[78] The last of the series, *Before the Sun Rises,* is unarguably an exceptional work of literature with the mark of psychoanalytic influence.

Zoshchenko wrote the book in 1942, after his evacuation to Alma-Ata, where he lived at the same time as did Eisenstein. Many commentators have spoken of the noticeable relaxation of ideological pressure from the regime during the war. For a former combat officer, the war environment could provide the bravery he otherwise lacked. Whether it was the war or the therapeutic success of his self-treatment, Zoshchenko's pen was freed from both the idiocy of feuilletons and the prolixities of academic writing with which he had attempted to conceal the underlying anxiety in his previous book, *Youth Returned.*

Before the Sun Rises was written almost entirely by a free man—free in both senses of the word, political and psychological. The work had no equal in Soviet prose in its degree of freedom, psychological depth, and absolute clarity. At the same time, the work owed much to the literature of the symbolists, whom Zoshchenko knew personally, despite being fifteen years younger than Bely and Blok. Most of all, the structure and style of *Before the Sun Rises* are reminiscent of Rozanov's books: It contains the same self-assured and unstylized first-person storytelling; the same sincerity in conveying the author's own sexuality without appealing to the reader's; the same manner of breaking the text down into short chapters with elementary structure. Zoshchenko made no attempt to conceal his sympathies: The central part of the story bears the same title as Rozanov's most important work, *Fallen Leaves.*

The story is constructed as a chain of free associations, each of which is an isolated recollection. With their help, Zoshchenko delves, seeking the reasons for his melancholy. How can the unfortunate incident be found? One by one, he examines the recollections that cause him internal anxiety: "Anxiety, like the light of a photo flash, illuminates photographs of the past." Zoshchenko shows them to the reader one after the other, from the most recent to the very earliest. Women that seduced him; his father's death; battle portraits, scenes from daily life, commemorative sketches. There are no explanations for any of it. He goes still deeper, to age five and then two. But here the light fades, the author sees only emptiness and a world of chaos that disappears at the first touch of reason. Zoshchenko has no doubt that this is another world.

It is here, in the last part of the book, entitled *Up to Age Two,* that the author turns to scholars for understanding: physiologists of the Pavlovian school and Freudian analysts. The range, as we can see, is the very same as the one found in the explorations of Trotsky and Eisenstein. But

Zoshchenko, fully aware of his own neurosis, is concerned with a practical result. He introduces the reader to conditioned reflexes and tries to apply their laws to his own early childhood. He goes back to the village where he lived the first years of his life, but his melancholy intensifies, and he returns home in an awful state. Conditioned reflexes, and bromide, for that matter, are no longer any help to him. His sleep is haunted by nightmares. Before, he either did not dream or forgot his dreams right away. Now his eyes had barely closed before the visions began crowding in.

One doctor (it could have been our friend Dr. Margolis) told the author, "only through dreams will you make sense of your illness." He interpreted one dream, proclaiming that the author was suffering from sexual trauma. The author was indignant. The doctor declared: I interpreted the dream according to Freud. I am his student. And there is no more accurate science that would be helpful to you. The author consulted with other doctors. Among them was another faithful Freudian. This was an extremely intelligent doctor. The author almost became his disciple, but the doctor was a vociferous opponent of Pavlov. He interpreted every dream as the dream of an erotomaniac. And so the author continued his self-analysis, which alternated with popularized theoretical passages on the age-old theme, "Pavlov and Freud."

The Last Victory

The story is not over. Such an analysis, of course, could never be completed. The inability of self-analysis to tap the contents of one's own unconscious is one of the most elementary truths of the Freudian method. In the process of self-analysis, a person finds himself subject to the same distorting mechanisms that engender his symptoms and dreams. Only in contact with the conscious and unconscious of the other can authentic penetration of the self occur. Strangely enough, in Russia Bakhtin documented this truth brilliantly, even though he was critical about psychoanalysis in general, while it was forgotten in the texts of those who sympathized with Freud. In the works of Yermakov, Blonsky, and Trotsky, moments of awareness attracted far more attention than moments of transference, despite their equal importance for psychoanalysis. Incidentally, something similar was also characteristic of Russian symbolists: The transformation of the consciousness was understood as either an individual creative act or a collective theurgical action, but never as a dynamic process undertaken by a single person toward another in the struggle with resistance. Zoshchenko took the same route, rejecting psychoanalytic treatment from his "very intelligent" Freudian in favor of "Pavlovian" awareness of his own reflexive connections.

"That which is blocked can be uncovered. This block can be lifted by the light of logic, the light of higher consciousness." This was the meaning of

Zoshchenko's work, even in its socially useful sense. "After all, my texts speak of the victory of human reason, of science, and of the progress of consciousness. My work declaims the 'philosophy' of fascism, which says that the conscious brings countless misfortunes to mankind." It is surprising that Thomas Mann wrote almost the same thing to Jung's coauthor, Karl Kerenyi, in 1941: "Psychology is the means whereby myth may be wrested from the hands of the Fascist obscurantists to be 'transmuted' for humane ends."[79]

In the person of Zoshchenko, Russian culture and psychoanalysis once again crossed paths. Theirs was indeed a productive encounter, the result of which, this time, was directed against fascism in all its guises: *Before the Sun Rises* was not only an apologia of consciousness but also a testimony to the value of the individual, with all his sufferings, hopes, and strivings.

Precisely for this reason, the book became the target of special persecution by Party authorities. In 1946, the Central Committee of the Communist Party adopted a resolution "On the Journals *Zvezda* and *Leningrad*," turning its heavy ideological weaponry against two aging writers, living monuments to the Silver Age, Zoshchenko and Akhmatova. In the decree, Zoshchenko was referred to as the most "vulgar and idiotic man in literature," his most heinous crimes against the state having been "writing repulsive things like *Before the Sun Rises*." As Zhdanov said in a speech before the Central Committee: "It is difficult to find anything more disgusting in our literature than the morality preached by Zoshchenko in his novella *Before the Sun Rises*, where he portrays other people and himself as vile, lascivious beasts without shame or conscience."

The Central Committee resolution, by linking Zoshchenko to Akhmatova, put a symbolic end to the history of Russian modernism. The Russian writer who was closest to psychoanalysis found himself in company with the heiress to the Silver Age, in their common resistance to state terror. The ailing Zoshchenko managed to survive even the resolution of the omnipotent Central Committee. He was one of the very few who found in himself the courage and health to bear Party censure without dying or repenting, remaining true to himself. What he called psychoanalysis this time proved stronger than what Zhdanov and his colleagues called communism.

Conclusion

The history of psychoanalysis gives testimony to the penetrability of national borders by ideas. Freud's science of the individual gave rise to concepts that were equally well apprehended by and bore identical significance for different societies.[1] The fruits of human intellect—however specific and unique the milieu in which they blossom and ripen—often take on an extranational flavor in their mature stages; and yet the universality coveted by so many is attained by but a few.

One need only compare the history of psychoanalysis with that of Marxism to understand how incredibly complex is the transnational penetration of ideas and how deadly is their occasional perversion in the process. The intentions of the ideas' progenitors seem to have little effect on their destinies: Freud cherished few illusions in that regard and was plagued by many fears. Yet with each passing decade of the twentieth century, psychoanalysis has steadily expanded into an increasing number of national cultures, taking on particular characteristics unique to each case (in France, one finds an example of this process in the psychoanalysis of Jacques Lacan; and in the United States, in the unusually deep interpenetration of psychoanalysis and medicine). In Latin America, the last continent to be conquered by Freud's ideas, the downfall of each successive dictatorship invariably has been accompanied by a flowering of psychoanalysis. In sum, despite its long history of internal disagreements and divisions, psychoanalysis has maintained its essential traits. In striking contrast, the doctrine of Marx, who proclaimed the inevitability and universality of his goals, appears to be in fatal decline.

Psychoanalysis might aptly be compared to a comet transecting various solar systems: The comet is surrounded by a vacuum and encounters no similar objects as it pursues its course. Yet it is accompanied through space by gravitational and magnetic fields that distort its trajectory, whip its tail into a vortex, and sheer away clouds of vapor, which are left behind to find their own orbit in that solar system.

Psychoanalysis was so quickly and avidly adopted in turn-of-the-century Russia that my readers might well be perplexed by the later events recounted in this book: Could this really be the same Russia? Yes, indeed: In this country's extraordinary intellectual and political atmosphere, psychoanalysis underwent the greatest distortions it was ever to encounter in its development, and in the end it was almost unrecognizable. The peculiar characteristics of Russian culture, catalyzed by unique historical circumstances, produced an unprecedented intellectual amalgam, and psychoanalysis played a role in this process. The compactness of psychoanalytic doctrine, the clear demarcations between what psychoanalysis is and what it is not, afford us an unusually keen insight into the complex interplay of scientific concepts, spiritual values, and political forces that shaped the intellectual terrain of Russia in the twentieth century.

The evolution of Russian psychoanalysis was unique and multifaceted. In the area of theory, one of its most intriguing aspects is the line that can be traced from the Adlerian beliefs of Russian psychotherapists of the 1910s to the Trotskyism of Soviet analysts of the 1920s. The places occupied by sexuality in Freudian psychoanalytic theory and by transference in Freudian analytic practice were usurped in Russian theory and practice by questions of power and of consciousness. In clinical and applied work, the problems of consciousness and unconsciousness were assigned much greater importance than was transference, which was almost never mentioned by Soviet-era psychoanalysts, who had abandoned study of the sexual libido in their eagerness to discover other forces motivating the human psyche. Thus, psychoanalysis in Soviet Russia followed a trajectory exactly opposite to that pursued by the rest of the psychoanalytic world.

"I can confidently state that a strong and productive psychoanalytic movement could have developed in Russia, if the powers that be had not waged such an aggressive war against it," wrote Moisei Wulff, erstwhile president of the Russian Psychoanalytic Society, living in Berlin.[2] Today, in light of recent history and accumulated political experience, Wulff's statement seems oversimple. One cannot escape intellectual responsibility by blaming the authorities' ill will: In their struggle for political dominance, Russian psychoanalysts subjected themselves to the most dramatic of mental contortions. They were led astray by their own utopian illusions, failing to note the points of logical divergence between such dreams and what they knew of psychoanalysis. Adopting an attitude of hope and trust toward the new regime that was emerging, regenerated, alongside them, they found it most attentive and supportive—so long as it was peopled by those who were congenial to psychoanalysis.

From Tatiana Rosenthal to Ivan Yermakov, the work of Russian analysts was typified by the avoidance of all discussion of the libido, and at times by bold-faced hypocrisy on sexual matters. A rather comical example was Aron Zalkind, who so easily made the leap from Adlerian psychoanalysis to official repression of sexuality in the name of class rule. Other traditions, such as the enlightened eroticism of Lou Andreas-Salomé, Wilhelm Reich's sexual emancipation and social liberation, and Mikhail Bakhtin's conceptualization of discourse, were forgotten because they had no direct bearing on the problematics of power. In its earliest stages, the cult of power—the molten core around which the totalitarian consciousness revolved—sucked in all kinds of spiritual matter, including even that with which it was most incompatible, such as psychoanalysis.

The cult of power thus inevitably became a rite of death, regardless of the circumstances. This explains why, beginning with Sabina Spielrein, the theme of the death wish took on paramount significance for Russian analysts who were grappling with the same knotty problem that Solovyov and Ivanov had encountered—the culture of their homeland. Death and power made up the entire universe in which Russian psychoanalysis and its creatures had their being. Death and power were the elements constituting that black star with the gargantuan gravitational pull around which the comet of psychoanalysis revolved until it was at last sucked in, to commingle and fuse with dark oblivion.

The antinatural regime could achieve stability only by transforming the very nature of its human subjects; and this it strove mightily to do, commanding them hourly to perform the metamorphosis. Observing these machinations from a safe distance, the emigrant Fyodor Stepun wrote: "State despotism is terrifying not so much for its political limitations as for its educational and cultural impositions, its schemes to create a new man and a new humanity."[3] The idea of the "new man," which had been a central goal of Russian intellectuals from the symbolists of the 1900s to the pedologists of the 1930s, had become official government policy. Later, as the regime became progressively more liberal, the concept gradually lost all meaning; but it survived until the Brezhnev era, if only as an empty slogan.

Early Soviet psychoanalysis was unprecedentedly politicized and unusually close to the regime. The leadership of the Russian Psychoanalytic Society in the early 1920s consisted nearly entirely of Bolsheviks who planned to use psychoanalysis to their own ends. Moscow in the 1920s saw the organization of the State Psychoanalytic Institute (an otherwise unheard-of phrase in the history of psychoanalysis) and the Psychoanalytic Orphanage, a specialized establishment for the children of high-ranking party functionaries. Trotsky himself had a personal stake in psychoanalysis, assigning it a prominent place in his new political agenda; and none other than Stalin's son, Vasily (who would later become an alcoholic and an air force general), was among the children whose upbringing was overseen by the Psychoanalytic Orphanage.

But their close relationship to the regime saved neither psychoanalysts nor psychoanalysis. Just the opposite: The closer they moved to the center of power, the closer they came to death. Recall Adolf Ioffe, a patient of Adler's who later provided psychoanalysis to convicts in Siberian penal servitude. Ioffe committed suicide following the "liquidation of the Trotskyist opposition," among whose ranks he had figured prominently. Aron Zalkind died of a heart attack following the denunciation of his brainchild, pedology—the science of the "new man of the masses." Alexander Luria, one of the greatest psychologists of the Soviet period, began his career as academic secretary of the Russian Psychoanalytic Society and then left that post on the eve of the purges to work on developing a mechanical lie detector. Sabina Spielrein, who had discovered the death wish long before Freud, voluntarily returned to Bolshevik Russia and then remained behind in Nazi-occupied Rostov. Max Eitingon, one of the most inscrutable figures in intellectual history, personified power in international psychoanalysis.

In the history of psychoanalysis—that is, the history of ideas—the will to power that was described by Adler and never acknowledged by Freud was far removed from the death wish described by Spielrein and later rediscovered by Freud. The history of psychoanalysis—that is, the history of people—moves us to ask whether these two forms of desire are really so divergent. After all, both point us back toward Nietzsche. And following full circle, we sense a hidden, paradoxical logic: the cult of power . . . the service of death . . . the eros of the impossible.

Notes

Introduction

1. V. I. Ivanov, *Sobranie sochinenii v 4-kh tomakh* [Collected Works in Four Volumes] (Brussels, 1971), vol. 1, p. 825.

2. There is a body of specialized literature dealing with the perception of Nietzsche in Russia. Titles include: B. G. Rosenthal, ed., *Nietzsche in Russia* (Princeton: Princeton University Press, 1986); E. W. Clowes, *The Revolution of Moral Consciousness: Nietzsche in Russian Literature, 1890–1914* (DeKalb, Ill.: Northern Illinois University Press, 1988); R. Y. Danilevsky, "Russkii obraz Fridrikha Nitsshe (predistoriia i nachalo formirovaniia)" [The Russian Image of Friedrich Nietzsche (Prehistory and Early Formation)], in *Na rubezhe XIX i XX vekov* (Leningrad: Nauka, 1991), pp. 5–43; and B. G. Rosenthal, ed., *Nietzsche and Soviet Culture: Ally and Adversary* (Cambridge: Cambridge University Press, 1994).

3. A. Benois, *Moi vospominaniia* [Memoirs] (Moscow: Nauka, 1990), vol. 2, p. 48.

4. A. Grigoriev, *Vospominaniia* [Memoirs] (Moscow and Leningrad: Academia, 1930), p. 116.

5. A. A. Bogdanov, "Novyi mir" [New World], in *Voprosy sotsializma* [Issues in Socialism] (Moscow: Politizdat, 1990), p. 28.

6. *The Freud–Jung Letters*, ed. W. McGuire (London: Hogarth, 1974), p. 495.

7. S. Freud, *The Future of an Illusion* (New York: Norton, 1961), p. 9.

8. *The Letters of Sigmund Freud and Arnold Zweig*, ed. Ernst L. Freud (New York: New York University [NYU] Press, 1970), p. 25.

9. Nevertheless, Stalin- and Brezhnev-era ideologues were not alone in asserting that psychoanalysis was incompatible with Russian society. After emigrating, Alexander Pyatigorsky wrote that "Freudianism in all its permutations and stages . . . never was accepted by Russian culture"; see his article "O psikhoanalize iz sovremennoi Rossii" [On Psychoanalysis from Contemporary Russia], *Rossiia [Russia]*, no. 3 (Rome, 1977), pp. 29–50. Boris Groys based his otherwise outstanding reasoning on this misleading evaluation (see "Rossiia kak podsoznatel'noe Zapada" [Russia as the West's Subconscious], in *Utopiia i obmen* [Moscow: Znak, 1993], pp. 245–259).

10. M. G. Yaroshevsky, *Istoriia psikhologii* [History of Psychology], 2d ed. (Moscow: Pedagogika, 1976); A. V. Petrovsky, *Voprosy teorii i istorii psikhologii* [Problems in the Theory and History of Psychology] (Moscow: Pedagogika, 1984).

11. D. Joravsky, *Russian Psychology: A Critical History* (Oxford: Blackwell, 1989); L. Graham, *Science, Philosophy, and Behavior in the Soviet Union* (New York: Columbia University Press, 1987).

12. Among the most important works on the subject are J. Marti, "La Psychanalyse en Russie et en Union Soviétique de 1909 à 1930," *Critique* 346 (March 1976), pp. 199–236; H. Lobner and V. Levitin, "A Short Account of Freudism: Notes on the History of Psychoanalysis in the USSR," *Sigmund Freud House Bulletin* 2, no. 1 (1978), pp. 5–30; J.-M. Palmier, "La Psychanalyse en Union

Soviétique," in *Histoire de la psychanalyse*, ed. R. Jaccard (Paris: Hachette, 1982), vol. 2, pp. 213–270; E. Roudinesco, "Marxisme, psychanalyse, psychologie," chap. 1.2 in *Histoire de la psychanalyse en France*, vol. 2 (Paris: Seuil, 1986); A. Carotenuto, *A Secret Symmetry* (London: Routledge, 1984); J. L. Rice, "Russian Stereotypes in the Freud–Jung Correspondence," *Slavic Review* 41, no. 1 (Spring 1982): pp. 19–35; I. Maximov, "Histoire de la psychanalyse: La psychanalyse russe," *L'Ane*, no. 10 (1983), pp. 3–5; I. Manson, "Comment dit-on 'psychanalyse' en russe?" *Revue internationale du psychanalyse*, 1991, no. 4, pp. 407–422; A. Mikhalevitch, "Première implantation et rejet (1904–1930)," *Frénésie* 2, no. 7 (1989), pp. 125–146; M. Ljunggren, "The Psychoanalytic Breakthrough in Russia on the Eve of the First World War," in *Russian Literature and Psychoanalysis*, ed. Daniel Rancour-Laferriere (Amsterdam: Benjamin, 1989), pp. 174–191; M. Ljunggren, *The Dream of Rebirth: A Study of Andrej Belyj's Novel "Petersburg"* (Stockholm: Almqvist & Wiksell, 1982); M. Miller, "Freudian Theory Under Bolshevik Rule," *Slavic Review*, Winter 1985, pp. 625–646; M. Miller, "The Reception of Psychoanalysis and the Problem of the Unconscious in Russia," *Social Research* 57, no. 4 (1990), pp. 876–888; J. Rice, *Freud's Russia: National Identity in the Evolution of Psychoanalysis* (New Brunswick, N.J.: Transaction, 1993). Rice's important volume came out after my study was completed and published in Russian. There are important parallels and differences between the two books, which are especially relevant to the discussion in chapters 3 and 4 of mine.

13. E. Pfeiffer, ed., *Nietzsche, Rée, Salomé: Correspondance* (Paris: Presses Universitaires de France [PUF], 1979), p. 198.

14. S. Freud, "On the History of the Psychoanalytic Movement," in *The Standard Edition of the Complete Psychological Works of Sigmund Freud* (London: Hogarth, 1957), vol. 14, p. 66.

15. M. Bakhtin, *Dostoevsky's Poetics* (Ann Arbor: Ardis, 1973).

16. M. Bulgakov, *The Master and Margarita*, tr. Mirra Ginsburg (New York: Grove, 1967), p. 16.

Chapter One

1. There is a large and contradictory literature about the life of Lou Andreas-Salomé. This account is based on the following sources: L. Andreas-Salomé, *Ma Vie*, ed. E. Pfeiffer (Paris: PUF, 1977); R. Binion, *Frau Lou, Nietzsche's Wayward Disciple* (Princeton: Princeton University Press, 1968); H. F. Peters, *My Sister, My Spouse* (London, 1963); A. Livingstone, *Salomé: Her Life and Work* (New York: Moyer, 1984); P. Roazen, *Brother Animal: The Story of Freud and Tausk* (New York: NYU Press, 1986); and Biddy Martin, *Woman and Modernity: The (Life)-Styles of Lou Andreas-Salomé* (Ithaca: Cornell University Press, 1991).

2. Lou Andreas-Salomé, *Ma Vie*, p. 24.

3. For more detail on these events, see James Billington, *Fire in the Minds of Men: Origins of the Revolutionary Faith* (New York: Basic, 1980), pp. 492–495; and E. A. Pavliuchenko, *Zhenshchiny v russkom osvoboditel'nom dvizhenii* [Women in the Russian Liberation Movement] (Moscow: Mysl', 1988).

4. Livingstone, *Salomé*, p. 18.

5. Ibid., p. 22.

6. Ibid., p. 24.

7. Ibid., p. 26.

8. Ibid., p. 27.

9. Ibid., p. 30.

10. Letter from A. I. Herzen to M. K. Reichel of October 17, 1853, *Otryvki iz vospominanii M. K. Reichel i pis'ma k nei A. I. Gertsena* [Excerpts from the Memoirs of M. K. Reichel and Letters to Her from A. I. Herzen] (Moscow: Bukhgeim, 1909), p. 102.

11. Malwida von Meysenbug, *Memoiren einer Idealistin* (Frankfurt-am-Main, 1985), p. 342.

12. Ibid.

13. Livingstone, *Salomé*, p. 36.

14. I. K. Khmelevsky, "Patologicheskii element v lichnosti i tvorchestve Fridrikha Nitsshe" [The Pathological Element in the Personality and Work of Friedrich Nietzsche], a speech given at the meeting of the Society of Russian Physicians on February 22, 1903 (Kiev, 1904).

15. Letter from Freud to Paul Rée, March 21, 1882, in Peter Fuss and Henry Shapiro, eds., *Nietzsche: A Self-Portrait from His Letters* (Cambridge, Mass.: Harvard University Press, 1971), p. 59.

16. Friedrich Nietzsche, *Joyful Wisdom* (New York: Frederick Ungar, 1960).

17. Livingstone, *Salomé*, p. 40. (Rée called himself "Hüsung," a word from his local dialect.—Trans.)

18. Peters, *My Sister*, p. 120.

19. Letter from Freud to Peter Gast, July 13, 1882, in Fuss and Shapiro, eds., *Nietzsche*, p. 63.

20. Friedrich Nietzsche, Paul Rée, and Lou Andreas-Salomé, *Correspondance*, ed. E. Pfeiffer (Paris: PUF, 1979), pp. 153–154.

21. Ibid., pp. 135, 230.

22. Friedrich Nietzsche, *Thus Spoke Zarathustra* (Chicago: Gateway, 1957), p. 4.

23. Ibid., pp. 5–6.

24. E. Förster-Nietzsche, introduction to *Also sprach Zarathustra,* by Friedrich Nietzsche (Leipzig, 1922), p. xvii.

25. Written in 1884; cf. Peters, *My Sister*, p. 142.

26. Lou Andreas-Salomé, "Fridrikh Nitsshe v svoikh proizvedeniiakh," *Severnyi vestnik*, 1896, nos. 3–5.

27. V. Zhirmunsky, *Nemetskii romantizm i sovremennaia mistika* [German Romanticism and Contemporary Mysticism] (St. Petersburg, 1914), pp. 193, 13; V. Zhirmunsky, *Religioznoe otrechenie v istorii romantizma* [Religious Rejection in the History of Romanticism] (Moscow: Sakharov, 1919), p. 7.

28. Nietzsche, Reé, and Salomé, *Correspondance*, ed. E. Pfeiffer, p. 62. Vladimir Solovyov considered Nietzsche Lermontov's "closest heir." See V. Solovyov, *Stikhotvoreniia, estetika, literaturnaia kritika* (Moscow: Kniga, 1990), p. 444.

29. *Demon* was popular in Germany. In 1852–1876, the work was released in four different German translations and the Russian version was reprinted seven times in Germany. See *Lermontovskaia entsiklopediia* [The Lermontov Encyclopedia] (Moscow: Sovetskaia entsiklopediia, 1981), p. 393.

30. Mikhail Lermontov, "Demon," in Charles Johnston, *Rivers and Fireworks* (London: Bodley Head, 1980), p. 30.

31. Ibid., p. 36.

32. Ibid., p. 54.

33. Salomé's act, however, was fully in keeping with the *narodnik* tradition of unconsummated marriage, the early beginnings of which were signaled by Chernyshevsky's novel *What Is to Be Done?*—a tradition that remained important for several subsequent generations. See I. Paperno, *Chernyshevsky and the Age of Realism: A Study in the Semiotics of Behavior* (Stanford: Stanford University Press,

1988); and O. Matich, *Dialectics of Cultural Return: Zinaida Gippius' Personal Myth—Cultural Mythologies of Russian Modernism* (Berkeley: University of California Press, 1992), pp. 52–72.

34. Letter of May 9, 1926, in R. M. Rilke, B. Pasternak, M. Tsvetaeva, *Letters: 1926*, ed. Yevgeniy Pasternak (Orlando, Fla.: Harcourt-Brace, 1985), p. 81.

35. Letter of May 18, 1899, cited in K. Azadovsky, *Rilke und Russland* (Berlin-Weimar, 1986), p. 95.

36. The unpublished memoirs of S. N. Shil are kept at the Scientific Library of Moscow University, file 1004.

37. Lou Andreas-Salomé, "Russische Philosophie und Semitischer Geist," *Die Zeit*, no. 172 (January 15, 1898).

38. Friedrich Nietzsche, *Po tu storonu zla i dobra* [Beyond Good and Evil], in *Sochineniia v dvukh tomakh* (Moscow: Mysl', 1990), vol. 2, p. 370.

39. Boris Pasternak, *Safe Conduct: An Autobiography and Other Writings* (New York: New Directions, 1958), p. 13.

40. Rainer Maria Rilke, *Selected Works*, tr. J. B. Leishman (London: Hogarth, 1960), vol. 2, p. 67.

41. Peters, *My Sister*, p. 284.

42. Lou Andreas-Salomé, *Die Erotik* (Frankfurt, 1910).

43. *Sigmund Freud and Lou Andreas-Salomé: Letters,* ed. E. Pfeiffer (New York: Norton, 1985), p. 7.

44. See Livingstone, *Salomé,* p. 148.

45. See Roazen, *Brother Animal;* also Stefan Zweig, *Vrachevanie i psikhika* [Healing and the Psyche] (St. Petersburg: Gamma, 1992).

46. E. Jones, *The Life and Work of Sigmund Freud,* 3 vols. (New York: Basic, 1955).

47. Sigmund Freud, "Leonardo da Vinci and a Memory of His Childhood," in *The Standard Edition of the Complete Psychological Works of Sigmund Freud* (London: Hogarth, 1957), vol. 11, p. 69.

48. Ibid., p. 74.

49. Ibid., p. 69.

50. *The Freud–Jung Letters*, ed. W. McGuire (London: Hogarth, 1974), p. 478.

51. Paul Roazen, *Freud: Political and Social Thought* (London: Hogarth, 1969), pp. 84–85; R. L. Rudnytsky, *Freud and Oedipus* (New York: Columbia University Press, 1987), pp. 198–199.

52. Sigmund Freud, "Group Psychology and the Analysis of the Ego," in *The Standard Edition of the Complete Psychological Works of Sigmund Freud* (London: Hogarth, 1957), vol. 18, p. 67.

53. See Livingstone, *Salomé,* p. 152.

54. E. Jones, *The Life and Work of Sigmund Freud,* vol. 2, p. 421.

55. Paul Roazen, *Brother Animal.*

56. Ibid., p. 140.

57. L. Andreas-Salomé, *Mein Dank an Freud* (Vienna: Internationaler Psychoanalytischer Verlag, 1931), p. 19; L. Andreas-Salomé, *L'Amour du narcissisme* (Paris, 1980).

58. V. Solovyov, "Smysl liubvi" [The Meaning of Love], in *Sochineniia* [Works], vol. 2 (Moscow: Mysl', 1988).

59. According to Berdyaev, the Russian symbolist poets differed from Solovyov, whom they considered their teacher, in that they "believed in Sophia far more than in Christ"; incidentally, even Solovyov himself "allowed for the possibility of confusion in Sophia-ist moods." See Nikolai Berdyaev, "Smysl tvorchestva: Opyt

opravdaniia cheloveka" [The Meaning of Art: The Experience of Justifying Man's Existence], in *Sobranie sochinenii* [Collected Works], vol. 2 (Paris: YMCA, 1989).

60. V. Solovyov, "Ideia sverkhcheloveka" [The Idea of the Superman], in *Sochineniia* [Works] (Moscow: Mysl', 1988), vol. 2, pp. 626, 633.

61. V. Solovyov, "Smysl liubvi," in *Sochineniia*, vol. 2, pp. 516, 546.

62. Ibid., pp. 521, 522, 531.

63. L. Andreas-Salomé, "Russische Philosophie und Semitischer Geist."

64. L. Andreas-Salomé, "The Dual Orientation of Narcissism," *Psychoanalytic Quarterly* 31, no. 1 (1962), pp. 5, 28.

65. Ibid., p. 19.

66. Ibid., p. 10.

67. L. Andreas-Salomé, "Russische Dichtung und Kultur," *Cosmopolis* (August 1897), p. 574.

68. L. Andreas-Salomé, *Looking Back: Memoirs* (New York: Paragon, 1990), p. 35.

69. Livingstone, *Salomé*, p. 161; Biddy Martin, *Woman and Modernity: The (Life)-Styles of Lou Andreas-Salomé* (Ithaca: Cornell University Press, 1991), pp. 202–203.

70. L. Andreas-Salomé, *Looking Back*, p. 36.

71. Ibid., p. 38.

72. Ibid., p. 39.

73. Ibid., p. 38.

74. L. Andreas-Salomé, *Fenitschka,* ed. E. Pfeiffer (Frankfurt-am-Main: Ullstein, 1982), p. 45.

75. Ibid.

76. L. Andreas-Salomé, *Looking Back,* p. 88.

77. L. Andreas-Salomé, *Fenitschka.*

78. L. Andreas-Salomé, *Looking Back*, pp. 39–40.

79. Ibid., pp. 38–39.

80. See R. Fueloep-Miller, *Geist und Gesicht des Bolschewismus* (Zurich: Amathea, 1926), available in English translation as R. Fueloep-Miller, *The Mind and Face of Bolshevism* (New York: Harper, 1965).

Freud's article, "Dostoevsky and Patricide," contains a reference to Fueloep-Miller; see J. Rice, *Dostoevsky and the Healing Art* (Ann Arbor: Ardis, 1985), pp. 218–219.

81. L. Andreas-Salomé, *Looking Back*, p. 36.

82. Ibid., p. 39.

83. Ibid., p. 41.

84. Peters, *My Sister*, p. 283.

85. Livingstone, *Salomé*, p. 168.

86. Ibid.

87. *Sigmund Freud and Lou Andreas-Salomé: Letters,* ed. E. Pfeiffer, p. 32.

88. Ibid., p. 185.

89. Ibid., p. 57.

90. See Lou Andreas-Salomé, *Mein Dank an Freud.*

91. Livingstone, *Salomé*, p. 201.

92. Ibid., p. 203.

Chapter Two

1. A. Blok, "Est' igra: Ostorozhno voiti," in *Sobranie sochinenii* (Moscow: Khudozhestvennaia literatura, 1963), vol. 2, p. 181.

2. A. Benois, *Moi vospominaniia* [My Recollections] (Moscow: Nauka, 1990), vol. 1, p. 631; L. Mendeleeva-Blok, *Byli i nebylitsy* (Bremen, 1977), p. 29.

3. K. Mochulsky, *Andrei Bely: His Life and Works* (Ann Arbor: Ardis, 1977), p. 25.

4. F. Nietzsche, *Beyond Good and Evil*, p. 30.

5. F. Dostoevsky, *Biografiia, pis'ma, i zametki iz zapisnoi knizhki* (St. Petersburg, 1883), p. 373.

6. M. Bakhtin, *Problems of Dostoevsky's Poetics* (Ann Arbor: Ardis, 1973), pp. 49–50.

7. V. I. Ivanov, *Sobranie sochinenii* [Collected Works] (Brussels, 1987), vol. 4, p. 338.

8. V. Rozanov, "Opavshie list'ia" [Fallen Leaves], in *Uedinennoe* (Moscow: Politizdat, 1990), pp. 347, 148.

9. I. Annensky, "O sovremennom lirizme" [On Contemporary Lyricism], *Apollon*, 1909, vol. 3, p. 55.

10. L. Szilárd, "Neskol'ko zametok k ucheniiu Vyacheslava Ivanova o katarsise" [A Few Notes on Vyacheslav Ivanov's Study of Catharsis], in *Cultura i Memoria: Atti del terzo Simposio Internationale dedicato a Vjacheslav Ivanov*, vol. 2, *Testi in Russo* (La Nuovo Italia Editrice, 1986), p. 146.

11. N. Berdyaev, "Samopoznanie (Opyt filosofskoi avtobiografii)" [Self-Knowledge: The Experience of Philosophical Autobiography], in *Sobranie sochinenii*, vol. 1 (Paris: YMCA, 1989), pp. 167, 185.

12. V. Rozanov, "Opavshie list'ia."

13. V. A. Fateev, *V. V. Rozanov: Zhizn', tvorchestvo, lichnost'* [Rozanov: Life, Work, Personality] (Leningrad, 1991), p. 231.

14. V. Rozanov, *Liudi lunnogo sveta: Metafizika khristianstva* [Moonlight People: The Metaphysics of Christianity], 2d ed. (1913; reprint, Moscow: Druzhba narodov, 1990), pp. 73–74.

15. Ibid.

16. Ibid., p. 130.

17. Rozanov discussed "themes of Aphrodite" at great length with Alexander Benois, most of all confiding in him observations about his own wife. Benois recalled that there was no trace of tastelessness in Rozanov's comments, that they were marked with a combination of "sophisticated, subtle observation and almost childlike naïveté" (A. Benois, *Moi vospominaniia*, vol. 2, p. 249).

18. A. Sinyavsky, *Opavshie list'ia V. V. Rozanova* [Rozanov's *Fallen Leaves*] (Paris: Sintaksis, 1982), p. 33.

19. Freud, "Leonardo da Vinci," p. 101.

20. It is possible that Rozanov's ideas of homosexuality obliquely influenced Freud's interpretation of Leonardo da Vinci. In his essay on Leonardo da Vinci, Freud mentioned Merezhkovsky as one of his primary sources. Merezhkovsky, in turn, had been strongly influenced by Rozanov.

21. "Perepiska Rozanova i Gershenzona" [Correspondence Between Rozanov and Gershenzon], ed. V. Proskurina, *Novyi mir* 3, 1991, p. 231. The publisher is wrong in considering Weininger and Krafft-Ebing, whom Rozanov cited liberally, psychoanalysts.

22. D. H. Lawrence, *Selected Literary Criticism*, ed. A. Beel (New York: Viking, 1956), p. 253.

23. V. Rozanov, "Opavshie list'ia," p. 343.

24. V. Khodasevich, *Izbrannaia proza* [Selected Prose] (New York: Russica, 1982).

25. A. Bely, "O teurgii" [On Theurgy], *Novyi put'*, 1903, p. 9.

26. A. Bely, *Nachalo veka* [The Beginning of the Century] (Moscow, 1933), p. 276.

27. Bely recounted that Briusov practiced hypnosis as well as spiritualism: "He was never squeamish about the dubious atmosphere surrounding experiments in

hypnosis; . . . for a long while, he practiced hypnosis on me, Solovyov, and Ellis" (A. Bely, *Vospominaniia o Bloke* [Munich: Wilhelm Fink Verlag, 1969], p. 258).

28. Bely wrote, in early 1904: "Instead of the mystery, the brotherhood and sisterhood of which I had dreamed, there was mere romance. I was bewildered; more than that, I was stunned. . . . I had tried so hard to explain to Nina Ivanovna that Christ was between us; she agreed; and then, suddenly, this. My breakthrough to mystery, to 'theurgy' has been beaten back" (S. S. Grechishkin and A. V. Lavrov, "Biograficheskie istochniki romana Briusova 'Ognennyi angel'" [Biographical Sources of Briusov's Novel 'Fire Angels'], *Wiener Slawistischer Almanach*, 1978, vol. 1, p. 85). This story has been retold in detail many times. See also Konstantin Mochulsky, *Andrei Bely: His Life and Works*; Khodasevich, "Konets Renaty," in *Serebrianyi vek: Memuary* (Moscow: Izvestiia, 1990); Magnus Ljunggren, *The Dream of Rebirth: A Study of Andrej Belyj's Novel "Petersburg"* (Stockholm: Almqvist & Wiksell, 1982).

29. Cited in M. Ljunggren, *The Dream of Rebirth*, p. 138.

30. *The Freud–Jung Letters*, ed. W. McGuire (London: Hogarth, 1974), p. 226.

31. B. Vysheslavtsev, review of the first volume of Carl Jung's collected works on analytical psychology, *Put'*, February 20, 1930, pp. 111–113.

32. The idea that the story of Ivan Bezdomny is an encoded repetition of the Masonic initiation rite, a kind of "second birth," was articulated by Léna Szilárd in her talk "Bulgakov and the Symbolists," given at the International Colloquium on Bulgakov in Paris, June 1991.

33. A. Bely, *Pochemu ia stal simvolistom* (Ann Arbor: Ardis, 1982), p. 51.

34. A. Bely, *Vospominaniia o Bloke*, p. 117.

35. S. Averintsev, introduction to *Stikhotvoreniia i poemy* [Verse and Long Poems], by V. Ivanov (Leningrad: Sovetskii pisatel', 1978), p. 47.

36. A. Naiman, *Rasskazy ob Anne Akhmatovoi* [Stories of Anna Akhmatova] (Moscow: Khudozhestvennaia literatura, 1989).

37. N. Berdyaev, *Samopoznanie*, p. 177.

38. In *A. Blok: Novye materialy i issledovaniia, Literaturnoe nasledstvo* (Moscow: Nauka, 1982), vol. 3, p. 340.

39. Y. Gertsyk, *Vospominaniia* [Memoirs] (Paris: YMCA, 1973), p. 53.

40. S. Averintsev, introduction to *Stikhotvoreniia i poemy*, by V. Ivanov, p. 45.

41. V. Ivanov, "Daby v dushe chuzhoi," in *Stikhotvoreniia i poemy* (Leningrad: Sovetskii pisatel', 1976), p. 222. (Excerpt translated by Rebecca Ritke.)

42. N. Berdyaev, *Samopoznanie*, p. 172.

43. V. Ivanov, *Po zvezdam* [Stars] (St. Petersburg, 1909).

44. N. Berdyaev, *Samopoznanie*, p. 173.

45. N. Berdyaev, *Sobranie sochinenii* [Collected Works] (Paris: YMCA, 1990), vol. 4, p. 119.

46. V. Ivanov, *Po zvezdam*.

47. S. Bulgakov, *Avtobiograficheskie zametki* [Autobiographical Notes] (Paris: YMCA, 1946), p. 91.

48. Ivanov, *Po zvezdam*, pp. 99–100.

49. O. Mandelstam, *Kamen'* [Stone] (Leningrad: Nauka, 1990), pp. 206–207.

50. B. Zaitsev, *Dalekoe* [Distant] (Moscow: Sovetskii pisatel', 1991), p. 484.

51. V. Ivanov, "Da, sei pozhar," in *Stikhotvoreniia i poemy*, p. 285. (Excerpt translated by Rebecca Ritke.)

52. S. Averintsev, introduction to *Stikhotvoreniia i poemy*, by V. Ivanov, p. 45.

53. V. Ivanov, *Po zvezdam*, p. 153.

54. V. Ivanov, "Ni granei, ni godin," in *Stikhotvoreniia i poemy*, p. 132.

55. Ibid., p. 413.

56. Ibid., p. 125.

57. N. Berdyaev, "Smysl tvorchestva: Opyt opravdaniia cheloveka" [The Meaning of Creativity: The Experience of Justification of Man], in *Sobranie sochinenii*, vol. 2.

58. V. Ivanov, "Dukhovnyi lik slavianstva," in *Sobranie sochinenii*, vol. 4, p. 668.

59. W. J. McGrath, *Dionysian Art and Populist Politics in Austria* (New Haven: Yale University Press, 1974).

60. *The Freud–Jung Letters*, pp. 293–294.

61. Ibid., p. 293.

62. Ibid., p. 295.

63. C. G. Jung, *Essays on Contemporary Events* (London: Kegan Paul, 1947).

64. I. M. Kogan, "Weltuntergangserlebnis und Wiedergeburtsphantasie bei einem Schizophrenen," *Internationale Zeitschrift für Psychoanalyse*, 1932, 18, pp. 86–104.

65. L. Mendeleeva-Blok, *Byli i nebylitsy*, p. 50.

66. A. Blok, *Sochineniia*, vol. 2, pp. 476, 716.

67. V. Orlov, "Sny i iav" [Sleeping and Waking], in A. Blok, *Pis'ma k zhene* (Moscow: Nauka, 1876), p. 21.

68. "A. Blok: Novye materialy i issledovaniia," in *Literaturnoe nasledstvo* (Moscow: Nauka, 1980), vol. 92, part 1, pp. 358, 369, 394.

69. F. Stepun, *Byvshee i nesbyvsheesia* (New York: Chekhov, 1956), vol. 1, pp. 269–270.

70. A. Bely, *Nachalo veka*, p. 89.

71. M. Ljunggren, *The Dream of Rebirth*, p. 86.

72. L. Ivanova, *Vospominaniia: Kniga ob otse* [Memoirs: A Book About My Father] (Paris: Atheneum, 1990), p. 217.

73. V. Ivanov, "Anima," in *Iz istorii russkoi filosofskoi mysli kontsa XIX i nachala XX vekov: Antologiia* (Washington: Interlanguage Literary Associates, 1965), pp. 183–197; V. Ivanov, *Sobranie sochinenii*, vol. 4, pp. 367–385.

74. The sonnet "Porog soznaniia" [The Threshold of Consciousness] and the history of its dedication can be found in V. Ivanov, *Sobranie sochinenii*, vol. 3, pp. 562, 845.

75. L. Ivanova, *Vospominaniia*, pp. 217–218.

76. Leonid Ionin, personal communication.

77. L. Ginzburg, *Literatura v poiskakh real'nosti* [Literature in Search of Reality] (Moscow: Sovetskii pisatel', 1987), p. 221.

78. From the letters of C. G. Jung to E. K. Metner [in German], Archives of the Russian State Library (Moscow), fund 167, file 14, p. 62. These excerpts from the Jung–Metner correspondence were first published in *Eros nevozmozhnogo* (the Russian edition of this book). They now are available also in M. Ljunggren, *The Russian Mephisto: A Study of the Life and Work of Emile Metner* (Stockholm: University of Stockholm Press, 1994), pp. 213–230 [in German and in English]. Here, I have quoted from Ljunggren's English translation.

79. C. G. Jung, *Izbrannye trudy po analiticheskoi psikhologii*, ed. Emile Metner, 3 vols.: vol. 1, *Psikhologicheskie tipy* (Zurich: Musaget, 1929); vol. 2, *Libido, eia metamorfozy i simvoly*; vol. 3, *Opyt izlozheniia psikhoanaliticheskoi teorii i drugie stat'i* (Zurich: Psikhologicheskogo kluba, 1939).

80. A. Carotenuto, *A Secret Symmetry: Sabina Spielrein Between Freud and Jung* (London: Routledge, 1980), pp. 56, 124.

81. E. Metner, preface to *Izbrannye trudy po analiticheskoi psikhologii*, vol. 1.

82. B. Vysheslavtsev, review of C. G. Jung, *Izbrannye trudy po analiticheskoi psikhologii*, vol. 1, *Psikhologicheskie tipy*, *Put'* 20 (February 1930), pp. 111–113.

83. Letter from Jung to Metner, quoted in M. Ljunggren, *The Russian Mephisto,* p. 221.

84. M. Ljunggren, "The Psychoanalytic Breakthrough in Russia on the Eve of the First World War," in Rancour-Laferriere, ed., *Russian Literature and Psychoanalysis* (Amsterdam: Benjamin, 1989), pp. 174–191.

85. Y. Gertsyk, *Vospominaniia,* p. 154.

86. This is an allusion to the Russian idiomatic expression "behind seven locks," that is, something absolutely inaccessible.—Trans.

87. Y. Gertsyk, *Vospominaniia,* p. 154.

88. L. Ivanova, *Vospominaniia,* p. 63.

89. A. Bely, "Mezhdu dvukh revoliutsii," p. 312.

90. N. Berdyaev, "Koshmar zlogo dobra" [Nightmare of the Evil Good], *Put'* 4, June–July 1926.

91. I. Ilyin, *Religioznyi smysl filosofii: Tri rechi, 1914–1923* [The Religious Meaning of Philosophy: Three Speeches, 1914–1923] (Paris: YMCA), pp. 29–30.

92. Ibid., pp. 60–63.

93. I. A. Ilyin, *Aksiomy religioznogo opyta* [Axioms of Religious Experience] (Paris, 1953), vol. 1.

94. N. Poltoratsky, *Ivan Aleksandrovich Iliin: Zhizn', trudy, mirovozzrenie* [Ivan Alexandrovich Ilyin: Life, Work, Worldview] (New Jersey: Hermitage, 1989).

95. "Ustami Buninykh: Dnevniki" [From Bunin's Lips: Diaries], *Posev,* 1981, vol. 2, p. 239.

96. See Poltoratsky, *Ivan Aleksandrovich Iliin.*

97. A. Bely, *Nachalo veka,* p. 101.

98. John Malmstad, ed., "Andrei Bely i antroposofiia" (Andrei Bely and Anthroposophy], *Minuvshee* 8, 1989, p. 416.

99. N. A. Frumkina, L. S. Fleishman, "A. A. Blok mezhdu 'Musagetom' i 'Sirinom'" [Alexander Blok between 'Musaget' and 'Sirin'], in *Blokovskii sbornik,* vol. 2 (Tartu: Tartu University Press, 1972), p. 387.

100. F. Stepun, *Byvshee i nesbyvsheesia,* vol. 1, p. 269.

101. A. Bely, *Vospominaniia o Steinere* [Recollections of Steiner] (Paris, 1982), pp. 33–34.

102. V. N. Voloshinov, *Freudianism: A Marxist Critique* (New York: Academic Press, 1976).

103. N. Osipov, "Psychoanalysis of the Prejudices," *International Journal of Psychoanalysis,* vol. 4, 1932, p. 482.

104. Malmstad, "Andrei Bely i antroposofiia," p. 380.

105. I. Ilyin, *Religioznyi smysl filosofii,* p. 63.

106. V. Khodasevich, "Andrei Bely," *Serebrianyi vek: Memuary* (Moscow: Izvestiia, 1990), p. 217.

107. A. Bely, *Pochemu ia stal simvolistom,* p. 3.

108. Ibid., p. 8.

109. A. Bely, *Kotik Letaev,* trans. G. Janecek (Ann Arbor: Ardis, 1971), p. 3.

110. A. Steinberg, *Druz'ia moikh rannikh let* [Friends of My Early Years] (Paris: Sintaksis, 1991), p. 125.

111. V. Khodasevich, "Ableukhovy–Letaevy–Korobkiny," in *Izbrannaia proza,* pp. 151–181; and "Andrei Bely," *Serebrianyi vek,* pp. 207–227.

112. A. Bely, *St. Petersburg,* trans. J. Cournos (New York: Grove, 1959), pp. 80–81.

113. N. Berdyaev, *Smysl tvorchestva,* pp. 216–240.

114. *Pamyat'* 5 (1989).

115. N. Berdyaev, "Dukhovnye osnovy russkoi revoliutsii" [Spiritual Roots of the Russian Revolution], in *Sobranie sochinenii*, vol. 4, pp. 105, 201, 205.

116. B. Zaitsev, *Dalekoe*, p. 487.

117. Y. Gertsyk, *Vospominaniia*, p. 136.

118. N. Berdyaev, *Samopoznanie*, p. 84.

119. N. Berdyaev, *Smysl tvorchestva*, p. 426.

120. B. Vysheslavtsev, *Etika preobrazhennogo erosa* [Ethics of Eros Transformed] (Paris: YMCA, 1931), p. vi. His review "Religiozno-asketicheskoe znachenie nevroza" (*Put'* 5, 1926, pp. 100–102) also deserves attention. A brief overview of Freud's and Adler's ideas ends with the statement, "neuroses are punishment for sins."

121. Ibid.

122. Ibid., p. 69.

123. S. Frank, "Psikhoanaliz kak mirovozzrenie" [Psychoanalysis as a World-view], *Put'* 25, December 1930, pp. 22–50.

124. N. Lossky, "Dr. N. E. Osipov kak filosof" [Dr. N. E. Osipov as a Philosopher], in *Zhizn' i smert': Sbornik pamiati D-ra N. E. Osipova* (Prague, 1935), vol. 1, pp. 46–54.

125. N. Lossky, *Istoriia russkoi filosofii* [History of Russian Philosophy] (Moscow: Sovetskii pisatel', 1991), pp. 384–385.

126. Ibid., p. 384.

127. Lossky, "Dr. N. E. Osipov kak filosof," p. 51.

128. N. Baranova-Shestova, *Zhizn' L'va Shestova* [The Life of Lev Shestov] (Paris, 1983), vol. 1, p. 235.

129. Ibid., p. 242.

130. A. Steinberg, *Druz'ia moikh rannikh let*, p. 248.

131. Ibid.

132. This could have been the German translation of Shestov's book about Chekhov, *Tvorchestvo iz nichego* [Creation out of Nothing], or parts of his long treatise *Na vesakh Iova* [In Job's Balances], which came out a little later, in 1929, as excerpts of the latter were published separately in German.

133. E. Jones, *The Life and Work of Sigmund Freud* (New York: Basic, 1955), vol. 3, p. 140.

134. N. Baranova-Shestova, *Zhizn' L'va Shestova*, vol. 1, p. 22.

135. Ibid., vol. 2, pp. 62–63.

136. Ibid., vol. 2, pp. 207–208.

137. A. Blok, *Sochineniia v dvukh tomakh*, vol. 2, p. 564.

138. V. Khodasevich, "Konets Renaty," p. 179.

139. V. Khodasevich, *Izbrannaia proza*.

140. V. Khodasevich, "Konets Renaty," p. 179.

141. This document was discovered by Vera Proskurina. See V. Proskurina, "K izucheniiu literaturno-bytovogo konteksta tvorchestva V. Ivanova v 1915 (zhurnal *Bul'vary i perekrestki*: neizdannye materialy)," a paper presented at a colloquium dedicated to Vyacheslav Ivanov in Geneva in June 1992.

Chapter Three

1. E. Jones, *The Life and Work of Sigmund Freud*, vol. 2 (New York: Basic, 1955), p. 274.

2. P. Roazen, *Freud and His Followers* (New York: Knopf, 1975), p. 155.

3. K. Obholzer, *The Wolf-Man Sixty Years Later* (London: Routledge, 1980), p. 167.

4. E. Jones, *The Life and Work of Sigmund Freud,* vol. 2, p. 274.

5. S. Freud, "From the History of an Infantile Neurosis," in *Three Case Histories* (New York: Collier, 1963), p. 298. The basic sources on the Pankeev case are this monograph by Freud, which was written mainly in the winter of 1914–1915 and later fleshed out and annotated by the author before its publication; the memoirs of Pankeev himself; and several clinical descriptions produced by psychoanalysts who worked with Pankeev after Freud. Many of these writings are collected in M. Gardiner's book, *The Wolf-Man and Sigmund Freud* (London: Karnac Books, 1989). Another important source is a book of interviews with Pankeev conducted near the end of the 1970s (K. Obholzer, *The Wolf-Man Sixty Years Later*).

6. *Confession sexuelle d'un anonyme russe* (Paris: Usher, 1990). The text attracted Nabokov's high praise after it appeared in Havelock Ellis's *Psychology of Sex.*

7. Referring to Gorky's work *The Life of Klim Samgin.*—Trans.

8. E. Erikson, *Childhood and Society* (New York: Norton, 1950), p. 402.

9. For an analysis comparing Pankeev with Lermontov and his characters (particularly with the Demon), see E. Halpert, "Lermontov and the Wolf Man," *American Imago,* 1975, vol. 32, no. 4, pp. 315–329.

10. M. Gardiner, ed., *The Wolf-Man and Sigmund Freud: The Memoirs of the Wolf-Man* (New York: Basic, 1971).

11. A. Blok, "Pis'ma k zhene," in *Literaturnoe nasledstvo* (Moscow: Nauka, 1978), vol. 89, p. 112.

12. Gardiner, *The Wolf-Man and Sigmund Freud,* p. 50.

13. This brings to mind one of Freud's early theories, which he later abandoned: "In more than half of the severe cases of hysteria, obsessional neurosis, etc. which I have treated psychotherapeutically, I have been able to prove with certainty that the patient's father suffered from syphilis." This is an excerpt from *Three Essays on the Theory of Sexuality,* written by Freud in 1905. It was expurgated from later editions by the author. Cited in Roazen, *Freud and His Followers,* p. 110.

14. Gardiner, *The Wolf-Man and Sigmund Freud,* p. 137.

15. Freud, "From the History of an Infantile Neurosis."

16. Jones, *The Life and Work of Sigmund Freud,* vol. 2, p. 274.

17. Freud, "From the History of an Infantile Neurosis," p. 191.

18. Ibid., p. 192.

19. Gardiner, *The Wolf-Man and Sigmund Freud,* p. 173.

20. J. L. Rice, "Russian Stereotypes in the Freud–Jung Correspondence," *Slavic Review,* vol. 41, no. 1 (Spring 1982), pp. 13–35.

21. S. Freud, *The Complete Introductory Lectures on Psychoanalysis* (New York: Norton, 1966), p. 369.

22. O. Mandelstam, "Susal'nym zolotom goryat . . . ," in *Stone,* trans. R. Tracy (Princeton: Princeton University Press, 1981), p. 47.

23. It was unfortunately after completing this book that I learned of an important work by Nicholas Abraham and Maria Torok, *Cryptomanie: Le Verbier de l'Homme aux Loups* (Paris: Flammarion, 1976); tr. ed. with foreword by J. Derrida, *The Wolf Man's Magic Words* (Minneapolis: University of Minnesota Press, 1986). In this work, the story of the Wolf-Man is interpreted in a thoroughly unconventional manner. In a way, the suppositions in the authors' analysis of the case coincide with mine, but they come to completely different conclusions. The authors take the fact that Pankeev was multilingual as the starting point in decoding his dreams, and, in general, his entire life. The verbal material left by the patient and known today from Freud's German transcription is "played back" in Russian and English (one of Pankeev's governesses was English) and "translated" by consonance. For

example, the sound of the German word *wolf* is perceived by Russian ears, say the authors, as *gul'fik*, the Russian word for a kind of Renaissance jock-strap. This being so, the authors assert, one can assume that the childhood perception of the word *gul'fik*, along with its symbolic meaning, was pushed back into the subconscious, from whence it broke through into a distorted and "translated" (into German, and then into the language of images) dream about wolves. In the same dream, the authors read "walnut" (*orekh*) as akin to "sin" (*grekh*), and they see the row of old walnut trees as a row of long-forgotten sins. The content of the wolf dream, from the authors' point of view, is not the result of a Sergei peeping on his parents in the act, but of the child overhearing an argument between his Russian mother and English governess concerning his erotic games with his sister. This complicated analysis is flawed in that it stretches a whole series of points and allows a number of incongruities obvious to the Russian ear. For instance, the word *gul'fik*, although it appears in Russian dictionaries, is extremely rare and belongs to a lexical category that a child could not possibly have known. The authors attest that the word "six" (*shestero*), referring to the number of wolves, is consonant with the word "sister" (*sestra*), although the two words sound much less alike than one would think from reading dictionary transcriptions. Caught up in their own new reading method, the authors even see the name Rank, written in Cyrillic, embedded in Sergei's last name, even though this claim would then lead us to believe that Pankeev himself was the product of Freud's imagination during his conflict with Rank. In general, one gets the impression that playing with words in three languages provides unlimited possibilities that might serve to propel one's interpretation in any direction. However, the conclusion suggested by these authors is quite interesting. It has to do with Sergei's taboo on the word "rub" (*teret'*), which signified the games with his sister. The word was pushed back into the subconscious as a meaningless word-thing but later became the root of a plethora of Sergei's images, symptoms and actions: his attraction to women washing (in Russian, *rubbing*) floors, his trip to the *Terek* river in Georgia after his sister poisoned herself with mercury (*rtut'*), his choice of a lover with the name *Therese*, and his paranoia about the scar (a rubbed spot, according to the authors' interpretation) on his nose.

24. Obholzer, *The Wolf-Man Sixty Years Later*, p. 5.

25. Maxim Gorky was the pseudonym of Soviet literary figure Alexei Maximovich Peshkov.—Trans.

26. E. Erikson, *Childhood and Society* (New York: Norton, 1950), p. 353.

27. Ibid., p. 368.

28. Ibid., p. 369.

29. Incidentally, Freud characterized Pankeev's nanny in the same way that Pushkin's Arina Rodionovna is described in Russian schoolbooks: as "an uneducated old woman of peasant birth, with untiring affection for him. He served her as a substitute for a son of her own who had died young." (Freud, "From the History of an Infantile Neurosis," p. 196.)

30. V. Rozanov, "Opavshie list'ia," in *Uedinennoe* (Moscow: Politizdat, 1990), pp. 184 and 351.

31. A. Bely, *Na rubezhe dvukh stoletii* (Moscow: Khudozhestvennaia literatura, 1989), p. 184.

32. Sergey Diaghilev (1871–1929) was the impresario of the *Ballets Russes* and the editor of the Russian modernist journal *Mir iskusstva* (World of Art).—Trans.

33. S. Freud, "From the History of an Infantile Neurosis," p. 232.

34. Ibid., p. 256.

35. Ibid., pp. 303, 284.

36. *The Freud–Jung Letters*, ed. W. McGuire (London: Hogarth, 1974), p. 494.

37. Letter of October 19, 1920, in *Letters of Sigmund Freud*, ed. E. Freud (New York: Basic, 1960), p. 333.

38. Ibid.

39. S. Freud, "Dostoevsky and Patricide," in *Collected Papers* (New York: Basic, 1959), vol. 5, p. 222.

40. Freud, "From the History of an Infantile Neurosis," p. 313.

41. Ibid., p. 312.

42. Ibid., p. 294.

43. Ibid., p. 251.

44. Ibid., p. 257.

45. Ibid., p. 311.

46. Ibid., p. 260.

47. A. Blok, *Sochineniia v dvukh tomakh* (Moscow: Khudozhestvennaia literatura, 1955), vol. 2, p. 653.

48. A. Blok, *Selected Poems*, tr. Alex Miller (Moscow: Progress, 1981), pp. 320–321.

49. Ibid.

50. Blok, *Pis'ma k zhene*, p. 112.

51. M. Chekhov, *Literaturnoe nasledie* [Literary Heritage] (Moscow: Iskusstvo, 1986), vol. 1, p. 184.

52. A. Bely, *Na rubezhe dvukh stoletii*, p. 194.

53. F. Stepun, *Byvshee i nesbyvsheesia* (New York: Chekhov, 1956), vol. 1, p. 319. Compare E. V. Barabanov, "Russkaia filosofiia i krizis identichnosti," *Voprosy filosofii*, no. 8, 1991, pp. 102–116.

54. C. Tomlinson, *Versions from Fyodor Tyutchev, 1803–1873* (London: Oxford University Press, 1960), p. 44.

55. C. Fourier, *The Utopian Vision of Charles Fourier: Selected Texts on Work, Love and Passionate Attraction*, tr. J. Beecher and R. Bienvenu (Columbia: University of Missouri Press, 1983), p. 353.

56. Obholzer, *The Wolf-Man Sixty Years Later*, p. 139.

57. Ibid., p. 137.

58. Gardiner, *The Wolf-Man and Sigmund Freud*, p. 89.

59. Ibid., p. 88.

60. Paraphrase of Gardiner, *The Wolf-Man and Sigmund Freud*, p. 89.

61. See Obholzer, *The Wolf-Man Sixty Years Later*.

62. Freud, "From the History of an Infantile Neurosis," p. 316.

63. *Freud–Andreas-Salomé: Letters*, p. 80.

64. Freud, "From the History of an Infantile Neurosis," p. 192.

65. Ibid., p. 316.

66. Roazen, *Freud and His Followers*, p. 172.

67. Gardiner, *The Wolf-Man and Sigmund Freud*, p. 129.

68. Ibid., p. 328.

Chapter Four

1. E. Jones, *The Life and Work of Sigmund Freud* (New York: Basic, 1955), vol. 1, p. 3.

2. Ibid., vol. 1, p. 338.

3. Ibid., vol. 2, p. 14.

4. *Letters of Sigmund Freud*, ed. E. L. Freud (New York: Basic, 1960), p. 177.

5. L. O. Darshkevich, *Kurs nervnykh boleznei* (A Course on Mental Illnesses), 3 vols. (Kazan, 1904–1917).

6. Ibid., vol. 3, p. 549.

7. One important source of knowledge about Russia was a book by a professional Slavicist who was connected to Freud: René Fueloep-Miller: *The Mind and Face of Bolshevism* (New York: Harper, 1965); the original German edition was published in Zurich in 1926. Fueloep-Miller's travelogue gave a shockingly original glimpse of the Russian revolution; the author, who had written earlier about Rasputin and Dostoevsky, emphasized the religious and, particularly, sectarian roots of Bolshevism. Fueloep-Miller was the editor of Freud's essay "Dostoevsky and Patricide" and might well have influenced the conception of the work. For more on this connection, see J. Rice, *Dostoevsky and the Healing Art* (Ann Arbor: Ardis, 1985), pp. 218–219.

8. S. Freud, *Gesammelte Werke, Nachtragsband* [Complete Works of Sigmund Freud, Supplement] (Frankfurt-am-Main, 1987), p. 669.

9. E. Jones, *The Life and Work of Sigmund Freud*, vol. 1, p. 403.

10. J. L. Rice, *Dostoevsky and the Healing Art*, p. 217. Russian associations accompanied the idea of the death wish even later. In 1923, psychoanalyst Wilhelm Reich, who tried to combine analysis and Marxism (see chapter 7), wrote an article in which he developed his ideas about the death instinct. According to Freud, Reich's assertion that the death wish was a product of the capitalist system was senseless. Although he recommended the article for publication, Freud attached a critical response in which he denied any involvement of psychoanalysis in politics. Eitingon, however, prevented the publication of this critical response, while his close associate Siegfried Bernfeld announced that the note's publication would be tantamount to a declaration of war on Soviet Russia (E. Jones, *The Life and Work of Sigmund Freud*, vol. 2, p. 166).

11. Letter from Freud to Stefan Zweig of October 19, 1920, in *Letters of Sigmund Freud*, p. 333.

12. M. P. Polosin, "N. E. Osipov: Biograficheskii ocherk na osnove biograficheskikh zapisok" [N. E. Osipov: A Biographical Essay Based on Biographical Notes], in *Zhizn' i smert'* [Life and Death], eds. A. L. Bem, F. N. Dosuzhkov, and N. O. Lossky (Prague, 1935), vol. 1, p. 11.

13. *The Freud–Jung Letters*, ed. W. McGuire (London: Hogarth, 1974), p. 283.

14. Fyodor Stepun, *Byvshee i nesbyvshees'ia* (New York: Chekhov, 1956), vol. 1, p. 316.

15. L. M. Rosenstein, "O sovremennykh psikhiatricheskikh techeniiakh v Sovetskoi Rossii," in *Psikhogigieniicheskie i nevrologicheskie issledovaniia*, ed. L. M. Rosenstein (Moscow: Narkomzdrav, 1928), pp. 115–121.

16. J. Marti, "La psychanalyse en Russie et en Union Soviétique de 1909 à 1930," *Critique* 346, 1976, p. 201.

17. L. M. Rosenstein, "O sovremennykh psikhiatricheskikh techeniiakh v Sovetskoi Rossii."

18. M. P. Polosin, "N. E. Osipov: Biograficheskii ocherk na osnove avtobiograficheskikh zapisok," p. 11.

19. I. Yermakov, "V. P. Serbsky: Nekrolog" [Obituary of V. P. Serbsky], *Psikhonevrologicheskii vestnik*, August 2–4, 1917.

20. S. Freud, "On the History of the Psycho-Analytic Movement," in *The Standard Edition of the Complete Psychological Works of Sigmund Freud*, vol. 14, p. 33.

21. E. Jones, *The Life and Work of Sigmund Freud*, vol. 2, p. 110.

22. *A Psycho-analytic Dialogue: The Letters of Sigmund Freud and Karl Abraham, 1907–1926* (London: Hogarth, 1965), p. 82.

23. L. Y. Droznes, *Zadachi meditsiny v bor'be s sovremennoi nervoznost'iu* (Odessa, 1907), p. 15.

24. *The Freud–Jung Letters*, p. 263.

25. Rumors that Bekhterev was killed after his psychiatric diagnosis of Stalin circulated in psychiatric and Kremlin circles beginning in the 1930s. Such legends are documented in L. Shatunovskaya, *Zhizn' v Kremle* [Life in the Kremlin] (New York: Chalidze, 1982), pp. 180–184; A. Antonov-Ovseenko, *The Time of Stalin* (New York, 1983), p. 254; A. Vaksberg, *Stalin's Prosecutor: The Life of Andrei Vyshinsky* (New York: Grove, 1990), pp. 41–42. Many prominent Soviet psychiatrists were convinced of the veracity of these rumors, including even the most conservative minded, such as A. V. Snezhnevsky, A. A. Lichko, and V. N. Timofeev. Bekhterev's students also believed the story, including Vladimir Myasishchev and Samuil Mnukhin; as did the Bekhterev family, including his granddaughter, Academician Natalia Bekhtereva. A survey of later accounts can be found in F. D. Volkov, *Vzlet i padenie Stalina* [The Rise and Fall of Stalin] (Moscow: Spektr, 1992), pp. 294–295. For intellectual history, this oral tradition is important. During the glasnost period, however, the question was often debated in its more concrete dimensions; physicians and historians discussed the circumstantial evidence pointing toward Bekhterev's poisoning, such as the incomplete official diagnosis of cause of death and the fact that the requisite autopsy was never performed (*Literaturnaia gazeta*, 12/9/87 and 9/28/88; *Ogonek*, 1988, no. 11, p. 7; *Meditsinskaia gazeta*, 11/11/88). The evidence is not conclusive in the juridical sense, but we are not in court. Naturally, Bekhterev's diagnosis does not mean that Stalinist policy on the whole can be interpreted in psychiatric terms (a critical overview of this theme can be found in D. Rancour-Laferriere, *The Mind of Stalin: A Psychoanalytical Study* [Ann Arbor: University of Michigan Press, 1988], ch. 2; and in W. Laqueur, *Stalin: The Glasnost Revelations* [London: Unwin Hyman, 1990], pp. 134–135).

26. The names of Russian psychiatrists have taken more than their share of abuse. One Moscow institute that for many years was the center of extrajudicial psychiatric repression bears Serbsky's name. Another institute in Leningrad specializing in psychotherapeutic methods and "appeal to personality" is named for Bekhterev.

27. V. Khodasevich, *Izbrannaia proza* [Selected Prose] (New York: Russica, 1982).

28. B. I. Nikolaevsky, *Russkie masony i revoliutsiia* [Russian Masons and the Revolution], ed. Y. Fel'shtinsky (New York: Chalidze, 1990).

29. E. Jones, *The Life and Work of Sigmund Freud*, vol. 2, p. 286.

30. N. Osipov, "O 'panseksualizme' Freida," *Zhurnal nevropatologii i psikhiatrii imeni S. S. Korsakova* 5–6, pp. 747–760.

31. A. O. Edelstein, *Psikhiatricheskie s'ezdy i obshchestva za polveka (1887–1931)* (Moscow: Medgiz, 1948), p. 46.

32. I. Maximov, "L'Histoire de psychanalyse en Russie," *L'Ane*, 1983, 10, pp. 3–5.

33. Y. Kannabikh, "Evoliutsiia psikhoterapevticheskikh idei v XIX veke"; N. Osipov, "O psikhoanalize"; N. Vyrubov, "K voprosu o geneze i lechenii nevroza trevogi kombinirovannym gipnoanaliticheskim metodom," *Psikhoterapiia* 1, 1910.

34. S. Freud, "Group Psychology and the Analysis of the Ego," in *The Standard Edition of the Complete Psychological Works of Sigmund Freud*, vol. 18, p. 89.

35. S. Freud, "On the History of the Psycho-Analytic Movement," in *The Standard Edition of the Complete Psychological Works of Sigmund Freud*, vol. 14, p. 16.

36. O. Feltsman, "K voprosu o sushchnosti gipnoza po sovremennym pred-stavleniiam," *Psikhoterapiia* 3, 1910, pp. 125–132.

37. O. Mandelstam, "Egipetskaia marka," in *Shum vremeni* (Leningrad: Priboi, 1928), pp. 138–143.

38. In 1910, Pevnitsky, like Osipov, Feltsman, and others, embarked on a tour of the European centers of psychotherapy. He met Freud, Jung, Bleuler, and Dubois and presented a paper, "Manifest Phobias as Symbols of a Patient's Hidden Phobia," in Paris, where little, if anything, was known about psychoanalysis. The paper was delivered at the Paris Society of Hypnology and Psychology on January 18, 1911, and published in the journal *Sovremennaia psikhiatriia* [Modern Psychiatry] 1, 1910. Also relevant to our analysis of the Russian situation are reports that Pevnitsky made immediately upon his return, to the Society of Petersburg Psychiatrists ("Several Cases of Psychoanalysis," January 29, 1911) and the Society of Normal and Pathological Psychology ("Personal Impressions of Psychotherapeutic Schools in the West," February 1, 1911).

39. A. Pevnitsky, "O psikhoanalize pri lechenii alkogolikov," *Psikhoterapiia* 1, 1912, pp. 21–28.

40. N. Vavulin, "Snovideniia pri svete nauki," *Novyi zhurnal dlia vsekh* 1, 1913, pp. 79–86.

41. A. Pevnitsky, "O psikhoanalize pri lechenii alkogolikov."

42. N. V. Krainsky, "Pedagogicheskii sadizm" [Pedagogical Sadism], *Sovremennaia psikhiatriia*, 1912, vol. 6, pp. 655–659.

43. Ibid.

44. *Sovremennaia psikhiatriia*, 1912, vol. 7, and 1913, pp. 77–80. After emigrating, Krainsky published a brochure in which he accused Tolstoy of facilitating the Russian revolution (N. Krainsky), *Lev Tolstoi kak iurodivyi* [Leo Tolstoy as God's Fool] (Belgrade: Russkaia tipografiia, undated), as well as a collection of bitter memoirs (N. Krainsky, *Bez budushchego: Ocherki po psikhologii revoliutsii i emigratsii* [Without a Future: Outlines of the Psychology of Revolution and Emigration] [Belgrade, 1931]; the affair with Kosakovsky is not mentioned there.

45. *Mikhail Chekhov: Literaturnoe nasledie* [Mikhail Chekhov: Literary Heritage] (Moscow: Iskusstvo, 1986), vol. 1, p. 184.

46. Ibid., p. 176.

47. K. Stanislavsky, "Rabota aktera nad soboi," *Sobranie sochinenii* (Moscow: Iskusstvo, 1989), vol. 2, pp. 436–437.

48. N. Yevreinov, *Fotobiografiia: S materialov, sobrannykh A. Yevreinovoi*, ed. E. Proffer (Ann Arbor: Ardis, 1981).

49. N. Yevreinov, *Proiskhozhdenie dramy: Pervobytnaia tragediia i rol' kozla v istorii ee vozniknoveniia* (Petrograd: Petropolis, 1921); N. Yevreinov, *Azazel i Dionis* (Petrograd: Academia, 1924).

50. N. Yevreinov, *Teatr dlia sebia* [Theater for Oneself] (Petrograd, 1915), vol. 1.

51. N. Yevreinov, "Teatroterapiia" [Theater Therapy], *Zhizn' iskusstva*, October 9–10, 1920.

52. See J. E. Kombs and M. W. Mansfield, eds., *Drama in Life* (New York: Hastings House, 1976).

53. N. Yevreinov, *P'esy iz repertuara "Krivogo Zerkala,"* 3 (Petrograd: Academia [undated]); see also D. Zolotnitsky, *Zori teatral'nogo Oktiabria* (Leningrad: Iskusstvo, 1976), p. 161.

54. S. Eisenstein, *Izbrannye proizvedeniia* (Moscow: Iskusstvo, 1964), vol. 1, p. 308.

55. N. Yevreinov, *Teatr dlia sebia* (Petrograd, 1917), vol. 3, p. 34.

56. A. Kashina-Yevreinova, *Podpol'e geniia: Seksual'nye istochniki tvorchestva Dostoevskogo* (Petrograd: Tret'ia strazha, 1923).

57. N. Yevreinov, *Taina Rasputina* (Petrograd: Byloe, 1924).

58. N. Yevreinov, *Samoe glavnoe* (Petersburg: Gosudarstvennoe, 1921).

59. Yevreinov's Azazel served as a direct prototype for Bulgakov's Azazello, by occupation as well as name. Yevreinov cited the apocryphal *Book of Enoch*, according to which Azazel is a "seducer of women who teaches them to enhance their physical aspect by means of rouge and ceruse" (N. Yevreinov, *Azazel i Dionis*, p. 167). In *The Master and Margarita: A Comedy of Victory* (Birmingham: University of Birmingham Press, 1977, p. 32), Lesley Milne suggests that Bulgakov's character harks back to Enoch via Yevreinov.

60. N. Yevreinov, *Teatr u zhivotnykh (o smysle teatral'nosti s biologicheskoi tochki zreniia)* (Petrograd: Kniga, 1924), p. 10.

61. M. Shaginyan, *Svoia sud'ba* (Moscow: Frenkel', 1923).

62. A. Zalkind, "Individual'no-psikhologicheskii analiz 3-kh sluchaev somnambulizma," *Psikhoterapiia* 3, 1914, p. 130.

63. A. Carotenuto, *A Secret Symmetry: Sabina Spielrein Between Freud and Jung* (London: Routledge, 1980), p. 125.

64. "Letopis' zhizni i tvorchestva M. A. Chekhova," in *Mikhail Chekhov: Literaturnoe nasledie* (Moscow: Iskusstvo, 1986), vol. 2.

65. M. Wulff, "Opyt psikhoanaliticheskogo razbora sluchaia psikhonevrologicheskogo zabolevaniia," *Sovremennaia psikhiatriia*, 1914, vol. 8, pp. 197–225.

Chapter Five

1. From Sabina Spielrein's diary, date unknown; cited in A. Carotenuto, *A Secret Symmetry: Sabina Spielrein Between Freud and Jung* (London: Routledge, 1980), p. 3.

2. C. Weizmann, *V poiskakh puti* [In Search of a Path] (Jerusalem: Biblioteka Alii, 1983), vol. 1, p. 60.

3. Ibid.

4. Carotenuto, *A Secret Symmetry*, p. 140.

5. *The Freud–Jung Letters*, ed. W. McGuire (London: Hogarth, 1974), p. 7.

6. Ibid., pp. 8–9.

7. Carotenuto, *A Secret Symmetry*, p. 120.

8. From the diary of Sabina Spielrein, August 27, 1909. Cited in Carotenuto, *A Secret Symmetry*, p. 120.

9. *The Freud–Jung Letters*, pp. 12–13.

10. Ibid., p. 72.

11. Ibid.

12. A. Pushkin, "A Little Bird," in *Pushkin Threefold*, trans. Walter Arndt (Ann Arbor: Ardis, 1972), p. 183.

13. A. Pushkin, "The Captive," in *Selected Works in Two Volumes*, trans. Irina Zheleznova (Moscow: Progress, 1974), vol. 1, p. 21.

14. Ibid.

15. *The Freud–Jung Letters*, p. 82.

16. E. Jones, *The Life and Work of Sigmund Freud* (New York: Basic, 1955), vol. 2, p. 112.

17. From Sabina Spielrein's diary, September 21, 1909. Cited in Carotenuto, *A Secret Symmetry*, p. 6.

18. *The Freud–Jung Letters*, p. 89.

19. Ibid., p. 90.

20. J. Rice, "Russian Stereotypes in the Freud–Jung Correspondence," *Slavic Review* 41, no. 1 (Spring 1982), pp. 13–35.

21. *The Freud–Jung Letters*, p. 90.

22. Ibid.

23. Ibid., p. 95.

24. Ibid.

25. Ibid., p. 207.

26. From the diary of Sabina Spielrein, August 28, 1909. Cited in Carotenuto, *A Secret Symmetry*, p. 5.

27. *The Freud–Jung Letters*, p. 210.

28. Contemporary legend had it that Jung was a direct descendant of Goethe.

29. *The Freud–Jung Letters*, p. 212.

30. Ibid., p. 135.

31. Carotenuto, *A Secret Symmetry*, p. 91.

32. *The Freud–Jung Letters*, pp. 225–227.

33. Ibid., p. 226.

34. From the diary of Sabina Spielrein, cited in Carotenuto, *A Secret Symmetry*, p. 5.

35. *The Freud–Jung Letters*, p. 228.

36. Ibid., pp. 230–231.

37. Ibid., p. 145.

38. A. de Mijolla, "Quelques figures de la situation de 'supervision' en psychanalyse," *Etudes Freudiennes* 31, May 1989, pp. 117–130.

39. Carotenuto, *A Secret Symmetry*, p. 114.

40. *The Freud–Jung Letters*, p. 232.

41. Ibid., p. 235.

42. Carotenuto, *A Secret Symmetry*, p. 92.

43. Ibid., p. 94.

44. Ibid., p. 99.

45. Sigmund Freud, "Observations on Transference-Love," in *The Standard Edition of the Complete Psychological Works of Sigmund Freud* (London: Hogarth, 1958), vol. 12, p. 162.

46. Ibid., p. 161.

47. Ibid., p. 165.

48. Ibid.

49. Ibid.

50. Lydia Ginzburg told a similar anecdote from Soviet life: "Malevich was dying of cancer. For a long time, a doctor visited him at home. The doctor neither cured him nor even attempted to effect a cure (Malevich was hopelessly ill), but Malevich taught him to appreciate leftist painting." Quoted from Lydia Ginzburg, *Literatura v poiskakh real'nosti* [Literature in Search of Reality] (Moscow: Sovetskii pisatel', 1987), p. 242.

51. From the diary of Sabina Spielrein, September 11, 1910. Cited in Carotenuto, *A Secret Symmetry*, p. 11.

52. *The Freud–Jung Letters*, pp. 236–237.

53. Ibid.

54. Ibid.

55. Carotenuto, *A Secret Symmetry*, pp. 114–115.

56. *The Freud–Jung Letters*, p. 238.

57. Ibid., p. 241.

58. C. G. Jung, "Freud and Psychoanalysis," *Collected Works* (Princeton: Princeton University Press, 1961), vol. 4, p. 166.

59. From the diary of Sabina Spielrein, around 1909. Cited in Carotenuto, *A Secret Symmetry*, pp. 107–108.

60. S. Spielrein, "Die Destruction als Ursache des Werdens," *Jahrbuch für psychoanalytische und psychopathologische Forschungen*, vol. 4 (1912), pp. 465–503.

61. Carotenuto, *A Secret Symmetry*, p. 48.

62. Alexander Pushkin's "Song of Oleg the Wise" (1822) was a poetic rendering of the legend from the Primary Chronicle of ancient Rus'. According to the story, a medieval Russian prince named Oleg was told by soothsayers that his favorite horse would be the cause of his death, so he ordered the animal taken away. Many years later, the horse died, and Oleg went to view his old friend's bones. The prince stepped on the horse's skull, and a deadly snake slithered out and bit him. The prince died.—Trans.

63. Spielrein, "Die Destruction als Ursache des Werdens."

64. *The Freud–Jung Letters*, p. 494.

65. S. Freud, "Civilization and Its Discontents," *The Pelican Freud Library* (New York: Penguin, 1985), p. 311.

66. S. Freud, *Beyond the Pleasure Principle*, in *The Standard Edition of the Complete Psychological Works of Sigmund Freud* (London: Hogarth, 1955), vol. 18, p. 55.

67. Roazen, *Freud and His Followers* (New York: Knopf, 1975), p. 290.

68. Spielrein, "Die Destruction als Ursache des Werdens."

69. See C. Jung, *Psychology of the Unconscious: A Study of the Transformations and Symbolisms of the Libido, a Contribution to the History of the Evolution of Thought*, tr. Beatrice Hinkle (New York: Dodd, Mead, 1946).

70. P. Federn, review of Spielrein, "Die Destruction als Ursache des Werdens," *Internationale Zeitschrift für Ärztliche Psychoanalyse*, 1913, no. 1, pp. 92–93. Spielrein certainly was not alone in focusing on this "mystical modality." By 1910, Max Weber and his Heidelberg circle (which included the young György Lukács and Frieda Gross, the widow of Freudian dissident Otto Gross) were inspired by "Slavic mysticism," and specifically by the reading of Tolstoy, Dostoevsky, and Solovyov in German translation, as well as by contacts with the Russian student community. (In characteristic fashion, a depressed Weber once said that if he ever held a seminar again he would accept only Russians, Poles, and Jews.) Fyodor Stepun, a Heidelberg student and a prominent Russian religious philosopher, was mentioned as belonging to this milieu (Arthur Mitzman, *The Iron Cage: An Historical Interpretation of Max Weber* [Transaction, 1985], pp. 272–275).

71. V. Ivanov, *Po zvezdam* (St. Petersburg, 1909), p. 64.

72. Ibid., p. 413.

73. A. Bely, "Epopeia," *Vospominaniia o A. A. Bloke* (Munich: Wilhelm Fink, 1969).

74. Later, the idea of the death instinct became quite widespread among Russian analysts. Osipov based his later works on the concept (see chapter 6). At the meeting of the Russian Psychoanalytic Society held in May 1926, Vinogradov of Kiev related the story of a young woman who had committed suicide by self-immolation. Vinogradov interpreted the case as an example of the destructive instinct. In November 1927, Dr. Holz of Moscow, who worked as a physician during the recent Crimean earthquake, reported on the mental reactions of those who lived through the disaster. She singled out those individuals who evidenced indifference to danger. According to Holz, surveys of these people revealed their unconscious attraction to death.

75. Sigmund Freud, *Beyond the Pleasure Principle*, pp. 58–59.

76. Ibid., p. 59.
77. P. Roazen, *Freud and His Followers*.
78. Carotenuto, *A Secret Symmetry*, p. 115.
79. *The Freud–Jung Letters*, p. 447.
80. Ibid., p. 469.
81. Ibid., p. 470.
82. Ibid., p. 500.
83. Ibid., p. 495.
84. Ibid., p. 210.
85. Ibid., p. 293.
86. Ibid., p. 296.
87. Ibid., pp. 490–492.
88. Ibid., pp. 492–493.
89. Ibid., p. 492.
90. Ibid., pp. 526–527.
91. Ibid., p. 529.
92. Ibid., pp. 534–535.
93. Ibid., p. 535.
94. Carotenuto, *A Secret Symmetry*, p. 118.
95. Ibid., pp. 119–120.
96. Ibid., p. 190.
97. Ibid., pp. 116–117.
98. Ibid., p. 71.
99. Ibid., pp. 116–117.
100. Ibid., pp. 120–121.
101. Ibid., pp. 82–85.
102. Ibid., p. 112.
103. Ibid., pp. 121–122.
104. Ibid., p. 145.
105. Ibid.
106. Rice, "Russian Stereotypes in the Freud–Jung Correspondence," p. 3.
107. S. Spielrein, "On the Origin and Development of Speech," *International Journal of Psychoanalysis*, 1920, no. 1, p. 359.
108. S. Spielrein, "Quelques analogies entre la pensée de l'enfant, celle de l'aphasique et la pensée subconsciente," *Archive de psychologie*, 1923, no. 18, pp. 305–322.
109. S. Spielrein, "Die Zeit im unterschwelligen Seelenleben," *Imago*, 1993, no. 9, pp. 300–317.
110. J. Piaget, "La psychanalyse et ses rapports avec la psychologie de l'enfance," *Bulletin de la Société A. Binet*, 1920, no. 20, pp. 18–34 and 41–58.
111. S. Spielrein, "Die drei Fragen," *Imago*, 1923, no. 9, pp. 260–263.
112. S. Spielrein, "Kinderzeichnungen bei offenen und geschlossenen Augen," *Imago*, 1931, no. 16, pp. 259–291.
113. Carotenuto, *A Secret Symmetry*, p. 119.
114. Ibid., pp. 57, 184.
115. S. Spielrein, "L'Automobile: Symbole de la puissance mâle"; "Rêve et vision des étoiles filantes," *International Journal of Psychoanalysis*, 1923, no. 4, pp. 128–132.
116. Carotenuto, *A Secret Symmetry*, p. 126.
117. Ibid., p. 74.
118. Ibid., p. 127.
119. Obholzer, *The Wolf-Man Sixty Years Later* (London: Routledge, 1980), p. 48.

120. M. I. Spielrein, personal communication.

121. I. N. Spielrein, D. I. Reitynbarg, and G. O. Netsky, *Yazyk krasnoarmeitsa* [The Language of a Red Army Soldier] (Moscow, 1928).

122. I. N. Spielrein, "O Peremene imen i familii: Sotsial'no-psikhologicheskii etiud" [On Change in First and Last Names: A Sociopsychological Study], *Psikhotekhnika i psikhofiziologiia truda*, 1929, no. 4, pp. 281–285.

123. M. I. Spielrein, personal communication.

124. *International Journal of Psychoanalysis*, 1924, vol. 5, p. 258.

125. Central State Archives of Russia, fund 2307, section 9, file 222, p. 1.

126. Central State Archives of Russia, fund 2307, section 23, file 13, pp. 19–20.

127. Central State Archives of Russia, fund 259, section 9a, file 3, p. 159.

128. Central State Archives of Russia, fund 2307, section 23, file 13, pp. 19–20.

129. The rough draft is in the personal collection of A. R. Luria.

130. See Vygotsky's autobiography, published in A. A. Leontiev, *L. S. Vygotsky* (Moscow: Prosveshchenie, 1990).

131. R. van der Veer and J. Valsiner, *Understanding Vigotsky: A Quest for Synthesis* (Oxford: Blackwell, 1991).

132. In his *List of Works* for 1915–1923 there are only short literary reviews, a manuscript on Hamlet, and unpublished speeches for teachers' conferences (see L. S. Vygotsky, *Sobranie sochinenii v 6 tomakh* [Collected Works in Six Volumes] [Moscow: Pedagogika, 1984], vol. 6, p. 366).

133. *International Journal of Psychoanalysis*, 1929, vol. 10, p. 562.

134. S. Freud, *Beyond the Pleasure Principle*, p. 55.

135. J. Piaget, "Kommentarii k kriticheskim zamechaniiam L. S. Vygotskogo" [Commentary on the Critical Comments of L. S. Vygotsky], *Khrestomatiia po obshchei psikhologii* (Moscow: Izd. MGU, 1981), pp. 188–193.

136. For a psychoanalytical reading of Vygotsky's works, see A. Wilson and L. Weinstein, "An Investigation into Some Implications of a Vygotskian Perspective on the Origins of the Mind," *Journal of the American Psychoanalytic Association*, 1992, vol. 40, pp. 349–380, 725–760.

137. The interview was conducted in 1990.

138. In Russia, the Christmas tree is called a "New Year's tree." Generally considered a nondenominational symbol, the New Year's tree is often erected in Jewish homes as well as Christian ones during the winter holidays.—Trans.

Chapter Six

1. K. Tsetkin, *O Lenine* [On Lenin] (Moscow, 1955), p. 44.

2. S. Yermolinsky, *Iz zapisok raznykh let* [From the Notes of Various Years] (Moscow: Iskusstvo, 1990), p. 38.

3. N. Mandelstam, *Vtoraia kniga* [The Second Book] (Moscow, 1990), p. 67.

4. A. Voronsky, "Freidizm i iskusstvo" [Freudism and Art], *Krasnaia nov'*, 1925, book 7, p. 260.

5. F. Stepun, "Mysli o Rossii" [Thoughts About Russia], *Sovremennye zapiski*, 1924, vol. 19, p. 324.

6. N. Gumilev, *Sobranie sochinenii v 4 tomakh* [Collected Works in Four Volumes] (Moscow: Terra, 1991), vol. 2, pp. 101, 104.

7. V. Shklovsky, *Sentimental'noe puteshestvie* [Sentimental Journey] (Moscow: Novosti, 1990), p. 76.

8. K. Chukovsky, *Dnevnik, 1901–1929* [Diary, 1901–1929] (Moscow: Sovetskii pisatel', 1991), pp. 275–277. Chukovsky worked in one of the State Publishing

House's offices, and probably read "Beyond the Pleasure Principle," which first came out in Russian translation in 1925.

9. N. A. Bogomolov, "Vokrug 'Foreli'" [Around "The Trout"], in *Mikhail Kuzmin i russkaia kul'tura 20-go veka* (Leningrad, 1990), p. 208.

10. L. S. Vygotsky and A. Luria, introduction to the Russian translation of "Beyond the Pleasure Principle" in Sigmund Freud, *Psikhologiia bessoznatel'nogo* [Psychology of the Unconscious] (Moscow: Prosveshchenie, 1989), p. 29.

11. Another example:
There once was a student in Leningrad,
Who lived by Freud's teachings, and messed things up bad.
He rode in the trolley but forgot to pay,
It was because of a meeting he skipped yesterday.
He blew his whole fortune at the drop of a hat,
A colic in childhood was the cause of all that. . . .
(N. Traugott, personal communication, 1992).

12. *International Journal of Psychoanalysis,* 1922, vol. 3, p. 514.

13. Literally, "Mountain Pass." A literary group that coalesced in 1923–1924 around the journal *Krasnaia nov'*. Some prominent members were Mikhail Svetlov, Eduard Bagritsky, and Andrei Platonov.—Trans.

14. G. Belaya, *Don-Kikhoty 20-kh godov* [Don Quixotes of the 1920s] (Moscow: Sovetskii pisatel', 1989).

15. O. Mandelstam, *Slovo o kul'ture* [A Word on Culture] (Moscow: Sovetskii pisatel', 1989).

16. Cited in G. Belaya, *Don-Kikhoty 20-kh godov,* pp. 124–125.

17. *Proletarskie kul'turno-prosvetitel'skie organizatsii:* the Proletarian Cultural and Educational Organizations, founded in 1917 by Bogdanov and Lunacharsky to develop a distinctly proletarian literature and art.—Trans.

18. G. Belaya, *Don-Kikhoty 20-kh godov,* pp. 124–125.

19. See *Kratkaia literaturnaia entsiklopediia* (Moscow, 1962), vol. 1, p. 1047. A member of the Russian Social-Democratic Workers' Party from 1904 onward, Voronsky was the creator and editor in chief of the first Soviet literary journal, *Krasnaia nov'*. He was a member of the Trotskyist opposition in 1925–1928, later arrested, readmitted to the Communist Party after a confession, and arrested for the last time in 1937.

20. G. Belaya, *Don-Kikhoty 20-kh godov,* pp. 124–125.

21. *Kak my pishem* [How We Write] (Leningrad: Izd. Pisatelei, 1930), p. 437.

22. Y. Zamyatin, *Sochineniia* (Moscow: Kniga, 1988), p. 575; this fragment was published by E. Barabanov.

23. The Serapion Brothers was a literary group that emerged in 1921 and included Konstantin Fedin, Nikolai Tikhonov, Mikhail Zoshchenko, among others. They espoused creative pluralism and discussed literary craftsmanship at their meetings. The group disintegrated in 1929.—Trans.

24. Vsevolod Ivanov, *Vozvrashchenie Buddy—Chudesnye pokhozhdeniia portnogo Fokina—U* [The Return of Buddha, The Wondrous Travels of Fokin the Tailor, and U] (Moscow: Pravda, 1991), pp. 150–152.

25. Ibid.

26. Ibid., pp. 187, 423, 386, 302.

27. Y. Zamyatin, *Sochineniia,* p. 437.

28. A. Platonov, "Schastlivaia Moskva" [Happy Moscow], *Novyi mir,* 1991, no. 9, pp. 21, 40.

29. *Nietzsche in Russia* (Princeton: Princeton University Press, 1986).

30. Pitirim Sorokin said of Kollontay that "the woman's revolutionary enthusiasm is nothing other than indirect gratification of her nymphomania" (Pitirim Sorokin, "Boinia: revoliutsiia 1917 goda" [Slaughterhouse: The Revolution of 1917], in *Chelovek, Tsivilizatsiia, Obshchestvo* [Man, Civilization, and Society] [Moscow: Politizdat, 1992], p. 236).

31. For the debate around Kollontay's essay, see A. Kollontay, "Dorogu krylatomu erosu," *Molodaia gvardiia*, 1923, no. 3; P. Vinogradskaya, "Voprosy morali, pola, byta i tov. Kollontay," *Krasnaia nov'*, 1923, no. 6, pp. 179–214; A. Lunacharsky, "Moral' i svoboda," *Krasnaia nov'*, 1923, no. 7, p. 134.

32. L. Ginzburg, *Literatura v poiskakh real'nosti* [Literature in Search of Reality] (Moscow: Sovetskii pisatel', 1987), p. 156.

33. O. Mandelstam, *Slovo o kul'ture*, p. 200.

34. See the research of S. Fitzpatrick, "Sex and Revolution: An Examination of Literary and Statistical Data . . . ," *Journal of Modern History*, no. 50 (1978), pp. 253–278.

35. Ibid.

36. L. Ginzburg, *Literatura v poiskakh real'nosti*, p. 158. ("I say, let it be Vanechka": In other words, Ginzburg observed a shift in authors' interest and involvement in psychoanalysis from adults to children.—Ed.)

37. *Internationale Zeitschrift für Psychoanalyse* 7, 1921, p. 385.

38. T. K. Rosenthal, "Stradanie i tvorchestvo Dostoevskogo," *Voprosy izucheniia i vospitaniia lichnosti* (Petrograd) 1, 1919, pp. 88–107.

39. In her 1923 book on Dostoevsky (see chapter 4), A. Kashina-Yevreinova maintained the opposite: that Dostoevsky's epilepsy became aggravated in prison. The application of psychoanalysis to Dostoevsky was also discussed in 1924 by Boris Griftsov (B. A. Griftsov, *Psikhologiia pisatelia* [The Psychology of the Writer] [Moscow: Khudozhestvennaia literatura, 1988]). Some time later, the same question was addressed by Yermakov (see below), whose archives contain the unpublished manuscript of a book on Dostoevsky.

40. Rosenthal, "Stradanie i tvorchestvo."

41. In 1927, Odessa doctor Yakov Kogan wrote in the introduction to his translation of a book by Anna Freud: "In the Institute of Pediatric Examination . . . psychoanalytical observation is a mandatory part of the general research done on all of the children" (Y. M. Kogan, foreword to *Vvedenie v tekhniku detskogo psikhoanaliza* [Introduction to the Technique of Child Psychoanalysis] by Anna Freud [Odessa, 1927]). It is likely that this statement was inaccurate, even as early as at the time of Tatiana Rosenthal's death.

42. *International Journal of Psychoanalysis* 1, 1920, p. 208.

43. A. R. Luria, "Puti razvitiia sovetskoi psikhologii: Po sobstvennym vospominaniiam" [Paths of Development in Soviet Psychology: According to His Own Recollections], transcript of a March 25, 1974, speech to the Moscow Section of the Soviet Psychological Society, from the archives of Elena Luria.

44. Luria's letters are in the Freud archives in the United States and will not be available to researchers until the year 2000. Freud's brief replies can be found in the archives of E. A. Luria in Moscow.

45. Central State Archives of Russia, fund 2307, section 23, file 13, p. 23.

46. Central State Archives of Russia, fund 2307, section 2, file 412, p. 1; also in these archives is the Charter of the Russian Psychoanalytic Society, adopted on September 30, 1922, as well as the model of the organization's official stamp: Central State Archives of Russia, fund 2307, section 1, file 294, pp. 4–7.

47. I. I. Glivenko, G. G. Weisberg, O. Y. Schmidt, I. D. Yermakov, M. V. Wulff, Y. V. Kannabikh, P. P. Blonsky, A. A. Sidorov, A. G. Gabrichevsky, V. A. Nevsky, N. G. Uspensky, S. T. Shatsky, A. K. Voronsky, and Dr. Beloborodov (Central State Archives of Russia, fund 2307, section 1, file 294, p. 7).

48. For a history of the ministry of education, see Sheila Fitzpatrick, *The Commissariat of Enlightenment* (Cambridge: Cambridge University Press, 1970).

49. L. Ivanova, *Vospominaniia: Kniga ob otse* [Memoirs: A Book About My Father], ed. J. Malmstad (Paris: Atheneum, 1990), p. 81.

50. Central State Archives of Russia, fund 298, section 1, file 1, p. 135.

51. This side of Schmidt's multifaceted career remains underestimated by historians. Loren Graham, who dedicated a whole section of his book to Schmidt (Loren Graham, *Science, Philosophy and Behavior in the Soviet Union* [New York: Columbia University Press, 1987]), did not even mention his psychoanalytical interests.

52. M. I. Davydova and I. D. Yermakov, *Psikhologicheskii zhurnal* [Psychological Journal], 1989, vol. 10, no. 2, pp. 156–159; M. I. Davydova, "Nezavershennyi zamysel: K istorii izdaniia trudov Z. Freida v USSR" [Unfinished Project: On the History of the Publication of the Works of Sigmund Freud in the USSR], *Sovetskaia biografiia*, 1989, no. 3, pp. 61–64. Yermakov's daughter, M. I. Davydova, holds his personal archives.

53. *Pod znamenem Marksizma*, 1929, nos. 10–11, p. 12.

54. I. D. Yermakov, "O beloi goriachke," *Psikhonevrologicheskii vestnik*, January 1917, no. 1, p. 91.

55. For more on Shatsky, see V. I. Malinin and F. A. Fradkin, *S. T. Shatsky: Rabota dlia budushchego* (Moscow: Prosveshchenie, 1989).

56. Ibid., pp. 91–99, 24.

57. See A. F. Losev, *Iz rannikh proizvedenii* [From His Early Works] (Moscow: Pravda, 1990), p. 3.

58. P. P. Blonsky, "Kak ia stal pedologom i imenno takim, kakim stal" [How I Became a Pedologist, and the Kind That I Am], in I. I. Rufim, ed., *P. P. Blonsky v ego pedagogicheskikh vyskazivaniiakh* [P. P. Blonsky in His Pedagogical Statements] (Moscow: Rabotnik prosveshcheniia, 1928); also published in P. P. Blonsky, *Izbrannye pedagogicheskie i psikhologicheskie sochineniia* [Collected Pedagogical and Psychological Works] (Moscow: Pedagogika, 1979), vol. 1, pp. 30–39.

59. P. P. Blonsky, "Ocherki detskoi seksual'nosti" [Outlines of Infantile Sexuality], in *Izbrannye pedagogicheskie i psikhologicheskie sochineniia*, vol. 1, pp. 202–277.

60. C. Read, *Culture and Power in Revolutionary Russia* (New York: St. Martin's, 1990), p. 135.

61. N. Mandelstam, *Vtoraia kniga*, p. 51.

62. Cited in M. Chudakova, *Zhizneopisanie Mikhaila Bulgakova* (Moscow: Kniga, 1988), p. 242.

63. J. Marti, "La psychanalyse en Russie et en Union Soviétique de 1909 à 1930," *Critique*, 1976, no. 346.

64. A. R. Luria, "Puti razvitiia sovetskoi psikhologii."

65. Ibid.

66. *International Journal of Psychoanalysis*, 1923, vol. 4.

67. Ibid., pp. 240–241.

68. *International Journal of Psychoanalysis*, 1923, vol. 3, p. 241.

69. The fact of this trip is known to us from the Schmidts' travel documents, held in the Central State Archives of Russia, fund 2307, section 9, file 222, p. 19.

70. Cited in J. Marti, "La psychanalyse en Russie et en Union Soviétique," p. 220.

71. M. I. Astvatsaturov, *Psikhoterapiia i psikhoanaliz* (Leningrad, 1924), p. 54.

72. *International Journal of Psychoanalysis*, 1924, vol. 5, p. 258.

73. *International Journal of Psychoanalysis*, 1929, vol. 10, p. 562.

74. Several different curriculum proposals for the State Psychoanalytic Institute are on file in the Ivan Yermakov archives.

75. *International Journal of Psychoanalysis*, 1924, vol. 5, p. 258.

76. V. Schmidt, "Education psychanalytique en Russie," *Temps modernes*, March 1969; M. Higgins and C. Raphael, eds., *Reich Speaks of Freud* (London: Condor, 1967). An analysis of the reaction of the International Psychoanalytic Association to Vera Schmidt's experience can be found in E. Roudinesco, *Histoire de la psychanalyse en France*, vol. 2, p. 55.

77. "Psikhoanaliticheskii institut-laboratoriia 'Mezhdunarodnaia Solidarnost'," in the archives of I. D. Yermakov. Further referred to as "The Yermakov Report."

78. Kept in the Central State Archives of Russia.

79. "The Yermakov Report."

80. Ibid.

81. A. R. Luria, *Puti razvitiia sovetskoi psikhologii*; Luria's account is corroborated by his interview with M. G. Yaroshevsky. See M. G. Yaroshevsky, "Vozvrashchenie Freida," *Psikhologicheskii zhurnal*, 1988, vol. 9, no. 6, pp. 129–138.

82. "The Yermakov Report."

83. *International Journal of Psychoanalysis*, 1922, vol. 3, p. 520.

84. J. Marti, "La psychanalyse en Russie et en Union Soviétique."

85. Central State Archives of Russia, fund 298, section 45, file 45, pp. 50–52.

86. Ibid.

87. Central State Archives of Russia, fund 298, section 1, file 1, p. 49.

88. Y. P. Sharapov, *Iz istorii ideologicheskoi bor'by pri perekhode k NEPu* [From the History of the Ideological Struggle During the Transition to the NEP] (Moscow: Nauka, 1990), p. 57.

89. Central State Archives of Russia, fund 2306, section 1, file 2101, p. 164.

90. Central State Archives of Russia, fund 259, section 86, file 81.

91. Central State Archives of Russia, fund 298, section 1, file 58, pp. 109–110.

92. Central State Archives of Russia, fund 2306, section 1, file 2168, p. 75.

93. Central State Archives of Russia, fund 259, section 9a, file 3, p. 159.

94. Central State Archives of Russia, fund 2307, section 9, file 222, p. 19.

95. Cited in J. Marti, "La psychanalyse en Russie et en Union Soviétique."

96. Central State Archives of Russia, fund 2307, section 9, file 222, pp. 36–37.

97. Ibid., p. 39.

98. N. N. Traugott, personal communication, September 1992.

99. Central State Archives of Russia, fund 2307, section 9, file 222, pp. 66–67.

100. Ibid., p. 82.

101. Marti, "La psychanalyse en Russie et en Union Soviétique."

102. Personal conversation with M. I. Davydova, 1990.

103. Central State Archives of Russia, fund 2307, section 9, file 222, p. 60.

104. Ibid., p. 76.

105. Central State Archives of Russia, fund 298, section 1, file 58, p. 110.

106. Central State Archives of Russia, fund 259, section 9a, file 3, p. 159.

107. Found in the archives of I. D. Yermakov.

108. *International Journal of Psychoanalysis*, 1929, vol. 6, p. 245.

109. *International Journal of Psychoanalysis*, 1928, vol. 9, p. 143.

110. M. Miller, "Freudian Theory Under Bolshevik Rule," *Slavic Review* (Winter 1985), p. 641.

111. B. Khersonsky, introduction to *Tolkovanie snovidenii* [Interpretation of Dreams] by Sigmund Freud, trans. Y. M. Kogan (Odessa, 1991).

112. I. A. Perepel, *Psikhoanaliz i fiziologicheskaia teoriia povedeniia* [Psychoanalysis and the Physiological Theory of Behavior], introduction by A. A. Ukhtomsky (Leningrad, 1928), p. 132.

113. M. V. Wulff, "Po povodu nekotorykh psikho-patologicheskikh iavlenii u avtobusnykh shoferov" [On Several Psychopathological Phenomena in Bus Drivers], in *Psikhologigienicheskie i nevrologicheskie issledovaniia* (Moscow, 1928), pp. 194–200.

114. Boris Pilnyak, *Rasplesnutoe vremia* [Splashed Time] (Moscow: Sovetskii pisatel', 1990), p. 144.

115. In 1929, Luria met with Horace Meyer Kallen, an American philosopher and Zionist who was then visiting the USSR. The translation of Luria's book that came out soon afterward in the United States bore a dedication to Kallen (Aleksandr R. Luriia, *The Nature of Human Conflicts; or Emotion, Conflict, and Will, an Objective Study of Disorganization and Control of Human Behavior* (New York: Liveright, 1932). The book contained, among other things, some curious argumentation for and against psychoanalysis. In 1963, Luria was more than willing to affirm his previous affection for psychoanalysis to another American guest. See Lewis S. Feuer, "Freud's Ideas in the Soviet Setting: A Meeting with Aleksandr Luriia," *Slavic Review,* 1987, vol. 46, no. 1, pp. 106–112.

116. *International Journal of Psychoanalysis,* 1929, vol. 10, p. 515.

117. E. Perepel, "The Psychoanalytic Movement in the USSR," *Psychoanalytic Review,* 1939, vol. 26, p. 299.

118. J. L. Rice, "Russian Stereotypes in the Freud–Jung Correspondence," p. 34.

119. E. Perepel, "The Psychoanalytic Movement."

120. Personal conversations with N. N. Traugott and L. A. Chistovich, 1991.

121. A. I. Belkin, "Freid: Vozrozhdenie v SSSR?" [Freud: Reborn in the USSR?], preface to S. Freud, *Izbrannoe* [Selected Works of Sigmund Freud] (Moscow: Vneshtorgizdat, 1989), pp. 19–20.

122. Ibid.

123. Information on the Russian translations of Freud is provided in an essay by I. Manson, "Comment dit-on 'psychanalyse' en russe?" *Revue internationale de l'histoire de psychanalyse,* 1991, no. 4, pp. 407–422.

124. The transcript of the May 6, 1922, meeting of the Psychoanalytic Club for the Study of Artistic Creativity may be found in the archives of I. D. Yermakov, in Moscow.

125. I. D. Yermakov, *Etiudy po psikhologii tvorchestva A. S. Pushkina* [Sketches on the Psychology of A. S. Pushkin's Works] (Moscow-Petrograd: GIZ, 1923); I. D. Yermakov, *Ocherki po analizu tvorchestva N. V. Gogolia* [Outlines of the Analysis of N. V. Gogol's Works] (Moscow-Petrograd: GIZ, 1924).

126. Yermakov, *Ocherki po analizu tvorchestva N. V. Gogolia,* p. 171.

127. N. Berdyaev, *Dukhi russkoi revoliutsii.*

128. A. Akhmatova, "Kamennyi gost' Pushkina" [Pushkin's Stone Guest] in *Sochineniia* (Moscow: Panorama, 1990), vol. 2, p. 84.

129. I. Ehrenburg, *Neobychainye pokhozhdeniia Julio Jurenito i ego uchenikov* [The Extraordinary Adventures of Julio Jurenito] (Moscow: GIZ, 1923).

130. Osipov's obituary was published in the *Internationale Zeitschrift für Psychoanalyse,* 1934, no. 20, p. 277. Books that came out later include: A. L. Bem, F. N. Dosuzhkov, and N. O. Lossky, eds., *Zhizn' i smert'* (Prague, 1935); A. L. Bem, *Dostoevskii: Psikhoanaliticheskie etiudy* (Berlin, 1938), dedicated to the memory of

N. E. Osipov. See also Osipov's article "Dvoinik: Peterburgskaia poema Dostoevskogo (zametki psikhiatra)" in *O Dostoevskom*, ed. A. L. Bem (Prague, 1929), vol. 1.

131. M. P. Polosin, "N. E. Osipov: Biograficheskii ocherk na osnove avtobiograficheskikh zapisok," in A. L. Bem, F. N. Dosuzhkov, and N. O. Lossky, eds., *Zhizn' i smert'*, vol. 1, pp. 9 and 11.

132. Ibid., p. 12.

133. N. O. Lossky, "N. E. Osipov kak filosof" [Osipov as a Philosopher], in *Zhizn' i smert'*, vol. 1, p. 52.

134. F. N. Dosuzhkov, "N. E. Osipov kak psikhiatr" [Osipov as a Psychiatrist], in *Zhizn' i smert'*, vol. 1, p. 33.

135. N. E. Osipov, "Strashnoe u Gogolia i Dostoevskogo" [The Frightful in Gogol and Dostoevsky], *Zhizn' i smert'*, p. 134.

136. Ibid., p. 127.

137. N. E. Osipov, "Strakh smerti," cited in Dosuzhkov, "Nevroz boiazni, strakh smerti i strakh prividenii" [The Neurosis of Fear, Fear of Death and Fear of Ghosts], in *Zhizn' i smert'*, vol. 2, p. 127.

138. Ibid., p. 134.

139. N. E. Osipov, "Revoliutsiia i son" [Revolution and Dreams], *Nauchnye trudy Russkogo narodnogo universiteta v Prage*, vol. 4, 1931, pp. 175–203.

140. Letter of August 11, 1930, from Osipov to M. P. Polosin, cited in M. P. Polosin, "N. E. Osipov," p. 17.

141. Osipov, "Revoliutsiia i son," p. 188.

142. Osipov, "Strashnoe u Gogolia i Dostoevskogo," p. 131.

143. Bem, Dosuzhkov, and Lossky, eds., *Zhizn' i smert'*.

Chapter Seven

1. The reader may wish to refer to the following analyses of the ideological debates surrounding Freudomarxism: M. Miller, "Freudian Theory Under Bolshevik Rule," *Slavic Review*, Winter 1985, pp. 625–646; M. Miller, "The Reception of Psychoanalysis and the Problem of the Unconscious in Russia," *Social Research 57*, no. 4 (1990), pp. 876–888; E. Roudinesco, *Histoire de la psychanalyse en France* (Paris: Seuil, 1986), vol. 2, pp. 50–71; A. Mikhalevitch, "Première implantation et rejet," *Frénésie*, no. 7, 1989, pp. 125–146; D. Joravsky, *Russian Psychology: A Critical History* (Oxford: Blackwell, 1989); and A. V. Petrovsky, *Voprosy istorii i teorii psikhologii* [Issues in the History and Theory of Psychology] (Moscow: Pedagogika, 1984), pp. 111ff.

2. E. Jones, *The Life and Work of Sigmund Freud* (New York: Basic, 1955), vol. 3, p. 16.

3. B. Naarden, "Marx and Russia," *History of European Ideas*, vol. 12, no. 6 (1990), pp. 783–797.

4. James L. Rice, "Dostoevsky and Freud's Russia," presentation given at a symposium in Ljubljana on July 26, 1989.

5. M. Krull, *Sigmund, Fils de Jacob* (Paris: Gallimard, 1983.)

6. *Freud and Andreas-Salomé: Letters*, ed. E. Pfeiffer (New York: Norton, 1985), p. 75.

7. The reference here is to *Civilization and Its Discontents*. See *The Letters of Sigmund Freud and Arnold Zweig*, ed. E. L. Freud (New York: NYU Press, 1970), p. 21.

8. E. Kurzweil, *The Freudians* (New Haven: Yale University Press, 1989), p. 286.

9. C. G. Jung, *Dream Analysis* (London: Routledge, 1984), p. 175.

10. For more discussion of the intersection between psychoanalysis and left-leaning political movements in the West, see: H.-P. Gente, *Marxismus, Psychoanalyse, Sexpol* (Frankfurt-am-Main, 1970); C. Lasch, "The Freudian Left and the Cultural Revolution," *New Left Review,* no. 129, September 1981, pp. 23–34; B. Richards, *Images of Freud* (London: Dent, 1989); P. Roazen, *Freud and His Followers* (London: Allen, 1976); E. Roudinesco, *Histoire de la psychanalyse en France,* vol. 2 (Paris: Seuil, 1986); E. Kurzweil, *The Freudians* (New Haven: Yale University Press, 1989); B. Harris and A. Broack, "Otto Fenichel and the Left Opposition in Psychoanalysis," *Journal of the History of Behavioral Sciences,* no. 27 (April 1991), pp. 157–165.

11. *Marx et Lenine, Freud et Lacan: Colloque de la Découverte Freudienne* (Presses Universitaires du Mirail, 1991).

12. Notation of November 7, 1912, in L. Andreas-Salomé, *In der Schule bei Freud: Tagebuch eines Jahres, 1912–1913* (Zurich, 1958), p. 25. Alfred and Raisa Adler had four children. The eldest daughter Valentina went off to Soviet Russia to build communism, was arrested in 1937, and perished in the gulag in 1942. Their other daughter, Alexandra, like Anna Freud, became the inheritor of her father's psychological ideas and the president of the International Association of Individual Psychology (S. Gardner and G. Stevens, *Red Vienna and the Golden Age of Psychology, 1918–1938* [New York: Praeger, 1992], p. 131).

13. F. Eros, "'Instincts' and the 'Forces of Production': The Freud-Marx Debates in Eastern and Central Europe," paper presented at the Sixth European CHEIRON meeting in Brighton, England, September 2–6, 1987.

14. Paul Federn, *Zur Psychologie der Revolution* (Vienna: Die Österreichische Volkswirt, 1919).

15. This document is missing from all known Soviet archives. Here it is cited from the research of a French historian, who relied on émigré sources: J. Marti, "La psychanalyse en Russie et en Union Soviétique de 1909 à 1930," *Critique,* no. 46 (1976), p. 230.

16. B. Bykhovsky, "O metodologicheskikh osnovaniiakh psikhoanaliticheskogo ucheniia Freida" [On the Methodological Basis of Freud's Psychoanalytical Doctrine], *Pod znamenem marksizma,* no. 12, 1923.

17. A. B. Zalkind, *Ocherki kul'tury revoliutsionnogo vremeni* [Outlines of the Culture of the Revolutionary Era] (Moscow, 1924).

18. L. Trotsky, "Kul'tura i sotsializm" [Culture and Socialism], *Sochineniia* (Moscow, 1927), vol. 21, pp. 430 and 260.

19. M. A. Reisner, "Problemy psikhologii i teorii istoricheskogo materializma" [Issues in Psychology and the Theory of Historical Materialism], *Vestnik sotsialist-icheskoi akademii,* 1923, no. 3; M. A. Reisner, "Freid i ego shkola o religii" [Freud and His School on Religion], *Pechat' i revoliutsiia,* 1924, no. 2.

20. *Psikhologiia i Marksizm* (Leningrad, 1925).

21. L. S. Vygotsky, "Istoricheskii smysl psikhologicheskogo krizisa" [The Historical Meaning of the Psychological Crisis], in *Sobranie sochinenii* (Moscow: Pedagogika, 1982), vol. 1, p. 331. A current view of the correlation between Vygotsky and psychoanalysis can be found in A. Wilson and L. Weinstein, "Psychoanalysis and Vygotskian Psychology," *Journal of the American Psychoanalytical Association,* 1992, vol. 40, no. 2, pp. 349–380, and no. 3, pp. 725–760.

22. "Deiateli SSSR i revoliutsionnogo dvizheniia Rossii" [Public Figures in the USSR and the Russian Revolutionary Movement], *Entsiklopedicheskii slovar' Granat* (1927; reprint, Moscow: Sovetskaia entsiklopediia, 1989), pp. 152–156. The memoirs of Ioffe's wife, who worked in Moscow as Trotsky's personal secretary, are also intriguing (M. M. Ioffe, *Vospominaniia* [Tel Aviv: Vremia i my, 1977]).

23. L. Trotsky, "Ioffe," in Y. Fel'shtinskii, ed., *Portrety revoliutsionerov* (Benson, Vt.: Chalidze, 1988), pp. 370–376.

24. On March 6, 1907, Adler spoke on Ioffe's case at the meeting of the Vienna Psychoanalytic Society (*Minutes of the Vienna Psychoanalytic Society* [New York: International University Press, 1962], vol. 1, pp. 139–143). From this presentation we know quite a number of curious details of Ioffe's fears and dreams, but Adler said nothing of his revolutionary ideas. Two years later, on March 10, 1909, Adler gave a talk before the same society "On the Psychology of Marxism" (*Minutes of the Vienna Psychoanalytic Society*, vol. 2, pp. 173–178), in which the ideological influence of Trotsky and Ioffe is evident. For more on the development of Adler's political views, see S. Gardner and G. Stevens, *Red Vienna and the Golden Age of Psychology, 1918–1938*.

25. Letter from Trotsky to academician I. P. Pavlov [in Russian], in L. Trotsky, *Sochineniia* [Works] (Moscow, 1927), vol. 21, p. 260.

26. Trotsky, "Ioffe."

27. Ibid.

28. I. Deutscher, *Trotskii v izgnanii* [Trotsky in Exile] (Moscow: Politizdat, 1991), pp. 214, 254, 284. For example, in May 1935 Trotsky was reading Fritz Wittels's book on Freud and commented on it in his journal with an expert tone, "A poor little book by a jealous student" (L. Trotsky, *Dnevniki i pis'ma* [Journals and Letters] [New York: Ermitazh, 1990], p. 119).

29. Trotsky, "Ioffe."

30. A. A. Ioffe, "Po povodu bessoznatel'nogo v zhizni individuuma" [On the Unconscious in the Life of the Individual], *Psikhoterapiia*, 1913, no. 4, pp. 234–238.

31. The Smolny Institute in St. Petersburg served as the Bolshevik headquarters during the October revolution.—Trans.

32. Trotsky, "Ioffe," p. 371; L. Trotsky, *Moia zhizn'* [My Life] (Moscow: Panorama, 1991), p. 217.

33. Trotsky, "Ioffe," pp. 373–374.

34. See V. I. Lenin, *Polnoe sobranie sochinenii* [Complete Works] 5th ed. (Moscow, 1963), vol. 52, pp. 99–101. (Tseka is the acronym for Tsentral'nyi komitet, the Central Committee of the Communist Party.—Trans.)

35. V. A. Shishkin, *Tsena priznaniia* [The Price of Recognition] (St. Petersburg: Nauka, 1991), p. 107.

36. Y. Fel'shtinskii, "Trotsky," in *Portrety revoliutsionerov*, pp. 384–402.

37. Ibid.

38. Ibid.

39. Ibid.

40. Ibid.

41. L. Trotsky, *Literature and Revolution* (Ann Arbor: University of Michigan Press, 1960), pp. 254–255.

42. L. Trotsky, "O kul'ture budushchego" [On the Culture of the Future], in *Sochineniia*, vol. 21, p. 110.

43. L. Trotsky, *Literature and Revolution*, p. 254.

44. L. Trotsky, "A Few Words on How to Raise a Human Being," in *Problems of Everyday Life and Other Writings on Culture and Science* (New York: Monad, 1973), p. 140.

45. K. Mannheim, *Man and Society in an Age of Reconstruction* (London: Routledge and Kegan Paul, 1980), p. 217.

46. Trotsky, *Literature and Revolution*, p. 255.

47. L. Trotsky, "A Few Words on How to Raise a Human Being," p. 140.

48. L. Trotsky, *Leon Trotsky Speaks* (New York: Pathfinder, 1972), p. 269.

49. Chrezvychainyi komitet, the "extraordinary committee," was a predecessor of the KGB.—Trans.

50. V. Samoilov and Y. Vinogradov, "Ivan Pavlov i Nikolai Bukharin," *Zvezda*, 1989, no. 10.

51. N. I. Bukharin, "O mirovoi revoliutsii, nashei strane, kul'ture i prochem (Otvet professoru I. Pavlovu)" [On the Global Revolution, Our Country, Culture, and So Forth (Reply to Professor I. Pavlov], *Krasnaia nov'*, 1924, nos. 1–2; the article was condensed and reprinted in N. I. Bukharin, *Metodologiia i planirovanie nauki i tekhniki* [The Methodology and Planning of Science and Technology] (Moscow: Nauka, 1989), pp. 225–259.

52. Letter from Trotsky to academician I. P. Pavlov [in Russian], in L. Trotsky, *Sochineniia*, vol. 21, p. 260.

53. M. G. Yaroshevsky, "Vozvrashchenie Freida" [The Return of Freud], *Psikhologicheskii zhurnal*, 1988, no. 9, pp. 129–138.

54. S. N. Davidenkov, *Evoliutsionno-geneticheskie idei v nevropatologii* [Evolutionary and Genetic Ideas in Neuropathology] (Leningrad: GIDUV, 1947), p. 153. Another example is the experiments done in 1934 that combined the study of complex conditioned reflexes among children with the Jungian associative experiment (N. N. Traugott and V. K. Faddeeva, "O vliianii zatrudnennogo ugasheniia pishchedobyvatel'nykh uslovnykh refleksov na obshchee i rechevoe povedenie rebenka," in *Na puti k izucheniiu vysshikh form neirodinamiki rebenka* (Moscow: Gosudarstvennoe meditsinskoe izd. 1934), pp. 316–405.

55. Trotsky's letter gave birth to a legend: The authors of a book on Pavlov (V. Samoilov and A. Mozzhukhin, *Pavlov v Peterburge–Petrograde–Leningrade* [Pavlov in St. Petersburg–Petrograd–Leningrad] [Leningrad: Lenizdat, 1988], p. 266), quoting the letter apparently from memory, ascribed the following words to Trotsky: "I studied psychoanalysis with Freud for eight years." However, I located no documentary evidence of such a text, and while Trotsky might have known Freud, he was not his patient or student. The original letter is still in the archives of the Pavlov Commission of the Russian Academy of Sciences in St. Petersburg. The versions of the letter in Trotsky's *Complete Works* and in Pavlov's personal archives correspond, so there is no reason to doubt their authenticity.

56. L. Trotsky, *Literature and Revolution*, p. 220.

57. G. Malis, *Psikhoanaliz kommunizma* [Psychoanalysis of Communism] (Kharkov: Kosmos, 1924), pp. 24, 74–79.

58. E. Jones, *The Life and Work of Sigmund Freud*, vol. 3, p. 185.

59. M. Higgins and C. M. Raphael, eds., *Reich Speaks of Freud* (New York: Noonday, 1967), p. 115.

60. "Leon Trotsky and Wilhelm Reich: Five Letters," *International Socialist Review*, 1967, no. 5.

61. Letter from Sergey Eisenstein to Wilhelm Reich, in L. Ionin, ed., *Sotsiologicheskie issledovaniia*, 1977, no. 1, pp. 176–179.

62. Higgins and Raphael, eds., *Reich Speaks of Freud*, p. 49.

63. W. Reich, "Die Stellung der Psychoanalyse in der Sowjetunion," *Die psycho-analytische Bewegung*, 1929, no. 4, pp. 359–368.

64. M. Wulff, "Zur Stellung der Psychoanalyse in der Sowjetunion," *Die psycho-analytische Bewegung*, 1930, no. 1, pp. 70–75.

65. W. Reich, *Mass Psychology of Fascism* (New York: Simon and Schuster, 1970).

66. M. Higgins and C. M. Raphael, eds., *Reich Speaks of Freud*, p. 114.

67. E. Jones, *The Life and Work of Sigmund Freud*, vol. 3, p. 191.

68. P. Roazen, *Freud and His Followers*, p. 333; J. Chemonni, *Freud et le sionisme* (Paris: Solin, 1988), p. 156.

69. *The Freud–Jung Letters*, ed. W. McGuire (London: Hogarth, 1974), p. 90.

70. E. Jones, *The Life and Work of Sigmund Freud*, vol. 2, p. 161.

71. P. Roazen and B. Swerdloff, eds., *Heresy: Sandor Rado and the Psychoanalytic Movement* (Northvale, N.J.: Aronson, 1995), p. 101.

72. *Freud–Andreas-Salomé: Letters*, ed. E. Pfeiffer (New York: Norton, 1985), p. 179.

73. E. Jones, *The Life and Work of Sigmund Freud*, vol. 2, p. 145.

74. Cited in Roazen, *Freud and His Followers*, p. 330.

75. *Internationale Zeitschrift für Psychoanalyse*, 1931, vol. 17, p. 283.

76. Sidney L. Pomer, "Max Eitingon," in Franz Alexander et al., eds., *Psychoanalytic Pioneers* (New York: Basic, 1966), pp. 51–62.

77. E. Roudinesco, *Histoire de la psychanalyse en France*, vol. 1, p. 157.

78. E. Jones, *The Life and Work of Sigmund Freud* (New York: Basic, 1955), vol. 3, p. 165.

79. Ibid., p. 182.

80. The Palestinian Society initially numbered six members, four of whom—Eitingon himself, Moisei Wulff, E. Shalit, and A. Smelyanskaya—were Russians (J. Chemonni, *Freud et le sionisme*).

81. Roazen and Swerdloff, eds., *Heresy*, p. 110.

82. P. Broue, "La main-d'oeuvre 'blanche' de Stalin," *Cahiers Léon Trotsky*, December 1985, no. 24, pp. 75–84; J. J. Dziak, *Chekisty: A History of the KGB* (New York: Heath, 1987); S. Schwartz, "Intellectuals and Assassins: Annals of Stalin's Killerati," *New York Times Book Review*, January 24, 1988, pp. 3 and 30–31. For the fierce polemic around this article, see T. Draper, "The Mystery of Max Eitingon," *New York Times Book Review*, April 14, 1988; replies by Stephen Schwartz and Vitaly Rappoport, another reply by Draper, a letter by Walter Laqueur (*New York Times Book Review*, June 16, 1988), and a roundup analysis by Robert Conquest (*New York Times Book Review*, July 3, 1988). Max Eitingon's defenders, relying on information received for the most part from his descendants, convincingly demonstrated that the German psychoanalyst Eitingon and the Soviet intelligence officer Eitingon were not brothers. Other aspects of this story remain, it seems to me, open to further discussion. The information from Sandor Rado on the sources of Max Eitingon's fortune was not brought to bear in the 1988 debate. It is difficult to agree with Draper's easy explanation of Eitingon's financial relations with the Skoblins, writing the money off to pure philanthropy: The unusual magnitude of these donations was established by the Paris trial and confirmed by Plevitskaya's prison journal, which is kept in the Filonenko Papers at the Bakhmeteff Archive, Rare Book and Manuscript Department of the Columbia University Library. Neither was Draper able to explain the story of the "Green Bible," the book containing secret codes, although he admitted that the Skoblins received it from Max Eitingon. In all, the polemic around this affair seems far too charged with family and professional interests. Pavel Sudoplatov, Naum Eitingon's former boss, also denied that the German doctor participated in NKVD operations. As proof he offered a story of recent contact with Eitingon's relatives and a reference to Draper's "model research." However, Sudoplatov suggested that Max Eitingon's London heirs and Leonid Eitingon's Moscow heirs still consider each other "distant relatives" (P. Sudoplatov and A. Sudoplatov, *Special Tasks: The Memoirs of an Unwanted Witness—A Soviet Spymaster* [Boston: Little, Brown,

1994], p. 37). On the whole I agree with Robert Conquest: There is no proof that Max Eitingon was a Soviet agent; however, there are sufficient grounds for such a hypothesis. "In many cases while in strict law we would need complete proof, history often has to go without such certainty" (R. Conquest, "Max Eitingon, Another View," *New York Times Book Review,* July 3, 1988.
    83. The NKVD was the immediate predecessor of the KGB.—Trans.
    84. V. Rappaport and Y. Alekseev, *Izmena rodine: Ocherki po istorii Krasnoi armii* [Betrayal of the Motherland: Outlines of Red Army History] (London: Overseas, 1989), pp. 502–504. This book, published by dissident historians in 1985 in English and later in Russian, contains more complete background on Naum Eitingon; his brother, a Berlin doctor, is also mentioned. New information about General Eitingon's activities will probably continue to emerge and captivate our imaginations. On July 31, 1991, the newspaper *Izvestiia* stated that "right up until the 1950s, the General was directly linked to the KGB's secret chemical laboratory, where various poisons were developed to be used against 'enemies of the people' slated for elimination. For this connection, he was sentenced to a long prison term after Beria's condemnation."
    85. *Glavnoe razvedyvatel'noe upravlenie* [Main Intelligence Directorate] (GRU), the organ of Soviet military intelligence.—Trans.
    86. See N. Grant, "A Thermidorian Amalgam," *Russian Review,* July 1963, vol. 22.
    87. A. A. Mosolov, *Pri dvore poslednego imperatora* (St. Petersburg: Nauka, 1992), p. 83.
    88. *The Freud–Jung Letters,* p. 89.
    89. J. J. Dziak, *Chekisty: A History of the KGB.*
    90. The diary can be found in the Filonenko Papers, Bakhmeteff Archive, Rare Book and Manuscript Department, Columbia University. See also V. Maksimova, "Delo Plevitskoi" [The Plevitskaya Affair], *Moskovskii nabliudatel',* 1993, nos. 2–3, pp. 59–72. In her diary, Plevitskaya recorded the events that took place during the criminal investigation. On January 17, 1938, she wrote that Y. F. Semyonov, editor in chief of the Paris-based newspaper *Vozrozhdenie,* had been called to testify. Semyonov stated that the Skoblins became acquainted with the "Bolsheviks" in 1920 at Max Eitingon's house in Berlin. When asked to name his source, Semyonov implicated Ivan Lukash, whom Eitingon had commissioned to write Plevitskaya's memoirs, *Dezhkin Karagod.* Plevitskaya continued: "Semyonov went on talking at length about the Eitingons' fur trade with the Bolsheviks, how the furs were bought up in Siberia and then shipped off to London." For her part, Plevitskaya wondered: "What does international trade have to do with Miller's disappearance? I informed S[emyonov] that our friend M. E. Eitingon was a learned psychiatrist and took no interest either in international trade or in politics." Elsewhere, Plevitskaya described Eitingon in these words: "He's educated, rich—what use would he have for the Bolsheviks? . . . We've been friends for 15 years. They've given us material support" (p. 27). At the inquest, Plevitskaya denied any intimate association with Eitingon, but readily confirmed that the émigré Lukash was writing her memoirs and that Eitingon was paying him. She tried to use the latter fact as evidence of Eitingon's innocence: "The contents of my book," Plevitskaya said, were such that no "Communist sympathizer or operative" would support the effort financially (p. 27). Plevitskaya affirmed that Eitingon had come to Europe after emigrating to Palestine (p. 28) and that after Miller disappeared she had spent the night at the apartment of L. I. Raigorodsky, a relative of Eitingon's in Paris (p. 23). Raigorodsky, for his part, denied that Max Eitingon was a participant in the Miller affair or in the family's trade with the USSR. Also brought into evidence during the trial were letters from

the renowned psychoanalysts Princess Marie Bonaparte and Dr. R. Loewenstein, who gave testimony to Eitingon's upstanding character. Further witness to the circumstances surrounding the trial is provided by documents connected with Plevitskaya's attorney, Maximilian Filonenko, which are found in the personal archives of Georgii Polyansky. Polyansky wrote (February 12, 1939) that, according to Filonenko's wife, the attorney was convinced Plevitskaya was guilty and was trying to get her to confess. To accomplish the latter, Filonenko had told her that Skoblin had called him from the Soviet envoy's residence in Paris, where he had holed up. Plevitskaya supposedly broke down under this pressure and admitted to collaborating with the NKVD. "After she confessed, Plevitskaya begged Max [Filonenko] to appeal directly to the Soviet envoy to procure whatever funds were necessary in order to secure her pardon." Moreover, Filonenko reportedly had said that Plevitskaya assumed from the very start that he was under the direct orders of the Soviet envoy (see the G. A. Polyansky folder in the Filonenko Papers, Bakhmeteff Archive). Even more interesting was the way in which Plevitskaya talked Filonenko into representing her: "'Money is no object'—after all, she said, money just flies right out of Palestine and into her pockets" (Letter from Barbara Shakhovskaya, Filonenko's wife, to Polyansky, September 29, 1937). Finally, Plevitskaya herself wrote to Filonenko from prison December 19, 1938, pleading with him to "have a talk with the Russian bigwigs," especially Raigorodsky, in order to procure the means for her defense.

91. N. Berberova, *Kursiv moi* [In My Own Hand] (Munich: Fink, 1972).

92. "Deiateli SSSR i revoliutsionnogo dvizheniia Rossii," in *Entsiklopedicheskii slovar' Granat* (Moscow, 1989), p. 452; see also Shishkin, *Tsena priznaniia*, p. 134.

93. S. Schwartz, "Intellectuals and Assassins: Annals of Stalin's Killerati."

94. N. Baranova-Shestova, *Zhizn' L'va Shestova* [The Life of Lev Shestov] (Paris, 1983), vol. 2.

95. V. Samoilov and Y. Vinogradov, "Ivan Pavlov i Nikolai Bukharin," p. 108.

96. N. Berdyaev, *Samopoznanie*, p. 172.

97. N. Berberova, *Kursiv moi*, p. 165.

98. E. Jones, *The Life and Work of Sigmund Freud*, vol. 2, p. 166.

99. A. Steinberg, *Druz'ia moikh rannikh let* [Friends of my Early Years], ed. G. Niva (Paris: Sintaksis, 1991), p. 248.

100. Trotsky's two children, who emigrated with him, died under circumstances that might lead one to suspect their physicians of causing their deaths. In 1938, Trotsky's son Lev Sedov died in a Russian surgical clinic in Paris; and Russian historians generally concur that General Eitingon's team took part in his death (although Sudoplatov denied it in *Special Tasks*, p. 83). On January 5, 1933, Trotsky's daughter Zinaida Volkova committed suicide. She had been undergoing psychoanalysis in Berlin (I. Deutscher, *Trotskii v izgnanii*, p. 214). Nothing more specific is known about the circumstances surrounding her death, and, unlike her brother's death, they attracted little attention. When she perished, Zinaida's analysis had been going on for over a year. She had made it out of Russia in 1930 and suffered from depression. Trotsky, taking advantage of his connections and constricted by his limited funds, managed to arrange for her to meet with a certain psychoanalyst, who according to the memoirs of Trotsky's secretary, "spoke Russian fluently" (J. van Heijenoort, *With Trotsky in Exile: From Prinkipo to Coyoacan* [Cambridge, Mass.: Harvard University Press, 1978], p. 35; see also D. Volkogonov, *Trotskii* [Moscow: Novosti, 1992], vol. 2, p. 157). In February 1932, Zinaida was deprived of the right of reentry into the USSR, as was the rest of the Trotsky clan. Despite this, her psychoanalyst, supposedly for medical reasons, firmly recommended that she return to

her homeland. As Trotsky wrote in an open letter to Stalin: "Psychiatrists have declared unanimously that only her immediate return home to normal conditions, to family and labor might save her. But your decree has snatched away this very possibility" (L. Trotsky, "Po povodu smerti Z. L. Volkovoi" [Concerning the Death of Z. L. Volkova], *Biulleten' oppozitsii,* March 1933, pp. 29–30). The creation of this double bind brought the patient to the brink of despair. Trotsky could have been right when he blamed his daughter's death (and later his son's) on Stalin, viewing them as acts of political vengeance. Zinaida's therapist might not have been Max Eitingon himself (since he hardly ever practiced), but it was certainly one of his close associates. It is difficult to imagine that in Berlin of 1931–1932 there might be Russian-speaking, pro-Soviet analysts who were *not* connected to Eitingon. Volkova's letters are kept in the Trotsky Archives, Houghton Library, Harvard University. They reveal astonishing details: Zina suffered from an incestuous delusion. On the peak of it, she was convinced that her father had fallen in love with her, that they were engaged in some kind of erotic liaison and that, after the treatment, she would be reunited with him. Trotsky forwarded some of the letters that he received from Zina to her analyst in Berlin. Subsequently the analyst informed Zina about it. This eventually brought Zina to her final decision.

101. A. Steinberg, *Druz'ia moikh rannikh let,* pp. 248–252.

102. Letter from M. Gershenzon to L. Shestov, June 16, 1924, *Minuvshee,* no. 6, p. 302.

103. We know this fable also from Steinberg's retelling.

104. A. Steinberg, *Druz'ia moikh rannikh let,* p. 249.

105. L. Trotsky, Speech to the First All-Union Congress of Scientific Workers, *Sochineniia,* vol. 21, p. 262.

106. V. Shklovsky, *Sentimental'noe puteshestvie* [Sentimental Journey] (Moscow: Novosti, 1990), p. 197.

107. W. H. Auden, "Psychology and Art Today," in E. Kurzweil and W. Phillips, eds., *Literature and Psychoanalysis* (New York: Columbia University Press, 1983), p. 130.

108. A. Falk, "Freud and Herzl," *Midstream,* January 1977, p. 19.

109. Ibid.

Chapter Eight

1. *Pedologicheskaia entsiklopediia* (Moscow, 1929), vol. 3.

2. L. S. Vygotsky, "K voprosu o pedologii i smezhnykh s nei naukakh" [On the Question of Pedology and Similar Sciences], *Pedologiia,* 1931, no. 3.

3. P. Efrussi, *Uspekhi psikhologii v Rossii* [The Successes of Psychology in Russia] (Petrograd, 1923), p. 7.

4. V. M. Bekhterev, "Sub'ektivnyi ili ob'ektivnyi metod v izuchenii lichnosti" [Subjective or Objective Method in the Study of Personality], *Molodaia gvardiia,* 1924, no. 5; V. N. Osipova, "Shkola V. M. Bekhtereva i pedologiia" [The School of V. M. Bekhterev and Pedology], *Pedologiia,* 1928, no. 1, pp. 10–26. For more on the history of the creation of the Pedological Institute and on V. T. Zimin, see I. Guberman, *Bekhterev: Stranitsy zhizni* [Bekhterev: Pages from a Life] (Moscow, 1977).

5. N. Nikitin, "Estestvennaia nauka o cheloveke i sotsializm" [The Natural Science of Man and Socialism], *Pod znamenem marksizma,* 1933, no. 6, p. 217. Dneprostroi, a dam and hydroelectric power plant on the Dnieper river, was a massive early Soviet construction project that later came to symbolize the monumental achievements of communism.

6. P. P. Blonsky, *Pedologiia* (Moscow: Rabotnik prosveshcheniia, 1925).

7. L. S. Vygotsky, "Psikhotekhnika i pedologiia" [Industrial Psychology and Pedology], *Psikhotekhnika i psikhofiziologiia truda*, 1931, nos. 2–3, p. 173.

8. I. N. Spielrein, "Psikhotekhnika v SSSR v poslednie gody" [Industrial Psychology in the USSR in Recent Years]. *Pod znamenem marksizma*, 1930, no. 5, p. 136.

9. "Iz rechei N. K. Krupskoi, N. I. Bukharina, A. V. Lunacharskogo, i N. A. Semashko po osnovnym voprosam pedologii: 1 Pedologicheskii s'ezd" [From the speeches given by N. K. Krupskaya, N. I. Bukharin, A. V. Lunacharsky, and N. A. Semashko on basic issues in pedology at the First Pedological Conference], *Na putiakh k novoi shkole*, 1928, no. 1, p. 10.

10. A. B. Zalkind, "O metodologii tselostnogo izucheniia v pedologii" [On the Methodology of Comprehensive Study in Pedology], *Pedologiia*, 1931, no. 2, p. 3.

11. N. A. Rybnikov, *Yazyk rebenka* [The Language of the Child] (Moscow-Leningrad, 1926), p. 15.

12. I. S. Kon, *Rebenok i obshchestvo* [The Child and Society] (Moscow: Pedagogika, 1988).

13. A. Blok, "Intelligentsiia i revoliutsiia" [Intelligentsia and Revolution], in *Sobranie sochinenii* (Moscow, 1962), vol. 6, p. 12.

14. Bekhterev, "Sub'ektivnyi ili ob'ektivnyi metod v izuchenii lichnosti."

15. V. Samoilov and Y. Vinogradov, "Ivan Pavlov i Nikolai Bukharin," *Zvezda*, 1989, no. 10.

16. N. I. Bukharin, "O mirovoi revoliutsii, nashei strane, kul'ture i prochem (Otvet professoru I. Pavlovu)" [On Global Revolution, Our Country, Culture, and Other Things (Reply to Professor Pavlov)], *Krasnaia nov'*, 1924, no. 1, pp. 170–178, and no. 2, pp. 105–119; reprinted in condensed form in N. I. Bukharin, *Metodologiia i planirovanie nauki i tekhniki* (Moscow: Nauka, 1989), pp. 225–259.

17. "From the speeches given by N. K. Krupskaya, N. I. Bukharin, A. V. Lunacharsky, and N. A. Semashko on basic issues in pedology at the First Pedological Conference" [in Russian], *Na putiakh k novoi shkole*, 1928, no. 1, p. 10.

18. Ibid.

19. Ibid.

20. Ibid., p. 14.

21. P. P. Blonsky, *Pedagogika* (Moscow, 1922), p. 31.

22. "From the speeches given by N. K. Krupskaya, N. I. Bukharin, A. V. Lunacharsky, and N. A. Semashko on basic issues in pedology at the First Pedological Conference" [in Russian], *Na putiakh k novoi shkole*, 1928, no. 1, p. 10.

23. M. V. Wulff, "Fantaziia i real'nost' v psikhike rebenka" [Fantasy and Reality in the Child's Psyche] (Odessa, 1926), p. 24.

24. S. Freud, *The Future of an Illusion*, pp. 7–8.

25. Ibid., p. 8.

26. N. K. Krupskaya, "Sistema Teilora i organizatsiia raboty sovetskikh uchrezhdenii" [Taylor's System and the Organization of Work in Soviet Institutions], *Krasnaia nov'*, 1921, no. 1, pp. 140–145.

27. E. Yenchman, *Vosemnadtsat' tezisov o teorii novoi biologii* [Eighteen Theses on the Theory of New Biology] (Rostov-on-the-Don, 1920; Pyatigorsk, 1920), p. 17; E. Yenchman, *Teoriia novoi biologii i marksizm* [The Theory of the New Biology and Marxism], 2d ed. (Petrograd, 1923).

28. "Avtobiograficheskaia proza M. S. Al'tmana" [The Autobiographical Prose of M. S. Altman], *Minuvshee*, 1990, no. 10, pp. 208, 220. Ivanov's poem dedicated to Altman can be found in Vyacheslav Ivanov, *Stikhotvoreniia* [Poetry] (Leningrad: Sovetskii pisatel', 1978), p. 295.

29. N. I. Bukharin, "Yenchmaniada (k voprosu ob ideologicheskom pererozhdenii)" [The Yenchmaniad (On the Question of Ideological Degeneration)], *Krasnaia nov'*, 1923, no. 6, pp. 145–178; if one is to believe Yenchman himself, he enjoyed the support of Pokrovsky and Timiryazev, both senior members of the Academy.

30. M. Levidov, "Organizovannoe uproshchenie kul'tury" [The Organized Simplification of Culture], *Krasnaia nov'*, 1923, no. 1, p. 318.

31. I. Khodorovsky, "Osnovnye cherty sovremennogo sostoianiia narodnogo prosveshcheniia v RSFSR" [The Basic Features of the State of Popular Education in the RSFSR], *Krasnaia nov'*, 1923, no. 7, p. 140.

32. Ibid.

33. P. O. Efrussi, *Uspekhi psikhologii v Rossii* [The Success of Psychology in Russia] (St. Petersburg, 1923).

34. "From the speeches given by N. K. Krupskaya, N. I. Bukharin, A. V. Lunacharsky, and N. A. Semashko on basic issues in pedology at the First Pedological Conference" [in Russian], *Na putiakh k novoi shkole* [On the Means Toward a New School], 1928, no. 1, p. 10.

35. Khodorovsky, "Osnovnye cherty sovremennogo sostoianiia narodnogo prosveshcheniia v RSFSR."

36. L. Ginzburg, *Literatura v poiskakh real'nosti*, p. 230; an expressive description of this intelligentsia is provided in Ginzburg's essay "Eshche raz o starom i novom (pokolenie na povorote)" [Once More on the Old and the New (A Generation at the Turning Point)], published in *Tynianovskii sbornik: Vtorye tynianovskie chteniia* (Riga: Zinatne, 1986), pp. 132–140.

37. Taken from "Pedagogicheskaia Moskva," a reference calendar for 1923, p. 435.

38. N. A. Rybnikov, "Pedologicheskie uchrezhdeniia respubliki" [Pedological Institutions of the Republic], *Pedologiia*, 1928, no. 1, p. 181.

39. *Pedologiia*, 1931, no. 4, p. 103.

40. A. I. Lipkina, personal communication, 1987.

41. S. S. Molozhavy, "Testirovanie i pedagogicheskii protsess" [Testing and the Pedagogical Process], *Prosveshchenie na transporte*, 1927, no. 2, p. 22.

42. M. A. Levina, "Contributions to the debate," *Pedologiia*, 1932, no. 4.

43. A. B. Zalkind, "K voprosu o sushchnosti psikhonevrozov" [On the Question of the Essence of Psychoneuroses]; and "Individual'no-psikhologicheskii analiz trekh sluchaev somnambulizma" [Individual-psychological Analysis of Three Cases of Somnambulism], *Psikhoterapiia*, 1913, no. 3.

44. Zalkind, "K voprosu o sushchnosti psikhonevrozov," p. 178.

45. *Spisok meditsinskikh vrachei* [Directory of Medical Physicians] (Moscow: Narkomzdrav, 1925).

46. A. B. Zalkind, *Ocherki kul'tury revoliutsionnogo vremeni* [Outlines of the Culture of the Revolutionary Period] (Moscow, 1924), p. 29.

47. A. B. Zalkind, "O iazvakh v VKP(B)," in *Ocherki kul'tury revoliutsionnogo vremeni* (Moscow, 1924).

48. A. B. Zalkind, *Polovoi vopros v usloviiakh sovetskoi obshchestvennosti* [The Sexual Question in the Conditions of Soviet Society] (Leningrad, 1926).

49. G. Dayan, "Vtoroi psikhonevrologicheskii s'ezd" [The Second Psychoneurological Conference], *Krasnaia nov'*, 1924, no. 2, p. 155.

50. A. B. Zalkind, "Psikhonevrologicheskie nauki i sotsialisticheskoe stroitel'stvo" [Psychoneurological Sciences and Socialist Construction], *Pedologiia*, 1930, no. 3, pp. 309–322.

51. Announcement published in *Pedologiia*, 1931, no. 1, p. 69.

52. A. B. Zalkind, "Differentsirovka na pedologicheskom fronte" [Differentiation on the Pedological Front], *Pedologiia*, 1931, no. 3, p. 11.

53. N. K. Krupskaya, "Contributions to the debate," *Pedologiia*, 1932, no. 4, p. 103.

54. A. B. Zalkind, "O metodologii tselostnogo izucheniia v pedologii" [On the Methodology of Research Synthesis in Pedology], *Pedologiia*, 1931, no. 2.

55. M. G. Yaroshevsky, personal communication, 1987.

56. A. Bely, "O teurgii" [On Theurgy], *Novyi put'*, 1903, no. 9.

57. D. Azbukin, "Psikhologiia shkol'nikov v nachale Oktyabr'skoi revoliutsii" [The Psychology of Schoolchildren at the Beginning of the October Revolution], *Pedologicheskii zhurnal*, 1923, no. 3, pp. 60–72.

58. L. S. Geshelina, "Sreda i sotsial'no-biologicheskaia kharakteristika sovremennogo doshkol'nika" [The Environment and Sociobiological Characteristics of the Contemporary Preschooler], *Pedologiia*, 1928, no. 1, pp. 113–136.

59. I. A. Perepel, *Freidizm i ego akademicheskaia oppozitsiia* [Freudianism and Its Academic Opposition] (Leningrad [published by author], 1936), p. 19.

60. Y. I. Kazhdanskaya, "Sotsial'no-politicheskie predstavleniia detei—shkol'nikov pervogo kontsentra trudovykh shkol goroda Odessy," *Pedologiia*, 1928, no. 2, p. 94.

61. This was the date of the "Bloody Sunday" massacre, which sparked the first Russian revolution in 1905.—Trans.

62. N. A. Rybnikov, "Ideologiia sovremennogo shkol'nika" [The Ideology of the Contemporary Schoolchild], *Pedologiia*, 1928, no. 1, pp. 150–158; N. A. Rybnikov, *Derevenskii shkol'nik i ego idealy: Ocherki po psikhologii shkol'nogo vozrasta* [The Rural Schoolchild and His Ideals: Outlines of School-age Psychology] (Moscow, 1916).

63. P. V. Arkhangel'skii, "Derevenskii shkol'nik i trud" [The Rural Schoolchild and Labor], *Pedologiia*, 1928, no. 2, pp. 110–135.

64. R. G. Vilenkina, "K kharakteristike nastroeniia rabochego podrostka" [Toward a Description of the Mood of the Working-class Teen], *Pedologiia*, 1930, no. 1, pp. 81–97.

65. E. Kol'man, "Pis'mo tovarishcha Stalina i zadachi fronta estestvoznaniia i meditsiny" [Comrade Stalin's Letter and the Tasks on the Natural Sciences and Medical Front], *Pod znamenem marksizma*, 1931, nos. 9–10, p. 169. The author of this virulent article, one of the organizers of the deadly debates of those years, would later emigrate and publish his memoirs under the title *My ne dolzhny byli tak zhit'* [We Shouldn't Have Lived Like That] (New York: Chalidze, 1982).

66. *Pedologiia*, 1931, no. 1, p. 4.

67. *Pravda*, July 5, 1936.

68. See Petrovsky, "Zapret na kompleksnoe issledovanie detstva," pp. 131–132.

69. *Sbornik prikazov i rasporiazhenii po Narkomprosu RSFSR* [Collected Decrees and Orders of the RSFSR Ministry of Education], 1936, no. 15, p. 4.

70. *Sbornik prikazov i rasporiazhenii po Narkomprosu RSFSR*, 1936, no. 23, p. 17.

71. A. S. Bubnov, *Osnovnye napravleniia bor'by za pod'em sovetskoi shkoly i pedagogicheskogo obrazovaniia* [Basic Directions in the Struggle for the Improvement of the Soviet School System and Pedagogical Education] (RSFSR Ministry of Education, 1936), p. 27; I. M. Kogan, ed., *Dobit' do kontsa pedologiiu* (Leningrad: Oblono, 1936), pp. 68–70.

72. M. G. Yaroshevsky, "Stalinizm i sud'by sovetskoi nauki" [Stalinism and the Fates of Soviet Science], in *Repressirovannaia nauka* (Leningrad: Nauka, 1991).

Chapter Nine

1. S. Freud and W. C. Bullitt, *Thomas Woodrow Wilson: A Psychological Study* (Boston: Houghton Mifflin, 1967).

2. Many books have been written about Bullitt, notably B. Farnsworth, *William C. Bullitt and the Soviet Union* (Bloomington: Indiana University Press, 1967); and W. Brownell and R. N. Billings, *So Close to Greatness: A Biography of William C. Bullitt* (New York: Macmillan, 1987). Bullitt's correspondence with Roosevelt has also been published: Orville H. Bullitt, ed., *Personal and Secret: Correspondence Between F. D. Roosevelt and W. C. Bullitt* (Boston: Houghton Mifflin, 1972).

3. S. Freud and W. C. Bullitt, *Thomas Woodrow Wilson*, p. 253. See also: *The Bullitt Mission to Russia*, testimony before the U.S. Senate Committee on Foreign Relations by W. C. Bullitt (1919; Hyperion, 1977).

4. W. Brownell and R. N. Billings, *So Close to Greatness*, p. 105.

5. S. Freud and W. C. Bullitt, *Thomas Woodrow Wilson*, p. 271.

6. W. C. Bullitt, *It's Not Done* (New York, 1926). The title of this novel on the life of American socialists alludes, curiously enough, to Chernyshevsky's novel *What Is to Be Done?*

7. W. Brownell and R. N. Billings, *So Close to Greatness*, p. 113.

8. Letter of December 7, 1930, from Freud to Arnold Zweig, in *The Letters of Sigmund Freud and Arnold Zweig*, tr. W.D.R. Scott (London: Hogarth, 1970), p. 25.

9. S. Freud and W. C. Bullitt, *Thomas Woodrow Wilson*, p. vi.

10. Even though some postulates of this book appear naive, they are comparable to later attempts at Wilson's psychobiography. See: A. L. George and J. L. George, *Woodrow Wilson and Colonel House: A Personality Study* (New York, 1956); Alexander L. George, "Some Uses of Dynamic Psychology in Political Biography: Case Materials on Woodrow Wilson," in Fred I. Greenstein and Michael Jerver, eds., *A Source Book for the Study of Personality and Politics* (Chicago: Markham, 1971), pp. 78–98.

11. S. Freud and W. C. Bullitt, *Thomas Woodrow Wilson*, p. viii.

12. Ibid., p. 254.

13. George Kennan, *Memoirs, 1925–1950* (New York: Pantheon, 1967), p. 79.

14. Ibid., pp. 81–82.

15. "Reminiscences of H. A. Wallace," Office of Oral History at Columbia University, Part 5, pp. 893 and 429.

16. "Reminiscences of J. P. Warburg," Office of Oral History at Columbia University, Part 4, p. 894.

17. Ibid., p. 429.

18. A. I. Utkin, *Diplomatiia Franklina Ruzvel'ta* [The Diplomacy of Franklin Roosevelt] (Sverdlovsk: Izd. Ural'skogo Universiteta, 1990), p. 47.

19. W. Brownell and R. N. Billings, *So Close to Greatness*, p. xi.

20. C. W. Thayer, *Bears in the Caviar* (Philadelphia: Lippincott, 1950), p. 156.

21. Elena Bulgakova, *Dnevnik Eleny Bulgakovoi* [Elena Bulgakova's Diary] (Moscow: Knizhnaia palata, 1990), p. 95.

22. Other Bulgakov scholars also have suggested that the Spring Festival at the American embassy served as a prototype of Satan's Rout. See V. Chebotareva, "Prototip bulgakovskoi Margarity" [The Prototype for Bulgakov's Margarita], *Literaturnyi Azerbaidzhan*, 1988, no. 2, pp. 117–118; L. Parshin, "Velikii bal u sa-

tany" [Satan's Ball], *Nauka i zhizn"* 10, 1990, pp. 93–99; B. V. Sokolov, *Roman M. Bulgakova "Master i Margarita"* [Bulgakov's Novel *Master and Margarita*] (Moscow: Nauka, 1991), p. 121; V. Losev and L Yanovskaya, "Kommentarii," in *Dnevnik Eleny Bulgakovoi.* In his book *Chertovshchina v amerikanskom posol'stve v Moskve ili 13 zagadok Mikhaila Bulgakova* [Deviltry in the American Embassy, or the 13 Riddles of Mikhail Bulgakov] (Moscow: Knizhnaia palata, 1991), Leonid Parshin drew on details about the embassy reception contained in Elena Bulgakova's diaries. The author reiterated the conclusion about the connection between Satan's ball in the novel and the embassy reception. His further analysis took a path different from the one I have taken here: Following in Elena Bulgakova's footsteps, Parshin reconstructed a historical prototype of Baron Maigel, one of the Muscovites in the novel.

23. V. Losev and L. Yanovskaya, "Kommentarii," in *Dnevnik Eleny Bulgakovoi,* p. 359.

24. O. H. Bullitt, ed., *Personal and Secret,* pp. 116–117.

25. C. W. Thayer, *Bears in the Caviar,* p. 156.

26. Ibid., p. 158.

27. C. W. Thayer, *Diplomat* (New York: Harper, 1959), pp. 230–231.

28. C. W. Thayer, *Bears in the Caviar,* p. 162.

29. O. H. Bullitt, ed., *Personal and Secret,* p. 116.

30. Mikhail Bulgakov, *The Master and Margarita,* tr. Michael Glenny (New York: Harper & Row, 1967), p. 269.

31. Those Bulgakov scholars who have found numerous prototypes of each pair at the ball do not, however, comment on the idiosyncrasy of their peculiar gathering. To the best of my knowledge, only Mikhail Kreps has paid attention to this problem, coming to different conclusions from mine here (see Mikhail Kreps, *Bulgakov i Pasternak kak romanisty* [Bulgakov and Pasternak as Novelists] [Ann Arbor: Hermitage, 1984], p. 79).

32. Bulgakov, *The Master and Margarita,* pp. 267–268.

33. L. Parshin, *Chertovshchina v amerikanskom posol'stve.*

34. V. Losev and L. Yanovskaya, "Kommentarii," p. 359.

35. Ibid.

36. Bulgakov, *The Master and Margarita,* p. 294.

37. W. Brownell and R. N. Billings, *So Close to Greatness,* p. 143.

38. O. H. Bullitt, ed., *Personal and Secret,* p. 65.

39. "Reminiscences of H. A. Wallace," p. 2057.

40. W. Brownell and R. N. Billings, *So Close to Greatness,* p. 176.

41. B. Farnsworth, *William C. Bullitt and the Soviet Union,* p. 153.

42. M. Chudakova, *Zhizneopisanie Mikhaila Bulgakova* [The Life of Mikhail Bulgakov] (Moscow: Kniga, 1988), p. 340.

43. Ibid., p. 350.

44. *Dnevnik Eleny Bulgakovoi,* pp. 77–78.

45. Ibid., p. 86.

46. The Collection of Manuscripts of the Institute of Russian Literature (Pushkinskii Dom), fund 369, file 351.

47. Ibid., file 307.

48. Bulgakov, *The Master and Margarita,* p. 383.

49. *Dnevnik Eleny Bulgakovoi,* pp. 48–49.

50. Intourist was the Soviet state travel agency for foreign visitors, which provided a wide variety of services.—Trans.

51. *Dnevnik Eleny Bulgakovoi,* p. 63.

52. C. W. Thayer, *Bears in the Caviar*.
53. *Dnevnik Eleny Bulgakovoi*, p. 68.
54. Ibid., pp. 113, 114, 118.
55. Ibid., pp. 96, 92, 97.
56. W. Brownell and R. N. Billings, *So Close to Greatness*, p. 176.
57. *Dnevnik Eleny Bulgakovoi*, p. 92.
58. Ibid., p. 107.
59. Ibid., p. 114.
60. Ibid., p. 117.
61. Ibid., p. 118.
62. Ibid., pp. 60–61.
63. Ibid., p. 74.
64. M. Chudakova, *Zhizneopisanie Mikhaila Bulgakova*, p. 407.
65. *Dnevnik Eleny Bulgakovoi*, p. 74.
66. L. Yanovskaya, *Tvorcheskii put' Mikhaila Bulgakova* [Mikhail Bulgakov's Creative Path] (Moscow: Sovetskii pisatel', 1983), pp. 265, 277. Vulis, who knew Bulgakov's circle of friends, believed that Woland's prototype was Stalin. The case for this does not seem very convincing (A. Vulis, *Roman M. Bulgakova Master i Margarita* [Moscow: Khudozhestvennaia literatura, 1991]).
67. Kreps, *Bulgakov i Pasternak kak romanisty*, p. 164.
68. A. Barkov pinpointed the action of the novel as taking place in May–June 1936, relying on a number of indirect indications (A. Barkov, "O chem govoriat paradoksy" [What Paradoxes Tell Us], *Literaturnoe obozrenie* 5, 1991, p. 66).
69. "Reminiscences of H. A. Wallace," p. 1677.
70. Cited in M. Chudakova, *Zhizneopisanie Mikhaila Bulgakova*, p. 164.
71. M. Bulgakov, *Journal confisqué* (Paris: Solin, 1992).
72. Bulgakov, *The Master and Margarita*, pp. 120–121.
73. Ibid., p. 121.
74. Vyacheslav Ivanov, *Sobranie sochinenii* [Collected Works] (Brussels, 1987), vol. 4, p. 153.
75. Bulgakov, *The Master and Margarita*, p. 205. The experiments of Professor Woland and his retinue at the Variety Theater, as well as some other scenes from *The Master and Margarita* (the confiscation of foreign currency on stage in Nikanor Ivanovich's dream, Koroviev's tricks, and so on) seem a practical extrapolation of Yevreinov's ideas on monodrama and the theatricalization of life, the continuation of his train of thought in a different format (see chapter 4).
76. Bulgakov, *The Master and Margarita*, pp. 124–125.
77. Ibid., p. 125.
78. *Bezdomny* is the Russian word for "homeless."—Trans.
79. Osip Mandelstam, *Slovo i kul'tura* [Discourse and Culture] (Moscow: Sovetskii pisatel', 1987), p. 200.
80. Letter from S. L. Tseitlin to Bulgakov dated April 10, 1938. Collection of Manuscripts of the Institute of Russian Literature (Pushkinskii Dom), fund 369, file 502. Tseitlin ended his letter with a pun alluding to Woland: "Should you wish to use your consultant (without quotation marks) in future, I will be glad to assist you."
81. *Dnevnik Eleny Bulgakovoi*, pp. 85–86.
82. Ibid., p. 108.
83. M. Chudakova, *Zhizneopisanie*, pp. 354, 356.
84. William Bullitt, *It's Not Done* (New York: Harcourt Brace, 1926).
85. Bulgakov, *The Master and Margarita*, p. 380.

86. Ibid., pp. 380–381.

87. Boris Gasparov, in his classic article ("Iz nabliudenii nad motivnoi strukturoi romana Bulgakova *Master i Margarita*" [From Observations of the Motivational Structure of Bulgakov's Novel *The Master and Margarita*], *Slavica Hierosolymitana*, 1978, no. 3, pp. 198–251), constructed a logic matrix, into which he fit the characters of the novel and their prototypes. According to Gasparov's conclusions, the novel developed on three historical planes: ancient Jerusalem, the beginning of the nineteenth century, and Moscow of the 1930s. The characters were projected into each of these historical strata, changing their appearance but preserving continuity. Gasparov conjectured that Woland's equivalents were Afrany in Jerusalem and the opera Mephistopheles in the early nineteenth century. Furthermore, he concluded: "Most of the Muscovite characters . . . have corresponding prototypes as their main projections. It is therefore natural to investigate the question whether Woland also has such a prototype." Analyzing the text, Gasparov noted that Woland's Moscow prototype must be the "famous foreigner" who "is feared . . . and even suspected of being a spy. At the same time he is expected to voice his approval of the new Moscow and Muscovites" (pp. 237–238). Gasparov investigated the problem deductively, but lacked the historical data to complete this section of his matrix. He mentioned several Western writers who visited Soviet Moscow as possible prototypes for Woland. It seems, however, that Bullitt as we know him fits this role much better than H. G. Wells or André Gide. The correlation between Gasparov's logical prediction and the historical facts that became known after the publication of Elena Bulgakova's diaries is a rare and inspiring episode in the humanities.

88. Bulgakov, *The Master and Margarita*, pp. 373–374.

89. M. Kreps mused that since the Master received a promise that he would be able to write his novels, walk under the cherry blossom with Margarita, and listen to Schubert, "we can only guess what the light looks like if mere peace is so attractive" (M. Kreps, *Bulgakov i Pasternak kak romanisty*, p. 93).

90. Bulgakov, *The Master and Margarita*, p. 373.

91. Mikhail Bulgakov, *Pis'ma* [Letters] (Moscow: Sovremennik, 1989), p. 213.

92. A. Schwartz, *Zhizn' i smert' Mikhaila Bulgakova* [Life and Death of Mikhail Bulgakov] (Ann Arbor: Hermitage, 1988), p. 91.

93. J. E. A. Curtis's characterization of Woland alluded to the diplomatic profession, but he had an entirely different power structure in mind: "Woland figures in the novel as a kind of plenipotentiary ambassador from the supernatural realm" (J. E. A. Curtis, *Bulgakov's Last Decade: The Writer as Hero* [Cambridge University Press, 1987], p. 173). Overall, the connection between Bulgakov and Bullitt has been underestimated by scholars, and the context of emigration often has been significantly downplayed. See also: Ellendea Proffer, *Bulgakov: Life and Work* (Ann Arbor: Ardis, 1984); Andrew Barratt, *Between Two Worlds: A Critical Introduction to The Master and Margarita* (Oxford: Clarendon, 1987); M. Chudakova, *Zhizneopisanie Mikhaila Bulgakova* (Moscow: Kniga, 1988); Lesley Milne, *Mikhail Bulgakov: A Critical Biography* (Cambridge: Cambridge University Press, 1990).

94. M. Chudakova, *Zhizneopisanie*, p. 462.

95. V. Vilenkin, "Nezabyvaemye vstrechi" [Unforgettable Encounters], in *Vospominaniia o Mikhaile Bulgakove* (Moscow: Sovetskii pisatel', 1988), p. 298.

96. Bulgakov, *The Master and Margarita*, p. 281.

97. Ibid., p. 251.

98. W. Brownell and R. N. Billings, *So Close to Greatness*, p. 196.

99. Ibid., p. 183.

100. On Bullitt's policy in France, see William W. Kaufmann, "Two American Ambassadors: Bullitt and Kennedy," in G. A. Craig and F. Gilbert, eds., *The Diplomats* (Princeton: Princeton University Press, 1981), pp. 649–681.

101. W. Brownell and R. N. Billings, *So Close to Greatness*, p. 256.

102. In his postwar books, Bullitt speculated about geopolitics, about America's role in the world, and about the world government of the near future.

103. "Reminiscences of H. A. Wallace," p. 3486.

Chapter Ten

1. *Vekhi: Sbornik statei o russkoi intelligentsii*, 2d ed. (Moscow, 1909), p. 81.

2. V. Rozanov, *Apokalipsis nashego vremeni*—Mimoletnoe. Moscow: Respublika, 1994.

3. Kolyma is a region of Siberia in which many prison labor camps are situated.

4. V. Shalamov, "Novaia proza" [New Prose], *Novyi mir,* 1989, no. 12, pp. 3 and 61.

5. V. Ivanov, *Dionis i pradionisiistvo* [Dionysus and Pre-Dionysianism] (Baku, 1923), p. 157.

6. V. Nabokov, "Chto vsiakii dolzhen znat'" [What Everyone Should Know], in *Priglashenie na kazn': Rasskazy* (Moscow: Kniga, 1989), p. 412. This is a short satirical piece advertising a patented formula called "Freudianism for Everyone" (pp. 393–395).

7. N. Y. Mandelstam, *Vospominaniia* [Memoirs] (Moscow: Kniga, 1989), p. 126.

8. M. Bakhtin, *Estetika slovesnogo tvorchestva* [The Aesthetics of Speech Genres] (Moscow: Iskusstvo, 1986), p. 331.

9. V. Adrianova-Perets, "Simvolika snovidenii Freida v svete russkikh zagadok" [Freud's Dream Symbolism in Light of Russian Riddles], in *Akademiku N. Ya. Marru* (Moscow: AN SSSR, 1935), pp. 497–505. I am grateful to academician D. S. Likhachev for pointing out this source.

10. V. V. Ivanov, *Ocherki po istorii semiotiki v SSSR* [Outlines on the History of Semiotics in the USSR] (Moscow: Nauka, 1976).

11. S. Eisenstein, *Izbrannye proizvedeniia v 6 tomakh* [Collected Works in Six Volumes] (Moscow: Iskusstvo, 1964), vol. 1, pp. 82 and 657.

12. *Eizenshtein v vospominaniiakh sovremennikov* [Eisenstein in the Recollections of His Contemporaries] (Moscow, 1978), p. 204.

13. S. Eisenstein, *Izbrannye proizvedeniia*, vol. 1, p. 657.

14. Ibid., p. 415.

15. Ibid., p. 305.

16. Ivanov, *Ocherki po istorii semiotiki*, p. 93.

17. Marie Seton, *Sergei M. Eisenstein* (London: Dennis Dobson, 1952), p. 134.

18. Ivanov, *Ocherki po istorii semiotiki*, pp. 113–114.

19. Ibid., p. 113.

20. S. Eisenstein, *Izbrannye proizvedeniia*, p. 657.

21. Ibid., p. 508.

22. Ibid., p. 85.

23. Ibid.

24. Ibid., p. 657.

25. I. Montegu, *With Eisenstein in Hollywood* (New York: International Publishers, 1967), p. 105.

26. Eisenstein, *Izbrannye proizvedeniia*, p. 83.

27. Montegu, *With Eisenstein in Hollywood*, p. 345.

28. K. Clark and M. Holquist, *Mikhail Bakhtin* (Cambridge, Mass.: Harvard University Press, 1984), p. 117.

29. M. Bakhtin, *Estetika slovesnogo tvorchestva*, pp. 329–330.

30. M. Bakhtin, *Problemy poetiki Dostoevskogo* [Problems of Dostoevsky's Poetics] (Moscow: Sovetskaia Rossiia, 1979), p. 48.

31. Ibid.

32. V. Ivanov, "Mysli o simvolizme" [Thoughts on Symbolism], *Trudy i dni*, 1912, no. 1, p. 6.

33. V. N. Voloshinov, *Freidizm: Kriticheskii ocherk* [Freudianism: A Critique] (Moscow: Gosudarstvennoe, 1927), p. 118.

34. See V. V. Ivanov, *Ocherki po istorii semiotiki v SSSR*; V. V. Ivanov, "Znachenie idei M. M. Bakhtina o znake, vyskazyvanii i dialoge dlia sovremennoi semiotiki" [The Meaning of M. M. Bakhtin's ideas of the Symbol, Expression, and Dialogue for Contemporary Semiotics], in *Trudy po znakovym sistemam* (Tartu, 1973), vol. 6; and Clark and Holquist, *Mikhail Bakhtin*. Another point of view can be found in G. S. Morson and C. Emerson, "The Disputed Texts," in *Rethinking Bakhtin* (Evanston: University of Chicago Press, 1989).

35. Bakhtin, *Estetika slovesnogo tvorchestva*, pp. 394–404.

36. V. V. Ivanov, "Znachenie idei M. M. Bakhtina."

37. V. Kozhinov and S Konkin, "Mikhail Mikhailovich Bakhtin: Kratkii ocherk zhizni i deiatel'nosti" [Mikhail M. Bakhtin: A Short Outline of His Life and Career], in *Problemy poetiki i istorii literatury* (Saransk, 1973).

38. K. Clark and M. Holquist, *Mikhail Bakhtin*.

39. Bocharov, "Ob odnom razgovore i vokrug nego," *Novoe literaturnoe obozrenie*, 1993, 2, p. 75.

40. Y. Etkind, *Zapiski nezagovorshchika* [Notes of a Nonconspirator] (London: Overseas Publications, 1977), p. 257.

41. V. N. Voloshinov, *Freudianism: A Marxist Critique* (New York: Academic, 1976), p. 8.

42. Ibid., p. 10.

43. Ibid., p. 11.

44. Ibid., p. 86.

45. Ibid., p. 77.

46. Ibid.

47. V. N. Voloshinov, "Marksizm i filosofiia iazyka" [Marxism and the Philosophy of Language], in *Osnovnye problemy sotsiologicheskogo metoda v naukakh o iazyke* (Leningrad, 1929).

48. J. V. Stalin, *Marksizm i voprosy iazykoznaniia* [Marxism and Issues in the Science of Language] (Moscow, 1949).

49. Bakhtin, *Estetika slovesnogo tvorchestva*.

50. J. Lacan, *Ecrits* (Paris: Point, 1975); "L'Ethique de la psychanalyse," in *Le Seminaire 7* (Paris: Seuil, 1986).

51. Voloshinov, *Freudianism: A Marxist Critique*, p. 79.

52. Ibid., p. 86.

53. Ibid., p. 87.

54. M. Bakhtin, *Problemy poetiki Dostoevskogo*.

55. M. Bakhtin, *Estetika slovesnogo tvorchestva*, p. 339.

56. M. Bakhtin, "Avtor i geroi v esteticheskoi deiatel'nosti" [Author and Character in Aesthetic Activity], in *Estetika slovesnogo tvorchestva*.

57. M. Bakhtin, *Estetika slovesnogo tvorchestva*, p. 339.

58. M. Bakhtin, *Problemy poetiki Dostoevskogo*, p. 50.

59. M. Bakhtin, *Estetika slovesnogo tvorchestva*, pp. 333, 345.

60. *The Freud–Jung Letters*, ed. W. McGuire (London: Hogarth, 1974), p. 535.

61. Ibid.

62. In Russian philosophy, a historical overview of the problem can be found in M. S. Kagan, *Mir obshcheniia* [The World of Communication] (Moscow: Politizdat, 1988).

63. M. Bakhtin, *Problemy poetiki Dostoevskogo*, p. 65.

64. M. Bakhtin, *Estetika slovesnogo tvorchestva*, p. 328.

65. Ibid., p. 393.

66. M. Bakhtin, *Tvorchestvo Fransua Rable i narodnaia kul'tura srednevekov'ia i Renessansa* [The Work of François Rabelais and the Popular Culture of the Middle Ages and Renaissance] (Moscow: Khudozhestvennaia literatura, 1990).

67. Ibid., p. 167.

68. Ibid., p. 356.

69. M. Bakhtin, *Estetika slovesnogo tvorchestva*, p. 394.

70. Ibid., p. 402.

71. S. S. Averintsev, "Bakhtin, smekh, khristianskaia kul'tura" [Bakhtin, Laughter, Christian Culture], *Rossiia/Russica*, 1988, no. 6, pp. 119–130.

72. Ibid.

73. Ibid.

74. O. Mandelstam, *Slovo i kul'tura* [Word and Culture] (Moscow: Sovetskii pisatel', 1987), pp. 255 and 200.

75. M. Zoshchenko, *Izbrannye proizvedeniia v dvukh tomakh* [Selected Works in Two Volumes] (Leningrad: Khudozhestvennaia literatura, 1968).

76. I. Metter, *Ne porastet byl'em* [It Won't Become Overgrown with Fact] (Leningrad: Sovetskii pisatel', 1989), p. 635.

77. Collection of manuscripts of the Institute of Russian Language and Literature of the Russian Academy of Sciences, M. M. Zoshchenko Archives, fund 501, section 2, file 16.

78. M. Zoshchenko, *Vozvrashchennaia molodost'* [Youth Returned], *Golubaia kniga* [The Blue Book], *Pered voskhodom solntsa* [Before the Sun Rises] (Leningrad: Khudozhestvennaia literatura, 1988).

79. Letter of February 18, 1941 from Thomas Mann to Karl Kerenyi, in *Mythology and Humanism: The Correspondence of Thomas Mann and Karl Kerenyi*, tr. A. Gelley (Ithaca: Cornell University Press, 1975), p. 100.

Conclusion

This chapter was translated by Rebecca Ritke.

1. The transnational character of psychoanalysis was amusingly confirmed by Igor' Shafarevich, an aggressive anti-Semite who nonetheless made recourse to Freud in his analysis of socialism as a manifestation of the death instinct (see I. Shafarevich, *Sotsializm kak iavlenie mirovoi istorii* [Paris: YMCA, 1977]).

2. M. Wulff, "Zur Stellung der Psychoanalyse in der Sowjetunion," *Die psychoanalytische Bewegung*, no. 1 (1930), p. 75.

3. F. Stepun, *Byvshee i nesbyvsheesia* (New York: Chekhov, 1956), vol. 1, p. 276.

About the Book
and Author

Marxism was not the only Western idea to influence the course of Russian history. In the early decades of this century, psychoanalysis was one of the most important components of Russian intellectual life. Freud himself, writing in 1912, said that "in Russia, there seems to be a veritable epidemic of psychoanalysis." But until Alexander Etkind's *Eros of the Impossible*, the hidden history of Russian involvement in psychoanalysis has gone largely unnoticed and untold.

The early twentieth century was a time when the craving of Russian intellectuals for world culture found a natural outlet in extended sojourns in the West, linking some of the most creative Russian personalities of the day with the best universities, salons, and clinics of Germany, Austria, France, and Switzerland. These ambassadors of the Russian intelligentsia were also Freud's patients, students, and collaborators. They exerted a powerful influence on the formative phase of psychoanalysis throughout Europe, and they carried their ideas back to a receptive Russian culture teeming with new ideas and full of hopes of self-transformation.

Fascinated by the potential of psychoanalysis to remake the human personality in the socialist mold, Trotsky and a handful of other Russian leaders sponsored an early form of Soviet psychiatry. But, as the Revolution began to ossify into Stalinism, the early promise of a uniquely Russian approach to psychoanalysis was cut short. An early attempt to merge medicine and politics forms final chapters of Etkind's tale, the telling of which has been made possible by the undoing of the Soviet system.

The effervescent Russian contribution to modern psychoanalysis has gone unrecognized too long, but *Eros of the Impossible* restores this fascinating story to its rightful place in history.

Alexander Etkind is professor of the history of ideas and Russian literature in the European University, St. Petersburg, Russia, and a visiting fellow in the Woodrow Wilson Center in Washington, D.C.

Index